LEARNSMART ADVANTAGE WORKS

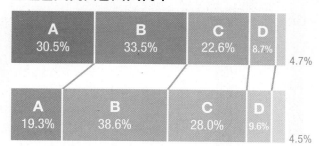

LEARNSMART®

A	B	C	D	
30.5%	33.5%	22.6%	8.7%	4.7%

A	B	C	D	
19.3%	38.6%	28.0%	9.6%	4.5%

Without LearnSmart

More C students earn B's

*Study: 690 students / 6 institutions

Over 20%
more students
pass the class
with LearnSmart

*A&P Research Study

LEARNSMART® Pass Rate - 70%

Without LearnSmart Pass Rate - 57%

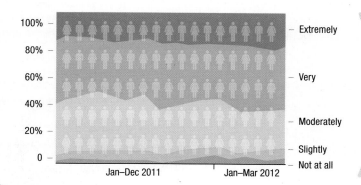

- Extremely
- Very
- Moderately
- Slightly
- Not at all

100% 80% 60% 40% 20% 0

Jan–Dec 2011   Jan–Mar 2012

More than 60%
of all students agreed
LearnSmart was a
very or extremely
helpful learning tool

*Based on 750,000 student survey responses

> **AVAILABLE**
> *ON-THE-GO*

How do you rank against your peers?

Let's see how confident you are on the questions.

What you know (green) and what you still need to review (yellow), based on your answers.

COMPARE AND CHOOSE WHAT'S RIGHT FOR YOU

	BOOK	LEARNSMART	ASSIGNMENTS	
connect	✓	✓	✓	LearnSmart, assignments, and SmartBook—all in one digital product for maximum savings!
connect Looseleaf	✓	✓	✓	Pop the pages into your own binder or carry just the pages you need.
connect Bound Book	✓	✓	✓	The #1 Student Choice!
SMARTBOOK® Access Code	✓	✓		The first and only book that adapts to you!
LEARNSMART® ADVANTAGE Access Code		✓		The smartest way to get from a B to an A.
CourseSmart eBook	✓			Save some green and some trees!
create™	✓	✓	✓	Check with your instructor about a custom option for your course.

> Buy directly from the source at http://shop.mheducation.com.

Ninth Edition

Supervision

CONCEPTS AND SKILL-BUILDING

Samuel C. Certo
Steinmetz Professor of Management
Crummer Graduate School of Business
Rollins College

SUPERVISION: CONCEPTS AND SKILL-BUILDING, NINTH EDITION

Published by McGraw-Hill Education, 2 Penn Plaza, New York, NY 10121. Copyright © 2016 by McGraw-Hill Education. All rights reserved. Printed in the United States of America. Previous editions © 2013, 2010, and 2005. No part of this publication may be reproduced or distributed in any form or by any means, or stored in a database or retrieval system, without the prior written consent of McGraw-Hill Education, including, but not limited to, in any network or other electronic storage or transmission, or broadcast for distance learning.

Some ancillaries, including electronic and print components, may not be available to customers outside the United States.

This book is printed on acid-free paper.

1 2 3 4 5 6 7 8 9 0 RMN/RMN 1 0 9 8 7 6 5

ISBN 978-0-07-772061-2
MHID 0-07-772061-x

Senior Vice President, Products & Markets: *Kurt L. Strand*
Vice President, General Manager, Products & Markets: *Michael Ryan*
Vice President, Content Design & Delivery: *Kimberly Meriwether David*
Managing Director: *Susan Gouijnstook*
Director: *Michael Ablassmeir*
Lead Product Developer: *Ann Torbert*
Product Developer: *Gabriela Gonzalez*
Marketing Manager: *Elizabeth Trepkowski*
Director, Content Design & Delivery: *Terri Schiesl*
Full-Service Manager: *Faye Schilling*
Content Project Managers: *Melissa M. Leick, Kristin Bradley, and Judi David*
Buyer: *Susan K. Culbertson*
Interior Design: *Tara McDermott*
Cover Design: *Studio Montage, St. Louis, MO*
Cover Image: Getty Images/RF
Compositor: *Aptara®, Inc.*
Typeface: *10/12 Palatino*
Printer: *R. R. Donnelley*

All credits appearing on page or at the end of the book are considered to be an extension of the copyright page.

Library of Congress Cataloging-in-Publication Data

Certo, Samuel C.
    Supervision : concepts and skill-building / Samuel C. Certo.—Ninth edition.
        pages cm
    ISBN 978-0-07-772061-2 (alk. paper)
    ISBN 0-07-772061-X (alk. paper)
    1. Supervision of employees.   I. Title.
    HF5549.12.C42 2016
    658.3'02—dc23   2014034047

The Internet addresses listed in the text were accurate at the time of publication. The inclusion of a website does not indicate an endorsement by the authors or McGraw-Hill Education, and McGraw-Hill Education does not guarantee the accuracy of the information presented at these sites.

www.mhhe.com

To all of my supervisor friends who
have helped sharpen my thoughts
about how they work!

As with all previous editions, this book prepares students to be supervisors. Supervision continues to be more exciting or challenging than at any other time in our history! Dealing with modern issues like sustainability, a multicultural workforce, social media, and alternative energy supplies provides challenging and stimulating everyday tests for modern supervisors. Competent supervisors have a central role in helping modern organizations to appropriately deal with such critical factors. As a result, competent supervisors are of utmost importance to modern organizations and to society as a whole.

Supervision: Concepts and Skill-Building helps students learn what it takes to be a successful supervisor in today's complex work world. The focus of this new edition continues the tradition of presenting both traditionally proven and cutting-edge supervision concepts as practical tools for meeting present-day supervision challenges. In addition, this text furnishes students with an even richer mix of practical supervision concepts and real-life examples that illustrate how modern supervisors handle contemporary problems. Carefully studying supervision concepts and their relationship to real-world, practical examples throughout this text will greatly enhance a student's chances of gaining success and personal rewards as a supervisor.

Overview of this New Text

Words can't express my thankfulness for your kind words and encouragement over the years. *Supervision* has helped hundreds of thousands of students across the globe to prepare for supervisory roles in organizations. The persistent success of this book continues to reinforce my opinion that a high-quality supervision text must contain important theoretical yet practical material as well as facilitate the student learning and instructional processes. The following sections outline in detail how this new edition presents important, practical supervision theory and accomplishes this facilitation.

The Foundation

This ninth edition, like all previous editions, is built on a solid theoretical foundation. To generate this original foundation, surveys were sent to instructors of supervision courses as well as supervisors nationwide to gather information about what would be needed to develop the highest-quality supervision learning package available in the marketplace. The main themes generated from the results of this survey were summarized and presented to focus groups around the country for refinement and expansion. Supervision professors and practicing supervisors then acted as individual reviewers to help fine-tune the book as it developed. Figure A, on the following page, depicts the focus of various professionals during the development of this text.

The Ninth Edition—Sustaining A Successful Tradition

Supervision: Concepts and Skill-Building is divided into five main parts: "What Is a Supervisor?" "Modern Supervision Challenges," "Functions of the Supervisor," "Skills of the Supervisor," and "Supervision and Human Resources." The following sections describe the parts and chapters of the ninth edition.

FIGURE A | *Supervision:* The Professional Team

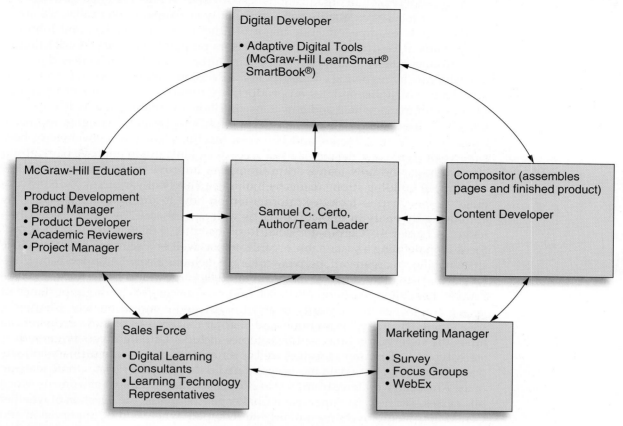

The professional team involved in building this text is extensive. Samuel Certo, the author and team leader, works with the product developers who manage the product and brand, the digital product developers who assemble the adaptive digital tools like McGraw-Hill LearnSmart® and SmartBook®, the compositors who typeset the pages and assemble the final product, the marketing managers who coordinate surveys and focus groups, and the digital learning consultants and learning technology representatives who make up the sales force.

The Core of this Revision

Naturally, the heart of this edition continues the tradition of incorporating current trends in supervision-related research as well as examples of what constitutes more present day challenges for supervisors. Focus on these more modern supervision challenges includes coverage on topics like sustainability, energy management, the green movement, and Internet applications including the use of social media. Rest assured that this new edition is NOT a trendy view of supervision. Instead, this new edition furnishes students with a realistic view of the traditional view of supervisions, modern challenges supervisors face, and the relationship between the two that must be maintained if a supervisor is to be successful in today's world. The following sections highlight several changes for each part of this new edition in more detail.

Part One, "What Is a Supervisor?" consists of the first chapter, "Supervision: Tradition and Contemporary Trends." Chapter 1 opens with a new "A Supervision Challenge" that focuses on ensuring customer satisfaction at Wegmans' supermarkets. Among other topics, this chapter introduces the concept of sustainability and shows how apps for mobile workers can help supervisors to control company activities through mobile devices. This chapter aims at providing the student with a thorough introduction to supervision before embarking on a more detailed study of the supervision process.

Part Two, "Modern Supervision Challenges," covers areas in which supervisors will have to meet important contemporary organizational challenges. Chapter 2,

"Ensuring High Quality and Productivity," depicts how quality and productivity can affect supervision in organizations. The revised "A Supervision Challenge" for this chapter focuses on quality and productivity at a supermarket called Shearer's Foods. Timely examples include major product recalls at Johnson and Johnson, using iPads at Hadronics to help supervisors pinpoint activities contributing to poor product quality, and how a hospital in Burbank, California, increased quality of health care by involving employees in the decision-making process. Coverage in this chapter includes updates on productivity trends and coverage of Deming's 14 points for management and how they contribute to building quality in organizations, as well as a discussion of lean enterprise philosophy and a six sigma approach. Chapter 3, "Groups, Teams, and Powerful Meetings," includes coverage of how supervisors can use social media like Facebook or LinkedIn to improve work group effectiveness, and how teamwork training can improve performance, as well as coverage of building strong teams by building an array of various skills. New coverage in this chapter includes information on how to promote inclusiveness by embracing diversity in the workplace as well as a revised "A Supervision Challenge." Chapter 4, "Corporate Social Responsibility, Ethics, and Sustainability," focuses on defining a sustainable organization as well as discussing how to achieve sustainability in organizations. New coverage includes a new "A Supervision Challenge" that discusses unethical behavior at Wells Fargo branches despite the corporations' heavy emphasis on ethics as well as a discussion of the importance of giving employees the authority to act ethically and compassionately. Chapter 5, "Managing Diversity," is an important chapter that focuses on how diversity can affect the supervision process. Major topics include defining diversity, prejudice, stereotypes, sexism, and ageism as well as differentiating between primary and secondary diversity. New data has been entered describing the racial/ethnic makeup of the American workforce from 1990 to 2020, as well as the number of women-owned businesses. The new "A Supervision Challenge" focuses on the question of whether Generation Y employees are unfairly stereotyped, whereas the "Supervision and Ethics" and "Supervision and Diversity" features have both been revised to reflect current information.

Part Three, "Functions of the Supervisor," contains four chapters. Chapter 6, "Reaching Goals: Plans and Controls," combines the planning and control functions of a supervisor. Discussion of DuPont's corporate vision along with strategic goals provides students with a practical example. A revised "A Supervision Challenge" identifies the ways that Meijer, Inc, helps supervisors identify top performers and make corrections for those who fall short while a new "Supervisory Skills" focuses on planning, scheduling, and spending for supervisors in the construction industry. Chapter 7, "Organizing and Authority," opens with a new "A Supervision Challenge" that focuses on a recent trend to replace hierarchical organizational structure with a holacracy and the pros and cons of this choice. Coverage also includes tall versus flat organizations, as well as learning organizations. A new "Practical Advice for Supervisors" for this chapter explores safety and effectiveness of night workers. A new "Supervision and Diversity" illustrates how Walgreens was able to both improve efficiency and accommodate workers with disabilities at high-tech distribution center. While a new "Supervisory Skills" describes many of the myths about delegation and how to overcome them to be a more effective supervisor. This chapter also includes a discussion of organizational structure, span of control, and delegation. Chapter 8, "The Supervisor as Leader," has a new "A Supervision Challenge" that uses as example from Kraft Foods to illustrate how company history can be used to inspire employees. New coverage also focuses on various approaches to leadership, how desirable leadership traits vary in different cultures around the world, and how to be a good, ethical role model to employees. Chapter 9, "Problem Solving, Decision Making, and Creativity," gives students insights about the kinds of problems and decisions that supervisors face, as well as possible steps for solving problems and making decisions. For practical supervision insights in these areas the new "A Supervision Challenge" discusses the issue of retaining employees in high-stress jobs such as being a 911 dispatcher. Additionally, a new "Supervision and Ethics" probes the question of what unethical decisions you might find ways to justify while a new "Supervisory Skills" delves into how to be a decisive person and make decisions to solve problems. Sections on how to think creatively and using social media to generate new ideas are also included in this chapter.

Part Four, "Skills of the Supervisor," discusses important abilities that supervisors must have to be successful. These abilities include "Communication: Theory and Modern Media" (Chapter 10), "Motivating Employees" (Chapter 11), "Problem Employees: Counseling and Discipline" (Chapter 12), "Managing Time and Stress" (Chapter 13), and "Managing Conflict and Change" (Chapter 14). This section is filled with new, updated examples of how supervisors maneuver in these skill areas. Chapter 10 opens with a new "A Supervision Challenge" on using iPads for business communication at Hadronics. New coverage focuses on includes avoiding generalizing about people based on their culture, updated data about daily media consumption, a revised "Supervisory Skills" that discusses using graphs and charts to communicate visually, and information about social media, their use in business networking, and their potential hazards to your career. Additionally, a revised "Supervision and Diversity" explores the issues of an employee feeling different from other employees and the potential negative consequences of those feelings. New coverage for Chapter 11 includes a new "A Supervision Challenge" that focuses on using gamification to make work and training activities more appealing and, potentially, more effective. Another point of the chapter can be found in a revised "Supervision and Ethics" that emphasizes that flexible arrangements must be fair and not take advantage of employees. New coverage also includes discussion of how to work with your employees to develop traits that will ready them for promotions as well as why it is important to make sure that your employees receive the credit for the work they do. Chapter 12 opens with a new "A Supervision Challenge" that discusses a court case by a troubled employee against Chevron. Additionally, the chapter contains updated data on absenteeism, workplace violence, and theft in the workplace. New coverage includes acceptable social media behavior for professionals and how to provide constructive criticism regardless of your personal feelings toward someone. Chapter 13 begins with a new "A Supervision Challenge" that focuses on relieving stress in the workplace. It also features a revised "Practical Advice for Supervisors" about how to use mobile devices to save time and a new "Supervision and Ethics" that addresses the issue of treating employees ethically when their jobs involve risks. Added coverage on the relationship between stress and performance has also been added. Chapter 14's "A Supervision Challenge" tackles the issue of being in a supervisor in the midst of corporate changes, such as reorganizations or buyouts, and the challenges those situations bring. New coverage discusses how to understand and manage a multigenerational workforce. Additional new coverage focuses on implementing change in a work group and encouraging employees to "unfreeze."

Again in this edition, "Appendix A: Organizational Politics" follows Part Four. This appendix continues to provide students with a special and unique vehicle for learning about the impact of politics on supervision in modern organizations. The material provides a clear definition of organizational politics and discusses various levels of political action as well as political tactics. Also emphasized is a related topic called impression management, along with special coverage of how to manage organizational politics.

The text concludes with Part Five, "Supervision and Human Resources." Beginning this part, Chapter 15, "Selecting Employees," overall, focuses on the process of choosing the right person to fill an open position and the sources, methods, and legal issues that must be considered. Added new coverage includes a fresh

"Supervision and Diversity" that discusses promoting diversity in a small business setting. Chapter 16, "Providing Orientation and Training," discusses the process of orienting new employees, developing skills in employees, and evaluating training methods. This edition includes a new "A Supervision Challenge" that illustrates the fact that successful supervisors make companies successful—and that proper training can lead to successful supervisors. New data on the types of training U.S. companies are investing in is included in this chapter. Additionally, new topics include the need to retrain employees, the benefits of life-long learning, information on certification training, and a discussion of some popular apps to keep your brain active and agile. Chapter 17, "Appraising Performance," opens with a revised "A Supervision Challenge" that uses a YMCA in Rochester, New York, to illustrate how performance appraisals can be made to matter to employees and to the organization. Overall, the chapter discusses the importance of a systematic performance appraisal and provides several appraisal methods. It includes a focus on how performance appraisal goals should match up with employee ambitions, the relationship between employee performance appraisal and employee effort expended in the job, and the importance of gathering appropriate data to be used in performance appraisals. New material included in a revised "Supervision: New Trends" illustrates how social media can make it easier for employees to receive frequent performance appraisal feedback. Additionally, a completely new "Supervisory Skills" discusses how a self-appraisal can be used as a tool for career advancement.

The text ends with Appendix B and Appendix C. Appendix B, "Supervision Laws: Health and Safety, Labor Relations, Fair Employment" focuses on practical legal information relevant to successful supervision. Appendix C, "The Supervisor's Career Path: Finding a Career that Fits," is a rich career resource for students regarding finding that first job, perhaps a supervision job, as well as managing a career. It emphasizes important topics such as setting career goals, preparing for a job search, and interviewing essentials. Internet resources are pinpointed from which students can get help with self-assessments of their personality and skills, résumé building, job-hunting resources, and how to evaluate a good job offer. This appendix is designed to be a vital topic for course discussion as well as a valuable reference guide as students actually begin and manage their careers.

Overview of Text Learning System

Each chapter in this edition continues the tradition of making the study of supervision interesting, enjoyable, effective, and efficient. As you will see, the list of individual pedagogy elements in this new edition has changed somewhat in order to improve the overall pedagogic impact of the book. Each pedagogy component in this new edition is described in the following sections.

One of the main changes for this edition is a dramatic update in book design as a pedagogy tool—a part of the learning system. To heighten student involvement and engagement with the text, this edition features a new color scheme, more photos, updated figures, and a more reader-friendly layout.

New Design!

Certo, Supervision, 9e, is enhancing student engagement through a new visually captivating design. Students will be drawn into the content and remain captivated by the bold colors, layout, and industry photos.

Chapter Outlines

The chapter outlines provided at the beginning of each chapter are tools students can use to preview the chapters and review the materials before testing. These outlines also can be used to help students understand the relationship of certain topics to other chapter topics.

Learning Objectives

The key points of a chapter's content are highlighted in learning objectives at the beginning of the chapter. The learning objectives serve as a guide for previewing as well as reviewing concepts to be learned.

A Supervision Challenge

Each chapter opens with a vignette, entitled "A Supervision Challenge," which is an episode about an actual supervisor on the job. Each "Supervision Challenge" has a corresponding discussion exercise section at the end of the chapter entitled "Meeting the Challenge" (see below for details). Almost all chapter-opening incidents are new to this edition to keep students current with challenges that modern supervisors face.

Margin Definitions

Key terms are defined in the margins. Students can use these definitions to test their understanding of the terms and find the places where important concepts are discussed.

Supervision Examples

Many examples of supervisors in action are nested within each chapter. Students are able to enrich their study of chapter content by seeing examples of how the concepts being studied arise in real organizations or in the lives of real supervisors.

Learning Highlights

Several extended real-world illustrations depicting supervisors meeting daily challenges are boxed off in each chapter. These illustrations have been carefully chosen and placed within chapters to help make learning via this text more interesting, more applicable, and more lasting. As a result of this highlights program, this book is rich with real-world supervisory experiences. In addition, these highlights have been extensively updated or, in many cases, wholly replaced for this edition. The types of highlights appearing throughout the book are described below:

Supervision and Ethics

This feature is designed to illustrate the vital role that ethics plays in being a supervisor. Virtually every phase of supervisory activity can be affected by ethical issues. For example, the new "Supervision and Ethics" feature in Chapter 4 talks of the need for employees to be given the authority to act ethically and compassionately.

Supervisory Skills

This feature shows students how supervisors use skills to meet current challenges as they conduct their work. These boxes are designed to give students the most current examples available. For instance, the new box in Chapter 14 focuses on the ways supervisors can "unfreeze" their employees and implement necessary changes within their work group.

Practical Advice for Supervisors

This feature highlights practical guidelines that can help students be successful supervisors. Chapter 12 contains a fresh and thorough look at ways to provide constructive criticism.

Supervision and Diversity

Each of these features illustrates an important diversity issue related to the chapter content and emphasizes how modern supervisors can deal with the issue. A new example in Chapter 15 discusses how supervisors can bring diversity to even a small business.

Supervision: New Trends

This feature focuses on developing trends in how supervisors do their jobs. Themes for this feature throughout the book largely focus on new technology available to supervisors that will make them more efficient and effective. Developing technologies like social media and video conferencing are highlighted but not overemphasized.

Summary

Learning objectives are recapped at the end of each chapter via brief summaries of the chapter concepts. This unique format allows students to review what they've learned from each learning objective.

Photos, Figures, and Tables

Photographs, illustrations, and tables are used extensively to clarify and reinforce text concepts.

Key Terms

Each chapter includes a list of key terms. Reading this list can help students review by testing their comprehension of the terms. The number of the page on which a term is first defined is also included in the glossary at the end of the book. These terms are highlighted throughout the book as margin definitions.

Review and Discussion Questions

These questions test understanding of the chapter concepts. They can be used independently by students or by instructors as a method of reviewing the chapters.

Skills Module

Skills modules at the end of each chapter reflect a commitment to emphasize student skills in applying supervision concepts. Each module contains a number of elements that instructors can use as a formal part of a course to develop students' application abilities. Students also can use the elements independently. Each skills module is divided into two parts: concepts and skill-building.

Part One: Concepts

This skills module section focuses on helping students clarify and retain the supervision concepts studied in the chapter. The section contains a summary organized by chapter learning objectives, a list of key terms along with reference page numbers where students can review the meanings of the terms, and review and discussion questions that students can study independently or that instructors can use as the basis for classroom discussion.

Part Two: Skill-Building

This section focuses on helping students develop abilities in applying chapter concepts to solve supervision problems. This section contains:

Meeting the Challenge. This activity asks students to respond to questions by applying the chapter's concepts to the opening scenario. For instance, the new opening scenario for Chapter 7, "How Do You Get Things Done When There Are No Managers?" is based on activities at a real-life company—Zappos. The "Meeting the Challenge" feature for this chapter asks students to discuss the challenges this company and its employees will face as changes to work groups are implemented.

Problem-Solving Case. Next, each chapter contains a short case that further applies the chapter's concepts to various supervision situations. Specially designed questions for each case ask students to focus on solving a supervision problem. For example, the case in Chapter 12, "Suspensions of Lexington, Kentucky, Police Officers," asks students to determine the right of the police department to discipline its officers for misconduct while they are off duty.

Assessing Yourself. Each chapter contains a short, engaging self-assessment quiz, which helps students see the kinds of supervisors they can be. For example, Chapter 5, "Managing Diversity," presents a questionnaire students can use to explore their age bias. Discussion questions accompanying the quizzes help students more fully explore the self-assessment results to build better insights about themselves. In the Chapter 5 skills module, for example, students are asked to generate a list of common prejudices people might have against older workers.

Class Skills Exercises. A skills exercise is an activity specifically designed to help students develop supervision skills. Each skills module contains two exercises that vary in format and design. Some exercises are designed to be completed by individuals, whereas others are designed to be completed as groups. Most exercises can be used either in class or out of class. For example, the skills exercises for Chapter 6 focus on developing goal-setting skills and controlling skills.

Glossary

Terms and definitions are gathered from each chapter and listed at the end of the book in the glossary, which provides ready reference for students and instructors. To encourage student review, the text pages on which the terms are defined and discussed are included.

McGraw-Hill Connect

McGraw-Hill's Connect Management offers a number of powerful tools and features to make managing assignments easier, so you can spend more time teaching. Students engage with their coursework anytime from anywhere in a personalized way, making the learning process more accessible and efficient. Connect Management optimizes your time and energy, enabling you to focus on course content and learning outcomes, teaching, and student learning.

LearnSmart
The Smartest Way to Get from B to A

No two students are alike. Why should their learning paths be? LearnSmart uses revolutionary adaptive technology to build a learning experience unique to each student's individual needs. It starts by identifying the topics a student knows and does not know. As the student progresses, LearnSmart adapts and adjusts the content based on his or her individual strengths, weaknesses, and confidence, ensuring that every minute spent

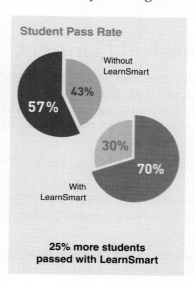

Grade Distribution

Without LearnSmart: A 19.3%, B 38.6%, C 28.0%
With LearnSmart: A 30.5%, B 33.5%, C 22.6%

58% more As with LearnSmart

Student Pass Rate

Without LearnSmart 43%, 57%
With LearnSmart 30%, 70%

25% more students passed with LearnSmart

studying with LearnSmart is the most efficient and productive study time possible.

LearnSmart also takes into account that everyone will forget a certain amount of material. LearnSmart pinpoints areas that a student is most likely to forget and encourages periodic review to ensure that the knowledge is truly learned and retained. In this way, LearnSmart goes beyond simply getting students to memorize material—it helps them truly retain the material in their long-term memory.

SmartBook
A Revolution in Reading

SmartBook™ is the first and only adaptive reading experience designed to change the way students read and learn. It creates a personalized reading experience by highlighting the most impactful concepts a student needs to learn at that moment in time. As a student engages with SmartBook, the reading experience continuously adapts by highlighting content based on what the student knows and doesn't know. This ensures that the focus is on the content he or she needs to learn, while simultaneously promoting long-term retention of material. Use SmartBook's real-time reports to quickly identify the concepts that require more attention from individual students—or the entire class.

Interactive Applications
A Higher Level of Learning

Interactive Applications offer a variety of automatically graded exercises that require students to apply key concepts. Whether the assignment includes a drag & drop, video case, sequence, and case analysis, these applications provide instant feedback and progress tracking for students and detailed results for the instructor.

Self Assessment

Provides students with insight into their personal beliefs, values, skills, and interests in relation to the content covered in the text. These are assignable directly through Connect.

McGraw-Hill Connect

McGraw-Hill Education reinvents the textbook learning experience for today's students with *Connect*, providing students with a cost-saving alternative to the traditional textbook. A seamless integration of a media rich eBook and *Connect, Connect* provides all of the *Connect* features plus the following:

- A web-optimized eBook, allowing for anytime, anywhere online access to the textbook.
- Powerful search function to pinpoint and connect key concepts in a snap.
- Highlighting and note-taking capabilities as well as access to shared instructors' notations.

Sam Certo's *Supervision: Concept's and Skill Building* 9th edition offers you a complete package to prepare you for your course.

McGraw-Hill Connect

McGraw-Hill *Connect* strengthens the link between faculty, students, and course-work, helping everyone accomplish more in less time.

Efficient Administrative Capabilities

Connect offers you, the instructor, auto-gradable material in an effort to facilitate teaching and learning.

Reviewing Homework

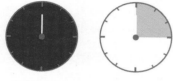

60 minutes
without Connect → 15 minutes
with Connect

Giving Tests or Quizzes

60 minutes
without Connect → 0 minutes
with Connect

Grading

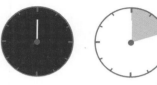

60 minutes
without Connect → 12 minutes
with Connect

Student Progress Tracking

Connect keeps instructors informed about how each student, section, and class is performing, allowing for more productive use of lecture and office hours. The progress tracking function enables instructors to:

- View scored work immediately and track individual or group performance with assignment and grade reports.
- Access an instant view of student or class performance relative to learning objectives.
- Collect data and generate reports required by many accreditation organizations, such as AACSB.

Instructor Library

Connect's instructor library serves as a one-stop, secure site for essential course materials, allowing you to save prep time before class. The instructor resources found in the library include:

- **Instructor's Manual** conveniently provides instructors with an overview of each chapter, covering key terms, learning objectives, lecture notes, and supplemental exercises to use both inside and outside the classroom.
- **Test Bank** conveniently provides instructors with an overview of each chapter, covering key terms, learning objectives, lecture notes, and supplemental exercises to use both inside and outside the classroom. The Test Bank questions are categorized by topic, learning objective, level of difficulty, Bloom's Taxonomy, and accreditation standards (e.g., AACSB).
- **PowerPoint Presentations** A full suite of color **PowerPoint** slides distills key concepts and objectives from each chapter in the book.
- **Manager's HotSeat** videos are an especially important resource. In today's business world, it is important for a supervisor to be aware of situations that may arise with employees. These 10 segments show how a real manager handles difficult, unscripted situations in the workplace. These improvised scenarios reveal how issues such as diversity in hiring, sexual harassment, organizational change, and project management really shape the way business is done. These videos are

the perfect way to expose students to the interpersonal side of supervisory work in organizations. Students are able to view the segments and answer integrated questions as they watch.

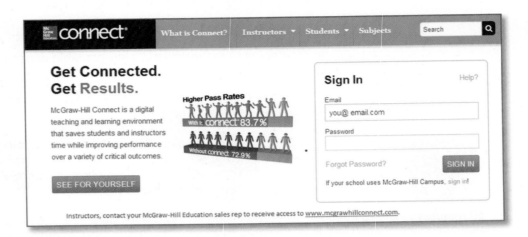

Create

Instructors can now tailor their teaching resources to match the way they teach! With McGraw-Hill Create, **www.mcgrawhillcreate.com,** instructors can easily rearrange chapters, combine material from other content sources, and quickly upload and integrate their own content, like course syllabi or teaching notes. Find the right content in Create by searching through thousands of leading McGraw-Hill textbooks. Arrange the material to fit your teaching style. Order a Create book and receive a complimentary print review copy in three to five business days or a complimentary electronic review copy via e-mail within one hour. Go to **www.mcgrawhillcreate.com** today and register.

Tegrity Campus

Tegrity makes class time available 24/7 by automatically capturing every lecture in a searchable format for students to review when they study and complete assignments. With a simple one-click start-and-stop process, you capture all computer screens and corresponding audio. Students can replay any part of any class with easy-to-use browser-based viewing on a PC or Mac. Educators know that the more students can see, hear, and experience class resources, the better they learn. In fact, studies prove it. With patented Tegrity "search anything" technology, students instantly recall key class moments for replay online or on iPods and mobile devices. Instructors can help turn all their students' study time into learning moments immediately supported by their lecture. To learn more about Tegrity, watch a two-minute Flash demo at **http://tegritycampus.mhhe.com.**

Blackboard® Partnership

McGraw-Hill Education and Blackboard have teamed up to simplify your life. Now you and your students can access *Connect* and Create right from within your Blackboard course—all with one single sign-on. The grade books are seamless, so when a student completes an integrated *Connect* assignment, the grade for that assignment automatically (and instantly) feeds your Blackboard grade center. Learn more at **www.domorenow.com.**

McGraw-Hill Campus™

McGraw-Hill Campus is a new one-stop teaching and learning experience available to users of any learning management system. This institutional service allows faculty and students to enjoy single sign-on (SSO) access to all McGraw-Hill Education materials, including the award-winning McGraw-Hill *Connect* platform, from directly within the institution's web site. With McGraw-Hill Campus, faculty receive instant access to teaching materials (e.g., eTextbooks, test banks, PowerPoint slides, animations, learning objects), allowing them to browse, search, and use any instructor ancillary content in our vast library at no additional cost to instructor or students.

In addition, students enjoy SSO access to a variety of free content (e.g., quizzes, flash cards, narrated presentations) and subscription-based products (e.g., McGraw-Hill *Connect*). With McGraw-Hill Campus enabled, faculty and students will never need to create another account to access McGraw-Hill products and services. Learn more at **www.mhcampus.com.**

Assurance of Learning Ready

Many educational institutions today focus on the notion of *assurance of learning,* an important element of some accreditation standards. *Supervision* is designed specifically to support instructors' assurance of learning initiatives with a simple yet powerful solution. Each test bank question for *Supervision* maps to a specific chapter learning objective listed in the text. Instructors can use our test bank software, EZ Test and EZ Test Online, to easily query for learning objectives that directly relate to the learning outcomes for their course. Instructors can then use the reporting features of EZ Test to aggregate student results in similar fashion, making the collection and presentation of assurance of learning data simple and easy.

AACSB Tagging

McGraw-Hill Education is a proud corporate member of AACSB International. Understanding the importance and value of AACSB accreditation, *Supervision* recognizes the curricula guidelines detailed in the AACSB standards for business accreditation by connecting selected questions in the text and the test bank to the six general knowledge and skill guidelines in the AACSB standards. The statements contained in *Supervision* are provided only as a guide for the users of this textbook. The AACSB leaves content coverage and assessment within the purview of individual schools, the mission of the school, and the faculty. While the *Supervision* teaching package makes no claim of any specific AACSB qualification or evaluation, we have within *Supervision* labeled selected questions according to the six general knowledge and skills areas.

McGraw-Hill Customer Experience Group
Contact Information

At McGraw-Hill Education, we understand that getting the most from new technology can be challenging. That's why our services don't stop after you purchase our products. You can e-mail our Product Specialists 24 hours a day to get product training online. Or you can search our knowledge bank of Frequently Asked Questions on our support website. For Customer Support, call **800-331-5094** or visit **www.mhhe.com/support.** One of our Technical Support Analysts will be able to assist you in a timely fashion.

Acknowledgments

As the author, the many years of success of *Supervision: Concepts and Skill-Building* have been very gratifying. As with any book, however, the success of this book has been due, in very large part, to the hard work and commitment of many respected colleagues. I am pleased to be able to acknowledge the input of these professionals. For this edition, several colleagues should be recognized for valuable ideas and thoughts:

Joseph Adamo
Cazenovia College

Dr. Patricia Beckenholdt
University of Maryland University College

Trinidad M. Callava
University of Miami

Raven Davenport
Houston Community College

Laura De La Cruz
Dona Ana Community College New Mexico State University

Marilee Feldman
Kirkwood Community College

Terika L. Haynes
Fayetteville Technical Community College

Pearl Ivey
Central Maine Community College

Linda Koffel
Houston Community College NW

Mitchell Lautenslager
Fox Valley Technical College

Dr. John Mago
Anoka Ramsey Community College

Connie Nichols
Odessa College

David Reva
Kalamazoo Valley Community College

Dean D. Saunders
San Jacinto Community College

Margene E. Sunderland
Fayetteville Technical Community College

Mary Lynn Tripp
Wisconsin Indianhead Technical College

Mary Vogl-Rauscher
Moraine Park Technical College

In addition, a continuing, special thanks to the experts who have provided feedback over the years:

Raymond Ackerman
Amber University

Rex Adams
Southside Virginia Community College, Daniels

Musa Agil
Cape Fear Community College

Linda Alexander
Southeast Community College, Lincoln

Dave Alldredge
Minnesota School of Business

Gemmy Allen
Mountain View College

Scott Ames
North Lake College

E. Walter Amundsen
Indiana University Southeast

Paul Andrews
Southern Illinois University

Lydia Anderson
Fresno City College

Solimon Appel
College for Human Services

Bob Ash
Rancho Santiago College

Glenda Aslin
Weatherford College

Bob Baker
Caldwell Community College

James Bakersfield
North Hennepin Community College

L. E. Banderet
Quinsigamond Community College

Robert Barefield
Drury College, Springfield

Laurence Barry
Cuyamaca College

Perry Barton
Guinnett Area Technical College

Lorraine Bassette
Prince George Community College

Vern Bastjan
Fox Valley Technical College

Becky Bechtel
Cincinnati Technical College

Kenneth Beckerink
Agricultural and Technical College

Gina Beckles
Bethune-Cookman College

Jim Beeler
Indiana Vocational and Technical College, Indianapolis

Robert Bendotti
Paradise Valley Community College

Jim Blackwell
Park College

Carrie Blair
College of Charleston

David Bodkin
Cumberland University

Arthur Boisselle
Pikes Peak Community College

Robert Braaten
Tidewater Community College

James Brademas
University of Illinois, Urbana

Suzanne Bradford
Angelina College

Richard Braley
Eastern Oklahoma State College

Janis Brandt
Southern Illinois University

Stanley Braverman
Chestnut Hill College

Duane Brickner
South Mountain Community College

Dick Brigham
Brookhaven College

Arnold Brown
Purdue University North Central

Eugene Buccini
West Connecticut State University

Gary Bumbarner
Mountain Hope Community College

Kick Bundons
Johnson County Community College

Bill Burmeister
New Mexico State University

Randy Busch
Lee College

Oscar S. Campbell
Athens State College

Marjorie Carte
D. S. Lancaster Community College

Joseph Castelli
College of San Mateo

Win Chesney
St. Louis Community College at Meramac

James Chester
Cameron University

William Chester
University of the Virgin Islands

Michael Cicero
Highline Community College

Jack Clarcq
Rochester Institute of Technology

Charles Clark
Oklahoma City Community College

Sharon Clark
Lebanon Valley College

Virgil Clark
Sierra College

Jerry Coddington
Indiana Vocational and Technical College, Indianapolis

Bruce Conners
Kaskaskia College

Ronald Cornelius
University of Rio Grande

Gloria Couch
Texas State College Institute

Darrell Croft
Imperial Valley College

Joe Czajka
University of South Carolina

Beatrice Davis
Santa Fe Community College

James Day
Grambling State University

Richard De Luca
University of Hawaii, Kapiolani Community College

Edwin Deshautelle, Jr.
Bloomfield College

Richard Deus
Louisiana State University at Eunice

Ruth Dixon
Sacramento City College

Mike Dougherty
Milwaukee Area Technical College

Leroy Drew
Diablo Valley College

Janet Duncan
Central Maine Technical College

Ron Eads
City College of San Francisco

Acie B. Earl, Sr.
Black Hawk College

Todd Ecklund
Minnesota School of Business

Patrick Ellsberg
Lower Columbia College

Earl Emery
Lower Columbia College

Tracy Ethridge
Tri-County Technical College

Roland Eyears
Baker College, Flint

Tom Falcone
Central Ohio Technical College

James Fangman
Wisconsin Technical College

Medhat Farooque
Central Arizona College

Jim Fatina
Indiana University

Dr. Anthony Favre
Mississippi Valley State University

Janice M. Feldbauer
Austin Community College

Jack Fleming
Triton College

Lee Fleming
Moorpark College

Charles Flint
San Jacinto College Central

Toni Forcioni
Montgomery College, Germantown

Laurie Francis
Mid State Technical College

Cheryl Frank
Inver Hills Community College

Connie French
Los Angeles City College

Larry Fudella
Erie Community College South

William Fulmer
Clarion University of Pennsylvania

Carson Gancer
Kalamazoo Valley Community College

Autrey Gardner
*Industrial Technology Department,
Warren Air Force Base*

David Gennrich
Waukesha County Technical College

Brad Gilbreath
New Mexico State University

Sally Gillespie
Broome Community College

Catherine Glod
*Mohawk Valley Community
College*

Tim Gocke
Terra Technical College

Richard Gordon
Detroit College of Business, Dearborn

Greg Gorniak
*Pennsylvania State University,
Behrend*

William G. Graham
Palm Beach Community College

Valerie Greer
University of Maryland

James Grunzweig
Lakeland Community College

James Gulli
Citrus College

Peter J. Gummere
Community College of Vermont

Thomas Gush
College of DuPage

Bill Hamlin
Pellissippi State Technical College

Willard Hanson
Southwestern College

James Harbin
East Texas State University

Carnella Hardin
Glendale College

Scott Harding
Normandale Community College

Louis Harmin
Sullivan County Community College

LeeAnna Harrah
Marion Technical College

Lartee Harris
West Los Angeles College

Edward L. Harrison
University of South Alabama

Paul Hedlund
Barton County Community College

Dr. Douglas G. Heeter
Ferris State University

Kathryn Hegar
*Indiana Vocational and Technical,
Terre Haute*

J. Donald Herring
State University of New York—Oswego

Charles A. Hill
UC—Berkeley Extension

Gene Hilton
Mountain View College

Jean Hiten
Brookhaven College

Roger Holland
Owensboro Community College

Larry Hollar
Cerritos College

Russ Holloman
Catawba Valley Community College

Joshua Holt
Ricks College

Tonya Hynds
Augusta College

Robert Ironside
Indiana University at Kokomo

Ruby Ivens
Lansing Community College

Ellen Jacobs
North Lake College

Debbie Jansky
Milwaukee Area Technical College

Bonnie Jayne
College of St. Mary

Bonnie Johnson
Fashion Institute of New York

Sue Jones
Odessa College

Iris Jorstad
Waubonsee Community College

Vincent Kafkaa
Effective Learning Systems

Ronald C. Kamahele
University of Alaska—Anchorage

Jack E. Kant
San Juan College

Sarkis Kavooyian
Bryant & Stratton

Bernard Keller
Delaware Technical and Community College

Robert Kemp
Pikes Peak Community College

James Kennedy
Angelina College

Howard Keratin
Peralta Laney College

James Kerrigan
Fashion Institute of Technology

Scott King
Stonehill College

Jay Kingpin
EI Centro College

Edward Kingston
University of South Florida

Ronald Kiziah
Piedmont Virginia Community College

Mary Lou Kline
Caldwell Community College

Russell Kunz
Collin County Community College, Spring Creek

Sue Kyriazopoulous
DeVry Institute of Technology

Bryan Lach
Alamance Community College

Mitchell Lautenslager
Fox Valley Technical College

Karen Lavender-Edwards
Lansing Community College

Joyce LeMay
Saint Paul College

Les Ledger
Central Texas College

Allen Levy
Macomb Community College Center

Corinne Livesay
Mississippi College

Thomas Lloyd
DeVry Institute of Technology

Barbara Logan
Westmoreland County Community College

Rosendo Lomas
Albuquerque Technical-Vocational Institute

Frances Lowery
Lawrence Technical University

Henie Lustgarten
Brewer State Junior College

Paul D. Lydick
Paul D Camp Community College

Alvin Mack
University of Maryland

Jon Magoon
Everett Community College

Marvin Mai
Santa Rosa Junior College

John Maloney
College of DuPage

Joseph Manno
Empire College

Gary Marrer
Glendale Community College

Lynda Massa
Santa Barbara Business College

Noel Matthews
Front Range Community College

Edward Mautz
Montgomery College

Ron Maxwell
EI Camino College

Kim McDonald
IPFW

Robert McDonald
Central Wesleyan College

Tim McHeffey
Suffolk County Community College

William McKinney
University of Illinois, Urbana

Joseph McShane
Gateway Technical Institute, Kenosha

Raymond Medeiros
Southern Illinois University

Unny Menon
California State Polytechnic University

Dorothy Metcalfe
Cambridge Community College Center

Eugene Meyers
Fashion Institute of Design and Merchandising, Los Angeles

Charles Miller
Western Kentucky University

Dr. Diane Minger
Cedar Valley College

David Molnar
NE Wisconsin Technical College

Daniel Montez
South Texas College

Dominic A. Montileone
Delaware Valley College

Wayne Moorhead
Delaware Valley College

Peter Moran
Brown Mackie College

Ed Mosher
Wisconsin Indianhead Technical College

Donald Mossman
Laramie County Community College

John Mudge
Concordia College

James Mulvihill
Mankato Technical Institute

David W. Murphy
Madisonville Community College

Hershel Nelson
South Central Technical College

John Nugent
Polk Community College

Randy Nutter
Montana Technical College

Sylvia Ong
Scottsdale Community College

Cruz Ortolaza
Geneva College

Smita Jain Oxford
Commonwealth College

Joseph Papenfuss
Catholic University of Puerto Rico

Mary Papenthien
Westminster College, Salt Lake City

John Parker
Milwaukee Area Technical College

Martha Pickett
Casper College

Sarah T. Pitts
Christian Brothers University

Steven Pliseth
University of Wisconsin, Platteville

Barbara Pratt
Sinclair Community College

Robert Priester
Community College of Vermont

Barbara Prince
Madison Area Technical College

John Pryor
Northern Nevada Community College

Marcia Ann Pulich
University of Wisconsin—Whitewater

Margaret Rdzak
Cardinal Stritch College

William Redmon
Western Michigan University

Arnon Reichers
Ohio State University

Charles Reott
Western Wisconsin Technical Institute

Peter Repcogle
Orange County Community College

Richard Rettig
University of Central Oklahoma

Harriett Rice
Los Angeles City College

Robert Richardson
Iona College

Charles Riley
Tarrant County Junior College

Richard Riley
National College

Michael Rogers
Albany State College

Robert Roth
City University, Bellevue

Larry Runions
North Carolina Vocational Textile

Henry Ryder
Gloucester County College

Larry Ryland
Lurleen B. Wallace Junior College

Mildred Sanders
Jefferson State Community College

Don Saucy
*University of North Carolina—
Pembroke*

Duane Schecter
Muskegon Community College

S. Schmidt
Diablo Valley College

Ralph Schmitt
Macomb Community College South

Irving Schnayer
Peralta Laney College

Greg Schneider
Waukesha County Technical College

Arthur Shanley
Milwaukee School of Engineering

Margie Shaw
Lake City Community College

Allen Shub
Northwestern Illinois University

Pravin Shukla
Nash Community College

Clay Sink
University of Rhode Island

Dr. Leane B. Skinner
Auburn University

Ron Smith
DeKalb Institute of Technology

Steve Smith
Mid State Technical College

Wanda Smith
Ferris State University

Carl Sonntag
Pikes Peak Community College

Marti Sopher
Cardinal Stritch College

Jerry Sparks
*St. Louis Community College at
Florissant Valley*

David Spitler
*Cannon International Business
College*

Richard Squire
Central Michigan University

Dick Stanish
Northwest Technical College

Gene Stewart
Tulsa Junior College

George Stooks
*State University of New
York—Oswego*

John Stout
Brookhaven College

Art Sweeney
University of Scranton

Sally Terman
Troy State University

Sherman Timmons
Scottsdale Community College

Don Tomal
University of Toledo

Donna Treadwell
University of Arkansas at Little Rock

Ron Tremmel
Johnson County Community College

Guy Trepanier
Rend Lake College

John Tucker
Iona College

Bill Tyer
Purdue University

Robert Ulbrich
Tarrant County Junior College

Diann Valentini
Parkland College

Steven Vekich
Fashion Institute of Technology

Susan Verhulst
Des Moines Area Community College

Michael Vijuk
Washington State Community College

Charles Wall
William Rainey Harper College

Obviously, the professionals at McGraw-Hill deserve special recognition. I was fortunate enough to have a fine editor on this project. Michael Ablassmeir took on this project with enthusiasm and vigor. Gabriela Gonzalez was the invaluable product developer of this new edition project. She monitored all project activities and ensured their timely completion. Several others at McGraw-Hill were indispensable in making this edition a reality. These professionals include: Melissa Leick, Susan K. Culbertson, and Sumit Makarh.

Orlando businessman Charles Steinmetz, a longtime leader in the pest-control industry, has taught me many practical lessons about supervision over the years. My observing Chuck as a member of his board of directors was an invaluable learning opportunity for me. Chuck and his wife, Lynn, established the Steinmetz Chair in Management to bolster scholarship at the Roy E. Crummer Graduate School of Business at Rollins College. I feel much honored to be the first holder of the Steinmetz Chair of Management and hope to relate to students the keen business acumen and high moral and ethical standards that have made Charles Steinmetz a world-class entrepreneur and manager.

From a personal viewpoint, every author needs love and support from a caring family. My family is nothing but the best in this regard. My wife and best friend, Mimi, leads the way with constant encouragement and even more importantly, is my moral compass.

Most of all, I'm very grateful for gifts from God that enable me to carry out projects of this nature.

Samuel C. Certo

DR. SAMUEL C. CERTO is the Steinmetz Professor of Management and a former dean at the Roy E. Crummer Graduate School of Business at Rollins College. He has been a professor of management for over 20 years and has received prestigious awards, including the Award for Innovative Teaching from the Southern Business Association, the Instructional Innovation Award granted by the Decision Sciences Institute, and the Charles A. Welsh Memorial Award for outstanding teaching at the Crummer School. Dr. Certo has received the Bornstein and Cornell awards at Rollins College for the significant contribution of his scholarship in enhancing the worldwide reputation of Rollins College.

His numerous publications include articles in journals such as *Academy of Management Review, Journal of Experiential Learning and Simulation,* and *Training.* He also has written several successful textbooks, including *Modern Management: Concepts and Skills.* Professional books published include *The Strategic Management Process* and *Digital Dimensioning: Finding the E-Business in Your Business.* Several of his books have been translated into languages like Chinese, Portuguese, Spanish, and Croatian for distribution throughout the world.

Dr. Certo's recent study has focused on leadership and wisdom. His new book *Chasing Wisdom: Finding Everyday Leadership in Business and Life* emphasizes combining Biblical and business principles to enhance organizational success.

A past chairman of the Management Education and Development Division of the Academy of Management, he has been honored by that group's Excellence of Leadership Award. Dr. Certo also has served as president of the Association for Business Simulation and Experiential Learning, as associate editor for *Simulation & Games,* and as a review board member of the *Academy of Management Review.* His consulting experience has been extensive, with notable experience on boards of directors.

Brief Contents

Contents

part three | Functions of the Supervisor   140

Chapter 6
Reaching Goals: Plans and Controls   140

Chapter 7
Organizing and Authority   174

Chapter 14
Managing Conflict and Change 378

part five | Supervision and Human Resources 418

Chapter 15
Selecting Employees 418

Supervision
CONCEPTS AND SKILL-BUILDING

chapter one | Supervision: Tradition and Contemporary Trends

learning objectives

After you have studied this chapter, you should be able to:

1.1 Define what a supervisor is.

1.2 Summarize research findings that have led to basic ideas of what managers should do.

1.3 Describe the basic types of supervisory skills.

1.4 Describe how the growing diversity of the workforce affects the supervisor's role.

1.5 Identify the general functions of a supervisor.

1.6 Explain how supervisors are responsible to higher management, employees, and co-workers.

1.7 Describe the typical background of someone who is promoted to supervisor.

1.8 Identify characteristics of a successful supervisor.

A Supervision Challenge

WEGMANS' SUPERVISORS, SERVICE, AND SUCCESS

Ever wonder what qualities set successful companies apart from others? Often, it's a matter of supervision. In 2014, a survey of *Consumer Reports* readers identified Wegmans as the best supermarket chain in the United States. When comparing Wegmans to other supermarkets, customers rated it superior in service, perishables, prices, and cleanliness. Wegmans' supervisors play a big role in the company's successful ratings, especially when it comes to providing customer service, which Wegmans believes to be the cornerstone of the supermarket's success. As a result, when hiring supervisors and all other personnel, the importance of customer service is written into every job description and considered in every interview. It is not surprising, after such emphasis, that Wegmans' customers expressed such favorable reviews of the service they receive during their shopping experiences. If Wegmans focuses on customer service so heavily, the supermarket needs employees who will make this their primary goal. This is where supervisors come in. They make it a priority to ensure that customers acquire the best supermarket experience possible.

One way that a front-end supervisor strives to keep customers coming back is by monitoring checkout lanes. If wait times become too long, the supervisor must find a solution. Sometimes it is a matter of assigning another employee to open an additional checkout lane. Other times, the supervisor will be the one to hop on the register to help or even bag groceries or run back to a product display to check the price of an item. No job is too small, especially since customers who see the supervisor making efforts to expedite the checkout process are more likely to return, trusting that Wegmans values their time and money.

Front-end supervisors also have to stay available for any questions or concerns that arise. These include queries from employees and customers. A new cashier may need help looking up a produce code, a customer service associate may need supervisory approval for a return. Likewise, a customer may need help finding a product or navigating a cumbersome aisle. Simply being accessible for questions makes the supervisor stand out in regards to customer service commitment. Consider this: a man is shopping with his two young, fussy children and cannot find the appropriate brand of formula. If the supervisor is available to help, this shopper could easily ask for assistance and be on his way. If no associate appears available to help, this shopper may very well leave the store without making a purchase.

Ultimately, while all Wegmans employees are expected to ensure great customer service, much responsibility falls upon the shoulders of the supervisors. They are, after all, often the first person that a customer sees when they walk in, and the last person they see when they leave. Further, supervisors are usually the person that customers will ask for help or share their frustrations with. Regardless of whether supervisors are working at the service desk, training new employees, bagging groceries, or just walking across the store, they are constantly looking for opportunities to improve the customers' shopping experiences, and, hence, constantly reinforcing Wegmans' successful commitment to customer service.

1. How can supervisors encourage employees to be equally committed to customer service?

2. What personality traits do you think a Wegmans supervisor should have in order to best perform job responsibilities?

Sources: Based on Paige Cooperstein, "Consumer Reports Reveals the 10 Best Supermarkets in America," *Business Insider*, March 28, 2014, http://www.businessinsider.com/best-supermarkets-in-america-2014-3; "Northborough, MA Wegmans—Front End Service Team Leader Full-Time (Hourly Assistant Front End Manager / Night Manager)," *US Jobs*, 2012, http://americjobs.blogspot.com/2013/09/northborough-ma-wegmans-front-end.html#.U0VKItzD_KI; "How to be a smarter supermarket shopper: Learn how to get more from your store. Plus, Ratings of 55 grocers nationwide," *Consumer Reports Magazine*, 2014, http://www.consumerreports.org/cro/magazine/2014/05/how-to-be-a-smarter-supermarket-shopper/index.htm.

supervisor
A manager at the first
level of management

Wegmans' supervisors' commitment to employees and customers is significant because supervisors are critically important to their organizations. Supervisors inspire employees to do their best. By motivating employees to perform at their peak, the supervisor enables an organization to benefit from their commitment, talent, and enthusiasm.

A **supervisor** is a manager at the first level of management, which means the employees reporting to the supervisor are not managers. The Taft-Hartley Act embellishes this definition by indicating that a supervisor is "any individual having authority, in the interest of the employer, to hire, transfer, suspend, lay off, recall, promote, discharge, assign, reward or discipline other employees, or responsibility to direct them, or to adjust their grievances, or effectively to recommend such action, if in connection with the foregoing the exercise of such authority is not of a merely routine or clerical nature, but requires the use of independent judgment."[1] Many different kinds of organizations need supervisors. Figure 1.1 reprints actual advertisements for a variety of supervisory jobs.

The basic job of a manager is to see that an organization meets its goals, yet there are distinctions. For the top executives of an organization, managing is about making sure that the organization's vision and business strategy will allow it to meet its goals through the years ahead. Managing at the supervisory level means ensuring that the employees in a particular department are performing their jobs so that the department will contribute its share to accomplishing the organization's goals. Usually, supervisors focus on day-to-day problems and goals to be achieved in one year or less. This chapter introduces what supervisors do and what skills and characteristics they need to be effective.

Supervision: A Historical Perspective

LO1.1 ▶ Define what a supervisor is.

In studying supervision, keep in mind that present-day theories about how to be a supervisor are based upon management and supervision research findings that have continuously evolved over many years. Management research findings are

FIGURE 1.1 | A Sampling of Supervisory Positions to Be Filled

These job advertisements illustrate the need to read advertisements carefully to determine if you would or would not be a good fit for a position. Not all of them have "supervisor" in the title, but each requires supervisory skills.

Advertising PRODUCTION MANAGER
Electronic desktop production agency seeks self-starting, problem-solving Production Manager to supervise catalogue/retail page construction in Mac platform. Minimum 5-7 yrs. experience in managing production and personnel required. Service bureau background a plus.

AUTOMATIC SCREW MACHINE SECOND SHIFT SUPERVISOR
Established growing suburban manufacturer looking for qualified individual to supervise second shift of manufacturing operations. Must have knowledge and experience on multiple/single spindle machines. Enjoy excellent working conditions in a new plant. Very good salary and full benefit package.

CHIEF PHYSICAL THERAPIST
Rural health care consortium has an immediate opening for a licensed physical therapist to develop a progressive, sophisticated therapy delivery system. The ideal candidate should understand sound management principles and possess strong assessment and clinical skills. Candidate must also be willing to assume department leadership. Competitive salary and benefit package.

SECRETARIAL SUPERVISOR
Large law firm seeks Secretarial Supervisor to join our secretarial management team. Responsibilities include orienting, coordinating, and evaluating a secretarial staff of approximately 200. Previous law firm experience (supervisory or secretarial) preferred. Ideal candidate will be able to work well with a variety of personalities in a demanding, fast-paced environment. We offer state-of-the-art technology, an excellent benefits package and salary commensurate with experience.

SALES MANAGEMENT
Our growing organization is seeking an experienced Sales Management candidate to lead our expanding Color Copier Department. The successful candidate will have 3-5 years sales management experience in planning, organizing, hiring, and motivating a team of sales professionals. Previous sales experience, account development techniques, and vertical market success are required. Familiarity with printing, graphic arts, office equipment or other related industry experience helpful.

ASSISTANT DIRECTOR OF HOUSEKEEPING
Large luxury hotel is accepting resumes for an Assistant Director of Housekeeping. College degree and 4-5 years of Housekeeping Management experience required. Preferred applicants will have experience as a Director of Housekeeping for a small to medium size hotel or Assistant Director at a large hotel. Must have excellent administrative and supervisory skills.

important since supervision is management at the lowest level of the organization. Clearly, some early management research findings related to supervision are just as important today as when the actual research was conducted. A few of these early research findings are introduced next. More detail on this research, as well as more recent research, is integrated and discussed throughout.

LO1.2 ▶ Summarize research findings that have led to basic ideas of what managers should do.

Supervisors Should Focus on Efficiency

Frederick W. Taylor (1856–1915) is often referred to as the "father of scientific management." Taylor believed that in order to improve efficiency, it is important to consider the best way in which a job could be completed. By applying scientific knowledge to the study of production, it was feasible to maximize efficiency.

While working at the Bethlehem Steel Company, Taylor studied the best way to maximize efficiency for employees whose sole responsibility involved shoveling materials. As he observed the workers while they were performing their job, Taylor considered several factors. First, what kinds of shovels worked best with what materials? Second, was it most productive for workers to shovel 5, 10, 15, 20, 30, or 40 pounds at a time? Third, how quickly can a shovel be pushed into a pile of materials and then pulled out properly loaded? Fourth, how much time is required to swing a shovel backward in order to throw the given horizontal distance at a given height? Taylor also considered the size of each worker, the weight of the materials, and the distance that the materials were to be thrown. He then developed a detailed plan that described the conditions under which employees could be most efficient. Three years after his plan was implemented, the total number of shovelers was reduced from 600 to 140, and the average number of tons shoveled per worker per day rose from 15 to 59. Also, wages increased and the cost of handling a ton of material dropped significantly. Clearly, the application of science to the study of production can result in maximal employee efficiency.

Supervisors Should Focus on Functions to Be Performed

Henri Fayol (1841–1925), a French industrialist, is often regarded as the pioneer of administrative theory. The ideas that he generated relative to general management principles are still considered to be important among contemporary thinkers. Mr. Fayol asserted that all managers have primary management functions to perform in organizations. More detailed information about these functions follows later. These functions include:

- Planning—setting goals for an organization, and developing an overall strategy for achieving the goals.
- Organizing—assigning tasks to specific members of the organization.
- Leading—motivating the employees of the organization to achieve the tasks that were given to them, as well as handling conflicts as they arise.
- Controlling—overseeing the various tasks that are being completed and ensuring that they are done in the expected manner; making sure that things go as planned.

Supervisors Should Focus on People

Because they deal directly with employees and have knowledge about an organization's customers, supervisors emphasize a people orientation. This focus recognizes that the quality of an organization is often affected by the quality of interactions among its members. Consistent with this approach is the idea that supervisors must recognize that above all, their employees should be treated in a humane fashion. Abraham Maslow (1908–1970), a pioneering psychologist who is perhaps the best-known

The physical safety of workers is one of the most basic considerations for employers.

contributor of the people focus, recognized that people have different sets of needs that are met in a hierarchical pattern. The most basic needs of any human being are physiological needs, such as food and shelter. Once those needs are met, then safety needs must be considered. Safety needs include security of job, family, health, and property. Next on the hierarchy are needs related to love and belonging, including friendship, family, and intimate relationships. The fourth level of the hierarchy includes esteem needs, including self-esteem and confidence. The final part of the hierarchy includes self-actualization, which includes an attitude of acceptance, a lack of racial biases, and creativity. Based upon Maslow's findings, supervisors must help workers to satisfy their personal needs while being productive in organizations.

LO1.3 ▸ Describe the basic types of supervisory skills.

Types of Supervisory Skills

Although a supervisor in a Pizza Hut restaurant and a supervisor in a Ford Motor Company factory work in very different environments, the skills they need to be successful fall into the same basic categories. These categories of skills are used by all levels of managers in all kinds of organizations. Skills developed during a beginning supervisory job will prove useful in every job held throughout a management career.

Classic Understanding of Management Skills

For many years, experts have considered managers' success dependent on three basic categories of skills: technical, human relations, and conceptual. In addition, the application of those skills requires a fourth skill: decision making.

technical skills
The specialized knowledge and expertise used to carry out particular techniques or procedures

Technical skills are the specialized knowledge and expertise used to carry out particular techniques or procedures. A United Way fundraiser's ability to persuade executives to write big checks is a technical skill. A mechanic's ability to bring an automobile engine back to life relies on technical skills. Other technical skills may involve bookkeeping, selling, and many other types of work. To be "technical," skills do not have to be mechanical or scientific; they can involve any work-related technique or procedure.[2]

human relations skills
The ability to work effectively with other people

Human relations skills are the skills required to work effectively with other people. These skills include the ability to communicate with, motivate, and understand people. Supervisors use their human relations skills to impress their superiors, inspire employees, defuse conflicts, get along with co-workers, and succeed in many other ways.

conceptual skills
The ability to see the relation of the parts to the whole and to one another

Conceptual skills involve the ability to see the relationship of the parts to the whole and to one another. For a supervisor, conceptual skills include recognizing how the department's work helps the entire organization achieve its goals and how the work of various employees affects the performance of the department as a whole.

decision-making skills
The ability to analyze information and reach good decisions

Decision-making skills involve the ability to analyze information and reach good decisions. Someone with strong decision-making skills can think objectively and creatively. Chapter 9 provides a more detailed look at how to make decisions effectively.

The relative importance of each type of skill depends on the level of management. As shown in Figure 1.2 on the following page, human relations skills are important at every level of management. However, supervisors rely more on

FIGURE 1.2 | Relative Importance of Types of Skills for Different Levels of Managers

The degree to which you need technical skills, conceptual skills, and decision-making skills varies with the level of management. Human relations skills, however, are almost equally significant at all levels of management.

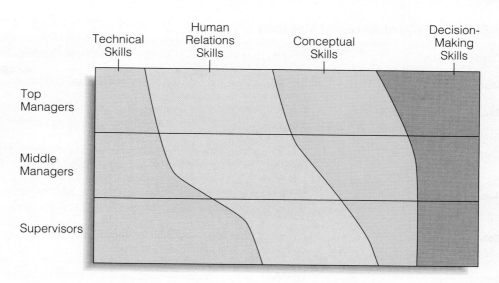

technical skills than do higher-level managers because employees who have a problem doing their jobs go to the supervisor and expect help. Also, top managers tend to rely more on decision-making skills simply because they tend to make more complex decisions.

Modern View of Management Skills

Expanding on the classic view of management skills, current thinkers have taken a fresh look at the activities a manager typically performs.[3] This way of thinking starts with a list of activities and then identifies the skills required to carry out those activities successfully. The typical manager's activities fall into three groups:

1. *Task-related activities:* Efforts to carry out critical management-related duties, such as planning, setting objectives for employees, and monitoring performance.
2. *People-related activities:* Efforts to manage people, such as by providing support and encouragement, recognizing contributions, developing employees' skills, and empowering employees to solve problems.
3. *Change-related activities:* Efforts to modify components of the organization, such as monitoring the environment to detect a need for change, proposing new tactics and strategies, encouraging others to think creatively, and taking risks to promote needed changes.

These activities frequently come together in today's fast-moving business environment. Contemporary business demands such as *sustainability* (operating with a minimal impact on the environment) and *social media* (online tools for sharing information) call for new ways of working. Often, managers are at the front lines of understanding how these changes will result in new tasks, enabling employees to develop the needed skills, and encouraging them to embrace change in order to help their companies and careers thrive.

To carry out these activities, supervisors and other managers rely on a diverse set of skills, including those listed in Table 1.1 on the following page. Situations vary, so individual supervisors may need skills beyond those listed here.

To develop the variety of skills needed to be a good supervisor, you should learn and practice the concepts discussed in this book. Get to know good supervisors and managers and observe how they handle situations. Supervisors who continually develop their skills in each area are the ones most likely to be promoted to higher levels of management.

TABLE 1.1 | Skills of Successful Managers

Clarifying roles	Assigning tasks; explaining job responsibilities, task objectives, and performance expectations
Monitoring operations	Checking on the progress and quality of the work; evaluating individual and unit performance
Short-term planning	Determining how to use personnel and other resources to accomplish a task efficiently; determining how to schedule and coordinate activities efficiently
Consulting	Checking with people before making decisions that affect them; encouraging participation in decision making; using the ideas and suggestions of others
Supporting	Being considerate; showing sympathy and support when someone is upset or anxious; providing encouragement and support when a task is difficult or stressful
Recognizing	Providing praise and recognition for effective performance, significant achievements, special contributions, and performance improvements
Developing	Providing coaching and advice; providing opportunities for skill development; helping people learn how to improve their skills
Empowering	Allowing substantial responsibility and discretion in work activities; trusting people to solve problems and make decisions without getting approval first
Envisioning change	Presenting an appealing description of desirable outcomes that the unit can achieve; describing a proposed change with enthusiasm and conviction
Taking risks for change	Taking personal risks and making sacrifices to encourage and promote desirable change in the organization
Encouraging innovative thinking	Challenging people to question their assumptions about the work and consider better ways of doing it
External monitoring	Analyzing information about events, trends, and changes in the external environment to identify threats and opportunities for the work unit

LO1.4 ► Describe how the growing diversity of the workforce affects the supervisor's role.

Supervising a Diverse Workforce

Good human relations skills are especially important in today's environment because of the increasing diversity of the U.S. workforce.[4] In 1980, just over half (51 percent) of the workforce consisted of white men;[5] this group's share of the workforce is expected to fall to 42.8 percent by 2020.[6] While the share of white men in the workforce declines, the share of black, Hispanic, and Asian workers is expected to rise. (See the accompanying "Supervision and Diversity" to learn more about Hispanics, the largest ethnic group.) Women are entering the workforce at almost the same rate as men, and they now make up more than 47 percent of the adult labor pool.[7] In addition, the segment aged 55 years and over is expected to represent more than 25.2 percent of the U.S. population by 2020.[8]

Opportunities and Challenges

Together, these changes mean that supervisors can expect to have more employees who are female, nonwhite, and experienced—perhaps senior citizens holding a job after retirement. Consider Al Aurilio, who supervises workers sorting scrap materials that arrive at the warehouse of Pacific Iron and Metal Company, located in Seattle, Washington. With more than 60 years of experience at the company, Aurilio has become an expert in the metal composition of the items to be sorted, and he willingly shares his knowledge with employees.[9] As described in subsequent

SUPERVISION AND DIVERSITY

THE LARGEST ETHNIC MINORITY GROUP

Hispanics—immigrants and descendants of immigrants from Latin America—have become the largest ethnic minority group in the United States. More than 1 in 10 U.S. workers are Hispanic, and their share of the workforce is expected to grow. That means many supervisors will have Hispanic employees in the coming years.

A wide variety of Americans wear the label Hispanic. Their origins are diverse, and they include both well-paid professionals and entry-level workers at the low end of the wage scale. The majority of them trace their roots to Mexico, almost one-tenth have a Puerto Rican heritage, and Cubans are the third largest group.

While the broad ethnic group "Hispanic" actually includes great diversity, supervisors may benefit from recognizing some cultural norms that are common among Hispanic workers. One is a tendency to stress personal relationships. Hispanic workers may rely heavily on personal contacts to locate a new job and may respond well to goals and rewards set for the whole group. They generally appreciate face-to-face instruction and hands-on training to learn new skills. Hispanic workers may talk with one another while working more than workers from some other cultures do.

However, the supervisor may discover that Hispanic workers do not talk much to the supervisor. This difference expresses another value that is often stressed in Hispanic communities: respect for authority. A supervisor might find that many Hispanic employees do exactly as directed, no more and no less, out of respect for the supervisor's authority in directing them. If the supervisor is hoping employees will offer suggestions and try new ways of working, the supervisor may have to ask specifically for such behavior. Of course, describing expectations clearly is a helpful skill for supervisors to use with employees of any cultural background.

Sources: Based on Nestlé Professional, "The Hispanic Workforce," *Mix*, www.nestleprofessional.com, accessed November 7, 2008; and EthnoConnect, "Ten Myths about Latina Workers," *EthnoConnect News*, www.ethnoconnect.com, accessed November 7, 2008.

In any workplace, there is likely to be a diverse group of employees. This requires supervisors to be able to work with a wide variety of people.

chapters, this growing diversity enables supervisors to draw on a greater variety of talent and gain insights into more perspectives than ever before.

Diversity is not a new issue. A tremendous wave of immigration that ended in the early part of the 20th century brought the immigrant population in the United States to 15 percent of the total U.S. population. The inflow of immigrants then subsided until the final decade of the 20th century, and this latest surge continued until its peak in 2006. Today almost one in six workers are immigrants. Of the immigrants coming to the United States today, the share with a college degree has been rising, especially in the eastern United States. Immigrant workers without a high school diploma tend to be concentrated in the western states.[10]

Although diversity is not a new issue, the even greater diversity expected in the U.S. workforce of the future—coupled with laws and policies intended to ensure fair treatment of various groups—requires supervisors to work successfully with a much wider variety of people. Some of the people from other backgrounds may be the supervisor's own managers, partly owing to today's global economy. When Mike Burch took a job as maintenance supervisor in a then-new Honda Power Equipment Manufacturing plant in North Carolina, management of the Japanese-based company expected him to learn Honda's ways of operating. Burch, who had barely traveled outside his home state, flew to Japan to experience firsthand Honda's emphasis on cleanliness and safety. At first, the experience felt strange, but Burch came to respect his Japanese bosses. More than 20 years later, Burch says working for people from another culture has made him more open-minded about people in general. That trait helps Burch manage the diverse group of employees now reporting to him.[11]

Subtle Discrimination

Today hardly anyone would say that it is all right to discriminate or that a manager should be allowed to give preference to employees of the manager's race or sex. However, subtle forms of discrimination persist in every workplace, and everybody holds some stereotypes that consciously or unconsciously influence their behavior.[12] The subtle discrimination that results may include ignoring the input from the only woman at a meeting or mistaking an African-American professional for someone with a less prestigious job.

Supervisors and other managers can use several tactics to improve attitudes:

- Have employees work with someone who is different, which gives the employees a chance to educate themselves about the customs and values others hold.

- Use the kind of behavior they expect employees to exhibit, including demonstrating respect for others.

- Question negative stereotypes. When an employee makes an offensive comment, point out the damage it does, and ask the employee to avoid such remarks in the future.

Unfortunately, many supervisors still work for organizations that fail to see the advantages of hiring and developing a diverse workforce. Even in an organization whose management is not committed to these goals, supervisors can provide advice and coaching to female and nonwhite employees, helping them get along in the organization. Supervisors also can make a point of learning about the individual employees in the department, such as what motivates them and what their career goals are. Throughout this book, you will find more specific ideas for meeting the diversity challenge as it relates to the chapter topics.

General Functions of the Supervisor

LO1.5 ▶ Identify the general functions of a supervisor.

Jennifer Plotnick is a supervisor of her city's board of education. Her responsibilities include ensuring that the employees in her department are doing a good job, preparing a budget for her department, making sure not to spend more than the budgeted amounts, explaining to employees what they are expected to do, and justifying to her manager why she needs to add people to her department in the following year. In contrast, supervisors in other settings may spend most of their time enabling employees to do their jobs and handle fewer responsibilities than Plotnick.

planning
Setting goals and determining how to meet them

Although settings and degrees of responsibility may differ, supervisors and other managers carry out the same types of functions. To describe these common activities, management experts categorize them as planning, organizing, staffing, leading, and controlling. The management functions are illustrated in Figure 1.3, which shows that all of the activities should be directed toward enabling employees to deliver high-quality goods and services, whether to customers of the organization or to colleagues in another department.

FIGURE 1.3 | Functions of Supervisors and Other Managers

All the managerial functions are equally important and contribute to a firm's ability to deliver a high-quality good or service.

Planning

Common sense tells us that we do our best work when we know what we are trying to accomplish. The supervisor's job includes determining the department's goals and the ways to meet them. This is the function of **planning**. Sometimes a supervisor has a substantial say in determining the goals themselves, whereas another supervisor must focus on how to achieve goals set by higher-level managers.

As mentioned previously, the supervisor's job is to help the organization meet its goals. Organizational goals are the result of planning by top managers. The purpose of planning by supervisors, then, is to determine how the department can contribute to achieving the organization's goals. This includes planning how much money to spend—and, for a retailer or sales department, how much money to bring in—what level of output to achieve, and how many employees will be needed. Computer technology has made new planning tools possible as well. Chapter 6 discusses planning in greater detail.

Organizing

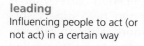

organizing
Setting up the group, allocating resources, and assigning work to achieve goals

Once the supervisor figures out what needs to get done, the next step is to determine how to set up the group, allocate resources, and assign work to achieve those goals efficiently. This is the function of organizing.

Somebody has to decide how to set up the overall organization, creating departments and levels of management. Of course, few supervisors have much of a say in those kinds of decisions. At the supervisory level, organizing usually involves activities such as scheduling projects and assigning duties to employees (or, as will be discussed subsequently, enabling employees to carry out these organizing tasks). In addition, modern supervisors are increasingly responsible for setting up and leading teams of workers to handle special projects or day-to-day operations. Virtual teams rely on electronic communication to function effectively when team members and supervisors are widely separated. Chapter 7 discusses organizing in greater detail, and Chapter 3 addresses leading a team.

Staffing

staffing
Identifying, hiring, and developing the necessary number and quality of employees

The supervisor needs qualified employees to carry out the tasks that he or she has planned and organized. The activities involved in identifying, hiring, and developing the necessary number and quality of employees are known as the function of staffing. Whereas an operative (nonmanagement) employee's performance is usually judged on the basis of the results that the employee has achieved as an individual, a supervisor's performance depends on the quality of results that the supervisor achieves through his or her employees. Therefore, staffing is crucial to the supervisor's success. The various activities of the staffing function are addressed in Chapters 15–17.

Leading

leading
Influencing people to act (or not act) in a certain way

Even if the supervisor has the clearest and most inspired vision of how the department and its employees should work, this vision will not become a reality unless employees know and want to do their part. The supervisor is responsible for letting employees know what is expected of them and inspiring and motivating employees to do good work. Influencing employees to act (or not act) in a certain way is the function of leading. Good leadership is even more important for supervisors in this time of rapid change, fueled by the widespread use of the Internet and other technologies.

Organizing draws heavily on the supervisor's conceptual skills, but leading requires good human relations skills. The supervisor needs to be aware of and use behaviors that employees respond to as he or she desires. Chapter 8 includes a more detailed discussion of leading. Other chapters discuss the ways in which supervisors influence employees to act, such as by communicating (Chapter 10), motivating (Chapter 11), and disciplining (Chapter 12).

Supervisors are responsible for many things including planning, organizing, staffing, leading, controlling, and training others.

SUPERVISION: NEW TRENDS

MOBILE APPS FOR TRACKING WORKERS

In some businesses today, it is not possible for supervisors to keep an eye on all their employees because the employees' jobs take them out on the road, serving customers directly. That's the case with companies that send employees to stores to set up promotional displays and stock shelves. Providing top-quality service requires that employees have realistic schedules and easy access to the materials they need, so they can arrive at each store on time to carry out their assignments.

In the past, controlling in that kind of situation required countless phone calls, mounds of paperwork, and wasted time as the supervisor waited for employees' progress reports. For example, an employee might visit 10 stores, set up a display in each store, take a digital photo of each display, jot down notes about the work, and then head home to spend a few hours transferring all the notes and photos to a computer. Today, mobile devices like smartphones and tablet computers provide an avenue for supervisors to get up-to-theminute information about employees' performance. So the same employee can visit a store, open a tablet app, tap in answers to survey questions, use the tablet to take a photo, and let the app send the data immediately to the supervisor. The flow of information enables supervisors to step in immediately when situations require help,

as when employees can't find display materials or are running behind schedule.

Mobile apps for traveling employees also include data from global positioning systems (GPS). Natural Insight has created an app called WorkTrak that verifies whether employees are at their assigned locations at scheduled times. If an employee's GPS coordinates diverge from the employee's assigned location, the system sends a warning to the employee. If the employee doesn't check in, the system alerts the supervisor to contact the employee and troubleshoot the problem. If someone else needs to be sent to a store, the GPS shows the supervisor which other employees are nearest to that location. The system also automatically keeps track of employees' mileage, so they don't have to fill out logbooks.

A quick search of the Android and Apple marketplaces reveals countless apps for mobile workers—time trackers, time sheets, GPS mobile trackers, and various mobile employee self-service apps that allow employees to stay connected to their company's systems, applications, and products (SAP) information from anywhere and at any time.

Source: Based on Julie Gallagher, "Upward Mobility," *Supermarket News,* September 12, 2011, downloaded from Business & Company Resource Center, http://galenet.galegroup.com.

Controlling

controlling
Monitoring performance and making needed corrections

The supervisor needs to know what is happening in the department. When something goes wrong, the supervisor must find a way to fix the problem or enable employees to do so. Monitoring performance and making needed corrections is the management function of **controlling.** Today, technology may help supervisors carry out this responsibility more accurately and therefore more fairly. In call centers, for example, computers monitoring phone calls may use a technique called "speech analytics" to flag calls in which the characteristics of the voices indicate that the employee is having difficulty with a customer and may need assistance or coaching. Supervisors can deliver computerized training targeting specific weaknesses agents right at their desks, so they can improve without having someone stand over them and criticize. When employees believe that help and feedback are related to their true skills and performance, they are more motivated to improve.[13] For another high-tech example of controlling, see "Supervision: New Trends."

Another aspect of controlling relates back to planning. A good supervisor does not just plan to meet goals. A good supervisor finds ways to best utilize the people and the equipment available in order to meet or exceed goals. Monitoring the progress and performance of the employees being supervised—controlling and making adjustments as necessary—allows a supervisor to revise plans when needed and to be a catalyst within an organization to ensure forward movement.

In an increasing number of organizations, the supervisor is not supposed to control by dictating solutions. Instead, the supervisor is expected to provide employees with the resources and motivation to identify and correct problems themselves. In these organizations, the supervisor is still responsible for controlling, but he or she works with others to carry out this function. Chapter 6 discusses these and more traditional principles of controlling in more detail.

Relationships among the Functions

Notice that Figure 1.3, on page 10, shows the management functions as a process in which planning comes first, followed by organizing, then staffing, then leading, and finally controlling. This order occurs because each function depends on the preceding function or functions. Once the supervisor has planned what the department will do, he or she can figure out the best way to organize work and people to accomplish those objectives. Then the supervisor needs to get the people in place and doing their jobs. At that point, the supervisor can direct their work and inspire their efforts. The results are then evaluated by the supervisor to ensure that the work is getting done properly. During the controlling function, the supervisor may wish to revise some goals, at which point the whole process begins again.

Of course, real-life supervisors do not spend one week planning, then one week organizing, and so on. Instead, they often carry out all the management functions during the course of a day. For example, a patient care coordinator in a hospital might start the day by checking the nurses' performance (controlling), then attend a meeting to discuss the needs of the patients (planning), and then help resolve a dispute between a nurse and a physical therapist (leading). Thus, Figure 1.3 is a very general model of managing that shows how the functions depend on one another, not how the supervisor structures his or her work.

Typically, supervisors spend most of their time leading and controlling, because they work directly with the employees who are producing or selling a product or providing support services. Planning, staffing, and organizing take up less of a supervisor's time. In contrast, higher-level managers are responsible for setting the overall direction for the organization; thus, they spend more time on planning and organizing.

Responsibilities of the Supervisor

LO1.6 ▶ Explain how supervisors are responsible to higher management, employees, and co-workers.

Dan Bobinski, director of the Center for Workplace Excellence in Boise, Idaho, recalls talking to a former secretary who had two very different supervisors. The first supervisor was extremely effective. She demonstrated concern for all the secretaries in her group, understood their work, trained them in new tasks, and then gave them wide latitude to do their jobs. Then the first supervisor left and was replaced with an inexperienced supervisor. The new supervisor was unfamiliar with the secretaries' work, but rather than admit a need to learn, she simply handed over one task after another until the exhausted and frustrated secretaries looked for jobs elsewhere. According to Bobinski, the second supervisor could have avoided this failure by taking responsibility for learning about employees, including their needs and goals, and for learning more about how to fulfill the responsibilities of a supervisor.[14]

An employee who becomes a supervisor assumes all the responsibilities listed in Table 1.2 (on the following page). In summary, though supervisors have more power than nonmanagers, they also have many responsibilities—to higher management, to employees, and to co-workers.

Types of Responsibilities

Supervisors are responsible for carrying out the duties assigned to them by higher-level managers. This includes giving managers timely and accurate information for planning. They should look for ways their group can contribute to achieving the organization's larger goals, such as reducing energy use or learning to communicate with customers using the modern technology they prefer (for example,

TABLE 1.2 |
Responsibilities of Supervisors

Sources: Nolo.com, "When You're the Boss," reprinted at www. workingwoman.com/wwn/article. jsp?contentId=513&ChannelID=210; Rona Leach, "Supervision: From Me to We," *Supervision*, February 2000, p. 8.

- Recognize the talents of each subordinate.
- Share your vision of where the organization wants to go.
- Treat employees with dignity and respect.
- Conduct necessary meetings efficiently and ensure they accomplish their intended tasks.
- Keep your staff informed and up to date.
- Be accessible to those under your supervision.
- Conduct periodic evaluations of your group's progress.
- Provide an opportunity for employees to evaluate you.
- Praise your staff for their accomplishments.
- Keep in touch with your industry.
- Be able to perform the duties of those you supervise.
- Keep a sense of humor.
- Be fair.
- Follow proper hiring practices.
- Know the law as it applies to your company and your job.
- Adhere to workplace safety rules and regulations.
- Keep accurate employee records.
- Avoid sexual harassment and discrimination based on gender, age, race, pregnancy, sexual orientation, or national origin.
- Know how to fire an employee without violating his or her rights.

video chat services like Skype or microblogs like Twitter). They also must keep their managers informed about the department's performance. Supervisors are expected to serve as a kind of linchpin, or bridge, between employees and management. Thus, their responsibilities include building morale and carrying employee concerns to the relevant managers.

Some supervisors may question the notion that they have a responsibility to their employees. After all, the employees are responsible for doing what the supervisors say. Nevertheless, because supervisors link management to the employees, the way they treat employees is crucial. Supervisors are responsible for giving their employees clear instructions and making sure they understand their jobs. They must look for problems and correct them before employees' performance deteriorates further. They also need to treat their employees fairly and speak up for their interests to top management.

Finally, supervisors are responsible for cooperating with their co-workers in other departments. They should respond promptly when a co-worker in another department requests information. They should share ideas that will help the organization's departments work together to accomplish common goals. And supervisors should listen with an open mind when co-workers in other departments make suggestions about improving the way things are done. When supervisors learn from one another's ideas, the whole organization benefits, and the supervisors have the satisfaction of working together as members of a team.

Responsibilities and Accountability

accountability
The practice of imposing penalties for failing to adequately carry out responsibilities and providing rewards for meeting responsibilities

Whatever the responsibilities of a particular supervisor, the organization holds the supervisor accountable for carrying them out. Accountability refers to the practice of imposing penalties for failing to carry out responsibilities adequately, and it usually includes giving rewards for meeting responsibilities.[15] Thus, if customer service supervisor Lydia Papadopoulos effectively teaches the telephone representatives on her staff to listen carefully to customers, the company might reward her with a raise. In contrast, a higher-level manager who gets frustrated with a supervisor who fails to provide information about what is happening in the department might eventually fire the supervisor for not carrying out this responsibility.

LO1.7 ▶ Describe the typical background of someone who is promoted to supervisor.

Becoming a Supervisor

Most supervisors start out working in the department they now supervise. Because technical skills are relatively important for first-level managers, the person selected to be supervisor is often an employee with a superior grasp of the technical skills needed to perform well in the department. The person also might have more seniority than many other department employees. Good work habits and leadership skills are also reasons for selecting an employee to be a supervisor. Sometimes a company will hire a recent college graduate to be a supervisor, perhaps because the person has demonstrated leadership potential or a specialized skill that will help in the position.

Making the shift from co-worker to supervisor can be difficult and will require human relations and conceptual skills.

Unfortunately, none of these bases for promotion or hiring guarantee that a person knows how to supervise. A hotel employee promoted to a supervisory position, for instance, might be at a loss for ways to motivate those who now report to her. Likewise, when Carol Hymowitz took on her first supervisory role as *The Wall Street Journal*'s Pittsburgh bureau chief, she had to develop her human relations skills. She recalls that in her first week on the job, an inexperienced reporter asked for feedback on her writing. Hymowitz immediately began pointing out all the areas for improvement. The reporter's expression of dismay showed Hymowitz "that if I wanted creative and hard-working employees, I needed to keep my style in check and make sure that I applauded my staff's strengths as much as I targeted their weaknesses."[16]

Becoming a supervisor marks a big change in a person's work life. The new supervisor suddenly must use more human relations and conceptual skills and devote more time to planning ahead and keeping an eye on the department's activities. Also, a change occurs in the supervisor's relationships with the employees in the department. Instead of being one of the crowd, the supervisor becomes a part of management—even the target of blame or anger when employees resent company policies. All these changes are bound to lead to some anxiety. It is natural to wonder whether you are qualified or how you will handle the problems that surely will arise.

Preparing for the Job

One way to combat the anxiety is to prepare for the job. A new supervisor can learn about management and supervision through books and observation. He or she can think about ways to carry out the role of supervisor. More important than friendliness are traits such as fairness and a focus on achieving goals. A supervisor

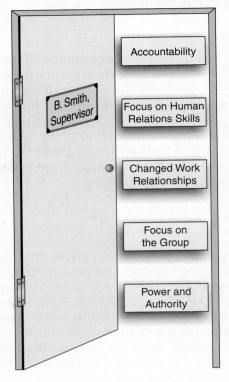

FIGURE 1.4 | What Awaits the New Supervisor?

Obtaining a supervisory position is not reaching a destination, it is the beginning of a journey that will require the use of many skills and talents, some of which may not yet be fully developed.

can also strive to learn as much as possible about the organization, the department, and the job. To see what awaits a new supervisor, refer to Figure 1.4.

Once on the job, a supervisor needs to continue the learning process. More important than understanding the layout of the workplace is learning about the employees in the department or work group. Who are the quiet but productive workers, for example, and who are the unofficial leaders? To get to know employees, a supervisor can talk to his or her own manager and read performance appraisals, but the most reliable sources of information are the employees themselves. Particularly in the early days on the job, a supervisor should take time to discuss goals with employees and observe their work habits.

A supervisor may learn that one or more employees had been candidates for the supervisor's job and therefore may be jealous. One constructive approach that a supervisor might take to this problem is to acknowledge the other person's feelings, ask for the employee's support, and discuss his or her long-term goals. An important aspect of this approach is that the supervisor is helping employees meet or exceed their own goals. For example, a sales supervisor can help a potentially jealous salesperson increase sales. Most employees will regard someone who helps them make more money as a better manager.

Obtaining and Using Power and Authority

To carry out his or her job, a supervisor needs not only knowledge but also power (the ability to do certain things) and authority (the right to do certain things). To acquire power upon assuming the job of supervisor, it may help to have the new supervisor's boss make an official announcement of the promotion. When accepting the job, a supervisor can ask his or her boss to announce the promotion at a meeting of the employees. There the supervisor can take the opportunity to state his or her expectations, desire to work as a team, and interest in hearing about work-related problems.

A new supervisor should not rush to make changes in the department but instead should first understand how the department works and what employees expect. Making changes quickly and without seeking their input can alienate employees and put them on the defensive. The supervisor can build support for change by introducing it gradually after inviting suggestions when appropriate.

For more ideas on becoming a supervisor, see "Practical Advice for Supervisors." Also, many chapters in this book will provide ideas that will help with this transition. For example, Chapter 7 discusses the delegation of authority, and Chapter 14 covers the sources and types of power, along with more information about managing change.

connect SELF-ASSESSMENT 1.1

Is Supervising Right for You?

Now that you understand a little about the scope and responsibilities of the position of supervisor, it's time to ask yourself "Is this the right position for me? Do I have what it takes to be a successful supervisor?" This assessment will help you determine whether or not you will be happy as a supervisor.

PRACTICAL ADVICE FOR SUPERVISORS

BECOMING A SUPERVISOR

Often, a new supervisor takes on his or her position as the result of a promotion. That means the supervisor's relationships with others in the department will change. How do you maintain positive working relationships with people when you are now responsible for ensuring they get their work done correctly and efficiently? Here are some suggestions for making the transition smoothly:

- *Set limits on your behavior.* Some kinds of behavior that co-workers commonly engage in—gossiping, grumbling about work, choosing friends—will interfere with your role as supervisor. Employees are counting on you to be fair and objective. If some employees expect favors based on friendship, they are not true friends.

- *Don't be a "rescuer."* Instead of jumping in to get the work done whenever a problem arises, teach the employees in your group to do the tasks you once handled. Training can be harder than doing the job yourself, but it builds a stronger work group.

- *Figure out how to measure success.* How can you tell if each person is succeeding in terms of quality, cost, and timeliness? As a supervisor, you need to see when employees are on track toward meeting their goals and when you need to step in.

- *Communicate with everyone.* Make a point of talking to each member of your work group so that you can understand each person's goals and everyone knows what your expectations are. Show employees how each person's efforts benefit the whole group.

- *Be firm.* Sometimes employees "test" a new supervisor to see if rules and standards will be enforced. If that happens, you will need to make it clear that you are serious about the whole group's success.

- *Learn from others.* Get to know other supervisors and managers who will share the wisdom gained from their experience.

Sources: Based on Brandi Britton, "Making the Move from Peer to Supervisor," *Los Angeles Business Journal*, October 10, 2005; Ed Lisoski, "From Peer to Supervisor," *Supervision*, May 2005, both downloaded from Business & Company Resource Center, http://galenet.galegroup.com. Lisa Quast, "8 Tips to Transition from Co-Worker to Manager," *Forbes*, http://www.forbes.com/sites/lisaquast/2013/09/30/8-tips-to-transition-from-co-worker-to-manager/.

LO1.8 ▶ Identify characteristics of a successful supervisor.

Characteristics of a Successful Supervisor

Unfortunately, many of us have worked for someone who seemed to stifle our best efforts or angered us with unfair decisions. Many of us also have worked for a supervisor who taught us new skills, inspired us to do better than we thought possible, or made us look forward to going to work each day. What is behind the success of this second category of supervisors? Figure 1.5 (on the following page) illustrates some characteristics of successful supervisors. Complete the Assessing Yourself exercise on pages 22–23 to see whether supervising is a good fit with your current traits and interests.

A successful supervisor has a *positive attitude*. Employees tend to reflect the attitudes of the people in charge. When the supervisor's attitude toward work, the organization, and change required by modern trends is positive, employees are more likely to be satisfied with and interested in their work. In addition, managers and co-workers prefer working with someone who has a positive attitude.

Successful supervisors are *loyal*. As a part of the management team, they must take actions that are best for the organization. This responsibility may include making decisions that are unpopular with employees. In such situations, supervisors must recognize that taking on a supervisory job means they cannot always be "one of the gang."

Successful supervisors are *fair*. Supervisors who play favorites or behave inconsistently will lose the support and respect of their employees and not be able to lead effectively. Also, when supervisors make assignments and decisions on the basis of whom they like best, they will not necessarily make the assignments and decisions best suited to the organization. Another aspect of being fair is to follow the rules yourself. The supervisor can set a good example, for instance, by being on time and refraining from doing personal tasks on the job or taking supplies home.

FIGURE 1.5 | Characteristics of a Successful Supervisor

Successful supervisors are those that bring a number of useful personal characteristics to the job or who can acquire the skills they need.

Supervisors also need to be *good communicators.*[17] Employees and bosses alike depend on the supervisor to keep them informed of what is happening. Employees who receive clear guidance about what is expected of them will not only perform better but also be more satisfied with their jobs. Good communication also includes making contact with employees each day and listening to what they have to say. Chapter 10 takes an in-depth look at the communications skills that supervisors need to develop.

To be successful, supervisors must be *able to delegate*, that is, give their employees authority and responsibility to carry out activities. Since supervisors tend to have excellent technical skills, delegating may be a challenge. They may resist giving an assignment to an employee who may not carry it out as easily or as well as they, the supervisors, could do. Nevertheless, supervisors cannot do the work of the whole department. So, they must assign work to employees. Equally important, a supervisor should give employees credit for their accomplishments. This, in turn, makes the supervisor look good; the employees' successes show that the supervisor is able to select and motivate employees as well as delegate effectively. Chapter 7 discusses delegation in greater detail.

Finally, a successful supervisor must *want the job*. Some people are happier carrying out the technical skills of their field, whether it is carpentry, respiratory therapy, or financial management. People who prefer this type of work to the functions of managing will probably be happier if they turn down an opportunity to become a supervisor. In contrast, people who enjoy the challenge of making plans and inspiring others to achieve goals are more likely to be effective supervisors.

About This Book

This book introduces the many kinds of activities supervisors must carry out to accomplish their overall objective of seeing that employees contribute toward achieving the organization's goals. Part One is devoted to a broad view of the supervisor's role. Chapter 1 serves as an introduction to the general activities and responsibilities of supervisors.

Part Two describes the challenges modern supervisors face in meeting their responsibilities. The ever higher expectations of customers, business owners, and the general public have made high quality at low cost a necessary concern of employees at all levels, including the supervisory level. Therefore, Chapter 2 addresses how supervisors can understand and carry out their role in maintaining and constantly improving quality and productivity. Chapter 3 covers groups and teamwork, reflecting the increasingly common role of the supervisor as a team leader. Supervisors (and others in the organization) also must consider the ethical implications of their decisions, the topic of Chapter 4. The value of diversity is the topic of Chapter 5.

Part Three takes a deeper look at the supervisory functions introduced in this chapter. Chapter 6 discusses how supervisors use planning and controlling to enable their work groups to reach goals and objectives. Chapter 7 covers the function of organizing, including supervisors' use of delegation to share authority and responsibility. Chapter 8 examines the supervisor's role in carrying out the management function of leading. Chapter 9 explains how supervisors can be effective at creatively solving problems and making decisions.

Part Four describes the skills needed by supervisors in all kinds of organizations. Individual chapters cover the ways supervisors can communicate, motivate their employees, supervise "problem" employees, manage time and stress, and handle conflict and change. These skills are important at all levels of management and in all types of organizations. A special appendix follows this part and emphasizes how supervisors can negotiate and handle organizational politics.

The last part of this book addresses activities related to managing the organization's human resources: its employees. Chapter 15 covers the supervisor's role in selecting new employees. Chapter 16 discusses the process of training new and current employees. Chapter 17 describes how supervisors appraise employees' performance.

Finally, an end-of-book appendix introduces some of the many government laws and regulations that guide supervisors' roles and decisions with regard to human resources. It focuses on health and safety issues, labor relations, and fair employment practices.

Throughout the book, the chapters include special features designed to help you apply the principles of supervision to the practice of supervising real people in a real organization. These features include "Practical Advice for Supervisors" and "Supervisory Skills," which discuss actual examples of modern supervisory challenges—creativity, innovation, and teamwork—as well as provide practical tips for effective supervision. "Supervision and Diversity" feature boxes demonstrate how the diverse workforce of the future is already affecting the lives of supervisors. "Supervision: New Trends" feature boxes provide examples of how contemporary trends in society and technology are shaping the supervisor's role. "Supervision and Ethics" feature boxes illustrate how supervisors are able to meet the demands of their job in an ethical manner. Each chapter opens with "A Supervision Challenge"—a case that shows how real supervisors and organizations have approached the issues covered in the chapter and solved common problems in the workplace.

An end-of-book notes section, divided by chapter, provides source and additional reading material for various topics covered within the chapters. The glossary at the end of this text provides a quick reference to all key terms. For review, each definition is followed by the number of the page where the boldfaced key term is defined.

The Skills Modules at the end of each chapter contain self-assessments, skill-building exercises, role-playing exercises, and information applications. Within this section is also a reflection back to "A Supervision Challenge" as well as an additional "Problem-Solving Case." These exercises allow you to use the concepts from the text and develop leadership abilities.

Skills Module

PART ONE: CONCEPTS

Summary

1.1 Define what a supervisor is.

A supervisor is a manager at the first level of management. That is, the employees reporting to the supervisor are not themselves managers.

1.2 Summarize research findings that have led to basic ideas of what managers should do.

Frederick Taylor showed that supervisors and other managers can improve efficiency by directing how employees carry out their work. Henri Fayol

pioneered administrative theory, which identified four management functions: planning, organizing, leading, and controlling. Abraham Maslow is among the best known of the human behavior experts who emphasized meeting employees' basic human needs.

1.3 Describe the basic types of supervisory skills.

According to the classic model, the basic supervisory skills are technical, human relations, conceptual, and decision-making skills. Technical skills are the specialized knowledge and experience used to carry out particular techniques or procedures. Human relations skills enable the supervisor to work effectively with other people. Conceptual skills enable the supervisor to see the relation of the parts to the whole and to one another. Decision-making skills are needed to analyze information and reach good decisions. A more recent model identifies skills needed to succeed in task-related, people-related, and change-related activities. These skills include clarifying roles, monitoring operations, and planning for the short-term; consulting, supporting, recognizing, developing, and empowering employees; and envisioning change, taking risks, encouraging innovative thinking, and monitoring externally.

1.4 Describe how the growing diversity of the workforce affects the supervisor's role.

Compared with the current makeup of the U.S. workforce, an increasingly large share of employees will be female, nonwhite, and older. As a result, supervisors in the future will typically manage a more diverse group of employees. This reality means that supervisors can benefit from a greater variety of talents and viewpoints, but it also requires them to draw on more sophisticated human relations skills than in the past.

1.5 Identify the general functions of a supervisor.

The general functions of a supervisor are planning, organizing, staffing, leading, and controlling. Planning involves setting goals and determining how to meet them. Organizing is determining how to set up the group, allocate resources, and assign work to achieve goals. Staffing consists of identifying, hiring, and developing the necessary number and quality of employees. Leading is the function of getting employees to do what is expected of them. Controlling consists of monitoring performance and making needed corrections.

1.6 Explain how supervisors are responsible to higher management, employees, and co-workers.

Supervisors are responsible for doing the work assigned to them by higher management and for keeping management informed of the department's progress. They link higher management to employees. Supervisors are responsible for treating employees fairly, making instructions clear, and bringing employee concerns to higher management. Supervisors also are responsible for cooperating with co-workers in other departments. Organizations hold supervisors accountable for meeting these various responsibilities.

1.7 Describe the typical background of someone who is promoted to supervisor.

Most supervisors begin as employees in the department they now supervise. They usually have superior technical skills and may have seniority or demonstrate leadership potential.

1.8 Identify characteristics of a successful supervisor.

A successful supervisor is usually someone who has a positive attitude, is loyal, is fair, communicates well, can delegate, and wants the job.

Key Terms

supervisor, *p.* 4
technical skills, *p.* 6
human relations skills, *p.* 6
conceptual skills, *p.* 6

decision-making skills, *p.* 6
planning, *p.* 10
organizing, *p.* 11
staffing, *p.* 11

leading, *p.* 11
controlling, *p.* 12
accountability, *p.* 15

Review and Discussion Questions

1. What are some ways that a supervisor's job is similar to those of managers at other levels? How does a supervisor's job differ from those of other managers?

2. Imagine that you have just been promoted to supervise the cashiers in a supermarket. List the specific technical, human relations, conceptual, and decision-making skills you think you might need to succeed at this job. How might you develop them continually to achieve the job of store manager?

3. Identify whether each of the following skills relates most to task-related, people-related, or change-related activities.

   a. The ability to communicate well with one's manager.

   b. The ability to evaluate whether sales clerks are delivering polite and timely service.

   c. The ability to plan a safety training program for the housekeeping staff.

   d. The ability to involve employees in making good scheduling decisions to accommodate their vacation preferences.

   e. The ability to see how new technology can help the department meet its goals.

   f. The ability to teach an employee how to machine a part without unnecessary changes in the setup of equipment.

4. Population trends suggest that the workforce will become increasingly diverse. What are some advantages of greater diversity? What challenges does it pose to the supervisor?

5. What are the basic functions of a supervisor? On which functions do supervisors spend most of their time?

6. What responsibilities do supervisors have to each of these groups?

   a. Higher management.

   b. The employees they supervise.

   c. Co-workers in other departments.

7. Emma has just been promoted to an office manager position in a small real estate office. Some of the people she will supervise are her former peers; she is aware that one of them also applied for the office manager's job. How can Emma prepare for her new position? What might be the best way to approach the co-worker who did not get the manager's job?

8. What are some ways a new supervisor can use power and authority effectively?

9. List the characteristics of a good supervisor. In addition to the characteristics mentioned in the chapter, add any others you believe are important. Draw on your own experiences as an employee and/or supervisor.

Notes

1. See "National Labor Relations Act," 1954, www.nlrb.gov.

2. For more about the importance of technical skill, see Sylvia Hysons, 2008, "The role of technical skill in perceptions of managerial performance," *The Journal of Management Development*, 27, p. 275.

3. Gary Yukl, Angela Gordon, and Tom Taber, "A Hierarchical Taxonomy of Leadership Behavior: Integrating a Half Century of Behavior Research," *Journal of Leadership and Organizational Studies* 9, no. 1 (Summer 2002), pp. 15–32.

4. For recent information regarding the importance of diversity in the workplace, see Ellen Curtis and Janice Dreachslin, 2008, "Integrative literature review: Diversity management interventions and organizational performance: A synthesis of current literature," 7, p. 107.

5. U.S. Census Bureau, *Statistical Abstract of the United States: 2008*, table 570, accessed at www.census.gov/compendia/statab.

6. Ibid.; and Bureau of Labor Statistics, "Employment outlook: 2010–2020: Labor force projections to 2020: a more slowly growing workforce," Table 4, http://www.bls.gov/opub/mlr/2012/01/art3full.pdf.

7. Ibid.; and Bureau of Labor Statistics, "Labor Force Statistics from the Current Population Survey: Demographics," Table 11, www.bls.gov/cps/cpsaat11.pdf, last modified February 19, 2014.

8. Ibid.; and Bureau of Labor Statistics, "Employment outlook: 2010–2020: Labor force projections to 2020: a more slowly growing workforce," Table 4, http://www.bls.gov/opub/mlr/2012/01/art3full.pdf.

9. Lisa Chiu, "The Iron Man of 4th Avenue South," *Seattle Times*, April 4, 2006, http://community.seattletimes.nwsource.com/archive/?date=20060404&slug=longtimer04.

10. Sabrina Tavernise, "Immigration to U.S., after Dip, Is Back Up," *New York Times*, December 16, 2010, http://www.nytimes.com; Chris Churchill, "Tired, Poor No Longer," *Times Union (Albany, NY)*, June 19, 2011, http://www.timesunion.com; and Matthew Hall, Audrey Singer, Gordon F. De Jong, and Deborah Roempke Graefe, "The Geography of Immigrant Skills: Educational Profiles of Metropolitan Areas," Brookings Institution, *State of Metropolitan America*, no. 34, June 9, 2011, http://www.brookings.edu.

11. Robert Boyer, "Workers Reflect on 25 Years of Honda," *Times-News (Burlington, NC)*, June 8, 2008, downloaded from Business & Company Resource Center, http://galenet.galegroup.com.

12. For more information about the ramifications of subtle discrimination, see Sik Hung Ng, 2007, "Language-based discrimination: Blatant and subtle forms," *Journal of Language and Social Psychology*, 26, p. 106.

13. Tracey E. Schelmetic, "Fairness: An Underestimated Principle in the Call Center," *Customer Interaction Solutions*, May 2008, http://www.thefreelibrary.com/Fairness%3A+an+underestimated+principle+in+the+call+center.-a0179705558.

14. Dan Bobinski, "Young Managers Must Compensate for Less Experience," *Idaho Business Review*, August 2, 2011, http://idahobusinessreview.com/2011/08/02/young-managers-must-compensate-for-less-experience/.

15. For further information about the importance of accountability, see Angela Hall, Michael Bowen, Gerald Ferris, Todd Royle, and Dale Fitzgibbons, 2007, "The accountability lens: A new way to view management issues," *Business Horizons*, p. 405.

16. Carol Hymowitz, "Effective Management Remains an Art Steeped in Good Relationships," *The Wall Street Journal*, August 11, 2008, http://online.wsj.com.

17. For more information related to the importance of effective communication, see Paul Nelissen and Marine van Selm, 2008, "Surviving organizational change: How management communication helps balance mixed feelings," *Corporate Communications*, 13, p. 306.

PART TWO: SKILL-BUILDING

Meeting the Challenge

Reflecting back to page 3, consider some of your own experiences shopping in grocery stores. Did you notice any actions that made your shopping trip smoother or more pleasant? What would you suggest the store change about its supervisors' responsibilities? How could interacting with supervisors at your store and supervisors like those at Wegmans affect your impression of the stores and the likelihood that you would shop there again? With your group, come up with a list of tasks beyond those mentioned in the example on page 3 that you feel a supervisor should be responsible for completing or overseeing.

Problem-Solving Case: Refereeing the Referees of the Atlantic Coast Conference

When basketball teams from Duke, Georgia Tech, and the other 13 members of the Atlantic Coast Conference (ACC) play, most eyes are on the players and the scoreboard. Some avid fans also watch the referees, sometimes challenging their calls. Few would notice one important observer: John Clougherty, supervisor of the ACC's officials.

To carry out his job, Clougherty attends dozens of games every season and watches the rest on DVDs at home. At the ready is a legal pad, on which he takes notes about the number of fouls called on each team and data about particular calls he needs to discuss later with individual officials. When they make a mistake, Clougherty lets them know right after the game. In fact, quick feedback is one of this supervisor's priorities. Right after he became supervisor, he began requiring that each game be recorded on DVD and that a disc be delivered to the officials minutes after the end of the game. If there is a disagreement about a call and Clougherty is at the game, he might review the recording immediately with the officials. The information also helps him communicate effectively with team coaches.

Clougherty uses his DVD recordings as an important resource for teaching the referees. Occasionally, they also provide a record in support of disciplinary actions. For example, during a game between Florida State and Duke, a crew of officials improperly called a technical foul on a Florida State basketball player and then failed to review the play on the courtside monitor. Clougherty responded with a suspension.

In addition to training and discipline, Clougherty is also responsible for hiring. He has brought several new officials to ACC games. For his hiring expertise, he draws on his extensive experience: "After 30 years [as a college referee], I think I have a pretty good eye for talent." In fact, he has plenty of firsthand experience. During those 30 years of officiating, Dougherty worked at a dozen Final Four games and four national title games.

1. Which supervisory skills seem to be most important to Clougherty's job? Why?
2. What types of responsibilities does he undertake?
3. How important do you think Clougherty's experience as a referee was in preparing him to be a supervisor? Other than that work experience, what experiences and qualities do you think would be important for someone to succeed in Clougherty's job? Do those experiences and qualities apply to most supervisory jobs?

Sources: Ed Miller, "ACC Official Supervisor, a Relatively Thankless Job" (Norfolk, Va.) *The Virginian-Pilot*, March 6, 2006, http://hamptonroads.com/2006/03/acc-official-supervisor-relatively-thankless-job, accessed February 27, 2014.

Assessing Yourself

Is Supervising Right for You?

Answer each of the following questions Yes or No.

	Yes	No
1. Do you consider yourself a highly ambitious person?	___	___
2. Do you sincerely like people and have patience with them?	___	___
3. Could you assume the responsibility of decision making?	___	___
4. Is making more money very important to you?	___	___

5. Would recognition from others be more important to you than taking pride in doing a detailed job well? ____ ____

6. Would you enjoy learning about psychology and human behavior? ____ ____

7. Would you be happier with more responsibility? ____ ____

8. Would you rather work with problems involving human relationships than with mechanical, computational, creative, clerical, or similar problems? ____ ____

9. Do you desire an opportunity to demonstrate your leadership ability? ____ ____

10. Do you desire the freedom to do your own planning rather than being told what to do? ____ ____

Total ____ ____

Give yourself 1 point for each Yes answer. If your score is 6 or more, you might be happy as a supervisor. If your score was 5 or less, you should think hard about your preferences and strengths before jumping into a supervisory job.

Source: From *Supervisor's Survival Kit: Your First Step*, by Elwood N. Chapman. Copyright © 1993 Pearson Education Inc. Reprinted by permission of Pearson Education Inc., Upper Saddle River, NJ.

Class Skills Exercise

Recognizing Management Skills

Which of the five management functions would you rely on in each of the following situations? Discuss your choices in class.

1. One of your employees is chronically late for work.
2. Your department has switched to a new e-mail service, and some people are having difficulty making the change.
3. Your manager has asked you to have your staff complete a special project without incurring any overtime.
4. It is time to prepare your department's budget for the coming year.
5. Your team's productivity is not meeting the standards the team set.

Building Supervision Skills

Defining Your Role as Supervisor

Instructions

1. Imagine you are the supervisor in each scenario described below, and you must decide which supervisory function(s) you would use in each.
2. Many of the scenarios require more than one function. The "Answers" column lists the number of functions your answer should include. Mark your answers using the following codes:

Code	Supervisory Function	Brief Description
P	Planning	Setting goals and determining how to meet them
O	Organizing	Determining how to set up the group, allocate resources, and assign work to achieve goals
S	Staffing	Identifying, hiring, and developing the necessary number and quality of employees
L	Leading	Getting employees to do what is expected of them
C	Controlling	Monitoring performance and making needed corrections

3. As a class, compare and discuss your answers and the reasoning you used in determining them.

Scenarios

Your group's work is centered on a project that is due in two months. Although everyone is working on the project, you believe that your subordinates are involved in excessive socializing and other time-consuming behaviors. You decide to meet with the group to have the members help you break down the project into smaller subprojects with mini deadlines. You believe that this will help keep the group members focused on the project and that the quality of the finished project will then reflect the true capabilities of your group.

Your first impression of the new group you will be supervising is not too great. You tell your friend at dinner after your first day on the job: "Looks like I got a babysitting job instead of a supervisory job."

Your boss asks your opinion about promoting Andy to a supervisory position. Andy is one of your most competent and efficient workers. Knowing that Andy lacks leadership skills in many key areas, you decide not to recommend him at this time. Instead you tell your boss you will work with Andy to help him develop his leadership skills so that the next time an opportunity for promotion occurs, Andy will be prepared to consider it.

You begin a meeting of your work group by letting the members know that a major procedure the group has been using for the past two years is being significantly revamped. Your department will have to phase in the change during the next six weeks. You proceed by explaining the reasoning management gave you for this change. You then say, "Take the next 5 to 10 minutes to voice your reactions to this change." The majority of comments are critical of the change. You say, "I appreciate each of you sharing your reactions; I, too, recognize that all change creates problems. However, either we can spend the remaining 45 minutes of our meeting focusing on why we don't want the change and why we don't think it's necessary, or we can work together to come up with viable solutions to solve the problems that implementing this change will most likely create." After five more minutes of an exchange of comments, the consensus of the group is that they should spend the remainder of the meeting focusing on how to deal with the potential problems that may arise from implementing the new procedure.

You are preparing the annual budget allocation meetings to be held in the plant manager's office next week. You decide to present a strong case to support your department's request for money for some high-tech equipment that will help your employees do their jobs better. You will stand firm against any suggestions of budget cuts in your area.

Early in your career you learned an important lesson about employee selection. One of the nurses on your floor unexpectedly quit. The other nurses pressured you to fill the position quickly because they were overworked even before the nurse left. After a hasty recruitment effort, you made a decision based on insufficient information. You regretted your quick decision during the three months of problems that followed, until you finally had to discharge the new hire. Since that time, you have never let anybody pressure you into making a quick hiring decision.

Source: This team-building exercise was prepared by Corinne Livesay, Bryan College, Chattanooga, Tennessee.

Answers

(four functions)
1. _____

(three functions)
2. _____

(one function)
3. _____

(three functions)
4. _____

(one function)
5. _____

(two functions)
6. _____

Building Supervision Skills

Leading a Team

In Chapter 1 ("Supervision: Tradition and Contemporary Trends"), you learned two ways to categorize the different skills that supervisors use to decide which skills apply in any given situation. Here, you will apply your knowledge of the classic skill categories to several team-building situations.

Instructions

Imagine that you are the supervisor in each of the following situations. Decide which of the following skills will best help you build a team: technical, human relations, conceptual, decision making. Each situation requires more than one skill.

1. As the supervisor of a group of production workers in a plant that manufactures parts for wind turbines, you have been asked by upper management to join a team of supervisors from different departments. Your objective will be to investigate ways to improve the time required to fill large orders from major customers. Which two skills do you think will be most important to you on this team?

2. You supervise 20 telephone operators on the night shift for an online store. You used to be an operator yourself, so you know a great deal about the job. Management has been pressing you and other supervisors to reduce the amount of time operators spend on the telephone for each order. You believe that a potentially negative situation for your employees can be solved with a friendly competition between two teams of operators. There are no punishments for the team that comes in second, but there is a reward for the team that wins. Team members are encouraged to find new ways to reduce telephone time without reducing customer satisfaction. Which two skills do you think would be most important as you get your teams up and running?

3. You are a supervisor in the engineering department and a member of a team that includes people from production, finance, marketing, and engineering. After conducting marketing research, your team must determine whether to recommend that your company expand its operations overseas. Which three skills do you think would be most important in your contribution to the team?

chapter two | Ensuring High Quality and Productivity

learning objectives

After you have studied this chapter, you should be able to:

2.1 Describe the consequences suffered by organizations as a result of poor-quality work.

2.2 Compare product quality control and process control.

2.3 Summarize techniques for quality control.

2.4 Identify ways organizations measure their success in continuous quality improvement.

2.5 Identify constraints on productivity.

2.6 Describe how productivity and productivity improvements are measured.

2.7 Identify ways productivity may be improved.

2.8 Explain why employees have fears about productivity improvement and how supervisors can address those fears.

A Supervision Challenge

CONTRIBUTING TO HIGH QUALITY AND PRODUCTIVITY AT SHEARER'S FOODS

If you've ever picked up your supermarket's private-label pretzels or tortilla chips, the snacks you enjoyed might well have been made by Shearer's Foods in its Ohio factories. If so, those snacks came from a company that wants to deliver nothing short of perfection to its own employees, its consumers, and the stores where they shop. That expectation is expressed in the company's slogan, "Shearer Perfection in Every Bag." Shearer's interprets "perfection" widely: perfection in its products, in marketing and distribution support for stores, and in a corporate culture dedicated to the well-being of employees, their community, and the environment.

Shearer's continually adopts new procedures and technologies in efforts to ensure this high quality. Computer systems on the production lines provide a constant flow of data. Statistical readouts on touch screens display quality measures from a variety of sensors. For each production job scheduled, operators check a screen that uses images of a ticking alarm clock to specify which tasks are required for start-up, quality checks, and other procedures, as well as when each task must be completed. If a problem arises, the system notifies the responsible technician or supervisor, so that person can address the problem right away. Employees responsible for machinery keep abreast of operations by checking computer monitors displaying green icons for normal operation, blue for idle equipment, and red for problems such as a test that hasn't been performed.

The commitment to quality is inseparable from the company's drive to minimize costs and waste. After all, avoiding errors and problems in production will also eliminate costs associated with discarding substandard products. Shearer's regularly brings together employees to figure out how to improve processes by cutting out unnecessary activities, allowing for discussion opportunities and collaboration. And Shearer's takes its commitment to efficiency a step further than many other snack food producers by committing to environmental sustainability—that is, keeping energy consumption and resource use to the lowest possible levels. For example, in building its latest manufacturing facility, Shearer's looked for the highest-efficiency ovens and used chimneys that capture heat and recycle it into the plant's heating system and into heating water for cooking the corn used to make tortilla chips. The building also collects rainwater for flushing toilets.

In a company with these standards, supervisors and their employees are driven to constantly learn and improve. The requirements for a supervisory job at Shearer's Foods are extensive. Along with applying communications and problem-solving skills, production supervisors at Shearer's must be able to use knowledge of mathematics and statistics to meet goals for quality and efficiency. The company also looks for candidates who have experience with using computer technology and the latest techniques for ensuring high quality and productivity.

Keeping employees committed to maintaining perfection comes with its own challenges. Some employees may worry that constant improvements in quality and productivity could result in staff reductions. This concern is certainly warranted since the computer monitoring of production does minimize the number of employees needed to run the modern production lines. However, through dedication to perfection, sales will rise, providing the company with opportunities to expand its employee network. In fact, the growth of Shearer's productivity has led to increases in hiring, not firing. Still, the demands on supervisors remain.

1. Is this company's commitment to quality realistic? Explain.

2. How can supervisors get employees excited about constant improvement when change is hard?

Sources: Kevin T. Higgins, "Shearer's Foods Rethinks the Food Plant," *Food Engineering,* April 2011, pp. 33–48; Marina Mayer, "LEED-ing the Way," *Snack Food & Wholesale Bakery,* February 2011, pp. 26–32; Shearer's Foods, "About Us" and "Careers," http://www.shearersfoodsinc.com, accessed April 2, 2014.

TABLE 2.1|Dimensions of Quality

Source: Adapted from David A. Garvin, "Competing on the Eight Dimensions of Quality," *Harvard Business Review,* November–December 1987.

Dimension	Explanation
Performance	The product's primary operating characteristic, such as an automobile's acceleration or the picture clarity of a television set
Features	Supplements to the product's basic operating characteristics—for example, power windows on a car or the ceremony with which a bottle of wine is opened in a restaurant
Reliability	The probability that the product will function properly and not break down during a specified period; a manufacturer's warranty is often seen as an indicator of reliability
Conformance	The degree to which the product's design and operating characteristics meet established standards, such as safety standards for a baby's crib
Durability	The length of the product's life—for example, whether a stereo lasts for 5 years or 25 years
Serviceability	The speed and ease of repairing the product—for example, whether a computer store will send out a repairperson, service the computer in the store, or provide no maintenance service at all
Aesthetics	The way the product looks, feels, tastes, and smells, such as the styling and smell of a new car
Perceived quality	The customer's impression of the product's quality, such as a buyer's belief that an Audi is a safe and reliable car

Shearer's Foods seeks "perfection" by hiring employees and supervisors who "understand, appreciate, and share our commitment to continued and advancing excellence." And the company looks for ways to use its people, energy, and other resources as efficiently as possible. At Shearer's Foods and other companies, supervisors have a major role in helping keep quality high and costs low.

This chapter looks at the supervisor's role in ensuring high quality and productivity. Quality has different meanings depending on the kind of business and the customers served. However, a logical way to understand the meaning of *high quality* is to think of it as work that meets or exceeds customers' expectations. Table 2.1 describes eight possible measures for the quality of goods or services. **Productivity** is the amount of results (output) an organization gets for a given amount of inputs (see Figure 2.1). Thus, productivity can refer to the amount of acceptable work employees do for each dollar they earn or the number of acceptable products manufactured with a given amount of resources.

productivity
The amount of results (output) an organization gets for a given amount of inputs

Many of the supervisor's activities, including planning, leading, and controlling are directed toward improving quality and productivity. This chapter considers the supervisor's role in making these improvements. It begins with a description of the consequences of poor quality and then introduces types of quality-control efforts. The chapter explains how managers at all levels can measure whether they are improving quality and meeting high-quality standards. Next, this chapter takes a deeper look at the meaning and measurement of productivity. It concludes by describing ways that supervisors can participate in efforts to improve productivity.

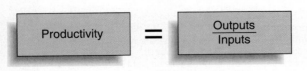

FIGURE 2.1 | The Productivity Formula

A simple way of visualizing productivity is as a formula in which it is equal to the output achieved for a given amount of input.

Consequences of Poor Quality

Like employees at all levels, supervisors must care about quality. They must care because poor quality limits the organization's access to resources and raises its costs.

Limited Resources

When the quality of an organization's goods or services is poor, the whole organization suffers. As word spreads about problems with the product, customers look for alternatives. The organization develops a negative image, which drives away customers and clients. The organization loses business and therefore revenues, and it also has more difficulty attracting other important resources. An organization with a poor reputation has a harder time recruiting superior employees and borrowing money at favorable terms.

The goal of call centers is to provide immediate customer service, but many companies are finding out that this is only successful when the employees taking calls are properly trained and supported.

Many firms know that the potential for lost business is a major reason to invest in quality. Dell established itself as a market leader by selling high-quality computers at a low cost, thanks to its efficient operations. Unfortunately, the drive to be efficient began to move the company away from customer satisfaction. In particular, many customers became frustrated with Dell's call centers. One reason: Many service reps were trained to solve only one category of a problem, so almost 45 percent of calls had to be transferred from the agent who answered the call to someone with the knowledge needed to help the customer. Richard L. Hunter, brought in to improve Dell's customer service, called the situation "terrible," explaining that it was comparable to "delivering materials to the wrong factory 45 percent of the time." Worse, to slow the tide of calls from customers, Dell tried removing its toll-free service number from its Web site. Customers' reactions showed up in Dell's declining market share and slumping customer satisfaction ratings. To improve the situation, Hunter borrowed factory methods such as giving each call center employee a colored flag to raise whenever he or she needs help, along with training to equip service reps to solve a wider range of problems.[1] Today, Dell runs a "lean" call center, which you will learn more about later.

Higher Costs

Poor-quality work can also lead to high costs. Some managers might think it is expensive to ensure that things are done right the first time. But the reality is that businesses spend billions of dollars each year on inspections, errors, rework, repairs, customer refunds, and other costs to find and correct mistakes. Attracting new customers costs several times more per customer than keeping existing customers satisfied, so marketing costs are higher too. Thus, poor quality often results in much wasted time and materials, in addition to requiring that unacceptable items be fixed or discarded. If the problems remain undetected until after the goods have been sold, the manufacturer may have to recall its products for repair or replacement. In addition, poor goods and services may result in lawsuits by disgruntled or injured customers.

Unfortunately, sometimes companies feel so much pressure to boost profits by reducing costs that they trim quality-control efforts, only to suffer major costs of poor quality. In a 15-month period, Johnson & Johnson issued more than 11 major product recalls covering products as varied as contact lenses, hip implants, and contaminated batches of popular drugs including Tylenol, Benadryl, and Zyrtec. In addition, families of a group of women who died while using a birth-control patch made by J&J filed a lawsuit against the company. Besides bearing the lost sales, legal costs, and administrative costs (the artificial-hip recall alone was said to cost hundreds of millions of dollars), J&J took a huge hit to its reputation for being a company that consumers could trust with their health and their children's well-being. Former J&J insiders blamed management, telling reporters that J&J had lost sight of its past commitment to putting quality control ahead of costs.[2]

Also costly, in terms of money, damaged reputations, and harm to consumers, have been problems with tainted products from food manufacturers. For example, reports of salmonella bacteria in serrano and jalapeño peppers in 2008 frightened U.S. consumers (as the illness itself sickened more than 1,400) and caused restaurants around the nation to cancel orders for produce. That same year, the United States witnessed its largest-ever recall of beef: 143 million pounds suspected of contamination with *E. coli* bacteria. As companies obtain more of their ingredients from overseas and use a wider variety of additives, keeping track of the food supply's quality becomes a difficult challenge. But when a mistake can send people to the hospital, companies cannot afford to let quality slide.[3]

Types of Quality Control

LO2.2 ▶ Compare product quality control and process control.

quality control
An organization's efforts to prevent or correct defects in its goods or services or to improve them in some way

Because of the negative consequences of poor quality, organizations try to prevent and correct such problems through various approaches to quality control. Broadly speaking, **quality control** refers to an organization's efforts to prevent or correct defects in its goods or services or to improve them in some way. Some organizations use the term *quality control* to refer only to error detection, whereas *quality assurance* refers to both the prevention and the detection of quality problems. However, this chapter uses *quality control* in the broader sense because it is the more common term.

Whichever term is used, many organizations—especially large ones—have a department or employee devoted to identifying defects and promoting high quality. In these cases, the supervisor can benefit from the expertise of quality-control personnel. Ultimately, however, the organization expects its supervisors to take responsibility for the quality of work in their departments.

In general, when supervisors look for high-quality performance to reinforce or improvements to make, they can focus on two areas: the *product* itself or the *process* of making and delivering the product. Figure 2.2 illustrates these two orientations.

Product Quality Control

product quality control
Quality control that focuses on ways to improve the product itself

An organization that focuses on ways to improve the product itself is using **product quality control**. For example, employees in a print shop might examine a sample of newsletters or envelopes to look for smudges and other defects. A city's park district might consider ways to upgrade its playground equipment or improve the programs it offers senior citizens.

Computer technology can greatly improve product quality control. Morton Metalcraft Co. of Morton, Illinois, makes sheet-metal components for farm and industrial vehicles such as John Deere backhoes. Morton employees work with a computer system that uses digital photos, drawings, and key dimensions of products to create software routines for checking the quality of the entire product and its subsections. To cope with last-minute design changes by customers, Morton has programmed the system with customized routines that enable a change in

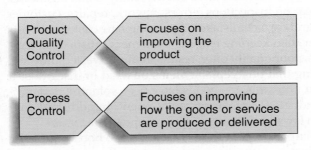

FIGURE 2.2 | Types of Quality Control

To improve quality, a supervisor can choose to focus on the product, the process, or both.

SUPERVISION: NEW TRENDS

HADRONICS GIVES SUPERVISORS IPADS FOR BETTER PROCESS CONTROL

In recent years, computers have been shrinking, which makes them more practical for supervisors whose jobs keep them moving to be near employees. For example, at Hadronics' Cincinnati, Ohio, factory, the four production supervisors carry iPad tablet computers so they can spot and troubleshoot problems before defects or downtime result.

The decision to buy iPads for supervisors came after the company had struggled to help them share information. Hadronics makes precision, customized parts for printing equipment. Depending on a particular customer's needs, parts travel through some combination of processes in the grinding and finishing department and the plating department. One supervisor oversees each of those departments, supported by a machinery supervisor and a quality control supervisor. To fulfill orders on time and without defects, they need to coordinate activities with each other and with the details of each work order and the status of the needed machinery. But most of the time, the supervisors were working away from each other and from any employees who needed help. Time was lost as supervisors and employees spent much of the day hunting for each other. Employees were reluctant to report problems because they didn't want to leave their posts to find their supervisor.

One source of this difficulty, ironically, was that supervisors were distracted by the computer information system that was delivering performance data. The shop control software reported part specifications, machine status, and schedules for work processes, but the information was sent to the supervisors' computers at their desks. Whenever supervisors wanted to look up or enter information, they had to leave the area where the work was taking place in order to use their computers. When the supervisors or employees ran into problems, they would shout to one another across the room, often misinterpreting messages and making errors as a result.

Hadronics initially tried a low-tech solution that involved signal flags, but the supervisors often missed flags, and employees hated to draw attention to their problems in such a visible way. So the company investigated ways to make the computerized performance data more portable. Smart phones are portable, but their screens are too small for this type of application. So Hadronics tried giving an iPad to the supervisor of its grinding and finishing department. Before long, he was so efficient in staying on top of situations in his department that the company bought iPads for the other three supervisors. Now they spot, diagnose, and fix problems right on the shop floor. Employees no longer overlook inspections, products ship on time, and when processes result in quality problems, supervisors change them on the spot so the issues do not recur.

Sources: Based on Emily Probst, "iPads Keep Supervisors on the Shop Floor," *Modern Machine Shop,* April 18, 2011, http://www.mmsonline.com/articles/ipads-keep-supervisors-on-the-shop-floor, accessed March 11, 2014.

as little as five minutes. The system has cut inspection time too. Inspecting the cab of a John Deere backhoe used to take two operators 4.5 hours; now one operator can do it in less than 45 minutes.[4]

Process Control

process control
Quality control that emphasizes how to do things in a way that leads to better quality

An organization might also consider how to do things in a way that leads to better quality. This focus is called **process control**. The print shop, for example, might conduct periodic checks to make sure its employees understand good techniques for setting up the presses. The park district might ask the maintenance crew to suggest ways to keep the parks cleaner and more attractive. In this way, the park district can improve the process by which the crew members do their job.

As with product quality control, process control can be improved with the use of computer technology. For an example of how one company has improved quality by using modern computer applications to streamline processes, see "Supervision: New Trends."

A broad approach to process control involves creating an organizational climate that encourages quality. From the day they are hired, employees at all levels should understand that quality is important and that they have a role in delivering high quality. In the city park district example, managers and employees might consider ways to be more responsive to citizens' input. The greater responsiveness, in turn, could enable park district employees to recognize ways to serve the community better.

Process control techniques can be very effective. At Accurate Gauge and Manufacturing, based in Rochester Hills, Michigan, process control is an important part of the company's efforts to plan for quality and correct the causes of defects in the precision parts it manufactures for heavy equipment and commercial and automotive vehicles. Quality teams meet weekly to prevent problems, but some process improvements are responses to problems. Even when a failure occurred in a product line the company was preparing to phase out, engineering manager Mark Tario led efforts to correct the process by setting up procedures for operators to check both pressure and position simultaneously as the parts were being produced. In addition to impressing the customer with this extreme commitment to quality, the effort established a process that became the standard procedure for making other defect-free parts.[5]

<table>
<tr><td>**LO2.3** ▶ Summarize techniques for quality control.</td><td colspan="2"># Methods for Improving Quality</td></tr>
</table>

Within this broad framework, managers, researchers, and consultants have identified several methods for ensuring and improving quality. Today most organizations apply some or all of these methods, including statistical quality control, the zero-defects approach, employee involvement teams, Six Sigma, lean process improvement, and total quality management. Table 2.2 summarizes these techniques.

In choosing a method—or, more commonly, applying the methods selected by higher-level management—supervisors must remember that a technique alone does not guarantee high quality. Rather, quality-control processes work when the people who use them are well motivated, understand how to use them, and exercise creativity in solving problems. Providence Health & Services, a hospital in Burbank, California, increased employee understanding and motivation by involving them in deciding how to improve quality of care. In the pharmacy department, staff members planned how to reduce errors in filling prescriptions. By studying performance measures, they determined that the biggest cause of mistakes was distractions resulting from cluttered workspaces and people wandering into the

TABLE 2.2 | Quality Improvement Methods

Statistical quality control	Looking for defects in outcomes selected through a sampling technique
Statistical process control	Using statistics to monitor production quality during the production process
Zero-defects approach	All employees delivering such high quality that goods and services are free of problems
Employee involvement teams	Setting up teams of employees to identify and solve quality-related problems
Six Sigma	Using a formal process in which teams study processes and correct problems to limit defects to 3.4 per million operations
Lean process improvement	A practice that considers any costs other than a cost that adds value for the customer to be wasteful and, hence, something to be eliminated
Total quality management	Focusing the whole organization on continuously improving every business process so it satisfies customers

Setting and maintaining procedures and expectations enable pharmacists to stay organized and efficient.

pharmacy. The pharmacy staff rearranged the work area to reduce clutter, set specific hours for visitors, and developed new procedures for picking up prescriptions. Two months later, a review of performance measures indicated that medication errors had plunged 47 percent.[6] Showing employees that quality procedures make a measurable difference is another important way to build support for quality control.

Statistical Quality and Process Control

It rarely makes economic sense to examine every part, finished good, or service to ensure it meets quality standards. For one thing, that approach to quality control is expensive. In addition, examining some products, such as packages of cheese or boxes of tissues, can destroy them. As a result, unless the costs of poor quality are so great that every product must be examined, most organizations inspect only a sample. Looking for defects in parts, finished goods, or other outcomes selected through a sampling technique is known as **statistical quality control**.

statistical quality control
Looking for defects in parts or finished products selected through a sampling technique

The most accurate way to apply statistical quality control is to use a random sample. This means selecting outcomes (such as parts or customer contacts) in a way that each has an equal chance of being selected. The assumption is that the quality of the sample describes the quality of the entire lot. Thus, if 2 percent of the salad dressing bottles in a sample have leaks, presumably 2 percent of all the bottles coming off the assembly line have leaks. Or if 65 percent of customers surveyed report they were treated courteously, presumably about 65 percent of all customers feel that way.

statistical process control (SPC)
A quality-control technique using statistics to monitor production quality on an ongoing basis and making corrections whenever the results show the process is out of control

Rather than wait until a process is complete to take a random sample, the operators of a process can use statistics to monitor production quality on an ongoing basis. This quality-control technique is known as **statistical process control (SPC)**. The operator periodically measures some aspect of what he or she is producing—say, the diameter of a hole drilled or the correctness of an account number entered into a computer—then plots the results on a control chart such as the simplified one shown in Figure 2.3. The middle line in the chart shows the value that represents the standard—in this case, the mean (average). Above and below the mean value are lines representing the acceptable upper and lower limits. When a measured value falls between these limits, the operator may assume the process is working normally. When a value falls outside these limits, the operator can take steps to correct the process.[7] SPC gives the operator great control over maintaining quality, so quality control does not need to be assigned to specialized personnel. That is one reason SPC is popular today, especially in manufacturing firms.

In summary, statistical quality control is the application of statistical and analytical tools to monitor the outputs of a process. Statistical process control, on the other hand, is the application of statistical and analytical tools to control the inputs of a process.

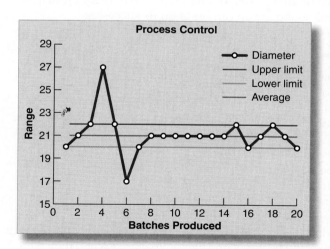

FIGURE 2.3 | Chart of Statistical Process Control
With statistical process control, as long as the process stays within set limits, no action is required. When the process exceeds a limit, then changes are made to the process inputs to bring the process back within the limits.

Zero-Defects Approach

A broad view of process quality control is that everyone in the organization should work toward the goal of

zero-defects approach
A quality-control technique based on the view that everyone in the organization should work toward the goal of delivering such high quality that all aspects of the organization's goods and services are free of problems

delivering such high quality that all aspects of the organization's goods and services are free of problems. The quality-control technique based on this view is known as the **zero-defects approach.** An organization that uses the zero-defects approach provides products of excellent quality not only because the people who produce them are seeking ways to avoid defects but also because the purchasing department is ensuring a timely supply of well-crafted parts or supplies, the accounting department is seeing that bills get paid on time, the human resources department is helping find and train highly qualified personnel, and so on.

Thus, in implementing a zero-defects approach, managers and employees at all levels seek to build quality into every aspect of their work. Employees work with supervisors and other managers to set goals for quality and identify areas where improvement is needed. Management is responsible for communicating the importance of quality to the whole organization and rewarding high-quality performance.

Employee Involvement Teams

employee involvement teams
Teams of employees who plan ways to improve quality in their areas of organization

Recognizing that the people who perform a process have knowledge based on their experiences, many organizations directly involve employees in planning how to improve quality. Many companies set up **employee involvement teams** such as quality circles, problem-solving teams, process improvement teams, or self-managed work groups. The typical employee involvement team consists of up to 10 employees and their supervisor, who serves as the team leader. In this role, the supervisor schedules meetings, prepares agendas, and promotes the participation and cooperation of team members. (The next chapter describes general principles of teams, including the role of the team leader.)

The team meets periodically, usually at least once or twice a month for an hour or two during the workday. At these meetings, participants examine areas where quality needs improvement, and they develop solutions. The problems discussed may be identified by management or operative employees. In either case, the problems should be related to the employees' everyday work, because this is where they have the greatest expertise. In a typical process, the members of the team might take the following steps (see Figure 2.4 on the following page):

1. Identify quality problems related to the employees' areas of responsibility.
2. Select the problems to focus on first. A newly formed group may find it helpful to focus on simple problems so the group can build on its successes.
3. Analyze the problem to identify its causes.
4. Identify possible solutions and select one to recommend to management.

Depending on the organization's policies, one or more managers usually must approve the recommendations of the employee involvement team. Once a recommendation is approved, the appropriate people in the organization must implement it. The team should follow up on the implementation to ensure that the problem actually was solved.

Quality and productivity have steadily improved at General Cable Corporation's factory in Moose Jaw, Saskatchewan, Canada, through the efforts of employee teams. Production teams seek improvements in costs and quality, saving the company hundreds of thousands of dollars a year. On the basis of their firsthand experience, production workers can identify solutions as simple as adjusting the running speeds for machinery. For example, slowing the speed of the factory's triple extrusion process cut scrap costs in half. Ray Funke, the facility's production manager when they were named as one of *Industry Week's* Best Plants, credited employee participation and the free flow of information with the company's successes. All of General Cable's employees receive data about production and financial performance so that they can identify problems and see the impact of solutions. Said Funke, "People leave here [at the end of the day] thinking there's something we can improve on."[8]

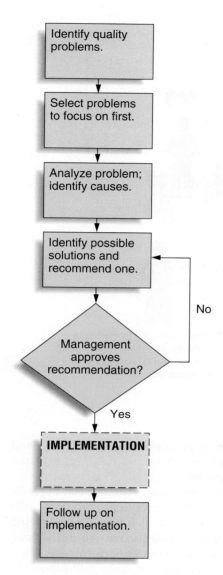

FIGURE 2.4 | Typical Procedure for an Employee Involvement Team

The general steps for an employee involvement team include identifying the problem, the causes of the problem, and possible solutions to the problem.

Six Sigma
A process-oriented quality-control method designed to improve the product or service output to 99.9997 percent perfect

As at General Cable, employee involvement teams are most likely to succeed if supervisors apply the principles of problem solving (described in Chapter 9) and the guidelines for supervising groups (discussed in Chapter 3). In addition, successful teams typically have the characteristics shown in Figure 2.5 on the following page. Employee involvement teams must have support from supervisors and higher-level managers, and the participants should have the skills necessary to contribute. To get the group off to a good start, the organization should provide training at the first meeting or meetings. Skills to teach might include problem-solving techniques, approaches to quality improvement, and methods for leading a group discussion and encouraging participation. Finally, employee involvement teams are most successful when all group members are eager to participate. For that reason, it is a good idea to make membership in the team voluntary.

Six Sigma

Applying the terminology and methods of statistical quality control and the strong commitment of the zero-defects approach, manufacturers and other companies have used a quality-control method they call **Six Sigma**. This is a process-oriented quality-control method designed to reduce errors to 3.4 defects per 1 million *operations,* which can be defined as any unit of work, such as an hour of labor, completion of a circuit board, a sales transaction, or a keystroke. (*Sigma* is a statistical term defining how much variation there is in a product. In the context of quality control, to achieve a level of six sigma, the output of operations would be 99.9997 percent perfect.) Along with the basic goal of reducing variation from the standard to almost nothing, Six Sigma programs typically include a rigorous analytical process for anticipating and solving problems to reduce defects, improve the yield of acceptable products, increase customer satisfaction, and deliver best-in-class organizational performance. These improvements, in turn, boost profits.[9]

In the mid-1980s Motorola became the first U.S. company to institute a large-scale Six Sigma program, and the firm now teaches Six Sigma concepts and courses to other organizations. General Electric also offers its customers high-level instruction in Six Sigma methods. GE's first effort, undertaken by GE Medical Systems, brought the quality program to a handful of health care customers and resulted in more than $94 million in benefits.[10] McKesson, which provides the health care industry with medicines, supplies, and information technology services, has used Six Sigma to improve the way its accounts receivable department collects payments from customers.[11]

Six Sigma is highly structured and emphasizes costs and profits.[12] An organization forms process improvement teams and trains employees to become Black Belts, who act as liaisons with upper management. The Black Belts, who are usually well-regarded and technically competent product or line personnel, help the teams define problems, measure defects, use statistics to analyze the reasons for defects, set priorities, develop and test a plan to solve each problem, and institute ongoing control measures to keep the problem from coming back.

Lean Enterprise Philosophy

The lean enterprise philosophy, sometimes also called lean manufacturing or lean production, generally refers to one of two approaches. One approach focuses on improving the flow of work through a production process. Any interruptions in flow indicate areas of quality problems. Correcting these areas leads to less waste and an improved process. The other lean approach refers to continually identifying

FIGURE 2.5 |
Characteristics of Successful Employee Involvement Teams

Successful employee involvement teams consist or people that both wish to participate and who have problem-solving skills. They also need to have support from higher-level managers.

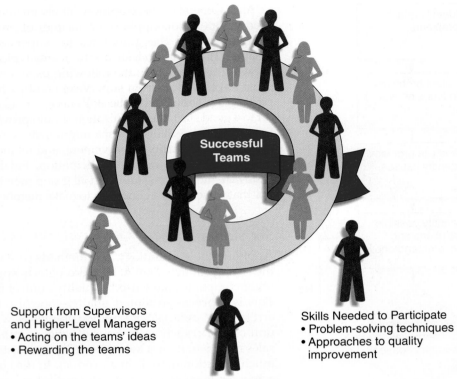

Support from Supervisors and Higher-Level Managers
• Acting on the teams' ideas
• Rewarding the teams

Skills Needed to Participate
• Problem-solving techniques
• Approaches to quality improvement

Desire to Participate

and eliminating waste through the use of a variety of assessment, scheduling, and production control tools. If applied appropriately, waste is eliminated, production time is reduced and, consequently, costs are reduced.

An example of the implementation of the lean philosophy can be seen in Dell's call center. As mentioned earlier in this chapter, Dell had problems in the way calls were routed through their technical support agents and, as a result, were seeing low customer satisfaction ratings and were losing market share. An individual, Richard L. Hunter, was brought in to improve Dell's call center performance. What he found was that Dell had too many network sites and too many call queues. In their quest to reduce the costs of technical support, Dell had created a large number of small, narrowly defined call queues and then were unable to get customers to the right queue 45 percent of the time. To fix these issues, Hunter made a structural change, reducing the number of network sites. He also dramatically reduced the number of call queues. With these changes, the need for call transfers was reduced to 18 percent and the time customers spent on hold dropped from an average of seven to eight minutes to one minute. Said Hunter, "I'm a huge proponent of lean and Six Sigma—which are staples of manufacturing. So we applied lean techniques to the call center, applied Six Sigma disciplines, and now run them like call factories."[13]

Total Quality Management

total quality management (TQM)
An organization-wide focus on satisfying customers by continuously improving every business process for delivering goods or services

Bringing together aspects of other quality-control techniques, many organizations have embraced the practice of **total quality management (TQM)**, an organization-wide focus on satisfying customers by continuously improving every business process for delivering goods or services.[14] Some of the leading users of TQM are Federal Express, Hewlett-Packard, Motorola, 3M, Westinghouse, and Xerox Business

Products and Systems. The objective of TQM is to meet or exceed customer expectations. Thus, it is not a final outcome but an ongoing commitment by everyone in the organization. For example, Weyerhaeuser Company's insurance department, which serves other departments within the forest products firm, adopted TQM principles. In weekly classes, the department's 12 members learned how to work in small teams to evaluate risk management software, improve departmental record-keeping, and accomplish other departmental goals. The teams plan and evaluate their quality efforts and run brainstorming sessions with outside vendors and internal customers to find ways to improve their services.[15]

Today, most companies accept the basic idea of TQM—that everyone in the organization should focus on quality. Three experts who played important roles in spreading this idea are Philip B. Crosby, W. Edwards Deming, and Joseph M. Juran.

- Crosby, known worldwide as a quality expert, pioneered the quality movement in the United States. To achieve product quality, Crosby maintains, the organization must be "injected" with certain ingredients, much as a vaccination serum is intended to keep a person healthy. These ingredients are integrity, systems that measure quality, communications about progress and achievements, operations that educate suppliers and employees in delivering quality, and policies supporting the organization's commitment to quality.

- Deming taught statistical quality control in Japan shortly after World War II and became an important contributor to quality-improvement efforts there for decades before his emphasis on total quality became widely discussed in the United States. Deming emphasizes that to achieve product quality, the organization must continually improve not only the product's design but also the process of producing it. Organizations that put into practice Deming's 14 Points for Management (summarized in Table 2.3 on page 38) demonstrate a commitment to his vision of transformed companies delivering top quality.

- Like Deming, Juran taught quality concepts to the Japanese. He emphasized the view that management should seek to maintain and improve quality through efforts on two levels: the organization as a whole and individual departments in the organization.

A basic strategy for implementing TQM is to use groups, such as employee involvement teams, to identify and solve problems. Another is to review criteria for improving quality (such as the categories for the Baldrige Award, described subsequently) and then seek to meet those criteria. Typically, these efforts address the processes used for delivering goods and services, not just the products themselves. In addition, these efforts address the entire flow of activities and participants that Deming saw as being related to delivering quality to customers: suppliers, receipt and testing of materials, production processes, product inspection, product distribution, customers, market research, and design and redesign of the product, based on the research results.

Because TQM strategies call for the involvement of employees at all levels, the organization needs to educate employees about why quality improvement is needed and how the TQM process will work. Supervisors can help a TQM effort succeed by behaving as if quality is important. Among TQM users, this commonly is called "walking the talk." For example, if everyone is to receive training in quality improvement, supervisors who walk the talk will participate fully in the training sessions, even if they have other important matters to which to attend.

Total quality management requires that employees at all levels focus on meeting or exceeding the expectations of their customers. This principle assumes that everyone has a customer to serve. A salesclerk and a nurse can easily identify their "customers," but even the back-office personnel at a manufacturer are delivering

TABLE 2.3 | Deming's 14 Points for Management

Source: W. Edwards Deming Institute, "Theories & Teachings," http://deming.org/theman/theories/fourteenpoints, accessed March 5, 2014.

1. Create constancy of purpose toward improvement of product and service, with the aim to become competitive and to stay in business, and to provide jobs.

2. Adopt the new philosophy. We are in a new economic age. Western management must awaken to the challenge, must learn their responsibilities, and take on leadership for change.

3. Cease dependence on inspection to achieve quality. Eliminate the need for inspection on a mass basis by building quality into the product in the first place.

4. End the practice of awarding business on the basis of price tag. Instead, minimize total cost. Move toward a single supplier for any one item, on a long-term relationship of loyalty and trust.

5. Improve constantly and forever the system of production and service, to improve quality and productivity, and thus constantly decrease costs.

6. Institute training on the job.

7. Institute leadership . . . . The aim of supervision should be to help people and machines and gadgets to do a better job. Supervision of management is in need of overhaul, as well as supervision of production workers.

8. Drive out fear, so that everyone may work effectively for the company . . . .

9. Break down barriers between departments. People in research, design, sales, and production must work as a team, to foresee problems of production and in use that may be encountered with the product or service.

10. Eliminate slogans, exhortations, and targets for the work force asking for zero defects and new levels of productivity. Such exhortations only create adversarial relationships, as the bulk of the causes of low quality and low productivity belong to the system and thus lie beyond the power of the work force.
    • Eliminate work standards (quotas) on the factory floor. Substitute leadership.
    • Eliminate management by objective. Eliminate management by numbers, numerical goals. Substitute leadership.

11. Remove barriers that rob the hourly worker of his right to pride of workmanship. The responsibility of supervisors must be changed from sheer numbers to quality.

12. Remove barriers that rob people in management and in engineering of their right to pride of workmanship [for example, annual or merit ratings and management by objective].

13. Institute a vigorous program of education and self-improvement.

14. Put everybody in the company to work to accomplish the transformation. The transformation is everybody's job.

services to someone. Satisfying customers requires knowing who they are. They may be the people who buy the company's products; the taxpayers who support the government agency; or the other employees in the organization who use the reports, advice, or other support prepared in a given department.

For the government of Erie County, New York, efforts at continuous improvement are focused on helping citizens use the county's services more efficiently. For example, the county determined that a resident typically needed two and a half weeks to arrange for a permit to rent a picnic shelter after trading phone calls and mailing a check. Getting information was so cumbersome that the county was renting only 30 percent of its reservable sites. Employees sat down with computer experts and determined that an online process could answer residents' questions and collect money in just 25 minutes at the county's Web site. The improved quality of service from the reworked system would boost revenues for the county and help citizens gain full use of the amenities for which their tax dollars pay.[16]

Quality Standards

LO2.4 ▶ Identify ways organizations measure their success in continuous quality improvement.

How can supervisors and others in the organization know whether they are satisfying their internal or external customers? How can they tell whether they are using practices likely to foster high quality? To answer such questions, supervisors and other managers set standards using the guidelines for the Baldrige Award, ISO 9000 standards, benchmarking, and a focus on customer value.

The **Baldrige Performance Excellence Program** is an annual award administered by the U.S. Commerce Department's National Institute of Standards and Technology (NIST) and given to the organization that shows the highest quality performance as measured by seven categories:[17]

Baldrige Performance Excellence Program
An annual award administered by the U.S. Department of Commerce and given to the company that shows the highest quality performance in seven categories

1. Leadership
2. Strategic planning
3. Customer and market focus
4. Measurement, analysis, and knowledge management
5. Human resource focus
6. Process management
7. Results

All competitors for the award receive feedback that recommends areas for further improvement. Many organizations, whether or not they apply for the award, use the Baldrige evaluation categories to assess their own performance. The Baldrige programs have served as the basis for almost 60 international and more than 44 state-sponsored quality awards.

Participation in the Baldrige and other award programs is increasing. Since its beginning more than 25 years ago, more than 1,600 applications have been submitted for the Baldrige Award Program, and attendance at the related Quest for Excellence conference has grown. One reason for participating is the effort to improve business performance. Award recipients generally perform well, including higher market share.[18]

ISO 9000
A series of standards adopted by the International Organization for Standardization to spell out acceptable criteria for quality systems

Another measure of success in quality management is ISO 9000 certification. **ISO 9000** is a series of standards adopted by the International Organization for Standardization to spell out acceptable criteria for quality systems. To be certified, an organization is visited by independent audit teams; if the auditors determine that the key elements of the standards are in place, they issue a certification of compliance. (Note that they are evaluating quality processes, not product quality.) Organizations seek ISO 9000 certification for a number of reasons. A customer may require it as a condition of doing business, or a nation's government may require it of organizations selling in that nation. As more businesses become certified, those that want to remain competitive will have to be certified as well.[19]

benchmarking
Identifying the top performer of a process, then learning and carrying out the top performer's practices

Managers at all levels can evaluate their success in improving quality by comparing their processes and results with those at other departments and organizations. This practice is known popularly as **benchmarking**: identifying, learning, and carrying out the practices of top performers. The term first referred to the practice of comparing the products and processes at one's own company with those that are the best in the world. For example, General Mills observed a NASCAR pit crew to get ideas for speeding up changes in Betty Crocker production lines.[20] Although this might seem like an activity for higher-level managers, supervisors can apply the technique to their own department's operations or even to their own career and management style.

NASCAR pit crews serve as examples of how to work quickly while maintaining quality.

value
The worth a customer places on a total package of goods and services relative to its cost

These quality-improvement practices can make the organization effective at whatever it does, yet they may not assess whether employees are doing what customers *want*. For example, an accounting department might use the zero-defects approach so well that it produces a year's worth of reports without a single error. But if the reports do not contain information useful to the recipients, has the department done high-quality work? Recognizing this principle, an increasing number of organizations have concluded that they need to provide a context for their efforts at quality improvement. In other words, quality improvement should be directed at a larger goal: to deliver greater customer value. In this sense, value refers to the worth the customer places on what he or she gets (the total package of goods and services) relative to the cost of acquiring it.

Quality improvement directed toward value begins when the organization's employees communicate with customers to determine their needs and wants. Customers may be evaluating a lot more than whether a product adheres to specifications; value may include timely delivery, helpful customer service, low need for maintenance, and information that helps them fully benefit from using the company's services.[21] The information about what customers want defines what the organization should focus on doing.

Guidelines for Quality Control

As with the other responsibilities of supervisors, success in quality control requires more than just picking the right technique. The supervisor needs a general approach that leads everyone involved to support the effort to improve quality. To develop such an approach, the supervisor can start by following the guidelines illustrated in Figure 2.6.

Prevention versus Detection

It is almost always cheaper to prevent problems from occurring than it is to solve them after they happen; designing and building quality into a product is more efficient than trying to improve the product later. Therefore, quality-control programs should not be limited to the detection of defects. Quality control also should include a prevention program to keep defects from occurring. One way to prevent problems is to pay special attention to the production of new goods and services. In a manufacturing setting, the supervisor should see that the first piece of a new product is tested with special care, rather than wait for problems to occur down the line. Also, when prevention efforts show that employees are doing good work, the supervisor should praise their performance. Employees who are confident and satisfied are less likely to allow defects in goods or services.

FIGURE 2.6 | Guidelines for Quality Control
To achieve quality requires the coordination of a number of different aspects of business.

Standard Setting and Enforcement

If employees and others are to support the quality-control effort, they must know exactly what is expected of them. This calls for quality standards. In many cases, the supervisor is responsible for setting quality standards as well as for communicating and enforcing them. These standards should have the characteristics of effective objectives detailed in Chapter 6: They should be written, measurable, clear, specific, and challenging but achievable. Furthermore, those standards should reflect what is important to the client.

Baptist Hospital Inc. (BHI), located in Florida, and a previous Baldridge Performance Excellence Program winner, has clear and specific goals for quality service. They begin with BHI's Standards of Performance, which all employees must read and agree to follow. The standards govern employee attitudes, appearance, service to patients, commitment to co-workers, and other aspects of a hospital worker's job. Employees also are taught what to say in different situations to convey an attitude of helpfulness. For example, if an employee sees a hospital visitor who appears lost, the employee is supposed to say, "May I take you to where you are going?" And BHI tracks a variety of performance measures, including quality of clinical care, medication errors, patient satisfaction, employee morale, and percentage of revenue devoted to caring for poor patients. BHI's performance on these measures exceeds community and national norms.[22]

In communicating standards, a supervisor should make sure employees know why quality is important. Employees should receive specific information about the costs of poor quality and the benefits of excellent quality. For example, if employees know how much it costs to make a component or win a new customer, they can understand the costs of remaking a defective component or alienating a customer. In addition, employees must understand the difference between poor quality and excellent quality. One way to do this is to use examples. In teaching a new employee how to manufacture a part, a supervisor could show a sample of a part that meets specifications and one that does not.

To enforce the standards, a supervisor must participate in inspecting the quality of goods and services that employees produce. This process may entail examining a random sample of parts, accompanying a salesperson on sales calls, or visiting the workplace where employees interact with customers. The timing of these inspections should be unpredictable enough that employees cannot adjust their performance because the supervisor will be checking up on them that day. When an inspection uncovers a quality problem, the supervisor should inform the responsible employees immediately. Then they should begin solving the problem. The appropriate response may include apologizing to customers as well as fixing a problem within the organization. Demanding a quick response demonstrates the importance of quality. For the enforcement of standards to be effective, the employees must know that management is serious about quality. A catchy slogan posted on bulletin boards, inscribed on buttons, or taped to cash registers is meaningless unless supervisors and other managers pay attention to these principles, reward employees for following them, and live up to them themselves.

LO2.5 ▶ Identify constraints on productivity.

The Productivity Challenge

Stiff competition from around the world is forcing U.S. businesses to pay attention to productivity. In addition, citizens' opposition to paying higher taxes is forcing governments to make their operations more productive. To help improve productivity, supervisors must understand why it is important and what limits an organization's productivity.

Trends in Productivity in the United States

When the productivity of organizations in a country is improving, people benefit. They can get goods and services at lower prices or with lower taxes than they otherwise could. Employers tend to pay higher wages and salaries to workers who

FIGURE 2.7 |
Productivity in the United States: Manufacturing Workers

Source: Data from U.S. Department of Labor, Bureau of Labor Statistics, "Major Sector Productivity and Costs," accessed March 6, 2014, http://data.bls.gov/cgi-bin/dsrv?pr.

[a]To track productivity, the Bureau of Labor Statistics measures percentage changes in output and compensation from one quarter to the next. The index compares the current quarter with 2009 (which is an index of 100). For example, an index of 50 would be half the 2009 level, and an index of 200 would be twice the 2009 level. [b]To determine the unit labor cost, the compensation per hour is divided by the output per hour.

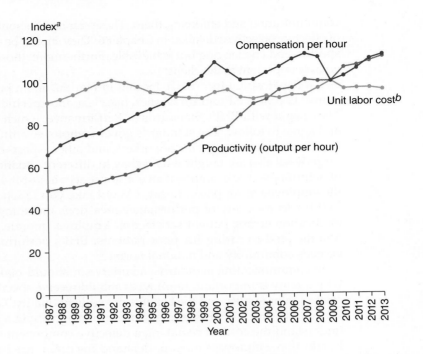

are more productive. People also have access to more and better goods and services. Because of these benefits, statisticians track productivity trends in various countries.

The amount of goods and services produced by the average U.S. worker remains higher than that for most other industrialized nations. Comparing the value of goods and services produced with an hour of labor, on average, U.S. workers produced more than their counterparts in most other developed nations, including Mexico, Japan, and Germany.[23] (Workers in Belgium, the Netherlands, Ireland, and Norway, produced more per hour worked.) As Figure 2.7 shows, manufacturing output per hour in the United States has been rising over the last two decades. The earnings of manufacturing workers have grown along with their output. Businesses pay more for more productive workers, so unit labor costs (compensation divided by output) have stayed near the index year throughout most of the period.

Constraints on Productivity

When you read about ways to improve productivity, keep in mind that several constraints limit the impact of a supervisor or even a higher-level manager. Supervisors and other managers should be aware of these constraints so that they can either plan ways to overcome them or set realistic goals within them. Some of the most important constraints on productivity are management limitations, employee attitudes and skills, government regulations, and union rules.

Management Limitations

Operative employees will contribute to improve productivity only if they believe management is truly committed to this objective. Too often, however, employees believe management is more interested in the next quarter's profits than in producing high-quality goods or services as efficiently as possible. Employees become frustrated, especially when managers seem to ignore their ideas.

The most important way supervisors can overcome this constraint is to set a good example. Supervisors should demonstrate by their actions and words that they are interested in the department's productivity. This behavior includes seeing that the job is done right the first time, as well as using resources wisely, which, on a personal level, includes being well organized. Supervisors also must communicate instructions clearly and plan carefully so that employees are able to live up to managers' expectations. Furthermore, supervisors should listen to employees' concerns and ideas about improving productivity. If the organization has a formal program for submitting ideas, supervisors can offer to help employees write down or explain their suggestions. In organizations that allow or expect employee participation in planning and decision making, supervisors should encourage this participation.

Employee Attitudes and Skills

Improving productivity requires changes. People have a natural tendency to resist change because it is challenging and often frightening (see Chapter 14). Employees who fear or resent productivity improvements will not be motivated to make the changes work. Part of a supervisor's job is to identify employee attitudes and, when necessary, help employees take a more positive view. (The last section of this chapter addresses this issue in greater detail.)

One attitude that many supervisors are encountering today, especially among young employees, is an expectation they will have access to the Internet at all times. Many organizations limit access to certain kinds of Web sites, such as games and social networking, and many employees resent those limitations. Typically, employers that block access are concerned that time on Facebook or Twitter is a distraction that hurts productivity. In fact, one study concluded that banning employees from Facebook at work would result in a 1.5 percent productivity improvement—a small percentage perhaps, but at a large firm, it could represent many dollars.[24] Others argue that social networking lets people maintain important social connections and share information that can help them function more effectively. Whatever the company's policy, the supervisor's role is to cultivate a positive attitude so employees will be as productive as possible with the available tools.

Employees' skills also influence how effective productivity-building efforts will be. When an organization wants each member to contribute more, each member must either work faster or do the job differently. Some employees can perform new tasks or do their jobs in a new way with little or no training. Other employees understand only one way of working. When employees want to change but don't know how, supervisors can overcome this constraint by providing more training. When employees are unwilling or unable to learn, this constraint is more difficult to overcome.

Government Regulations

Businesses and other organizations in the United States are regulated in many areas, including payment of overtime wages, disability compensation, environmental pollution, building codes, minimum safety standards, and child labor. Following these regulations costs money, but the laws reflect the values of the majority in our society. For example, it might be cheaper to hire children to assemble electronic components, but few people want to return to the days of children laboring long hours within factory walls. Likewise, scrubbers on power-company smokestacks cost money, but clean air to breathe is essential. Even when government regulations seem illogical or unreasonable, an organization can face serious penalties for ignoring or disobeying them. Thus, the proper role of supervisors and other managers is to know these regulations and seek ways to improve productivity without violating the law.

Union Rules

Union contracts typically specify rules for what tasks particular employees may do, what hours they may work, and how organizations may use them. Sometimes, an organization's managers see a way to improve productivity that violates one of these rules. For example, it might be more efficient to have two employees learn each other's jobs so that they can get the work done even when one of them is away or busy. However, the union contract might contain a rule against this.

When employers and unions collaborate on a solution, they can overcome such constraints, although the process usually takes time. If an organization explains how everyone will benefit from the changes, the union may agree to revise the contract, especially if the alternative is employee layoffs. Even though a supervisor can propose changes, it is not part of a supervisor's job to remove these constraints. Supervisors must do their best to get work done as efficiently as possible under the existing work rules.

LO2.6 ▶ Describe how productivity and productivity improvements are measured.

Measuring Productivity

The basic way to measure productivity is to divide outputs by inputs (see Figure 2.1 on page 28). In other words, productivity is the amount of output produced with the inputs used. Table 2.4 provides examples of inputs and outputs for several types of organizations. The productivity equation can compare the output and input for an individual, a department, an organization, or even an entire country's paid workforce. The remaining discussion focuses on the direct concern of supervisors with the productivity of their department and their individual employees.

By applying basic arithmetic to the formula for productivity, the supervisor can see what has to change for productivity to increase. The right side of the equation is a fraction. Remember that when the top (numerator) of a fraction gets bigger, the number becomes greater. When the bottom (denominator) of a fraction gets bigger, the number becomes smaller. For example, 3/2 is greater than 1/2, and 1/5 is less than 1/3. To increase productivity, a supervisor needs to increase outputs, reduce inputs, or both. Consider an employee who processes 96 driver's license applications in an eight-hour day at the secretary of state's office. One way to measure this employee's productivity is 96/8, or 12 applications per hour (see Figure 2.8 on the following page). A supervisor might note that a more experienced employee can process 20 applications per hour, so by this measure, the first employee is less desirable and might require more training, better motivation, or just more experience.

But the organization is also interested in the cost of the employee. So the supervisor might measure the input as the employee's cost per day (hourly wage times number of hours). If the employee earned $6 per hour, the productivity measure would be 96/($6 × 8), or 2 (see Figure 2.8). If the employee who processes

TABLE 2.4 | Examples of Inputs and Outputs

Source: Adapted from Samuel C. Certo, *Modern Management*, 6th ed., Allyn & Bacon, 1994.

Organization	Inputs	Outputs
Bus line	Buses; gas, oil, and other supplies; terminals; drivers; ticket sellers; managers; tickets; schedules; funds; data	Transportation services to passengers
Manufacturing firm	Trucks; plants; oil, rags, and other supplies; raw materials; purchased parts; production workers; supervisors; engineers; storekeepers; bills of material; inventory records; production schedules; time records; funds; data	Goods for use by customers
Hospital	Ambulances; hospital rooms; beds, wheelchairs, X-rays; receptionists; administrators; nurses; doctors; medicines; drugs; splints, bandages, food, and other supplies; medical charts; funds; data	Health care services to patients
Police force	Cars and vans; offices; police officers; forms; handcuffs, radios, guns, office supplies, and other supplies; office furniture; equipment for forensic research; uniforms; funds; data	Protection of public safety

FIGURE 2.8 | Productivity Measurement

Productivity measures the number of items produced per hour. Costs, however, must also be factored in to determine if a more productive person who earns more per hour actually saves the company money.

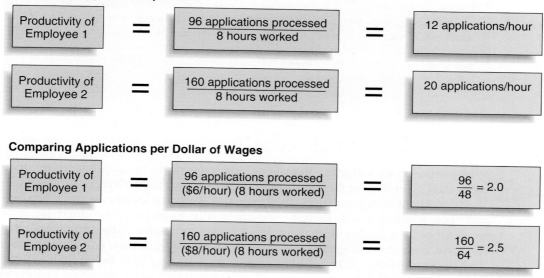

Comparing Applications per Hour

| Productivity of Employee 1 | = | 96 applications processed / 8 hours worked | = | 12 applications/hour |

| Productivity of Employee 2 | = | 160 applications processed / 8 hours worked | = | 20 applications/hour |

Comparing Applications per Dollar of Wages

| Productivity of Employee 1 | = | 96 applications processed / ($6/hour) (8 hours worked) | = | $\frac{96}{48} = 2.0$ |

| Productivity of Employee 2 | = | 160 applications processed / ($8/hour) (8 hours worked) | = | $\frac{160}{64} = 2.5$ |

FIGURE 2.9 | Quantity without Quality Does Not Boost Productivity

Productivity is more than just a measure of units produced per hour. Productivity is also a measure of the quality of what is produced.

Source: Keith Goldstein/Getty Images.

20 applications per hour earns $8 per hour, that employee's productivity would be 160/($8 × 8), or 2.5. Thus, the more experienced employee is more productive, even considering the higher wage rate.

In this example, high productivity offsets the high cost of labor, but in practice, some companies have difficulty competing because productivity gains lag behind rising compensation. The airlines industry is one arena in which this is true. What once was a lucrative market for all carriers has become highly competitive as many low-cost carriers have emerged. In addition, the ability of individuals to search for and purchase their own tickets online has put a downward pressure on airline "per seat" prices. This, in turn, has led to lower revenues for the airlines. Increasing productivity of employees is, therefore, one tool that airlines have tried to use to maintain or increase their profits. It has not, however, been successful. Massachusetts Institute of Technology's (MIT's) Airline Data Project has been tracking a variety of components of the airline industry since 1995. What they found is that, though employee productivity has increased 73 percent between 1995 and 2012, the productivity per dollar of employee compensation has actually decreased 13 percent in the same timeframe.[25]

The output measured in the productivity formula is only goods and services of acceptable quality. A rude salesclerk and a production worker making defective components are not really productive. In these cases, the productivity formula would include only the number of correctly made components or the amount of sales made courteously and accurately. The gemologist in Figure 2.9 closely examines a diamond using a loupe to ensure quality.

---

connect SELF-ASSESSMENT 2.1

Test Your Personal Productivity

Supervisors' personal behaviors affect their individual productivity. In turn, supervisors' personal productivity affects the productivity of those they supervise. Employees watch their supervisors for examples of acceptable and desirable behavior at work. Therefore, it is important for you to model productivity for your workers. This assessment will help you assess your personal productivity and identify those behaviors that may be keeping you from being as productive as you could be.

LO2.7 ▶ Identify ways productivity may be improved.

Improving Productivity

When supervisors and other managers look for ways to boost productivity, they often start by looking at their costs per unit of output. Productivity improves when the department or organization can do as much work at a lower cost and when output rises without a cost increase. Another way to improve productivity is to improve process quality so that employees work more efficiently and do not have to spend time correcting mistakes or defects. Mistakes, errors, and rework are a drag on productivity. Poor quality can slow the output of both individuals and the firm as a whole. For that reason, one of the supervisor's most important tasks is to think of and implement ways to get the job done right the first time.

Many of the quality-control strategies introduced in this chapter, such as Six Sigma, zero defects, and employee involvement, apply to productivity improvement. For example, in 2003, 3M Corporation began using Six Sigma as its primary method for improving process and product quality. Beginning with processes in its factories and then turning to the efficiency of other processes, such as finance and customer service, 3M used Six Sigma and other programs to cut about $300 million from its costs in 2003 and 2004.[26] Since then, 3M has adapted their methodology and now use a Lean Six Sigma approach to achieve operational excellence in a number of their services.[27] In contrast, however, 3M found that Six Sigma was not entirely beneficial in the Research and Development (R & D) division. It was perceived to restrict innovation, a necessary component of R & D, and so was removed from that division.[28] The point of the 3M example is that Six Sigma and other quality benchmarks must be considered in the specific context of each organization. Things that work well at some companies or divisions will not necessarily work well at others. Furthermore, quality initiatives may have a ceiling after which they decline. Imitating others because of their success does not always lead to good results.[29]

Because of their direct contact with employees, supervisors play an important part in most of these initiatives. Supervisors can increase their own and their team's or group's productivity by understanding the goals of quality programs and their own role in achieving those goals. Through leadership and motivation, they can help employees contribute to quality goals. Finally, they can use their specific knowledge of the tasks and processes their teams perform to find unique ways to contribute to productivity.

To lower costs, supervisors can use a number of strategies. (See the basic alternatives summarized in Figure 2.10 on the following page.) These strategies are not mutually exclusive. Supervisors can get the greatest productivity by using as many of these strategies as will work. In deciding which strategies to use, supervisors should consider which will appeal to higher-level management, which will be acceptable to employees, and which involve areas within their control.

An important part of many of these strategies is encouraging and using employees' ideas for saving money. Operating the machines, preparing the reports, and

FIGURE 2.10 | Cost-Control Strategies

Supervisors can employ a number of different tactics to control costs or drive them down.

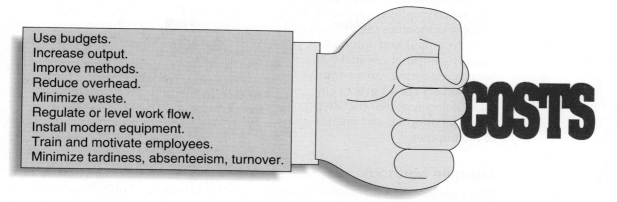

Use budgets.
Increase output.
Improve methods.
Reduce overhead.
Minimize waste.
Regulate or level work flow.
Install modern equipment.
Train and motivate employees.
Minimize tardiness, absenteeism, turnover.

COSTS

serving clients or customers gives employees a close-up view of how things are done, enabling them to see the shortcomings of the organization's way of doing things. For instance, Philips Lighting charged employees with finding ways to operate more efficiently and reaped the rewards of ideas generated throughout the company. A team of packaging workers figured out how to reduce the time a lamp spends waiting to be packed from one or two days to just 15 minutes. At the same time, they determined they could pack them as well with less cardboard, and the reduction in packaging volume means the company can ship the same amount of product in 44 percent fewer trucks. Maintenance workers at the Philips plant in Salina, Kansas, improved maintenance manuals and procedures, making the workplace safer even as they increased the amount of time machinery is running properly.[30]

Use Budgets

Not surprisingly, before a supervisor can make intelligent decisions about how to trim costs, he or she has to know where the money is going. The most important source of such information is budget reports, described in Chapter 6. By reviewing budget reports regularly, a supervisor can see which categories of expenses are largest and identify where the department is spending more than it budgeted. Then a supervisor should spend time with workers, observing how they use the department's resources, including their time. The process of gathering information about costs and working with employees to identify needed improvements is part of a supervisor's control function.

Increase Output

Remember that the numerator in the productivity equation (output/input) represents what the department or organization is producing. The greater the output at a given cost, the greater the productivity. Thus, a logical way to increase productivity is to increase output without boosting costs.

Sometimes, by applying themselves, people can work faster or harder. Servers in a restaurant may find they can cover more tables, and factory production workers may find they can assemble more components. Of course, it is not always possible to increase output without sacrificing quality. Also, this method of improving productivity often makes employees unhappy. A supervisor who wants to boost productivity by increasing output must first ensure that the new output goals are reasonable, perhaps by including employees in the decision-making process. A supervisor must also communicate the new goals carefully, emphasizing any positive aspects of the change. For example, a supervisor might mention that if employees are more productive, the organization has a chance to remain competitive without layoffs. In the end, improving productivity by increasing output works only when employees are motivated to do more (see Chapter 11).

Some companies use technology to ensure productivity. Software programs that monitor e-mail and Internet usage have many uses, including applications that identify computer use that is not work related or that violates company rules. Electronic monitoring can also provide basic productivity measures such as how long order takers spend processing each customer order. The American Management Association reported that 76 percent of employers were using some form of electronic monitoring, and one-fourth of companies had fired an employee for misuse of the Internet.[31]

Improve Methods

There are only limited ways of doing the same thing better or faster. Reviewing and revamping the way things are done is the basic principle of *reengineering*. Process control techniques for improving quality also can improve productivity. Kato Engineering, located in Mankato, Minnesota, used a process called *kaizen*, in which teams map the details of each work process, looking for ways to eliminate waste. The manufacturing company improved productivity in office procedures as well as factory operations. Now Kato answers requests for quotes in one-sixth the original time and processes order changes in 2 hours instead of 24.[32]

A potentially powerful approach to improving methods is to give employees more control over the way they work. Much of the growth in productivity in the 1990s came from efforts such as getting production ideas from nonmanagement employees and linking rewards to high performance.[33] Similarly, designing jobs to include variety and responsibility makes the jobs more interesting, which should motivate employees to deliver higher quality as well as work harder.

Like managers at all levels, supervisors should be constantly on the lookout for ways to improve methods. Some ideas will come from supervisors themselves. (Chapter 9 provides suggestions for creative thinking.) Employees often have excellent ideas for doing the work better because they see the problems and pitfalls of their jobs. Supervisors should keep communication channels open and actively ask for ideas.

Reduce Overhead

overhead
Expenses not related directly to producing goods and services; examples are rent, utilities, and staff

Many departments spend more than is necessary for **overhead**, which includes rent, utilities, staff support, company cafeteria, janitorial services, and other expenses not related directly to producing goods and services. Typically, an organization allocates a share of the total overhead to each department based on the department's overhead expenses. However, a supervisor can periodically look for sources of needless expenses, such as lights left on in unoccupied areas or messy work areas that mean extra work for the janitorial staff. By reducing these costs to the company, a supervisor ultimately reduces the amount of overhead charged to his or her department.

Staff departments in particular can be guilty of contributing too much to the cost of overhead by generating unnecessary paperwork. Supervisors and their employees who produce or handle reports and forms should evaluate this paperwork, whether hard copy or electronic, to make sure it is needed. Another way to reduce the amount of paper is to make sure that when a procedure calls for a form with several parts, all the parts are actually used.

Minimize Waste

Waste occurs in all kinds of operations. A medical office may order too many supplies and wind up throwing some away or taking up unnecessary storage space.

SUPERVISION AND ETHICS

HIGH-TECH SCHEDULING IN STORES: IS IT FAIR?

In the competitive retail market, a company's success can depend on the quality of the service they provide. At the same time, a big part of the cost of running a store is the salesforce. If salespeople are standing around or just tidying the shelves, their productivity sinks. In order to cut costs, countless retail chains are investing in software that helps them calculate just how many people are needed to keep the merchandise moving at any given time of day or day of the week. Companies including Limited Brands, Gap, Williams-Sonoma, Ann Taylor, and GameStop are using these workforce management systems.

According to the companies that sell the software, it can cut a store's labor costs by at least 5 percent and increase productivity by at least 15 percent. But from some employees' viewpoint, workforce management software does this at a high cost to them. For example, because store traffic rises and falls throughout the day, the most effective software divides the day into shorter shifts, so peak staffing occurs only during peak shopping times. But that means some employees have to rush to work for just a few hours' pay and then either commute frequently or make do with less income. Workers' pay also may vary more from week to week as the scheduling system tinkers with their hours.

When workforce management systems were first being developed and put into use, some employees find the automation uncomfortably impersonal. Computer systems are more apt to schedule employees based on their past performance, with the top sellers assigned to the busiest times of day, and without consideration of non-work activities and commitments. That boosts store profits, at least in the short term, but it becomes harder for less-experienced employees to build their skills and can lead to disgruntled employees.

Today's workforce management systems offer real-time information that allow supervisors and staff to easily adapt to ever-changing situations. This allows retailers to provide a flexible workforce that can provide outstanding service to their customers at the least cost possible.

While supervisors may still have to handle some worker complaints of unfairness of scheduling decisions, the benefits to the company are clear and employees can be empowered with the knowledge that the workforce management systems is placing them at the right place and at the right time to best serve the consumer.

Source: Based on Vanessa O'Connell, "Retailers Reprogram Workers in Efficiency Push," *The Wall Street Journal*, September 10, 2008, http://online.wsj.com; Liz Moughan, "Innovating with Workforce Management," *NRF Stores*, August 2012, downloaded from Kronos, http://www.kronos.com/showAbstract.aspx?id=17545&rr=0&Lang Type=1033&ecid=ABEA-56QT5S, accessed March 10, 2014.

---

idle time, or downtime
Time during which employees or machines are not producing goods or services

Waiting by the printer for each page of a print job is an example of idle time.

detour behavior
Tactics for postponing or avoiding work

A factory may handle materials in a way that produces a lot of scrap. A sales office may make unnecessary photocopies of needlessly long proposals, contributing more to landfills than to the company's profits.

A costly form of waste is idle time, or downtime—time during which employees or machines are not producing goods or services. This term is used most often in manufacturing operations, but it applies to other situations as well. In a factory, idle time occurs while a machine is shut down for repairs or workers are waiting for parts. In an office, idle time occurs when employees are waiting for instructions, supplies, a computer printout, or a response to a question they asked the supervisor. In both settings, idle time may occur because jobs and work processes are poorly designed. Productivity consultant Edgar Burnett visited a factory that assigned six operators to six machines. Their work involved periodically monitoring the machine's output and feeding in materials about every 40 minutes. Burnett quickly determined that one operator could run two machines without difficulty. Similarly, Burnett observed a receptionist who spent less than three hours a day on tasks related to receiving visitors. The company solved the problem of the receptionist's idle time by training her to perform clerical tasks as well.[34] In service businesses, an important way to minimize idle time is to schedule just enough employees to perform the service at any given time. To learn more about the challenges of scheduling employees fairly, see the "Supervision and Ethics" feature.

Another form of wasted time results from detour behavior, which is a tactic for postponing or avoiding work. Employees and their supervisors use a wide variety of detour behavior: A supervisor enjoys a cup of coffee and the newspaper before

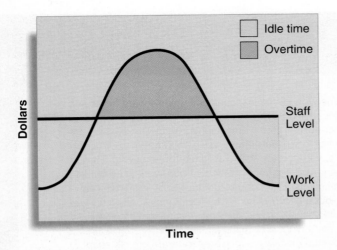

FIGURE 2.11 | The Costs of Uneven Work Flow

Arranging for an even work flow will cut down on staff idle time as well as costly overtime.

turning to the day's responsibilities or an employee stops by a colleague's desk to chat. Detour behavior may be especially tempting when a person's energy is low or a person is facing a particularly challenging or unpleasant assignment. (The opposite of detour behavior is effective time management, discussed in Chapter 13.)

Wasted time may be an even more important measure of lost productivity than wasted costs. For office employees, a major cause of wasted time is spam—messages that are unrelated to work, unwanted, and often distasteful or fraudulent. Organizations are countering the problem with filtering software that searches messages and attachments for viruses and worms, inappropriate content, and other signals that a message is likely to be spam. They also are training employees to be more wary about opening e-mail attachments from unknown senders.

Supervisors should be on the alert for wasted time and other resources in their department. They can set a good example for effective time management and make detecting waste part of the control process (see Chapter 6). Often, employees are good sources of information on how to minimize waste. The supervisor might consider holding a contest to find the best ideas.

Regulate or Level the Work Flow

An uneven flow of work can be costly (see Figure 2.11). When work levels are low, the result is idle time. When the department faces a surge in demand for its work, employees have to work extra hours to keep up. As a result, the department may have to pay workers overtime rates—one and a half or two times normal wages—during peak periods. In addition, people get tired, so they are rarely as efficient during overtime hours as they are during a normal workday. If a supervisor can arrange to have a more even work flow, the department can be staffed appropriately to get the job done during normal working hours, and fewer employees will be idle during slow periods.

A supervisor can take several steps to regulate departmental work flow:

1. A supervisor should first make sure that adequate planning has been done for the work required.

2. A supervisor may also find it helpful to work with his or her manager and peers or form teams of employees to examine and solve work-flow problems. Cooperation can help make the work flow more evenly or at least more predictably. For example, a manager who travels extensively may assign a great deal of work upon her return, not realizing that she is clustering deadlines instead of spreading them out for an even work flow. The sales department may be submitting orders in batches to the production department instead of submitting them as soon as they are received.

3. If the work flow must remain uneven, a supervisor may find that the best course is to use temporary employees during peak periods, an approach that can work if the temporary employees have the right skills.

Install Modern Equipment

Work may be slowed because employees are using worn or outdated equipment. If that is the case, a supervisor may find it worthwhile to obtain modern equipment. Although the value of installing modern equipment is obvious for manufacturing departments, many other workplaces can benefit from using modern equipment,

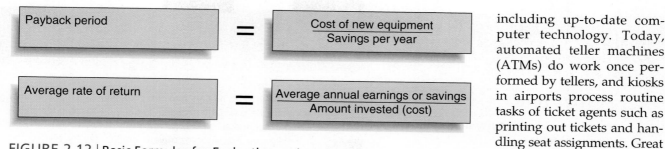

FIGURE 2.12 | Basic Formulas for Evaluating an Investment

The payback period and the average rate of return are two key calculations used by companies to determine if an investment is practical.

including up-to-date computer technology. Today, automated teller machines (ATMs) do work once performed by tellers, and kiosks in airports process routine tasks of ticket agents such as printing out tickets and handling seat assignments. Great Clips, a chain of hair salons known for their inexpensive and quick haircuts, does not require or accept appointments. It is first come, first served based upon checking in at the counter in the store. Recently, however, they began offering the option to check in online from a computer or smartphone. The application allows customers to check the wait time at nearby locations and then to "check in" at the store of their choice—adding their name to the wait list. Customers can then gauge when to arrive at the store, using the interim time in whatever way they like, and they don't have to spend time sitting in the lobby. It also benefits the franchises because it allows them to gauge the number of clients to expect so that they can move staff around or change their schedules to meet the customer demands.[35]

In deciding to buy new equipment or recommending its purchase, a supervisor needs to determine whether the expense will be worthwhile. One way to do this is to figure out how much money per year the new equipment will save in terms of, for example, lower repair costs, less downtime, and more goods produced. Then compute the number of years before the savings will offset the cost of buying the equipment, a time known as the **payback period**. A payback period is computed according to the first formula shown in Figure 2.12. Thus, if a computer system will cost $120,000 and is expected to save the office $40,000 per year, the payback period is three years ($120,000/$40,000 per year). Higher-level management or the finance department usually has an opinion on what payback period is acceptable for the organization.

payback period
The length of time it will take for the benefits generated by an investment (such as cost savings from machinery) to offset the cost of the investment

average rate of return (ARR)
A percentage that represents the average annual earnings for each dollar of a given investment

Another way to evaluate whether an investment is worthwhile is to find its **average rate of return (ARR)**. The ARR is a percentage that represents the organization's average annual earnings for each dollar of a given investment. An ARR of 15 percent means that each dollar invested yields income (or savings) of 15 cents a year. A basic formula for ARR is the second equation in Figure 2.12. For the computer system in the previous example, the ARR would be the $40,000 annual savings divided by the $120,000 cost, or 0.33—a 33 percent return. To determine whether this return is acceptable, a supervisor compares it with what the money spent could earn in another form of investment. Again, higher-level management or the finance department usually has established standards for this measure.

Payback period and ARR, as described here, are only two simple ways to evaluate investments. Other, more complex methods consider factors such as the timing of payments and earnings. Software is available to compute payback periods, ARR, and other analyses of the financial worthiness of an investment.

Train and Motivate Employees

To work efficiently, employees need a good understanding of how to do their jobs. Thus, a basic way to improve productivity is to train employees. As you will see in Chapter 11, training alone does not lead to superior performance; employees also must be motivated to do good work. In other words, employees must want to do a good job. Motivation is a key tactic for improving productivity because employees carry out most changes and are often in the best position to think of ways to achieve their objectives more efficiently (see "Supervisory Skills: Motivating").

SUPERVISORY SKILLS

MOTIVATING

Pride Fuels Productivity Improvements at General Motors

Researchers at the University of Pennsylvania studied productivity at 3,000 companies. They learned that when companies spent an amount equal to 10 percent of their revenues on capital improvements such as machinery and computer systems, their productivity grew by an average of 3.9 percent. But when companies spent a comparable amount for employee development, productivity rose much more: 8.5 percent. The lesson: Employees matter.

Supervisors can influence productivity by motivating their employees to contribute their ideas and efforts toward improved output and efficiency. A dramatic example of motivated employees making a difference occurred in Wilmington, Delaware in the mid-1990s. General Motors decided to close a factory there because it was less productive than other GM plants. Executives traveled to the plant and announced to the assembled workers that the plant would be closed and said, "There is nothing you can do to affect this decision." After the executives left, the plant manager appealed to their pride: "There may be nothing we can do to affect this decision, but . . . we can make them feel really stupid! Because they are going to be closing the best plant in General Motors!"

The workers were inspired by this appeal to their pride. Teams of workers and managers identified ways to improve quality and reduce costs. Union leaders cooperated with the factory's management in the improvement effort. The company provided weekly information about quality and costs. Within two years, the factory became GM's lowest-cost producer, and its cars had the company's lowest warranty costs. The company reversed its decision to close the plant. Now, whenever the Wilmington factory faces a difficult challenge, managers motivate employees by recounting this experience.

Over the years since this episode with General Motors, the need for ongoing employee training and development has become increasingly clear to organizations. Recent years have seen continual growth in the investment in training. In fact, from 2010 to 2011 there was a 9.5 percent growth in spending on employee development, with employees averaging 15.3 hours of training. 2012 and 2013 saw additional growth in this arena.

In addition to providing and promoting training, supervisors can apply the lessons of GM's Wilmington plant by emphasizing pride of achievement, rather than just monetary rewards. Look for and point out the group's successes. Pass on the enthusiasm by telling your group's success stories again and again.

Sources: John A. Byrne, "How to Lead Now: Getting Extraordinary Performance When You Can't Pay for It," *Fast Company,* August 1, 2003, http://www.fastcompany.com/46966/how-lead-now, accessed March 10, 2014; "Bersin & Associates' New Research Finds Organizations Spending Significantly More on Employee Development to Combat Skills Gap in the Labor Market," January 16, 2012, http://www.bersin.com/News/Content.aspx?id=15142, accessed March 10, 2014; Doug Harward, "Key Trends for 2012: New Era of Personal Learning is Transforming the Training Industry," December 9, 2011, https://www.trainingindustry.com/articles/10-trends-for-2012.aspx, accessed March 10, 2014; Doug Harward, "Key Trends for 2013: Sustainability & the Changing Role of the Learning Leader," https://www.trainingindustry.com/ezine/current-issue/key-trends-for-2013-sustainability-and-the-changing-role-of-the-learning-leader.aspx, accessed March 10, 2014.

Minimize Tardiness, Absenteeism, and Turnover

Lack of motivation is often the problem underlying time lost to tardiness and absenteeism. When employees dislike their jobs or find them boring, they tend to use excuses to arrive late or not at all. Lost time is costly; in most cases, the organization is paying for someone who is not actually working. In addition, other employees may be unable to work efficiently without the support of the missing person. As a result, minimizing absenteeism and tardiness is an important part of the supervisor's job. (Chapter 12 provides some guidelines for this task.)

Absenteeism may be the first step to leaving the company. The employee misses more and more days, then finally quits. The rate at which employees leave an organization is known as turnover. High turnover is expensive, because the organization must spend a lot of money to recruit and train new employees. Therefore, an important part of controlling costs is to keep good employees by making the organization a place they want to stay. A few years ago at Costco, for example, labor costs as a percentage of sales (that is, dollars spent on labor divided by dollars of goods sold) were *lower* than at Walmart, even though

turnover
The rate at which employees leave an organization

Costco's wages were higher than Walmart's. Costco's higher wages helped keep employee turnover much lower than at Walmart, where it costs $2,500 to hire and train a new worker. And Costco's motivated employees helped its stores sell more per square foot. Thus, Costco earned more profits per employee than Walmart did.[36] Recent research also indicates that the degree to which employees feel supported by their organization and supervisor can play an important role in whether they choose to leave their current job. In general, when an employee is feeling unsupported by his or her organization or supervisor, that employee is more likely to look for a new employment opportunity. Therefore, as a supervisor, it is important to be aware of how supported your employees feel about their relationship with you and the company as a whole.[37] Supervisors can also minimize turnover by applying the principles of motivation, described in Chapter 11.

Employee Fears About Productivity Improvement

LO2.8 ▶ Explain why employees have fears about productivity improvement and how supervisors can address those fears.

During a speech to the National Association of Manufacturers, then Dallas Federal Reserve Bank President Robert D. McTeer Jr. told the following story: "At the rate you're going with productivity improvements, the factory of the future may have only two employees: a man and a dog. The man's job will be to feed the dog. The dog's job will be to keep the man from touching the equipment."[38] Indeed, some organizations have very few production employees. Denver-based Inflow Inc. automated its Web-hosting services to the point that only two or three employees are needed to run its 20,000-square-foot facilities.[39] Some observers expect that the Internet will eventually link not just pieces of factory equipment but also factories themselves, and perhaps even entire supply chains.

A highly productive organization is in an ideal position to thrive and grow. Thus, employees can benefit from productivity improvements. This is true especially when efforts to boost productivity focus on improving the quality of processes rather than simply cutting payroll costs. Even so, many employees react with fear when managers start talking about improving productivity.

Employees may have good reason to be fearful. Many have experienced or heard of cost reductions leading to less overtime pay, more difficult work, and even layoffs. Today's business news is full of stories about *outsourcing* (contracting with specialists to perform business functions) and *offshoring* (arranging for lower-cost workers in other countries to handle jobs that had been performed in the United States). When layoffs occur, the people who are left behind often have to struggle to keep up with the work that still has to be done.

Supervisors must respond to these fears. Most important, they must be prepared with information. A supervisor who does not understand the types of changes to be made and the reasons for them should discuss the matter with his or her manager as soon as possible. After obtaining a clear view of the organization's plans and goals, a supervisor should present this information to the employees. In doing so, a supervisor should emphasize what the benefits will be and avoid dwelling on the negatives. Sometimes productivity improvements such as automation or improved work processes make jobs more interesting, as in the case of bank tellers after deposits and withdrawals became automated. Often in today's competitive global business environment, productivity improvement is simply necessary for survival.

At ArvinMeritor Inc.'s manufacturing facility in Asheville, North Carolina, some managers and supervisors were initially unenthusiastic when the company brought in consultants to improve efficiency. But orders for the company's axles were falling, and profits were diving too. Support for the effort built as supervisors and production workers learned how to carry out programs for making production leaner and continuously improving methods. The Asheville facility has since saved millions of dollars through greater efficiency, and customer satisfaction improved as well. The factory even became so competitive on costs that it began to fill orders that had been going to a Mexican facility.[40]

When a supervisor gives information about productivity improvement, employees should have an opportunity to ask questions. The supervisor who cannot answer some of the questions should promise to get answers—and then do so. On its own, information will not make employees enthusiastic about a productivity program, but uninformed employees almost certainly will suffer from low morale.

In Chapter 14, we look more closely at how supervisors can help employees cope with the fears and related challenges that accompany productivity improvements and other types of change.

Skills Module

PART ONE: CONCEPTS

Summary

2.1 Describe the consequences suffered by organizations as a result of poor-quality work.

Poor-quality work gives an organization a negative image, which drives away customers and makes it harder to recruit superior employees and borrow money. Poor-quality work also can lead to higher costs associated with attracting customers, inspecting for and correcting defects, replacing defective products, and defending against lawsuits.

2.2 Compare product quality control and process control.

Both types of quality control involve preventing and detecting quality-related problems. Product quality control focuses on ways to improve the product. Process control focuses on how to do things in a way that results in higher quality.

2.3 Summarize techniques for quality control.

Statistical quality control involves looking for defects in parts or finished products selected through a sampling technique. In statistical process control, the operator takes samples during the process, plots the results on a chart, and makes corrections when the chart indicates the process is out of control. The zero-defects approach holds that everyone in the organization should work toward the goal of delivering such high quality that all aspects of the organization's goods and services are free of problems. Employee involvement teams plan ways to improve quality in their areas of the organization. In periodic meetings, team members examine needs for improvement and develop solutions. Six Sigma is a structured approach in which teams define problems in work processes and identify solutions that bring defects down to 3.4 per million. The lean enterprise philosophy refers to either improving the flow of work through a production process or continually identifying and eliminating waste through the use of a variety of assessment, scheduling, and production control tools. Total quality management is an organization-wide focus on satisfying customers by continuously improving every business process involved in delivering goods or services. Thus, TQM is a continuous process that unfolds gradually and focuses on satisfying customers.

2.4 Identify ways organizations measure their success in continuous quality improvement.

Organizations compare their practices and performance with various sets of guidelines. They may compete for the Baldrige Performance Excellence Program or assess their performance using its evaluation categories. They may seek certification for meeting the standards of ISO 9000. Also, they may compare their performance with that of organizations that excel in particular areas—a practice known as benchmarking. To ensure that any of these methods are focused on the right measures, the organization can set performance standards in terms of customer value. Focusing on preventing quality problems is cheaper than detecting them. Supervisors and other managers should set, communicate, and enforce standards for quality control. The organization should insist on high quality from its suppliers inside and outside the organization. Supervisors and higher-level managers should provide valued rewards for high-quality work.

2.5 Identify constraints on productivity.

Productivity is the amount of results (output) an organization gets for a given amount of inputs such as labor and machinery. Management limits productivity when it does not seem truly committed to improving it. Employee attitudes and skills limit productivity when employees are unable or unwilling to meet on organizations that limit their productivity to achieve other objectives. A union contract may contain work rules that limit productivity.

2.6 Describe how productivity and productivity improvements are measured.

To measure productivity, divide the amount of outputs by the amount of inputs. Outputs are the amount of work done or goods and services produced, assuming that these are of acceptable quality. Inputs may be measured as dollars, hours, or both. Productivity increases when output increases, input decreases, or both.

2.7 Identify ways productivity may be improved.

Two ways to improve productivity are to control quality and to control costs. Controlling quality

involves minimizing defects or errors. Controlling costs involves producing the same amount of goods or services at a lower cost or producing more at the same cost. A supervisor may increase output by having people or machines work faster or harder. A more effective approach may be to improve methods, that is, to get things done more efficiently. The supervisor may identify ways to reduce overhead and minimize waste, including idle time and wasted physical resources. Regulating or leveling the work flow can make staffing more efficient. Installing modern equipment reduces costs when the new equipment is more efficient. To cut costs related to personnel, a supervisor should see that workers receive adequate training and motivation, and he or she should take steps to minimize tardiness, absenteeism, and turnover.

2.8 Explain why employees have fears about productivity improvement and how supervisors can address those fears.

Many employees are fearful of productivity improvements because many organizations make such changes through layoffs and extra work for the remaining employees. Supervisors can respond by keeping employees informed about the organization's plans, emphasizing the benefits, and listening to employees.

Key Terms

productivity, *p. 28*
quality control, *p. 30*
product quality control, *p. 30*
process control, *p. 31*
statistical quality control, *p. 33*
statistical process control (SPC), *p. 33*
zero-defects approach, *p. 34*
employee involvement teams, *p. 34*

Six Sigma, *p. 35*
total quality management (TQM), *p. 36*
Baldrige Performance Excellence Program, *p. 39*
ISO 9000, *p. 39*
benchmarking, *p. 39*
value, *p. 40*

overhead, *p. 48*
idle time/downtime, *p. 49*
detour behavior, *p. 49*
payback period, *p. 51*
average rate of return (ARR), *p. 51*
turnover, *p. 52*

Review and Discussion Questions

1. Brand X Corporation seeks to be the lowest-cost maker of lawn chairs and toboggans. To keep costs down, management tells the production department, "Keep that assembly line moving. We have an inspector on staff to catch the mistakes later." What are the consequences Brand X Corporation is likely to experience as a result of this approach to manufacturing?

2. What is the difference between product quality control and process control? Give an example of each. (If possible, use examples from a job you have held.)

3. Define the zero-defects approach to quality control. Do you think zero defects is attainable? Why or why not?

4. Michelle LeVerrier supervises a group of tellers at a bank. The bank manager has asked her to lead an employee involvement team designed to improve the processes of serving individual customers at the teller windows. The four steps the team must take are to (*a*) identify quality problems in the specific area of responsibility, (*b*) select one problem to focus on, (*c*) analyze the problem, and (*d*) identify solutions and select one to present to management. How might Michelle use this four-step procedure to conduct her first team meeting?

5. What is total quality management (TQM)?

6. Imagine that you are the supervisor responsible for a pharmacy. You have received a few

complaints about mistakes in customers' prescriptions. To improve the quality of service delivered by the pharmacists, you can concentrate on (*a*) doing a better job of catching errors in the future or (*b*) doing a better job of avoiding errors. Which approach would you choose? Explain.

7. Frank Ouellette works at a government agency in which neither managers nor employees seem to worry about how long it takes to complete an assignment. Should Frank's co-workers be concerned about productivity? Why or why not?

8. Anna Holt, a supervisor in a boot manufacturing plant, just received a memo from her manager informing her that productivity on her shift must increase by 10 percent during the next fiscal quarter. However, when she recently approached her manager about upgrading two of the machines, she was turned down. In addition, she knows that her employees' union will balk at an increase in the number of boots her group must produce in a given shift. What constraints on productivity does Anna face? How might she attempt to resolve them?

9. At the claims-processing office for All-Folks Insurance, 25 employees process 2,500 claims a day. The claims-processing office for Purple Cross Insurance uses a state-of-the-art computer system, and its 15 employees process 3,000 claims a day.

   a. Which office is more productive?

   b. At which office would you expect employees to be paid more? Why?

   c. Suppose that half the claims processed by the employees at Purple Cross contain errors and all of the claims processed at All-Folks are done correctly. Which office would you say is more productive? Why?

10. Where can supervisors get information to help them determine costs?

11. How would you expect employees to respond to each of these efforts to cut costs?

    a. A plan to increase output by scheduling fewer rest breaks.

    b. A plan to increase output by hiring someone to bring supplies to workers, rather than having them get their own supplies.

12. Rachel Roth supervises a shift of workers who manufacture ski clothing. Because of its seasonal nature, the work flow tends to be uneven, and Rachel feels that this hurts productivity. What steps might Rachel take to try to regulate the work flow in her department?

13. A maintenance supervisor learned that installing a type of high-efficiency light bulb in the building can save the organization $1,000 a year. Replacing the light bulbs with the new ones would cost about $2,500.

    a. What is the payback period for this replacement?

    b. What is the average rate of return?

    c. Do you think this is a worthwhile investment? Why or why not?

14. How does high turnover hurt productivity? What can a supervisor do to minimize turnover?

15. Why do employees sometimes resist productivity improvements? How can supervisors prepare for and respond to employee attitudes?

Notes

1. Louise Lee, "Dell: Facing Up to Past Mistakes," *BusinessWeek*, June 18, 2006, http://www.businessweek.com/stories/2006-06-18/dell-facing-up-to-past-mistakes, accessed March 11, 2014.

2. David Voreacos, Alex Nussbaum, and Greg Farrell, "Johnson & Johnson's Quality Catastrophe," *Bloomberg BusinessWeek*, March 31, 2011, http://www.businessweek.com/magazine/content/11_15/b4223064555570.htm#p1; and Mina Kimes, "Why J&J's Headache Won't Go Away," *Fortune*, August 19, 2010, http://money.cnn.com/2010/08/18/news/companies/jnj_drug_recalls.fortune/, accessed March 11, 2014.

3. Nick Zubko, "The Secret Ingredients in Food Safety," *Industry Week*, October 9, 2008, http:// www.industryweek.com/companies-amp-executives/secret-ingredients-food-safety, accessed March 11, 2014; and Kent Garber, "Food Safety's Dirty Little Secret," *U.S. News & World Report*, September 10, 2008, http://www.usnews.com/news/national/articles/2008/09/10/food-safetys-dirty-little-secret, accessed March 11, 2014.

4. Mary Connelly, "Ford Works with Suppliers to Ensure Quality Standards," *Automotive News*, April 30, 2001, p. 36.

5. Maggie McFadden, "Quality Management: The Quality Is in the Process," *Quality*, June 1, 2006, http://www.qualitymag.com/articles/84762-quality-management-the-quality-is-in-the-process, accessed March 5, 2014.

6. John M. Buell, "Lean Six Sigma and Patient Safety: A Recipe for Success," *Healthcare Executive*, March/April 2010, pp. 26–35.

7. For more information about how statistical process control can be used in organizational settings, see Mattias Elg, Jesper Olsson, and Jens Dahlgaard, "Implementing statistical process control: An organizational perspective," *The International Journal of Quality and Reliability Management*, 2008, p. 545.

8. John S. McClenahen, "General Cable Corp.: IW Best Plants Profile 2005" *Industry Week*, September 12, 2005, http://www.industryweek.com/companies-amp-executives/general-cable-corp-iw-best-plants-profile-2005.

9. "Six Sigma—Overview," The Quality Portal, www.thequalityportal.com/q_6sigma.htm, accessed March 5, 2014.

10. Gregory T. Lucier and Sridhar Seshadri, "GE Takes Six Sigma beyond the Bottom Line," *Strategic Finance*, May 2001, pp. 40–46.

11. "How McKesson Leverages Six Sigma to Drive AR Process Enhancements," *Managing Credit, Receivables and Collections*, October 2010, pp. 1–4.

12. To learn more about how six sigma has affected management practices, see Xingxing Zu, Lawrence Fredendall, and Thomas Douglas, "The evolving theory of quality management: The role of Six Sigma," *Journal of Operations Management*, 2008, pp. 630–650.

13. Richard Owen and Laura L. Brooks, PhD, *Answering the Ultimate Question: How Net Promoter Can Transform Your Business*, John Wiley & Sons, November 2008.

14. For a recent description of total quality management, see Therese Joiner, "Total quality management and performance: The role of organization support and co-worker support," *The International Journal of Quality and Reliability Management*, 2007, p. 617.

15. Roberto Ceniceros, "Insurance Department Takes Team Approach to Quality," *Business Insurance*, April 29, 2001, http://www.businessinsurance.com/article/20010429/AWARDS03/10003807.

16. Matthew Spina, "Renting County Park Shelters to Become Easier," *Buffalo News (Buffalo, N.Y.)*, June 12, 2008, http://www.highbeam.com/doc/1P2-21677005.html.

17. National Institute of Standards and Technology, "Fact Sheet: Malcolm Baldrige National Quality Award," NIST Web site, www.nist.gov/public_affairs/factsheet/mbnqa.cfm, accessed March 5, 2014.

18. National Institute of Standards and Technology, "Fact Sheet: Malcolm Baldrige National Quality Award," NIST Web site, www.nist.gov/public_affairs/factsheet/mbnqa.cfm, accessed March 5, 2014; David Drickhamer, "Continuous Improvement—Beating the Baldrige Blues," *Industry Week*, December 21, 2004, http://www.industryweek.com/companies-amp-executives/continuous-improvement-beating-baldrige-blues; National Institute of Standards and Technology: Baldrige FAQs: "Baldrige Award Recipients," NIST Web site, http://www.nist.gov/baldrige/about/faqs_recipients.cfm, accessed March 26, 2014.

19. For a recent description of how ISO relates to a company's financial status, see Mary Benner and Fracisco Veloso, "ISO 9000 practices and financial performance: A technology coherence perspective," *Journal of Operations Management*," 2008, p. 611.

20. Pallavi Gogoi, "Thinking Outside the Cereal Box," *BusinessWeek*, July 27, 2003, http://www.businessweek.com/stories/2003-07-27/thinking-outside-the-cereal-box.

21. John R. Brandt, "Competing beyond Quality," *Industry Week*, December 21, 2004, http://www.industryweek.com/planning-amp-forecasting/brandt-leadership-competing-beyond-quality.

22. National Institute of Standards and Technology, "2003 Award Winner: Baptist Hospital Inc.," NIST Web site, www.nist.gov, accessed March 5, 2014; Baptist Health Care, "Standards of Performance," Baptist Health Care Web site, www.ebaptisthealthcare.org/BHC/Standards.aspx, accessed March 5, 2014.

23. Organisation for Economic Co-operation and Development, "Income and Productivity Levels," *OECD Factbook 2008*, http://www.oecd.org/statsportal/.

24. "Yammering Away at the Office," *The Economist*, January 28, 2010, http://www.economist.com/node/15350928.

25. "Airline Data Project," MIT Global Airline Industry Program, http://web.mit.edu/airlinedata/www/default.html, accessed April 22, 2014.

26. John S. McClenahen, "New World Leader," *Industry Week*, December 21, 2004, http://www.industryweek.com/companies-amp-executives/new-world-leader, accessed March 8, 2014.

27. 3M Manufacturing Services: Lean Six Sigma, http://solutions.3m.com/wps/portal/3M/en_WW/DrugDeliverySystems/DDSD/technology-solutions/manufacturing-services/operational-excellence/lean-six-sigma/, accessed March 8, 2014.

28. Vrushali Soni, "Six Sigma at 3M, Inc. Case Study," Management Paradise, http://www.managementparadise.com/VrushaliSoni/documents/3722/six-sigma-at-3m-inc-case-study/, accessed March 26, 2014.

29. Stephen J. Mezias and Alan B. Eisner, "Modes of Interorganizational Imitation and the Transformation of Organizational Populations," Advances in Strategic Management, 1999, 16, pp. 113–130, http://pages.stern.nyu.edu/~smezias/Modes_of_Interorganizational_Imitation.pdf, accessed March 26, 2014.

30. Michael Strand, "Philips Turns to 'Lean Manufacturing,'" *Salina Journal (Salina, Kan.)*, August 15, 2008, downloaded from Business & Company Resource Center, http://galenet.galegroup.com.

31. American Management Association (AMA), "2005 Electronic Monitoring & Surveillance Survey: Many Companies Monitoring, Recording, Videotaping—and Firing—Employees," news release, May 18, 2005, AMA Web site, www.amanet.org.

32. Tonya Vinas, "Best Practices—Spreading the Good Word," *Industry Week*, December 21, 2004, http://www.industryweek.com/companies-amp-executives/best-practices-spreading-good-word, accessed March 8, 2014.

33. "What's Lifting Productivity," *BusinessWeek*, May 23, 2004, http://www.businessweek.com/stories/2004-05-23/whats-lifting-productivity, accessed March 8, 2014.

34. Raymond Dreyfack, "Treasure Chest: Money-Saving Ideas for the Profit-Minded Supervisor," *Supervision*, December 1, 2001, downloaded from Business & Company Resource Center, http://galenet.galegroup.com.

35. "Great Clips Launches Industry's 1st Online Check-In Service," Great Clips web site, April 15, 2011, http://www.greatclips.com/about-us/press-room/online-check-in-04-15-11, accessed March 26, 2014.

36. Stanley Holmes and Wendy Zellner, "Commentary: The Costco Way," *BusinessWeek*, April 11, 2004, http://www.businessweek.com/stories/2004-04-11/commentary-the-costco-way, accessed March 10, 2014.

37. For more information about factors that reduce turnover, see Carl Maertz, Rodger Griffeth, Nathanael Campbell & David Allen, "The effects of perceived organizational support and perceived supervisor support on employee turnover," *Journal of Organizational Behavior*, 2007, 1059–1075.

38. Darnell Little and Adam Aston, "Even the Supervisor Is Expendable," *BusinessWeek*, July 22, 2001, http://www.businessweek.com/stories/2001-07-22/even-the-supervisor-is-expendable, accessed March 10, 2014.

39. Steve Hamm, Spencer E. Ante, Andy Reingardt, and Manjeet Kripalani, "Services: To Stay Competitive, Companies Are Finding New Ways to Automate Operations, Reuse Technology, and Streamline Processes," *BusinessWeek*, June 20, 2004, http://www.businessweek.com/stories/2004-06-20/services, accessed March 10, 2014.

40. Philip Siekman, "The Struggle to Get Lean," *Fortune*, January 12, 2004, http://money.cnn.com/magazines/fortune/fortune_archive/2004/01/12/357931/, accessed March 10, 2014.

PART TWO: SKILL-BUILDING

Meeting the Challenge

Reflecting back on page 27, discuss how it might have felt to be a production or maintenance supervisor when Shearer's Foods was preparing to build and operate its new energy-efficient facility. If you were a supervisor, would you have welcomed or resented the drive to be efficient in every way? Why? Working as a group, summarize three ways in which a Shearer's supervisor could support the company's efforts to reach "perfection" in quality and productivity. For ideas, review the management functions and skills introduced in Chapter 1.

Problem-Solving Case: Fast Food Is All about Service

David Drickhamer, former editorial research director for *Industry Week* magazine, told about a stop he made to buy lunch for his hungry child. They were running errands, so Drickhamer pulled into the drive-through lane of a fast-food restaurant.

The customer experience began when Drickhamer pulled up to the ordering station and heard a recorded message urging him to try the chain's new chicken sandwich. He ordered a child's meal featuring chicken pieces and a dipping sauce.

Drickhamer drove up to the cashier's window. Jon, the cashier, asked him to please wait while he left to get new batteries for the headset through which he received orders. Jon returned a minute later and requested payment—but for the wrong total amount. While he had been away getting the batteries, two more orders had come in, so Jon tried to figure out how to make his computer return to Drickhamer's order. Jon apologized and called for a supervisor to help. The supervisor walked over and wordlessly corrected the order on the computer. Jon took the payment and made change as he entered the next customer's order.

Drickhamer pulled up to the next window to receive his food. There, a woman named Mary asked his choice of dipping sauce. He replied "None" as he looked inside the bag. Seeing that no napkins were included (even though this was a child's meal that usually comes with a sauce), he requested napkins—twice. She, like Jon, was wearing a headset and didn't reply.

Drickhamer remained at the pickup window, waiting for napkins. A few seconds later, the window opened again. A third employee was there, ready with the next customer's order. Drickhamer repeated his request for napkins. The third employee handed over the napkins, and Drickhamer drove away with a contented passenger in the backseat.

1. What forms does quality take in a fast-food restaurant? That is, what aspects of the food, service, atmosphere, and so on do you consider to be acceptable in terms of quality, and what would exceed your expectations?

2. Productivity efforts in a fast-food restaurant often involve behind-the-scenes work in the kitchen. But in describing his experience, Drickhamer emphasizes that in a service business, production includes interactions with the customer. Identify one or two places in this case study where productivity could have been better.

3. Working alone or in a group, draw a diagram of the work process described in this case study. In your diagram, show what materials each employee needed, as well as what each employee provided to the customer. Evaluate where the process could be improved, based on the information given and any experiences you have with fast-food restaurants. Finally, prepare a list of actions to improve the quality and productivity of this work process. As directed by your instructor, submit the diagram and list as a written report or present your findings to the class.

Source: Based on David Drickhamer, "Continuous Improvement—Fine-Tuning the Fast Food Lane," *Industry Week*, December 21, 2004, http://www.industryweek.com/companies-amp-executives/continuous-improvement-fine-tuning-fast-food-lane, accessed March 10, 2014.

Assessing Yourself

Test Your Personal Productivity

Place a check mark next to each of the activities you do or habits you have formed. The more check marks, the more productive you can be.

_____ 1. I complete tasks right away, without procrastinating.

_____ 2. I take notes during meetings and conversations to avoid misunderstanding and omissions.

_____ 3. I plan tomorrow's work today by writing a few notes before quitting time.

_____ 4. I prioritize my tasks, tackling the most important or most difficult ones first every day.

_____ 5. I keep a follow-up file.

_____ 6. I plan realistic deadlines, allowing time for delays.

_____ 7. I keep my workspace or desk neat and uncluttered.

_____ 8. I delegate wherever possible and reasonable to my assistant and/or my subordinates.

_____ 9. I limit the number and length of phone calls and monitor my own use of the Internet.

_____ 10. I am not afraid to say no in order to protect the time I have available for the job.

Pause and Reflect

1. Do supervisors need to be even more productive than people they supervise? Why or why not?

2. How can I use my time better in the future?

Source: Quiz from Ted Pollock, "Increasing Personal Productivity," *Supervision*, March 2001. Reprinted by permission of © National Research Bureau, 320 Valley Street, Burlington, IA 52601.

Class Skills Exercise

Defining and Measuring Quality of Service

Because roughly 8 out of every 10 jobs in this country are in the service sector, it is important to understand the significance of providing quality customer service. This exercise is designed to help you apply what you learned in this chapter to a service-sector job.

Instructions

1. Form groups of two or three people. Identify a work setting where customer service is critical. The place should be one with which all of you are familiar. It might be a workplace where one of you has worked or at least been a customer (e.g., retail store, post office, bank, hospital, university, resort, restaurant).
2. Identify a specific job title for the work setting (e.g., waiter/waitress, nurse, clerk at the university bookstore, shoe salesperson at a store).
3. Review some of the principles covered in this chapter (see Exhibit A). Select those that are appropriate to the job you have identified, and develop specific customer service guidelines for the employees.

EXHIBIT A

- Process control
- Zero-defects approach
- Employee involvement teams
- Philip Crosby's five ingredients for quality (integrity, systems, communications, operations, and policies)
- Benchmarking
- Prevention versus detection
- Standard setting and enforcement
- The role of suppliers
- Rewards for quality
- Dimensions of quality (performance, features, reliability, conformance, durability, serviceability, aesthetics, and perceived quality from Table 2.1)

4. Now select principles appropriate for a supervisor of employees in the job you have identified, and develop some supervisory guidelines that focus on customer service. For example, how should the supervisor monitor performance to determine that employees are practicing the quality service standards you have established?
5. Share your group's efforts with the class by presenting a written statement that includes work setting, job title, principles from Exhibit A and how your group applied them to the job, and principles from Exhibit A and how your group applied them to the supervisor.

Source: This team-building exercise was prepared by Corinne Livesay, Bryan College, Chattanooga, Tennessee.

Building Supervision Skills

Improving Performance

Divide the class into groups of four to six people. Each group receives the following materials: 20 index cards, a roll of tape, a pair of scissors, and a felt-tipped pen. To complete the exercise, the groups may use these supplies and no others.

The instructor specifies how much time the groups will have to complete the project (10 or 15 minutes). When the instructor gives the signal to begin, each group is to use the materials provided to construct a house. The teams may use the materials in any way they see fit, but they may not use additional materials of their own.

When time is up, someone from each group brings the group's house to a table or other designated location in the classroom. The instructor appoints five class members to serve on a panel of judges. They rate each house on a scale of 1 to 5 (with 5 representing the highest quality). The judges' scores are totaled, and the house with the highest score is deemed the winner of this quality contest. Finally, the class discusses the following questions:

- On what basis did the judges rate the quality of the houses? How many of the criteria in Table 2.1 did they use?
- How did your group decide on a way to make its house? How well did your group work together to produce the house?
- Given your group's experience and the information about how the judges arrived at their scores, how would you want to improve the quality of your house if you could repeat the exercise? Are your changes process improvements or product improvements?
- Which team was most productive? Why? Did it use methods that could have helped the other groups? How could you have improved the productivity of your team?

chapter three | Groups, Teams, and Powerful Meetings

A Supervision Challenge

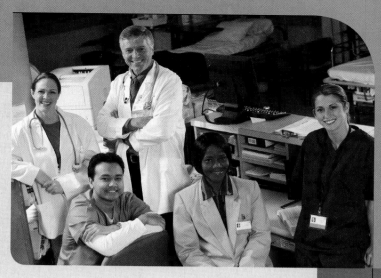

A CHRISTIANA HOSPITAL DEPARTMENT CAN'T SUCCEED WITHOUT COOPERATION

In a hospital operating room, teamwork can literally be a life or death matter. That teamwork extends beyond the surgical team of doctors, nurses, and technicians to include behind-the-scenes support from groups such as a sterile processing department (SPD), which is responsible for ensuring that clean, correct instruments are available for each surgical procedure. Proficiency from the SPD team is critical to maintaining smooth proceedings and quality patient care. Unfortunately for Christiana Hospital of Newark, Delaware, however, the support from SPD was becoming unreliable. Flustered employees were rushing at the end of each shift to assemble carts of supplies, but items were often missing or defective, causing delays for the surgical teams.

The solution? Taking teamwork to the next level. The hospital created problem-solving teams that combined directors, managers, nurses, supervisors, and employees from the SPD department and operating rooms. The team members were charged with identifying the sources of the problem and determining what changes were needed to achieve excellent service.

When employees from different areas came together, it helped everyone see that the problem had many causes—some were the result of poorly established and executed SPD procedures, and others stemmed from factors beyond the control of the SPD staff. For example, there was a gap between SPD staffing levels and workloads. Doctors performed most operations between 9 a.m. and 5 p.m., when SPD staffing levels were high; however, used instruments were being returned to SPD in the evening as shifts were changing. The problem-solving teams drew up new rules to get more of the instruments back to SPD earlier. In addition, SPD supervisors adjusted staffing levels so that enough SPD employees would be available during the busiest times. The teams also convinced hospital administrators to increase instrument inventory, putting an end to shortages.

Improved communication played a role in the solution, too. SPD staff had suffered from poor morale as they tried with repeated failure to meet performance targets. Employees working different shifts felt in so much conflict that they frequently left unfinished work for the next shift to complete. SPD supervisors recognized these conditions and led the way in changing attitudes. They encouraged their employees to contribute their ideas for improving processes so that everyone could feel pride in meeting higher standards. They also implemented new half-hour meetings at shift changes to coordinate work and improve communication. These efforts led to decreased conflict between employees and an increased sense of collaboration and team building.

Through the supervisors' openness and encouragement, the SPD was able to learn from its failures and come together as a team. As the SPD staffers learned, it is important to be able to discuss challenges and come together to resolve them. These events show that effective procedures carried out by collaborative teams—and individuals who know that they can voice their opinions—produce strong outcomes in the operating room and the hospital setting more broadly. An effective process and a positive work environment help to ensure quality patient care.

At Christiana Hospital, SPD supervisors served as both members of the problem-solving teams and leaders of their shifts. As you study this chapter, think about the benefits of approaching problems as a team. Are there also challenges in team building and teamwork? What possibilities for greater success from a team effort can be realized if a team is well designed and well led?

Sources: Based on Rick Dana Barlow, "Rediscovering Excellence after Being Lost in Transition," *Healthcare Purchasing News*, September 2008, downloaded from Business & Company Resource Center; Gheorghe H. Popescu "Factors That Influence Management Development in Healthcare Organizations," *Economics, Management, and Financial Markets* 8.4 (2013), 172–177.

It is unlikely that Christiana Hospital would have made equally successful improvements without the guidance of its problem-solving teams. Aisha Mootry also appreciates the importance of working with others at her organization, a media agency called Tapestry. When Mootry was promoted from media planner to media supervisor, she realized she would have to manage a complex set of working relationships, including those with the pair of media planners she supervises, her own manager, and her colleagues handling other functions and client groups at Tapestry. Mootry sums up every supervisor's challenge this way: "There are many layers of relationships that need to be managed."[1] A central fact of life for supervisors is that much of their work and almost all of their goals involve getting work done in groups.

group
Two or more people who interact with one another, are aware of one another, and think of themselves as a unit

To define that term formally, a **group** is two or more people who interact with one another, are aware of one another, and think of themselves as a group. In today's business world, these groups include both those who work together in person as well as those who work together virtually using the various tools made available courtesy of the Internet. The supervisor must see that groups of employees work together to accomplish objectives. An increasing number of organizations are expanding group efforts by forming teams. As leaders or members of a team, supervisors help plan and carry out a variety of activities. Many group and team efforts take place in meetings.

This chapter covers how the supervisor can work effectively as a leader and member of a team or other group. Some general characteristics of groups—why people join them, what kinds of groups operate in the workplace, how groups can be described, and how they develop—are described. Then efforts to build employee participation through the use of teamwork are discussed, and the basic benefits of teamwork and ways supervisors can lead teams effectively are outlined. Finally, the chapter provides guidelines for holding meetings.

Reasons for Joining Groups

LO3.1 ▶ Explain why people join groups.

The opening of Colors restaurant in New York City came as a sign of rebuilding after a national tragedy. About half of the restaurant's 50 workers had been employees of Windows on the World, the famed restaurant near the top of the World Trade Center. After the bombing of the center in 2001, Windows employees who survived the attack confronted the grief of losing dozens of co-workers as well as their workplace and their own jobs. A group of former Windows employees joined other investors to start Colors, an establishment whose name reflects the ethnic diversity of the cuisine and the staff, which includes immigrants from over 20 nations. Executive chef Raymond Mohan not only runs the kitchen but also coaches the employee–owners in their role as restaurant investors. Mohan says, "Everyone has an opinion about how [Colors] should be run. . . . I try to make sure that they're doing things in a safe, healthy, and efficient way." An obvious reason to invest in and work for Colors is to pursue a career in the restaurant business. But for some employees, the relationships mean more. Bartender Patricio Valencia calls his co-workers from Windows "my second family."[2]

This example suggests that people belong to groups for many reasons. Sometimes group membership simply goes along with being an employee. In particular, all employees are members of the organization that employs them, most are part of a division

Sometimes a workplace, such as a restaurant, can be a home away from home for employees.

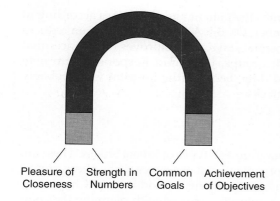

FIGURE 3.1 | What Draws People to Groups?

People are drawn to groups, whether work-related or purely social, for a variety of reasons.

Pleasure of Closeness   Strength in Numbers   Common Goals   Achievement of Objectives

or department, and some also join a union when they go to work for a particular company. At other times, employees join a group because their supervisor or some other manager asks them to do so. In such cases, an employee may join the group to advance his or her career or simply to avoid going against the manager's wishes. Finally, an employee may join a group because being a member satisfies his or her personal needs. The most common personal reasons for joining a group include the following, which are also illustrated in Figure 3.1:

- *Closeness*—Being members of the same group builds ties among people. Friendships generally result from the shared experiences that come from membership in some kind of group, such as a class at school or a bowling team.
- *Strength in numbers*—Having ties to others gives people confidence they may lack when they act alone. Their sense of confidence is well founded. In an organization, a group of people tends to be more influential than one person acting alone.
- *Common goals*—When people have a goal to meet, they can get moral and practical support by working with or alongside others who have similar goals.
- *Achievement of personal objectives*—Membership in a group can help people achieve personal objectives in a variety of ways. The time spent with group members can be enjoyable. Membership in certain groups can enhance a person's prestige. In a related vein, group membership can satisfy people's desire to feel important.

Groups in the Workplace

LO3.2 ▶ Distinguish types of groups that exist in the workplace.

As mentioned previously, all the employees of an organization form a group. On a practical level however, most organizations are too large for all their members to interact with one another. Therefore, except at very small organizations, most employees cluster into smaller groups. Some examples are departments, task forces, and groups that meet for lunch to play cards, do needlework, or talk about baseball. References to groups in this chapter generally mean these small groups, that is, groups small enough that all members interact with one another.

To fully benefit from the various groups in an organization, the supervisor needs to be able to identify them. The first step is to recognize the various categories of an organization's groups. Then the supervisor can apply several principles for building cooperation on the part of the groups.

Functional and Task Groups

functional groups
Groups that fulfill ongoing needs in the organization by carrying out a particular function

task groups
Groups that are set up to carry out a specific activity and then disband when the activity is completed

Some groups fulfill ongoing needs in the organization by carrying out a particular function, such as producing goods, selling products, or investing funds. These are called **functional groups.** For example, a hospital's accounting department has the ongoing responsibility for keeping accurate records of the flow of money into and out of the organization. In most cases, a functional group is one that appears on a company's organization chart.

Other groups, called **task groups,** are set up to carry out a specific activity, and they disband when that activity has been completed.[3] A task group also may be formed for a task that is ongoing. For example, Piedmont Medical Center in Rock Hill, South Carolina, set up a Rapid Response Team to respond to cardiac arrests (heart attacks) among patients. Whenever a nurse senses that a person has conditions associated with a heart attack, he or she pages for the team to respond. The team—which includes a critical-care nurse, respiratory therapist, critical-care doctor, and nursing supervisor—evaluates the patient and intervenes according to the symptoms observed. One team member, Dr. Bill Alleyne, says the team reduces the need for intensive care, shortens hospital stays, and improves the chances that patients will survive.[4] Like many task groups, the Rapid Response Team may operate for years with no definite end date, because the hospital will probably always have patients at risk for heart attacks.

Formal and Informal Groups

formal groups
Groups set up by management to meet organizational objectives

The examples of functional and task groups are also types of **formal groups.** These are groups set up by management to meet organizational objectives. Thus, these groups result from the management function of organizing (introduced in Chapter 1). A customer service department and a committee charged with planning the company picnic are formal groups.

informal groups
Groups that form when individuals in the organization develop relationships to meet personal needs

Other groups result when individuals in the organization develop relationships to meet personal needs. These are **informal groups.** Figure 3.2, on the following page, shows two informal groups in a small store. Perhaps the china department manager and four clerks like to jog after work; they might find themselves jogging together. Eventually they could build friendships around this shared activity. Most employees welcome the opportunity to be part of informal groups because these groups help satisfy social needs. The friendships established within the group can make work more enjoyable.

Informal subgroups can develop among members of a formal group when the formal group fails to meet some personal needs. For example, when some group members feel angry at the group's leader or uncertain about whether they really belong, they may form a subgroup. Subgroups may also form when some group members feel uncomfortable with the way they are expected to behave; for example, they might be expected not to express their feelings. In such a situation, the people who form a subgroup may feel more comfortable with the other members of the subgroup.

Members of a formal group might create an informal group by spending time together beyond the formal group setting. Exercising together could be an example.

Teamwork in an Organic Organization

An organic organization is one in which, at least in theory, there is very little hierarchy. Each employee is multi-talented and has the diverse skills and flexibility to perform a variety of tasks. In such an organization the workers all are on the same level, communication is a network of connections, and there are few rigid procedures. An organic organization has group leadership, dramatically improved teamwork, and, consequently, can more easily adapt to changes in the business environment or marketplace. The weakness of this type of organization is that it requires cooperation from all the members, which in the real world does not always occur.

Various companies have experimented with this type of organization. One notable example was Google who, in 2002, implemented an organic organization that was absent of engineering managers in efforts to facilitate a more streamlined process for idea development. This "flat" organization experiment ended within a few months, largely due to the realization that managers contribute beyond overseeing and delegating. Managers were critical in fostering collaboration and communication between employees and aiding employees in prioritizing tasks. Though Google stepped away from the completely "flat"

FIGURE 3.2 | Formal and Informal Group Structures

An organizational chart shows the formal relationships among employees and makes it possible to identify the functional groups within an organization. These are represented by the solid lines in this chart. Informal groups often form among employees to fulfill social needs. In this chart, the informal associations are indicated by the dotted lines.

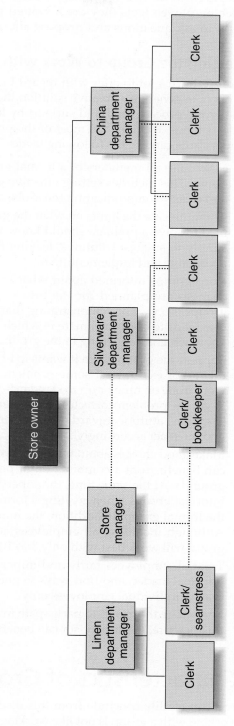

······· Informal links.

Source: From Samuel C. Certo, Human Relations Today: Concepts and Skills (New York: McGraw-Hill), p. 259.

approach, they did lower the number of supervisor and management positions. This grants the employees more authority. They are encouraged to share their ideas and suggestions, but also recognize that before doing so, they must be prepared to defend their ideas with data and sound reasoning. Consequently, each employee feels they are a valued part of the team and that they have the right to ask questions and propose alternatives.[5]

LO3.3 ▶ Discuss how supervisors can get groups to cooperate with them.

Getting the Group to Work with You

Groups have a lot to offer with regard to decision making and problem solving. A group can generate a creative solution that a single person might not think of, and the group process can build support by letting people make decisions about what affects them. To make the most of the potential benefits of working with groups, supervisors can use the following tactics.

- Make sure all members of a formal group know what they can and should be doing. This includes setting effective group objectives (described in Chapter 6) and clearly communicating those objectives.
- Communicate the limits on what the group can do. For example, a group assembled to solve a problem should know whether it is to implement the solution or simply to suggest solutions, leaving to the supervisor the task of choosing an alternative and implementing it.
- Keep groups informed about what is happening in the organization and what changes are planned for the future. Making the effort to communicate with groups is a way of demonstrating that they are important to the organization. It also tends to create a climate in which group members readily let the supervisor know what is happening in the group.
- Support the group when it wants to bring legitimate concerns to higher management. For example, if some problem is keeping employees from getting their work done on time or up to standards, the supervisor should do what is possible to get the problem corrected. However, this does not mean adopting an "us versus them" attitude toward management. The supervisor is a part of management and must act accordingly.
- Make good choices about whom to assign to the group. In many cases, the group can benefit from a combination of people with a variety of strengths or backgrounds. At the same time, the supervisor needs to be careful about splitting up informal groups when creating a formal one; doing so could hurt morale within the formal group. In addition, the number of group members can be important. Although including all employees is sometimes important, for many tasks a group will work best with only 5 to 10 members.
- Treat all employees fairly and impartially, respect the position of the group's informal leader, and find ways to give rewards to the group as a whole, rather than to individual employees only.
- Encourage the group to participate in solving problems. As a result of following this practice, the supervisor can benefit by receiving the group's support.

LO3.4 ▶ Describe characteristics of groups in the workplace.

Characteristics of Groups

You can readily conclude from this discussion and from personal experience that working with a group is not like working alone. Social scientists have summarized a number of group characteristics, including ways to describe them, how effective they are, and what pressures they place on individuals. Supervisors who are aware of this theoretical information can use it to understand what is happening in a group situation. They can decide whether the group is effectively supporting the achievement of

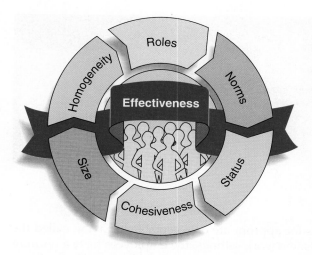

FIGURE 3.3 | Ways to Describe Groups

Groups can have a number of different characteristics. For a group to be effective, people with different personal traits must come together and fill the necessary roles within the group.

roles
Patterns of behavior related to employees' positions in a group

role conflicts
Situations in which a person has two different roles that call for conflicting types of behavior

organizational objectives or if supervisors need to step in and make changes.

When looking at how groups are the same or different, it helps to consider some basic ways of describing them. Some of the most useful characteristics include roles, norms, status, cohesiveness, size, homogeneity, and effectiveness—which are illustrated in Figure 3.3.

Roles

The character taken on by each actor in a play is the actor's role. In an organization's groups, the various group members also take on roles, or patterns of behavior related to their position in the group. Some common roles that you may have encountered or even held include the (formal or informal) leader of a group, the scapegoat, the class clown, and the person to whom others take their problems.

What leads a person to take on a role? Sometimes a person's formal position in an organization dictates a certain role. For example, as described in Chapter 1, certain kinds of behavior are expected of a supervisor. Another source of a person's role is a combination of the person's beliefs about how he or she ought to behave and other people's expectations about how that person will act. For example, if Anne displays empathy toward a colleague who is going through a divorce, she may eventually find that many people in the department come to her for advice when a problem arises. If she continues to respond with sympathy and concern, she may take on a role in which she hears other people's troubles but is expected not to complain herself. Similarly, if Stuart makes wisecracks during a couple of meetings, group members may start expecting to hear jokes and funny remarks from him on a regular basis.

The kinds of roles people select serve different purposes. People may take on a role, such as leader or organizer, that helps the group get its work done. Or they may take on a role that holds the group together—the person who can be counted on to smooth ruffled feathers whenever conflicts arise among group members. Finally, group members may take on roles that help them meet personal needs. Thus, Stuart may be making jokes to cover up his own discomfort with being a group participant.

Awareness of roles is important because recognizing them can help the supervisor encourage desirable behavior or bring about a change in undesirable behavior. The supervisor would probably want to include an informal group's leader in planning how to carry out a change in policy. A supervisor who finds an employee's wisecracks to be a distraction during meetings needs to understand that other people may be encouraging this employee's behavior. Thus, to get the employee to stop, the supervisor will have to end the encouragement of the wisecracks as well as the wisecracks themselves.

Sometimes supervisors also have to resolve problems involving role conflicts, situations in which a person has two different roles that call for conflicting types of behavior. Suppose, for example, that several employees have been members of a volleyball team for a number of years. At work, one of them is promoted to be supervisor of the others, with the expectation that he will end the goofing off that has been common in the department. The supervisor's role as teammate conflicts with his role as strict supervisor. The way the supervisor resolves this conflict—which role he chooses—will influence his performance as a supervisor as well as his relationship with the employees.[6]

Norms

norms
Group standards for appropriate or acceptable behavior

Groups typically have standards for appropriate or acceptable behavior, called the group's norms.[7] For instance, in some work settings, the employees have a norm of doing only what is expected of them and no more. They may fear that if they do an exceptional amount of work, management will expect that much from them every day. A new employee eager to develop a strong work record could anger the others if he or she violates the norm by doing "too much." Other norms may be stated rather than implied; for example, an organization expects everyone to arrive at work on time.

When a member of the group violates a norm, the group responds by pressuring the person to conform. Formal groups have procedures for handling violations of norms that are group policies, such as arriving at work on time. With unofficial norms, a typical first step would be for someone to point out to the violator how he or she is expected to behave. If that does not work, the group may resort to shutting the person out, ridiculing the person, or even threatening him or her with physical harm.

Employees whose norm is doing no more than is required have a norm that hurts the organization. When a supervisor finds that a group of employees seems to be behaving in a way that works against the achievement of organizational objectives, the supervisor could investigate whether these employees are following some norm of an informal group. This might be the case if half a dozen employees in the department regularly leave work 15 minutes early. One way to change this kind of norm is to look at the way the organization treats the behavior. Perhaps the organization or supervisor does not properly reward those who do follow the rules. In trying to persuade employees to change or ignore an informal group's norm, the supervisor must remember that violating norms carries negative consequences for group members.

Status

status
A group member's position in relation to others in the group

A group member's status is his or her position relative to others in the group. Status depends on a variety of factors, including the person's role in the group, title, pay, education level, age, race, and sex. Thus, in one group, the person with the highest status might be a man who is the tallest and owns a cottage by a lake. The others find this person's presence impressive and hope for invitations to the cottage, so his status is high.

Status is important to supervisors because group members with the highest status have the most effect on the development of group norms. Group members with lower status tend to pattern their behaviors after those of high-status members. A supervisor who wants to reinforce or change group norms will have the greatest success by focusing on the high-status members of the group.

Cohesiveness

cohesiveness
The degree to which group members stick together

The degree to which group members stick together is known as cohesiveness. A cohesive group has members who want to stay with the group even during periods of stress. They abide by group norms even when under pressure to follow other norms.

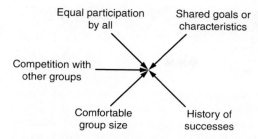

Equal participation by all

Shared goals or characteristics

Competition with other groups

Comfortable group size

History of successes

FIGURE 3.4 | Situations in Which Groups Stick Together

Many factors have an impact on a group's cohesiveness and, consequently, how well a group functions.

Groups that are cohesive work harder than others and are more likely to accomplish their objectives. Thus, when a group's objectives support those of the organization, the supervisor will want the group to be cohesive.[8] As summarized in Figure 3.4, the supervisor can foster cohesiveness in several ways:

- By emphasizing to group members their common characteristics and goals. A supervisor of a research department might point out proudly that this is a select group of talented individuals working on an important project.
- By emphasizing areas in which the group has succeeded in achieving its goals. A history of successes, such as accomplishing tasks or increasing the status of members, tends to improve cohesiveness.
- By keeping the group sufficiently small—ideally no more than eight members—so that everyone feels comfortable participating. When a larger number of employees report to a single supervisor, he or she might want to support the formation of more than one group.
- By encouraging competition with other groups. In contrast, cohesiveness diminishes when group members are competing with one another.
- By encouraging less active members to participate in group activities. Groups tend to be more cohesive when everyone participates equally.

Size

An organization's groups may vary widely in size. As few as two people can form a group. Up to 15 or 16 group members can get to know and communicate well with one another. Beyond 20 members, however, informal subgroups tend to form.

Big groups typically operate differently from small ones. Small groups tend to reach decisions faster and rely less on formal rules and procedures. Also, quiet group members are more likely to participate in a small group. If group processes seem overly cumbersome—for example, if the group tends to take too long to reach decisions—the supervisor might consider dividing the group into subgroups of about 8–12 members. A bigger group might make sense when a lot of work needs to get done and the individual group members can work independently most of the time.

Homogeneity

homogeneity
The degree to which the members of a group are the same

The degree to which the members of a group are the same is known as **homogeneity.** Thus, a *homogeneous* group is one in which group members have a lot in common. When group members have many differences, the group is said to be *heterogeneous.*[9] Group members can be alike or different according to age, sex, race, work experience, education level, social class, personality, interests, and other characteristics.

The members of a homogeneous group enjoy a number of benefits. Perhaps the most significant is that people feel most comfortable around others who are like themselves. This may be the reason that homogeneous groups offer better cooperation among members, greater satisfaction, and higher productivity, at least for simple tasks.

At the same time, the U.S. workforce is becoming more diverse. For complex, creative tasks, a heterogeneous group can perform better than a homogeneous one because group members offer a variety of skills, experience, and viewpoints. The heterogeneous group as a whole has broader skills and knowledge, and it can examine problems from different points of view.

SUPERVISION: NEW TRENDS

HOW SOCIAL NETWORKING IS MAKING GROUPS MORE EFFECTIVE

Social networking, made famous by Facebook and LinkedIn, is an easy way for people to send messages, photos, and thoughts to family, friends, and colleagues. Most of us have heard the biggest downside of this software: that the public nature of the Internet spreads around information that is better kept private. But computer users at many companies have also seen the huge upside: helping people find each other and share valuable content. Therefore, more and more companies are setting up *private* social networks and encouraging their employees to log in, find coworkers with common interests, and share what they know, so everyone can build connections and work more effectively.

One way social networking can build effectiveness is by helping employees select the best people to meet a need. Just as people set up a profile on Facebook to describe their hometown, relationship status, interests, and more, employees in a corporate social network can set up a profile detailing their work experiences, skills, and interests. A supervisor trying to start up a new project could search the network to find the others in the organization who have done something similar and can offer advice. Then he or she might search profiles of the employees in his or her department to verify that employees selected for the project have the right mix of backgrounds and skills.

Social networking tools also can help group members communicate more effectively. Group members can easily post documents and messages about projects they are working on. Status updates—as simple as "Away from my desk" or as detailed as "Researching ideas for reducing the error rate on Line B"—can help employees find each other, know when not to interrupt, or identify when might be a good time to jump in and help with a task. Employees can post status updates or use microblogs (like tweets on Twitter) to provide additional information about what they are doing

and what ideas and trouble they are encountering. Instant messages offer easy back-and-forth as well.

Social networking sites can also be set up with widgets—small, embedded software programs—that let users record and display progress on projects. Charts and graphics can help supervisors and employees easily see whether they are on schedule or need to press harder to complete specific tasks. And when a project is complete, the collection of status updates, instant messages, shared documents, and other communications at the site can be saved as a record of the project. Supervisors can use the information for appraising performance or planning new projects so that future group performance is even more effective.

IBM is one company that has leveraged social networking to increase communication and collaboration between employees all over the world. To that end, they created Beehive, an internal social network, which has gained momentum in the years since its implementation and now supports over 30,000 employees. Employees can use this network in three different ways. They can connect with other employees they have met on projects, at company meetings, and so on, as well connecting with other employees that have similar areas of expertise. Another use is brainstorming and collaboration with other employees about projects. Last, Beehive can be used by all employees to pass ideas and information on to upper level employees/managers that they usually do not have a connection with or access to.

Sources: Adapted from Matthew Sarrel, "Tapping the Positive from Social Networks for Collaboration," *eWeek*, November 9, 2010, pp. 22–26; http://www.eweek.com/c/a/Messaging-and-Collaboration/Tapping-the-Positive-from-Social-Networks-for-Enterprise-Collaboration-563243/, accessed March 12, 2014; "From Social Networks to Collaboration Networks: The Next Evolution of Social Media for Business," *Forbes*, September 9, 2011, http://www.forbes.com/sites/karlmoore/2011/09/15/from-social-networks-to-collaboration-networks-the-next-evolution-of-social-media-for-business/, accessed March 17, 2014.

Effectiveness

The preceding characteristics of groups can affect whether a particular group is effective—that is, whether it achieves what it has set out to do. To the supervisor, a group's effectiveness is one of its most important characteristics. In general, the organization's formal groups should be as effective as possible. The supervisor wants informal groups to be effective only to the extent that they support organizational goals. For example, a company softball team that builds morale and improves working relations is properly effective. A clique that hurts morale among the employees who feel left out is not supporting organizational objectives.

Today, more and more organizations are improving group effectiveness by giving employees access to tools that help them collaborate online. Modern supervisors have to keep up with the latest in social networking so they can use those tools to find people where they are these days: on the Internet. "Supervision: New Trends" describes some of the collaboration tools that are becoming important in organizations.

Teams

team
A small group whose members share goals, commitment, and accountability for results

Organizations today are increasingly looking for ways to involve employees in decision making and problem solving. For a growing number of organizations, teamwork is the means to employee involvement. A **team** is a small group whose members share goals, commitment, and accountability for results. When most organizations form a team, someone is appointed to be team leader. Often the team leader is a supervisor, and the team consists of operative employees.

Being an effective team leader draws on many of the same skills required of an effective supervisor. The team leader needs excellent communication skills, patience, fairness, and good rapport with team members. In addition, because the purpose of the team is to draw on the expertise of all team members, the team leader will need to rely most on a leadership style that encourages involvement. (For more on this type of leadership, see Chapter 8.)

self-managing work teams
Groups of 5 to 15 members who work together to produce an entire product

In the 1970s, it became popular to form teams in which employees suggested ways to improve the quality of their work. More recently, organizations have expanded their use of teams by creating **self-managing work teams**. These are groups of 5 to 15 members who work together to produce an entire product. The team members rotate jobs, schedule work and vacations, and make other decisions affecting their area of responsibility. At the Center for Creative Leadership, based in Greensboro, North Carolina, the library staff functions as a self-managed work team. The library team meets weekly to make decisions such as establishing a budget, scheduling staff, setting goals for the team, and planning special projects. Team members meet individually with upper management regarding their pay and performance.[10]

LO3.5 ▶ Identify the stages that teams pass through as they develop.

Stages of Team Development

A team typically must pass through several stages of development before it becomes fully productive. It is important for managers to be patient as a team moves through these different stages. It often takes some time for teams to become effective as a unit. Following are the five stages that teams work through en route to becoming effective.

Forming

Forming is the first stage of the team development process in which the team members become acquainted with one another and oriented to the idea that they are part of a team. During this phase of team development, members will explore what is expected of them as part of the team, as well as the different strengths of the other team members.

The initial forming stage of team development is often accompanied by stress and uncertainty. Team members attempt to grasp what their role is on the team, what other members' roles are on the team, and what the overarching goals are for the team. Supervisors should allow time for thorough exploration of these topics, as groups will often not be successful unless the aforementioned topics have been discussed.

Storming

Storming is the second stage of team development. Storming describes a period of conflict in which group members assert their different roles on the team. This period of group development is also often perceived as stressful, largely because group members try to delineate exactly what each member's specific role will be. Supervisors are encouraged to allow team members to express their feelings and opinions related to their role in the group. It's important for supervisors to highlight the long-term goal of the team in order to most effectively facilitate this stage of team development.

Norming

Norming is the third stage of team development. Norming is characterized by agreement among team members. During this stage, there is understanding of what each person's role in the team is, and team members generally feel as though their voices have been heard by the other members. There is not as much conflict in this stage of team development. Supervisors are encouraged to help their teams develop effective norms and values that will help the team ultimately meet its goal.

Performing

Performing is the fourth stage of team development. Performing is characterized by solving organizational problems and meeting assigned challenges. It is during this stage that the team becomes productive, largely because it has developed through the previous three stages. It is important for supervisors to reinforce team members throughout this stage of productivity. Rewarding team members will encourage further team success.

Adjourning

Adjourning is the fifth stage of team development. Once the team has met all of its goals, it is appropriate for the team to disband. This stage of team development is not required for every team, given that some teams meet for indefinite periods of time. When this stage is appropriate, though, it is normal for team members to feel a sense of loss as team members often find being part of a team to be rewarding. It is important for supervisors to make this transition as seamless as possible, and to assure team members that new and exciting challenges await them in the future.

LO3.6 ▶ Explain why teamwork is important.

Benefits of Teamwork

A basic benefit of using work teams is that they enable the organization to increase its usage of the insights and expertise of all its employees. In the marketing area, some companies are setting up sales teams that combine technical and sales experts to better address the needs of their major customers. For example, many high-tech and Internet firms combine experts in hardware, software, and technical support to help customers fully use the hardware and software they buy. IBM is encouraging its brilliant scientists to join sales experts in teams that call on potential clients. Sometimes the scientists on these teams need guidance in learning how to communicate effectively with business executives. IBM computer scientist Baruch Schieber, for example, says, "I used to believe that you could solve everything using math." Eventually, he recognized that equations were not the most persuasive way to show managers how IBM could solve their problems. When he joined a team working with Boston Coach, Schieber saw that math could solve the problem of scheduling the company's limousines. But he took his time listening to Boston Coach's headquarters employees before he explained that he could use the company's data to build a computer system that would allow drivers to pick up more customers each day.[11]

Teams can also serve as motivators. Employees who participate in planning and decision making are more likely to take responsibility for the quality of what they do. They also tend to be more enthusiastic about their work. Responsible, enthusiastic employees are more likely to work hard and deliver high quality.

Ultimately, motivating employees and drawing on their strengths should enhance the performance of the organizations that use self-managing work teams. For example, economists Derek Jones and Takao Kato found performance improvements at a manufacturing facility that introduced teamwork.[12] The company, which the researchers nicknamed PARTS to protect its privacy, set up eight-member production teams to meet weekly for problem solving and to get employees more involved in making decisions to improve quality. Because PARTS phased in teamwork gradually, Jones and Kato could compare the performance of team members versus nonmembers. In the months after the startup of teamwork, team members' efficiency improved while the efficiency of the other employees declined. Quality—measured as a lower rejection rate for defective parts—improved for both groups, but teams might have played a role. Often, when teams improved a process, other employees could adopt or benefit from their innovations. For example, when one team improved the labeling of spare parts so that finding the correct parts was easier, everyone used the new labeling system. A challenge remained for supervisors; however, the performance advantage of the team members later slipped. Evidently, team formation is only a first step, and supervisors must also lead teams effectively and motivate employees to continue excelling, as described in Chapter 11.

LO3.7 ▶ Describe how the supervisor can lead a team so that it is productive.

Leading the Team

Whether an organization's teams achieve the benefits of teamwork depends in part on the teams' leaders. Broadly speaking, the goal of a team leader is to develop a productive team. Experts in teamwork have linked team productivity to the team characteristics described in Table 3.1 (on the following page). In general, these characteristics describe a team whose members want to participate, share ideas freely, and know what they are supposed to accomplish. Some ways to develop this kind of team include communicating often to be sure everyone understands the goals and reviews what is working well and what needs to change. Team leaders need to be good role models—trustworthy, cooperative, and team oriented. When the supervisor's role involves team leadership, he or she may want to get training in coaching, conflict management, and other skills to help team members work together effectively.[13]

Coaching the Team

The team leader who can stimulate high-quality performance is one who focuses on enabling team members to do their best. *Enabling* in this context means providing employees with the resources they need to do their job and removing obstacles that interfere with their work (e.g., procedures that slow employees down without adding value from the customer's perspective). Providing resources includes making sure employees have the training they need to be effective team members. Besides technical skills, employees on teams may need training in interpersonal skills such as conflict resolution. In addition, supervisors should acquaint themselves with the strengths that the members themselves bring to the team. Just as on a sports team, not everyone will excel in the same areas, but the team succeeds when all the players are placed in their positions of strength.[14] Say, for example, your most productive worker never speaks up during team meetings, even though you were hoping to develop leadership by having everyone take a turn at running the meetings. If training and encouragement do not make a difference, it might be wisest to shift your focus to developing her strengths and get her insights outside of meetings.

TABLE 3.1 | Team Characteristics Associated with Team Productivity

Characteristic	Description and Significance
Openness and honesty	These are signs that group members trust one another. Tact and timing also are important.
Leadership that does not dominate	The leader is flexible, changing with conditions and circumstances.
Decisions made by consensus	The leader will sometimes have to make a decision alone or reject suggestions, but all team members should have a voice in making many decisions, not simply a vote without the full opportunity to be heard.
Acceptance of assignments	Team members should willingly take on the tasks that must be done, then do them correctly and on time. Team members should view work as a cooperative effort, helping each other out as needed.
Goals that are understood and accepted	Goals give the team purpose and direction. Team members should view accomplishing them as the team's primary purpose.
Assessment of progress and results	Team members should focus on results.
Comfortable atmosphere	Some conflict can stimulate desirable action and change, but there should be a basic level of cooperation.
Involvement and participation	Team members should be involved in the work of the group. When a team member is reluctant to speak up at meetings, the leader should seek his or her input during or outside the meeting.
Debate and discussion	If everyone agrees all the time, it may signify that team members are unable or unwilling to contribute.
Atmosphere of listening	Team members should listen to one another, even when they disagree.
Access to information	All team members need to know what is happening.
Win–win approach to conflict	Team members should work to resolve conflicts in ways that let everyone be a winner.
Relatively low turnover	Members of a team must have close relationships, which is impossible when the team's membership keeps changing.

Sources: Adapted from Edward Glassman, "Self-Directed Team Building without a Consultant," *Supervisory Management,* March 1992, p. 6; Louis V. Imundo, "Blueprint for a Successful Team," *Supervisory Management,* May 1992, pp. 2–3.

By enabling teams to excel and empowering them to make decisions, team leaders are coaching employees. For example, instead of simply telling employees what to do, coaches ask questions that help them decide how to handle a situation.

The team leader encourages team members by expressing understanding and appreciation of their ideas and feelings. In place of criticism, the coach initiates discussions about "how we can do it better next time." The coach also pays attention to how team members interact, recognizing when it is time to wrap up a discussion and when to promote balanced participation from team members.

This style of leading may seem to leave a supervisor with less power than one who gives directions and checks up on performance. However, coaching enables the supervisor to build on the strengths and expertise of the whole group. The likely result is a stronger position for everyone, including the supervisor.

Team building activities help to foster collaboration and communication.

team building
Developing the ability of team members to work together to achieve common objectives

Selection of Team Members

A team leader may be charged with selecting either candidates for jobs that involve teamwork or existing employees to participate in a team devoted to a particular task. In either case, the supervisor should look for people who work well with others. If the team is to include people from several departments, the team leader should talk to other supervisors and employees to learn which employees would do best on the team.

Team Building

Once the team leader knows who will be on the team, he or she must develop the group's ability to work together to achieve common objectives. This process is known as team building. Team building includes several activities: setting goals, analyzing what needs to be done and allocating work, examining how well the group is working, and examining the relationships among the team members.

At some organizations, a consultant with expertise in team building carries out this process. However, hiring someone often is too expensive, especially for small organizations. When the supervisor is responsible for team building, he or she can carry out that responsibility at regular team meetings. At the end of a meeting, the supervisor can devote some time to asking team members how well they thought

SUPERVISORY SKILLS

PROMOTING INCLUSIVENESS

EMBRACING DIVERSITY IN THE WORKPLACE

Many companies have divisions all over the world and even companies that only have U.S. offices may very well have employees from different parts of the world. With a global economy and a more mobile workforce comes an increasingly diverse workforce. A good supervisor needs to be aware of the strengths of this diverse workforce and use these strengths to the advantage of the company. As Douglas M. Stayman, associate dean for MBA programs at Cornell University, noted in a diversity training session: Diversity fosters creativity and awareness of diverse points of view and is critically important to avoid cultural blunders. "An organization won't be successful if it doesn't embrace the diversity of different people," Stayman said.

Supervisors can cultivate an inclusive work environment by employing the following strategies:

- *Be a role model. Lead by example.* Supervisors need to understand diversity and inclusion and be open to different perspectives, value the opinions of others, and make everyone feel comfortable in the workplace.

- *Support employees.* Being inclusive means supporting people of varied backgrounds. Work to understand employees' strengths and skills and, as much as possible, try to make work schedules flexible to accommodate their outside interests and personal lives.

- *Treat employees equitably.* Each employee needs to be provided the same opportunities, training, and pay.

- *Provide diversity and inclusion training.* Learning about other cultures and practicing cross-cultural communication is essential for employees as well as supervisors.

- *Include "inclusiveness" in your business goals.* Cultivate an atmosphere of inclusion by including specific, concrete plans in your business goals.

- *Motivate employees to be inclusive.* Let employees know that inclusive behavior is one of the criteria on which they will be evaluated.

- *Avoid common pitfalls.* One common pitfall is believing that certain culture groups are good at certain tasks—perhaps to the exclusion of other tasks. This might cause a supervisor to miss an employee's full potential. Supervisors must also avoid the pitfall of talking more with or spending more time with the employees with whom they share similar backgrounds or interests. It is important for supervisors to get to know each of their employees personally.

Source: Yuezhou Huo, "Creating an atmosphere of inclusiveness in the workplace," October 2012, Cornell EnterpriseOnline, http://www2.johnson.cornell.edu/alumni/enterprise/fall2013/index.cfm?action5inside&inside_id542&item53, accessed March 17, 2014.

the meeting worked and whether they think they developed a creative solution. Participants can rate how well the meeting went in terms of whether everyone participated, whether they felt the others heard them, and whether the meeting had a successful outcome.

Drawing on her experience as a library manager, Debbie Schachter notes that team building is not so much about clever games and expensive retreats as it is about ensuring that team members understand their proper roles and responsibilities. She advises supervisors to make sure that all team members understand the purpose of any team-building efforts. The exercise can be simply a way for team members to understand each other better, without awkwardness and embarrassment.[15] Consultant Jim Jenkins holds a similar view. He says team building need not take the expensive forms that are so widely reported, such as outdoor obstacle courses, well-known motivational speakers, or even late-night parties. Rather, effective ways to build strong working relationships may be as simple as 15-minute weekly sessions that focus on respectful dialogue.[16]

Communication in Teams

The way the team leader communicates with other team members will influence the success of the team. In general, the team leader should create a climate of trust and openness and encourage team members to collaborate. The team leader also should acknowledge disagreement, not squelch it. To determine whether you already have a communication style that would make you an effective team leader or if you need to make some changes to fill that role, complete the Assessing Yourself exercise at the end of this chapter.

Team leaders need this kind of communication style because successful teamwork requires open and positive communication among team members. Feeling able to express one's viewpoint and knowing how to do so constructively are essential for reaping the benefits of diverse viewpoints.

Of course, effective communication is not just a matter of being pleasant; sometimes the supervisor has to get everyone focused on the issue at hand. And some situations call for firmness. At Autoliv, North America's factory in Tremonton, Utah, a work team was assigned to figure out a way to increase capacity without the time and significant expense of adding to its facilities. At its first meeting, the team spent two hours on the same complaint: there was no possible way to meet the team's objective. However, the team leader insisted, "There is a way, and we will not leave until we figure it out." Eventually, forced to focus on a solution, the team members came up with a wide variety of creative ideas that solved the problem.[17]

Rewards

For teams to remain productive, members must be rewarded appropriately. The organization should reward the entire team for its accomplishments instead of emphasizing individual rewards. At Zircoa Inc., which makes industrial ceramics, rewards are a good fit with the company's emphasis on teamwork. Beginning with job interviews, conducted by pairs of employees, the focus is on whether a person functions well as part of a team. When teams meet their goals, supervisors are empowered to deliver group rewards such as tickets to a concert or coupons for a meal at a local restaurant. Also, employees are encouraged to suggest cost-cutting measures, and when an idea succeeds, everyone is paid a share of the gain.[18] (For more on group incentives, see Chapter 11.)

Team members also are likely to value different rewards; therefore, the rewards should be varied enough that everyone feels motivated. For example, the typical salesperson is motivated by money, whereas technical people might be more interested in recognition and promotion. Thus, one approach might be to use the company's basic incentive plan and ask the team members to reach a consensus on what additional reward they would enjoy receiving for a specific accomplishment.

Powerful Meetings

Much of the work of teams and other groups occurs in meetings. When groups plan, solve problems, and reward successes, they usually do so in a meeting. Although the supervisor's role may be that of either participant in or leader of the meeting, this chapter emphasizes the latter. The principles described here apply to other situations as well, but supervisors will have less ability to make improvements when someone else is conducting the meeting.

Reasons for Meetings

Meetings should take place when they serve a purpose. As obvious as this sounds, many supervisors and other managers hold meetings at a regularly scheduled time, whether or not they have something particular to accomplish. A supervisor who is thinking of calling a meeting should consider specifically what the meeting is intended to accomplish within the time allotted. Bob Mitchell, owner of Integrated Management Group, notes that supervisors at a construction site are usually expected to hold regular safety meetings with employees at the site, often using company-supplied training materials. But unless the supervisor ensures that the topic is relevant to the particular job site, employees will see the meetings as a waste of time.[19] And, of course, it goes without saying that a supervisor should not call a meeting at all for an illogical purpose such as making small matters seem important, trying to appear democratic, or rescuing a lost cause (e.g., building a groundswell of support for an idea the boss has vetoed).

There are several valid reasons for holding a meeting. One is to convey news to a group of people when their feedback is important. Conveying information in a meeting gives the supervisor a chance to see and respond to people's reactions to the news. A meeting is also appropriate when the supervisor wants the group to participate in decision making. (Chapter 9 describes the pros and cons of decision making in a group.) The supervisor may use meetings to prepare group members for a change and build support for that change. (Chapter 15 describes this process.) Meetings are especially important when some or all members of a group work in different locations—for example, when some employees telecommute, or work from home via computer connections. In this situation, employees don't have the chance encounters that lead them to trade ideas, feel encouraged, and build a sense of shared purpose. Technology is making meetings with telecommuters and remote employees more powerful, so they don't even need to travel to a central location. Employees with Webcams and videoconferencing software can see each other's faces on computer screens. Software programs such as Citrix GoToMeeting, Cisco TelePresence, Acrobat Connect Pro, and MS Office Live let users talk to one another, share and edit documents, view and mark up virtual whiteboards, and record meetings for future reference. A detailed, focused agenda, described in the next section, is especially important for online meetings, because it is harder for the meeting leader to pick up cues when participants become impatient or bored.[20]

Google, for example, regularly holds meetings that bring together salespeople, product managers, engineers, and employees serving particular industries to see how they can meet newly defined needs. In the words of former Google vice president and now Facebook COO Sheryl Sandberg, "We are in a constant mode of change, so we are in a constant mode of collaboration. . . . And when I think collaboration works best is when someone on the engineering side makes a customer point, and someone on the sales side makes a systems point." Then, Sandberg knows, the collaboration is helping everyone see the big picture.[21]

Formal versus Informal Meetings

Just as we discussed formal and informal groups, meetings may also be either formal or informal. A formal meeting, which we will discuss in greater detail in the following sections, is one that is scheduled, and typically has an agenda, which is shared with all attendees, to guide the specific goals of the meeting.

An informal meeting, on the other hand, may be one which occurs spontaneously or which takes place in a less formal location. Such a meeting would not have a distributed agenda, a scheduled start and end time, or any of the components that are typically associated with a formal meeting. Even though an informal meeting does not have the same components as a formal meeting, it is the supervisor's job to try to apply as many of the best practices of a formal meeting to an informal meeting as possible. Being prepared, keeping the meeting on topic, taking notes, restating or summarizing what has been discussed, and bringing the meeting to a timely close are all just as important in an informal meeting as a formal meeting. As you learn about the skills used in a formal meeting in the sections below, consider how these could be applied in an informal meeting setting.

Preparing for a Meeting

LO3.8 ▶ Discuss how to plan for effective meetings.

To prepare for a meeting, the supervisor should decide who is to attend and when and where to meet. When the purpose of a meeting is to convey information to the whole department, naturally the whole department should be invited. In many cases, however, the participants are to provide or evaluate information. In these cases, the supervisor should invite only those who have the needed information or expertise.

As much as possible, a meeting should be scheduled at a time that is convenient for all participants. Times that tend to cause problems are peak working hours and the last few hours before a weekend or holiday. However, if a meeting is supposed to be brief, it makes sense to schedule the meeting for a half-hour before lunch or quitting time.

The location of the meeting usually depends on the available facilities. For a very small meeting, the participants might be able to meet in the supervisor's office. Larger meetings can take place in a conference room. When the whole department is called, finding a big enough space can be a challenge. In general, it is more comfortable to meet casually in the work area than to squeeze a big group into a stuffy conference room.

agenda
A list of the topics to be covered at a meeting

One of the most basic preparation tasks is to draw up an agenda, a list of the topics to be covered at the meeting. A complete agenda specifies the meeting's date, time, location, and objectives, as well as the *items* on the agenda—that is, a list of a few topics for idea generation, discussion, and/or problem solving. For each agenda item, the planner should identify who will lead it, specify how the topic will be addressed (for example, delivering a report or leading a discussion that reaches a decision), and estimate how much time the item will require.[22] Figure 3.5, on the following page, is an agenda that was used at a meeting called by an editor to discuss the progress on this book. Notice that in addition to the topics to be covered, the agenda states the name of the group that is meeting, the location, the date, and the starting and ending times of the meeting.

FIGURE 3.5 | Sample Agenda

An agenda is a good way to make sure that everyone attending a meeting is aware of the time parameters as well as the specific topics to be discussed. The agenda should be distributed well in advance of the meeting so that everyone has time to prepare for discussions.

Team for *Supervision* Text

Sheraton O'Hare

June 24, 2015

8:30 a.m.–3:00 p.m.

1. Workbook (8:30–10:00)
   a.   Components and process
   b.   Possible sources of material
   c.   Tentative schedule
2. Remaining manuscript work (10:00–12:00)
   a.   Examples in text
   b.   Opening vignettes
   c.   End-of-chapter material
   d.   Changes based upon reviewer feedback
3. Working lunch (12:00–1:00)
4. Videos (1:00–2:00)
5. Ancillaries (2:00–3:00)
   a.   Components
   b.   Process

A well-crafted agenda is specific enough that participants can be well prepared. Breck England, a training product architect for FranklinCovey Company, is exasperated by one-word topics: "For instance, an agenda that simply says 'Budget.' What about the budget? How can you possibly prepare for that?"[23] England recommends agenda items that indicate an action, such as to prepare requests for next year's budget. Specific information on the agenda is also useful because some people invited to the meeting may see that they don't actually need to be there and can use their time more effectively. An employee who doubts that a meeting is important can check with his or her supervisor about which activities have priority.

The agenda should be distributed to all participants in time for participants to review it before the meeting and make any necessary preparations. In addition, the person calling the meeting should make sure that participants have received any other documents they might need so they are prepared to contribute. At the

PRACTICAL ADVICE FOR SUPERVISORS

GETTING READY FOR A MEETING

People hate wasting time, especially when they have challenging jobs with important goals to meet. So it's no wonder that effective meetings are a big force behind employees' satisfaction with their jobs. The following tips for meeting preparation will help you make all of your meetings productive:

- *Pinpoint your purpose.* Then make sure that a meeting is the best way to accomplish your purpose. A meeting is a great way for a group to generate ideas or solve a problem, but if you're just going to make announcements, it might be more efficient to send an e-mail. An exception would be if the person making the announcement is also interested in getting feedback or if the people receiving the announcement might have questions that should be addressed within the group.

- *Target your invitations.* Some meetings are designed to bring the whole work group together. But if you're tackling a specific problem, be selective about who gets an invitation. Consider who offers expertise on the subject and who has the power to make and implement decisions. If some parts of your agenda will interest only part of the group, consider scheduling two meetings with two agendas, so as not to waste anyone's time. Chemical manufacturer Chemtura started holding smaller but more frequent sales meetings, inviting participants with an interest in particular regions and products. Although managers attend more meetings, they find that these meetings are more productive than the larger assemblies used in the past.

- *Encourage "outside the box" thinking.* At some meetings it is useful to leave time in the agenda for open discussion on topics in the news, recent advancements in technology, or other innovations that might spark new ideas for the company. This also gives employees a chance to create synergy.

- *Write it down.* Prepare an agenda, and be sure it stays focused on the meeting's purpose. Give all participants a copy of the agenda in plenty of time for them to be prepared to participate. Assign someone to take notes during the meeting so that you'll have an accurate report of what happened.

Sources: Rebecca Aronauer, "Cure the Meeting Blahs: Tips to Make Your Meetings More Efficient and Productive," *Sales & Marketing Management*, June 2006; T. L. Stanley, "Make Your Meetings Effective," *Supervision*, April 2006, both downloaded from InfoTrac, http://web4.infotrac.galegroup.com; "Resuscitate Your Staff Meeting: 10 Strategies to Get Your Team Up and Running," Oasis Outsourcing, http://www.oasisadvantage.com/running-an-effective-staff-meeting, accessed March 16, 2014.

regular staff meetings of a Midwest computer manufacturer, participants receive a statement of each meeting's topic ahead of time so that they can research the issue. For example, a topic might be "What actions should we take to reduce scrap rates by 10 percent?" This topic requires research to make the meeting worthwhile. In some situations, each participant takes responsibility for a particular item on the agenda.[24]

For further guidance on meeting preparation, see "Practical Advice for Supervisors."

LO3.9 ▶ Provide guidelines for conducting effective meetings.

Conducting a Meeting

Meetings should begin promptly at the scheduled starting time—this is true for both in-person and virtual meetings. This practice demonstrates respect for all participants' schedules, and it encourages people to be on time. It helps to announce an ending time and end the meeting promptly at that time. When critical issues come up near the end of a meeting, the group can reach an agreement to extend the meeting or continue the discussion at another time.

To make sure meetings are as fruitful as possible, the supervisor can facilitate the discussion in several ways, which are summarized in Figure 3.6 (on the following page). One is to rephrase ideas that participants express. For example, if an employee on a printing company's health and safety committee says, "We've got to do something about the fumes in the shop," the supervisor might comment, "You're recommending that we improve ventilation." This type of response helps ensure that the supervisor and other participants understand

FIGURE 3.6 | Guidelines for Conducting a Meeting

Conducting a successful meeting, whether formal or informal, requires following some basic guidelines.

what has been said. Of course, the supervisor has to use this technique with care; participants might become annoyed if the supervisor sounds like their echo. Also, the supervisor should summarize key points often enough to make sure everyone is following the discussion. Times to summarize include at the conclusion of each agenda item, at the end of the meeting, and at times when people have trouble following the discussion.

The supervisor should be careful not to dominate the discussion; instead, he or she should make sure that everyone has a chance to participate. Having everyone sit around a table or in a circle makes people feel more involved. Some people find it easier than others to speak up during a meeting. The person leading the meeting is responsible for encouraging everyone to contribute, a task that can be as simple as saying, "Mary, what do you think about the suggestions that have been proposed so far?" Another way to encourage participation is to appoint different employees to take turns as discussion leaders. This is a way to offer leadership training and demonstrate trust in employees.[25]

Quieting participants who are monopolizing a discussion can be a more delicate matter. One approach is to begin with someone other than the talkative person, then go around the table and hear each person's views on some topic. Also, the supervisor could have a one-on-one talk with the person monopolizing discussions, letting the person know his or her contributions are important but that the lengthy discourse is unnecessary.

Throughout the meeting, the supervisor should take notes on what is being decided. This helps the supervisor summarize key points for participants. In addition, it helps the supervisor recall what actions are to be taken later and by whom.

When it is time for the meeting to end, the supervisor should help bring it to a close. A direct way to do this is to summarize what has been covered, state what needs to happen next, and thank everyone for coming. For example, at the end of a meeting called to decide how to make the company's purchasing decisions more efficient, the supervisor might say, "We've selected three interesting possibilities to explore. Max will research the costs of each, then we'll meet back here in two weeks to select one." Then the supervisor's job becomes one of following up to make sure that plans are carried out. As in the example, following up may include planning another meeting.

SELF-ASSESSMENT 3.2

How do You Communicate as a Team Leader?

When leading meetings or just in daily communication with your workers, there are many communication pitfalls. Luckily, you can identify problems in your communication style and improve your communication ability. This assessment will help you do just that. Later, in Chapter 10, you will learn a great deal more about communication.

Overcoming Problems with Meetings

A frequent complaint about meetings is that they waste time because participants stray from the main topic and go off on tangents. Thus, an important job for the supervisor is to keep the discussion linked to the agenda items. When a participant begins discussing an unrelated topic, the supervisor can restate the purpose of the meeting and suggest that if the topic seems important, it could be covered in another meeting.

In steering the discussion back on course, it is important to avoid ridiculing the participants and to respect their efforts to contribute. The supervisor can do this by focusing on the effects of particular kinds of behavior instead of on the personalities of the participants. For example, if a participant tends to interrupt when others are speaking, the supervisor should not say, "Don't be so inconsiderate." A more helpful comment might be, "It's important that everyone in our group have a chance to state his or her ideas completely. Interruptions discourage people from participating."

Other problems arise because the meeting leader and participants have failed to prepare for the meeting. If there is no agenda, the discussion may ramble aimlessly. If someone failed to bring necessary background information, the participants may be unable to make plans or reach decisions, and the meeting will be unproductive. These kinds of problems lead to frustration and anger among participants who feel they are wasting precious time. The solution is to follow the guidelines described previously, including the creation and distribution of an agenda well before the meeting. When the supervisor is prepared to lead the meeting but others are unprepared to participate, the supervisor should probably consider rescheduling the meeting.

Skills Module

PART ONE: CONCEPTS

Summary

3.1 Explain why people join groups.

People may join a group because membership in that group goes along with being an employee. (All employees are members of the organization that employs them.) Employers may ask employees to join particular groups such as committees or task forces. An employee also may join a group because doing so satisfies personal needs such as closeness, common goals, and achievement of personal objectives.

3.2 Distinguish types of groups that exist in the workplace.

Functional groups fulfill ongoing needs in the organization by carrying out a particular function. Task groups are set up to carry out a specific activity and disband when the activity is completed. Formal groups are set up by management to meet organizational objectives. Informal groups result when individuals in the organization develop relationships to meet personal needs.

3.3 Discuss how supervisors can get groups to cooperate with them.

The supervisor should make sure all members of a formal group know what they can and should be doing. The supervisor also should keep groups informed about what is happening in the organization and what changes are planned. The supervisor should support the group when members want to bring legitimate concerns to higher management. When the supervisor is responsible for setting up a group, he or she should combine people with a variety of strengths and backgrounds but avoid separating members of informal groups. Finally, general principles of effective supervision apply to supervising groups as well as individuals.

3.4 Describe characteristics of groups in the workplace.

Group members have various roles, or patterns of behavior related to their position in the group. Group members are expected to follow norms, or the group's standards, for appropriate or acceptable behavior. The status of each group member depends on a variety of factors, which may include his or her role in the group, title, pay, education level, age, race, and sex. Some groups are more cohesive than others; that is, the members of some groups are more likely to stick together in the face of problems. Groups may vary widely in terms of size, with subgroups likely to form in groups of more than 20 members. Homogeneity refers to the extent to which group members are the same. All these characteristics can influence the effectiveness of a group. In general, a supervisor wants a group to be effective when its goals support the achievement of organizational goals.

3.5 Identify the stages that teams pass through as they develop.

In the first stage, called forming, the team members become acquainted with one another and oriented to the idea that they are part of a team. The next stage, storming, is a period of conflict as group members assert various roles. During norming, the third stage, team members arrive at agreement about each team member's role, and the level of conflict subsides. During the performing stage, the team emphasizes problem solving and is at its most productive. Teams that have met all their goals may then disband; this stage, called adjourning, does not apply to every team.

3.6 Explain why teamwork is important.

Teams bring employees together to collaborate on solving problems and making decisions. By using teams, the organization can draw more fully on the insights and expertise of all its employees. Teams also can motivate employees by giving them a say in how things are done. As a result, organizations that use teams can benefit from improved performance, which

is measured by higher quality and greater productivity and profits.

3.7 Describe how the supervisor can lead a team so that it is productive.

If building the team includes selecting team members, the supervisor should include people who work well with others. The supervisor should adopt a coaching role, enabling employees by providing them with the resources they need and removing any obstacles in their way. Then the supervisor builds the team by helping it set goals, analyzing what needs to be done and allocating the work, examining how well the group is working, and examining the relationships among team members. The supervisor can increase the success of the team through effective communication that creates a climate of trust and encourages collaboration. The supervisor should see that teams receive group rewards valued by team members.

3.8 Discuss how to plan for effective meetings.

The supervisor should hold a meeting only when there is a valid reason for doing so. He or she should schedule the meeting at a convenient time and plan who is to attend and where the meeting will take place. The supervisor should create an agenda, which lists the topics to be covered at the meeting. The agenda should be distributed to all participants far enough in advance that they can be prepared to contribute at the meeting.

3.9 Provide guidelines for conducting effective meetings.

Meetings should start and end promptly. The supervisor should facilitate the discussion through such means as rephrasing what participants say and summarizing key points without dominating the discussion. The supervisor should make sure that everyone participates in the discussion, take notes of what is being decided, and keep the discussion on track by reminding participants of the topic under consideration. After the meeting, the supervisor should follow up to make sure plans are carried out.

Key Terms

group, *p. 64*
functional groups, *p. 65*
task groups, *p. 65*
formal groups, *p. 66*
informal groups, *p. 66*
roles, *p. 69*

role conflicts, *p. 69*
norms, *p. 70*
status, *p. 70*
cohesiveness, *p. 70*
homogeneity, *p. 71*
team, *p. 73*

self-managing work teams, *p. 73*
team building, *p. 77*
agenda, *p. 80*

Review and Discussion Questions

1. Think of your current job or the most recent job you held. (If you have never been employed, consider your role as a student.)

   a. Of what groups are you a member? For example, what organization employs you? In which division or department do you work? Are you a member of any informal groups?

   b. Why did you join each of these groups?

2. State whether each of the following groups is formal or informal. Then state whether it is a functional group or a task group.

   a. Six employees who have decided on their own to research the possibility of establishing an onsite day care facility.

   b. The board of directors of a major corporation.

   c. Three employees who decide to plan a birthday celebration for a co-worker.

   d. Software developers at an educational publisher.

3. Joseph Dittrick is a supervisor in the marketing department of a toy manufacturer. He is responsible for leading a group of employees in finding ways to improve a problematic product. In what ways can Joseph encourage the group to be as effective as possible?

4. Why do supervisors need to know about each of the following characteristics of groups?

   a. Roles of group members.

   b. Status of group members.

5. Yolanda Gibbs supervises employees in the reference department of a public library. Her team meets once a month to discuss ways to improve the quality of services delivered at the library. Yolanda wants the team to be cohesive so that its members will work hard. How can she encourage the cohesiveness of this group?

6. A supervisor observes that the members of a committee seem to spend a lot of time complaining and have trouble focusing on the issues the committee was formed to address. How can the supervisor help the committee move into the performing stage of team development?

7. Peter Wilson is a supervisor who also leads a team that has been working on revamping an old product—snow saucers—to make them seem new and more attractive to a new generation of customers. The team includes both design and salespeople. What type or types of rewards might Peter consider for his team members if the project is successful?

8. How can a supervisor at an organization with self-managing work teams help the organization avoid violations of federal labor law?

9. Bonnie First supervises respiratory therapists at a large community hospital. One day her manager said, "Your department used too much overtime again last week. I want you to propose a solution to this problem, and I think you need to involve the employees in finding the solution. Get back to me in a week with your ideas." To prepare for the next meeting with her manager, Bonnie decided she needed to hold a department meeting at 1:00 the next afternoon. She asked two therapists to spread the word about this meeting.

   At the meeting, Bonnie described the problem. To her disappointment, no one seemed to have any suggestions. She said, "Unless someone has a better idea, you're just going to have to help each other out more when someone is having trouble keeping up. And don't hesitate to ask me to pitch in, too."

   How could the supervisor have better planned this meeting?

10. As a supervisor, you have done everything you can to prepare for a meeting, including writing up and distributing an agenda. At the meeting, you have problems with two of the participants. Ken dominates the conversation, drifting off to subjects that are not on the agenda. Sheryl refuses to talk at all, even though you know she has read the agenda and probably has something insightful to contribute. What steps might you take to elicit more positive participation from Ken and Sheryl?

Notes

1. Sonja D. Brown, "Congratulations, You're a Manager!" *Black Enterprise,* April 2006, 36 (9) downloaded from Business & Company Resource Center, http://galenet.galegroup.com.

2. Stevenson Swanson, "Window of Opportunity Opens in N.Y.," *Chicago Tribune,* January 22, 2006, sec. 1, p. 9.

3. For more information about the role of positive attitudes in the success of a task group, see Alison Bianchi and Donna Lancianese, March 2007, "Accentuate the positive: Positive sentiments and status in task groups," *Social Psychology Quarterly,* pp. 7–26.

4. Julie Graham, "Hospital Team Works to Cut Cardiac Arrests," *(Rock Hill, S.C.) Herald,* July 4, 2006, downloaded from Business & Company Resource Center, http://galenet.galegroup.com.

5. David A. Garvin, "How Google Sold Its Engineers on Management," *Harvard Business Review,* December 2013, http://hbr.org/2013/12/how-google-sold-its-engineers-on-management/ar/1, accessed March 17, 2014.

6. For further understanding of the potential role conflicts that managers face, see Ajay Mehra and Mark Schenkel, June 2008, "The price chameleons pay: Self-monitoring, boundary spanning and role conflict in the workplace," *British Journal of Management,* 19(2), pp. 138–144.

7. For more information regarding how group norms might affect group cohesion, see Roderick Swaab, Katherine Phillips, Daniel Diermeier, and Victoria Medvec, June 2008, "The pros and cons of dyadic side conversations in small groups: The impact of group norms and task type," *Small Group Research,* 39(3), pp. 372–390.

8. For an understanding of how different tasks affect the cohesion of a group, see Martin Lea, Russell Spears, and Susan Watt, July/August 2007, "Visibility and anonymity effects on attraction and group cohesiveness," *European Journal of Social Psychology,* 37(4), pp. 761–773.

9. For more information about considerations for managers related to homogeneous versus heterogeneous groups, see Deborah Crown, August 2007, "The use of group and groupcentric individual goals for culturally heterogeneous and homogeneous task groups," *Small Group Research,* 38(4), pp. 489–508.

10. Jean Vollrath, "Operating as a Self-Managed Team," *Information Outlook,* July 2008, pp. 42–45.

11. Jim Jenkins, "Management Tools: Getting Up to Full Speed," *HRMagazine,* 51 (4) April 1, 2006, http://www.shrm.org/Publications/hrmagazine/EditorialContent/Pages/0406managementtools.aspx, accessed March 12, 2014.

12. Derek C. Jones and Takao Kato, January 1, 2011, "The Impact of Teams on Output, Quality, and Downtime: An Empirical Analysis Using Individual Panel Data," *Industrial and Labor Relations Review,* 64 (2), 215–240, http://digitalcommons.ilr.cornell.edu/cgi/viewcontent.cgi?article=1463&context=ilrreview, accessed March 12, 2014.

13. Patricia M. Buhler, "Managing in the New Millennium: Are You a Team Player?" *SuperVision,* March 1, 2006, downloaded from Business & Company Resource Center, http://galenet.galegroup.com; Thomas Capozzoli, "How to Succeed with Self-Directed Work Teams," *SuperVision,* February 2006, downloaded from InfoTrac, http://web2.infotrac.galegroup.com.

14. Garold L. Markle, "The Weakness Trap," *SuperVision,* July 2010, pp. 19–20.

15. Debbie Schachter, "Building a Team: It's Not Just about Those Exercises," *Information Outlook,* September 2008, downloaded from Business & Company Resource Center, http://galenet.galegroup.com.

16. Jim Jenkins, "Management Tools: Getting Up to Full Speed," *HRMagazine,* 51 (4) April 1, 2006, http://www.shrm.org/Publications/hrmagazine/EditorialContent/Pages/0406managementtools.aspx, accessed March 12, 2014.

17. Mark Newton, "The Big Picture: Leadership Insights from the *IW* Best Plants," *Industry Week,* October 9, 2008, www.industryweek.com/lean-six-sigma/big-picture-leadership-insights-iw-best-plants-autoliv-north-america-continues-improv, accessed March 12, 2014.

18. Myra Orenstein, "Dream Team," *Inside Business,* September 2008, http://www.ibmag.com/Main/Archive/Dream_Team_10586.aspx, accessed March 12, 2014; Zircoa: About Us, http://www.zircoa.com/other/about.zircoa.html, accessed March 13, 2014.

19. Bob Mitchell, "Playing It Safe," *Electrical Construction & Maintenance,* May 1, 2008, http://ecmweb.com/content/playing-it-safe, accessed March 12, 2014.

20. "The Wonder of Webinars," *Accountancy,* January 2010, pp. 48–49; Darleen DeRosa, "Hello, Is Anybody Out There? Six Steps to High-Impact V-Meetings," *T1D,* August 2011, pp. 28–29.

21. Julia Chang, "The World According to Google," *Sales & Marketing Management,* April 4, 2006, downloaded from InfoTrac, http://web4.infotrac.galegroup.com.

22. Kimberly Douglas, "Ten Pitfalls of Pitiful Meetings and How to Fix Them," American Management Association, August 5, 2010, http://www.amanet.org/training/articles/Ten-Pitfalls-of-Pitiful-Meetings1and-How-to-Fix-Them.aspx, accessed March 12, 2014; Dennis Sowards, "More than Five Ways to Improve Meetings," *Contractor,* June 1,

2011, http://contractormag.com/columns/ sowards/five-ways-improve-meetings-0611, accessed March 12, 2014.

23. Heather Stewart, "Lean, Mean Meetings: Combat Boredom in the Boardroom," *Utah Business*, October 1, 2008, http://www.utahbusiness.com/

articles/view/lean_mean_meetings, accessed March 12, 2014.

24. David K. Lindo, "You Can Make It Better," *Super-Vision*, April 1, 2004, downloaded from InfoTrac, http://web4.infotrac.galegroup.com.

25. Ibid.

PART TWO: SKILL-BUILDING

Meeting the Challenge

Reflecting back on page 67, imagine that you were a sterile processing department (SPD) supervisor at Christiana Hospital, assigned to one of its problem-solving teams. Consider that your team would also include hospital managers, nurses, and employees and that some team members would be from the operating room, while others would represent SPD. With your group, discuss and identify several possible sources of conflict on this team. Suggest some ways that an SPD supervisor could help the team move beyond conflict (the storming stage) and toward constructive solutions. Also, identify ways that your participation on the team could help you lead your employees in SPD.

Problem-Solving Case: Peer Groups Help Eastman Kodak Employees Resolve Disputes

When employees have difficult disagreements at Eastman Kodak Company, they can get help from a team of their peers. Kodak offers a peer/ management dispute-resolution process. Frontline and management employees volunteer to serve as panelists who hear complaints and recommend solutions. Generally, they offer to serve because they are attracted to this approach to problem solving and they want to help; many think of themselves as eligible because they consider themselves good leaders, listeners, or problem solvers.

The peer/management dispute-resolution process brings together a panel of employees and managers, with the employees being in the majority. The panel cannot change company policies or work rules. Rather, they address whether the people in the situation they are reviewing were correctly applying company policies and rules. Kodak agrees that it will abide by the panel's decision; the employee who brings the complaint need not abide by the decision and may pursue other remedies.

Peer/management review is part of a larger conflict-resolution system at Kodak. The system's former director, Mary Harris, said the ability to choose peer/management review added to employees' satisfaction.

Some managers, however, were nervous when Kodak introduced peer/management review. The company had to reassure them that they would not be punished if a review panel overruled decisions they had made. Rather, the company explained that the process was a resource available to managers and employees alike. Experience with the process convinced Don Franks, an operations manager at the Kodak Park manufacturing facility. An employee used the process to challenge a decision Franks had made. Franks explains that he initially "wasn't too thrilled" to have one of his decisions publicly questioned, but he felt "ready for help" in resolving the problem with the employee. In the end, the panel upheld Franks's decision, and the employee was satisfied. Franks believes the employee would have continued to question the decision if the procedure had not been in place to give the issue an airing.

Harvey Caras, whose consulting firm helped Kodak set up the peer review system, says only a small percentage of supervisors need to be convinced that the system will benefit them. And in Caras's experience, they see the benefits after they understand how the system will work. He tells about the manager of a manufacturing plant who told him the dispute-resolution process has been a positive learning experience. According to Caras, the manager said, "Every time we get overruled [by a panel], we learn something that helps us make this a better place to work."

At Kodak, then supervisor Patrick Teora had participated in several panels. He found that employees from the shop floor contributed a valuable firsthand perspective, and the managers who participated contributed to gaining a grasp of required documents and procedures. He believed the two kinds of participants worked well as a team because all the team members took their role seriously. Teora also discovered that serving on a panel made him a better supervisor. Because he's "not crazy about someone picking apart my decision," he was more careful about how he used his authority.

1. What challenges could arise from bringing together employees and managers to work as a group on a dispute-resolution panel? How can Kodak address these challenges?

2. To staff its peer/management review panels, Kodak requests volunteers. What are some advantages and disadvantages of using volunteers instead of another approach, such as hiring people for the job or requiring employees to participate?

3. Imagine you are the leader of a peer/management panel such as the one described in this case. Your panel is being asked to hear an employee's complaint that her supervisor unreasonably turned down her request to participate in a training program. Prepare an agenda for the panel's meeting to hear the complaint. Whose viewpoints will you need to hear? How will you ensure that all those viewpoints are heard? How will you set up the meeting to ensure that the whole panel participates in the decision?

Source: Margaret M. Clark, "Making Peer Review Work" *HRMagazine*, January 2004, http://www.shrm.org/Publications/hrmagazine/Editorial Content/Pages/0104clark_work.aspx, accessed March 17, 2014.

| Assessing Yourself | **How Do You Communicate as a Team Leader?** |

In response to each item, circle the number that reflects what you never do (1), rarely do (2), often do (3), or always do (4). Be honest with yourself. Your answer should reflect your own perceptions of your communication skills. When you have finished, total your score. The higher your score, the better communicator you likely are. If you have a low score, look at the questions you rated as a 1 or 2 and focus on finding ways to improve those scores.

Message Preparation

1.	When I'm preparing to communicate, I think about the goal of my communication.	1	2	3	4
2.	I plan carefully before I send a message or meet with someone.	1	2	3	4
3.	I think about the point of view and feelings of the person or people I am communicating with.	1	2	3	4
4.	I ask for and then consider the advice of other people.	1	2	3	4

Message Delivery

5.	When delivering my message, I express myself with conviction.	1	2	3	4
6.	I speak openly and candidly, making it clear when I am expressing feelings or opinions versus facts.	1	2	3	4
7.	I make connections between my message and the larger goals of my organization.	1	2	3	4
8.	I provide the information my group needs, including information that might come from other sources.	1	2	3	4

9. My message makes clear any actions that need to be taken.	1	2	3	4
10. I make the key points clear and verify that those receiving my message understand what I am saying.	1	2	3	4

Message Reception

11. When people disagree with me, I listen to what they have to say and do not respond immediately.	1	2	3	4
12. When people talk, I listen attentively. (Attentive listening means not thinking of other things or trying to formulate my response while someone is talking to me.)	1	2	3	4
13. I keep an open mind when speaking and being spoken to.	1	2	3	4
14. I value receiving constructive feedback and use it to improve my communication skills.	1	2	3	4
15. When I am spoken to, I confirm my understanding by repeating what I have heard.	1	2	3	4

Pause and Reflect

1. When is it helpful to be task-oriented? When is it better to focus on getting contributions from the whole team?
2. Why can disagreement be beneficial in teams?
3. How can I encourage people to express their thoughts when we disagree? How can I express my own disagreements in a constructive way?

Class Skills Exercise

Meeting Participation Skills

A key characteristic of any effective meeting is participants who know how to listen. Write a list of dos and don'ts for being a good listener in a meeting, and share your ideas with the class. Here are a few to get you started: *Do:* Be alert, concentrate on the speaker, and avoid making hasty judgments about what is said. *Don't:* Interrupt, talk to others in the room, or let your feelings about the speaker get in the way.

Building Supervision Skills

Evaluating Team Performance

In working with teams, most managers believe in the following axiom: "None of us is as smart as all of us." Let's see if this axiom holds true for this exercise.

Instructions

1. Perform this part of the exercise on your own. When your instructor starts the clock, you will have two minutes to fill in the U.S. state names on Chart 1 (on page 92). The first letter of each of the 50 states is provided. Write the state name out in full; do not use abbreviations. Do not talk among yourselves during this step.

2. Form teams of three to five students to work on Chart 2 (on page 93). Your team should select someone to record your group's list. Without looking back at the first chart you completed, your group will have two minutes to fill in the second chart. Speak quietly among yourselves so that other teams will not overhear your answers.

3. Your instructor will read the 50 state names so that you may check your answers. Then fill in the information about your team's performance.

Chart 1: Working alone

Number of correct answers for each team member: _____ _____ _____ _____

Chart 2: Working in teams

Number of correct answers your team completed: _____

How many members of your team got the same or a better score on Chart 1 than the group got on Chart 2? _____

Questions for Discussion

1. How many individual students, working alone, did as well or better than students working in one of the teams?

2. Benefiting from the collective knowledge of a group to help solve a problem is but one advantage to working in groups. Name some other advantages of working in an effective group or team that normally cannot be realized when individuals work alone.

Source: Prepared by Corinne Livesay, Bryan College, Chattanooga, Tennessee.

CHART 1 |
Working Alone

1. A	26. M
2. A	27. N
3. A	28. N
4. A	29. N
5. C	30. N
6. C	31. N
7. C	32. N
8. D	33. N
9. F	34. N
10. G	35. O
11. H	36. O
12. I	37. O
13. I	38. P
14. I	39. R
15. I	40. S
16. K	41. S
17. K	42. T
18. L	43. T
19. M	44. U
20. M	45. V
21. M	46. V
22. M	47. W
23. M	48. W
24. M	49. W
25. M	50. W

(continued)

CHART 2 |
Working in Teams

1. A	26. M
2. A	27. N
3. A	28. N
4. A	29. N
5. C	30. N
6. C	31. N
7. C	32. N
8. D	33. N
9. F	34. N
10. G	35. O
11. H	36. O
12. I	37. O
13. I	38. P
14. I	39. R
15. I	40. S
16. K	41. S
17. K	42. T
18. L	43. T
19. M	44. U
20. M	45. V
21. M	46. V
22. M	47. W
23. M	48. W
24. M	49. W
25. M	50. W

chapter four | Corporate Social Responsibility, Ethics, and Sustainability

learning objectives

After you have studied this chapter, you should be able to:

4.1 Define corporate social responsibility and the tenets of the Davis model.

4.2 Define ethics, and explain how organizations specify standards for ethical behavior.

4.3 Identify benefits of ethical behavior and challenges that make ethical behavior more difficult in the modern workplace.

4.4 Discuss the impact of cultural differences on ethical issues.

4.5 Describe major types of ethical behavior that supervisors should practice.

4.6 Outline ways to make ethical decisions.

4.7 Provide guidelines for supervising unethical employees.

4.8 Define whistle-blowers, and describe how the supervisor should treat such employees.

4.9 Describe how supervisors can contribute to achieving sustainability.

A Supervision Challenge

ETHICAL SALES

Like other companies, Wells Fargo is a business where sales are important. Sales from within the branch—from checking accounts, to overdraft protection, to lines of credit and more—are a key factor in Wells Fargo's success. In order to secure these sales, Wells Fargo relies heavily on its employees to connect with customers and sell them these services and products, and these services and products themselves can actually be very beneficial for customers. For example, a customer with a checking account might genuinely benefit from opening a savings account in order to prevent the risk of a check bouncing. This means less stress about monitoring the balance of the checking account. A customer who has several ties to a bank is also more likely to stay with that bank than a customer with only one account at the bank, so this becomes a win-win situation: The customer gets quality services or products and the bank gets a satisfied customer who will keep coming back.

The challenge arises when tellers become too overwhelmed by the pressure to make sales. Recently, bank tellers and their supervisors have been coming forward to criticize the high-pressure sales environment at Wells Fargo. It seems that in efforts to makes sales and meet quotas, many employees resorted to unethical behavior, often out of fear of losing their jobs.

In December 2013, the *Los Angeles Times* investigated these accusations of unethical behavior at Wells Fargo. Tellers had set quotas, and supervisors were expected to ensure that these quotas were met. This created a stressful work environment for everyone. Tellers stayed late, attended additional training or call sessions, and felt threatened with job termination if they did not meet their sales quotas. Supervisors coached coworkers to help them make sales, but they also felt the pressure of lagging numbers. If their tellers did not meet quotas then the supervisor was held responsible for not enforcing the standards set for their team. Working conditions became unbearable for many.

The pressure of sales was so intense that some tellers began manipulating customers and taking actions customers did not agree to. Employees trying to meet their sales goals friends and family members to open accounts. Credit cards were ordered for customers who did not authorize them. One teller supervisor, who requested anonymity during the investigation, even discovered that a woman who was homeless was convinced to open six checking and savings accounts, which would cost $39 each month in fees. The woman had only come to the bank to open a free account where she could have her disability benefits directly deposited. The supervisor helped the woman cancel the unnecessary accounts, but

the moment stands out as one where the ethics of the bank employees were becoming obviously questionable due to the panic of making sales.

Amidst all of these stories, Wells Fargo did attempt to rectify the unethical behavior. In October 2013, 30 employees were fired for opening fake accounts to meet their sales quotas. Further, Wells Fargo has emphasized its formal code of ethics which is 18 pages long; the supervisor's role is clearly defined under "Manager and Leadership Responsibilities" and lists several expectations including two key responsibilities:

- "Be an example of ethical behavior."
- "Make team members understand that profit is not more important than ethics."

If ethics was so heavily emphasized by Wells Fargo, why did so many unethical actions occur? How could the company and supervisors have helped to prevent other employees from feeling so overwhelmed and, hence, justified in their wrongful behavior? As you continue reading this chapter, consider the ethics of setting and meeting sales quotas and the supervisor's role in monitoring ethical behavior when the temptation to succeed becomes so heavily emphasized.

1. Is it the bank's fault if employees resort to unethical means of meeting sales quotas?

2. How could a supervisor affect the sales culture at Wells Fargo?

Sources: Based on Scott Reckard, "Wells Fargo's pressure-cooker sales culture comes at a cost," *Los Angeles Times,* December 21, 2013, http://www.latimes.com/business/la-fi-wells-fargo-sale-pressure-20131222,0,5474088.story?page=1#axzz2yxzwm8qk, accessed April 17, 2014; Mark Calvey, "Wells Fargo fires 30 employees over fake new accounts," *San Francisco Business Times,* October 7, 2013, http://www.bizjournals.com/sanfrancisco/blog/2013/10/wells-fargo-fired-employees-los-angeles.html?page=all, access April 17, 2014; "Wells Fargo Team Member Code of Ethics and Business Conduct," *Wells Fargo,* January 2014, https://www08.wellsfargomedia.com/downloads/pdf/about/team_member_code_of_ethics.pdf, accessed April 17, 2014.

As the story about setting quotas at Wells Fargo indicates, many decisions that supervisors make are more complicated than a choice between right and wrong. In business, as in our daily lives, we make choices that affect other people in complex ways. To help you make choices that consider the impact on others, this chapter covers the roles of corporate social responsibility and ethics in the workplace. The chapter begins by discussing corporate social responsibility and then distinguishing ethical behavior from unethical behavior. Next, guidelines describe how supervisors should behave ethically. The chapter also explains how to handle the challenges of supervising unethical employees and employees who report unethical or illegal behavior in the organization. The final section of the chapter looks at how thinking about corporate social responsibility and ethical obligations along with profits has led business leaders to pursue sustainability.

LO4.1 ▶ Define corporate social responsibility and the tenets of the Davis model.

corporate social responsibility
Managerial obligation to take action that protects and improves the welfare of society and the organization's interests

Fundamentals of Corporate Social Responsibility

Corporate social responsibility is the managerial obligation to take action that protects and improves both the welfare of society as a whole and the interests of the organization. Supervisors are responsible for meeting goals not only within their organization but also those for the benefit of society.

Many areas exist in which a supervisor can strive to meet an organizational goal and benefit society at the same time. One such area would be a supervisor working to meet the organizational goal of producing high-quality products. Producing high-quality products not only helps to increase the marketability of company products but simultaneously benefits society by providing reliable products. Another example would be a construction supervisor who is attempting to meet the organizational goal of building new houses for the poor under a contract with the city. The supervisor not only is helping to meet company obligations under the contract but is simultaneously transforming the organization's community into a more socially satisfying place.

The Davis Model of Corporate Social Responsibility

Keith Davis, a theorist in the area of corporate social responsibility, has developed a model by which businesses can become more socially responsible.[1] The model consists of the following five propositions:

1. *Social responsibility arises from social power.* Businesses have a significant impact on societal issues such as environmental pollution and minority employment. Because businesses have this social power, it is important for them to act in socially responsible ways.

2. *Business shall operate as a two-way open system, with open receipt of inputs from society and open disclosure of its operations to the public.* Because businesses have power, they must listen to the public to understand what can be done to improve society as a whole. This is a two-way street, though, and society must also be able to listen to businesses about their ideas about how to improve society.

3. *The social costs and benefits of an activity, product, or service shall be thoroughly calculated and considered in deciding whether to proceed with it.* Business decisions should not simply be focused on the degree of economic profit to be earned. There are other factors, including societal consequences, which need to be considered when making decisions about the direction of a business.

4. *The social costs related to each activity, product, or service shall be passed on to the consumer.* Businesses need to earn money in order to keep providing services to society. They should not be expected to continually lose money in order to improve society. Therefore, consumers must be ready to buy services from businesses to help them maintain operational functions.

5. *Business institutions, as citizens, have the responsibility to become involved in certain social problems that are outside their normal areas of operation.* According to the Davis model, businesses need to help solve societal issues that may be outside their normal realm of action. In theory, as societal issues are solved, businesses will see increased profits, which will strengthen the argument for businesses taking action to solve societal problems.

Overall, a supervisor must act in a way that supports the accomplishment of the corporate social responsibility mission of his or her organization. The following sections build on the topic of corporate social responsibility by discussing ethics, giving supervisors insights about what ethics is, and, as a result, helping them determine how supervisors should function.

LO4.2 ▶ Define ethics, and explain how organizations specify standards for ethical behavior.

ethics
The principles by which people distinguish what is morally right

Ethics in the Workplace

One way of promoting social responsibility in organizations is teaching supervisors about the importance of ethics. In general, **ethics** refers to the principles people use to distinguish what is morally right.[2] For example, most people would agree that cheating is wrong, or at least they would agree that it is unethical to cheat an elderly widow out of her life savings. Many decisions about ethics are more difficult. For example, is it cheating or just clever to pad an expense report or take advantage of a supplier's mistake in totaling a bill? The Assessing Yourself quiz on page 115 is a chance for you to examine your own standards of ethical behavior. To get an accurate score, be honest with yourself!

Some people say that "business ethics" is an oxymoron—that is, a contradiction in terms. Can businesspeople behave ethically, and if so, should they? One view is that profitability should be the overriding concern of business. This view makes it easy to behave ethically unless an ethical choice is also costly to the organization. Another view is that organizations and their employees have an obligation to behave ethically, even if doing so cuts into short-term economic advantages. The implication is that we are all better off if organizations and individuals consider the common good.

As a supervisor, you will be looking for ethical behavior in your employees and also making sure you contribute to an environment that encourages ethical actions. Research suggests that such efforts do make a difference. A recent survey by the Ethics Resource Center found that 41 percent of employees in business and government have observed unethical conduct (down from 55 percent in 2007), but 37 percent kept that information to themselves. At the same time, the most important factor in whether companies have a strong ethical culture is whether supervisors demonstrate ethical behavior and reinforce employees' ethical actions.[3] Employees have many opportunities to observe supervisors' concern for ethics: one survey found that when employees speak up about ethical lapses, they most often make that report to their supervisor (see Figure 4.1 on the following page).

LO4.3 ▶ Identify benefits of ethical behavior and challenges that make ethical behavior more difficult in the modern workplace.

Benefits of Ethical Behavior

In addition to being morally right—a phrase that is not typically used in the business world as it is tied more to religious beliefs and one's internal

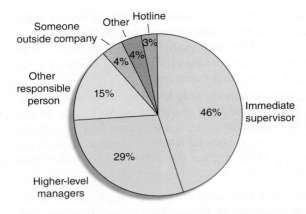

FIGURE 4.1 | Where Employees Report Ethical Lapses

Research by the Ethics Resource Center found that the majority of employees who report unethical behavior do so to their immediate supervisor or to higher-level managers. This puts supervisors in the unique position of being responsible for upholding their company's standards.

Source: Ethics Resource Center, "Reporting: Who's Telling You What You Need to Know, Who Isn't, and What You Can Do about It," Supplemental Research Brief, September 2010, http://www.ethics.org/page/nbes-supplemental-research-briefs, accessed March 17, 2014.

Boeing is a company that has suffered from multiple counts of unethical behavior and scandals.

conscience—ethical behavior offers potential advantages to the organization. To be known as an ethical individual or organization is a satisfying way of maintaining a reputation for high standards. Ethics distinguishes right from wrong and guides conduct. In a study of hundreds of salespeople, those who perceived that their organization maintained high ethical standards were more likely to trust their supervisor and be satisfied with their job, and salespeople who trusted their supervisor were more likely to plan to stay with the company.[4] Achieving this type of ethical climate is mostly a matter of day-to-day practices. For example, employees expect their supervisor to be fair. One way to demonstrate fairness involves performance reviews. Supervisors can give fair performance appraisals by setting clear, measurable standards, making sure employees know and understand these standards, and scoring performance objectively according to the standards.[5]

Ethical behavior is part of a range of behaviors that ensure an organization's long-term health and success. For a business, that success shows up in the performance of the company's stock. Some investors go out of their way to select companies with a good track record of ethical behavior. Jim Huguet, an investment manager, built a high-performing portfolio of stocks by looking at various performance measures including the companies' "corporate governance"—systems for ensuring that the leaders put the company's success ahead of enriching themselves.[6] A number of investment firms, including Calvert Funds, Domini Social Investments, and Pax World Funds, list ethical behavior as one of their criteria for choosing stocks. Analysts at such firms are likely to steer away from companies that have been fined by government regulators, have been audited by supposedly independent firms that are also earning fees for consulting, or pay executives more than $10 million per year.[7]

Ethical behavior can also improve the organization's relations with the community, which tends to attract customers and top-notch employees. Children's clothing company Hanna Andersson is well known for its concern for the community. That concern is expressed through charitable giving of a portion of its profits and the Hannadowns program for donating its clothing, which is durable as well as beautiful. The company also pays employees for working up to 16 hours a year as volunteers in their communities. Co-founder Gun Denhart says, "Businesses, like people, don't live in a vacuum. You can't have a healthy company in an unhealthy community."[8] As well as earning approval, ethical behavior tends to reduce public pressure for government regulation—a situation that most managers would view as beneficial.

In contrast, the costs of unethical behavior can be high. Organizations whose employees are unethical may lose respect, customers, and qualified employees who are uncomfortable working in an environment that compromises their moral standards. Unethical and illegal behavior caused the downfall of many companies, including Enron and Tyco. Others, among them Boeing and Martha Stewart Living Omnimedia, have struggled to recover from scandals.

Unethical behavior has personal consequences as well. Federal employees who accept gifts that fall outside federal government regulations can be suspended, demoted, or even fired. Employees who cheat or steal from their employer may wind up in jail. Even if legal, activities that are against company policy can result in firing. And at the most basic level, a person who behaves unethically has to live with that knowledge day in and day out. Thomas S. Murphy, who once served as chief executive officer of Capital Cities/ABC, says that some of the best advice he ever received was his father's counsel: "Doing the wrong thing is not worth the loss of one night's sleep."[9]

Challenges to Ethical Behavior

Despite these implications, the restructurings, cutbacks, and layoffs of recent years have made ethical behavior harder to encourage. With greater responsibilities, supervisors and other managers in restructured or downsized organizations cannot monitor employees' day-to-day behavior. At the same time, the uncertainty of the work environment has made many employees afraid of being ethical when doing so conflicts with other goals. Fudging numbers on performance records or producing shoddy merchandise to keep costs down is tempting, if the alternative is to be laid off for failing to meet cost or performance goals. Hard-pressed employees need flexibility, authority, and ethical leadership to create an environment in which to make principled decisions. For an example of a circumstance in which ethical and compassionate decision making lead to better customer service, see "Supervision and Ethics."

Other challenges arise from the supervisor's environment. For example, sometimes an organization places so much emphasis on measuring productivity, sales, or some other goal that employees doubt they will be rewarded for pursuing other

SUPERVISION AND ETHICS

EMPLOYEES NEED AUTHORITY TO ACT ETHICALLY AND COMPASSIONATELY

We have all heard stories of the customer service representatives of a company who are so bound by their organizations "rules" that they are unable or unwilling to apply common sense to a situation. While organizations have policies in place so that employees have clear guidelines on how to behave in a variety of situations, they are not meant to paralyze employees or to take away their authority to make good decisions. The employees of United Airlines apparently understand this distinction and were, therefore, able to make the choice to go above and beyond what they were required to do in order to assist a customer in need.

On January 24, 2013, San Francisco resident Kerry Drake was at the airport anxious to visit his dying mother in Lubbock, Texas. In order to get there, he first had to fly from San Francisco to Houston. And, unfortunately, this flight was delayed by 30 minutes. This delay made it unlikely that he would make the connecting flight to Lubbock—the last flight of the day. Consequently, he would likely not get to see his mother before she passed away.

The flight attendants on the San Francisco to Houston flight saw how distraught he was and learned about his situation. One comforted him and another conveyed the information to the flight's pilot. Unbeknown to Drake, the pilot used his radio to call Houston to see if anything could be done to assist the man.

When Drake landed in Houston, he rushed to the terminal to catch his flight to Lubbock, but it was clear that he would be too late for the connecting flight. To his great surprise, however, when he got to the terminal, the gate agent called out his name with a smile and ushered him on to the waiting plane to Lubbock. The airport employees, pilots, and flight attendants had decided to delay the flight by the 15 or so minutes that Drake needed in order to make the connection. Because of the actions of the United Airlines employees, Drake did make it to his mother's bedside before she passed away later that night.

Should employees bend rules to assist their customers under special circumstances? Do businesses as well as individuals have an ethical duty to help people in need? Fortunately for Drake, the United Airlines employees felt that they had the authority and latitude to make a decision to assist a customer in need.

Sources: Based on Scott Stump, "Airline Holds Flight to Help Man Reach Dying Mother's Bedside," *TODAY Travel*, March 6, 2013, http://www.today.com/travel/airline-holds-flight-help-man-reach-dying-mothers-bedside-1C8727586, accessed April 2, 2014; Katia Hetter, "United Airlines delays flight for man to see dying mother," *CNN Travel*, March 10, 2013, http://www.cnn.com/2013/03/06/travel/united-flight-delay-dying-mother/, access April 22, 2014.

goals, including high ethical standards. This is particularly a problem when employees do not have access to all the resources they need to meet their goals. These circumstances may have contributed to questionable actions taken by a security officer in a Target store. In a performance review, the officer's supervisor had told him he needed to increase the number of suspects he apprehended. That call for improvement may have been on the officer's mind when he saw a man conceal some merchandise and walk toward an exit. When the suspect neared the exit, the security officer put his hand on the man's arm to stop him. As the suspect struggled to get away, a nearby shopper saw the incident, approached, and heard the officer ask for help. The witness got involved, was stabbed by the suspect, and later sued. The way the security officer handled the situation broke several of Target's policies, which included working in pairs to apprehend suspects. However, the store had no other officers on duty at the time the incident occurred.[10] It seems unethical for a security officer to let a bystander become involved in a dangerous situation, but the pressure to meet performance targets without adequate support surely made a bad choice more likely.

On a more mundane level, a supervisor may simply find that tolerating lapses of ethics leads employees to behave in increasingly unacceptable ways. For example, if the supervisor looks the other way when employees take home small items like pencils or screws, employees may eventually start "borrowing" bigger items.

Differing Measures of Ethical Behavior

LO4.4 ▶ Discuss the impact of cultural differences on ethical issues.

code of ethics
An organization's written statement of its values and rules for ethical behavior

How can supervisors meet these challenges to ethical behavior? A good starting point is to seek guidance from the organization's **code of ethics**, if it has adopted one. This is an organization's written statement of its values and rules for ethical behavior.[11] For instance, Figure 4.2 shows the credo for Johnson & Johnson Corporation. This code of ethics is useful because it clearly outlines the company and employee responsibilities.

Meeting high ethical standards is especially challenging for those who work with people from more than one culture, because ethical standards can vary from culture

FIGURE 4.2 | The Johnson & Johnson Credo (Statement of Beliefs)

Most companies have a written statement of beliefs (a credo) or a code of ethics to guide and direct the behavior of all employees.

Source: Johnson & Johnson, "Our Credo," corporate Web site, www.jnj.com/sites/default/files/pdf/jnj_ourcredo_english_us_8.5x11_cmyk.pdf, accessed March 17, 2014.

We believe our first responsibility is to the doctors, nurses and patients, to mothers and fathers and all others who use our products and services. In meeting their needs everything we do must be of high quality. We must constantly strive to reduce our costs in order to maintain reasonable prices. Customers' orders must be serviced promptly and accurately. Our suppliers and distributors must have an opportunity to make a fair profit.

We are responsible to our employees, the men and women who work with us throughout the world. Everyone must be considered as an individual. We must respect their dignity and recognize their merit. They must have a sense of security in their jobs. Compensation must be fair and adequate, and working conditions clean, orderly and safe. Employees must feel free to make suggestions and complaints. There must be equal opportunity for employment, development and advancement for those qualified. We must provide competent management, and their actions must be just and ethical.

We are responsible to the communities in which we live and work and to the world community as well. We must be good citizens—support good works and charities and bear our fair share of taxes. We must encourage civic improvements and better health and education. We must maintain in good order the property we are privileged to use, protecting the environment and natural resources.

Our final responsibility is to our stockholders. Business must make a sound profit. We must experiment with new ideas. Research must be carried on, innovative programs developed and mistakes paid for. New equipment must be purchased, new facilities provided and new products launched. Reserves must be created to provide for adverse times. When we operate according to these principles, the stockholder should realize a fair return.

to culture. In a study comparing values of professionals in the United States, Canada, and Mexico, respondents from all the countries agreed that honesty is one of the most important qualities for representing ethical standards in business. However, only Canadian professionals included loyalty among the top three values, and only Mexican professionals put compromise in the top three.[12] Even when ideals match, people in different parts of the world may accept different standards of behavior from businesspeople. Transparency International tracks perceived levels of corruption, such as bribery of public officials, and finds a wide variation in the amount of corrupt practices people observe from country to country. As shown in Figure 4.3, people in Denmark, New Zealand, Finland, and Sweden observe very little corruption. In contrast, corruption is common in Sudan and North Korea. In addition to allowing for the comparison of the perception of corruption levels between countries, Transparency International also allows for comparisons for any given country from year to year. For example, from 2010 to 2013, Iraq improved in the rankings (moving from 175 to 171) though its score did not change significantly (moving from 15 to 16).

FIGURE 4.3 | A Sampling of Countries' Perceived Corruption Levels

While the Corruption Perceptions Index generated scores for 177 countries, this chart shows a sampling of those countries. Clearly perceptions of perceived levels of public sector corruption—and, likely, real levels of corruption—vary greatly around the world.

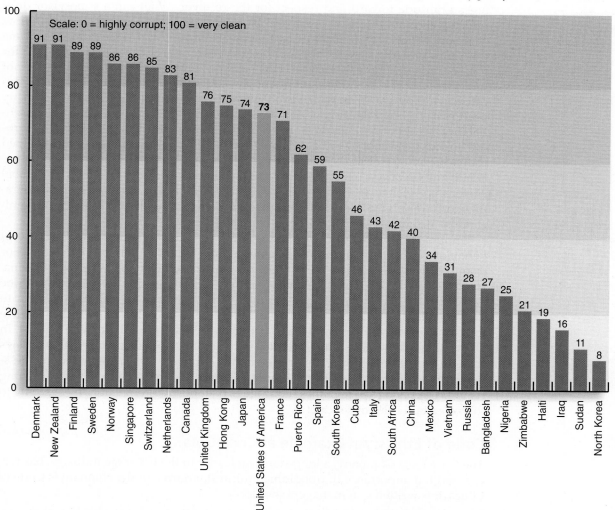

Source: Data taken from "Transparency International Corruption Perceptions Index 2013, www.transparency.org/cpi2013/results, accessed March 17, 2014." Reprinted with permission.

The difference is that the scores of other countries, such as Afghanistan which dropped from 14 to 8 in the same years, moved them lower than Iraq. The United States generally performs about the same; it had a 75 rating in 2003, a 3 in 2007, 71 in 2010, and a 73 in 2013. This usually places the United States around twentieth in the world.[13]

If an organization does business in a country where corruption is expected, employees can have more difficulty meeting high standards. They may find it easiest to close deals and obtain government approvals if they go along with local expectations for making payoffs. Some manufacturers with international operations have even set aside funds for this type of payment. However, this type of conduct not only violates U.S. and European laws, but also sends mixed messages about what the company expects of its people. Research by the Corporate Executive Board found that in countries such as India and China, employees are often unsure whether they are seeing misconduct. Supervisors and their companies do well to establish clear corporate values and business-related standards that employees can understand and of which they can be proud.[14]

One reason for perceived differences in corruption levels is that gift giving in the workplace can have different meanings from one culture to another. In the United States, the giving of gifts often is interpreted as bribery, an attempt to buy influence. However, in many parts of the world, giving a gift is the proper way to indicate one's gratitude toward and respect for the receiver. What can a supervisor do if refusing a gift might insult the giver? Most important, the supervisor must follow company policy, and in many cases, that means turning down the gift. At the same time, however, the supervisor should explain carefully and politely the reason for not accepting the gift. If a supervisor has immigrant employees who might not understand U.S. views about gift giving, this might be an area about which to educate all employees before such a problem arises. Find out if there are any company policies or codes of ethics covering the situation. Following these policies is essential for all employees, including supervisors, and provides a way to show that turning down a gift is not meant as an insult to the giver. Some companies have helped individuals make ethical choices in an international context by signing the voluntary United Nations Global Compact. The compact includes principles of global citizenship, such as working against extortion and bribery. So far, over 7,000 organizations from 145 countries have signed the compact; of these, 309 are U.S. organizations, including Nike and General Electric.[15]

Understanding cultural differences also can help businesspeople interpret behavior so they can arrive at agreements that are acceptable on both sides. For example, Western ideals tend to focus on individual behavior, whereas in China, standards are based more on context, including relationships. In other words, one person's duty to another depends on the nature of their relationship, say, father to son or supervisor to employee. People doing business in China find that they have to begin by getting to know one another and establishing a relationship of trust. In China, that relationship of trust is likely to count for more than any particular laws that are on the books, but may or may not be enforced. So, an American businessperson in China might respect Chinese values by taking time to develop trusting relationships and expect Chinese colleagues to honor Western values by agreeing to follow certain rules of conduct.[16]

Code of Ethics: An Example at Coca-Cola

The Coca-Cola Company, a long-standing leader in the beverage industry, has recognized the importance of upholding ethical standards. In the company's Code of Ethics, it is written that managers should:

- Ensure that the people you supervise understand their responsibilities under the Code and other Company policies.

- Take opportunities to discuss the Code and reinforce the importance of ethics and compliance with employees.
- Create an environment where employees feel comfortable raising concerns.
- Consider conduct in relation to the Code and other Company policies when evaluating employees.
- Never encourage or direct employees to achieve business results at the expense of ethical conduct or compliance with the Code or the law.
- Always act to stop violations of the Code or the law by those you supervise.[17]

By writing a Code of Ethics, the Coca-Cola Company has demonstrated the importance of upholding ethical standards in the workplace.

Integrity Policy: GE's Citizenship

General Electric has made a commitment to perform with integrity through its "The Spirit & The Letter" guiding policy document. This commitment is instilled in every employee and is cited as a "nonnegotiable expectation of behavior." Available in over 30 languages, all GE employees have access to this 60-plus page document that includes, among other things, a code of conduct, compliance policies, and "what-if" scenarios. Recognized as one of the world's most renowned compliance programs, "The Spirit and The Letter" is supported by a system of policies, processes, training, and communications. Every employee is made aware of exactly what the expectations are regardless of where in the world they work.[18]

LO4.5 ▶ Describe major types of ethical behavior that supervisors should practice.

Ethical Behavior of Supervisors

If supervisors wish to see a high standard of ethical behavior in the workplace, they must behave ethically themselves. Supervisors in particular must exhibit important dimensions of ethical behavior including loyalty, fairness, and honesty (see Figure 4.4).

As a leader, a supervisor is expected to be loyal to the organization, to his or her manager, and to his or her subordinates (see Chapter 8). When these loyalties conflict, ethical dilemmas result. These loyalties also may come into conflict with the supervisor's self-interests. If supervisors are seen by others in the organization to put their own interests first, they will have difficulty earning the loyalty, trust, and respect of others.

Fairness is another important trait of a supervisor. Employees expect to be treated evenhandedly. They resent it if the supervisor plays favorites or passes the blame for mistakes on to them. In some cases, their resentment can breed unethical responses that make the situation even worse. One office employee admitted to a newspaper reporter how he used to get revenge against a bullying boss: The employee noticed that his supervisor was unusually devoted to his collection of pens. Sensing vulnerability, the employee began replacing the pens, one at a time, with nonworking models. Then he discovered that if he snuck a pen from the desk and drew a line through a dab of Superglue, he could return the same pen to the desk, and the mystified boss would no longer be able to use it. While the employee's revenge was certainly unethical in its own right, it enabled him to feel he was playing a kind of game to even the score.[19]

FIGURE 4.4 | Important Dimensions of Ethical Behavior by Supervisors

There are a variety of dimensions to ethical behavior. As a leader in the company, supervisors are expected to model these behaviors for their employees and each other.

nepotism
The hiring of one's relatives

Supervisors may find it harder to be fair—or to convince others that they are fair—when they supervise their own relatives. Therefore, supervisors may find it wise to avoid **nepotism,** the hiring of one's own relatives.[20] A related problem can arise when supervisors accept a gift from a supplier or someone else who may wish to influence their judgment. Even if a supervisor is sure about remaining objective in the acceptance of cash, lavish entertainment, or other gifts, other people may question whether the supervisor can be fair. When supervisors place themselves in such a position, management tends to doubt their ability to exercise good judgment.

Honesty includes several types of behavior by the supervisor. First, when employees make a suggestion or accomplish impressive results, the supervisor should be sure that the employees get the credit. Pretending that other people's accomplishments are your own is a type of dishonesty. So is using the company's resources for personal matters. For example, a supervisor who spends work time chatting with friends on the phone or who takes supplies home for personal use in effect is stealing what belongs to the organization. Furthermore, the supervisor is demonstrating that such behavior will be overlooked, thus encouraging employees to be equally dishonest. Finally, supervisors should be honest about what the organization can offer employees.

■ CONNECT SELF-ASSESSMENT 4.1

Assessing Your Ethical Decision Making Skills

Every decision has some ethical question involved in it. These issues may be small, large, seem non-existent, or appear overwhelmingly complex. It is important not only to understand your organization's ethical code, but also your own sense of ethics. This assessment will help you understand how you apply ethics in your decisions.

LO4.6 ▶ Outline ways to make ethical decisions.

Making Ethical Decisions

Assuming that it is desirable to choose ethical behavior and to help employees do so, the challenge is to decide what action is ethical in a particular situation and then determine how to carry it out.[21] There are no hard-and-fast rules for making ethical decisions. In some cases, two possibilities might seem equally ethical or unethical. Perhaps someone will get hurt no matter what the supervisor decides. In addition, as discussed previously, people from different cultures may have different measures of ethical or unethical behavior. "Practical Advice for Supervisors" on the following page offers recommendations for making decisions when faced with this kind of dilemma.

Sometimes the supervisor can promote ethical decision making by involving others in the process. When the group discusses the issue, group members can offer their perspectives on the situation and the underlying values. Discussing the ethical implications of the decision can help the supervisor see consequences and options that he or she might not have thought of alone. (Chapter 9 provides further guidelines for group decision making.)

Deciding what behavior is ethical does not always end an ethical dilemma. Employees are sometimes afraid that doing what is ethically right will cause their performance to suffer and may even cost them their jobs. However, supervisors can help alleviate these concerns. Employees respond when supervisors and higher-level managers model ethical behavior and include ethical standards in performance discussions and rewards (even as simple as praising ethical actions).

PRACTICAL ADVICE FOR SUPERVISORS

RECOMMENDATIONS FOR MAKING DECISIONS

In some situations, the ethical course of action is obvious. But how can supervisors decide what to do when the alternatives are a mixture of benefits and harm, greed and good? One way to practice thinking ethically is to react to these tricky situations by asking yourself three basic questions:

1. *Would you accept this from your kids?* Think about how you would justify each course of action you are considering. Now imagine that your child is offering you this same justification (if you don't have children, try to imagine that you do). Would your rationale, coming from a child, sound like a valid reason for going ahead with the idea? Sometimes in the business world, excuses come down to "everyone is doing it" or "I won't get caught." Most parents would not accept that kind of reasoning from a child; as an adult, you can certainly find better guidelines for how to act.

2. *Will it make you happier?* This question assumes that you can experience the greatest long-term happiness by being the best person—supervisor, co-worker, parent, spouse, citizen, and so on—you can be. Think about how you will feel when you are living with the consequences of your choice.

3. *Can you carry out the action without forcing or manipulating others to go along?* If you have to trick an employee or twist someone's arm to get that person to cooperate with an action, it may be a red flag that something is wrong. If you have to use the power of your position as supervisor to force your employees to carry out your decision, you are taking away their dignity and ability to reason as humans can and should do. Certainly, as a supervisor, you have rights and duties to direct work, and there are consequences of employees' choices. But if you have to coerce people, it tends to signal that you are not using your power as ethically as you might.

Sources: Kyle Scott, "Business Ethics: Do What's Right, or What's Right Now?" *Supervision*, July 2011, 72 (7), pp. 8–9; Laura Bruck, "Business Ethics: Shades of Grey," Material Handling & Logistics, May 13, 2011, http://mhlnews.com/labor-management/business-ethics-shades-grey, accessed March 17, 2014.

LO4.7 ▶ Provide guidelines for supervising unethical employees.

Supervising Unethical Employees

It is tempting to ignore the unethical behavior of others, hoping they will change on their own. However, the problem usually gets worse as the unethical employee sees that he or she can get away with the behavior. Consequently, when the supervisor suspects that an employee is behaving unethically, the supervisor needs to take prompt action. Figure 4.5 summarizes the steps to take.

The first step is to gather and record evidence. The supervisor needs to be sure that unethical behavior is actually occurring. For example, if the supervisor suspects that one or more employees are padding their expense accounts, the supervisor regularly should review expense reports. As soon as the supervisor sees something that looks odd, he or she should ask the employee about it. After confronting the employee with the evidence, the supervisor should follow the organization's disciplinary procedure. (Discipline is discussed in Chapter 12.)

FIGURE 4.5 | Steps to Take When an Employee Is Suspected of Unethical Behavior

Having a plan in place to address any potential unethical behavior of employees can make a difficult situation a bit easier to handle.

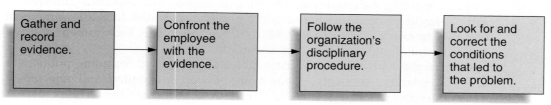

After dealing with the specific problem, the supervisor should try to understand what conditions contributed to this problem. That effort can help the supervisor avoid similar ethical lapses in the future. In analyzing why an employee has behaved unethically, consider whether you have created a climate for ethical behavior in the department. Have you set a good example through your own ethical behavior? Are the rewards for productivity so great that they tempt employees to cut ethical corners? Do the employees hear messages that say the organization cares only about achievements, such as, "I don't care how you get it done, just do it"? Research by the Corporate Executive Board has found that employees are most likely to behave with integrity in an organization where employees feel comfortable speaking up, trust their co-workers, have a good relationship with their supervisor, give and receive open communication, experience organizational justice, sense a positive tone at the top of the company, and are clear about what the organization expects them to do to meet ethical standards.[22]

LO4.8 ▶ Define whistle-blowers, and describe how the supervisor should treat such employees.

whistle-blower
Someone who exposes a violation of ethics or law

Treatment of Whistle-Blowers

Someone who exposes a violation of ethics or law is known as a whistle-blower. Typically, a whistle-blower brings the problem first to a manager in the organization.[23] If management seems unresponsive, he or she then contacts a government agency, the media, or a private organization. The whistle-blower's hope is that the negative publicity will spur the organization to do the right thing. Of course, the negative publicity also can damage the organization. This is one reason why supervisors should respond carefully and appropriately when employees come to them with complaints. (To learn more about responding appropriately, see "Supervisory Skills.")

A whistle-blower's report may be embarrassing as well as costly to the organization. Nevertheless, whistle-blowers are protected by federal laws, the laws of several states, and some recent court decisions. For example, federal laws protect employees who make complaints pertaining to violations of antidiscrimination laws, environmental laws, and occupational health and safety standards. For example, the Sarbanes-Oxley Act forbids employers from retaliating against an employee who reports possible accounting, auditing, or reporting misdeeds that deceive investors. Thus, in general, employers may not retaliate against someone for reporting a violation. Suppose an employee files a complaint of sexual harassment; the organization may not react by firing the employee who complained.

Many laws are in place to protect whistle-blowers, but some still suffer from exposing their company and others are still hesitant to come forward.

In addition, under a Civil War–era law that was little used until the late 1980s, whistle-blowers who report on companies that are cheating the government stand to receive up to 30 percent of whatever money the company ultimately pays as a penalty for the fraud. The number of cases filed by whistle-blowers under the False Claims Act jumped from 66 in 1987 to 533 in 1997, and the cases filed each year continues to be high (574 in 2010). Recoveries under the False Claims Act since 1987 have totaled more than $30 billion, with anywhere from 15 to 30 percent awarded to the whistle-blowers. In a dramatic recent case, Scantibodies Laboratory CEO Thomas Cantor filed a whistle-blower lawsuit claiming that a parathyroid hormone assay test sold by one of his competitors, Quest Diagnostics, was faulty and was resulting in dialysis patients being overdosed with expensive and harmful drugs—leading to preventable surgeries and earlier deaths. In a 2011 settlement, Quest Diagnostics agreed to pay $302 million to the U.S. Government and was forced to shut down its diagnostics test subsidiary.[24]

Despite these protections, whistle-blowers often suffer for going public with their complaints. Typically, the whistle-blower is resented and rejected by co-workers and may be demoted or terminated. Even when the courts agree that the whistle-blower was treated unlawfully, it can take years for that person to be compensated by the organization or even appreciated by the public. Even when a whistle-blower keeps his or her job, there are consequences. Daniel Thobe blew the whistle at DPL Inc., a utility company. Thobe informed DPL's audit committee that he had concerns about the company's financial reporting and corporate governance. The committee hired an independent law firm to investigate, and the lawyers agreed with some of Thobe's concerns. Three top executives resigned, and DPL promised to strengthen its financial controls. Even though Thobe was protected by the Sarbanes-Oxley Act and kept his job, he faced the embarrassment of scathing criticism by DPL's executives during the investigation. And like other whistle-blowers who keep their jobs, Thobe is in the awkward position of working for a company he is known to have subjected to an investigation.[25] Because of these consequences—and out of fairness to one's employer—a would-be whistle-blower should try to resolve problems within the organization before blowing the whistle.

Today, many organizations are protecting ethics-minded employees and themselves with hotlines that make it easier to report and resolve ethical disputes within the organization. Cabela's, a retailer specializing in products for outdoor recreation, works with an outside firm that operates its hotline. The hotline operator has someone respond to each call within 48 hours, so the caller knows that his or her concerns were heard. The operator also provides Cabela's managers with quarterly reports, which they use to identify problem areas. For example, if several complaints come from a particular store, that fact may signal a need for managers at that store to receive training in an area of weakness.[26]

A supervisor's general attitude toward whistle-blowing should be to discourage reports of wrongdoing when they are motivated simply by pettiness or a desire to get back at someone. Yet, when someone does complain, the supervisor should investigate the complaint quickly and report what will be done. This lets employees know that their complaints are taken seriously and that the supervisor wants to handle them fairly and appropriately. The supervisor should bear in mind that the typical whistle-blower is not simply a troublemaker but a person with high ideals and competence. Keeping communication flowing and responding to

SUPERVISORY SKILLS

COMMUNICATING

Careful Listening Makes Whistle-Blowing Unnecessary

No one enjoys listening to people whine and complain, but sometimes a complaining employee is a blessing in disguise. An employee with a complaint may have important information about a problem that needs to be corrected. Even if the complaint is misguided, an employee who believes that a concern was ignored may turn into a whistle-blower, potentially causing great expense and embarrassment.

This situation is especially relevant to supervisors. Research by the Ethics Resource Center has found that employees who report misconduct are most likely to go to their immediate supervisor. Fewer turn to higher-level managers or their human resources department.

What should a supervisor do if an employee is complaining? Eric M. Heath, whose responsibilities at East Boston Savings Bank include training supervisors, says supervisors should listen carefully and provide "no-fault feedback." That means the supervisor doesn't jump to conclusions but instead asks open-ended questions about what the employee observed. The supervisor should treat the complainer with respect and thank him or her for the information. If the situation is ethical and in accord with business goals, the supervisor should, if possible, explain the reasons. If the situation calls for a response beyond what the supervisor can do, the supervisor should refer the employee to someone who can help.

Source: Based on Carolyn Hirschman, "Giving Voice to Employee Concerns," *HRMagazine*, August 1, 2008, 53 (8), http://www.shrm.org/Publications/hrmagazine/EditorialContent/Pages/0808hirscman.aspx, accessed March 17, 2014.

problems will allow the organization to find solutions without the costs and embarrassment of public disclosure. Finally, engaging in ethical behavior can eliminate the need for whistle-blowing—and the other negative fallout of misconduct—in the first place.

Sustainability

LO4.9 ▶ Describe how supervisors can contribute to achieving sustainability.

At a growing number of organizations, supervisors are not only expected to make ethical decisions and support efforts at social responsibility, they are also engaged in helping to make their organization *sustainable.* When Chapter 1 introduced the theme of sustainability, it focused on one important aspect: efforts to minimize the organization's impact on the natural environment. To express that goal in a simplified way, if organizations operate using less energy, less of the world's natural resources, and with less waste, they can keep on making their products available without using up what the planet can provide.

But in the way that business leaders think about being sustainable today, sustainability is much more: it represents an organization's ability to meet its present needs without compromising the ability of future generations to meet their needs.[27] That concern for the future requires managers at all levels to think broadly about the organization's impact on the natural environment, its workers, its investors, and the communities where it operates and serves customers.

sustainability
An organization's ability to meet its present needs without compromising the ability of future generations to meet their needs

Sustainable Organizations

In an organization that is sustainable, managers make decisions aimed at balancing present needs against the needs of future generations in three areas: the economy, the environment, and society.[28] Economic concerns include producing only what customers will demand and generating a fair profit for the company's investors. Environmental concerns include conserving natural resources and minimizing pollution and energy use. Societal concerns include protecting and caring for the communities where the organization's workers and customers live. This kind of sustainable organization can continue to flourish into the future because it is profitable, has an ongoing source of natural resources, has a steady supply of workers and customers, and is valued by the communities where it operates.

Thinking broadly beyond this year's profits may seem overly complicated. Business experts, however, believe that improving sustainability tends to increase productivity and stimulate innovation. For these and other reasons, sustainable organizations are well positioned to remain profitable.[29]

Achieving Sustainability

Efforts to achieve sustainability take place in every department and at every level of an organization. Supervisors can play important roles in identifying areas for improvement and leading their employees to implement changes that will make the organization more sustainable. Figure 4.6 on the following page summarizes basic steps that organizations can take to achieve sustainability.

The effort to become sustainable starts with goal setting. Supervisors and their employees need to know that the organization is striving for sustainability and what sustainability means for their particular organization. At a chemical company, sustainability goals may emphasize efforts to reduce hazardous waste. A restaurant may focus on its energy usage, the sources of the food it serves, and opportunities for its employees to share the benefits of healthful eating with families in the community.

FIGURE 4.6 | Steps toward Sustainability

Achieving sustainability is not something that happens over night or that can be achieved by doing just one thing correctly; it requires a series of continuous choices and steps toward that goal.

Set sustainability goals

Reward contributions to sustainability

Hire people with sustainability skills

Track progress toward sustainability

Making recycling available at public parks allows more people to contribute to minimizing energy usage.

In Highlands Ranch, Colorado, the Parks, Recreation and Open Space (PROS) Team charged its supervisors with finding ways to reduce the agency's impact on the environment. The supervisors studied their areas of operations to see if they could reduce pollution, waste, and energy and water usage while increasing the quality of the services they provide. With this goal in mind, supervisors came up with a variety of ideas that the PROS Team implemented, such as adding hybrid and electric vehicles to the fleet, reusing water for irrigation, placing recycling bins at ball fields, installing solar-powered locks and lights and waterless urinals in park restrooms, and establishing a policy that vehicles are to be turned off, not idled, when employees make stops.[30]

Attaining goals, of course, requires people with the right abilities. Therefore, becoming sustainable requires people who can think creatively about economic, environmental, and societal concerns. In a sustainable organization, supervisors who are involved in hiring decisions should be on the lookout for creative thinkers who care about their community. Organizations pursuing sustainability also may hire experts to lead these efforts. Supervisors should commit themselves to learning from these experts and encouraging their employees to learn as well.

Achieving and maintaining sustainability requires ongoing commitment at all levels, so organizations need to reward employees for contributing to sustainability. As we will see in Chapter 11, there are many ways that organizations reward employees with money, promotions, recognition, and more. Supervisors generally do not establish reward programs for the company, but they still have the ability to reward good performance through praise, encouragement, and interesting assignments. Even more powerful than any of these rewards, supervisors also can communicate how employees' efforts are benefiting the team, the company, customers, and the surrounding community. People are strongly committed to doing work that matters.

Finally, organizations should track progress toward meeting their sustainability goals. People want to know that their efforts succeed, and management must know whether initiatives are successful or in need of revision. In the previous example of the PROS Team in Highlands Ranch, several measures point toward success. The government there determined that water conservation had saved 24 million gallons of water, reducing costs by $24,000. The no-idle rule for drivers saved an amount of fuel equivalent to 20 travel miles per vehicle. Altogether, the PROS Team estimates that its sustainability efforts are saving taxpayers $250,000 a year.[31]

Skills Module

PART ONE: CONCEPTS

Summary

4.1 Define corporate social responsibility and the tenets of the Davis model.

Corporate social responsibility is the managerial obligation to take action that protects and improves both the welfare of society as a whole and the interests of the organization. The Davis model of corporate social responsibility asserts that (1) social responsibility arises from social power, (2) businesses shall operate as a two-way open system, (3) costs and benefits of a product should be considered when deciding whether or not to proceed, (4) costs can be passed on to the consumer, and (5) businesses should be involved in social problems that are outside their normal areas of operation.

4.2 Define ethics, and explain how organizations specify standards for ethical behavior.

Ethics refers to the principles by which people distinguish what is morally right. Organizations are particularly concerned about ethical behavior because modern technology has made the potential consequences of unethical behavior enormous. Recognizing the importance of preventing ethical lapses, many organizations have adopted a code of ethics. Codes of ethics provide guidelines for behavior and support top management's assertion that they care about ethical behavior.

4.3 Identify benefits of ethical behavior and challenges that make ethical behavior more difficult in the modern workplace.

To be known as an ethical organization is a satisfying way of maintaining a reputation for high standards. When customers, clients, and suppliers see that they are treated ethically, they are more likely to want to work cooperatively with the organization and do their best for it. Ethical behavior can also improve community relations, attracting customers and qualified employees. Unethical behavior, in contrast, can cause an organization to lose both respect and the best employees (who may be uncomfortable working for an unethical organization). Unethical behavior may even land employees and managers in jail if they break the law.

An uncertain work environment can make ethical behavior harder to encourage. Fear of losing one's job can lead employees to cooperate with unethical activities sponsored by others, so it is important for supervisors to foster a climate that encourages ethical behavior.

4.4 Discuss the impact of cultural differences on ethical issues.

In some cases, ethical standards and behavior vary among cultures. The biggest risk of operating in the most corrupt countries is potential shifts in the political winds. One reason for perceived differences in levels of corruption is that gift giving in the workplace is interpreted differently from country to country. The supervisor should always follow company policy but do so carefully and politely in order not to offend members of another culture.

4.5 Describe major types of ethical behavior that supervisors should practice.

Supervisors should be loyal to the organization, their manager, and their subordinates. Supervisors should treat others, especially employees, fairly. Ways to dispel any doubts about one's fairness are to avoid nepotism and decline gifts from suppliers and others seeking influence. Finally, supervisors should be honest, which includes giving subordinates credit for their accomplishments and avoiding personal use of the company's resources.

4.6 Outline ways to make ethical decisions.

There are no hard-and-fast rules for making ethical decisions, but asking some essential questions can help. The supervisor can promote ethical decision making by involving others in the thought process. Discussing the ethical implications of the decision can help the supervisor see consequences and options that he or she might not have thought of alone.

4.7 Provide guidelines for supervising unethical employees.

When the supervisor believes an employee is doing something unethical, he or she should take immediate action. The supervisor first should gather and record evidence. Then the supervisor should confront the employee with the evidence and follow the organization's disciplinary procedure. After dealing with a specific problem, the supervisor should try to understand what conditions contributed to the problem and then seek to correct those conditions.

4.8 Define whistle-blowers, and describe how the supervisor should treat such employees.

Whistle-blowers are people who expose a violation of ethics or law. They are protected from retaliation by federal and state laws as well as recent court decisions. The supervisor should discourage reports of wrongdoing when they are motivated simply by pettiness or a desire for revenge. However, when someone does complain, the supervisor should quickly investigate the complaint and report what will be done. This lets employees know that their complaints are taken seriously. Keeping communication flowing and responding to problems ultimately allows the organization to find its own solutions.

4.9 Describe how supervisors can contribute to achieving sustainability.

Sustainability represents an organization's ability to meet its present needs without compromising the ability of future generations to meet their needs. In a sustainable organization, supervisors and higher-level managers make decisions aimed at balancing present needs against the needs of future generations in three areas: the economy, the environment, and society. Supervisors can identify areas for improvement and lead their employees to implement changes that will make the organization more sustainable as it sets sustainability goals, hires people with sustainability skills, rewards contributions to sustainability, and tracks its progress toward sustainability.

Key Terms

corporate social responsibility, *p.* 96

ethics, *p.* 97

code of ethics, *p.* 100

nepotism, *p.* 104

whistle-blower, *p.* 106

sustainability, *p.* 108

Review and Discussion Questions

1. Allstate Insurance Company expresses its commitment to "be a great corporate citizen" in three areas: (1) valuing "inclusive diversity," so that employees "engage people with honesty, caring and integrity"; (2) helping communities through volunteer activities and monetary contributions; and (3) demonstrating "a passion to lead positive change in this country." (For details, see Allstate's Corporate Responsibility Report at www.allstate.com/corporate-responsibility.aspx.)

   a. Imagine you are a supervisor at Allstate. Suggest a few ways you could help carry out Allstate's commitment to corporate social responsibility.

   b. How, if at all, might these activities benefit Allstate?

2. What are some benefits of ethical behavior? What are some challenges to ethical behavior?

3. Gift giving in the workplace is interpreted differently from culture to culture. What can a supervisor do if his or her company prohibits accepting gifts but a customer from another culture insists on offering one?

4. In what ways can loyalty create conflict for a supervisor?

5. How should a supervisor practice honesty in the workplace?

6. In each of the following situations, what would have been the ethical thing for the employee or supervisor to do? What criteria did you use to decide? What would you have done in that situation? Why?

   a. Upon being hired, a new employee offers his supervisor confidential information about his former employer's marketing plan for a new product. The two companies have competing product lines.

   b. The associate editor of a magazine learns that a particularly newsworthy individual wants to be paid to grant an interview with the magazine. The magazine's policy is never to pay for interviews, but the editor knows she could "bury" the expense elsewhere in her budget. She desperately wants the story; she knows it will be good for both the magazine and her career.

7. Devon Price supervises a crew of maintenance workers. One day a secretary at the company took him aside and asked, "Do you know that Pete [a member of the crew] has been taking home supplies like nails and tape to work on personal projects?" What should Devon do?

8. Assume that Pete, the maintenance worker in question 7, was discovered pilfering supplies and was disciplined. Upset, he decides to act on some safety problems he has observed and complained about, and he reports them to the local office of the Occupational Safety and Health Administration (OSHA). When Devon, Pete's supervisor, finds out that the department will be investigated by OSHA, he is furious. It seems as though Pete is nothing but a troublemaker. What should Devon do?

9. As the supervisor of a small business's accounting department, you are responsible for a group of five employees who work in an office at computers. These employees keep track of the money the company earns and spends, and they process the documents for paying employees and suppliers and for collecting money from customers. Your company has recently announced a new commitment to sustainability. How can you, as the accounting supervisor, contribute to sustainability?

Notes

1. Keith Davis, "Five Propositions for Social Responsibility," *Business Horizons* (June 1975): 19–24.

2. For more reading about ethics and the potential consequences associated with unethical behavior, see "Brian English, Climate for ethics, and occupational-organisational commitment conflict," *Journal of Management Development*, 2008, 27 (9), pp. 963–975.

3. Paula J. Desio, "More Protection for Whistle-blowers? Or More Ethical Culture?" *Ethics Today*, October 28, 2008, www.ethics.org/ethics-today/1008/policy-report.html, accessed March 17, 2014; Ethics Resource Center, "2013 National Business Ethics Survey," www.ethics.org/nbes/, accessed March 17, 2014.

4. Jay Prakash Mulki, Fernando Jaramillo, and William B. Locander, "Effects of Ethical Climate and Supervisory Trust on Salesperson's Job Attitudes and Intentions to Quit," *Journal of Personal Selling and Sales Management*, Winter 2006, 26 (1), pp. 19–26, downloaded from Business & Company Resource Center, http://galenet.galegroup.com. A survey with similar results is reported in Ethics Resource Center, "National Business Ethics Survey: How Employees View Ethics in Their Organization, 1994–2005," www.ethics.org, July 17, 2006.

5. Gary Dessler, "How to Fine-Tune Your Company's Ethical Compass," *Supervision*, April 2006, 67 (4), p. 15, downloaded from InfoTrac, http://web2.infotrac.galegroup.com.

6. James M. Clash, "Vintage Names," *Forbes*, June 7, 2004, http://www.forbes.com/forbes/2004/0607/164.html, accessed March 17, 2014.

7. G. Jeffrey MacDonald, "A Quest for Clean Hands," *The Christian Science Monitor*, February 9, 2004, www.csmonitor.com/2004/0209/p14s01-wmgn.html, accessed March 17, 2014.

8. T. L. Stanley, "The Ethical Manager," *Supervision*, May 2006, 67 (5), p. 10, downloaded from InfoTrac, http://web2.infotrac.galegroup.com; Hanna Andersson, "Associates in the Community," http://hannaanderssoncareers.silkroad.com/hannaanderssonext/About_Us/in_the_community.html, accessed March 17, 2014.

9. Mindy Grossman, "The Best Advice I Ever Got: Thomas S. Murphy," *Fortune*, April 30, 2008, http://money.cnn.com/galleries/2008/fortune/0804/ gallery.bestadvice.fortune/10.html, accessed March 17, 2014.

10. "Creating Checks and Balances to Curb Numbers' Corrupting Influence," *Security Director's Report*, November 2010, pp. 1, 7, 10–12; "Five Ways to Avoid a $500,000 Jury Award," *Security Director's Report*, November 2010, pp. 1, 13–15.

11. For a recent empirical review of the usefulness of developing a code of ethics, see Brad Long and Cathy Driscoll, "Codes of Ethics and the Pursuit of Organizational Legitimacy: Theoretical and Empirical Considerations," *Journal of Business Ethics*, 2008, 77 (2), pp. 173–189.

12. "Ethics in the U.S., Canada, and Mexico: Who Would You Want to Do Business With?" news release, PR Newswire, June 6, 2006, http://www.prnewswire.com/news-releases/ethics-in-the-us-canada-and-mexico-who-would-you-want-to-do-business-with-55924402.html, accessed March 17, 2014.

13. "Persistently High Corruption in Low-Income Countries Amounts to an 'Ongoing Humanitarian Disaster,'" Transparency International, September 22, 2008, www.transparency.org/news/pressrelease/20080922_persistently_high_corruption_in_low_income_countries, accessed March 17, 2014; Corruptions Perceptions Index 2010, Transparency International, http://www.transparency.org/cpi2010/results, accessed March 19, 2014; Corruptions Perceptions Index 2013, Transparency International, http://www.transparency.org/cpi2013/results, accessed March 19, 2014.

14. Jonathan Katz, "Schooled by Scandals," *Industry Week*, March 14, 2011, http://www.industryweek.com/corporate-responsibility/schooled-scandals, accessed March 17, 2014; James Fitzmaurice, "Corporate Integrity in Emerging Markets" Corporate Executive Board Blogs, October 12, 2011, http://www.executiveboard.com/blogs/corporate-integrity-in-emerging-markets-should-we-use-the-same-standard/, accessed March 17, 2014.

15. Participants & Stakeholders, United Nations Global Compact, last updated May 29, 2013, http://www.unglobalcompact.org/ParticipantsAndStakeholders/Index.html, accessed March 19, 2014.

16. Gail Dutton, "Do Strong Ethics Hurt U.S. Global Competitiveness?" *World Trade*, March 2, 2008, downloaded from General Reference Center Gold,

http://find.galegroup.com; and Li Yuan, "Building Trust, Chinese-Style," *The Wall Street Journal*, April 25, 2008, http://online.wsj.com/news/articles/SB120897959046739075, accessed March 17, 2014.

17. The Coca-Cola Company, Our Company: Governance & Ethics, http://www.coca-colacompany.com/our-company/governance-ethics/governance-ethics, accessed March 17, 2014.

18. The Spirit & The Letter, GE Citizenship, http://www.gecitizenship.com/reports/spirit-letter/, accessed March 19, 2014.

19. Jim Martin, "Bad Bosses: Memories That Leave a Mark," *Erie (PA) Times-News*, July 17, 2011, http://www.goerie.com/apps/pbcs.dll/article?AID5/20110717/BUSINESS05/307179989/-1/BUSINESS, accessed March 17, 2014.

20. For more information on nepotism, see Frank Chervenak and Laurence McCullough, "Is Ethically Justified Nepotism in Hiring and Admissions in Academic Health Centers an Oxymoron?" *The Physician Executive*, September–October 2007, pp. 42–45, http://net.acpe.org/Resources/PEJ/2007/September_October/Chervenak.pdf, accessed March 17, 2014.

21. For tips on making ethical decisions, see Domènec Melé, "Integrating ethics into management," *Journal of Business Ethics*, 78 (3), March 1, 2008, pp. 291–297.

22. Phaedra Brotherton, "Corporate Integrity Pays Off in Better Performance," *T + D*, January 19, 2011, 65 (1), p. 24.

23. For further information about this topic, see Mathieu Bouville, "Whistle-Blowing and Morality," *Journal of Business Ethics*, September 2008, 81 (3), pp. 579–585, http://mathieu.bouville.name/education-ethics/Bouville-whistle-blowing.pdf, accessed March 17, 2014.

24. Taxpayers Against Fraud, "The 1986 False Claims Act Amendments: A Look at Twenty-five years of Effective Fraud Fighting in America," www.taf.org/public/drupal/TAF-fca-25anniversary_12(1).pdf, accessed March 17, 2014.

25. Phyllis Plitch, "Blowing the Whistle," *The Wall Street Journal*, June 21, 2004, http://online.wsj.com/article/0,,SB108749986209440359,00.html, accessed March 17, 2014.

26. Carolyn Hirschman, "Giving Voice to Employee Concerns," *HRMagazine*, August 1, 2008, 53 (8), http://www.shrm.org/Publications/hrmagazine/EditorialContent/Pages/0808hirscman.aspx, accessed March 17, 2014.

27. United Nations, *Report of the World Commission on Environment and Development*, United Nations General Assembly Resolution 42/187, December 1987. See also David A. Lubin and Daniel C. Esty, "The Sustainability Imperative," *Harvard Business Review* 88 (5), May 2010, http://hbr.org/2010/05/the-sustainability-imperative/ar/1, accessed March 17, 2014; Jeffrey Pfeffer, "Building Sustainable Organizations: The Human Factor," *Academy of Management Perspective*, February 1, 2010, 24 (1), pp. 34–35, http://amp.aom.org/content/24/1/34.abstract, accessed March 17, 2014.

28. Vince Luchsinger, "Strategy Issues in Business Sustainability," *Business Renaissance Quarterly*, Fall 2009, 4 (3), pp. 163–174; Mark Hollingworth, "Building 360 Organizational Sustainability," *Ivey Business Journal*, November/December 2009, http://iveybusinessjournal.com/topics/global-business/building-360-organizational-sustainability#.UyeVavldWSo, accessed March 17, 2014.

29. Michael S. Hopkins, "Eight Reasons (You Never Thought Of) That Sustainability Will Change Management," *MIT Sloan Management Review*, Fall 2009, 51 (1), pp. 27–30, http://sloanreview.mit.edu/article/8-reasons-you-never-thought-of-that-sustainability-will-change-management/, accessed March 17, 2014; Daniel C. Esty and Andrew S. Winston, *Green to Gold* (New Haven, CT: Yale University Press, 2006); Ram Nidumolu, C. K. Prahalad, and M. R. Rangaswami, "Why Sustainability Is Now the Key Driver of Innovation," *Harvard Business Review*, September 2009, http://hbr.org/2009/09/why-sustainability-is-now-the-key-driver-of-innovation/, accessed March 17, 2014.

30. "2011 Sustainability Champion Awards," *Colorado Biz*, March 3, 2011, pp. C7–C10, http://www.cobizmag.com/articles/2011-sustainability-champion-awards, accessed March 17, 2014.

31. Ibid., p. C12.

PART TWO: SKILL-BUILDING

Meeting the Challenge

Reflecting back to p. 95, consider the challenges faced by Wells Fargo and its employees. How did those challenges lead to unethical behavior? Did supervisors foster unethical behavior? How can a supervisor encourage sales without also encouraging unethical behavior? With your group, make a list of the things you would have done as a supervisor who witnessed employees conducting business in an unethical manner.

Problem-Solving Case: Scrap Metal Trips Up Stamford Supervisors

In the city government of Stamford, Connecticut, the Office of Operations has many responsibilities for maintaining the city's quality of life. The agency is charged with garbage collection and recycling, managing the city's vehicles and buildings, sewage treatment, maintaining city roads and parks, conducting building inspections, managing the construction of public buildings, and more. In carrying out some of these activities, employees of the Office of Operations generate or acquire scrap metal. And the question of what to do with that metal, unfortunately, became an ethical stumbling block for some of the agency's employees and their supervisors.

The scenario was something like this: At the end of a construction, repair, or demolition job, scrap metal such as old road signs and metal poles would be left at the site. Workers then had to dispose of it somehow. Supervisors established an informal practice in which the workers would take the metal to a private dealer, sell it, and take the cash payment to their supervisor, often without a receipt. Some employees even set up their own scrapping businesses and sold the scrap to their businesses.

The supervisors would collect the money and keep it in a "petty cash" jar or in a locked desk or safe. They would spend this fund on employees and their departments, paying for food, Christmas parties, funeral cards, and supplies for work. The practice continued for at least 30 years until a complaint led to a police investigation and an audit of the agency's books. A maintenance worker told a local newspaper reporter, "As long as I've been here, whoever the boss was got the money. That's what they told us to do, and they were the bosses." One employee reportedly told a police officer later that he had sold scrapped plows for more than $3,000 and kept the cash until the next day to "safeguard" the money until a supervisor became available to take it.

When the practice was disclosed, there was a public outcry, objecting that the sale of city-owned scrap metal for cash to benefit employees off the books was a misuse of public property and an abuse of the public trust. After investigators spent months trying to trace the cash received, placed in the funds, and spent at supervisors' discretion, they concluded that it would be impossible to ever know how much money had been raised and spent. However, it seemed that no rules had been violated and no laws had been broken. The supervisors had used the money to benefit employees and their department, not themselves. The mayor suspended the director of the Office of Operations for three weeks without pay, and two supervisors caught engaging in the practice were suspended for two weeks without pay.

In the months after the practice of selling scrap was exposed, the city began selling twice as much scrap metal through official channels. As a result, revenues to the city increased by $60,000. Meanwhile, city officials established clearer policies for the disposal of scrap. From then on, no city official was allowed to accept payments in cash, and whenever an employee wants to sell city property, that sale must first be approved by the city's purchasing agent.

1. Officials found no grounds to say that selling scrap and using the proceeds for employees and the department was *illegal*, but they did treat it as *unethical* behavior. What was unethical about this activity? Who was harmed by it?

2. What conditions in Stamford's Office of Operations might have contributed to this unethical conduct? What could the supervisors have done to ensure more ethical handling of scrap metal?

3. Review the definition of *sustainability* and the description of sustainable organizations. In what way(s) did the handling of scrap metal contribute to making the Office of Operations a sustainable organization? What behavior worked against sustainability? How might the agency's supervisors contribute to sustainability in the future?

Sources: Angela Carella, "'Failure of Management' in Scrap Flap," *Connecticut Post*, August 1, 2011, http://www.ctpost.com/default/article/Angela-Carella-Failure-of-management-in-scrap-1682958.php, accessed March 14, 2014; Angela Carella, "Board Differs on What Will End Scrap Flap," *Connecticut Post*, July 28, 2011, http://www.ctpost.com/default/article/Angela-Carella-Board-differs-on-what-will-end-1629210.php, accessed March 17, 2014; Kate King, "Stamford Workers Respond to Allegations of Scrap Metal Thefts," *Connecticut Post*, July 31, 2011, http://www.ctpost.com/default/article/Stamford-workers-respond-to-allegations-of-scrap-1665, accessed March 17, 2014; Kate King, "Pavia Disciplines Trio over Scrap Metal," *Connecticut Post*, July 26, 2011, http://www.ctpost.com/default/article/Pavia-disciplines-trio-over-scrap-metal-1588165.php, accessed March 17, 2014; City of Stamford Web site, http://www.ci.stamford.ct.us, accessed October 18, 2011 March 17, 2014.

Assessing Yourself

How Ethical Is Your Behavior?

The following list is taken from a survey of 1,300 workers who said they had engaged in unethical activities. Check the activities you would do or consider doing, and rate yourself using your own values (there is no score!). If you wish, you can compare your standards with those of the respondents at the end.

    _____   **1.** Cut corners on quality control.

    _____   **2.** Covered up incidents.

    _____   **3.** Abused or lied about sick days.

    _____   **4.** Lied to or deceived customers.

    _____   **5.** Put inappropriate pressure on others.

    _____   **6.** Falsified numbers or reports.

    _____   **7.** Dismissed or promoted an employee unfairly.

    _____   **8.** Lied to or deceived superiors on serious matters.

    _____   **9.** Withheld important information.

    _____ **10.** Misused or stole company property.

    _____ **11.** Engaged in or overlooked environmental infractions.

    _____ **12.** Took credit for someone's work or idea.

    _____ **13.** Discriminated against a co-worker.

    _____ **14.** Abused drugs or alcohol.

    _____ **15.** Engaged in copyright or software infringement.

    _____ **16.** Lied to or deceived subordinates on serious matters.

    _____ **17.** Overlooked, paid, or accepted bribes.

    _____ **18.** Had extramarital affair with business associate.

    _____ **19.** Abused an expense account.

    _____ **20.** Abused or leaked proprietary information.

    _____ **21.** Forged name without person's knowledge.

    _____ **22.** Accepted inappropriate gifts or services.

    _____ **23.** Filed false regulatory or government reports.

    _____ **24.** Engaged in insider trading.

Percentage of original respondents who admitted to each infraction: (1) 16%, (2) 13%, (3) 11%, (4) 9%, (5) 7%, (6) 6%, (7) 6%, (8) 5%, (9) 5%, (10) 4%, (11) 4%, (12) 4%, (13) 4%, (14) 4%, (15) 3%, (16) 3%, (17) 3%, (18) 3%, (19) 2%, (20) 2%, (21) 2%, (22) 1%, (23) 1%, (24) 1%.

Source: From Henry Fountain, "Of White Lies and Yellow Pads," *The New York Times,* July 6, 1997. Copyright © 1997 The New York Times. Reprinted with permission.

Pause and Reflect

1. Are your answers a good measure of how ethical you are? Can you think of any other behaviors that should be on this list?

2. Should a supervisor be held to higher ethical standards than the supervisor's employees?

3. In what areas of conduct are you most ethical? In what areas do you think your standards should improve?

Class Skills Exercise

Supervising Unethical Employees

Each student should complete the survey in Figure 4.7 anonymously, circling all the answers that apply. The instructor then tabulates the results and distributes them for discussion during the next class session.

For each item in the survey, discuss the following questions:

- Which answer or answers were selected by most students?
- What is the justification for the answers selected?
- If you were the supervisor of an employee who acted in this way, how would you respond (assuming that you observed the behavior)?
- If your supervisor learned that you had acted in the way indicated by the survey response, how do you think your career would be affected?

Source: This exercise is based on a suggestion submitted by James Mulvihill, Mankato, MN.

Building Supervision Skills

Decision Making

One way to make ethical decisions is to ensure that your decisions follow your organization's code of ethics. In this exercise, you will develop an example of such a decision.

As a team, agree on a code of ethics to study. You can choose an organization that interests you and visit its Web site to look for a code of ethics or a values statement. Or you can use the hyperlinks in "The Index of Codes," published online by the Illinois Institute of Technology's Center for the Study of Ethics in the

FIGURE 4.7 | Survey for Class Exercise

Which of the following actions would you take? Circle the letters of as many choices as apply to you.
1. Put false information in your résumé: — a. If necessary to get a job. b. Only about minor details. c. If most people are doing it. d. Never.
2. Tell a competing company secrets about your employer's product or procedures: — a. To land a job with the competitor. b. In exchange for $100. c. In exchange for $1 million. d. Never.
3. Cheat on a test used as the basis for promotion: — a. If you have a family to support. b. If you think the test is unfair. c. If your co-workers are doing it. d. Never.
4. Use the office copier: — a. To make a copy of your dentist's bill. b. To make six copies of a report that is related to charitable work you do. c. To make 50 copies of your résumé. d. Never for copies unrelated to work.
5. Pad your expense account for a business trip: — a. If you believe you are underpaid. b. Only for small amounts that the employer won't miss. c. Only when you are experiencing financial problems. d. Never.
6. Call in sick when you aren't sick: — a. If you're worn out from working on a big project. b. If your child is sick. c. If you need to recover from the weekend. d. Never.
7. Lie about your supervisor's whereabouts when he or she takes a long, liquid lunch: — a. Only if specifically instructed to do so. b. If the supervisor gives you a generous raise in return. c. Only when the person asking is your supervisor's superior. d. Never.

Professions (http://ethics.iit.edu/ecodes/). Another option is to use Johnson & Johnson's credo in Figure 4.2 on page 100.

Choose one of the principles in the code of ethics. Prepare a skit that illustrates that principle. Your skit should be about a workplace dilemma involving your chosen principle, showing how the people in the skit resolve the dilemma. If you can, base your skit on a work-related situation that at least one of your team members has experienced.

The teams will then take turns presenting their skits to the whole class. Have the class try to identify the ethical principle each skit illustrates. Finally, the class should vote on whether the solution presented in the skit actually follows the principle from the code of ethics.

chapter five | Managing Diversity

learning objectives

After you have studied this chapter, you should be able to:

5.1 Define diversity.

5.2 Discuss how the U.S. workforce is changing and its impact on the supervisor.

5.3 Differentiate among prejudice, discrimination, and stereotypes in the workplace.

5.4 Explain how sexism and ageism are barriers to diversity and how supervisors can be more aware of them.

5.5 Discuss how and why employers must accommodate employees' disabilities.

5.6 Describe some ways to communicate more effectively in the diverse workplace.

5.7 Describe the goals of diversity training.

5.8 List the most important recent legislation affecting diversity and its provisions.

A Supervision Challenge

ARE GENERATION Y EMPLOYEES UNFAIRLY STEREOTYPED?

Diversity comes in many shapes and sizes. We often think of race and gender as the primary forms of diversity, but diversity of age is also prevalent throughout the workforce today. Just as assumptions are often made about older employees, assumptions are also made about younger employees, particularly those who are part of Generation Y (Gen Y), also referred to the Millennial Generation. This generation includes people born between the 1980s and the early 2000s. And Gen Y employees are often subjected to stereotypes in the workplace. Supervisors may accept as fact that Gen Y workers are disloyal and lazy. These are common assumptions made. Supervisors may not even do this consciously; it is all too easy, however, to generalize and draw conclusions based on what you *think* you know.

To diffuse this potentially problematic situation, global food and beverage giant PepsiCo has worked to bring diverse generations together and to promote understanding and growth among its employees. To that end, PepsiCo has created a mentoring program called Conn3ct, which enables younger employees to share their ideas with more senior staff—with the knowledge that they will be heard and taken seriously, which is something Gen Y workers are said to strongly desire. PepsiCo also benefits from this program. It is able to use this young talent network to support its recruiting events and to help orient new, younger employees joining the company. One unanticipated, but perhaps equally important, benefit is that it also lets supervisors get to know their younger staff better and to see what they really have to offer. Supervisors can see that their younger employees do not always conform to the stereotypes.

What PepsiCo is finding through their mentoring program is also being borne out by recent data. Recent data shows that many of the negative views regarding Gen Y workers are misconceptions. Author Dan Schawbel found in a study for his book *Promote Yourself: The New Rules For Career Success,* that while managers may have a negative view of their Generation Y employees, those employees actually tend to have a positive view of their managers. Additionally, a recent study by Rutgers University showed that almost half of the students enrolled in school today are taking on more responsibility by paying their own way. This may be the result of their experiences growing up during the recession or of having parents whose finances suffered from the recession. In either case, the result is often a stronger work ethic and level of dedication. In another study, the Center for Women and Business at Bentley University found that the vast majority of Millennials believe that making a positive difference in the world is more important than professional recognition.

Negative traits that supervisors *think* they see in Gen Y employees may actually stem from a drive by these Gen Y workers to make a big impact, rather than a mere sense of entitlement. As Twitter employee Ryan Brown says, "Just because someone is younger doesn't mean they can't compete at a high level." It is not simply a question of ignoring the stereotypes, however. Some assumptions do correctly characterize the actions of younger employees. For example, many researchers agree that Gen Y employees tend to change jobs more often, staying on average only two years at one company. The reason for this transience is debated, however. Could it be that Gen Y employees are looking for places where there ideas are heard and their input is valued? If so, PepsiCo's Conn3ct program is certainly on the right track.

How can supervisors correctly adjust to the needs and motivations of diverse employees? Why is it important that they do so?

Sources: Based on Dan Schawbel, "You're Probably Wrong About Millennials," *Harvard Business Review Blog Network,* September 3, 2013, http://blogs.hbr.org; Jada A. Graves, "Millenial Workers: Entitled, Needy, Self-Centered?" *U.S. News & World Report,* June 27, 2012, http://money.usnews.com/money/careers/articles/2012/06/27/millennial-workers-entitled-needy-self-centered.

LO5.1 ▶ Define diversity.

What is Diversity?

PepsiCo's efforts to identify the values and meet the needs of different employee groups reflect the growing awareness of diversity in the workplace. Dealing successfully with cultural, ethnic, age, gender, and racial diversity is a lifelong process for most of us. However, being ready to work successfully in a multicultural environment is a goal supervisors can set immediately and work toward in every business encounter.

Our understanding of cultural diversity has matured in recent decades. The old "melting pot" model, in which immigrants were expected to assimilate their language and culture into the mainstream, has long since been left behind. The view today is that our diversity is our strength. We define **diversity** as the characteristics of individuals that shape their identities and the experiences they have in society.[1] Visible reminders and celebrations of our diverse heritage, such as Martin Luther King Jr. Day and Gay Pride celebrations, enrich and renew our society and our culture. Ensuring diversity within an organization offers supervisors the opportunity to make the best fit between the employee and the job, allowing varied points of view to be aired and improving decision making. Many forms of discrimination, in hiring and elsewhere in business practices, are illegal in the United States. Yet even if they were not, ethical considerations would encourage the supervisor to seek many kinds of diversity within his or her department or team.

Diversity is generally broken into two groups: primary diversity and secondary diversity, as illustrated in Figure 5.1. Primary diversity includes the more commonly thought of differences between people: age, ethnicity, gender, physical abilities/characteristics, race, and sexual orientation. These are things that cannot be changed; that an individual has no control over. The components of secondary diversity are the things that are perhaps not as often considered but that are integral to an individual's make up. They include education, employment history, family background, income, geographic location, marital status, military experience, and religion. The secondary dimensions of diversity are factors that an individual has some control over. For example, people can choose to alter their geographic location (secondary dimension), but they cannot choose to alter their age (primary dimension). Collectively, the primary and secondary dimensions of diversity are the things that allow forward-thinking employers to create a workforce that can generate new ideas, learn from each other, and form a cohesive team.

Businesses and governments are striving to acknowledge diversity in their communications and interactions with citizens, employees, and customers. Boston Goodwill, for example, has found valuable potential in workers with disabilities. The organization hired a man named Paul and trained him to do maintenance work. Before then, Paul had received public assistance because a learning disability had made it difficult for him to communicate, complete school, and find jobs. However, at Goodwill, Paul soon mastered maintenance and janitorial tasks. Eventually, he was promoted to night shift supervisor at the Barnes Federal Building. He is a patient leader of his crew of seven, and his attitude helps him keep employee turnover low.[2] In another example, Bank of America has been a leader in providing banking services in several languages, including Spanish, Mandarin, Cantonese, Taiwanese, and Vietnamese. Its services include the U.S.–Asia Banking Center,

diversity
Characteristics of individuals that shape their identities and the experiences they have in society

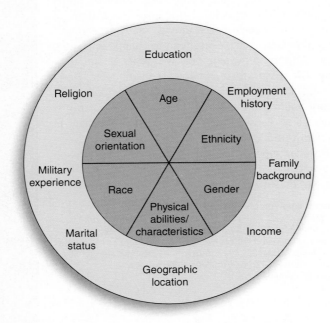

FIGURE 5.1 | The dimensions of diversity include both things that can be changed and things that cannot be changed.

established to serve customers with needs in both the United States and Hong Kong, and a self-managed 30-member team of bankers called the Chinese Banking Team, which operates from offices in the state of Washington.[3]

This chapter explores the challenges and opportunities related to workforce diversity, emphasizing how they affect supervisors. The chapter begins by summarizing some measures of America's increasing diversity. It then focuses on diversity-related challenges, such as prejudices and stereotypes. Finally, the chapter describes how supervisors can help organizations realize the advantages of diversity through communication, training, and the fulfillment of legal requirements.

---

connect SELF-ASSESSMENT 5.1

Appreciating and Valuing Diversity

Before you begin reading about various elements of diversity and challenges from diversity in organizations, take a few minutes to assess how you interact with individuals with backgrounds that differ from yours. This will benefit you by helping you prepare for your role as a supervisor. As the workplace continues to become more diverse, the successful supervisor will be one who is comfortable working with a variety of different types of individuals.

LO5.2 ▶ Discuss how the U.S. workforce is changing and its impact on the supervisor.

A Look at Our Diversity

The face of the United States is changing. This process is not new; the country was built on the concept of diversity as waves of immigrants and homesteaders arrived on its shores. Today, however, we recognize both subtle and obvious differences among employees at every organizational level. These differences call on all of a supervisor's management skills.

As recently as 1980, white men accounted for half of U.S. workers. Today, the participation of women in the workforce has risen to above 50 percent, and one survey found that women held half of all management, professional, and related occupations.[4] Mothers of young children in particular have entered the workforce as a permanent contingent at a rate that shows no sign of slowing. The workforce also is expected to continue to age, as some older workers postpone retirement to continue working and the first wave of the large generation commonly called baby boomers (those born between 1946 and 1964) reaches their 50s and 60s. The proportions of African Americans, Asian Americans, and Hispanics in the U.S. population and workforce are rising gradually and expected to continue to do so (see Figure 5.2 on the following page). Some of that increase is fueled by immigration. More than 16 percent of workers in the United States were born in another country. Of these foreign-born workers, over 38 percent are Hispanic, and over 28 percent are Asian.[5] These changes at work reflect overall trends in the U.S. population.[6] Supervisors will deal with older workers, telecommuters, flextime scheduling, ethnic holidays, and many other reflections of diversity that affect day-to-day operations in the workplace.

Other kinds of changes are occurring, although on a smaller scale. Advances in technology are enabling employees to customize their use of computers and telecommunications so that they can perform a variety of jobs. During the busy tax season, the Internal Revenue Service employs hundreds of disabled workers to answer phone requests from taxpayers, using computers equipped with such accommodations as

Diversity in the workplace has continued to expand since the 1980s when the U.S. workforce was dominated by white men.

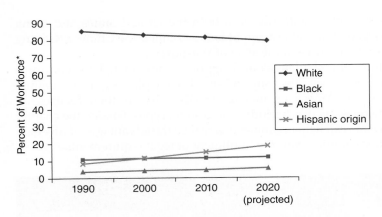

FIGURE 5.2 | The Changing Racial/Ethnic Makeup of the American Workforce, 1990–2020

The percentage of white workers in the U.S. workforce has been steadily declining over the last several decades—and is projected to continue to do so—while the percentage of Hispanic workers has increased significantly and the percentages of Asian and black workers has increased slightly.

*Percentages do not total 100% because racial groups and Hispanic origin are measured separately.

Source: Bureau of Labor Statistics, "Employment Outlook: 2010–20," news release, February 21, 2012, http://www.bls.gov/opub/mlr/2012/01/art3full.pdf, accessed March 20, 2014.

voice synthesizers that read information from the screen to blind users. Another productive blind worker is Janet Eckles, who answers telephone requests for a Spanish translator, a service provided by Language Line Services. Eckles also trains other employees, using a computer equipped with a program called Job Access with Speech, which lets her operate the computer via her keyboard and hear output read into an earpiece. The U.S. Defense Department uses a variety of adaptations, including speech recognition software, screen readers that print out screen text in Braille, and software that magnifies images on employees' computer screens.[7] However, in spite of these and other technologies, the employment rate of disabled men and women remains much lower than that of the overall labor force. Among the adults in the United States who have some type of disability, a little more than half held a job for at least part of the year, compared with almost 9 of 10 workers without a disability. Of those with a disability not rated as severe, 44 percent worked full-time for an entire year. The development of additional assistive technology is important, considering that 12 percent of the U.S. population has a severe disability, and the rate of disability is likely to increase as the population ages.[8]

Diversity also is influenced by local and international changes. The shifting fortunes of various regions in the United States, such as the so-called Rust Belt and California's famed Silicon Valley, draw workers to and from those areas in steady internal migrations. Events around the world, such as the breakup of the Soviet Union and the political and economic struggles of emerging nations, lead highly trained and sophisticated technical workers in many fields to the United States in search of employment. All these factors combine to raise the level of diversity that supervisors find in the workplace and increase opportunities to build a strong and flexible team.

Challenges to Working in a Diverse Society

LO5.3 ▶ Differentiate among prejudice, discrimination, and stereotypes in the workplace.

corporate culture
Beliefs and norms that govern organizational behavior in a firm

These trends are changing the way business firms operate. Supervisors today need new skills to communicate and collaborate effectively with a broader range of people. More generally, however, the awareness of differences of all kinds is creating changes in the way firms select, train, and motivate employees.[9] It also can have a profound impact on the corporate culture, or the beliefs and norms that govern organizational behavior in a firm.[10]

Over the last decade, Georgia-Pacific Corporation has made extra efforts to recruit and promote female employees. Seeking out female engineers and managers gives the paper goods company a larger pool of candidates for jobs in the industry, which has traditionally been male-dominated and usually operates in small towns. Employees sometimes have to adjust their thinking to suit the more diverse culture that results from bringing in nontraditional employees. One such example can be found in Lynda McCarty, who the company promoted to a job managing its sawmill in Prosperity, South Carolina. At first, McCarty was lonely in the town of a thousand people, many of whom wondered about the decision to put a woman in charge of the mill. McCarty, however, impressed her employees by working long hours, meeting their desire for new equipment and a break room, and displaying her toughness by insisting the employees clean up their coarse language. Georgia-Pacific managers reinforce the acceptance of female leaders by making a point to tell success stories like McCarty's.[11]

Prejudice and Discrimination

Efforts to appreciate diversity, such as those at Georgia-Pacific, are significant because negative attitudes and behaviors toward some groups continue to be a problem. One survey found that many employees—more than one-third of those surveyed—hear inappropriate sexual remarks at work. Almost 3 out of 10 hear ethnic and racial slurs.[12] Supervisors need to discourage these behaviors because they create a negative work environment for everyone.

prejudice
A preconceived judgment about an individual or group of people

Often, slurs are signs of prejudice, or a preconceived judgment about an individual or group of people. Prejudice can be a subtle force. We do not always recognize our own prejudices for what they are, even when they are affecting our behavior. For instance, suppose a supervisor has a position to fill. If the supervisor assumes that a female job applicant could not make sales calls at night, that an older worker is not as physically strong as a younger one, or that a working parent will abuse sick day privileges, he or she is making judgments on the basis of prejudice. When those judgments motivate business decisions related to hiring, appraisal, and promotion, they can be construed as discrimination.

discrimination
Unfair or inequitable treatment based on prejudice

Discrimination, unfair or inequitable treatment based on prejudice, is prohibited by law, as we discuss later in this chapter. The United States has been a nation of immigrants from its founding, although it has also borne the history of slavery. But the principles of religious and civic freedom extend deep into the U.S. legal system, beginning with the Constitution (1787) and the Emancipation Proclamation (1862–1863), continuing to the influential Civil Rights Act of 1964 and its later updates, and then to the Americans with Disabilities Act (1990). Specifically, Title VII of the Civil Rights Act of 1964 makes it illegal for an employer to discriminate on the basis of race, color, gender, religion, or national origin in making decisions regarding hiring, firing, training, discipline, compensation, benefits, classifications, or other terms or conditions of employment. For example, the courts held that an employee could sue a store after the employee complained that she was treated unfairly when she converted to Islam and began wearing a robe and head scarf. The employee said store managers complained about her clothing, changed her work hours without notice, and treated her disrespectfully. The employee also said other employees were treated differently and that her treatment was different because of her religion and its requirements. Thus, this employee's lawsuit was based on claims of religious discrimination.[13] To read more about how supervisors can help guard against religious discrimination at work, see "Supervision and Diversity" on the following page.

Legal consequences are only one cost of discrimination. A workplace tainted by prejudice and discrimination discourages and divides employees. If a supervisor treats employees unfairly for any reason, the outcome is never positive. The unfair treatment becomes widely known among employees, lowers morale and trust, and can eventually hurt productivity. Sometimes talented employees become so frustrated that they quit. The banking and finance industry is one that has a track record of women entering in large numbers but eventually leaving in frustration when they find hurdles to being promoted to management jobs. Patricia Cox recalls returning from a maternity leave to discover that her supervisor had passed her over for a challenging assignment that would have provided important career experience. Cox's supervisor assumed that because the job involved travel, Cox would not want the assignment when she had a baby. Cox had to explain that she would have preferred to have decided that for herself, and she later left that company for a management position at Charles Schwab.[14]

Supervisors have a responsibility to help guard against discrimination. Some types of discrimination are more obvious than others, and some are more easily

SUPERVISION AND DIVERSITY

AVOIDING RELIGIOUS DISCRIMINATION AT WORK

Charges of discrimination based on religion have been on the rise in the United States over the last decade. Although these claims are a small portion of all complaints, the fact that they are increasing is a concern for supervisors.

Sometimes problems arise because employees' religious practices require accommodations that affect others. For example, at a Tyson Foods chicken-processing facility, Muslim workers wanted a day off for one of their religion's major holidays, Eid al-Fitr. Initially, management gave them Eid in place of Labor Day, but this decision angered other workers who felt it was un-American to not celebrate Labor Day. Tyson, therefore, altered their initial plan and changed a paid birthday holiday to a personal day that workers could use for religious holidays if they wished. This seems to have been an agreeable decision to all.

Problems have arisen in other companies when workers ask for breaks to pray. For some jobs, this is a minor adjustment, but on an assembly line, everyone must take breaks at the same time to avoid disrupting the line.

Another kind of problem is the potential for harassment. Some religions encourage believers to spread the faith and seek converts. Workers who enthusiastically take on this religious duty could make other employees uncomfortable. At the extreme, they could cause workers to feel harassed and distracted from working effectively together. It is the responsibility of supervisors to maintain a positive work environment and forbid any kind of harassment.

Achieving a positive and harmonious work environment in which religions are accommodated without posing a hardship to the company requires supervisors to work with their company's management and their employees. For example, they should allow employees to express religious sentiments only if do not make others uncomfortable. The supervisor should forbid *all* forms of harassment. Likewise, they should try to accommodate all employees' religious needs, not favoring one group over another. If an employee says religion requires him or her to dress a certain way, pray or fast at certain times, and so on, the supervisor should listen first to the employee's own ideas for accommodating the religion without compromising work goals. A supervisor who does not see a reasonable way to accommodate a religious need should seek help from his or her manager and human resource department. Most importantly, the supervisor should be a role model for respecting all employees, regardless of their religion or lack of religion.

Sources: Based on Phred Dvorak, "Religious-Bias Filings Up," *The Wall Street Journal*, October 16, 2008, http://online.wsj.com; and Equal Employment Opportunity Commission, "Directives Transmittal: EEOC Compliance Manual Section 12—Religious Discrimination," no. 915.003, July 22, 2008, www.eeoc.gov.

countered than others. An important first step for any supervisor is to know and acknowledge his or her own prejudices. Once recognized, prejudices can be countered or even eliminated.

While it is all too easy to think that our past experiences with members of different ethnic, racial, or religious groups can be applied to those subordinates and co-workers we may meet in the future, generally they cannot. Believing they can is the source of prejudice. If, for instance, you assign workloads or responsibilities differently because you feel that "blacks have trouble keeping jobs" or "teenagers are unreliable," you are letting your prejudices control your business decisions. Aside from the ethical and legal problems of such beliefs, they can lead supervisors to make less-than-optimal use of a firm's resources and abuse the trust the firm has placed in them.

Stereotypes

Supervisors need to be aware of the many distinctions between U.S. culture and behavior and the norms of other countries. For example, the thumbs-up gesture in the United States is understood to mean okay or "all clear." In Iran, however, it is considered obscene. Bowing indicates respect in Japan, where smiling and nodding, important cultural expressions of politeness, do not necessarily signify agreement. In the United States, bowing is unknown, and when someone smiles and nods, Americans generally assume they concur with their statements.

Even time has a different value in certain cultures. In some cultures, it is considered rude or careless to act quickly in a business situation. The speed at which people speak and the number of times they consider it proper to repeat themselves also can vary from culture to culture.

What matters in dealing with racial and cultural differences is avoiding **stereotypes**, or generalized, fixed images of others. In other words, supervisors must always guard against generalizing what they believe or observe about a culture and using that to classify its members unfairly. Imagine, for instance, how you would respond to an employee or supervisor who said, "All Americans are aggressive and loud." Yet without much effort, you can probably think of similar negative statements you have heard about blacks, gays, elderly people, or the physically handicapped. Such stereotypes, usually based on false or incomplete information, prevent us from seeing people as individuals and treating them accordingly. Knowing that the Japanese revere their elders, for instance, or that Hispanic cultures are centered around the family, may enable a supervisor to understand why special tact is needed when delegating work to an older Japanese employee or why a Dominican worker might require time off during a parent's illness. It does not justify drawing erroneous conclusions based on stereotypes. Although avoiding stereotypes may take some effort, it is well repaid in improved interpersonal relationships and successful supervision of a diverse team.

A psychologist who consults with law firms and lawyers offers some insights into stereotyping.[15] First, stereotypes are often unintended, but they occur simply because human beings tend to put information into categories and to prefer things that are more familiar. Such normal patterns of processing information lead people to assume that those in the "other" group are more alike than they really are, while perceiving people in their own group as being distinct individuals. Supervisors should be aware of the pitfalls of relying on stereotypes, particularly commonly held assumptions about racial and cultural differences, and work to overcome them. Remaining aware that such stereotypes are outdated, and that they can lead to offensive behavior patterns, is an important first step toward removing them.

stereotypes
Generalized, fixed images of others

sexism
Discrimination based on gender stereotypes

Sexism

Women have long been a growing factor in the labor force, and their participation has changed the workplace in many ways. **Sexism**, or discrimination based on gender stereotypes, is a barrier to diversity that many employers have taken steps to combat and prevent. Whether it takes the form of sexist language, sexual harassment, or discrimination against gays or lesbians, sexism challenges the supervisor's efforts to ensure a fair and harmonious work environment.[16]

Although women are still a minority in top positions, as Figure 5.3 illustrates, more women head companies and divisions than ever before, and female entrepreneurs are making a strong mark on U.S. business. Corporations with female CEOs, chief operating officers, or heads of divisions include Kraft Foods, Archer-Daniels-Midland, The Coca-Cola Company, Xerox, and Nieman Marcus Stores. Small-business startups are more than twice as likely to be started by women as by men.[17] Many firms are developing

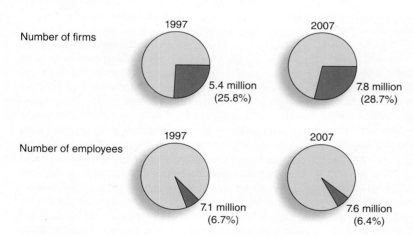

FIGURE 5.3 | Women-Owned Businesses: A Growing Share of the Total

The number of businesses owned by women has been growing in recent decades and, consequently, the share of workers employed by these businesses has grown as well.

Sources: Data from U.S. Census Bureau, *The 2012 Statistical Abstract of the United States,* Table 768, p. 507, www.census.gov; U.S. Census Bureau, "Summary of Findings: 2007," Survey of Business Owners: Women-Owned Firms, last updated June 7, 2011, http://www.census.gov.

Note: "Women-owned firms" are privately owned companies with more than 51 percent ownership by women.

flextime and work-at-home policies that make it easier for all workers—but particularly women, still the traditional caregivers for children and elderly relatives—to blend work and family responsibilities. Yet the number of single fathers with primary custody of their children has risen dramatically: from less than 300,000 in 1960 to 2.6 million in 2011. Single fathers represent almost one-quarter of the nation's single parents, whose special needs society and employers may be slow to recognize.[18]

Subtle use of language, such as the word *chairman* applied to a woman or *stewardess* instead of the gender-neutral *flight attendant,* is a form of sexism that conscientious supervisors can most readily overcome. More obvious sexism, such as passing over a woman for a physically demanding job, asking a pregnant job applicant about child care arrangements, or denying a promotion to a qualified woman, raises legal and ethical questions that a supervisor would have difficulty answering. Such actions are rarely, if ever, justified, although the difficulty women and minorities have experienced in rising through the corporate ranks is well-enough documented to be given a name. The "glass ceiling" refers to a certain level of responsibility to which many qualified applicants find themselves rising, and then no higher, despite their ability and willingness to contribute further to the goals of the firm. Changes for the better are occurring every day, but much progress remains to be made.

sexual harassment
Unwanted sexual attentions, including language, behavior, or the display of images

The most blatant form of sexism is **sexual harassment,** defined as unwanted sexual attentions, including language, behavior, or the display of images. Offenses have ranged from sexual jokes and displays of explicit pictures in the workplace to touching, sexual advances, and requests for sexual favors. In most cases of sexual harassment, women have been the victims and men the aggressors, but that need

SUPERVISION AND ETHICS

ROMANCE FOR SOME MAY BE HARASSMENT FOR OTHERS

Considering that people give some of their liveliest and most creative hours to the workplace, it is no wonder that romances sometimes are kindled between co-workers. However, when one of those romantic partners is a supervisor, sticky ethical situations can arise.

It is easy to see the problems when the supervisor is interested in romance but the employee being supervised merely wants a working relationship. If the supervisor issues an invitation to dinner, can the employee truly respond in a way that will not affect their relations at work? A flat "no" will hurt the supervisor's feelings, and the employee may worry that the supervisor will retaliate at work, perhaps in subtle ways such as failing to provide opportunities for training and promotions. If the employee gives an ambiguous answer, the supervisor might keep issuing invitations, and the employee would become increasingly uncomfortable. Either way, the supervisor now has a problem too. If the employee's work is unsatisfactory in any way, the supervisor will need to correct the employee, and the employee might interpret the supervisor's action as retaliation for refusing to date the supervisor. Thus, it becomes impossible for the supervisor to provide proper discipline.

But what if the employee is attracted to the supervisor? Even that apparently happy situation is full of problems. Other employees will inevitably find out about the romance and will be weighing every workplace decision to see if it is fair. More problems occur if and when the affair comes to an end. The employee might bring charges of sexual harassment, claiming that the relationship was unwanted or that the supervisor is retaliating against the employee for ending the affair.

Issues with workplace "romance"—whether mutually agreeable or not—have become such a significant issue that many companies now take preventative measures to avoid potential sexual harassment lawsuits. One such measure is to ask employees to sign a document stating that they are entering or in a relationship willingly. These "love agreements" or "Cupid contracts" typically include information on the corporation's sexual harassment policy and who to go to if problems are encountered. These contracts protect the company from a future lawsuit in which an employee might claim that they were coerced into a relationship, but they also protect employees from retaliation should the relationship end. With such a contract, signed by both parties, the employee has evidence that the relationship existed and could then show how, if it occurs, they were treated differently once the relationship ended.

While not all workplaces have romances and drama associated with it, it is always important for a supervisor to be fair, even if fairness limits some opportunities for romance.

Source: Based on Jonathan A. Segal, "Dangerous Liaisons," *HR Magazine,* 50 (12), December 1, 2005, Society for Human Resource Management, http://www.shrm.org/Publications/hrmagazine/EditorialContent/Pages/1205legaltrends.aspx, accessed April 10, 2014; Anne Fisher, "Why Your Office Romance is Your Employer's Business," *CNN Money,* June 7, 2013, http://management.fortune.cnn.com/2013/06/07/office-romance/, accessed April 10, 2014.

not be the case. No matter who is involved, sexual harassment is illegal, and experts advise supervisors to adopt a policy of "zero tolerance," take any complaints seriously, and investigate them at once. Some states, including Connecticut and California, require companies to train their supervisors in how to prevent sexual harassment. Even when not required by law, supervisors and their companies may request training to help them meet their ethical obligations and demonstrate that the supervisor and organization take the problem seriously.[19] Also, as described in the "Supervision and Ethics" feature, supervisors must be extremely cautious about entering into romantic relationships with individuals who work at the same company. These relationships often create awkward situations that may be considered unethical or even amount to a hostile environment for other employees.

Connect SELF-ASSESSMENT 5.2

Avoiding Age Bias

There are several generations working in organizations today: Baby Boomers, Gen X, Gen Y, and Millennials. You may find yourself working with or supervising workers who are much older than you. This very quick assessment will help you identify biases you may hold about older workers.

LO5.4 ► Explain how sexism and ageism are barriers to diversity and how supervisors can be more aware of them.

ageism
Discrimination based on age

Ageism

Your chances of someday supervising older workers are fairly high. The number of people aged 65 years and older in the U.S. labor force is growing for at least two reasons: The share of the population that is 65 years and older is growing, and more people in that age bracket have decided to continue working at least part-time.[20] Already, the share of older workers is greater than at any time since World War II, a trend that is expected to continue.

Although older workers offer significant experience, they sometimes encounter discrimination. They generally must look for work longer than younger adults, and research has found that older workers are more afraid of discrimination than of change.[21] Discrimination based on age is called **ageism**. Often, prejudices are at the root of ageism.[22] Some people expect older workers to perform less effectively, but evidence shows such negative expectations are often unfounded. One concern—that older workers cost more (because of their greater experience)—is true, but unlike the stereotypes, older workers are not absent more than young workers, are not necessarily harder to train, and are not just biding their time until retirement. In fact, many would like to receive training to advance their careers but find that employers are reluctant to invest as much in training older workers—and, significantly, that supervisors offer them less coaching and constructive feedback.[23] A survey by the Society for Human Resource Management found that older workers bring their employers a number of strengths, which are summarized in Figure 5.4.

FIGURE 5.4 | 10 Reasons to Hire Older Workers

Despite the prejudices that ageism supports, older workers offer many benefits and advantages to their employers.

Source: J. Collison, *SHRM/NOWCC/CED Older Workers Survey* (Alexandria, VA: Society for Human Resource Management, June 2003), cited in Nancy R. Lockwood, "The Aging Workforce: The Reality of the Impact of Older Workers and Eldercare in the Workplace," *HR Magazine*, December 2003, downloaded from InfoTrac, http://web5.infotrac.galegroup.com.

Number of Americans over 65

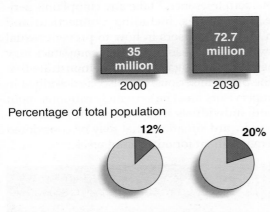

Percentage of total population

12%   **20%**

FIGURE 5.5 | Percentage of People over Age 65 in the United States, 2000 and 2030

With the total number of people over the age of 65 expected to continue to grow, as well as their percentage of the population, supervisors need to be prepared to work with older employees.

Source: U.S. Census Bureau, "U.S. Interim Projections by Age, Sex, Race, and Hispanic Origin," July 1, 2012, U.S. Census Bureau Web site, www.census.gov.

bona fide occupational qualification (BFOQ)
An objective characteristic required for an individual to perform a job properly

LO5.5 ▶ Discuss how and why employers must accommodate employees' disabilities.

disability
A physical or mental impairment that substantially limits a major life activity, a record of such an impairment, or being regarded as having such an impairment

As the baby-boomer generation ages, and as improvements in health care and nutrition allow for longer and healthier lives, older workers (both men and women) are sure to become a more common sight. The Age Discrimination in Employment Act (1967) makes it illegal to fail to hire, or fire, on the basis of age. When inexperienced younger workers are given preference over equally or better-qualified elders or when downsizing lets disproportionately more older (and often better-paid) workers go, ageism costs the organization the benefit of experience, perspective, and judgment that senior workers can bring. One company that appreciated the value of older workers was Borders Group, now a part of Barnes & Noble. The bookstore chain looked at performance statistics for its stores and discovered that stores with older workers "had much lower turnover, did better financially, [and] all the workers were happier," according to then senior vice president Dan Smith. So they began seeking out older workers as employees.[24]

In a few rare cases, such as the Federal Aviation Agency's limit of 64 years of age for airline pilots or acting roles that call for persons of very young or very advanced age, age represents what is called a bona fide occupational qualification (BFOQ), an objective characteristic required for an individual to perform a job properly. In all other cases, experts suggest that supervisors should beware of making decisions based on assumptions about age, such as that older employees are less physically capable or have failing eyesight that prevents them from performing well on the job. Tests that measure proven job qualifications, such as a vision test, can ensure that age is not being used as a discriminator and that valuable workers are not being overlooked or lost.

There is no longer a mandatory age for retirement, and many workers find it economically necessary to continue their careers. The Census Bureau estimates that 20 percent of the population will be over 65 years of age by 2030 (see Figure 5.5), and it is likely that many of those citizens will remain on the job. They will be a potent force, and many firms are prepared to train retirees who decide to return to work.

Generational studies are becoming increasingly common and can be used to provide a wealth of information to corporations and supervisors alike. Millennials (those born between 1980 and 1999) are the most studied generation to date.[25] Along with the Millennial Generation, generational studies can also be found for the GI Generation (those born between 1901 and 1924), the Silent Generation (born 1925–1946), the Baby Boom Generation (born 1946–1964), and Generation X (born 1965–1979). The Baby Boomers are often the subject of studies as there is such a large group of individuals who fall into this category. From these studies, you can learn anything from how likely someone in a specific age group is to use social media to how many tattoos or piercings they are likely to have.[26] While some of this information may not be directly useful in the workplace, it can provide much needed background and contextual information that a supervisor who is not of the same generation as their employees can use to better identify with them.

Accommodation of Disabilities

The Americans with Disabilities Act, written in 1990, was designed to protect the 43 million Americans that have one or more physical or mental disabilities. It is important to understand how "disability" is defined. A person is considered to have a disability "if s/he either has a physical or mental impairment that substantially limits one or more major life activities, has a record of such an impairment, or is regarded as having

qualified individual with a disability
person with a disability who, with or without reasonable accommodation, can perform the essential functions of a particular job

such an impairment."[27] Likewise, a **"qualified individual with a disability"** is defined as someone with a disability who, with or without reasonable accommodation, can perform the essential functions of the employment position that such individual holds or desires." If a job applicant with a disability is able to perform the necessary tasks to complete a prospective job, it is inappropriate not to hire them simply because they have a disability. Additionally, employers must provide reasonable accommodations to disabled persons, including making existing facilities readily accessible, modifying work schedules, and providing qualified readers or interpreters.

The Americans with Disabilities Act mandates the elimination of discrimination against individuals with disabilities. Employers are not allowed to deny an employment opportunity to a disabled job applicant who is an otherwise qualified individual. It is extremely important for supervisors to comply with the ADA and to convey to employees that it is inappropriate to discriminate against persons with disabilities. A supervisor's attitude about this topic permeates to employees, and it is important that all persons are treated with equal respect, regardless of their disability status. Upholding the Americans with Disabilities Act is an important step toward reducing bias and discrimination in the workplace.

Implications for the Supervisor

Supervisors can expect that their employees will be diverse in at least some of the ways described in this chapter. Figure 5.6 illustrates some possible sources of diversity in a work group. The supervisor's challenge is to build on the advantages of this diversity. Doing so requires effective communication that bridges cultural differences. Supervisors also can benefit from training in diversity and working closely with the company's human resource staff to learn how they and their employees must behave to obey laws related to workforce diversity.

Advantages of Diversity

Overcoming the challenges to supervising a diverse workforce can require consistent effort and a willingness to learn from mistakes, particularly for the new supervisor. But there are rewards, among them the confidence that such behavior is both ethical and fair. Other advantages for the individual supervisor are more concrete and include the opportunity to learn from the varied perspectives of those unlike ourselves, a better motivated and more loyal team of employees, enhanced communication skills, improved management ability, and enhanced opportunities for career advancement.

The firm as a whole can also benefit from a supervisor's successful efforts. Some advantages of diversity for the business organization are greater ability to attract and retain the best employees for the job, increased productivity, higher morale and motivation throughout the company, a more resilient workforce, greater innovation, reduced turnover, and enhanced performance leading to greater

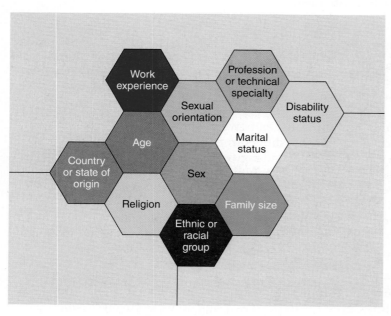

FIGURE 5.6 | Sources of Diversity in the Workplace
The diversity of a company's workforce provides some challenges, but also provides many advantages to the employer who can bring people with differences together into a cohesive working unit.

Allowing employees to telecommute is one way that supervisors can accommodate employees who need flexible schedules.

market share. For example, immigrant workers overcame obstacles to travel to the United States and find a job despite language barriers. Individuals with such a high success drive, energy level, and motivation have the potential to inspire the entire work group. They also may bring valuable ideas from their experiences in their country of origin.[28] Besides leading in ways that bring out the best in immigrant workers, supervisors can benefit the organization by being flexible with schedules and other work arrangements. Flexible work arrangements—often mentioned as a way to make the workplace "friendlier" to female employees—can deliver payoffs to all employees and the organization as a whole. After Chubb Insurance started giving employees flexibility in how they arrange their time, efficiency improved: employees contacted more customers per day and processed payments faster. In addition, because some employees chose to come in extra early while others preferred later hours, they stretched out the total time the company was available to customers each day.[29]

Even the best and most necessary efforts to manage diversity must be handled with care. Among the many challenges supervisors face in the newly diverse workplace is the task of adjusting job schedules and workloads to religious and ethnic holidays, family needs such as a sick child or an elderly parent needing temporary or ongoing care, and unique arrangements such as job sharing and telecommuting. Special equipment and training are sometimes needed to ease the stress of a disability in a capable employee or to tailor a workstation to an employee's physical needs. Bilingual employee manuals and the creation of benefit programs that offer medical coverage to life partners of either sex are other examples. Adjustments like these, while beneficial to the firm, can occasionally create dissatisfaction among other employees. Supervisors need to be aware that these problems also can occur and be prepared to deal with them.

Communication

LO5.6 ▶ Describe some ways to communicate more effectively in the diverse workplace.

Our attitudes toward others are perhaps nowhere as evident as in our communication with them. Communication in the workplace, therefore, is one area in which supervisors can serve as particularly good role models of managing diversity constructively.

Nonverbal communication is just as powerful in many contexts as the actual words we say, and body language differs from one culture to another (and even between genders) as much as spoken language does. It is important to try not to rely too much on generalizations about culture, because even within cultures, there are variations in behavior among individuals. But to draw some basic conclusions about how supervisors might best shape their communications with others, both managers and subordinates, we need to rely on a few simple statements. Keeping in mind that they do not reflect the real complexity of any foreign culture or of any individual, here are a few examples:[30]

- The Japanese value the ability to be physically still.
- Whites in North America interpret eye contact as a sign of honesty, while in many other cultures, eyes are dropped as a sign of respect to one's superiors.
- Americans tend to smile at everyone, while in Germany smiles are reserved for friends. The Japanese smile not just to express gladness but also to cover embarrassment and even anger.
- In Bulgaria, people nod their heads to signal no and shake their heads to mean yes.

- Latin Americans stand closer to people of the same sex than North Americans do, but North Americans stand closer to those of the opposite sex.
- In Asia, the Middle East, and South America, friends of the same sex can hold hands or walk arm-in-arm in public, while opposite-sex couples who touch in public are seen as slightly shocking.
- In North America, the person sitting at the head of a table is generally assumed to be the leader of the group unless that person is a woman, in which case observers tend to assume the leader is one of the men.

Nonverbal communication or body language seldom occurs without some accompanying words. Verbal communication, both written and spoken, offers many opportunities for bridging the gaps between cultures—just as many chances for us to fail to convey our intended meaning. One of the many ways in which supervisors can improve their communication with others in the diverse workplace of the future is to choose words with extra care, particularly when giving directions.

Many English words have more than one meaning, and the English language is full of slang, idioms, and borrowed expressions, such as "in the red," "out of left field," and "get the nod." These have the potential to mislead, confuse, and frustrate nonnative speakers of English and should be used with care, if at all. Doris West-Walkin, a former human resource consultant for Johns Hopkins Medical Institutions, observed the need to communicate carefully with the nurses her organization recruited from the Philippines. These employees spoke English but not the dialect and slang of their American-born colleagues. Thus, says West-Walkin, supervisors need to avoid using idioms like "Hit the call button" when they mean "Answer the patient's call button now!"[31]

Supervisors should also be aware that every industry has its own particular jargon and that specialized terms can pose particular problems. Publishing, for example, has its own specific meanings for such terms as *widow, orphan, register,* and *river.* Since even native speakers of English will find jargon unfamiliar at first, explanations of terms should be a standard part of orientation and training. When employees have a native language different from English, careful communication is even more important. Differences among employees also may affect the communication channels they select. Some employees may seek out their supervisor for a face-to-face conversation; others may be more comfortable putting their thoughts into writing. Choices of communication media differ notably among age groups. The "Supervisory Skills" feature on the following page offers some ideas for identifying and working with these age-related differences.

The point of all these examples is not that the supervisor must become an expert in other cultures. That would be an impossible and probably pointless goal. What these differences do suggest, however, is that it is most important not to make assumptions in communications with others, particularly regarding the way one's own words and actions are interpreted. Thinking before communicating, in order to understand the potential reaction to our words and gestures, is a good habit to foster. Checking for understanding is a simple but very effective way to ensure that we are conveying the meaning we intend.

LO5.7 ▶ Describe the goals of diversity training.

Diversity Training

To reap the full benefits of having a diverse workforce, supervisors first need to ensure that cultural differences are perceived by everyone as a positive force within the firm. Sometimes formal diversity training, such as a two- or three-day workshop, is needed to raise employee awareness of multiculturalism and help reduce such barriers to success as prejudice and stereotypes.[32] These programs are often credited with attracting minority recruits and raising sensitivity to differences among people. Improved communications skills are also a common goal of diversity

SUPERVISORY SKILLS

COMMUNICATING

Getting the Message across the Generation Gap

In a survey by the Society for Human Resource Management, more than two-thirds of respondents reported that conflict between the generations is an issue at their organization. Employees in different age groups tend to see the world somewhat differently, and those differences are especially likely to erupt in conflict when communication is poor. Here are some ideas for clear communication among supervisors and employees of different ages:

- Discuss what you expect from one another. Generation Y employees, born between 1981 and 1995, tend to be optimistic and enthusiastic, and they expect that their managers will be eager to act as mentors. Employees of older generations are more likely to expect these younger colleagues to rely on themselves. They might be willing to mentor a younger colleague, but they need to be asked, and the younger employee should not act as if this kind of help is an entitlement.

- Young employees also may need to hear the supervisor's expectations regarding e-mail. Generation Y workers opt for text messaging when they want a quick response and seldom think of e-mail as demanding a quick reply. Older workers, including supervisors, may assume that e-mail should be answered within a particular time frame, such as one day or less.

- Social media and mobile Internet devices are a part of everyday life for younger workers. Many of today's young workers are accustomed to sending and receiving frequent short messages, and they might feel disliked or unsupported if they go all day not hearing anything from their supervisor. With this in mind, supervisors can make a point of giving their employees (especially young employees) frequent daily feedback.

- Older workers are more likely to see frequent messaging as a series of interruptions. When they want to share information, employees born before 1965 tend to think in terms of face-to-face meetings. They value what they can learn from reading people's facial expressions, tone of voice, and body position. Younger employees and supervisors can improve communication with these workers by allowing time for face-to-face exchanges. More broadly, communicating through a variety of media raises the likelihood that all employees will get the message.

- Employees who grew up with the Internet assume that information is usually free and widely available. They expect to be kept in the loop when their team or organization is making changes. Supervisors can address this by sharing information whenever possible. It is a good practice in any case, because employees of all ages appreciate being well informed.

Source: Adrienne Fox, "Mixing It Up," *HR Magazine*, May 2011, pp. 22–27; Robert D. Ramsey, "Supervising an Intergenerational Work Force," *Supervision*, October 2011, pp. 16–18.

training, along with improving interpersonal and technical skills, increasing English proficiency, and facilitating mentoring. Some firms, however, have experienced a backlash against diversity training; problems include the reinforcement of group stereotypes and even lawsuits based on offensive statements made during "awareness raising" sessions. Appropriate controls and guidelines should accompany the training, which should be administered by professional trainers.

Despite the risks of stereotypes and awkward comments, diversity training is especially important for supervisors, because they interact directly with employees. Cultural anthropologists Thomas Kochman and Jean Mavrelis apply the tools of their field to identify patterns of group behavior that group members agree describe many of their members.[32] They find that such descriptions can be helpful for interpreting workplace interactions. For example, Kochman and Mavrelis have found that white men in corporations tend to have developed the idea that a person should be trusted unless that person has done something untrustworthy. People with this view can be puzzled when others distrust them on the grounds that trust is something a person must earn. Or to take another example, Kochman and Mavrelis have found that many black women were raised with the expectation that they should be strong and self-reliant. Women with this view may be competitive and speak up when they see a problem. Someone who is used to women protecting people's feelings might find the competitive behavior disturbing. Notice that these

Diversity training is particularly important for supervisors. The training is more effective when it is also embraced by top management.

statements do not describe *everyone* in a group, and they are quite different from an outsider's stereotypes (say, that white men feel entitled to what they have not earned or that black women are pushy). Learning from the work of social scientists and other experts can prepare a supervisor to think about situations more accurately.

When diversity is embraced by top management and built into policies and procedures that are fairly enforced, and when the goals of diversity training are continually reinforced within the corporate culture, it has the greatest chance of contributing to the company's goals. If such ideal support is lacking, supervisors can still support diversity by consistently setting a good example in their dealings with others. Such seemingly innocent practices as hiring only people who appear to fit into the "corporate culture" can lead supervisors to staff a firm with workers from similar backgrounds; with identical religious, ethnic, or racial characteristics; or from the same age bracket. Even if no legal actions are brought against such firms, they still are losing one of their best potential resources—the creativity and vitality that come from bringing people into contact with others from whom they can learn.

LO5.8 ▶ List the most important recent legislation affecting diversity and its provisions.

Legal Issues

A review of all the relevant employment law is beyond the scope of this text. Table 5.1 summarizes some major legislation that governs the areas of workplace

TABLE 5.1 | Some Important Equal Employment Opportunity Legislation

Legislation	Result
Title VII of 1964 Civil Rights Act, as amended	Created the Equal Employment Opportunity Commission; bars discrimination based on race, color, religion, sex, or national origin.
Equal Pay Act of 1963	Requires equal pay for men and women performing similar work.
Age Discrimination in Employment Act of 1967	Bars discrimination against those 40 years old and older because of age.
Vocational Rehabilitation Act of 1973	For jobs connected with the federal government, requires affirmative action to employ qualified handicapped persons and prohibits discrimination against them.
Pregnancy Discrimination Act of 1978	Bars discrimination in employment against women based on pregnancy, childbirth, or related conditions.
Vietnam Era Veterans' Readjustment Assistance Act of 1974	Mandates affirmative action in employment for veterans of the Vietnam War era.
Americans with Disabilities Act of 1990	Prohibits discrimination against disabled employees in the private sector and encourages reasonable accommodations for them.
Civil Rights Act of 1991	Places the burden of proof on the employer and allows for compensatory and punitive damages in discrimination cases.

diversity and that supervisors should know. These rules govern hiring, pay, promotion, and evaluation, all within the scope of the supervisor's responsibilities.

The Equal Employment Opportunity Commission (EEOC) was instituted by Title VII of the 1964 Civil Rights Act as amended in 1972. The EEOC consists of five members appointed by the president to serve a five-year term. This agency acts as the federal government's major means of enforcing equal employment opportunity laws and has the power to investigate complaints, use conciliation to eliminate discrimination when found, and file discrimination charges on behalf of an individual if needed. Individual states have also passed their own laws to fill perceived gaps in federal law.[34]

Since its inception, many Title VII complaints were found in favor of the employee. Employers did not take appropriate measures to protect the rights of employees and to curtail issues of discrimination. Two recent cases heard by the Supreme Court, however, have shifted the burden of proof more to the plaintiff. In one case, the Court stated that the plaintiff needed to prove that the "adverse employment action" occurred primarily because of the employer's motive to retaliate. In the other case, the definition of "supervisor" was called into question. The person who created a hostile racial environment for another employee did not have the power to change the employment status of the employee who filed the complaint. This person is therefore, in the eyes of the Court, not a supervisor to the plaintiff. Employer liability under Title VII only extends to individuals in supervisory positions.[35]

In both of these cases, the Court decided in favor of the employer. Strict interpretation of the law aside, however, as a supervisor, you should strive to create an equitable work environment for all employees so that it is not necessary to involve the judicial system.

Skills Module

PART ONE: CONCEPTS

Summary

5.1 Define diversity.

Diversity refers to the characteristics of individuals that shape their identities and the experiences they have in society. Racial, cultural, ethnic, age, gender, and other kinds of diversity are welcomed and considered as strengths in business organizations today.

5.2 Discuss how the U.S. workforce is changing and its impact on the supervisor.

The number of women and minorities in the workforce is increasing. The workforce is aging as well, and new technologies are integrating the disabled into the workforce with valuable skills and insights. Technical workers from abroad are bringing their expertise to many U.S. firms. All these changes offer supervisors both a challenge to their management skills and an opportunity to build a strong and flexible team of workers.

5.3 Differentiate among prejudice, discrimination, and stereotypes in the workplace.

Prejudice is a preconceived judgment about an individual or group of people. Discrimination is unfair or inequitable treatment based on prejudice. Stereotypes are generalized, fixed images we hold of others.

5.4 Explain how sexism and ageism are barriers to diversity and how supervisors can be more aware of them.

Sexism and ageism refer to discrimination against others on the basis of sex or age. Supervisors should be aware that sexism can be either subtle, as in sexist language, or blatant, as in sexual harassment, defined as unwanted sexual attentions including language, behavior, or the display of images. Sexual harassment is illegal. Ageism can cost the organization the benefit of experience, perspective, and judgment that older workers bring. Discrimination based on age is illegal except in the (rare) case of a bona fide occupational qualification (BFOQ).

5.5 Discuss how and why employers must accommodate employees' disabilities.

Employers may not discriminate in hiring or promoting a person with a disability who is able to perform the necessary tasks to complete a job. Additionally, employers must provide reasonable accommodations to disabled persons. Accommodations might include making existing facilities readily accessible, modifying work schedules, and providing qualified readers or interpreters. These practices avoid violating the Americans with Disabilities Act. They also are ethical and offer the benefits of workers who may be talented and highly committed to their jobs.

5.6 Describe some ways to communicate more effectively in the diverse workplace.

Supervisors can communicate more effectively by being aware that verbal and nonverbal communication varies in meaning across cultures. Avoiding slang and idioms, explaining technical jargon, and checking for meaning will help improve communication.

5.7 Describe the goals of diversity training.

Diversity training is intended to raise employee awareness of multiculturalism and help reduce such barriers to success as prejudice and stereotypes. Other goals include improved communications and interpersonal and technical skills.

5.8 List the most important recent legislation affecting diversity and its provisions.

Title VII of the 1964 Civil Rights Act, amended in 1972, created the Equal Employment Opportunity Commission (EEOC), which investigates and acts on complaints of discrimination. See Table 5.1 for a summary of recent legislation.

Key Terms

diversity, *p.* 120
corporate culture, *p.* 122
prejudice, *p.* 123
discrimination, *p.* 123
stereotypes, *p.* 125

sexism, *p.* 125
sexual harassment, *p.* 126
ageism, *p.* 127
bona fide occupational
qualification (BFOQ), *p.* 128

disability, *p.* 128
qualified individual with a
disability, *p.* 129

Review and Discussion Questions

1. What is diversity? How has its meaning changed?

2. Rasheen supervises the mail room for a large financial services firm. He has been told he will be attending a diversity training program next week. Rasheen believes that because he has recently hired three women from his native country, he does not need to know any more about diversity. As his supervisor, what would you say to Rasheen to prepare him for the training program?

3. Some research suggests that the increasing racial and cultural diversity in the United States is limited to the larger cities. How would you account for this trend? Does it suggest that only supervisors in these cities need be concerned about diversity?

4. Distinguish between prejudice and discrimination. How do stereotypes contribute to each?

5. Aaron, clerical supervisor for a health maintenance organization, wants to hire the best person for the receptionist job. Ramona, his manager, is doubtful that the candidate Aaron has selected will be capable because she uses a wheelchair. Ramona is concerned that other workers will have to spend a lot of time helping the receptionist get in and out of the office for lunch, breaks, and so on. How can Aaron ensure that his candidate will be an asset to the firm?

6. List as many English expressions as you can think of that might be confusing to a nonnative speaker of the language. Next to each, write a brief expression that conveys the same meaning with greater clarity.

7. Mariah's boss calls her "honey," although he refers to her co-workers as Jason, Rick, and Harrison. How can Mariah ask her boss to correct this situation?

8. Several members of your team are out ill, and you are falling behind your production schedule for the week. A new employee comes to you and asks for a half-day off for a religious holiday you have never heard of. What should you do?

9. What is the EEOC, and what are its responsibilities and powers?

Notes

1. Samuel C. Certo and Trevis Certo, *Modern Management: Concepts and Skills,* 11th ed. (Upper Saddle River, NJ: Prentice Hall, 2009), p. 83.

2. Goodwill Industries International, "Success Story: Night Shift Supervisor Overcomes Obstacles to Learning," What We Do pages, Goodwill Web site, www.goodwill.org, accessed July 25, 2006.

3. Bank of America, "Diversity & Inclusion," Culture, Inclusion, People page, Bank of America Web site, http://careers.bankofamerica.com/us/working-here/culture,-inclusion,-people#tab-diversity-recruiting, accessed on April 2, 2014.

4. Bureau of Labor Statistics, "*Women in the Labor Force: A Databook* Updated and Available on the Internet," news release, May 13, 2005, www.bls.gov.

5. Abraham T. Mosica Bureau of Labor Statistics, "Foreign-Born Workers in the U.S. Labor Force," Spotlight on Statistics, July 2013, www.bls.gov/spotlight/2013/foreign-born/home.htm.

6. See, for example, Elizabeth M. Grieco and Edward N. Trevelyan, "Place of Birth of the Foreign-Born Population: 2009," American Community Survey Brief 09-15 (U.S. Census Bureau, October 2010), http://www.census.gov; and Grayson K. Vincent and Victoria A. Velkoff, "The Next Four Decades: The Older Population in the United States, 2010 to 2050," Population Estimates and Projections P25-1138 (U.S. Census Bureau, May 2010), http://www.census.gov.

7. David S. Joachim, "Computer Technology Opens a World of Work to Disabled People," *New York Times,* March 1, 2006, www.nytimes.com; Grant Gross, "Technology Helps Disabled Workers," *PC World,* May 5, 2005, www.pcworld.com.

8. U.S. Census Bureau, "Facts for Features: Americans with Disabilities Act, July 26," news release, July 19, 2006, www.census.gov. See also K. C. Jones, "IBM Applies Technology for Disabled at Aging Baby Boomers," *TechWeb Technology News,* September 30, 2005, www.techweb.com.

9. For more information on how to infuse a sense of cohesion among diverse employees, see Christopher Ernst and Jeffrey Yip, March/April 2008, "Bridging Boundaries: Meeting the Challenge of Workplace Diversity," *Leadership in Action,* 28, pp. 3–6.

10. For further reading about corporate culture, see Volker Bach and Martin Whitehill, 2008, "The profit factor: How corporate culture affects a joint venture," *Strategic Change,* 17, p. 115.

11. Erin White, "Why Few Women Run Plants," *The Wall Street Journal,* May 1, 2006, http://online.wsj.com.

12. Kathy Gurchiek, "Slurs at Work Are on the Rise, Survey Finds," *HRMagazine,* June 2006, downloaded from InfoTrac, http://web2.infotrac.galegroup.com.

13. Mary-Kathryn Zachary, "Labor Law for Supervisors: Religion, Race and Dress Codes," *Supervision,* March 2006, downloaded from Business & Company Resource Center, http://galenet.galegroup.com.

14. E. J. Graff, "Is Banking Fair to Women?" *American Banker,* October 2011, pp. 20–25; Sasha Galbraith, "Creating 'Female-Friendly' Organizations," *Financial Executive,* April 2010, pp. 45–47.

15. Ellen Ostrow, "White-Male Culture of Big Firms Drives Women, Minorities Away," *Miami Daily Business Review,* June 24, 2008, downloaded from Business & Company Resource Center, http://galenet.galegroup.com.

16. For more information about a cross-cultural model of sexism, see I-Ching Lee, Felicia Pratto, and Mei-Chih Li, 2007, "Social relationships and sexism in the United States and Taiwan," *Journal of Cross-Cultural Psychology,* 38, p. 595.

17. Carol Hymowitz, "Women Swell Ranks as Middle Managers, but Are Scarce at Top," *The Wall Street Journal,* July 24, 2006, http://online.wsj.com; Melanie Lasoff Levs, "Next 20 Female CEOs, 2006," *Pink,* December 2005–January 2006, pp. 67–73.

18. Gretchen Livingston, "The Rise of Single Fathers: A Ninefold Increase Since 1960," Pew Research Social & Demographic Trends, July 2, 2013, http://www.pewsocialtrends.org/2013/07/02/the-rise-of-single-fathers/, accessed April 9, 2014.

19. "Training Can Keep Companies out of Court," *BusinessWeek Online,* March 9, 2006 (interview with Eli Kantor), downloaded at Business & Company Resource Center, http://galenet.galegroup.com.

20. David Wessel, "Older Staffers Get Uneasy Embrace," *The Wall Street Journal,* May 15, 2008, http://online.wsj.com.

21. R. Lockwood, "The Aging Workforce: The Reality of the Impact of Older Workers and Eldercare in the Workplace," *HRMagazine,* December 2003, http://www.ispi.org/pdf/suggestedReading/1LockwoodAging.pdf, accessed April 10, 2014.

22. For tips on how to combat the negative effects of ageism, see Catherine Webb, 2006, "Avoiding ageism at Coca-Cola: Company initiatives earn employer champion status," *Human Resource Management International Digest,* 14, p. 9.

23. Robert J. Grossman, "Keep Pace with Older Workers," *HR Magazine,* May 2008, www.shrm.org.

24. Ibid.

25. "The Millennial Generation Research Review," U.S. Chamber of Commerce Foundation, November 14, 2012, http://www.uschamberfoundation.org/MillennialsReport, accessed April 10, 2014.

26. "The Millennials: Confident. Connected. Open to Change." Pew Research Center, February 21, 2010, http://www.pewresearch.org/millennials/, accessed April 10, 2014.

27. See www.ada.gov for more information.

28. Robert D. Ramsey, "Supervising Employees with Limited English Language Proficiency," *Supervision*, June 2004, downloaded from InfoTrac, http://web5.infotrac.galegroup.com.

29. Galbraith, "Creating 'Female-Friendly' Organizations," p. 46.

30. These examples are taken from Kitty O. Locker, *Business and Administrative Communication*, 6th ed. (New York: Irwin/McGraw-Hill, 2003), pp. 297–300.

31. Donna M. Owens, "Multilingual Workforces," *HRMagazine*, September 2005, www.shrm.org.

32. For a modern approach to diversity training, see Carolyn Chavez and Judith Weisinger, 2008, "Beyond diversity training: A social infusion for cultural inclusion," *Human Resource Management*, 47 (2), pp. 331–350.

33. Annya M. Lott, "The Truth about Our Differences," *Black Enterprise*, July 2010, pp. 59–60.

34. Equal Employment Opportunity Commission, "Federal Equal Employment Opportunity (EEO) Laws," About EEO pages, EEOC Web site, www.eeoc.gov, last modified April 9, 2014; and William J. Wortel, "Avoiding State Law Pitfalls," *Employment Law Strategist*, June 1, 2008, downloaded from Business & Company Resource Center, http://galenet.galegroup.com.

PART TWO: SKILL-BUILDING

Meeting the Challenge

Reflecting back on page 120, consider the issue of diversity at PepsiCo. Begin by acknowledging that the members of your group may have different opinions on this subject. List the ways in which members of your group are diverse. Does it include several ethnic or racial groups and both sexes? Different age groups. How else are you "diverse"? As you continue the discussion, consider whether group members' different life experiences will help them see the situation in different ways, and try to listen carefully, especially to perspectives that are different from your own. Ideally, this process will help you understand the situations within companies more fully.

Discuss how Generation Y/Millenial workers' desire for engagement and meaningful work affects a supervisor's job. (You might also consider whether the statements about young workers are valid, and why or why not.) What might be harder about supervising such employees? What might be easier? When an employee demonstrates challenging behavior, what is the underlying cause and motivation? Does accommodating differences in age-related values make business sense? Ethical sense? Prepare a list of recommendations your group can agree on for supervising young workers. Then identify any suggested recommendations your group could not agree on.

Problem-Solving Case: Cultural Diversity in a Cookie Factory

Lori Madden, a teacher of Spanish, Portuguese, and Latin American culture, uses her cultural knowledge to help employers bridge language and cultural barriers with Spanish-speaking employees. One of her business clients was a cookie producer where about one-third of the line workers were Hispanic, mostly of Mexican origin. A union was attempting to organize the workers, and the company wanted to present its side of the decision more effectively. Looking at the longer term, the company also saw the union-organizing effort as a sign that it needed to ensure that workers were satisfied.

The manager who hired Madden as a consultant took her on a tour of the factory. During that time, a Spanish-speaking janitor approached Madden and asked her to translate a question: when would he get a raise? The manager could only remind the janitor of the company's wage structure and policies for granting raises, but the janitor already knew the policies. As she translated the exchange, Madden realized that something else was going on. The janitor was concerned about his family role. His wife also worked for the same company, but as an office worker, she earned more than he did. According to the janitor's cultural view of family roles, it was an embarrassment that he earned less than she did.

In this kind of situation, restating company policy would never lead to worker satisfaction.

The manager could not expect to change his employee's entire understanding of proper family roles. Nor could he violate company policy to make the employee happy. However, he could identify this janitor as an employee who would be highly motivated to work overtime or gain the skills that would qualify him for higher-paying positions at the factory.

This problem came as a surprise to the manager. Although he was able to bridge the language barrier with the janitor through an interpreter, the Hispanic employees generally did not speak up to air complaints or to put forward their opinions. They had a culturally based understanding that such behavior would be disrespectful. Madden's presence on the factory floor provided an opportunity for the janitor to raise the issue indirectly, as a question. Her cultural awareness gave her the insight that something lay behind the question, and she was able to probe for a greater understanding.

Besides playing this role as interpreter, Madden suggested other ways that the cookie company could create a more positive environment by addressing the needs and culture of its Hispanic employees. One step the company took was to create Spanish-language versions of instructions written for factory workers. Madden noted that translating English into Spanish was only part of the need: the instructions used highly technical language. Simplifying the writing in both languages would help all the factory workers understand instructions. She also encouraged the company to improve language skills by offering both Spanish instruction for supervisors and English instruction for the Hispanic workers. Furthermore, Madden noted that apprenticeship is a valued part of the Latin American work environment, so she encouraged the company to incorporate counseling or mentoring relationships into the development of employees.

Why go to all this trouble? The company where Madden consulted valued these employees. The manager who hired Madden described the Hispanic workers as typically hardworking, reliable, and willing to follow instructions. Of course, workers from other ethnic groups could also offer these or other strengths, but it was to the company's advantage to draw out the best from the talent it had.

1. In what ways would prejudice and stereotypes make it more difficult for the supervisors in this cookie business to improve relations with employees? How do the language differences contribute to the challenge?

2. The manager in this factory brought in a cultural expert to improve understanding of the Hispanic employees and enhance communication. Do you think this effort was more likely to improve communication or just reinforce prejudices? Why?

3. What else might supervisors in this factory do to improve the way the company manages diversity?

Source: Based on Lori Madden, "Creating a Happier, Healthier Hispanic Work Force," *EHS Today*, May 2011, pp. 46–49.

Assessing Yourself

Avoiding Age Bias

Place a 0 next to any statements you believe are true; write 10 for those you think are false.

_____ 1. Worker productivity declines with age.

_____ 2. Older employees are more expensive.

_____ 3. Older employees are more difficult to get along with.

_____ 4. Older employees are coasting until they can retire.

_____ 5. Older employees are prone to accidents and absenteeism.

_____ 6. Older employees can retire because they are financially secure.

_____ 7. Retraining older employees is more expensive because their future with the company is shorter than average.

Scoring: The higher your score, the less likely you are to be biased about an employee's age. All the statements are false.

Source: Adapted from Margaret J. Cofer, "How to Avoid Age Bias," *Nursing Management*, November 1, 1998, p. 11.

Pause and Reflect

1. Can you think of any other common prejudices about older workers?
2. Who are some older workers you know? Pick one or two, and consider what qualities they bring to their job. How well do they fit the seven stereotypes listed here?
3. How can you learn from your older co-workers? How can they learn from you?

Class Skills Exercise

Managing Diversity

Cultural Analysis Inventory

For each topic, there are two questions. Write brief responses to each. After you are finished, your instructor may wish to discuss your responses in class, or you may share them in small groups, or you may conduct a "culture hunt" by trying to find people in your class who answered the questions as you did.

1. Weddings
   a. What is the most important part of the wedding ceremony?
   b. What is the most important part of the reception?
2. Dinners
   a. Who carves the meat at large family dinners?
   b. Who clears the table at large family dinners?
3. Funerals
   a. What is the correct decision regarding "viewing" the remains?
   b. Where should a funeral be held?
4. Family
   a. What is the most important activity that your family does together?
   b. How far down the family tree does the obligation go to be responsible for a family member (e.g., lend money, take care of children, pay for food, let the person live with you temporarily)?
5. Ethnicity
   a. How does your family identify itself ethnically?
   b. What represents your family's cultural and ethnic identity? (For example, if you put "Hungarian," you might refer to a Hungarian lullaby or food that your family eats.)

Source: From Dan O'Haire and Gustav Friedrich, *Strategic Communication in Business and the Professions*, 2nd ed. Copyright © 1995 by Houghton Mifflin Company. Used with permission.

Building Supervision Skills

Providing Employee Orientation

Your work team is responsible for interviewing candidates for openings in the group and making hiring recommendations. For a current opening, you have interviewed several qualified people and decided which is the best. However, the candidate is quite young, and most of the members of your work group are in their 50s. Although they are impressed with the candidate's skills, you sense that they are reluctant to change the composition of the team so drastically. You are concerned that the workflow should continue without disruption and that the team spirit you have developed should remain high.

Assume the candidate is hired. Break into groups and brainstorm strategies for bringing the new person onto the team in such a way that the existing team members are accepting and welcoming.

chapter six | Reaching Goals: Plans and Controls

learning objectives

After you have studied this chapter, you should be able to:

6.1 Describe types of planning that take place in organizations.

6.2 Identify characteristics of effective objectives.

6.3 Define *management by objectives (MBO)* and discuss its use.

6.4 Discuss the supervisor's role in the planning process.

6.5 Explain the purpose of using controls.

6.6 Identify the steps in the control process.

6.7 Describe types of control and tools for controlling.

6.8 List characteristics of effective controls.

A Supervision Challenge

MEETING STANDARDS AT MEIJER INC.

Meijer Inc., a discount retail chain, has to keep costs down and efficiency up to deliver on its reputation for low prices. One target of these efforts is cashiers, who are expected to move customers through the lanes rapidly. The company has broken down the cashier's job into separate steps, such as greeting customers and scanning bulky items, and set standards for each. Software at the checkout terminals keeps track of how fast each cashier carries out each task and identifies which cashiers are failing to meet standards.

If a cashier scores less than 95 percent of the standard, the supervisor is supposed to make a change. The cashier might receive additional training or be assigned to a different job.

For cashiers, the monitoring makes them more concerned about how fast they work. Some have said they hurry customers along and avoid making eye contact that could encourage a customer to chat. Some say they feel stressed out. But a former manager for Meijer points out that posting information about employees' performance gives them a way to see whether they are meeting standards and showing who is excellent at the job. Some employees work best when they are working toward set goals.

One Meijer's cashier who says she usually meets or exceeds standards says she has a few tactics to help her beat the system. For example, the software allows more time for using a scanning gun, intended for large items, so this cashier uses it for items that don't really need it. She also frequently uses the terminal's "suspend" key, which pauses the system's timer. Obviously, these tactics don't improve how well the store is serving customers; they only help this employee with her score. This is a good example of why supervisor should not rely *solely* on these scores when evaluating their cashiers.

Another challenge in maintaining control through these cashier standards is loss prevention. Cashiers who are rushing to provide a speedy checkout might not request price checks on items that are missing tags. They may instead grab something comparable nearby and scan it as a substitute. Further, if a customer claims that there is a price contradiction, the cashier may be tempted to take their word for it rather than acquire the official confirmation. These small deviations from protocol can add up to inventory discrepancies and "shrink" or store losses. It is important, therefore, that the supervisor not allow cashiers to feel as though they should ignore all other standards just to be faster. Speed may be important, but so is accuracy and efficiency. If the end goal is to genuinely improve the service provided, cashiers need to know that they are expected to do more than race each other.

The cashier-monitoring system at Meijer can help supervisors identify top performers and make corrections when others fall short. It also raises some challenges, however, because it might take the cashiers' focus off making customers happy. The focus could easily become getting good scores on the system. As you study this chapter, consider the types of goals for cashiers that could help a store like Meijer succeed. How can a supervisor at a store ensure that cashiers meet those goals while still maintaining other standards and expectations?

Sources: Based on Vanessa O'Connell, "Stores Count Seconds to Trim Labor Costs," *The Wall Street Journal*, November 13, 2008, accessed April 17, 2014, http://online.wsj.com; Wren, "No Margin for Error: Loss Prevention in Grocery," *Bird's Eye View Advisories*, 2013, accessed April 17, 2014, http://www.wrensolutions.com/company/news/resources/no_margin_for_error.aspx.

The purpose of monitoring cashiers in Meijer stores is to ensure that they help the company reach its goals and objectives. Doing so requires knowledge of what these employees are supposed to accomplish and whether they are actually accomplishing it. Supervisors acquire that important knowledge by carrying out the functions of planning and controlling.

This chapter describes how supervisors can and should carry out those functions. The chapter begins with a description of how planning occurs in organizations, including the types of objectives and planning that are common. Next, the chapter discusses the supervisor's role as planner: setting and updating objectives and including employees in these processes. The second half of the chapter addresses the management function of controlling. It describes the process supervisors follow and some of the tools they use in controlling, as well as the characteristics of effective controls.

LO6.1 ▶ Describe types of planning that take place in organizations.

planning
Setting goals and determining how to meet them

Planning in Organizations

As you learned in Chapter 1, **planning** is the management function of setting goals and determining how to meet them. For supervisors, this process includes figuring out what tasks the department needs to complete to achieve its goals, as well as how and when to perform those tasks. For action-oriented people, planning can seem time consuming and tedious. But the need for planning is obvious, especially if you consider what would happen in an organization in which no one plans. For example, if a store did not implement planning, customers would not know when the store would be open, and employees would not know what inventory to order or when to order it. The location of the store might be an accident, with no marketing research to determine where business would be sufficient to generate a profit. The managers would not know how many employees to hire, because they would have no idea how many customers they would be serving. Clearly, this business would fail in the mission of providing its customers with high-quality service and merchandise.

Supervisors and other managers plan for several reasons. Knowing what the organization is trying to accomplish helps them set priorities and make decisions aimed at accomplishing their goals. The act of planning forces managers to spend time focusing on the future and establishes a fair way to evaluate employee performance. It helps managers use resources efficiently, thus minimizing wasted time and money. Time spent in planning a project can reduce the time required to carry it out. The total time for planning and execution can actually be shorter for a thoroughly planned project than for one started in haste.

Many inexpensive software packages can help supervisors plan projects efficiently. Templates that supervisors can customize for their own purposes lead the way through the various planning steps and help establish project phases and the order in which they need to be accomplished, project goals and deadlines, people and departments involved in the project, anticipated obstacles and action plans for overcoming them, and budgets and other resources.

Finally, the other functions managers perform—organizing, staffing, leading, and controlling—all depend on good planning. Before supervisors and other managers can allocate resources and inspire employees to achieve their objectives, and before they can determine whether employees are meeting those objectives, they need to know what they are trying to accomplish.

Supervisors rarely have much input into the way an organization does its planning. Rather, they participate in whatever process already exists. To participate constructively, supervisors should understand the process.

LO6.2 ▶ Identify characteristics of effective objectives.

objectives
The desired accomplishments of the organization as a whole or of part of the organization

goals
Objectives, often those with a broad focus

Objectives

Planning centers on the setting of goals and objectives. **Objectives** specify the desired accomplishments of the organization as a whole or of a part of it. According to one school of thought, **goals** are objectives with a broad focus. For example, an organization seeks to be the number one supplier of nursing home care by the end of next year. That would be considered a goal. In contrast, the accounting department seeks to have all invoices mailed within two weeks of a patient's departure; this is more specific and therefore an objective. This text, however, uses the term *objectives* in most cases and treats the terms *objectives* and *goals* as synonyms.

The photovoltaic cells on top of this roof will help the minimize energy usage. Installing photovoltaic cells is an example of a strategic objective.

No matter which term is used, an organization's goals identify what its people should be striving toward. At General Cable Corporation, management wanted to reduce an expensive problem: scrapped materials, which amounted to 4 percent of the company's cost of materials. After analyzing where most of the scrap was occurring, General Cable made sure that all employees saw and understood the charts pinpointing the problem areas. Then employees began looking for ways to reduce scrap by setting goals to fix problems in the costliest areas. Four years later, the scrap rate was down to 1.1 percent with a goal of 0.85 for the following year. Because General Cable makes sure equipment operators have information about where problems are occurring, these employees can contribute to meeting the scrap reduction goals.[1]

Strategic Objectives

Planning should begin at the top, with a plan for the organization as a whole. **Strategic planning** is the creation of long-term goals for the organization. These goals typically include the type and quality of goods or services the organization is to provide and, for a business, the level of profits it is to earn.[2]

strategic planning
The creation of long-term goals for the organization as a whole

DuPont's strategic objectives are guided by its corporate vision: "to find sustainable, innovative, market-driven solutions to solve some of the world's biggest challenges, making lives better, safer, and healthier for people everywhere." These noble ideas translate into a company that applies expertise in chemistry and its operations in more than 90 countries to sell chemicals, specialty plastics, and industrial materials. Staying ahead in these areas requires constant innovation, and the company has more than 75 research facilities in 12 countries. Strategic objectives include defining areas where investments in research have the greatest potential to deliver value in line with the corporate vision. For example, the company has recently focused on chemicals used in photovoltaics (the process of converting solar energy into electrical power) and high-temperature plastics for use in building lighter (and therefore more efficient) automobiles.[3]

Usually it is top managers who engage in strategic planning; in other cases, a planning department prepares objectives for approval by top management. Either way, the managers at the top decide where the organization should be going.

Operational Objectives

The objectives for divisions, departments, and work groups support the goals developed in strategic planning. These objectives, developed through **operational planning**, specify how the group will help the organization achieve its goals.[4] Operational planning is performed by middle managers and supervisors. Table 6.1, on the following page, summarizes the characteristics of strategic and operational planning.

operational planning
The development of objectives that specify how divisions, departments, and work groups will support organizational goals

Middle managers set objectives that will enable their division or department to contribute to the goals set for the organization. Supervisors set objectives that will enable their department or work group to contribute to divisional or departmental goals. For example, if the organizational objective for a bank is to increase profits by 8 percent next year, the goal of a branch located in a high-growth area might be to increase its own profits by 9 percent. At this branch, the vice president (supervisor) in charge of lending operations might have the objective of increasing loans to businesses by 15 percent. The head teller might have the objective of keeping customer waits to five minutes or less. (The good service is designed to support organizational objectives by attracting new customers to the bank.)

TABLE 6.1 | Characteristics of Strategic and Operational Planning

	Strategic Planning	**Operational Planning**
Planners	Top managers, possibly with a planning department	Middle managers and supervisors
Scope	Objectives for the organization as a whole	Objectives for a division, department, or work group
Time Frame	Long range (more than one year)	Short range (one year or less)

Operational objectives should get all employees focused on their role in supporting the company's strategy. Fire departments have established specific operational objectives for the group such as bringing a fire under control within 10 minutes after arrival of the first fire company and having all firefighters wear full personal protective equipment. Along with these objectives, goals for individual performance include such detailed measures as ensuring all firefighters are wearing seat belts, carrying the proper tools, and using hose lines.[5]

Notice in these examples that the objectives become more specific at lower levels of the organization, and planning tends to focus on shorter time spans. This is the usual pattern for planning in an organization. Thus, top managers spend a lot of their time thinking broadly over several years, whereas much of the supervisor's planning involves what actions to take in the current week or month.

Personal Objectives

In addition to planning for the department as a whole, each supervisor should apply good planning practices to his or her individual efforts. This includes determining how to help the department meet its objectives, as well as how to meet the supervisor's own career objectives. Another important application of planning is effectively managing the use of one's time. (Chapter 13 discusses time management.)

Characteristics of Effective Objectives

For objectives to be effective—that is, clearly understood and practical—they should have certain characteristics. As shown in Figure 6.1, they should be written, measurable or observable, clear, specific, and challenging but achievable.

Putting objectives *in writing* might seem like a nuisance, but doing so gives them importance; employees can see they are something to which managers have devoted time and thought. The people required to carry out the objectives can then look them up as a reminder of what they are supposed to be accomplishing, and they can take time to make sure they understand them. Finally, writing down objectives forces the supervisor to think through what the objectives say.

Making objectives *measurable* or at least observable provides the supervisor with a way to tell whether people are actually accomplishing them. Measurable objectives might specify a dollar amount, a time frame, or a quantity to be produced. Examples are the number of sales calls made, parts manufactured, or customers served. The words *maximize* and *minimize* are tip-offs that the objectives are not measurable. If the objective is to "maximize quality," how will anyone know whether maximum quality has been obtained? Instead, the objective might call for a defect rate of no more than 2 percent or for no customer complaints during the month. Other objectives that are difficult to measure are those that simply call for something to "improve"

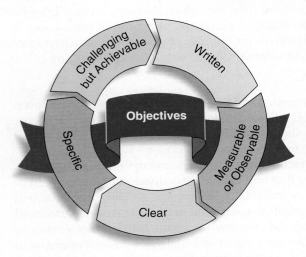

FIGURE 6.1 | Characteristics of Effective Objectives

For objectives to be clearly understood and practical, they need to have certain characteristics.

or "get better." The person writing the objective should specify a way to measure or observe the improvement.

When the supervisor needs other people to play a part in accomplishing objectives, those people must understand the objectives. Thus, it is easy to see why objectives should be *clear*. The supervisor can make sure the objectives are clear by spelling them out in simple language and asking employees whether they understand them.

Making objectives *specific* means indicating who is to do what and by what time to accomplish the objective. Specific objectives describe the actions people are to take and what is supposed to result from those actions. For example, instead of saying, "Computer files will be backed up regularly," a specific objective might say, "Each word-processing operator will back up his or her files at the end of each workday." Being specific simplifies the job of ensuring that the objectives are accomplished; the supervisor knows just what to look for. Also, specific objectives help employees understand what they are supposed to be doing.

Objectives that are *challenging* are more likely to stimulate employees to do their best than those that are not. However, the employees have to believe they are capable of achieving the objectives. Otherwise, they will become frustrated or angry at what seem to be unreasonable expectations. Most of us have had the experience of tackling a challenging job and enjoying the sense of pride and accomplishment that comes with finishing it. In setting goals, the supervisor should remember how stimulating and confidence building such experiences can be.

Mc Graw Hill Education **connect** SELF-ASSESSMENT 6.1

Assessing How Personality Type Impacts Your Goal-Setting Skills

Setting goals for yourself affects your own productivity. Helping your subordinate set effective goals is critical for individual, departmental, and organizational success. Your personality can influence how you look at planning and goal setting. This assessment uses elements from both your childhood and your present to give you a deeper understanding of your strengths and limitations as a goal-setter.

Policies, Procedures, and Rules

For example, to meet his objective of staffing his information systems department with top-quality employees, supervisor Bruce Frazzoli hired some people he used to work with at his former job. He was later embarrassed to be called on the carpet for violating his employer's policy that managers must work with the personnel department in making all hiring decisions. Frazzoli learned that supervisors and other managers must consider the organization's policies, procedures, and rules when setting objectives. The content of the objectives and the way they are carried out must be consistent with all three.

policies
Broad guidelines for how to act

Policies are broad guidelines for how to act; they do not spell out the details of how to handle a specific situation. For example, a firm might have a policy of increasing the number of women and minorities in its workforce. Such a policy does not dictate whom to hire or when; it merely states a general expectation. Figure 6.2 on the following page summarizes a dress code policy for an Ontario hospital.

procedures
The steps that must be completed to achieve a specific purpose

Procedures are the steps that must be completed to achieve a specific purpose. An organization might specify procedures for hiring employees, purchasing equipment, filing paperwork, and many other activities. Publishing company McGraw-Hill's management guidelines include suggested procedures for how to conduct performance appraisals and employment interviews. A supervisor may be responsible for developing the procedures for activities carried out in his or her own department.

FIGURE 6.2 | Provisions in a Hospital's Dress Code Policy

A dress code policy is just one example of a policy a business might have to provide to employees as a guideline for behavior.

Sources: Based on K. Cheung, "Hospital's Strict Dress-Code Policy Helps Patients Identify Clinical Staff," *Fierce Healthcare,* July 15, 2011, http://www.fiercehealthcare.com; Ottawa Hospital, "Dress Code," Corporate Policy and Procedure Manual, http://www.ottawahopsital.on.ca.

After Ottawa Hospital, located in Ontario, Canada, learned that patients were having trouble figuring out which workers were clinical staff members, the hospital prepared a dress code aimed at creating a more professional atmosphere and less confusion about roles. Here are some key points of that policy:

All Employees
- Dress in a manner that portrays a professional image and promotes patient confidence.
- Wear shoes that are clean and provide support, comfort, and protection against workplace injury.
- Wear hair in a way that it does not come into contact with the patient or obscure vision (for example, long hair must be pulled back).

Clinical Staff
- Dress according to the guidelines for their professional group.
- Wear personal protective garments such as scrubs and lab coats in designated areas but not outside the workplace.
- Limit hand jewelry to a smooth wedding band and/or a watch, and do not wear long, dangling jewelry.

Support Services Staff
- Wear clean employer-issued uniforms.
- Wear a pair of shoes dedicated for the workplace.

rules
Specific statements of what to do or not do in a given situation

action plan
The plan for how to achieve an objective

For example, a restaurant manager might spell out a cleanup procedure or a maintenance supervisor might detail the shutdown procedure for a piece of machinery. Procedures free managers and employees from making decisions about activities they carry out repeatedly.

Rules are specific statements of what to do or not do in a given situation. Unlike policies, they are neither flexible nor open to interpretation. For example, one rule at Excelitas Technology is that employees must wear safety goggles whenever they handle chemicals and when they weld, solder, drill, or cut wires. Restaurants have rules stating that employees must wash their hands before working. Rules of this kind are often imposed by law.

Action Plans

Objectives serve as the basis for action plans and contingency plans, as shown in Figure 6.3 on the following page. An **action plan** is a plan for how to achieve an objective. If you think of objectives as statements of where you want to go, then an action plan is a map that tells you how to get there.[6] For a successful trip, you need both kinds of information.

The supervisor creates an action plan by answering the questions *what, who, when, where,* and *how*:

- *What* actions need to be taken? Do sales calls need to be made, customers served in a certain way, goods produced? The supervisor should outline the specific steps involved.
- *Who* will take the necessary steps? The supervisor may perform some tasks, but many activities will be assigned to specific employees or groups of employees.
- *When* must each step be completed? With many types of processes, certain steps will determine when the whole project is completed. The supervisor should be particularly careful in scheduling those activities.
- *Where* will the work take place? Sometimes this question is easy to answer, but a growing operation may require that the supervisor plan for additional space. Some activities may require that the supervisor consider

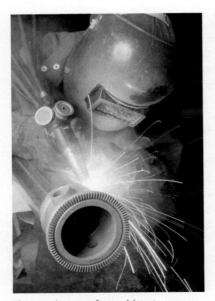

The requirement for welders to wear safety gear is an example of a rule.

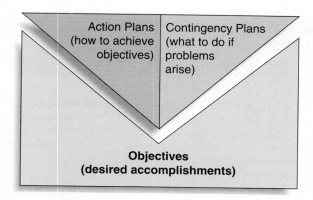

FIGURE 6.3 | Areas of Planning

Action plans and contingency plans are the tools used to meet desired objectives.

contingency planning
Planning what to do if the original plans don't work out

the arrangement of work on the shop floor or the arrangement of items in a warehouse or supply room.

- *How* will the work be done? Are the usual procedures and equipment adequate, or does the supervisor need to innovate? Thinking about how the work will be done may alert the supervisor to a need for more training.

Contingency Planning

A lot of people believe in Murphy's law: "If anything can go wrong, it will." Even those who are less pessimistic recognize that things do not always go as planned. A delivery may be delayed by a strike or a blizzard, a key employee may take another job, a "foolproof" computer system may crash. The sign of a good supervisor is not so much that the supervisor never has experienced these nasty surprises but that he or she is prepared with ideas about how to respond.

Planning what to do if the original plans do not work out is known as **contingency planning.** The wise supervisor has contingency plans to go with every original plan. In a warehouse, for example, employees meet objectives by working with increasingly sophisticated equipment such as lift trucks with onboard computers and conveyors that move packages past scanners or sensors that keep track of inventory. Supervisors in this environment need to plan for the necessary maintenance to keep this equipment running smoothly, but they also need contingency plans for what to do when a computer crashes or a machine or truck breaks down in spite of good maintenance. One part of the plan involves how the team will handle a breakdown: Will someone be trained to do basic repairs? What parts should be kept on hand so you do not have to wait for a technician to order them? Who should be called for repairs that are beyond the capabilities of employees? Another part of the contingency plan would include decisions about how to keep activities moving ahead without the equipment: Will the company rent equipment? Will it hire temporary workers to keep up while others are making repairs or working around a broken conveyor? How can employees keep track of inventory on paper if the computer crashes? Answering questions such as these ahead of time is easier than answering them in the midst of a crisis.[7]

One useful technique for contingency planning is to review all objectives, looking for areas where something might go wrong. Then the supervisor determines how to respond if those problems do arise. In today's organizations, many objectives involve getting work done with computers, often online. To learn more about the kinds of contingency plans that are needed for this type of work, see "Supervision: New Trends" on the following page.

Contingency planning is not always formal. It would be too time-consuming to create a written contingency plan for every detail of operations. Instead, the supervisor simply has to keep in mind how to respond if some details of the operation do not go as planned.

LO6.3 ▶ Define *management by objectives (MBO)* **and discuss its use.**

management by objectives (MBO)
A formal system for planning in which managers and employees at all levels set objectives for what they are to accomplish; their performance is then measured against those objectives

Management by Objectives

Many organizations use a formal system for planning known as **management by objectives (MBO),** a process in which managers and employees at all levels set objectives for what they are to accomplish. Their performance then is measured against those objectives.[8] Basically, MBO involves three steps:

1. All individuals in the organization work with their managers to set objectives, specifying what they are to do in the next operating period (such as a year).

SUPERVISION: NEW TRENDS

WHEN CLOUD COMPUTING GETS STORMY

Just about every computer user has experienced a need for contingency planning, and many of us have learned the hard way. Say a storm passes by, knocking out the electricity, or a laptop battery runs down, and the computer is suddenly out of power. If you haven't been saving your work, it's gone in a flash. Other mishaps include files being accidentally erased, disks becoming corrupted, or computers being infected with a virus. In each case, valuable data can be lost if a copy wasn't previously stored somewhere. Besides that, the owner of a nonfunctioning computer cannot work until a repair is made or a replacement (with the needed data) is found. A contingency plan for these problems helps the user recover faster.

Nowadays, additional complications—and solutions—are available in a popular trend called "cloud computing." Today that term broadly refers to computer work where some or all of the data processing or storage takes place away from the user's computer, in a service provider's server computers. The data travel back and forth between the servers and the users over the Internet.

On one level, cloud computing is often a part of contingency plans. For example, computer users might decide that storing data in the cloud is the best protection against loss of data. If the power goes out, a computer malfunctions, or a flood or fire destroys hardware, the user can still get the data from the remote servers.

On another level, cloud computing creates a need for more contingency plans. Most basically, a company that uses a cloud service to store and process important data is counting on the service provider to stay in business, protect the data adequately, and fix any bugs in the software. If the service fails at any of those, the company could be unable to do its work, and its ability to correct the situation is limited. Contingency planning for problems in the cloud therefore is at least as important as deciding how to protect data stored by the user.

Another type of problem involves protecting the security of confidential data. Suppose all your payroll data go to a service that stores the data and prepares employees' paychecks. That kind of service might be a tempting target for hackers. Likewise, people who choose the cloud service should ensure that it encrypts the data. Even then, a contingency plan is necessary, just in case security is breached.

It might seem pessimistic to think that high-profile cloud-computing services would allow these problems. But computer systems are so complex and hackers so clever that even the best companies trip up. Recently, for example, Amazon Web Services crashed, temporarily disabling Instagram, Vine, AirBnB, and the Flipboard mobile magazine app. In another example, Sony struggled to restore service after its customer database was hacked. Even the Gmail e-mail service, which has an impressive uptime of over 99 percent, may lose a customer trying to reach a Gmail user during the other 1 percent of the time.

Solid contingency plans ensure that critical activities continue when cloud computing gets stormy.

Sources: Brad Stone, "Another Amazon Outage Exposes the Cloud's dark Lining," *Bloomberg Businessweek,* August 26, 2013, http://www.businessweek.com/articles/2013-08-26/another-amazon-outage-exposes-the-clouds-dark-lining; Paul Engle, "An Improving Cloud," *Industrial Engineer,* August 2011, p. 20; Mike West, "Cloud Needs Contingency Plans," *Information Management,* July/August 2011, p. 21.

2. Each individual's manager periodically reviews the individual's performance to see whether he or she is meeting the objectives. Typically, these reviews take place two to four times a year. The reviews help the individual and the manager decide what corrective actions are needed, and they provide information for setting future objectives.
3. The organization rewards individuals on the basis of how close they come to fulfilling the objectives.

Figure 6.4 on the following page shows examples of objectives for employees at several levels of an organization using MBO. Notice that the sample objective for the nonmanagement employee supports the achievement of the supervisor's objective, which in turn supports the achievement of his or her manager's objective, and so on up the hierarchy. (In practice, of course, each person in the organization would have several objectives to meet.)

For the effective use of MBO, managers at all levels (especially top management) must be committed to the system. Also, the objectives they set must meet the criteria

FIGURE 6.4 | Sample Objectives in an Organization Using MBO

In a corporation using management by objectives, the broad objectives of the top-level managers become increasingly specific objectives for lower-level managers.

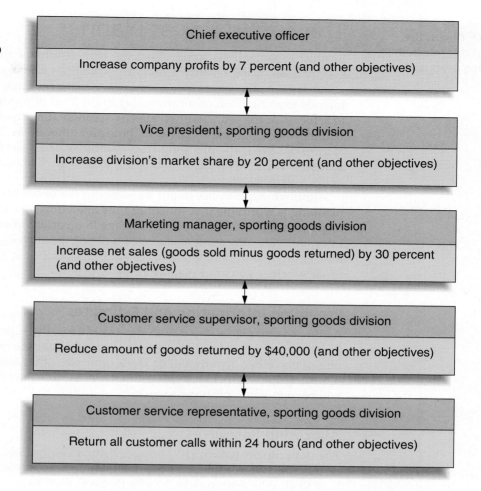

Chief executive officer

Increase company profits by 7 percent (and other objectives)

Vice president, sporting goods division

Increase division's market share by 20 percent (and other objectives)

Marketing manager, sporting goods division

Increase net sales (goods sold minus goods returned) by 30 percent (and other objectives)

Customer service supervisor, sporting goods division

Reduce amount of goods returned by $40,000 (and other objectives)

Customer service representative, sporting goods division

Return all customer calls within 24 hours (and other objectives)

for effective objectives described previously. For example, a salesperson would not be expected merely to "sell more" but to help develop specific objectives, such as "make 40 sales calls a month" and "sell 50 copiers by December 31." Finally, managers and employees must be able to cooperate in the objective-setting process.

Some people dislike MBO because setting and monitoring the achievement of objectives can be time-consuming and requires a lot of paperwork. However, the organization can benefit from involving employees in setting goals, which may lead to greater commitment in achieving them. Also, the employees can benefit from a system of rewards that is rational and based on performance rather than personality. In light of these advantages, a supervisor may want to use the MBO principles with the employees in his or her own department even if the organization as a whole has not adopted a formal MBO system.

For MBO to work effectively, this telesales employee would need to work with her supervisor and coworkers to determine exactly how many sales she is expected to make in a given amount of time.

LO6.4 ▶ Discuss the supervisor's role in the planning process.

The Supervisor as Planner

In most organizations, supervisors are responsible for the creation of plans that specify goals, tasks, resources, and responsibilities for the supervisor's own department. Thus, at the supervisor's level, objectives can range from the tasks he or she intends to accomplish on a certain day to the level of production the department is to achieve for the year. To be an effective planner, the supervisor should be familiar with how to set good objectives in these and other areas. The "Supervisory Skills" feature describes the planning responsibilities of supervisors in the construction industry. The general guidelines apply to similar challenges met by supervisors in many different settings.

Although supervisors might resist doing the necessary paperwork, thoughtful planning is worth the investment of time and effort. In carrying out their planning responsibilities, supervisors may engage in a variety of activities, from providing information to allocating resources, involving employees, coaching a team's planning effort, and updating objectives. (Take the Assessing Yourself quiz on page 170 to see whether you are a planner.)

Providing Information and Estimates

As the manager closest to day-to-day operations, the supervisor is in the best position to keep higher-level managers informed about the needs, abilities, and progress of his or her department or work group. For that reason, higher management relies on supervisors to provide estimates of the personnel and other resources they will need to accomplish their work.

Allocating Resources

The department for which the supervisor is responsible has a limited number of resources—people, equipment, and money. The supervisor's job includes deciding how to allocate resources to the jobs that will need to be done.

The process of allocating human resources includes determining how many and what kind of employees the department will need to meet its objectives. If the department's workload is expanding, the supervisor may need to plan to hire new employees. He or she also must plan for employee vacations and other time off, as well as for employee turnover.

The process of allocating equipment resources includes determining how much equipment is needed to get the job done. For example, does every bookkeeper need a personal computer, or will calculators be enough? The supervisor may find that the department needs to acquire more equipment. In that case, the supervisor must justify the request to buy or rent it by showing how it will benefit the organization.

Developing a Budget

budget
A plan for spending money

The process of allocating money resources is called *budgeting*. A **budget** is a plan for spending money. Many households use budgets to decide how much of each paycheck should go for housing, car payments, food, savings, and so on. Businesses use budgets to break down how much to spend on items such as wages and salaries, rent, supplies, insurance, and so on. These items would be part of an *operating budget*; big-ticket items such as machinery or a new building would more likely be accounted for separately as part of a *capital budget*.

Some organizations expect their supervisors to prepare a budget showing what they think they will need to spend in the next year to meet departmental goals or carry out a specific project. Table 6.2, on the following page, illustrates a sample budget for a machine shop project. The line items show different categories of

SUPERVISORY SKILLS

PLANNING

Planning: Planning, Scheduling, and Spending

The performance of the onsite supervisor is one of the most important components of a construction company's profits. The supervisor's planning and decision making, if done well, can help the company cope with the challenges of weather, suppliers, and labor unions. Because careful planning guides the onsite supervisor and directly impacts a project's time, cost, quality, and safety, making sure the supervisor has the appropriate training to do this job well is critical to a company's success.

The Associated General Contractors (AGC) of America recognizes the importance of planning and scheduling in the life of a construction supervisor. To meet the needs of the construction industry, they offer a Supervisory Training Program (STP) in which an entire unit is dedicated to planning and scheduling. Additionally, individual chapters of the AGC offer various locally sponsored training. One such program, offered by the Carolinas AGC, is the Project SuperVISION Education and Recognition Program for Construction Supervisors. A component of SuperVISION is "Effective Preplanning and Project Scheduling." This course teaches construction supervisors that a ". . . a construction project begins long before equipment and people come to the job site. Careful planning and scheduling before and during construction makes a job run smoothly and results in satisfied owners, subcontractors, suppliers, construction workers, and company managers."

So, what do construction supervisors need to do to meet the demands of planning and scheduling? James Adrian, a professor of civil engineering and construction and a consultant to the construction industry recommends listing each of the day's construction tasks in a worksheet. Next to each task, indicate the cost per unit for completing it. Then rate each task in three areas: (1) whether completing the task on time is critical to meeting the overall

schedule; (2) whether productivity risk—the chance that quality or efficiency will suffer if the supervisor is not involved—is high, low, or somewhere in between; and (3) whether the task is new or unfamiliar to the employees who will perform it. Finally, taking into account the costs and ratings, the supervisor ranks the tasks according to how much direct supervision will be needed. The supervisor should give the highest priority to tasks that have high costs, are critical to meeting the schedule, have high productivity risk, and are new or unfamiliar. High priority means the supervisor makes a point of observing the task and being available to help resolve problems.

Through working with supervisors on completing a planning worksheet, Adrian has discovered that many construction supervisors are unfamiliar with costs of materials and equipment. He demonstrated the significance of this problem to a group of students in a course on productivity. He took the group to a construction site to observe the work and note productivity problems. Everyone criticized the fact that a group of workers (who were paid more than $40 an hour) were taking a 15-minute break. But no one commented on a piece of equipment that stood idle for four hours. The students didn't think about it because none of them realized the rental cost of that equipment was more than $120 per hour.

The plans of good supervisors address both spending and scheduling. Busy and successful supervisors also need to maintain a practical view of planning how to efficiently allocate time for both workers and equipment.

Sources: ACG of America, "Supervisory Training Program," http://www.agc.org/cs/career_development/supervisory, accessed April 15, 2014; Carolinas ACG, "Project SuperVISION," http://www.cagc.org/edu_training/files/PSV_Brochure.pdf, accessed April 15, 2014; James Adrian, "Improving Your Supervisor's Work Day," *Pavement*, January 2006, http://www.forconstructionpros.com/article/10285523/improving-your-supervisors-work-day, accessed April 15, 2014.

expenses. The first column of figures contains the amounts budgeted for expenses in each category. The right-hand columns have the actual amounts spent each month in each category. The supervisor uses the actual amounts in controlling, which is described subsequently in this chapter.

In preparing a budget, the supervisor typically has rules and guidelines to follow. For example, one company may say that pay increases for the department as a whole must be no more than 5 percent of the previous year's budget for salaries. Another organization may specify a total amount that the department may spend, or it may give the supervisor a formula for computing the department's overhead expenses. On the basis of these guidelines, the supervisor then recom-

TABLE 6.2 | Sample Budget for a Machine Shop Project

Source: Adapted from *Industrial Supervision: In the Age of High Technology,* by David L. Goetsch. Copyright © 1992 Pearson Education, Inc. Reprinted by permission of Pearson Education, Inc., Upper Saddle River, NJ.

Budget Monitoring Report						
Organizational unit <u>Machine shop</u> Total parts needed <u>6,000</u> Parts per month projection <u>1,000</u>	Job number <u>1763</u> Parts produced to date <u>2,700</u> Current production per month <u>900</u>		Period <u>January–June</u> Remaining work <u>3,300</u> Difference <u>−100</u>			
Actual Expenditures						
Line Item	**Budgeted Amount**	**January**	**February**	**March**	**April**	**May**	**June**
Direct labor	$60,000	$10,000	$10,000	$10,000			
Indirect labor	5,400	900	900	900			
Material	13,200	2,195	3,156	1,032			
Operating supplies	3,000	1,200	0	296			
Equipment repair	5,400	0	0	3,600			
Total	**$87,000**	**$14,295**	**$14,056**	**$15,828**			

mends how much to spend in each area. In most cases, the supervisor and his or her manager review the budget. The supervisor must be willing to modify it when higher-level managers require a change.

Scheduling

scheduling
Setting a precise timetable for the work to be completed

The supervisor continually needs to think about how much work the department needs to accomplish in a given time period and how it can meet its deadlines. Setting a precise timetable for the work to be done is known as **scheduling.** This process includes deciding which activities will take priority over others and deciding who will do what tasks and when.

Many organizations expect supervisors to use one or more of the techniques and tools that have been developed to help with scheduling. Two of the most widely used techniques are Gantt charts and PERT networks. A **Gantt chart** is a scheduling tool that lists the activities to be completed and uses horizontal bars to graph how long each activity will take, including its starting and ending dates. The sample Gantt chart in Figure 6.5, on the following page, could be created by software that automatically fills in the chart using activity and schedule information entered on a spreadsheet.

Gantt chart
Scheduling tool that lists the activities to be completed and uses horizontal bars to graph how long each activity will take, including its starting and ending dates

program evaluation and review technique (PERT)
Scheduling tool that identifies the relationships among tasks as well as the amount of time each task will take

The **program evaluation and review technique (PERT)** is a scheduling tool that identifies the relationships among tasks and the amount of time each task will take. To use this tool, the planner creates a PERT network. For example, in Figure 6.6 on page 154, the circles represent the events that must occur to produce a film. The arrows between the circles represent the sequence of activities. The letter on each arrow refers to the activity that results in the corresponding event. Many PERT charts also include information about how long each task is expected to take. An important piece of information in a PERT network is the *critical path*—the sequence of tasks that will require the greatest amount of time. A delay in the critical path will cause the entire project to fall behind.

In addition to these tools, supervisors may use a computer to help with scheduling. Many project management software packages have been developed for this application.

FIGURE 6.5 | Sample Gantt Chart for a Building Project

A Gantt chart provides everyone involved in a project with a visual representation of exactly where things stand, what components are dependent upon others, what goals have been met, what is still to be completed, and the critical path of the project.

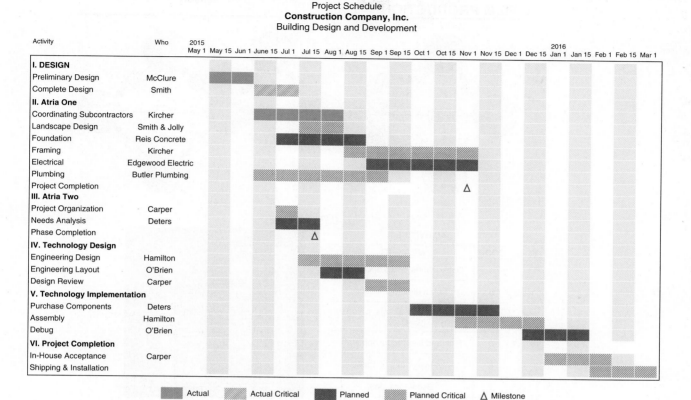

Involving Employees

To make sure that employees understand objectives and consider them achievable, supervisors may involve them in the goal-setting process. Employees who are involved in the process tend to feel more committed to the objectives, and they may be able to introduce ideas that the supervisor has not considered. In many cases, employees who help set objectives agree to take on greater challenges than the supervisor might have guessed.

One way to get employees involved in setting objectives is to have them write down what they think they can accomplish in the coming year (or month or appropriate time period). Then the supervisor discusses the ideas with each employee, modifying the objectives to meet the department's overall needs. Another approach is to hold a meeting of the entire work group at which the employees and supervisor develop objectives as a group. (Chapter 3 provides ideas for holding successful meetings.)

One organization where employees participate in setting objectives is the government of Yolo County, California. Department heads and other managers attend an annual retreat to establish an overall agenda for the coming year. Then supervisors meet with their employees to discuss the year's goals and ways the work unit can contribute to meeting the goals. When these group objectives are established and approved, employees contribute to the establishment of individ-

FIGURE 6.6 | PERT Scheduling Tool

Like a Gantt chart, a PERT chart provides a visual overview of a project and allows a supervisor to work through planning a project as well as to track a project as it progresses.

FILM PRODUCTION

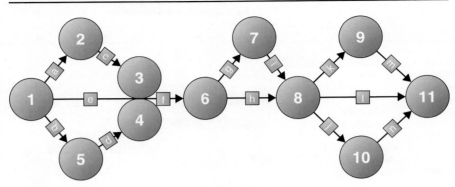

ACTIVITIES	
CODE	MEANING
a	Obtain funds, loans, investors
b	Solicit director interest
c	Draw up staff contracts, agree on salaries
d	Pick and hire production staff
e	Advertise, contact agents
f	Scout locations
g	Build sets
h, i	Film scenes
j	Pick a conductor, choose songs
k	Edit film
l	Write press releases, buy ads, create preview
m	Prescreen with audiences
n	Create soundtrack CD

EVENTS	
CODE	MEANING
1	Obtain script
2	Budget acquired
3	Talent hired
4	Production staff hired
5	Director signed contract
6	Locations picked
7	All sets final
8	Filming completed
9	Film edited
10	Soundtrack complete
11	Film released

Source: www.smartdraw.com/resources/examples/business/images/coded_pert_full.gif.

ual goals for particular tasks and projects. Although this goal-setting process is time-consuming, it helps keep employees more interested in and committed to their job requirements.[9]

Planning with a Team

In many applications of teamwork, teams, not individual managers, are charged with planning. In these cases, supervisors are expected not only to seek employee involvement in planning but also to coach their team in carrying out the planning function. This requires knowing and communicating a clear sense of what the plan should encompass and encouraging team members to cooperate and share ideas freely.

When teams draw on the many viewpoints and diverse experience of team members, they can come up with creative plans that dramatically exceed past performance. American Airlines turned to a team approach when it decided it could make its maintenance centers so efficient that the company could profitably sell maintenance services to other airlines. American formed teams of union and management employees to figure out how to raise the productivity of each maintenance center. At the center in Tulsa, one solution was to overhaul the basic approach to heavy maintenance. Under the traditional arrangement, an airplane would be parked in the hangar, and hundreds of workers would swarm over it, removing and replacing parts. The teams figured out it would be more efficient to set up three work areas and move each plane from one stage to the next. With suggestions from workers at all levels, the company redesigned the entire workplace, repositioning supervisors and rearranging parts and equipment to place them nearer to where they would be needed.[10] With these and other changes, American's Tulsa Maintenance Base is now able to use its aircraft maintenance operation to generate new revenue streams and to offer employees higher salaries and better benefits than many aircraft maintenance vendors.[11] (Chapter 3 provides a more detailed discussion of managing teamwork.)

Updating Objectives

Once the supervisor has set objectives, he or she should monitor performance and compare it with the objectives. (The control process will be described in the next section.) Sometimes the supervisor determines that objectives need to be modified.

When should supervisors update the objectives for their department or work group? They will need to do so whenever top management updates organizational objectives. Also, organizations with a regular procedure for planning will specify when supervisors must review and update their objectives.

LO6.5 ▶ Explain the purpose of using controls.

controlling
The management function of ensuring that work goes according to plan

The Supervisor as Controller

As you learned in Chapter 1, **controlling** is the management function of making sure that work goes according to plan. Supervisors carry out this process in many ways. Consider the following fictional examples:

- Bud Cavanaugh told his crew, "I expect the work area to be clean when you leave each day. That means the floors are swept and all the tools are put away."

- Once or twice each day, Maria Lopez took time to check the documents produced by the word-processing operators she supervised. Maria would look over a few pages each employee had produced that day. If one of the employees seemed to be having trouble with some task—for example, deciphering handwriting or preparing neat tables—Maria would discuss the problem with that employee.

- Sonja Friedman learned that citizens calling her housing department complained of spending an excessive amount of time on hold. She scheduled a meeting at which the employees discussed ways they could handle calls faster.

As shown in these examples, supervisors need to know what is going on in the area they supervise. Do employees understand what they are supposed to do, and can they do it? Is all machinery and equipment (whether a computer-operated milling machine or a cell phone) operating properly? Is work getting out correctly and on time?

To answer such questions, a supervisor could theoretically sit back and wait for disaster to strike. No disaster, no need for correction. More realistically, the supervisor has a responsibility to correct problems as soon as possible, which means that some way to *detect* problems quickly must be found. Detection of problems is at the heart of the control function.

By controlling, the supervisor can take steps to ensure quality and manage costs. Visiting the work area and checking up on performance, as Maria Lopez did, allows the supervisor to make sure that employees are producing satisfactory work. By setting standards for a clean workplace, Bud Cavanaugh reduced costs related to spending time looking for tools or to slipping on a messy floor. Sonja Friedman engaged her employees to improve work processes. In many such ways, supervisors can benefit the organization through the process of control.

LO6.6 ▶ Identify the steps in the control process.

standards
Measures of what is expected

The Process of Controlling

Although the specific ways in which supervisors control vary according to the type of organization and the employees being supervised, the basic process involves three steps. First, the supervisor establishes performance **standards,** which are measures of what is expected. Then the supervisor monitors actual performance and compares it with the standards. Finally, the supervisor responds, either by reinforcing success or by making some adjustment to bring performance and the standards into line. Figure 6.7 illustrates this process.

If the control system is working properly, the supervisor should be uncovering problems before customers and management discover them. This gives the supervisor the best opportunity to fix a problem in time to minimize damage.

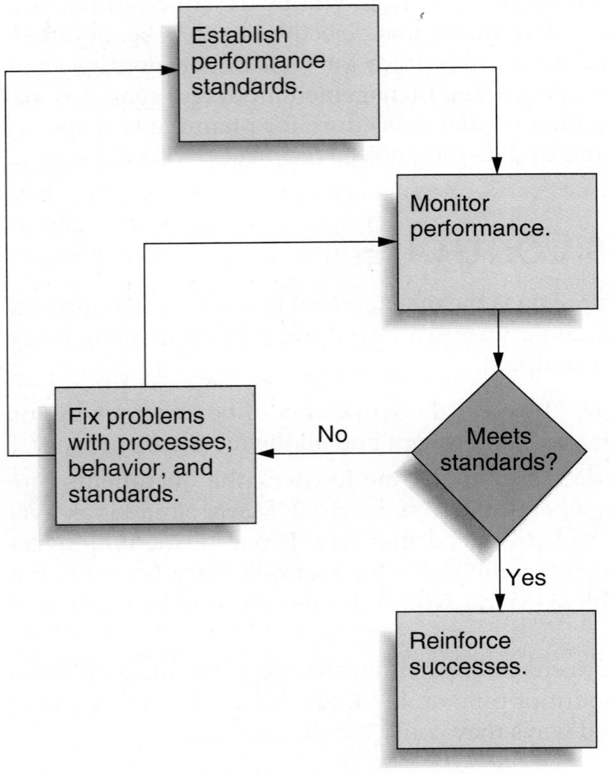

Establish Performance Standards

Performance standards are a natural outgrowth of the planning process. Once the supervisor knows the objectives employees are to achieve, he or she can determine what employees must do to meet those objectives. Assume that the objective of an eight-person telephone sales (telemarketing) office is to make 320 calls in a four-hour evening shift, resulting in 64 sales. To achieve this objective, each salesperson should average 10 calls an hour, with 2 in 10 calls resulting in a sale. Those numbers could be two of the office's performance standards.

Standards define the acceptable quantity and quality of work. (The measure of quantity in the example above is the number of telephone calls made; the number of sales measures the quality of selling, for example, turning a telephone call into a sale.) Other standards can spell out expectations for level of service, amount of money spent, amount of inventory on hand, level of pollution in the workplace, and other concerns. Ultimately, all these standards measure how well the department contributes to meeting the organization's objectives to serve its customers and—for a business—earn a profit.

The way supervisors set standards depends on their experience, their employer's expectations, and the nature of the work being monitored. Often, supervisors

FIGURE 6.7 | The Control Process

A proactive supervisor, with an efficient control system in place, can often catch and fix problems before they become costly, significant issues.

use their technical expertise to estimate reasonable standards. Past performance also is a useful guide for what can be expected. However, the supervisor must avoid being a slave to the past. In creating a budget, some supervisors assume that because they have spent a given sum in a given category in the past, that expense will be appropriate in the future. Sometimes there are better alternatives. Supervisors may have additional sources of information in setting performance standards. Equipment manufacturers and systems designers can provide information about how fast a machine or computer system will perform. Some companies arrange for time-and-motion studies to analyze how quickly and efficiently employees can reasonably work.

To be effective, performance standards should meet the criteria of effective objectives; that is, they should be written, measurable, clear, specific, and challenging but achievable. Standards also should measure dimensions of the goods or services that customers care about and that support the company's strategy. A sense of desperation evidently overwhelmed strategy at one financial-services company soon after the banking crisis. In a drive to cut costs, the institution gave its departments strict goals for expense reduction. The supervisor of the supply department decided to slash spending by declaring that no new orders would be accepted for three months. That made the department's goals achievable, but it created a serious dilemma for any other department if it ran out of paper or ink cartridges. The company's managers eventually figured out that they could get around the problem by trading supplies with one another—spending hundreds of dollars to ship office supplies between branches. The supply department met its budget goals, but the institution wasted a lot of money as a result.[12]

Not only should the supervisor have standards in mind, but the employees should also be aware of and understand those standards. In communicating performance standards, the supervisor should put them in writing so that employees can remember and refer to them as necessary. (Chapter 10 provides more detailed suggestions for communicating effectively.)

The supervisor should also be sure that the employees understand the rationale for the standards. It is human nature to resist when someone lays down restrictive rules, but the rules seem less a burden when they serve a purpose we can understand. Thus, if a law office's word-processing department has a standard to produce error-free documents, the department's supervisor can explain that it is part of the firm's plan to build a prestigious clientele by delivering an excellent product. With such an explanation, the word processors are less likely to feel overwhelmed by the stringent quality standard and more likely to feel proud that they are part of an excellent law firm.

Monitor Performance and Compare with Standards

Once performance standards are in place, the supervisor can begin the core of the control process: monitoring performance. In the example of the telephone sales force, the supervisor would want to keep track of how many calls each salesperson made and how many of those calls resulted in sales.

One way to monitor performance is simply to record information on paper or enter it into a computer, a task that can be done by the supervisor, the employees, or both. The telephone salespeople in the example might provide the supervisor with information to enter into a log such as the one shown in Table 6.3 on the following page. Some types of machinery and equipment have electronic or mechanical counting systems that provide an unbiased way to measure performance. For instance, the electronic scanners at store checkout stations can track how fast cashiers are ringing up merchandise.

A growing number of firms use forms of electronic monitoring to keep tabs on employees' performance. Some use software that tracks employees' use of

TABLE 6.3 | Sample Performance Record

Week of <u>November 12, 2012</u>
Performance Standard: <u>40</u> calls, <u>8</u> sales

Name	Number of Calls Completed	Number of Sales Made	Action
Forrest	32	6	Discuss slow pace of work.
French	41	8	Praise performance.
Johnson	39	7	None.
Munoz	47	9	Praise performance.
Peterson	38	8	Praise performance.
Spagnoli	50	7	Praise hard work; discuss how to turn more calls into sales.
Steinmetz	29	5	Discuss poor performance; discipline if necessary.
Wang	43	9	Praise performance.
Total	**319**	**59**	

the Internet. Others record the phone calls of customer service representatives. Electronic monitoring can be important for supervising employees who "telecommute," working from home or other locations away from the supervisor. Supervisors often worry about how to control the work of someone they cannot watch, so they may welcome the detailed information about employees' activities. However, it is also important to consider other ways of supervising remote workers. Supervisors need to focus on results more than activities, asking "What did you accomplish today?" rather than "What did you do today?" Supervisors of telecommuters also need superior listening skills so they can become aware of employees' concerns and problems expressed over the telephone, between the lines in e-mail, or even indirectly in the quality and type of work delivered.[13]

Of course, the monitoring must be efficient and accurate. In addition to using electronic monitoring, supervisors can get accurate information by observing workers directly. The supervisor's physical presence signals that the supervisor is interested in employees and what they are doing, and it makes the supervisor available to answer questions and help solve problems. An active supervisor not only checks on workers and ensures that they are meeting goals but also takes on many other roles, including teacher, safety officer, and advocate for employees.[14]

From a quality perspective, monitoring performance should include assessing whether customers are satisfied. In the case of groups that provide services to other employees in the organization, supervisors should ask those "internal customers" whether they are getting what they need when they need it. At Bristol-Myers Squibb Company, regular surveys ask whether employees are satisfied with in-house services such as housekeeping, grounds crews, and employee dining. The giant pharmaceutical company recently set up a team to improve the surveys so that they would use measures that are "actionable," meaning the department providing the services can use the results to identify types of changes that are needed.

For example, the survey about dining facilities used to ask for an overall rating, but an overall rating of "fair" or "excellent" doesn't suggest areas for improvement. The new surveys ask questions such as "Are the menu choices currently being offered meeting your dietary needs?"[15]

When monitoring performance, the supervisor should focus on how actual performance compares with the standards he or she has set. Are employees meeting standards, exceeding them, or falling short? Two concepts useful for maintaining this focus are variance and the exception principle.

variance
The size of the difference between actual performance and a performance standard

In a control system, variance refers to the size of the difference between actual performance and the standard to be met. When setting standards, the supervisor should decide how much variance is meaningful for control purposes. It can be helpful to think in terms of percentages. For example, if a hospital's performance standard is to register outpatients for lab tests in 10 minutes or fewer, the supervisor might decide to allow for a variance of 50 percent (five minutes). (In a manufacturing setting, a variance of 5 to 10 percent might be more appropriate for most standards.) As described in Chapter 2, some organizations strive for a standard of accepting zero defects.

exception principle
The control principle stating that a supervisor should take action only when variance is meaningful

According to the exception principle, the supervisor should take action only when the variance is meaningful. Thus, when monitoring performance in the previous example, the supervisor would need to take action only if outpatients spent more than 15 or fewer than 5 minutes registering for lab tests.

The exception principle is beneficial when it helps the supervisor manage his or her time wisely and motivate employees. A supervisor who did not tolerate reasonable variances might try to solve the "problem" every time an employee made one component too few or went over the budget for office supplies by the cost of a box of paper clips. In such a case, employees might become frustrated by the control system, and morale would deteriorate. At the same time, the supervisor would be too busy with trifles to focus on more significant issues.

Reinforce Successes and Fix Problems

The information gained from the control process is beneficial only if the supervisor uses it as the basis for reinforcing or changing behavior. If performance is satisfactory or better, the supervisor needs to encourage it. If performance is unacceptable, the supervisor needs to make changes that either improve performance or adjust the standard. The right-hand column in Table 6.3 lists some ways the telemarketing supervisor plans to respond to performance data.

reinforcement
Encouragement of a behavior by associating it with a reward

positive reinforcement
Presentation of something pleasant after a desired behavior has occurred

When employees are doing excellent work, customers are happy, and costs are within budget, the supervisor needs to reinforce these successes. Reinforcement means encouraging the behavior by associating it with a reward. In general, there are two types of reinforcement. Positive reinforcement involves the presentation of something pleasant after a desired behavior has occurred. An example of positive reinforcement in the workplace is verbal praise for a job well done. Praise from the supervisor for performance that meets standards not only gives the employee a good feeling but also clarifies what is expected. For exceptionally high performance, the supervisor also may reward the employee with a monetary bonus. The supervisor's actions will depend on company and union rules regarding superior performance.

negative reinforcement
Removal of something unpleasant after a desired behavior has occurred

The second type of reinforcement, negative reinforcement, involves the removal of something unpleasant after a desired behavior has occurred. For example, a supervisor might coach customer service employees on how to calm customers who are upset. As employees see that applying the supervisor's ideas puts an end to unpleasant customer behaviors such as shouting and complaining, the employees will feel reinforced to use those techniques more often.

Chapter 11 provides more background about reinforcement and other ideas for motivating employees.

When performance significantly falls short of standards, the supervisor should investigate. Below-standard performance is the sign of a problem—some factor in the organization that is a barrier to improvement. The supervisor's task is to identify the underlying problem. For example, if the supervisor in the telephone sales company learns that the group is not meeting its sales objectives, the supervisor could find out who is falling short of the sales goals: everyone or only one or two employees. If everyone is performing below standard, the problem may be that the sales force needs better training or motivation. Or the problem may lie outside the supervisor's direct control; the product may be defective or customers may lack interest for some other reason, such as poor economic conditions. If only one employee is failing to make sales, the supervisor needs to search for the problem underlying that employee's poor performance. Does the employee understand how to close a sale? Does the employee have personal problems that affect performance?

Poor performance itself is rarely a problem, but a symptom—an indication of an underlying problem. To use the information gained through controlling effectively, the supervisor needs to distinguish problems from symptoms. To see how this effort applies to one common situation, employee scheduling, see "Practical Advice for Supervisors." In the example of the Bristol-Myers Squibb survey described previously, the facilities department was surprised to learn that employees were dissatisfied with the menu variety offered in company cafeterias. The apparent problem was that menus had too few items. But before squeezing more offerings into the dining facilities, Ann McNally, the team leader responsible for the surveys, assembled a group of employees to talk about the problem. The employees in these groups described their busy days. When they

problem
A factor in the organization that is a barrier to improvement

symptom
An indication of an underlying problem

PRACTICAL ADVICE FOR SUPERVISORS

AVOIDING EXCESSIVE OVERTIME

The cost of overtime to a corporation can be significant. When employees who are paid on an hourly basis work overtime, they typically earn one and a half or two times their hourly wage. While occasionally working overtime to finish up an emergency or rush project may be an important way to keep customers happy, if workers are frequently putting in overtime hours, the extra expense is a symptom of an underlying problem. It is the supervisors job to investigate and determine where the problem lies and to develop solutions that reduce excessive overtime.

The supervisor should look for a pattern in the overtime hours. Are employees regularly working longer during certain peak periods? If so, it may be possible to schedule more employees for these times of heavy work. Or, it may be possible to get more done during slow times so that employees do not have to work longer when the demand picks up. Perhaps break times can be staggered so that work keeps flowing throughout the day.

Another possibility is that certain employees are the ones who consistently need to work overtime to complete their job responsibilities. In that case, the problem may be that assignments are not being divided appropriately among the employees so that each has an amount of work that can be accomplished during the workday or workweek. Or perhaps the work is divided appropriately but some employees need coaching, training, or better access to resources so that they can work efficiently. Defining this problem may require one-on-one meetings with employees, as well as careful observation of how they handle their jobs. Employees themselves may be able to suggest what needs to change.

By determining the underlying problem (or problems) that are leading to excessive overtime hours, a supervisor can take measures to reduce these hours. Reducing excessive overtime hours reduces company costs as well as leads to happier, more productive employees who are not consistently overworked.

Source: Based on Jack W. Reidenbach, "Overtime Overhaul: Questioning Leadership Planning," *Supervision*, September 2008, downloaded from Business & Company Resource Center, http://galenet.galegroup.com.

headed for the café to grab lunch, they did not study all the menu choices but just grabbed whatever they usually bought. The team determined that the complaint about menu variety was really a symptom of a communication and time problem. Employees needed to be able to see their alternatives at a quick glance. The department worked with its supplier of dining services to display alternatives differently and post menus online for employees to check ahead of time at their convenience. Adding more choices to the menu would have increased the company's costs without solving the real problem.[16]

Sometimes a problem underlying significant variance is that the standard is too low or too high. For example, if no employees on the telephone sales force are achieving the desired number of sales, the standards may be too high, given current economic or market conditions. In other cases, what the manager learns about performance may indicate that a standard is not measuring the right thing.

Fixing the problem may entail adjusting a process, the behavior of an individual employee, or the standard itself, as illustrated in Figure 6.8. For process and behavioral problems, supervisors can choose from among a number of possible actions:

- Develop new rewards for good performance.
- Train employees.
- Improve communications with employees.
- Counsel and/or discipline poor performers.
- Ask employees what barriers are interfering with their performance, then remove those barriers. (Common barriers include insufficient supplies or information, poorly maintained equipment, and inefficient work procedures.)

The best response to problems related to standards is to make the performance standard more appropriate. The supervisor may need to make the standard less stringent or more challenging.

Whatever actions the supervisor selects, it is important to give employees feedback soon after observing a deviation from the standard. This enables the employees to make changes before performance deteriorates further. A problem that has been allowed to continue is often harder to correct. For example, an employee may get into the habit of doing a task the wrong way or fall so far behind that it is impossible to catch up.

Modifying standards brings the control process full circle. With new standards in place, the supervisor is again ready to monitor performance.

FIGURE 6.8 | Tools for Fixing Performance Problems

There are several alternatives for supervisors when performance variances are detected.

Adjust Processes

Make processes simpler, more efficient, or more flexible.

Improve Behavior

Offer new rewards, better training, or clearer directions.

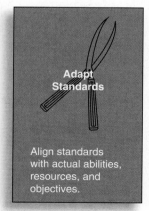
Adapt Standards

Align standards with actual abilities, resources, and objectives.

LO6.7 ▶ Describe types of control and tools for controlling.

feedback control
Control that focuses on past performance

concurrent control
Control that occurs while the work takes place

precontrol
Efforts aimed at preventing behavior that may lead to undesirable results

Types of Control

From the description of the control process, it might sound as though controlling begins when employees' work is complete: The employees finish their jobs, then the supervisor checks whether a job was done well. However, this is only one type of controlling. There are three types of control in terms of when it occurs: feedback control, concurrent control, and precontrol.

Feedback control is the type just described, that is, control that focuses on past performance. A supervisor reviewing customer comments about service is practicing feedback control. The customers provide information about the quality of service; the supervisor reacts by reinforcing or trying to change employee behavior.

The word *concurrent* describes things that are happening at the same time. Thus, concurrent control refers to controlling work while that work is being done. A restaurant manager who greets customers at their tables and visits the kitchen to see how work is progressing is practicing concurrent control. This supervisor is gathering information about what is going smoothly and what problems may be developing. The supervisor can act on any problems before customers or employees become upset. Another technique for concurrent control is statistical process control, described in Chapter 2.

Precontrol refers to efforts aimed at preventing behavior that may lead to undesirable results. Such efforts may include setting rules, policies, and procedures. A production supervisor might provide employees with guidelines about the detection of improperly functioning machinery. The employees can then request repairs before they waste time and materials on the machinery. Precontrol is one of the functions of the management philosophy known as total quality management (see Chapter 2).

Tools for Control

When considering how to monitor performance, the supervisor can start with some basic tools used by most managers. Gantt charts, discussed earlier in this chapter are an invaluable tool with which supervisors can closely monitor and control the progress and performance of a project. In addition, budgets and reports are common in most organizations. Finally, supervisors can benefit from personally observing the work.

Budgets

Creating a budget—a plan for spending money—is part of the planning process. In controlling, a budget is useful as a kind of performance standard. The supervisor compares actual expenses with the amounts in the budget.

Table 6.4, on the following page, is a sample budget report based on the example in Table 6.2. The first column shows each category of expenses for the machine shop project, which was scheduled to last for six months, from January through June. Thus, the six-month budget represents the total the supervisor expected to spend in each category for the project. This report was prepared on March 31 (halfway through the project), so one column shows what would be budgeted for half of the project. The adjacent column shows the amounts that actually were spent during the first three months. In the right-hand column appears the variance between the actual and budgeted amounts. In this case, the machine shop has a negative total variance because the project is $679 over budget for the first three months.

When using such a budget report for controlling purposes, the supervisor focuses on the variance column, looking for meaningful variances. In Table 6.4, the supervisor would note that the total unfavorable variance is due entirely to a large expense for equipment repair. The machine shop is otherwise under budget or exactly meeting the budget standards. Following the exception principle, the supervisor takes action when meaningful variance occurs. Typically, this involves

TABLE 6.4 | Budget
Report for a
Manufacturing Project

| Organizational Unit | Machine Shop | Job Number | 1763 | Date | March 31, 2012 |

Line Item	Six-Month Budget	Budgeted Year to Date (Jan.–Mar.)	Actual Year to Date (Jan.–Mar.)	Variance
Direct labor	$60,000	$30,000	$30,000	$0
Indirect labor	5,400	2,700	2,700	0
Material	13,200	6,600	6,383	217
Operating supplies	3,000	1,500	1,496	4
Equipment repair	5,400	2,700	3,600	–900
Total	**$87,000**	**$43,500**	**$44,179**	**–$679**

Source: Adapted from *Industrial Supervision: In The Age of Technology,* by David L. Goetsch. Copyright © 1992 Pearson Education, Inc. Reprinted by permission of Pearson Education, Inc., Upper Saddle River, NJ.

looking for ways to cut costs when the department goes over budget. The supervisor in the example will want to focus on avoiding further equipment breakdowns. Sometimes the supervisor can change the budget when a variance indicates that the budgeted figures were unrealistic.

Performance Reports

performance report
A summary of performance
and comparison with
performance standards

A well-structured report can be an important source of information. A **performance report** summarizes performance and compares it with performance standards. These reports can simply summarize facts, such as the number of calls made by sales representatives or the number of deliveries completed by delivery personnel, or they can be analytical; that is, they may interpret the facts.[17]

Most supervisors both prepare and request performance reports. Typically, the organization requires that the supervisor do a particular type of reporting of the department's performance. The supervisor's role is to prepare this report. Supervisors also may request that employees prepare reports for them. In that case, the supervisor can influence the type of reporting.

Consider the reporting needs at a company that sells electrical supplies to businesses. Warehouse supervisors would create reports about inventory levels and volume of orders filled each day or week. Sales supervisors would track the quantities and dollar volume of sales for each associate. Accounting supervisors would report on the amounts billed to and received from customers. Nowadays, many companies have computer software that collects the data from all parts of the organization, so managers can keep track of how the various units work together to meet goals such as fast order fulfillment and progress toward quarterly profits. For example, in Toms River, New Jersey, Good Friend Electric Supply uses an enterprise resource planning (ERP) system that processes order, inventory, shipping, and other data and flags problems so quickly that they can be solved even before a customer realizes something went wrong.[18]

When supervisors prepare or contribute data to performance reports, they should highlight and explain any variances from standards. Such explanations help with planning and problem solving. Useful reports clarify rather than conceal problems. Hiding performance problems can make it difficult for supervisors to convince managers that the group needs more resources or training.

As much as possible, supervisors should see that reports are simple and to the point. A table or log may be more useful than an essay-style report. Graphs can sometimes uncover a trend better than numbers in columns. Figure 6.9 shows how the

FIGURE 6.9 | Graph of Variances Determined from Table 6.3

Data from tables can be converted to graphs and charts that allow reports to be more quickly and easily understood.

Calls Completed—Variances from a Standard of 40

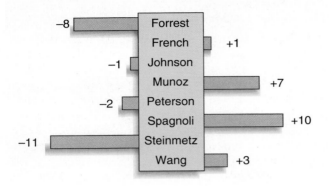

Sales Made—Variances from a Standard of 8

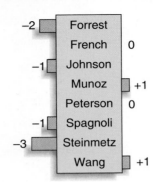

data from Table 6.3 (on page 158) can be converted into a graph. In this case, variances were first computed for the difference between each employee's performance and the performance standards. Notice how easy it is to tell from the graph the wide variation in the number of calls made by each employee. Does this mean some employees are working harder than others? Maybe, but remember the process of searching for a problem. It is also possible that some employees are better at keeping calls short and to the point.

Perhaps even more important is the supervisor's role in creating a climate that fosters full and accurate reporting. Supervisors can shape a favorable climate by actively seeking ideas from employees and being willing to listen to reports that something may be wrong.

The supervisor also should determine whether every report he or she is receiving is still useful. Many reports continue to be generated long after they have lost their usefulness. In deciding whether to continue using a report, the supervisor can consider whether it has the characteristics of effective controls, described at the end of this chapter.

Personal Observation

A supervisor who spends the entire day behind a desk reading budgets and reports is out of touch. An important part of controlling involves spending time with employees and observing what is going on. Management consultant Tom Peters has popularized this approach, which he calls "management by walking around." While engaged in this approach, the supervisor can listen to employees, help them discover better ways of doing their jobs, and make the changes necessary to help employees carry them out. For example, a nursing supervisor might observe that the nurses frequently spend time debating which demands to respond to first. The supervisor could discuss this with the nurses and help them develop criteria for setting priorities.

Personal observation can help the supervisor understand the activities behind the numbers in reports. However, the supervisor must be careful in interpreting what he or she sees. Often the presence of a supervisor causes workers to alter their behavior. Also, the supervisor must visit work areas often enough to be sure of witnessing routine situations, not just an unusual crisis or break in the action. At the same time, the supervisor must not spend so much time among employees that they feel the visits interfere with their work. How much time is the right amount to spend in management by walking around? The supervisor probably will have to rely on trial and error, weighing employee reactions and the amount of information obtained.

The inability to control through personal observation is a challenge of supervising employees who work at home. This issue is growing in importance as communications

The most successful telecommuters tend to be those who are highly motivated and communicative.

technology makes telecommuting possible for people with disabilities, working parents, and others who prefer to live further from urban centers or to not spend time commuting to an office. How can a supervisor make sure employees are not devoting their time to raiding the refrigerator and catching up on the latest soap operas? Freelance service provider oDesk.com addresses these concerns with the contractors in its network by using technology to keep tabs on workers. For example, monitoring systems can do random checks of what is on the telecommuting employee's computer screen, count how many keystrokes a worker has typed during a given period, and even take photos of the worker at the computer. However, employers are more often uncomfortable with that level of monitoring and prefer to rely on careful selection of telecommuters who work well independently. Tangela Hamilton, a supervisor for Working Solutions, considers her employees to be highly motivated and is mainly concerned about keeping the lines of communication open through e-mail, instant messaging, and voice mail so that she can resolve difficulties as soon as they arise.[19]

LO6.8 ▶ List characteristics of effective controls.

Characteristics of Effective Controls

No supervisor can keep track of every detail of every employee's work. An effective control system is one that helps the supervisor direct his or her efforts toward spotting significant problems. Normally, a supervisor has to use whatever control system higher-level managers have established. However, when making recommendations about controls or setting up controls to use within the department, the supervisor can strive for the following characteristics of effective controls: timeliness, cost effectiveness, acceptability, and flexibility.

Timeliness

The controls should be *timely,* enabling the supervisor to correct problems quickly enough to improve results. For example, an annual budget report does not let the supervisor adjust spending in time to meet the budget's goals. In contrast, monthly budget reports give the supervisor time to identify spending patterns that will pose a problem. If the supervisor's annual budget includes $500 to spend on overnight couriers but the department has already spent $200 by the end of February, the supervisor knows that work must be planned far enough ahead that materials can be sent by other, less expensive means.

Cost Effectiveness

The controls should be *economical.* In general, this means that the cost of using the controls should be less than the benefit derived from using them. In a supermarket, for example, an elaborate system designed to ensure that not a single item of inventory gets lost or stolen may not save the store enough money to justify the cost of the system.

Acceptability

The controls should be *acceptable to supervisors and employees.* Supervisors want controls that give them enough information about performance that they can understand what is going on in the workplace. Employees want controls that do not unduly infringe on their privacy. One area of controversy has been electronic monitoring of employee performance. For example, computers can track how many telephone calls operators handle and how much time they spend on each call. Electronic monitoring gives the supervisor a lot of information, including how much time operators spend going to the bathroom. Does this scrutiny enhance performance by encouraging employees to work hard, or does it merely lower morale and remove the incentive to take time to greet customers in a friendly way? The answer lies partly in the way supervisors use this information.

Employees also appreciate controls that focus on areas over which they themselves have some control. For example, a control that measures the number of units produced by an employee would be acceptable only if the employee always has the parts needed to produce those units. An employee whose performance looks poor because of an inventory shortage would feel frustrated by the control.

Flexibility

Finally, the controls should be *flexible.* This means the supervisor should be able to ignore variance if doing so is in the best interests of the organization. For example, in comparing expenditures to a budget, a supervisor should be aware of occasions when spending a little more than was budgeted actually will benefit the company. That might be the case when employees have to put in overtime to fill an order for an important customer. In the future, better planning might make it possible to avoid the overtime, but the immediate goal is to satisfy the customer.

One reason flexibility is important is that performance measures might be incompatible. For instance, employees may find it impossible to cut costs and improve quality at the same time. In that case, the supervisor may have to set priorities or adjust the control measures. Such actions are a type of planning, an example of how controlling and planning work together to help the organization reach its goals.

Skills Module

PART ONE: CONCEPTS

Summary

6.1 Describe types of planning that take place in organizations.

At the top level of an organization, managers engage in strategic planning, which is the creation of long-term goals for the organization. The plans for divisions, departments, and work groups are known as operational plans and are set by middle managers and supervisors. Operational plans support the strategic plan; they are more specific and focus on a shorter time frame. Supervisors also must apply good planning practices to their individual efforts.

6.2 Identify characteristics of effective objectives.

Effective objectives are written, measurable or observable, clear, specific, and challenging but achievable.

6.3 Define *management by objectives (MBO)* and discuss its use.

Management by objectives is a process in which managers and employees at all levels set objectives for what they are to accomplish, after which their performance is measured against those objectives. In MBO, all individuals in the organization work to set objectives, each employee's manager periodically reviews the employee's performance against the objectives, and the organization rewards individuals on the basis of how close they come to fulfilling the objectives. To use MBO effectively, managers at all levels of an organization must be committed to the system.

6.4 Discuss the supervisor's role in the planning process.

Supervisors are responsible for the creation of plans that specify goals, tasks, resources, and responsibilities for their own departments. Supervisors keep higher-level managers informed about the needs, abilities, and progress of their groups. They decide how to allocate resources to the jobs that need to be done, including creating budgets. Supervisors also engage in scheduling, using tools such as Gantt charts and PERT. When possible, they should involve employees in the planning process.

6.5 Explain the purpose of using controls.

By identifying problems in time for them to be corrected, controlling enables supervisors to ensure high-quality work and keep costs under control.

6.6 Identify the steps in the control process.

First, the supervisor sets and communicates performance standards in writing. The supervisor then monitors performance and compares it with the standards. Depending on whether performance is above, at, or below the standards, the supervisor reinforces successes or fixes problems. Fixing a problem may entail adjusting a process, the behavior of an employee, or the standard itself.

6.7 Describe types of control and tools for controlling.

Feedback control focuses on past performance. Concurrent control occurs while the work is taking place. Precontrol is aimed at preventing behavior that may lead to undesirable results. Gantt charts, budgets, performance reports, and personal observation are all tools for controlling.

6.8 List characteristics of effective controls.

Effective controls are timely, economical, acceptable to both supervisor and employee, and flexible.

Key Terms

planning, *p.* 142
objectives, *p.* 142
goals, *p.* 142
strategic planning, *p.* 143
operational planning, *p.* 143
policies, *p.* 145
procedures, *p.* 145
rules, *p.* 146
action plan, *p.* 146
contingency planning, *p.* 147

management by objectives (MBO), *p.* 147
budget, *p.* 150
scheduling, *p.* 152
Gantt chart, *p.* 152
program evaluation and review technique (PERT), *p.* 152
controlling, *p.* 155
standards, *p.* 156
variance, *p.* 159

exception principle, *p.* 159
reinforcement, *p.* 159
positive reinforcement, *p.* 159
negative reinforcement, *p.* 159
problem, *p.* 160
symptom, *p.* 160
feedback control, *p.* 162
concurrent control, *p.* 162
precontrol, *p.* 162
performance report, *p.* 163

Review and Discussion Questions

1. Why is it important for supervisors and other managers to plan?

2. Define policies, procedures, and goals. How does each relate to an organization's objectives?

3. Jill Donahue is the supervisor of the telephone operators who handle emergency calls from citizens and dispatch police, firefighters, and ambulances. One of her objectives for the coming year is to reduce the average time it takes for calls to be answered from 1 minute to 30 seconds. How can Jill create an action plan to achieve this objective? What questions must she answer? Suggest a possible answer for each question.

4. Assume you are the supervisor of the machine shop whose budget appears in Table 6.2.

   a. Modify the budgeted amounts to create a budget for a new project of the same size and type. Use the following assumptions and guidelines:

   - The organization says that direct labor costs may increase by no more than 6 percent.
   - You have been instructed to cut expenses for equipment repair by 10 percent.
   - You expect that materials costs will increase about 5 percent.

   b. What additional assumptions did you make to create the budget?

5. What is wrong with each of the following objectives? Rewrite each so that it has the characteristics of an effective objective.

   a. Improve the procedure for responding to customer complaints.

   b. Meet or exceed last year's sales quotas.

   c. Minimize the number of parts that are defective.

   d. Communicate clearly with patients.

6. What are some advantages of involving employees in the process of developing objectives? How can supervisors do this?

7. Your best friend just got promoted to a position as a supervisor and feels uncomfortable about "checking up on people." How can you explain to your friend why controlling plays an important role in helping the organization meet its goals?

8. What are the steps in the process of controlling?

9. How is the control process related to the management function of planning?

10. Bonnie Goode supervises the online support staff in the customer service department of a software company. The employees are expected to handle 50 phone requests for help per day (250 in a five-day work week). Every Monday, Goode receives a report of each employee's weekly performance relative to this standard. Her most recent report contained the following information

a. As supervisor, how should Goode respond to each employee's performance?

b. Is this control system an effective one for ensuring quality performance? Explain.

11. If failure to meet a performance standard indicates some type of underlying problem, how might the supervisor attempt to solve the problem?

12. Mildred Pirelli supervises salespeople in a department store. One day she walked around her department to observe the salespeople in action. She saw a salesperson approve a charge card purchase without following the company's policy of verifying the signature on the card.

a. How should Pirelli respond to this variance from company policy?

b. Should the way Pirelli obtained the information (personal observation) influence her choice of how to act? Explain.

13. Why do controls need to be timely and economical?

Employee	Mon.	Tues.	Wed.	Thurs.	Fri.	Total	Variance
Brown	10	28	39	42	16	135	−115
Lee	48	51	58	43	49	249	−1
Mendoza	65	72	56	83	61	337	87
Smith	53	48	47	40	45	233	−17

Notes

1. Jonathan Katz, "Snuffing Out Scrap," *Industry Week*, May 26, 2006, http://www.industryweek.com/quality/snuffing-out-scrap, accessed April 15, 2014.

2. For more information about strategic planning, see John Rudd, Gordon Greenley, Amanda Beatson, and Ian Lings, February 2008, "Strategic planning and performance: Extending the debate," *Journal of Business Research*, 61 (2), pp. 99–108.

3. Alan Murray, "Chemical Reaction," *The Wall Street Journal*, March 7, 2011, http://online.wsj.com (interview of Ellen Kullman); DuPont, "Our Company," http://www.dupont.com/corporate-functions/our-company.html, accessed April 15, 2014.

4. For an example of an operational plan, see Ajay Selot, Loi Kwong Kuok, Mark Robinson, Thomas Mason, and Paul Barton, January 2008, "A short-term operational planning model for natural gas production systems," *American Institute of Chemical Engineers Journal*, 54 (2), pp. 495–515.

5. Richard A. Mueller, "Fireball! Part Two: Defining a Win, Tie and Loss to Track Fire Service Quality," *Firehouse Magazine*, October 2008, downloaded from Business & Company Resource Center, http://galenet.galegroup.com.

6. To see a specific action plan related to leadership, see Anna Valerio, November/December 2006, "An Action Plan for Developing Women Leaders," *Leadership in Action*, 26 (5), p. 16, http://www.executiveleadershipstrategies.com/docs/Women-Leaders.pdf.

7. Don Kuzma, "Don't Plan for Repair—Plan for Maintenance," *Material Handling and Logistics*, May 2011, pp. 28–31, http://mhlnews.com/distribution/dont-plan-for-repair-plan-for-maintenance-0501, accessed April 15, 2014.

8. For a review of the MBO approach, see Conny Antoni, February 17, 2005, "Management by objectives: An effective tool for teamwork?", *The International Journal of Human Resource Management*, 16 (2), pp. 174–184.

9. Howard Newens, "The Fifth Dimension of Management: Make It Personal," *Government Finance Review*, October 2008, downloaded from Business & Company Resource Center, http://galenet.galegroup.com.

10 American Airlines, "Maintenance and Engineering Overview," http://www.aa.com/i18n/amrcorp/newsroom/maintenance-engineering.jsp, accessed April 15, 2014.

11. Mark Skertic, "American Airlines Gets into Maintenance Line," *Chicago Tribune*, June 25, 2006, sec. 5, pp. 1, 14, http://articles.chicagotribune.com/2006-06-25/business/0606250238_1_american-airlines-heavy-maintenance-maintenance-base, accessed April 15, 2014.

12. Tom Rieger, "Beware of Parochial Managers," *Gallup Business Journal*, May 26, 2011, http://businessjournal.gallup.com/content/147653/beware-parochial-managers.aspx, accessed April 15, 2014.

13. Jennifer Taylor Arnold, "Making the Leap," *HRMagazine*, May 2006, 51(5), http://www.shrm.org/Publications/hrmagazine/EditorialContent/Pages/0506SRarnold.aspx, accessed April 15, 2014.

14. Joel Levitt, "Active Supervision: Improve Shop Efficiency by 15 Percent," *Fleet Maintenance*, August 2005, downloaded from Business & Company Resource Center, http://galenet.galegroup.com.

15. "Taking the Guesswork out of Customer Satisfaction," *Food Management*, January 2006, http://food-management.com/business-amp-industry/taking-guesswork-out-customer-satisfaction, accessed April 15, 2014.

16. Ibid.

17. For a review of governmental performance, see Jerry Ellig, 2007, "Scoring government performance reports," *The Public Manager*, 36 (2), pp. 3–8, http://www.feiaa.org/files/File/TPM_v36_n2.pdf, accessed April 15, 2014.

18. Beth Badrakhan, "Data-Driven Quality," *Electrical Wholesaling*, February 2010, pp. 32, 35–36, http://ewweb.com/e-biz/data-driven-quality, accessed April 15, 2014.

19. Sue Shellenbarger, "Work at Home? Your Employer May Be Watching," *The Wall Street Journal*, July 31, 2008, http://online.wsj.com/news/articles/SB121737022605394845; and Christopher Musico, "There's No Place Like Home," *CRM Magazine*, October 2008, http://www.destinationcrm.com/Articles/Editorial/Magazine-Features/Theres-No-Place-Like-Home-50749.aspx, accessed April 15, 2014.

PART TWO: SKILL-BUILDING

Meeting the Challenge

Reflecting back on page 141, discuss Meijer's goals for cashiers and its system for monitoring their performance. Perhaps drawing on group members' own job experience, consider how supervisors and employees would react to such a system. Do the goals focus on the most important measures of success? How do you think employees would react to the system?

Assign one person in your group the role of a supervisor at a Meijer's store and one person the role of a cashier who is worried about his or her performance. Have them role-play a meeting to discuss how the cashier might improve.

After the role-play, discuss which goals the supervisor was focused on and which the employee was focused on. How will the supervisor's efforts to control performance affect the store's costs and the level of service received by its customers?

Problem-Solving Case: MBO Clarifies Objectives at Edward Don & Company

At Edward Don & Company, a distributor of supplies and equipment for the food service industry, employees in the credit department know what they are supposed to achieve. The reason is that the company's corporate credit manager, Jeff Ingalls, set up a management by objectives (MBO) program.

Ingalls meets with each staff member once a year to evaluate how well he or she met the previous year's objectives and set objectives for the coming year. He and the employee set five to seven objectives for the year. They may change the next year's goals based on past performance or new technology that will affect performance. Every three to six months, Ingalls meets again with employees to discuss whether they are making progress toward their goals. Even when employees can meet their objectives without Ingalls's help, meeting with them reminds the department that the objectives are important.

Objectives for credit department employees include quality, efficiency, and professional development. For example, the objectives for a credit analyst might involve keeping bad debt low relative to total loans made, approving at least a minimum number of new accounts, and learning computer skills. For collectors, objectives might include achieving a given increase in the percentage of accounts that are current (payments up-to-date), reducing the percentage for which payments are 90 days past due, and learning a new skill.

When an employee is failing to meet an objective, Ingalls and the employee discuss the problem and look for a way to resolve it. For example, an accounts receivable supervisor was having trouble with a goal that involved the accuracy with which the supervisor's employees recorded information. In an average month, the supervisor's employees made 40 to 50 errors for a transaction known as cash applications. The supervisor's objective called for a much lower error rate.

Ingalls and the supervisor set up a form on which the supervisor would record every cash application error. The supervisor recorded errors and identified the cause of each error. Most errors involved the employee receiving incorrect information or the employee receiving correct information but recording it incorrectly. To fix these basic problems, the supervisor met with each employee who made an error, discussed the source of the problem, and asked the employee to be more careful. This process demonstrated to the employees that their errors mattered. They responded by recording entries more carefully. Before long, cash application errors dropped to the range of 7 to 10 a month. As the department spent less time correcting errors, productivity improved, helping Ingalls meet his own objectives.

Ingalls says he prefers working for organizations that use MBO. He says MBO makes managing employees easier. Employees know what they are supposed to achieve, so Ingalls can let them focus on how to reach those objectives while he focuses on broader issues facing the credit department.

1. Without MBO, would it have been harder for Ingalls to detect and correct the problem the supervisor was having with cash application errors? Why or why not?

2. The examples of objectives for credit analysts and collectors include objectives for personal development through training. Why do you think Ingalls includes this category of goals? How, if at all, might they help Ingalls achieve his objectives for the credit department or contribute to the company's overall performance?

3. Write a personal development objective for yourself. Make sure it meets the criteria for effective objectives shown in Figure 6.1. Show your objective to a friend or classmate, and discuss with that person how you plan to achieve your objective.

Source: "MBO Improves Credit Department Performance," *Credit & Collection Manager's Letter*, April 1, 2003, downloaded from Business & Company Resource Center, http:// galenet.galegroup.com.

Assessing Yourself

Are You a Planner?

Answer each of the following questions with a Yes or No.

1. Do you decide the night before what to wear each day? _____
2. Do you buy birthday gifts at the last minute? _____
3. Do you divide up household chores with your roommates or family members? _____
4. When you receive a paycheck, do you designate certain portions of it for specific expenses? _____
5. At the beginning of the workday or school day, do you make a list of what you must accomplish? _____
6. Do you buy a big-ticket item because a friend has the same item and raves about it? _____
7. Do you start studying for final exams before the last week of classes? _____
8. When you purchase a new piece of electronic equipment, such as a computer or smartphone, do you read the instructions about how to use it? _____

9. Before taking a trip, do you look up driving directions or explore alternative routes? _____

10. When you have several projects to handle at once, do you first tackle the one that appeals to you most? _____

Scoring: Answering Yes to questions 1, 3, 4, 5, 7, 8, and 9 and No to questions 2, 6, and 10 indicates that you are a planner.

Pause and Reflect

1. Before you took this quiz, did you think of yourself as a careful planner? Did this quiz change your opinion?

2. Is planning more important for a supervisor than for an employee who is not in management? Why or why not?

3. Think of one or two planning tools you would like to try. When will you try them? How will you decide whether they are helping you?

Class Skills Exercise

Setting Goals

This exercise provides you with an opportunity to practice what you learned in this chapter. You will practice setting personal goals (objectives) that are written, measurable, specific, clear, and challenging.

Instructions

1. In the space provided on the following page, write four goals that are important for you to achieve during the remainder of this semester.

2. Some of the goals should be short term (maybe something you need to finish by the end of this week); others should have a longer time frame (maybe by the end of the semester).

3. Write your goal statement so you can check all four boxes (measurable, specific, clear, and challenging) as being represented. Provided here is a brief summary of each term:

   - *Measurable*—Provide a tangible way (dollar amount, time frame, or quantity) to determine whether you have reached your goal; avoid *maximize, improve,* and other terms that cannot be measured.
   - *Specific*—Describe the actions you will need to take to achieve your goal.
   - *Clear*—Use simple language.
   - *Challenging* (yet realistic and obtainable)—Choose motivating and stimulating goals that, when achieved, will give you a sense of pride and build your confidence.

4. Your four goals should represent several different areas; for example, academic, job, career, spiritual, family, financial, social, or physical goals. An example of a financial goal that meets all four criteria is "I will save 20 percent of every paycheck starting this Friday so I'll have enough to pay for my auto insurance when it comes due the last week of the semester." If you are having trouble meeting any of the four criteria in your personal goals, discuss your goal with a classmate or your professor to see if one of them can help you define that goal more clearly.

5. After successfully achieving each goal, write the date in the "Follow-up" column next to the goal.

Source: This class exercise was written by Corinne Livesay, Bryan College, Dayton, Tennessee.

Goal:	Follow-up
	(When you've achieved this goal, write the date here.)
✔ if statement is: Measurable ☐ Specific ☐ Clear ☐ Challenging ☐	

Goal:	Follow-up
	(When you've achieved this goal, write the date here.)
✔ if statement is: Measurable ☐ Specific ☐ Clear ☐ Challenging ☐	

Goal:	Follow-up
	(When you've achieved this goal, write the date here.)
✔ if statement is: Measurable ☐ Specific ☐ Clear ☐ Challenging ☐	

Goal:	Follow-up
	(When you've achieved this goal, write the date here.)
✔ if statement is: Measurable ☐ Specific ☐ Clear ☐ Challenging ☐	

Building Supervision Skills

Controlling a Yacht-Making Operation

Divide the class into groups of five or six members. One member of each group will act as the supervisor; the rest are employees. Because few real-life work groups get to choose their supervisor, the instructor might arbitrarily designate the supervisor in each group. The instructor provides each group with square sheets of paper; 6 × 6 inches is a good size.

1. Each person reviews instructions for making origami yachts shown in Figure 6.10 on the following page.
2. The supervisor in each group sets performance standards for making the yachts in 10 minutes. These should include quality as well as quantity standards. In setting the standards, the supervisor may use whatever information he or she can obtain; it is up to the supervisor whether to seek input from the group.

   At the same time, each employee estimates how many yachts he or she can make correctly in 10 minutes. The employee writes down this estimate but does not reveal it to the supervisor at this time.

FIGURE 6.10 | Instructions for Origami Yachts

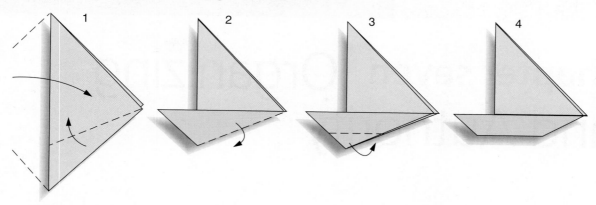

Source: Corinne Livesay of Bryan College, Dayton, Tennessee, supplied the origami instructions.

3. For 10 minutes, the employees make as many yachts as they can according to the instructions. During that time, the supervisor tries to monitor their performance in whatever way seems helpful. If employees seem to be falling short of the performance standard, the supervisor should try to find ways to improve performance. (This may include simply waiting patiently for skills to improve, if that seems most beneficial.)

4. After the 10 minutes have ended, determine how many yachts each group made and assess the quality of the work. As a class, discuss the groups' performance. Did each group meet its supervisor's performance standards? If not, was any variance significant? Based on their own estimates of how much they could do, do employees think their supervisor's standards were reasonable?

5. The class should also consider supervisors' efforts to take corrective action. Did supervisors intervene too much, or not enough? How did supervisors' attempts help or hurt employees' efforts? What does this experience reveal about the way supervisors should behave in the workplace?

chapter seven | Organizing and Authority

learning objectives

After you have studied this chapter, you should be able to:

7.1 Describe organization charts.

7.2 Identify basic ways in which organizations are structured.

7.3 Discuss the value of job descriptions.

7.4 Distinguish between line and staff authority and between centralized and decentralized authority.

7.5 Compare and contrast *authority, power, responsibility,* and *accountability*.

7.6 Identify the steps in the process of organizing.

7.7 Describe four principles of organizing.

7.8 Discuss why and how supervisors delegate.

7.9 Identify causes of reluctance to delegate.

A Supervision Challenge

HOW DO YOU GET THINGS DONE WHEN THERE ARE NO MANAGERS?

How are you able to supervise your team effectively and get things done? That is, where does your authority come from? Does it come from your position on the corporate organization chart, your expertise and experience, your management training, or some aspect of your personality? If you think that your power comes mainly from your position in the organization, then a recent corporate organizational trend may give you significant cause for concern.

Some companies are trying to eliminate corporate politics and bureaucracy by replacing the traditional hierarchical organizational structure with a holacracy. This method structures a company around the work that needs to be done, rather than around corporate departments with their command-and-control hierarchy. Holacracy was developed and trademarked by a company called HolacracyOne, and the concept is catching on among software startups and even large companies like Zappos, an online shoe and clothing store.

Zappos CEO Tony Hsieh announced that by the end of 2014 the company would be completely reorganized as a holacracy. Its 1,500 employees, including the CEO, will no longer have job titles or belong to functional departments. Managers, as a job function, will be eliminated, and the company will become "self-governing." Mr. Hsieh believes this structure is the only way for Zappos to remain nimble enough to adapt to the changing marketplace as the company grows.

Holacracy does provide some minimal organizational structure, however. Rather than departments, employees are organized into "circles" around functional areas, with each circle being self-governing. Instead of being accountable to the person above you in the organization chart, employees are accountable to each other.

To be clear, although holacracy eliminates the titles for supervisory employees, this does not mean there is no leadership. Leadership comes from the workers themselves, as individuals distinguish themselves by virtue of their ideas or efforts, and are endorsed by their peers. Some Zappos employees will serve as "Lead Links," which assign individual employees to particular roles, or reassign employees when necessary. But that is the extent of what Lead Links can do; they cannot tell people what to do.

This structure really impacts lower-level management strongly because most employees, particularly entry-level employees, are accustomed to reporting to a supervisor. It's somewhat easier to implement this at the management level where the discussion can be more abstract; but with supervisors and front-line employees the implementation needs to be extremely clear and concrete.

Most business experts are skeptical of holacracies at this point, noting that human beings naturally want to know where their own responsibility starts and ends. Author and leadership consultant Sally Helgesen says that in her experience, radical organizational change has the best chance of success when it comes from the bottom up, rather than being decreed from the top, because there is more complete buy-in throughout the organization. It's a good idea, then, to consider how to best accomplish the business's goals under different organizational methods.

As you study this chapter, think about how an organizational structure like holacracy would affect how (or even if) you supervise your employees. Do you think the holacracy Zappos is moving to will succeed? Can you become as a consensus leader in this type of organization and if so, how?

Sources: Based on Anna Rose Welch, "Zappos Embarks on Radical Restructuring Adventure Towards Holacracy," Integrated Solutions for Retailers, January 7, 2014, http://www.retailsolutionsonline.com and Sally Helgesen, "An Extreme Take on Restructuring: No Job Titles, No Managers, No Politics," strategy+business blog, February 11, 2014, http://www.strategy-business.com.

---

organizing
Setting up the group, allocating resources, and assigning work to achieve goals

In the opening story, the way work and responsibilities will be organized at Zappos will affect employees' ability to contribute to meeting the organization's goals. As you read in Chapter 1, **organizing** is the management function of setting up the group, allocating resources, and assigning work to achieve goals. By organizing, supervisors and other managers put their plans into action. When done well, organizing helps ensure that the organization uses its resources—especially human resources—efficiently. For this reason, a business that is well organized is in a better position to be profitable.

Managers in even the simplest organizations need to organize. If you were to set up a softball team, you would have to collect equipment, arrange for a place to play, find players, decide what position each is to play, and create a batting lineup. If you were operating a one-person business, you would have to decide where you would work, what activities you would need to accomplish, and whether you should contract with vendors to provide some services.

This chapter describes the ways organizations are structured and how supervisors organize. The process of organizing includes sharing authority and responsibility. The chapter explains how supervisors share both of these functions with the people who report to them.

The Structure of the Organization

Some of the most fundamental and far-reaching organizational decisions involve the structure of the organization as a whole. For example, top management could assign a manager authority for a particular product, a particular geographic region served by the organization, or a particular specialty such as sales or finance. Supervisors have little, if any, input into this type of decision. However, supervisors need to understand how they and their departments fit into the big picture, and that includes understanding the structure of the organization.

LO7.1 ▶ Describe organization charts.

Organization Charts

Businesspeople have come up with a standard way to draw the structure of an organization: the organization chart. These charts use boxes to represent the various positions or departments in an organization (usually just at management levels). Lines connecting the boxes indicate who reports to whom. Figure 7.1, on the following page, is an organization chart showing the structure of an international company. Note, for example, that someone is in charge of all North American operations, and someone is in charge of all international operations. These two managers report to the person who serves as president and chief operating officer of the entire company.

The positions at the top of an organization chart are those with the most authority and responsibility. Logically, the people in these positions are referred to as the top managers. By following the lines from the top managers down the chart to the lower levels, you can see which middle managers report to these top managers. In other words, the top managers are authorized to direct the work of the middle managers who report to them and are responsible for the performance of those middle managers. The bottom of the chart may show the first-level managers (or sometimes operative employees). Supervisors are not shown on the chart in Figure 7.1.

The number of levels in an organization from top management down to the operative employees describes the height of the organization. Organizations with much height are called *tall organizations,* and organizations with little height are usually called *flat.* Typically, in a flat organization, many people report to each manager. In that situation, employees tend to have a lot of decision-making authority and control over their work. When employees can handle the responsibility, a flat organization offers advantages: it is more flexible and responsive to customers than a tall organization. An extreme example of a flat organization is Basecamp (formerly known as 37signals), a software company located in Chicago. As the company grew, instead of adding managers to

FIGURE 7.1 | Organization Chart: An International Company

An organization chart provides a visual representation of the overall structure of a company.

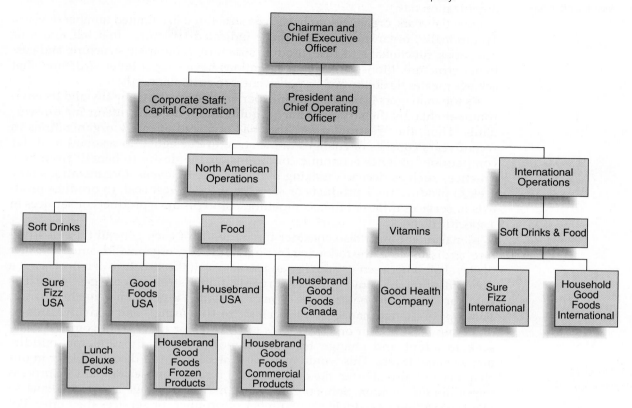

departments, it asked the departmental employees to find ways to manage their work themselves. Once, when the customer service department grew to three people, Basecamp tried hiring a team leader, who would measure performance and lead improvements. However, the company's founders later realized that the team members could more efficiently measure and improve their own performance. Therefore, the company eliminated the layer of management and planned for the department employees to take turns handling leadership tasks such as running meetings.[1]

Organization charts sometimes show only a portion of an organization. Like Figure 7.1, a chart may show only the top levels of management, or it may show a single division in a large company. Reading the titles of the people associated with each box gives an indication of the scope of a particular organization chart.

Being able to understand organization charts enables supervisors to figure out where they fit in the organization and where opportunities for future promotions might lie. Supervisors can see the variety of responsibilities held by others at their level in the organization. Knowing where they fit in helps supervisors determine how their department or group contributes to achieving the goals of the organization.

LO7.2 ▶ Identify basic ways in which organizations are structured.

department
A unique group of resources that management has assigned to carry out a particular task

Types of Structures

An organization with more than a handful of people works most efficiently when it is grouped into departments. A **department** refers to a unique group of resources that management has assigned to carry out a particular task, such as selling the company's products to customers in the Midwest, treating patients with cancer,

departmentalization
Setting up departments in an organization

or teaching mathematics. The way management sets up the departments—an activity called departmentalization—determines the type of structure the organization has.

Over the years, organizations have been structured in a limited number of ways. Traditionally, organization charts have indicated structures that fall into four categories: functional structure, product structure, geographic structure, and customer structure. More recently, organizations have sought other structures that achieve greater flexibility and responsiveness to customer needs.

As top managers learn from their experiences or as the company and its environment change, the structure may require minor adjustments or major overhauls. Thus, the "restructuring" that has occurred at many organizations in recent years consists of changes in the structure designed to respond to stiffer competition, tougher economic conditions, or the desire to benefit from new practices such as decision making by teams of employees. Organizations may seek to produce their products or services at the lowest cost, to produce products or services different than competitors, or to produce products or services in a specific niche.

Management must also consider the tradeoffs of each general type of structure, as discussed in the following sections, and every organization must consider the level of fit between its strategy and structure. If the structure of a firm is not a good fit with the strategy or an organization's strategy changes, then it is necessary to modify the structure of an organization to accommodate this change. This type of change management is called "restructuring," and it involves adapting components of an organization's structure. For example, a company may seek to adapt and change to become more organic by reducing middle-management layers. This would increase spans of control (discussed later in this chapter), but also shorten the decision time it takes for the company to process important information. Some organizations may also engage in change management by adding or reducing the number of products or services they offer. For example, General Electric has recently embraced a "culture of simplification" to simplify its operations and help it compete more effectively. This example of change management is intended to alter the organization's structure so that the company can better focus and adapt to its competitors in a dynamic and sometimes hostile market.

It is important to note that change management is a process that must be dealt with delicately. Employees generally resist efforts to change the organization. The organization's leadership can help improve change management initiatives by keeping employees informed of why changes are being made, and helping them understand their role after the intended change is completed.

Functional Structure

A functional structure groups personnel and other resources according to the types of work they carry out. For example, a business might have vice presidents of finance, production, sales, and human resources. Assigned to each vice president is the staff needed to carry out these activities. Figure 7.2 on the following page provides an example of a company with a functional structure. Wiss, Janney, Elstner Associates is an architectural firm in which one vice president is responsible for operations (that is, the work of all the architects and engineers who provide services to customers), and another is responsible for administration (that is, support services). Under the vice president of administration, the organization is divided into such functions as marketing and personnel. This structure is well-suited to centralized decision making and efficiency through economies of scale and specialization. It is not well-suited for dynamic environments where decisions must be made quickly and products or services customized.

FIGURE 7.2 | Functional Structure Partial organization chart for Wiss, Janney, Elstner Associates

The organization chart of a company with a functional structure reflects their grouping of personnel and resources according to the work that they do.

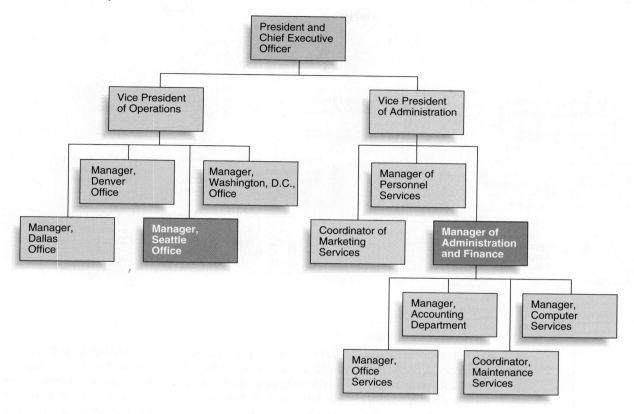

Product Structure

In an organization with a product structure, work and resources are assigned to departments responsible for all the activities related to producing and delivering a particular product (good or service). In an automobile business, there might be one department for each make of automobile. Colleges and universities are often departmentalized according to the subject matter taught. At the company shown in Figure 7.1, North American operations are departmentalized according to three product categories: soft drinks, food, and vitamins. Figure 7.3, on the following page, illustrates a product structure in the consumer and commercial banking division of a bank. Although a large bank's offerings are more widespread than would fit on the page, this partial organization chart shows that the division is structured according to the type of product, such as loans to consumers, commercial loans, various bank accounts, and so on.

Geographic Structure

A geographic structure results when an organization is departmentalized according to the location of the customers served or the goods or services produced. A manufacturing company might have a department for each of its factories scattered around the world. An insurance company might have a department for each of its 12 sales territories. The manager of each department would be responsible for producing and/or selling all the company's goods or services in that geographic region. At the architectural firm in Figure 7.2, operations are departmentalized on the basis of the cities where the offices are located: Dallas, Denver, Seattle, Washington, D.C., and other cities not shown.

FIGURE 7.3 | **Product Structure** Partial organization chart for a bank division

The organization chart of a company with a product structure reflects their grouping of personnel and resources according to the products they produce or service they provide.

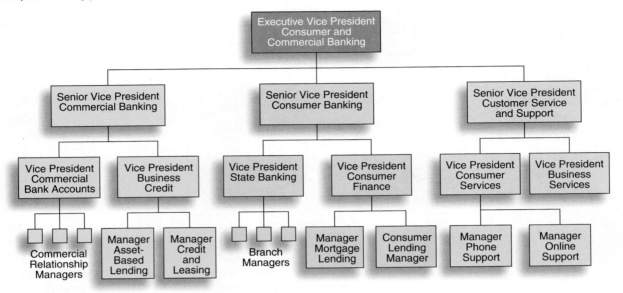

Customer Structure

A customer structure departmentalizes the organization according to the type of customer served. For example, an aerospace company might have different departments serving businesses, the military, and the space program. Rackspace, the founder of OpenStack®, the open-source operating system for the cloud, is based near San Antonio, Texas, and has a customer structure aimed at achieving its goal of giving customers "fanatical support." Various businesses, such as retailers and game sites, use Rackspace to handle the nuts and bolts of operating on the Internet. The company's customer service employees are grouped into teams, which include a leader, two or three account managers, and specialists in billing and technical support. Each team serves a set of customers of a particular size and complexity. When a customer calls with a problem requiring a specialist, that employee is seated near the one taking the phone call.[2]

Combinations

As you can see from the figures, organizations often combine the basic types of structures. Thus, Figure 7.1 combines geographic and product structures, whereas Figure 7.2 combines functional and geographic structures. A typical arrangement would be a large corporation with divisions for each of its product lines. Within each division, managers are assigned responsibility for carrying out a particular function, including sales and operations (that is, making goods or delivering services). Each sales department in turn is structured geographically.

Various combinations of structures occur when the organization forms teams of employees to meet objectives such as improving quality, developing products, or applying new technology. These teams may require diverse kinds of expertise, so the organization brings together people who perform different functions or work in different geographic areas. Often these teams of employees are grouped according to product or customer. For example, a team formed to develop a new type of speaker for a sound system might combine employees from the sales, engineering, and production functions under the umbrella of that new product. For a more in-depth discussion of forming and leading teams, see Chapter 3.

Organic Structures

The managers of many organizations consider the basic forms of departmentalization too rigid for a turbulent, highly competitive environment. Grouping people according to function or geographic area can create barriers that interfere with coordinating activities and sharing ideas. A rigid structure is rarely suitable for a very small organization. Such organizations typically have a highly organic structure, one in which the boundaries between jobs continually shift and people pitch in wherever their contributions are needed.

organic structure
Organizational structure in which the boundaries between jobs continually shift and people pitch in wherever their contributions are needed

Larger organizations, too, are seeking the flexibility of organic structures. They may do so by organizing around teams and *processes* (series of activities that deliver value to customers) or *projects* (groups of tasks with defined scope and ending points). Large-volume clinical laboratories sometimes use a process organization. Technicians specialize in performing certain categories of tests, especially those requiring extra training (e.g., genetic testing). But the specialized work can become boring, and it limits employees' chances to develop new skills and fill in for one another. Therefore, many other clinical labs rotate employees among workstations or assign employees to core groups that work wherever they are needed most.[3]

Research into the experiences of managers at seven large corporations found that a top challenge of this approach is that employees may become confused about the details of their roles and responsibilities.[4] As a result, managers at all levels, including supervisors, must take the time to be sure that all employees involved in a project or process have clear directions and a job description for their work on the particular project or process. If a supervisor is leading the team, the supervisor must be sure that all necessary roles have been assigned. Along with the usual roles, such as designing a product or setting up a production line, some teams may have unique goals requiring specially created roles.

A growing number of firms are creating "intrapreneurships," in which a small team or group within the company is given the resources to develop new ideas and new ventures without leaving the parent organization. In a variation of this approach, IBM set up teams for one-month projects to develop new customers, rather than new products. IBM's Corporate Service Corps assigns a group of 10 to 15 employees to serve businesses and nonprofit organizations in developing countries for free. Besides doing good for others, these teams are helping to build economic strength in places IBM hopes will become growth markets for its consulting and computing services. Service on one of these teams can be a tremendous way for an IBM supervisor or other employee to develop problem-solving skills, tackle interesting assignments, and build connections throughout the company, all while helping others. Since its launch in 2008, more than 2,400 employees have provided service in more than 30 countries.[5]

Like the organizations themselves, supervisors in these new structures must be flexible. They have to contribute wherever the organization currently needs their talents—a requirement that calls for continually knowing, updating, and communicating one's skills. They may have to identify how they can contribute to a particular project and then be ready to move to a new assignment when they no longer add value to the current one. In addition, supervisors in the new structures must rely more on human relations skills

These technicians might specialize in a particular area, or they could continually switch responsibilities for a more organic structure of work.

than on technical skills. Coaching a team or project group requires the ability to motivate, lead, and communicate as the team handles many project- or process-related decisions. This ability is especially needed for coaching teams that bring together people from a variety of functions.

Network Organizations

network organizations
Organizations that maintain flexibility by staying small and contracting with other individuals and organizations as needed to complete projects

A growing number of organizations are trying to stay flexible by staying small. Rather than adding employees to meet customer demands, these organizations, called **network organizations**, contract with other individuals and organizations as needed to complete specific projects.[6] In practice, this structure may involve *outsourcing*, or paying another organization to carry out a function. Insurance companies typically outsource the defense of lawsuits, after-hours call centers for loss reporting, and management of their investments.[7] In the last decade or so a form of outsourcing called *offshoring*, in which companies move departments from headquarters to cheaper overseas locations, has become common. Popular offshoring locations include India, China, and Eastern Europe, which have large numbers of engineers and scientists.[8]

Other organizations arrange *alliances*, or relationships based on partnership, including joint ventures, minority investments linked to contractual agreements, agreements to jointly fund research, and other, less formal arrangements. At the extreme is a *virtual organization*, in which a small core organization (maybe a single person) arranges alliances as needed to carry out particular projects. Hardinge Inc. used a virtual organization when it purchased Bridgeport Machines and moved Bridgeport's manufacturing line from Connecticut to Elmira, New York. Hardinge brought together key employees from Bridgeport Machine and Hardinge as well as experts from other companies. People from the JCIT Training Institute helped lay out the manufacturing flow. Participating suppliers included Zeller Electric and Skico (which makes component parts). This virtual team achieved the goal of moving the entire manufacturing process intact and setting it up in a way that improved quality and efficiency.[9]

Learning Organizations

learning organization
An organization that does well in creating, acquiring, and transferring knowledge and in modifying behavior to reflect new knowledge

In many organizations today, managers are realizing that their most significant assets are the knowledge and skills of their people. To make the most of these assets, managers may establish the conditions for building a **learning organization**. This term refers to an organization that does well in creating, acquiring, and transferring knowledge and in modifying behavior to reflect new knowledge.[10] Through the values rewarded, the computer systems set up, and the communications sent to employees, a learning organization signals that employees are expected to share ideas, solve problems together, and learn from their experience. When an organization instills these values and simplifies information sharing, employees can quickly help it respond when new opportunities and challenges arise. Examples of successful learning organizations include Honda, Corning, and General Electric.

LO7.3 ▶ Discuss the value of job descriptions.

Job Descriptions

Just as a clearly defined organization chart allows everyone within a company to know exactly who is responsible for what in an organization, clearly defined job descriptions allow those within the various organizational departments and positions to know exactly what are an individual's responsibilities. A good job description should be clear and should accurately define the company's needs. According to the U.S. Small Business Administration (SBA), the process of writing a job description usually begins with an analysis of the important facts about a job, including:[11]

- Individual tasks involved
- The methods used to complete the tasks
- The purpose and responsibilities of the job

- The relationship of the job to other jobs
- Qualifications needed for the job

With a good summary of these important facts in hand, a clear and accurate job description can be written. According to the SBA, job descriptions typically include:

- Job title
- Job objective or overall purpose statement
- Summary of the general nature and level of the job
- Description of the broad function and scope of the position
- List of duties or tasks performed critical to success
- Key functional and relational responsibilities in order of significance
- Description of the relationships and roles within the company, including supervisory positions, subordinating roles, and other working relationships

The last element listed is one that is key to ensuring that each person's role within the company's organizational structure is understood.

LO7.4 ▶ Distinguish between line and staff authority and between centralized and decentralized authority.

authority
The right to perform a task or give orders to someone else

Authority

When a supervisor assigns duties, he or she gives employees the authority to carry them out. Authority is the right to perform a task or give orders to someone else. The supervisor in turn has authority in certain areas, and his or her manager has even broader authority. Some common terms related to organizing and authority, and how those terms translate into everyday language, are shown in Table 7.1. Each is discussed in greater detail in the following sections.

Line, Staff, and Functional Authority

line authority
The right to carry out tasks and give orders related to the organization's primary purpose

The basic type of authority in organizations is line authority, or the right to carry out tasks and give orders related to the organization's primary purpose. Line authority gives a production supervisor at Deere & Company the right to direct a worker to operate a machine; it gives the head chef in a restaurant the right to direct the salad chef to prepare a spinach salad using certain ingredients. At the architectural firm represented in Figure 7.2, the manager of the Seattle office has line authority.

TABLE 7.1 | Everyday Meaning of Terms Related to Organizing

Source: Adapted from Brad Lee Thompson, *The New Manager's Handbook* (Burr Ridge, IL: Richard D. Irwin, Inc., 1995), p. 49.

Term	Everyday Meaning
Departmentalization	"Let's divide up the work."
Authority	"I (or you) get to decide how this is going to get done."
Responsibility	"I (or you) own this job; you can hold me accountable for it."
Accountability	"The buck stops here."
Unity of command	"No matter who else you work with, you are accountable to only one person."
Span of control	"There are limits to how many people a manager can effectively manage."
Delegation	"You have the responsibility and authority to accomplish this assignment."
Empowerment	"I trust you to perform these functions and accomplish these results; this means much more than just delegating a task to you."

staff authority
The right to advise or assist those with line authority

In contrast, staff authority is the right to advise or assist those with line authority. For example, the employees in the human resource department help other departments by ensuring that they have qualified workers. The quality-control manager at a manufacturing company helps the production manager see that the goods produced are of acceptable quality. In Figure 7.2, the manager of administration and finance has staff authority.

An amusing story from the Shark Tank column of *Computerworld* magazine illustrates the need for staff authority. According to this story, a technical support employee went to a company's payroll department in response to a complaint that the printer had jammed while printing payroll checks. As the tech support person approached the printer, the payroll clerk jumped in front of it, exclaiming that the tech person was not permitted to look at the checks. The tech employee wondered how it would be possible to fix the printer without approaching it. The payroll clerk replied, "You'll have to keep your eyes closed."[12] Obviously, this company's technical support employees need broad enough staff authority to work with their eyes open.

Conflicts often arise between line and staff personnel. Line personnel may feel that staff workers are meddling and do not understand their work or how important it is. Staff personnel may conclude that line personnel are resisting new ideas and do not appreciate the valuable assistance they are getting. Whether the supervisor has line or staff authority, he or she can benefit from being aware that these kinds of conflicts are common and trying to appreciate the other person's point of view.

functional authority
The right given by higher management to specific staff personnel to give orders concerning an area in which the staff personnel have expertise

Supervisors and other personnel with staff authority may also have functional authority. This is the right given by higher management to specific staff personnel to give orders concerning an area in which the staff personnel have expertise. For example, members of the accounting department might have authority to request the information they need to prepare reports. Or the human resource manager might have authority to ensure that all departments are complying with the laws pertaining to fair employment practices.

Centralized and Decentralized Authority

In some organizations, the managers at the top retain a great deal of authority; in others, management grants much authority to middle managers, supervisors, and operative employees. Organizations that share relatively little authority are said to be centralized; organizations that share a lot of authority are said to be decentralized.

These terms are relative. In other words, no organization is completely centralized or decentralized, but organizations fall along a range of possibilities from one extreme to another. An organization can even make changes in the degree to which it centralizes authority, depending on its strategic plan and goals. Even individual functions within an organization may make this type of change. Many corporations, including Agilent Technologies, AutoNation, and Cisco Systems, have made their finance operations more centralized and more decentralized at the same time. How can this be? The basic strategy is to identify which finance tasks, such as handling sales and payments, are routine. These repetitive tasks are centralized into one operation with one set of procedures, to make them as efficient as possible. Other finance tasks, such as planning what to spend to achieve long-range goals, are carried out by finance experts assigned to particular business units. These employees then can become experts in the particular businesses, helping their unit make better decisions.[13]

Supervisors who know whether their employer has a centralized or decentralized structure understand how much authority they can expect to have. Suppose a supervisor wants to expand the authority of her position so that she can make improvements in the department. This ambition probably will be viewed less favorably in a centralized organization than in a decentralized one.

LO7.5 ▶ Compare and contrast *authority*, *power*, *responsibility*, and *accountability*.

power
The ability to get others to act in a certain way

responsibility
The obligation to perform assigned activities

Power, Responsibility, and Accountability

It is easy to confuse authority with power, accountability, or responsibility. However, when used precisely, these terms do not mean the same thing. **Power** is the ability (as opposed to the right) to get others to act in a certain way. The supervisor's authority usually confers a degree of power; employees usually do what their supervisor asks them to do. However, some people have power that comes from sources other than their positions in the organization. Also, some people with authority have trouble getting others to act in the desired way. (Chapter 14 discusses power in greater detail.)

Responsibility is the obligation to perform assigned activities. People who accept responsibility commit themselves to completing an assignment to the best

PRACTICAL ADVICE FOR SUPERVISORS

ACCOUNTABILITY FOR THE SAFETY AND EFFECTIVENESS OF NIGHT WORKERS

A recent report by the Joseph Rowntree Foundation found that the quality of night-time care in residential homes for the elderly is suspect because there are generally no routine inspections of night-time staff and many are not adequately trained or supervised. In addition to receiving less training than day staff, the night staff felt undervalued and isolated from the running of the facility.

Workers at residential care facilities are not the only ones who need to work at night. There are many lines of work, such as security, law enforcement, manufacturing, construction, and hospital care, where employees are needed around the clock. Although these night shifts are necessary, they are at least 5 percent less productive. Additionally, evidence indicates that working at night is associated with fatigue, mood problems, and a higher rate of accidents. The risk of injury is elevated by as much as thirty percent. The problems are worse when the employees work rotating shifts—some shifts in the morning, others in the evening, and still others late at night. For these workers, the risk of having an accident is more than double that of straight day shift workers.

If an employee under these conditions falls asleep on the job, snaps at a customer, or loses focus and gets injured, who is responsible? Certainly, employees should take precautions to make sure they are prepared to do their jobs effectively. But the supervisor also is accountable for the group's performance and should make sure that employees have the resources and conditions necessary for workplace safety and effectiveness. Here are some suggestions for doing that:

- Be sure the department has enough personnel to cover all the shifts safely. People need days off to rest and for sick days and vacations, so the department needs about four crews to staff three shifts per day, seven days a week.
- Provide more supervision to ensure workers are more closely monitored.

- Avoid rotating shifts if at all possible. If workers have rotating shifts, schedule either 8-hour or 12-hour shifts. This ensures that shifts will start at the same time every day, so that workers' bodies can adjust more readily.
- Allow workers time to shift their circadian rhythm forward toward night shift. Give workers long, continuous time off, rather than a day or less at a time. For example, workers on 8-hour shifts might work two day shifts, two evenings, and two nights, then have two days off. Or workers on 12-hour shifts might work two days, then two nights, and then have four days off.
- Make work schedules as predictable as possible, so workers can plan ahead to meet needs for rest and personal relationships.
- Avoid assigning overtime to employees who work night or rotating shifts.
- Ensure that lighting is adequate—using full spectrum lighting where possible. Bright light signals the body that it should be alert.
- Avoid assigning complex tasks to night shift and schedule the most physically or mentally draining activities for the beginning of the shift if possible.
- Have more frequent breaks particularly during the dip in alertness in early morning.
- Encourage the company to establish a policy and quiet space for napping during break times. Short naps have been shown to improve alertness, judgment, and safety.
- Promote the use of carpooling and public transit to reduce the number of employees driving.

Sources: "When Guards Fall Asleep on Duty, Who's Truly at Fault?" Security Director's Report, July 2011, pp. 1, 11–13; "Coping Safely with Extended, Rotating, or Unusual Work Shifts," Safety Compliance Letter, no. 2529 (September 2011) pp. 7, 10; "Night-Time Practices Jeopardise Quality of Care in Residential Homes," Joseph Rowntree Foundation, http://www.jrf.org.uk/media-centre/night-time-practices-jeopardise-quality-care-residential-homes, accessed April 19, 2014; Dave Rebbitt, "Night shifts: Are they safe?," Canadian Occupational Safety, March 13, 2014, http://www.cos-mag.com/safety/safety-columns/3862-night-shifts-are-they-safe.html?print=1&tmpl=component.

of their ability. Of course, doing a good job is easier when you have the authority to control the necessary resources, including personnel. An important aspect of the supervisor's job therefore is to ensure that people have accepted responsibility for each of the tasks that the work group must complete—and that they clearly understand what those responsibilities are. The supervisor also must ensure that people have enough authority to carry out their responsibilities.

Employees who accept responsibility may be rewarded for doing a good job, and those who do not may be punished. This practice is called *accountability* (see Chapter 1). Assume an organization makes a supervisor responsible for communicating policies to his or her employees. Accountability means the supervisor can expect consequences related to whether that responsibility is met. Thus, accountability is a way of encouraging people to fulfill their responsibilities. For ideas on being accountable and responsible when scheduling employees for the night shift, see "Practical Advice for Supervisors."

The authority to transfer (delegate) responsibility to employees and hold them accountable adds to a supervisor's power. At the same time, even when a supervisor delegates, the supervisor remains accountable for employees' performance. Carley Roney, who founded the web site The Knot, aimed at couples planning weddings, learned this lesson when she had to balance leadership of her company with the demands of a second child in her family. Roney could no longer put the company first all the time, and she discovered that she could trust her staff members to do their work.[14] In a far sadder situation, a supervisor at Advanced Tent Rental learned about accountability after two workers were injured while taking down the support pole of a tent. The pole hit a live power cable, and both workers were injured; one eventually died. A court held the supervisor liable for failing to ensure there were no live power lines near the tent and failing to let the workers know about the danger. The supervisor might have thought it was acceptable to delegate the responsibility to be safe, but in fact, the supervisor was still accountable for their safety.[15]

---

connect SELF-ASSESSMENT 7.1

Identify Your Preferred Organizational Structure

Now that you know about many varieties of organizational structures, take a few minutes to think about what type of organization appeals to you most. In which type of structure do you think you would be most effective and most satisfied? This assessment will help you answer this question.

LO7.6 ▶ Identify the steps in the process of organizing.

The Process of Organizing

For a supervisor, organizing efforts are generally focused on allocating responsibilities and resources in a way that makes the department or work group operate effectively and efficiently. In addition, supervisors may want or need to set up teams (see Chapter 3). Whether the organizing job involves setting up a new company, restructuring an existing one, or deciding how to organize a department or team, the process should be basically the same. The supervisor or other manager should define the objective, determine what resources are needed, and then group activities and assign duties. This three-step approach leads to a structure that supports the goals of the organization, as illustrated in Figure 7.4 on the following page.

Define the Objective

Management activities should support the objectives developed during the planning process. In the case of organizing, the supervisor or other manager should

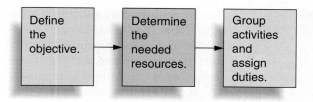

FIGURE 7.4 | The Process of Organizing

Organizing, regardless of the level within the company or the task to be accomplished, requires three basic steps.

begin by defining what objective the department or work group is supposed to be achieving. If the supervisor does not know, then he or she has not finished planning and should complete that job before trying to organize work. Walmart Stores operates more than 4,000 stores in the United States, so a big challenge is how to run stores profitably and develop high-potential employees when there is so much activity to manage. The company determined that it could do this best by giving regional managers better opportunities to develop their skills. So the company divided its U.S. stores into three geographic business units, called Walmart West, Walmart South, and Walmart North, each headed by an executive vice president. Each business unit is divided into regions headed by a general manager, and every region is divided into smaller markets, each headed by a director of stores serving that market. By creating separate business units and adding layers of management, the company reduced the number of people supervised by each of the higher-level managers, so efforts to develop regional managers can be more personal. It also created more management positions for store managers to move up to as their skills are developing.[16]

Determine the Needed Resources

The planning process also should give the supervisor an idea of what resources—including personnel, equipment, and money—are needed to achieve goals. The supervisor should review the plans and identify which resources are needed for the particular areas being organized.

SUPERVISION AND DIVERSITY

ACCOMMODATING WORKERS WITH DISABILITIES AND IMPROVING EFFICIENCY

Knowing that workers with disabilities and appropriate job skills can be highly dedicated and motivated, Walgreens designed the work and facility of its high-tech South Carolina distribution center to accommodate disabled workers. Walgreens saw a remarkable 20 percent increase in efficiency. Though 4 out of every 10 of the center's 800 employees have reported a physical or cognitive disability, productivity improved because the redesigned jobs are easier for everyone to carry out accurately.

According to Deb Russell, manager of outreach and employee services at Walgreens, the company focused on how to "make work more intuitive" without lowering standards for productivity. For example, while many warehouses might ask employees to type information with computer keyboards, Walgreens developed touch screens that display large symbols and pictures. Workers select images on the touch screen to complete various tasks. That means people who have difficulty reading and writing can handle jobs accurately. Also, the height of the workstations is adjustable, which makes them more comfortable for everyone—not just disabled workers—to use.

Because of Walgreens' success, many other companies, including Best Buy, Lowe's, and Toys R Us have adopted similar practices and have utilized programs that work to match companies looking to hire with disabled job-seekers. Lowe's has, in fact, sent leadership teams from around the country to the Walgreen's South Carolina facility to learn firsthand what is working. Subsequently, Lowe's has made modifications to their distribution facilities and is focusing recruiting efforts on people with disabilities.

Unfortunately, Americans with disabilities often still face a great deal of discrimination in the workplace and high rates of unemployment. Forward-thinking supervisors and companies can use the success stories of companies like Lowe's and Walgreens as examples of what they could achieve both in higher rates of efficiency, improved bottom lines, and making a significant difference in the lives of many individuals.

Sources: Susan J. Wells, "Counting on Workers with Disabilities," *HR Magazine*, April 2008, www.shrm.org; "Hiring Disabled Workers Can Make Companies More Efficient: Report," *Huffington Post*, August 22, 2012, http://www.huffingtonpost.com/2012/07/26/workers-with-disabilities_n_1707421.html, accessed April 19, 2014; Judy Owen, "Lowe's Ramps Up Disability Inclusion," *Forbes*, April 22, 2013, http://www.forbes.com/sites/judyowen/2013/04/22/lowes-ramps-up-disability-inclusion/, accessed April 19, 2014.

It's no secret that a strong portion of company success can be attributed to employees who are committed to customer service.

To achieve Ritz-Carlton's lofty goals that all of its customers be satisfied and return again, its managers have determined that they need employees committed to ensuring high quality. They also realize that every employee must be empowered to contribute to customer satisfaction. This responsibility in turn requires that employees have access to information about what customers want and how well the company's processes are working. Modern information systems help fulfill that need.

Group Activities and Assign Duties

The final step in the process is what most people think about when they consider organizing. The supervisor groups the necessary activities and assigns work to the appropriate employees. For example, the line leader in a small machine shop noticed that it was difficult to set priorities when a stack of work orders arrived from the company's office. So the line leader starts each day by reviewing the latest orders. She marks each order with a colored highlighter: green for rush jobs, yellow for orders that have a little longer to complete, and red for orders that aren't urgent. After organizing the work in this way, the line leader distributes the jobs among the various lines so they can keep work flowing smoothly.[17] At Walgreens, Lowe's, and many other companies, managers group activities and assign duties so that workers with disabilities can do certain jobs alongside nondisabled workers. To learn how, see "Supervision and Diversity."

To ensure that all the necessary responsibilities are assigned, the supervisor also can involve employees in this step of the organizing process. Employees are deeply involved in these decisions at Harley-Davidson's motorcycle plant in Kansas City, Missouri. Representatives from management and the union established an overall structure based on teamwork. Most of the work takes place in what the company calls *natural work groups* (NWGs), teams of up to 15 workers who handle all the tasks for specialized functions (painting, fabrication) or for assembling particular motorcycle models.[18] Each NWG decides how to meet its goals—for example, deciding how to arrange the machinery and equipment and solving quality problems. Workers in the NWG rotate through the group's various jobs so that they can fill in for one another as needed. The groups have authority for solving problems. For example, when a machine on the production line for welding frames broke down, the groups affected by the breakdown worked together to fix the machine and called in the next shift early to get caught up.[19]

The remainder of this chapter discusses how to carry out this third step of the organizing process.

LO7.7 ▶ Describe four principles of organizing.

Principles of Organizing

Supervisors, especially those who are new to the job, may be unsure how to group activities and assign duties. The task seems so abstract. Fortunately, management experts have developed some principles that can guide the supervisor: the parity principle, unity of command, chain of command, and span of control.

Parity Principle

parity principle
The principle that personnel who are given responsibility must also be given enough authority to carry out that responsibility

Parity is the quality of being equal or equivalent. Thus, according to the **parity principle**, personnel must have equal amounts of authority and responsibility. In other words, when someone accepts a responsibility, he or she also needs enough authority to be able to carry out that responsibility. If a head teller at a Citibank branch is responsible for providing high-quality customer service but does not have the authority to fire a surly teller, the head teller will find it difficult or impossible to carry out this responsibility.

Unity of Command

Meredith Buckle handled the maintenance jobs for a small office building. When building occupants experienced a problem, such as a leaky faucet or a cold office, they would call Buckle. Often, to get a faster response, they would call her repeatedly, complaining about how the problem was interfering with work. As a result, Buckle felt she could never keep everyone satisfied, and she had trouble deciding which jobs to do first.

unity of command
The principle that each employee should have only one supervisor

According to the principle of **unity of command**, each employee should have only one supervisor. Employees who receive orders from several people tend to get confused and aggravated. As a result, they tend to do poor work. It would have helped Buckle if the building manager had collected messages from the occupants and assigned the jobs to her along with a schedule for completing them.[20]

Sometimes a supervisor's manager violates this principle by directing the employees who report to the supervisor. This puts the employees in the awkward position of receiving directions from two people, and it puts the supervisor in the awkward position of needing to correct his or her manager's behavior. In this kind of situation, the supervisor might want to approach his or her boss with a tactful way to restore unity of command. The supervisor might say, for instance, "I've noticed that my team gets confused when you and I both give directions. I'd like to suggest that you let me know what you want, and I'll relay it to the team." Of course, the supervisor also should refrain from directing employees who report to someone else.

Chain of Command

In a chain, each link is connected to no more than two links, one on either side. In an organization, authority progresses like the links on a chain. Along this **chain of command**, authority flows from one level of management to the next, from the top of the organization to the bottom.

chain of command
The flow of authority in an organization from one level of management to the next

When someone skips a level, the principle of the chain of command is violated. For example, suppose that Fred Paretsky wants to take Friday off, but he suspects that the division manager will be more sympathetic to his request than his supervisor. So Paretsky goes directly to the division manager, who grants permission. Unfortunately, though the division manager does not know it, Paretsky's group will be understaffed on Friday because two other workers also will be absent. By violating the chain of command, Paretsky and the division manager have created a staffing problem that the supervisor could have avoided with a little planning. Similarly, in the preceding example of a supervisor's manager directing the supervisor's employees, the division manager is violating both the principles of chain of command and unity of command. In this situation, the division manager should ask the employee if they have discussed the issue with their immediate boss or if there is a reason they are not following the chain of command.

Taking every decision through every level of the organization can be time consuming and difficult, especially in an organization with many layers of management. The solution is to use common sense. For example, a request for information probably does not have to travel through every layer of management. In contrast, a decision that will affect the group's operations should probably pass through the chain of command.

Likewise, other exceptions to the chain of command rule, would be for situations in which the immediate boss is stealing or guilty of sexual harassment.

Working together, factors like *unity of command* and *chain of command* help to ensure that organization structure will be successful. Unity of command helps to eliminate factors within organization structure like complexity and confusion in the workplace. Chain of command helps to clarify issues like who should be giving direction in an organization and who should be taking it.

Span of Control

span of control
The number of people a
manager supervises

Clearly, keeping track of and developing the talents of one employee is easier than supervising 100 employees, but hiring a supervisor for every employee would be tremendously expensive. The number of people a manager supervises is known as the manager's **span of control**. The more people the manager supervises, the greater the span of control.

Today, spans of control have increased as organizations try to save money by eliminating management positions and empowering employees to make more decisions.[21] As shown in Figure 7.5, thinking about the ideal span of control has shifted over the years. First, mass production widened the span of control by simplifying and defining precise tasks. Then employee empowerment further widened the span of control by giving workers more say in decisions. Today's recommendation ranges from 15 to 25 employees, depending on the amount of supervision required; some kinds of organizations can have even wider spans. Sun Microsystems is an example of a traditional span of control, with work teams of up to 10 employees. In contrast, at the Gemesa cookie facility in Mexico, one manager supervises an average of 56 employees. The arrangement works because the company relies on self-managing work teams (described in Chapter 3).[22] This trend makes the supervisor's job more challenging than ever.[23] Modern supervisors need top-notch skills in communicating, motivating, and monitoring the performance of larger teams of workers.

In organizing, managers must be aware of how many people they can supervise effectively. Ideally, managers supervise as many people as they can effectively guide toward meeting their goals. That number depends in part on several factors that describe the work situation:[24]

- *Similarity of functions*—The more similar the functions performed by employees, the greater the span of control can be.
- *Geographic closeness*—The closer subordinates are physically, the greater the span of control can be.

FIGURE 7.5 | Recommended Spans of Control

The ideal number of people a supervisor should manage has changed in the last century.

Source: Based on "Span of Control," *The Economist,* November 9, 2009, http://www.economist.com.

- *Complexity and change*—The simpler and more familiar the functions performed by subordinates, the greater the span of control can be. Frequent or rapid changes can make jobs seem more difficult, so a smaller span of control is necessary.
- *Coordination*—Managers need a smaller span of control when they must spend a great deal of time coordinating the work of their subordinates with one another and with other groups. The less time they need to spend on coordination, the greater the span of control can be. In many organizations, information technology is making larger spans of control possible because employees easily can obtain the information they need and share information throughout the company.
- *Planning*—The less time a manager needs to spend on planning, the greater the span of control can be.
- *Availability of staff support*—The more staff specialists available to provide support in a variety of areas, the larger the span of control can be.
- *Performance standards*—If there are clear, objective standards for performance and employees are familiar with them, the span of control can be larger than in a situation where the supervisor continually must clarify what is expected of employees.

Characteristics of the managers and employees also are important. Managers may find that, as their experience grows, so does the number of people they can supervise effectively. Managers with strong skills in time management and decision making also are likely to be able to supervise more employees. As for employees, the better able they are to work independently, the greater their supervisor's span of control can be.

LO7.8 ▶ Discuss why and how supervisors delegate.

Delegating Authority and Responsibility

delegating
Giving another person the authority and responsibility to carry out a task

A recent nationwide survey of U.S. employees found that nearly half believed that their work demands prevented them from leading a healthy life. Two of the three top stressors mentioned were work and work–life balance, and one-quarter of the employees reported that they were more stressed than they were two years ago.[25] The concept of organizing implies that one person cannot do all the work of an organization. Even a one-person business usually contracts with outside people to provide some services. Giving someone else the authority and responsibility to carry out a task is known as **delegating**.[26] You can explore your delegation effectiveness by taking the Assessing Yourself quiz on page 200.

Benefits of Delegating

Whereas the performance of most nonmanagement employees is evaluated in terms of their individual accomplishments, a supervisor's performance is evaluated according to the achievements of the whole department. The department's output will be of the highest quality and the supervisor will look best when he or she draws on the expertise of employees. Supervisors in a steel mill appreciated the significance of this principle when they addressed a serious safety concern: many workers were not complying with lockout-tagout procedures, which ensure that hazardous equipment is safely shut down and will not be turned on during maintenance. The supervisors chose not to treat the matter as simply an issue of control, which would mean insisting that employees follow procedures or be disciplined. Rather, they delegated the problem solving to a group of employees, who worked with engineers and safety experts to determine the source of the problem and fix it. The group concluded that the existing safety procedures were hard to understand. By simplifying the process and clarifying the procedures, the group solved the problem of noncompliance—probably better than the supervisors could have done alone.[27]

In other examples, a production supervisor might establish a team of employees to devise ways to make the workplace safer. Those employees are likely to come up with more ideas than the supervisor could identify alone. Some employees might have backgrounds or areas of expertise that lead them to notice where improvements are needed—improvements that the supervisor might never have considered.

A supervisor who delegates also has more time for the jobs only a supervisor can do, such as planning and counseling. One way to think of this benefit of delegating is that it is an important tool for time management (discussed in Chapter 14). If the production supervisor in the example handled all aspects of safety, it could take weeks simply to identify and describe safety problems and solutions. That time might be better spent scheduling and arranging for employees to receive various types of training.

Likewise, a supervisor of a financial services company caused problems by failing to delegate. The company had placed a technical expert in charge of its information technology (IT). This manager knew a tremendous amount about computer hardware and put in long hours keeping the company's systems running smoothly. When the firm decided it should add a wider variety of systems to handle its business needs, the manager worked harder and harder to keep up with the mushrooming demands. He continued to try applying his own expertise, rather than delegating to the IT staffers. But he simply could not keep up with all the company's needs alone. Eventually, the company had to move the manager to a job without anyone to supervise, and a new manager was hired to delegate and focus on developing the knowledge of the people in the IT group.[28]

Delegating also has a beneficial effect on employees. Delegation of work gives employees a chance to develop their skills and their value to the organization. Depending on the kinds of tasks delegated, this additional responsibility can enhance their careers and their earning potential. It also can make employees' work more interesting. It is reasonable to expect that employees who are more interested in their work and more involved in meeting the organization's objectives are likely to do higher-quality work and remain with the organization longer. (This topic will be discussed in Chapter 11.) Thus, production employees who serve on the safety team might find that this added responsibility leads them to care more about the quality of their day-to-day work. Similarly, at Rubicon Oil Company, founder Greg Cushard discovered that the more involved he got in day-to-day meetings and details, the fewer ideas his employees were contributing. Cushard tried backing off and giving employees more problem-solving responsibility. Departments from sales to accounting to operations began to boost their performance. Not only were employees contributing more, but Cushard also noticed that giving them more latitude helped him identify which employees had the most to contribute to the company's success.[29]

Empowerment

These benefits of delegating explain why many organizations use employee involvement to improve the quality of their goods and services (see Chapter 2). In other words, they delegate decision-making authority and responsibility in a variety of areas to employees. This practice—called empowerment—is based on the expectation that employees will provide more insight and expertise than managers can provide alone and that this participation will make employees more committed to doing their best.

empowerment
Delegation of broad decision-making authority and responsibility

An empowered employee on a commercial banking team devised a new way to organize the team's work. She suggested team members consider specializing in particular types of clients, rather than tackling whichever assignment came in next. The team decided to try her idea temporarily. They found that with some adjustments, the plan made their work more interesting, and they were more committed to their tasks.[30]

FIGURE 7.6 | The Process of Delegating

Delegating is not a random assignment of jobs followed by waiting for them to be completed. It is a specific and logical process that includes following up.

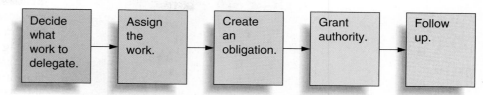

The Process of Delegating

When delegating effectively, the supervisor is not merely handing out jobs at random but should be following a logical process, as illustrated in Figure 7.6: deciding what work to delegate, assigning the work, creating an obligation, granting authority, and following up.

Decide What Work to Delegate

There are several ways to select which tasks to delegate. When an employee knows how to do a particular task better than the supervisor, delegation makes sense.[31] Another approach is to delegate simple tasks that employees clearly can handle. For example, a supervisor can have employees handle administrative duties. The supervisor also can delegate the tasks that he or she finds most boring. This approach can backfire, however, if employees perceive they always are chosen to do the dirty work. Tasks performed regularly are good candidates for delegation because it may be worth the effort to train employees to do them.

Of course, a supervisor should *not* delegate some tasks, including personnel matters and activities assigned specifically to the supervisor. Thus, the supervisor should not assign duties such as appraising performance and resolving conflicts. Likewise, if a sales supervisor's boss has asked her to fly to Vancouver to resolve a customer complaint, it would be inappropriate for the supervisor to delegate this assignment to someone else.

Assign the Work

The supervisor continues the delegation process by selecting employees to carry out the work. In delegating a particular task, the supervisor considers who is available and then determines which of them to assign. The decision may be based on who is best qualified or most efficient, or the supervisor may make assignments to provide training and development for employees who have shown potential. The supervisor also weighs the personalities involved, safety considerations, and any company policies or union rules that may apply. Supervisors can be most effective in carrying out this step when they know their employees well. Matching assignments to employee desires and skills can help the organization reap the full potential of its human resources. Based on her experience as a teller supervisor for WestStar Credit Union, branch manager Geraldine Albores advised, "Get to know each employee, know their strengths and weaknesses, then you can delegate."[32]

When two jobs must be done at the same time and the same person is best qualified to do both, the process of selecting an employee to do the work becomes complex. In such cases, the supervisor must set priorities. The supervisor must consider how important the particular task is to achieving the department's goals and serving customers. If priorities among jobs are unclear, the supervisor should check with his or her manager.

To finish the step of assigning work, the supervisor tells the designated employees what they are supposed to do. The supervisor must be sure that the employees understand what they are supposed to be doing and have the necessary knowledge and skills.

When supervisors delegate tasks to other employees, it's important that directions are clear and specific.

Clear directions are specific, but they should give employees some room to apply their knowledge and skills creatively. At the Toronto offices of the accounting and advisory firm Deloitte, when Karen Werger is delegating work on a client file to an employee, she first reviews each section of the file with the employee. She explains what the employee is supposed to do with each section and provides contact information for reaching the client. At another accounting firm, Fuller Landau, Suzanne Bertrand noticed that employees sometimes created problems by doing the easiest parts of a project first and then getting bogged down in the complex parts as the deadline nears. So when Bertrand delegated, she often set an early date when she wanted to review specific sections—the most complex ones—so there would be enough time left for addressing any difficulties.[33] To be sure employees understand an assignment, the supervisor can ask them to restate the assignment in their own words. (Chapter 10 provides more information about how to communicate clearly.) For more advice about delegating skills, see the "Supervisory Skills" box.

SUPERVISORY SKILLS

DELEGATING: OVERTHROWING THE MYTHS

For many supervisors, the great challenge of delegation is the feeling that the supervisor can do the job faster or better than the employees. Supervisors who feel this way are tempted to hover so much that employees never really learn to make decisions independently. Or at the other extreme, some supervisors are not sure how to lead and motivate, so they just assign duties and leave the results up to the employees. Of course, these employees are not really being supervised at all, and they may fall short of goals because they do not know how to succeed or they doubt that their efforts will be noticed and rewarded. Thus, the art of delegating involves knowing when to back off and when to become more involved. Delegating is a skill that can, and must, be learned in order to be an effective leader.

This is the premise of Brian Tracy's *Delegation & Supervision*. Tracy is a motivational speaker, business coach, and author. He proposes that the greatest challenge to delegating is overthrowing the myths about delegation. The myths are:

- There is not enough time to delegate.
- The staff is not competent enough.

- If you want it done right, you have to do it yourself.
- People will think you're not on top of things if you delegate to others.
- When you are good at something, you should do it yourself.

In reality, however, if a supervisor does not delegate tasks, there will not be enough time for that supervisor to accomplish what needs to be done. And employees will never become competent if they are not given the chance to try things, to make mistakes, and to learn from these mistakes. The failure of a supervisor to delegate means employees will not be equipped to handle their responsibilities and will become a bottleneck in the company's processes. Last, the belief that you, as a supervisor should stay on top of things or do them yourself because you are good, or better, than others, at them is actually an ego problem—and simply not true. Teaching and enabling others to do the things that we are good at, allows us to develop other skills—which, in turn, expands the capacity of the companies for which we work.

Sources: Based on ideas in Brian Tracy, *Delegation & Supervision*, Amacom, 2013; Dave McDonald, "Delegation & Supervision," August 8, 2013, Macarisms, http://macarisms.com/2013/08/28/delegation-supervision/, accessed on April 19, 2014.

Create an Obligation

When the supervisor makes an assignment, he or she needs to be sure the employee accepts responsibility for carrying it out. A supervisor can encourage employees to accept responsibility by involving them in making decisions and by listening to their ideas. Workers who feel involved are more apt to feel responsible. Supervisors cannot force employees to feel responsible, but fortunately, many employees willingly take on responsibility as a matter of course. In addition, by making employees accountable for their actions, supervisors lead them to accept responsibility.

Although the employee should accept responsibility for carrying out a task, this does not mean the supervisor gives up the responsibility for its proper completion. The organization still holds the supervisor accountable. Therefore, following delegation, both parties have responsibility for the work. The supervisor's job becomes one of ensuring that the employee has the necessary resources and that the task is completed and meets quality standards. The supervisor does so through the management function of controlling, described in the previous chapter.

Grant Authority

Along with responsibility, supervisors must give employees the authority they need to carry out their jobs. This is how supervisors follow the parity principle, discussed previously in this chapter. Thus, if a supervisor at Abbott Laboratories gives a researcher responsibility to carry out a particular procedure, the researcher must also be given the authority to obtain the materials and equipment needed to do the job.

Follow Up

After assigning duties and the authority to carry them out, the supervisor needs to give the employees some freedom to act independently and creatively. This does not mean the supervisor should abandon employees to succeed or fail on their own; after all, the supervisor is equally responsible for the success of the work. Therefore, it should be made clear to employees that the supervisor is available for guidance. The supervisor also should set forth a plan for periodically checking on the progress of the work. The supervisor may find that employees need additional information or help removing obstacles to success, or perhaps they simply need praise for the work they have done so far.

If an employee's performance of an unfamiliar task is less than perfect, the supervisor should not be discouraged from delegating in the future. Everyone needs time to learn, and disappointing performances may offer a chance for the supervisor to learn what is needed to strengthen an employee's skills. In addition, poor performance may have resulted from the way the work was delegated, not from a problem with the employee.

LO7.9 ▶ Identify causes of reluctance to delegate.

Reluctance to Delegate

Let's say a woman—we'll call her Ruby Singh—works late every night, reviewing all her employees' work and preparing detailed instructions for them to carry out the next day. Her own manager has suggested that she give the workers more freedom, which would save her a lot of time and probably increase their job satisfaction. However, Singh is afraid that if she does not keep close tabs on her employees, the department's performance will suffer.

Many supervisors are convinced that they are able to do a better job than their employees. They might even say, "If you want something done right, you have to do it yourself." Often they may be correct, particularly if their own promotion to a supervisory post resulted from high performance. Observing an employee making mistakes can be difficult, especially if the supervisor will look bad for allowing the mistake to occur.

These risks cause many supervisors to fear delegation. Psychologist Donna Genett speculates that this fear arises because "so many people move up to management on the basis of their own successes. When they get into management, a shift has to happen where their success comes from letting other people shine."[34] In other words, the organization needs supervisors to develop and coach employees so the employees can be more valuable to the organization. This requires delegation, even though learning may involve some mistakes.

In some cases, employees may really be unable to carry out jobs that they have been delegated. If so, the supervisor must consider ways to bring the workforce's talents into line with the department's needs. Perhaps employees need training or the department's hiring practices need improvement. (For more on selecting and training employees, see Chapters 15 and 16.)

As mentioned previously, delegating frees supervisors to concentrate on the tasks that they do best or that only they can do. Sometimes a supervisor is more comfortable being an expert at the employees' work than struggling with supervisory responsibilities such as motivating employees and resolving conflicts. However, the supervisor must overcome any discomfort or fear, because the organization needs supervisors who supervise.

Skills Module

PART ONE: CONCEPTS

Summary

7.1 Describe organization charts.

Organization charts are a standard way to draw the structure of an organization. Boxes represent the departments or positions, and connecting lines indicate reporting relationships. The positions at the top of the organization chart have the most authority and responsibility. If an organization chart has few levels, the organization is said to be flat.

7.2 Identify basic ways in which organizations are structured.

Unless they are very small, organizations are grouped into departments. An organization with a functional structure groups personnel and other resources according to the types of work they carry out. A product structure groups work and resources according to the product produced and delivered. In a geographic structure, the departments are set up according to the location of the customers served or the goods or services produced. A customer structure departmentalizes the organization according to the category of customer served.

Organizations now often combine the basic types of structures, particularly when teams of employees are formed to meet objectives such as improving quality or applying new technology. Those seeking flexibility often favor an organic structure—one in which boundaries between jobs continually shift and people pitch in wherever their contributions are needed. They may form network organizations, which contract with other individuals and organizations to complete specific projects (instead of adding permanent employees). They may also promote the acquisition and sharing of knowledge by creating a learning organization.

7.3 Discuss the value of job descriptions.

Job descriptions provide both employees and supervisors with clear information on what each person's role within the company's organizational structure should be.

7.4 Distinguish between line and staff authority and between centralized and decentralized authority.

Authority is the right to perform a task or give orders to someone else. Line authority is the right to carry out tasks and give orders related to the organization's primary purpose. Staff authority is the right to advise or assist those with line authority. When authority is centralized, it is shared by a few top managers; when authority is decentralized, it is spread among a greater number of people.

7.5 Compare and contrast *authority, power, responsibility*, and *accountability*.

Authority is the right to perform a task or give orders. Power is the ability (as opposed to the right) to get others to act in a certain way. Responsibility is the obligation to perform certain tasks. Accountability is the practice of imposing penalties for failure to adequately carry out responsibilities and giving rewards for success in meeting responsibilities. The authority to transfer responsibility to employees and hold them accountable adds to a supervisor's power. (However, a supervisor always is held accountable for his or her employees' performance.)

7.6 Identify the steps in the process of organizing.

To organize a department or work group, the supervisor should first define the objective of the department or work group, then determine what resources are needed. Finally, the supervisor groups activities and assigns duties to appropriate employees.

7.7 Describe four principles of organizing.

According to the parity principle, personnel with responsibility must also be given enough authority to carry out that responsibility. The principle of unity of command states that each employee should have only one supervisor. A chain of command is the flow of authority from one level of the organization to the next; most decisions and information should flow along the chain of command. Finally, supervisors and other managers should have an appropriate span of control; the best number of employees for a specific situation depends on a variety of factors.

7.8 Discuss why and how supervisors delegate.

Supervisors delegate to enhance the quality of the department's and supervisor's performance by drawing on the expertise of employees. Delegation also frees time for supervisory tasks. It may improve employee morale and performance by empowering them to make decisions in a variety of areas. To delegate, supervisors follow a five-step process: Decide what work to delegate, assign the work, create an obligation, grant authority, and follow up. When delegating, supervisors must make sure employees understand and are able to do the work, and they retain the responsibility to see that the work is done properly.

7.9 Identify causes of reluctance to delegate.

Many supervisors are reluctant to delegate because they believe no one else can do the job as well. They may not want to give up activities they enjoy. Some supervisors are more comfortable doing what their employees should be doing than carrying out supervisory responsibilities.

Key Terms

organizing, *p.* 175
department, *p.* 177
departmentalization, *p.* 178
organic structure, *p.* 181
network organizations, *p.* 182
learning organization, *p.* 182

authority, *p.* 183
line authority, *p.* 183
staff authority, *p.* 184
functional authority, *p.* 184
power, *p.* 185
responsibility, *p.* 185

parity principle, *p.* 189
unity of command, *p.* 189
chain of command, *p.* 189
span of control, *p.* 190
delegating, *p.* 191
empowerment, *p.* 192

Review and Discussion Questions

1. Emily Sanford has just been promoted to supervisor of the salespeople in the gift department at a department store. Which of the following organizing activities is she likely to carry out?
   a. Scheduling her employees' work hours.
   b. Forming a team of her employees to work on a promotional event within the department.
   c. Helping decide the best location for a new branch of the department store.
   d. Assigning an employee to sit at the bridal registry desk.
   e. Determining whether the department store should launch its own line of products.

2. What might be the best structure for each of the following organizations?
   a. A three-person company that sells complete, prepackaged gourmet dinners to specialty grocery stores.

   b. A small organization that supplies antique cars to movie studios.
   c. A manufacturer of windows, with offices in Toronto, Seattle, Miami, and Chicago.

3. What special attributes must supervisors have to be successful in some of the new types of organizational structures?

4. Which of the following supervisors have primarily line authority? Which have staff authority?
   a. The production supervisor at a publishing company, who is responsible for getting books typeset and printed.
   b. The housekeeping supervisor at a hospital.
   c. The word-processing supervisor at a law firm.
   d. The payroll department supervisor for a fire department.

5. In recent years, many organizations have become more decentralized. Typically this change involves eliminating middle management jobs and sharing more control with those at lower levels of the organization. How do you think this affects the role of supervisors in those organizations?

6. Does someone with authority always have power? Does a person who accepts responsibility necessarily have authority? Explain.

7. What are the steps in the process of organizing? How would they apply to the manager of an Olive Garden restaurant who needs to schedule employees? Explain in general how this supervisor could follow each step.

8. Describe each of the following principles of organizing:

a. Parity principle.
b. Unity of command.
c. Chain of command.

9. A production supervisor at a company that makes eco-friendly cleaning supplies learns about the factors that should influence the span of control. The supervisor believes that his own span of control is too large for him to supervise effectively. Is there anything a person in his position can do? If not, explain why. If so, suggest what he can try.

10. Harry Jamison, CPA, is planning to set up a business to prepare tax returns. Harry is the only person in the business, at least for now. Can he delegate any work? Should he? Explain.

11. What steps do you think a supervisor who is reluctant to delegate could take to overcome this discomfort?

Notes

1. Jason Fried, "Why I Run a Flat Company," *Inc.*, April 2011, http://www.inc.com.

2. Alison Overhold, "Cuckoo for Customers," *Fast Company*, June 2004, downloaded from InfoTrac, http://web2.infotrac.galegroup.com; "About Rackspace," Rackspace, http://www.rackspace.com/about/, accessed April 18, 2014.

3. Christopher S. Frings, "Addressing Management Issues," *Medical Laboratory Observer*, January 2003, downloaded from Business & Company Resource Center, http://galenet.galegroup.com; "About Rackspace," Rackspace, http://www.rackspace.com/about/, accessed April 18, 2014.

4. Thomas Sy and Laura Sue D'Annunzio, "Challenges and Strategies of Matrix Organizations: Top-Level and Midlevel Managers' Perspectives," *Human Resource Planning*, March 2005, downloaded from Business & Company Resource Center, http://galenet.galegroup.com. See also Lonnie Pacelli, "Making Many Units Whole," *Incentive*, January 2005, downloaded from Business & Company Resource Center, http://galenet.galegroup.com.

5. Carol Hymowitz, "IBM Creates Volunteer Teams to Cultivate Emerging Markets," *The Wall Street Journal*, August 4, 2008, http://online.wsj.com; "Corporate Service Corps," IBM, http://www.ibm.com/ibm/responsibility/corporateservicecorps/, accessed April 18, 2014.

6. For more information on network organizations, see Teck-Young Eng, 2007, "An investigation of internet coordination mechanisms in network organizations," *Journal of Interactive Marketing*, 21, p. 61.

7. Douglas McLeod, "Insurers Outsourcing Benefits Administration," *Business Insurance*, August 23, 2004, downloaded from Business & Company Resource Center, http://galenet.galegroup.com.

8. Simona Covel, "Eastern Europe Stakes Its Claim as Just the Right Site for Growth," *The Wall Street Journal*, September 8, 2004, http://online.wsj.com.

9. Patricia L. Smith, "Rebuilding an American Icon," *American Machinist*, June 2003, downloaded from Business & Company Resource Center, http://galenet.galegroup.com.

10. David A. Garvin, "Building a Learning Organization," *Harvard Business Review* 74, no. 4 (July 1993): 78. See also Leonel Prieto, "Some Necessary Conditions and Constraints for Successful Learning Organizations," *Competition Forum* 7, no. 2 (2009): 513–520.

11. "Hire & Retain Employees: Writing Effective Job Descriptions," The U.S. Small Business Administration, http://www.sba.gov/content/writing-effective-job-descriptions, accessed April 19, 2014.

12. "Wrong, Wrong, Wrong!" *Computerworld*, May 10, 2004, downloaded from Business & Company Resource Center, https://galenet.galegroup.com.

13. Don Durfee, "Striking a Balance," *CFO*, November 2005, downloaded from Business & Company Resource Center, http://galenet.galegroup.com.

14. "Follow These Leaders," *Fortune*, December 12, 2005.

15. "Advanced Tent Rental Ltd. and Supervisor Fined for Health and Safety Violations," *CNW Group*, May 31, 2006, downloaded from Business & Company Resource Center, http://galenet.galegroup.com.

16. "Wal-Mart Reorganizes U.S. Division," *Home Textiles Today*, February 8, 2010, p. 8; Wal-Mart Stores, "Corporate and Financial Facts," Fact Sheets, http://walmartstores.com/pressroom/factsheets, accessed November 2, 2011.

17. Chris Ortiz, "Lean Manufacturing as a Growth Creator," *Ceramic Industry*, August 2008, downloaded

from Business & Company Resource Center, http://galenet.galegroup.com.

18. For more information about natural work groups in the motorcycle industry, see P. Chansler, P. Swaimidass, and C. Cammann, 2003, "Self-managing work teams: An empirical study of group cohesiveness in 'natural work groups' at a Harley-Davidson Motor Company plant," *Small Group Research*, 34, pp. 101–120.

19. Michael Oneal, "Harley Enjoys Winning Cycle," *Chicago Tribune*, May 14, 2006, sec. 5, pp. 1, 9, 11.

20. Samuel C. Certo and S. Trevis Certo, Modern Management: Concepts and Skills, Upper Saddle River: New Jersey, 2014, p. 226.

21. For a recent review of challenges associated with span of control, see N. Theobald and S. Nicholson-Crotty, 2005, "The many faces of span of control: Organization structure across multiple goals," *Administration & Society*, 36, p. 648.

22. George Anders, "Overseeing More Employees with Fewer Managers," *The Wall Street Journal*, March 24, 2008, http://online.wsj.com.

23. Barbara Davison, "Management Span of Control: How Wide Is Too Wide?" *Journal of Business Strategy* 24, no. 4 (July–August 2003), downloaded from Business & Company Resource Center, http://galenet.galegroup.com.

24. The factors described in this paragraph are based on Harold Koontz, "Making Theory Operational: The Span of Management," *Journal of Management Studies*, October 1966, pp. 229–243; Davison, "Management Span of Control."

25. CCH Aspen Publishers, "Employees Blame Stress from Work, Finances, and Work/Life Balance for Lack of Healthy Lifestyle," *HR Management News & Information*, November 4, 2008, http://hr.cch.com.

26. For more information on delegation, see O. Swank & B. Visser, 2007, "Motivating through delegating tasks or giving attention," *Journal of Law Economics & Organization*, 23, p. 731.

27. Josh Williams, "Improving Management Support for Safety to Optimize Safety Culture," *Occupational Hazards*, June 2008, downloaded from Business & Company Resource Center, http://galenet.galegroup.com.

28. "When Good Managers Fail: The Law of Problem Evolution," *CioInsight*, May 18, 2005, downloaded from Business & Company Resource Center, http://galenet.galegroup.com.

29. Cari Tuna, "Micromanagers Miss Bull's-Eye," *The Wall Street Journal*, November 3, 2008, http://online.wsj.com.

30. Joseph A. Raelin, "Growing Group Leadership Skills," *Security Management*, June 2004, downloaded from Business & Company Resource Center, http://galenet.galegroup.com.

31. For a recent article describing the benefits of delegating, see C. Dai, T. Lewis, and G. Lopomo, 2006, "Delegating management to experts," *The Rand Journal of Economics*, 37, p. 503.

32. Michael Bartlett, "The Branch CEO," *Banking Wire*, November 17, 2005, downloaded from Business & Company Resource Center, http://galenet.galegroup.com.

33. Deena Waisberg, "How Are You Managing?" *CA Magazine*, March 2011, pp. 18–24.

34. Amy Alexander, "Let Yourself Delegate," *Greater Baton Rouge Business Report*, August 19, 2003, downloaded from Business & Company Resource Center, http://galenet.galegroup.com.

PART TWO: SKILL-BUILDING

Meeting the Challenge

Reflecting back on page 175, what sort of changes will both supervisors and front-line employees face in the coming months? What challenges will they face? How will work be delegated in these new work groups?

In your group, list the challenges you see facing Zappos' lead links in assigning work. Have three members of the group role-play a situation in which employees need to be reassigned because of a new product being released. One person should play the role of the lead link, one should be the employee being reassigned, and one should play the role of an employee who has an idea for what she believes is a better approach than reassigning employees. Are there principles of effective delegation that would help resolve this situation?

Problem-Solving Case: Is Thor Industries Organized for Growth?

Thor Industries is the largest maker of recreational vehicles in the world. If you have never heard of this company, that fact may have something to do with the way it is organized. The company's principal executive office is located in Elkhart, Indiana. Here, president and chief executive officer Bob Martin oversee the activities of a company that recently enjoyed more than $3.2 billion in sales.

The rest of the work occurs throughout North America at the company's 17 recreational vehicle (RV) factories. Thor makes RVs sold under many brand names, including Airstream, Keystone, Dutchmen, Outback, Four Winds, and General Coach.

Wade Thompson (deceased) and Peter Orthwein originally built Thor by purchasing RV and bus manufacturers and letting them operate independently. In effect the RV companies that Thor has acquired continue to compete with one another under the corporate umbrella. And brands within a division operate independently. At Keystone, for example, there are 29 brands, and they have separate factories, each with its own manager in charge of that brand. Within a facility, there are different functional groups, such as cabinetmaking, plumbing, electrical, and finishing. Each group has a floor leader. The leader and the group together have the responsibility to improve efficiency, including the authority to eliminate unproductive workers.

In addition to operating independently, the divisions are rewarded independently. The president of each division receives a portion of that division's pretax profits, and some of them earn more than the corporation's chief executive. The financial rewards at lower levels also are linked to performance. Factory workers in some cases are paid a rate based on the amount of production, rather than their hours worked. Also, the entire workforce at a facility earns a percentage of its sales. Each functional group within the facility—for example, plumbing or electrical— receives a given share of that amount.

This structure encourages innovation and customer service. The basic parts for any RV are essentially the same. Brands distinguish themselves by style, service, and special features. Thor executives believe that when each division handles its own sales, manufacturing, and research and development, they will have more incentive to outdo the other brands. Also, the smaller divisions can more readily hear and respond to customer feedback than a centralized corporation could. A Michigan dealer explains, "They don't have to go up this giant chain of command to get something done." In effect, this is the structure that General Motors (GM) once had, with different organizations for each of its makes. However, GM eventually became more centralized because it couldn't afford to continue duplicating so many functions.

What does this leave for Thor's chief executive to do? Primarily, Martin keeps track of the major financial measures. When a division is slipping, he gets involved.

1. Does this description of Thor Industries sound more like a functional, product, geographic, or customer structure, or some combination of these? Explain. Is Thor Industries highly centralized or decentralized? Explain.

2. Is Bob Martin a good example of a manager delegating authority? Why or why not?

3. Imagine you are a production supervisor in one of Thor's factories. Suggest how you would handle each of the following challenges within this company's organizational structure:

   a. You want to improve the quality of cabinet installation, and you would like to get ideas from supervisors at a division where the quality is very high.

   b. You want to cut the cost of electrical work by operating more efficiently—building the same number of RVs with fewer workers. You want the electrical team to accept responsibility for this challenge.

   c. You like to camp, and based on an idea you heard from some campers in a park you visited, you want to try building RVs with a new feature: computer workstations.

Sources: Jonathan Fahey, "Lord of the Rigs," *Forbes*, March 29, 2004, downloaded from Business & Company Resource Center, http://galenet.galegroup.com; Thor Industries, Annual Report 2013, http://ir.thorindustries.com/files/doc_financials/annual/Thor2013 AnnualReport.pdf; "Our History," Thor Industries, http://ir.thorindustries.com/about-thor/our-history/default.aspx, accessed April 20, 2014.

Assessing Yourself

Do You Delegate?

To test your delegating skills, answer the following questions with Yes or No.

1. Do you regularly work a lot of overtime? _____

2. Are you usually busier than the people you work with? _____

3. Must you often rush to meet deadlines? _____

4. Are you ever unable to complete important projects? _____

5. Are you too busy to plan or prioritize your work? _____

6. Do you return from vacation to find piles of unfinished business waiting for you? _____

7. Have you neglected training someone to take over your job on short notice? _____

8. Do you feel other people are taking breaks or leaving on time while you do their work for them? _____

9. Do you feel you are the only one who can do the job right? _____

10. Do you have difficulty expressing yourself? _____

The more Yes answers you give, the more likely it is that you have trouble delegating.

Source: Janet Mahoney, "Delegating Effectively," *Nursing Management,* June 1997, p. 62. Reprinted with permission of Lippincott Williams & Wilkins.

Pause and Reflect

1. When is it hardest for you to delegate?
2. When do you want others to delegate more to you?

Class Skills Exercise

Networking

Six Degrees of Separation

Some experts feel that no matter how an organization is designed, the key to efficiency is the creation of shortcuts between different levels of the firm. Studies have shown that it takes only a few such connections between well-connected individuals to make a very small world out of a large one. This is the idea that underlies the concept of "six degrees of separation," which originated in the work of Harvard social psychologist Stanley Milgram in the 1960s.

Milgram gave randomly selected people in Kansas and Nebraska each a letter addressed to someone they did not know in Massachusetts. He asked them to mail the letter to an acquaintance who would bring it closer to the target addressee. Each participant needed an average of only five intermediaries to make the connection.

Break into small groups and re-create Milgram's experiment as a thought exercise. Let one person in the group name a friend at a different school or university than the one you attend. Go around your group to see whether each person can mention someone who can lead you closer to your target friend. See whether you can at least reach the right campus, if not the person named, and compare notes with the other groups in your class to see how many "degrees of separation" were needed in the smallest and the largest chains.

Building Supervision Skills

Delegating

Organizing a Fund-Raising Team

Divide the class into teams of four to six members. Appoint a leader to act as supervisor for each team. Each team will hold the initial meeting to organize a fund-raising event for a cause of their choice. The teams should define their objectives, determine the needed resources, group activities, and assign duties. The supervisor should delegate whatever responsibilities he or she can, including asking for a volunteer to take notes at the meeting itself.

Before the end of class, a spokesperson for each team may report to the class on the effectiveness of the meeting: How quickly were objectives defined? How evenly were duties assigned? What was each member's responsibility? How efficient was the supervisor at delegating? Did some members seem to have more power than others?

chapter eight | The Supervisor as Leader

learning objectives

After you have studied this chapter, you should be able to:

8.1 Discuss the possible link between personal traits and leadership ability.

8.2 Explain democratic vs. authoritarian leadership.

8.3 Explain major leadership theories.

8.4 Identify criteria for choosing a leadership style.

8.5 Explain how supervisors can develop and maintain good relations with their employees, managers, and peers.

A Supervision Challenge

KRAFT LEADERS UNIFY EMPLOYEES

One of the critical roles of a supervisor is to serve as a leader for other employees. This becomes particularly important, and challenging, when supervisors are dealing with employees who are unhappy or discouraged.

When Kraft Foods acquired the Cadbury company, integrating the two companies was proving very challenging. Kraft Foods Inc, a global grocery manufacturing and processing conglomerate, had executed what was essentially a takeover of Cadbury, whose management was strongly opposed to the acquisition deal. When two bitter rivals finally end their rivalry in this way, emotions do not just turn off. However, for the acquisition to be successful, the Kraft management had to demonstrate leadership and show that they were integrating professionally and without bitterness.

When the acquisition deal closed, the Cadbury employees fundamentally distrusted Kraft. The Cadbury employees feared that Kraft would destroy their core values and diminish the quality of the Cadbury products. The Kraft employees resented such assumptions, which led to uncomfortable, less efficient work efforts. Kraft supervisors on the floor witnessed firsthand the way employees' attitudes influenced productivity and working conditions. They knew something needed to be done. These employees from two varying companies needed to see a form of leadership that could unite the workers and improve the working environment. Kraft supervisors and managers hit upon the idea to use corporate history to show that the two companies actually had pretty similar values and desires and should naturally work well together. If Cadbury employees were skeptical of Kraft, perhaps showing the long-standing leadership and quality of Kraft would help to show similarities between the two companies.

Kraft company archivists scoured the Kraft historical archives and realized that their company had several points in common with Cadbury. For example, both of the company's founders were very religious and embodied their companies with their faith; both companies had long histories—Cadbury was over a century old, and Kraft close to a century; and both companies had a deep commitment to providing high-quality products for their customers. Kraft created an intranet site to highlight the common themes the two companies shared in their histories. Company managers and supervisors reinforced these shared themes in subsequent communication with employees, and the effort was credited with smoothing the integration of Cadbury into Kraft.

This tactic worked because people naturally seek meaning in their work, and a shared history helps build a sense of purpose and unity. Employees want to feel part of a larger whole, something bigger than themselves, and we all want to work in a place that is consistent with our values and beliefs, where our work matters and makes a difference. Cadbury employees could feel confident that they were being led by supervisors who represented a high-quality company.

It took leadership from Kraft supervisors and managers to show Cadbury and Kraft employees that they held similar values and could work in unison. If this had not been done, the integration could well have fallen flat and led to mass employee resignations and overall unrest in the workplace. Supervisors had to figure out a way to smooth the merger before this happened.

As you study this chapter, think about other ways you might utilize leadership in situations involving unhappy employees. Can you use the leadership theories and principles from this chapter to avoid the pitfalls of using company history as a leadership tool? Consider these questions as you study this chapter.

Sources: Based on John T. Seaman Jr. and George David Smith, "Your Company's History as a Leadership Tool," *Harvard Business Review*, December 2012, http://hbr.org/2012/12/your-companys-history-as-a-leadership-tool/ar/1; Kraft, "About Us," http://www.kraftfoodsgroup.com/about/history/history.aspx, accessed April 23, 2014.

---

leading
Influencing people to act or not act in a certain way

When there is change within a company or challenging situations to be overcome, it may fall to the supervisors to help employees adjust to and cope with these situations. In other words, supervisors must be leaders. As you learned in Chapter 1, leading is the management function of influencing people to act or not act in a certain way.

This chapter explores what makes leadership work. The chapter describes a variety of leadership theories and provides criteria for matching a theory to a situation. Because leading mainly requires relationship skills, the chapter concludes with a discussion of how supervisors can relate effectively to the various people in an organization.

LO8.1 ▶ Discuss the possible link between personal traits and leadership ability.

Characteristics of a Successful Leader

What is the difference between a manager and a leader? According to consultant and author Paul Taffinder, "Managers seek and follow direction. Leaders inspire achievement." Management consultants Herb Greenberg and Patrick Sweeney say managing involves *implementing* ideas (putting them into action), whereas leading focuses on *initiating* ideas (getting them started). They cite the example of Skip Cimino, the president and chief executive officer of Robert Wood Johnson University Hospital Hamilton. In his career, Cimino discovered that leadership aims for "the willingness of individuals to want to step up, take responsibility, become accountable, accept risk and move forward."[1] A leader inspires that willingness by instilling in employees a sense of common purpose, a belief that together they can achieve something worthwhile.

Effective leaders are those who are able to influence follower attitudes and behaviors toward outcomes that are important for the organization. To find out whether people are natural leaders, social scientists have studied the personalities of effective leaders, looking for traits they hold in common. Presumably, such traits would be predictors of good leadership. Some traits that might be considered significant are the following:

- *Sense of responsibility*—A person who is promoted to a supervisory position is given responsibility for the work of others as well as for his or her own performance. Supervisors must be willing to take this responsibility seriously and be aware that they are responsible for their actions 24 hours a day, seven days a week. And as described in "Supervision: New Trends," on the following page, today's supervisors also must accept responsibility for their conduct online.
- *Self-confidence*—A supervisor who believes in his or her ability to get the job done will convey confidence to employees.
- *High energy level*—Many organizations expect supervisors to put in long hours willingly to handle the variety of duties that come with the job. Some supervisory positions also are physically challenging, requiring that the supervisor actively observe and participate in what is happening in the workplace.
- *Empathy*—In settling disputes, answering questions, and understanding needs, supervisors should be sensitive to the feelings of employees and higher management. Supervisors who have difficulty understanding what makes people tick will be at a disadvantage.

internal locus of control
The belief that you are the primary cause of what happens to yourself

external locus — its not my fault [handwritten note]

- *Internal locus of control*—An internal locus of control is the belief that you are the primary cause of what happens to yourself. People with an external locus of control tend to blame others or events beyond their control when something goes wrong. Those with an internal locus of control are thought to be better leaders because they try harder to take charge of events.
- *Sense of humor*—People with a good sense of humor are more fun to work with and work for (assuming they use appropriate humor—not racist or sexist anecdotes—and do not overuse rehearsed jokes that are unrelated to work).

Focusing on traits such as these, ask yourself whether you have leadership qualities. Also, determine whether you are CEO material by taking the Assessing Yourself quiz on page 223.

SUPERVISION: NEW TRENDS

USING SOCIAL MEDIA RESPONSIBLY

It's obvious that taking on a supervisory job changes a person's role and relationships at work. Because supervisors are managers, they are expected to lead effectively by modeling the kinds of behavior they want to see from employees on their team. In addition, supervisors are discovering that they also are responsible for conducting themselves appropriately online when they use social media such as Facebook, Twitter, and LinkedIn. Actions that might be tolerated or harmless coming from an operative employee are potentially disruptive and harmful from a supervisor.

At a minimum, employees say, it's awkward when a supervisor tries to connect with them on a social site such as Facebook. In a recent survey of U.S. workers, two-thirds rate these efforts to connect as being inappropriate. Many workers don't want to share the details of their social lives with their supervisor, but they might worry that if they turn down an invitation from the boss, it will harm their working relationship. If they accept an invitation anyway, the boss will see not only what the employees post, but also comments that friends and family post in reply. Some of those might not portray the employee in the best light, professionally speaking. Conversely, employees might see comments or pictures that do not reflect well on the boss's professional image, and that could make it more difficult for the supervisor to lead effectively in the future.

Another issue is that supervisors are responsible for meeting the standards of behavior expected of management.

Labor laws protect operative employees who complain to one another about working conditions and management behavior. As managers, supervisors have no such protection. Difficult situations arise if employees use social media to grumble and try to include the supervisor in those discussions. Supervisors may not participate and may not retaliate. In fact, some companies require that supervisors say only positive things about the company online. Likewise, suppose employees post jokes that could be offensive to co-workers in groups protected against discrimination. The supervisor's participation in the conversation could put the whole company at risk of being charged with creating a hostile working environment. Yet unlike a conversation that takes place among people at work, exchanges in social media give the supervisor little control over who joins in and what those people say.

Many supervisors conclude that they can best fulfill their responsibilities as leaders by separating their work and social networks on the Internet. In addition, they know that nothing is guaranteed to stay private forever on the Internet, so they post only pictures and comments that are consistent with the image they need to maintain at work.

Sources: Intermedia, "Don't Be Rude," news release, July 25, 2011, http://www.intermedia.net; "Twitter Scandal Generates Interest in What Constitutes Proper Policy," *HR Focus,* August 2011, pp. 1–4; John Alden and Chuck Rice, "Social Media Rules Pose Risks," *Atlanta Journal-Constitution,* October 30, 2011, http://www.ajc.com.

Although these traits sound plausible as the characteristics of a successful leader, results of various studies about leadership traits have been inconsistent. Some studies have found one set of traits to be significant, while others have identified a completely different set of traits. As a result, research has not established a clear link between personality traits and leadership success. Thus, if you have most of the traits described here, you may be a successful leader, but your success is not guaranteed. Also, if you have only a few of these traits, you need not be discouraged; you can still develop the skills that effective leaders use.

connect   SELF-ASSESSMENT 8.1

Do You Have What it Takes to be a Leader?

Leaders exist at all levels in an organization. As you move higher in an organization, the scope of your leadership impacts increases. However, you can be a leader in you earliest supervisory position. This assessment helps identify the qualities that will help you as a leader. You can use it to find those qualities you already have and can work to increase. It will also help identify qualities that may be hindering you as a leader so that you can work to eliminate or lessen these.

Leadership Theories

Anita O'Donnell runs a tight ship; she lays down the rules and tolerates no deviation from them. Greg Petersen focuses on what he perceives to be the needs of his employees; they in turn do good work out of loyalty to him. George Liang is an easygoing supervisor when the work is routine, but when a big order comes in, he turns tough.

If you have worked for more than one boss, chances are you have experienced more than one leadership style. O'Donnell, Petersen, and Liang illustrate only some of the possibilities. Some supervisors instinctively lead in a way they are comfortable with; others adopt their leadership style consciously. However, a supervisor who is aware of the basic types of leadership theories is probably in the best position to lead in ways that will get the desired results.

LO8.2 ▶ Explain democratic vs. authoritarian leadership.

authoritarian leadership
A leadership style in which the leader retains a great deal of authority

democratic leadership
A leadership style in which the leader allows subordinates to participate in decision making and problem solving

laissez-faire leadership
A leadership style in which the leader is uninvolved and lets subordinates direct themselves

Democratic vs. Authoritarian Leadership

One way to describe leadership styles is in terms of how much authority the leader retains. Do employees get to make choices and control their own work? Or does the supervisor make all the decisions? To describe the possibilities, management theorists refer to authoritarian, democratic, and laissez-faire leadership.

With authoritarian leadership, the leader retains a great deal of authority, making decisions and dictating instructions to employees. An example would be a military commander who expects unquestioning obedience.

Some supervisors share more authority than authoritarian supervisors do. With democratic leadership, the supervisor allows employees to participate in decision making and problem solving. A supervisor with a democratic style of leadership might have the staff meet weekly to discuss how to improve client relations. When a conflict arises, this supervisor asks the group to discuss possible solutions and select one.

At the opposite extreme from authoritarian leadership is laissez-faire leadership. A laissez-faire manager is uninvolved and lets employees do what they want. Supervisors are rarely, if ever, able to practice this style of leadership because the nature of the supervisor's job requires close involvement with employees.

Nor are many supervisors totally authoritarian or totally democratic. Most supervisors give employees some degree of freedom to do their jobs, but they still make some of the decisions for the department. Years ago, Robert Tannenbaum and Warren H. Schmidt drew a graph showing the continuum, or range of possibilities, for the degree of authority a manager can retain. This continuum, illustrated in Figure 8.1 on the following page, is still popular today as a way to picture the possibilities.

The Managerial Grid

Another way to look at differences in leadership styles is to consider what supervisors focus on in making decisions and evaluating accomplishments. In general terms, leaders may be task oriented or people oriented. A task-oriented leader is one who focuses on the jobs to be done and the goals to be accomplished. When the work gets done correctly and on time, a task-oriented leader is satisfied. On the other hand, a people-oriented leader is concerned primarily with the well-being of the people he or she manages. This type of leader emphasizes issues such as morale, job satisfaction, and relationships among employees.

Most organizations expect that their supervisors can combine some degree of task orientation with some degree of people orientation. A supervisor who tends to focus on getting out the work should remember to sometimes check how employees are feeling and getting along. A supervisor who regularly sticks up for employees' welfare should make sure that he or she also remembers to promote the organization's

FIGURE 8.1 | Possibilities for Retaining Authority

Very few supervisors are completely authoritarian or totally democratic, nor are many laissez-faire leaders. Most use approaches that fall somewhere on a continuum.

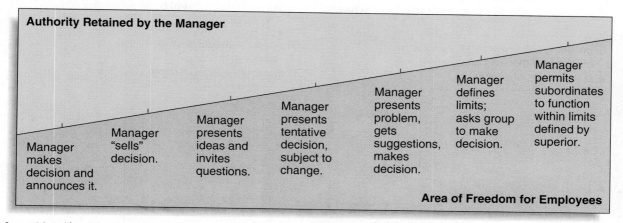

Source: Adapted from Robert Tannenbaum and Warren Schmidt, "How to Choose a Leadership Pattern," *Harvard Business Review*, May–June 1973.

goals. In practice, concern for employees' well-being is consistent with the idea that the organization's people are its most valuable assets. When supervisors help employees see their work as meaningful, give them the resources they need to get the job done, and express appreciation for their accomplishments, the supervisors are contributing to positive results at the same time they are making employees feel satisfied. An example is Cargill director Pete Wamsteeker, who says managing well is an important obligation that affects employees' lives: "I can't make mistakes with that. I really have an obligation to do it right, and I'm going to invest the time to do it right."[2]

Figure 8.2 on the following page identifies manager leadership styles. One axis shows the manger's concern for people, and the other axis shows the manager's concern for production. To apply this model of leadership, supervisors identify where their current styles of leadership fall in Figure 8.2, and then they determine what kinds of changes they need to make in order to adopt a better managerial style with a high concern for both people and production.

LO8.3 ▶ Explain major leadership theories.

Contingency Theories of Leadership

With all these possibilities, is there one best approach to leading employees? Should the supervisor consciously cultivate one leadership style? A common view is that the best style of leadership depends on the circumstances.

Fiedler's Contingency Model

One of the first researchers to develop such a theory—called a *contingency theory*—was Fred Fiedler. According to Fiedler, each leader has a preferred leadership style, which may be relationship oriented (i.e., people oriented) or task oriented. Whether relationship-oriented or task-oriented leaders perform better depends on three characteristics of the situation: leader–member relations, task structure, and the position power of the leader, as shown in Figure 8.3 on page 209. Leader–member relations refers to the extent to which the leader has the support and loyalty of group members. Task structure describes any specified procedures that employees should follow in carrying out the task. Position power refers to the formal authority granted to the leader by the organization.

FIGURE 8.2 | The Managerial Grid

A good supervisor balances a concern for people with a concern for production. Team management is a style of leadership in which job satisfaction, creativity, and productivity are usually the highest.

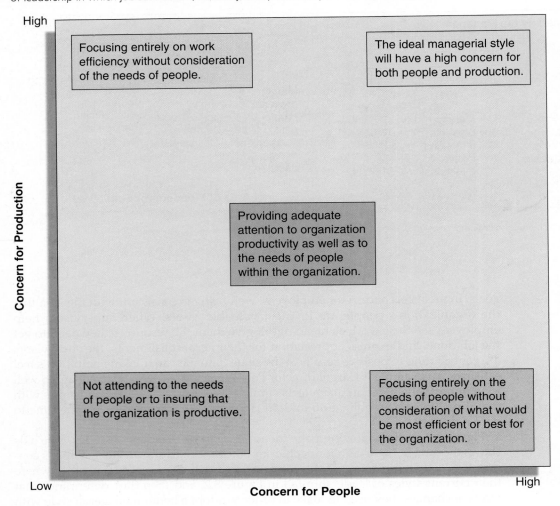

Fiedler recommends that a leader determine whether his or her preferred leadership style fits the situation. For instance, if a situation involves good leader–member relations, a structured task, and strong position power, the situation calls for a leader who is task oriented. If the leader's preferred style does not fit, Fiedler says, the leader should try to change the characteristics of the situation. In the preceding example, a relationship-oriented leader might try to make the task less structured; the result would be a situation in which the leader is likely to be more effective.

Life Cycle Theory of Leadership

Fiedler's work led others to develop their own contingency theories of leadership. For example, Paul Hersey and Ken Blanchard developed a model called the *life cycle theory*.

FIGURE 8.3 | Fiedler's Contingency Model of Leadership

The style of leadership that is best depends upon leader-member relations, task structure, and leader position power.

Leader–Member Relations	Good	Good	Good	Good	Poor	Poor	Poor	Poor
Task Structure	Structured	Structured	Unstructured	Unstructured	Structured	Structured	Unstructured	Unstructured
Leader Position Power	Strong	Weak	Strong	Weak	Strong	Weak	Strong	Weak
Which Leader Performs Better?	Task-Oriented Leader	Task-Oriented Leader	Task-Oriented Leader	Relationship-Oriented Leader	Relationship-Oriented Leader	Relationship-Oriented Leader	Task- or Relationship-Oriented Leader	Task-Oriented Leader

▢ Characteristics of the situation   ▢ Optimal leadership style for situation

Source: Adapted from Fred E. Fiedler, "Engineer the Job to Fit the Manager," *Harvard Business Review*, September–October 1965.

This model, like Fiedler's, considers the degrees to which managers focus on relationships and tasks. Unlike Fiedler's model, however, the Hersey-Blanchard theory assumes that the leader's behavior should adapt to the situation. Specifically, the leadership style should reflect the maturity of the followers, as measured by traits such as ability to work independently.

According to the Hersey-Blanchard life cycle theory, leaders should adjust their degree of task and relationship behavior in response to the growing maturity of their followers. As followers mature, leaders should move through the following combinations of task and relationship behavior:

1. High task and low relationship behavior.
2. High task and high relationship behavior.
3. Low task and high relationship behavior.
4. Low task and low relationship behavior.

Figure 8.4 shows how the choice of style changes over time in this model.

In special conditions, such as short-term deadlines, the leader may have to adjust the leadership style temporarily. However, Hersey and Blanchard maintain that this pattern of choosing a leadership style will bring about the most effective long-term working relationship between a leader and followers.

Path–Goal Theory of Leadership

The *path–goal theory of leadership* suggests that the primary activities of a leader are to make desirable and achievable rewards available to organization members who attain organizational goals and to clarify the kinds of behavior that must be performed to earn those rewards. The theory was originally developed by Robert House and later refined by House and Terence Mitchell.[3]

FIGURE 8.4 | Model of the Life Cycle Theory of Leadership

In the Hersey-Blanchard model, the behavior of the leader should adapt to the situation—changing with the maturity level of a follower changes.

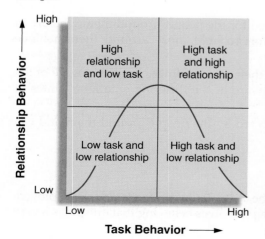

According to the theory of path–goal leadership, a leader should exhibit the following behaviors:

1. Directive behavior—Directive behavior involves telling followers what to do and how they are to do it. It is essential for a supervisor to be able to clearly communicate what is expected of followers and how they should complete their required tasks.

2. Supportive behavior—Supportive behavior involves recognizing that above all, followers are human beings. Therefore, it's important to be friendly and encouraging to followers.

3. Participative behavior—Participative behavior involves seeking input from followers about methods for improving business operations. For example, followers can often provide input as to what rewards would be desired upon completing tasks.

4. Achievement behavior—Achievement behavior involves setting a challenging goal for a follower to meet, and expressing confidence that the follower can meet this challenge. Ideally, a leader should assign a task that is challenging enough to stretch the follower, but not so challenging that the follower will be unable to complete the task.

Servant Leadership

Servant leadership involves putting other people's needs, aspirations, and interests above your own.[4] In fact, a servant leader deliberately chooses to serve other people. This seems paradoxical to many who believe that leaders should not be overly concerned about those who follow them. However, the servant leader's primary task is to serve the people around them, rather than lead. This selfless style of leadership has been written about since the 1970s, but it has been practiced for much longer. The founder of Christianity, Jesus Christ, is acknowledged by many as a servant leader. Jesus set an example to his followers on how to be a servant leader by washing others' feet and selflessly attending to those around him.

More recent research on servant leadership has indicated that a servant leader meets the following description:[5]

- *A good listener*—Servant leaders listen intently to the people who surround them. They take time to make sure that those surrounding them are heard and understood.
- *Empathic*—Not only do servant leaders hear the experiences of other people, but they are also attuned to the intellectual understanding of other peoples' thoughts and feelings.
- *Healing*—Servant leaders are concerned for the people around them who are in fragile states. They make much effort to help those around them achieve wellness.
- *Aware*—Servant leaders are aware of their surroundings. They are aware of the people around them, and they are aware of the differing emotional states of those around them.
- *Persuasive*—Servant leaders are respected by the people around them and can convince others of ideas.

Entrepreneurial Leadership

Entrepreneurial leadership is based on the attitude that the leader is self-employed. In other words, entrepreneurial leadership involves believing that one plays a very important role at a company rather than an unimportant one. For example, an entrepreneur acts as if losing money will result in personal financial loss and making money will result in additional financial income. An entrepreneurial leader skillfully fills the following roles[6]:

- Visionary. An entrepreneurial leader has a clear picture of how he/she would like to see their company grow in the future.
- Problem solver. Being able to solve problems, both big and small, is an essential skill for an entrepreneurial leader.
- Decision maker. Subordinates will often lose respect for their leaders if they are unable to make decisions. Entrepreneurial leaders are capable of making decisions when necessary.
- Risk taker. Making decisions about the future often involves risk. The entrepreneurial leader is comfortable with risk-taking and views it as a necessary component of being successful in business.

Approaches to Leadership

Leaders are important for many reasons and can influence followers in many ways. There are several broad approaches to leadership that summarize these influences; among these are spiritual leadership, authentic leadership, ethical leadership, transformational, and transactional leadership. Spiritual leadership reflects the extent to which leaders address the spiritual developmental needs of followers. Authentic leadership reflects the extent to which a leader stands by his or her values and provides true and accurate feedback to followers. Ethical leadership reflects the extent to which leaders possess an ethical and moral code and abide by those ethical standards. Transformational leaders focus on leading by influencing and developing their people. They view people as the means through which to accomplish the organization's objectives. Conversely, transactional leaders focus on leading by adhering to tasks. They view incentives and monitoring as effective means to ensure subordinates complete the organization's objectives. Although research suggests that most people prefer transformational leaders, the right type of leadership depends on the unique work context. Thus, the distinction between transformational and transactional leaders is truly a contingency approach.

LO8.4 ▶ Identify criteria for choosing a leadership style.

Choosing a Leadership Style

Viewing contingency theories as a whole provides some general guidelines for choosing a leadership style. To identify the most effective style, the supervisor should consider the characteristics of the leader, the subordinates, and the situation itself. Figure 8.5, on the following page, shows some key characteristics to weigh.

Characteristics of the Leader

Thanks to sources of variation such as personality type and cultural values, different leaders prefer different styles of leading. Whereas one supervisor might feel more comfortable backed up by a clear system of rules, regulations, and schedules, another might prefer to come up with creative approaches on the spur of the moment. One supervisor may like the results of involving employees in decision making, whereas another cannot get used to the time and effort this requires.

One common characteristic of good leaders is the ability to act as a good role model. One writer suggests that this is largely a matter of how the supervisor does the "little things" in relating to employees: arriving for meetings on time,

FIGURE 8.5 | Characteristics Affecting Choice of Leadership Style

Many elements are at play when choosing an effective leadership style—the task, the person leading, and the people being led.

Leadership Style

Leader Characteristics

- Values
- Confidence in employees
- Leadership strengths
- Tolerance for ambiguity

Subordinate Characteristics

- Need for independence
- Readiness to take responsibility
- Tolerance for ambiguity
- Interest in problem
- Understanding of and identification with goals
- Knowledge and experience
- Expectations

Situation Characteristics

- Type of organization
- Effectiveness of group
- Problem or task
- Time available

calling employees by name, returning e-mail and phone calls promptly, listening carefully, giving employees full credit for their accomplishments, avoiding waste (e.g., turning off the lights when leaving a room), and demonstrating respect by using good manners.[7] Together, these small acts add up to behavior that employees can and will respect.

To some extent at least, a supervisor gets the best results using the leadership style with which he or she feels comfortable. That comfort level depends on characteristics such as the following:

- *The manager's values*—What is most important to the supervisor in carrying out his or her job? Is it the department's contribution to company profits? The employees' or the manager's own growth and development? A manager concerned about developing employees is most likely to involve them in making decisions.

- *Level of confidence in employees*—The more confidence the supervisor has in employees, the more he or she will involve them in planning and decision making. For example, in the oncology unit of the Mayo Clinic, nursing supervisor Sherry Looker says her team of registered nurses "could run our unit." She says these "incredible" employees "have great critical thinking skills, are great patient advocates, and really work together as a team to provide the best care

Formally recognizing a job well done gives the employee a sense of accomplishment.

in the world to our patients."[8] It is easy to imagine that Looker would want to hear the ideas and opinions of such employees.

- *Personal leadership strengths*—Some supervisors have a talent for leading group discussions; others are better at quietly analyzing information and reaching a decision. Some are good at detecting employee wants and needs; others excel at keeping their focus on the numbers. Effective leaders capitalize on their strengths.

- *Tolerance for ambiguity*—When the supervisor involves employees in solving problems or making decisions, he or she cannot always be sure of the outcomes. Supervisors differ in their level of comfort with this uncertainty, which is called *ambiguity*.

Alice H. Eagly, a professor of psychology and of management and organizations at Northwestern University, reviewed more than 360 studies on gender and leadership. She found that the only significant difference between men and women in these studies was that women tended to be more democratic in their leadership style.[9] In many cases, this leadership style is supported by a view that the people in an organization are interdependent. A leader with this belief is more likely to respond to a problem by saying to employees, "Let's work out a solution together." To learn how leadership practices might also vary across cultures, see the "Supervision and Diversity" feature.

Characteristics of Subordinates

In selecting a leadership style, smart supervisors consider their employees as well as themselves. Employees who are at their most creative and productive when they have a lot of freedom will dig in their heels if their supervisor is authoritarian with them, even if that is the supervisor's natural leadership style. At the other extreme, employees who expect and rely on structure and direction will tend to drift and even become paralyzed if their leader has a laissez-faire or democratic style.

What should the supervisor look for in deciding the kind of supervision employees want? Here are some characteristics that should influence the choice:

- *Need for independence*—People who want a lot of direction will welcome authoritarian leadership.

- *Readiness to assume responsibility*—Employees who are eager to assume responsibility will appreciate a democratic or laissez-faire style of leadership.

- *Tolerance for ambiguity*—Employees who are tolerant of ambiguity will accept a leadership style that gives them more say in solving problems.

- *Interest in the problem to be solved*—Employees who are interested in a problem and think it is important will want to help solve it.

- *Understanding of and identification with goals*—Employees who understand and identify with organizational or departmental goals will want to play an active role in deciding how to meet those goals. Furthermore, the supervisor will find that such employees are reliable in carrying out their responsibilities. Employees who don't identify with goals may need more active direction and control from the supervisor.

- *Knowledge and experience*—Employees with the knowledge necessary to solve a problem are more apt to want to help find a solution. Furthermore, their input will be more valuable to the supervisor. Thus, someone who is new on the job will probably need a supervisor who engages in both task-oriented and relationship-oriented behavior, but the supervisor can become less involved as the employee gains experience.

SUPERVISION AND DIVERSITY

LEADING AROUND THE GLOBE

How do you know if a supervisor is being successful in a foreign country? Which leaders are the right ones to send to China or the Middle East? Can a successful leader in Russia also be successful in South America? What is the best way to prepare a leader for a new assignment in Canada?

To answer these questions and others, a recent study analyzed 30,576 leadership assessments from the following ten countries: Australia, Belgium, China, Denmark, India, Netherlands, Norway, Sweden, United Kingdom, and the United States. What they found, not surprisingly, was that leadership traits vary widely from country to country.

The prevailing differences in leadership were found between developed economies and emerging economies. In emerging economies (particularly India and China) successful leaders were those that used a hands-on approach to supervising employees. In these countries, there is a focus on the operational process and on monitoring individual performances. This likely stems from the need to get to market quickly and effectively in a fast-growing country. Companies are less concerned with the long-term or sustainability and more interested in quickly hiring, training, and managing individuals to meet the company's immediate needs. This makes for high demands from supervisors who are on the front line of training and managing employees.

Companies in midwestern Europe and the Nordic countries, by contrast, tend to more global thinkers and concerned with the long-term planning. Successful leaders in these countries focus on planning and communication and strive, along with those who work for them, toward the common good.

Successful supervisors and managers in the United States and the United Kingdom appear to take some lessons from both of these leadership styles and merge them together. While these leaders tend to demand a lot from those who work for them and focus on the execution of tasks, they also place a lot of accountability with the individual. They also tend to have a more "push-oriented" approach when it comes to change management.

This data supports what has long been anecdotal: Effective leadership varies from culture to culture. What this means is that it is very important to make sure that any leader given an assignment in a culture different than her own needs to be prepared for drastic differences in culture and the management style that is required to be effective in that culture.

This data also emphasizes the importance of developing leadership within a company and in the native culture. Bringing American management styles to other cultures will most likely not work. For example, the highest performing business of a global manufacturer of office products is in Russia. Within that organization, there is often rigorous debate and continuous questioning about the methods used and how to achieve the best numbers—a leadership model that would not likely be found in many U.S. businesses.

Last, the research supports the mindset that businesses need to consider the global marketplace as a community with individuals who have different values and perspectives. High performing companies let their companies and the leaders within them determine how best to optimize their employees for the market in which they operate. This involves upper-level managers through supervisors and sometimes even employees.

The researchers summarize that in leadership, like other business processes, companies need to think in terms of "global localization" or "glocalization" rather than "globalization." It is important to think about differences between locales and respect and reflect those differences.

Source: Josh Bersin, "How Does Leadership Vary Across the Globe?," *Forbes*, October 31, 2012, http://www.forbes.com/sites/joshbersin/2012/10/31/are-expat-programs-dead/, accessed April 22, 2014.

- *Expectations*—Some employees expect to participate in making decisions and solving problems. Others think that a supervisor who does not tell them what to do is not doing a good job.

Organizations that use self-managing work teams (see Chapter 3) generally encourage a variety of employee characteristics that are associated with the successful use of democratic leadership and a low degree of task-oriented behavior. They tend to train employees to assume extensive responsibility (or select such employees). They generally provide the team with information about issues to be handled and the performance of the organization and the team. This information should produce knowledgeable employees with an understanding of the problems

Teamwork and group discussions are a way that employees can practice self-management.

faced by the team. Finally, the members of a self-managing work team expect to be involved in making a wide variety of decisions. What is left for a leader to do? Much of importance: communicating a vision of the team's mission and fostering a climate in which team members contribute to and care about the success of the team and the organization.

Characteristics of the Situation

In addition to the personalities and preferences of the supervisor and subordinates, the situation itself helps determine what leadership style will be most effective. Several characteristics are important:

- *Type of organization*—Organizations often lend themselves to one leadership style or another. If the organization expects supervisors to manage large numbers of employees, a democratic leadership style may be time-consuming and relatively challenging. If higher-level managers clearly value one style of leadership, the supervisor may find it difficult to use a different style and still be considered effective. Lee Cockerell, who retired from his post as executive vice president of operations for Walt Disney Parks and Resorts in 2006, got his start in business as a waiter at the Hilton Hotel in Washington, D.C. A supervisor took a chance on hiring Cockerell, who had never been in such an upscale establishment, and then directed his every move to meet the hotel's exacting standards. Cockerell recalls that this supervisor's authoritarian but respectful leadership style was a necessary education in the standards of the company. Cockerell took a similar commitment to quality with him when he continued his career at Disney, where the attitudes and actions of frontline employees are what make each customer's experience memorable.[10]

- *Effectiveness of the group*—Regardless of the characteristics of individual employees, some groups are more successful in handling decisions than others. If a department, team, or other work group has little experience in making its own decisions, the supervisor may find that an authoritarian approach is easier to use. Supervisors should delegate decisions to groups that can handle the responsibility.

- *The problem or task*—The work group or individual employees can easily reach a solution to relatively simple problems, but the supervisor should retain greater control of complex or difficult problems. In addition to its difficulty, the supervisor should consider how structured a task is. A structured task— that is, one with a set procedure to follow—is best managed by an authoritarian leader. However, some tasks, such as generating ideas to improve customer service or planning the department picnic, are relatively unstructured. These tasks benefit from the employee involvement sought by a democratic, people-oriented leader.

- *Time available*—An authoritarian leader is in a position to make decisions quickly. Group decision making usually requires more time for discussion and the sharing of ideas. Thus, the manager should use a relatively democratic leadership style only when time allows for it.

For example, when Steven Preston took an executive post at the Small Business Administration, he recognized that the federal agency's situation included some daunting problems. The SBA was swamped with claims related to Hurricanes Katrina, Rita, and Wilma, which it was trying to handle using a computer system that was decades old—practically prehistoric in computer time. Employees were demoralized by the situation and just trying to get by from day to day. In this difficult situation, it was appropriate for Preston to dictate some actions. These included an upgrade of the computer system and rearrangement of work into a team structure, so that employees working in different functions could focus more on client needs, rather than functional procedures.[11] The team structure improved group effectiveness, and as the team members saw how their efforts helped clients, it improved employee morale as well. As the situation changed, Preston and the agency's supervisors could shift toward more democratic and more relationship-oriented leadership.

When employees and managers work in teams, a democratic leadership style is generally appropriate. Some management experts think that a coach is a good analogy for this leadership style. Coaches delegate responsibility to carry out operations, and they are willing to share authority. They focus on picking qualified people, helping them learn to do their jobs well, and inspiring peak performance. Nathan Helder applied this kind of approach to his landscaping company, Gelderman Landscaping. He wanted to improve productivity, but instead of imposing a lot of rules and restrictions on spending, he taught his managers about how their decisions affect the company's profits. Then he educated the foremen in his maintenance and construction divisions in how their crews contribute to profits. Armed with that information and the company's goals for productivity and growth, the foremen and their employees helped the company improve even through economically difficult times.[12]

LO8.5 ► Explain how supervisors can develop and maintain good relations with their employees, managers, and peers.

Leader Relationships

Leading is clearly an application of human relationship skills and is perhaps the most important measure of whether the supervisor excels at relations with his or her employees. Of course, supervisors need good relationship skills for other relationships as well. They need to work effectively with their manager and peers and be positive about themselves.

Most books about business focus on the technical skills of managing. How can a supervisor develop human relations skills? Ways to get along with almost anyone include projecting a positive attitude, taking an interest in other people, and helping out. In addition, the supervisor can take steps to work on each of the categories of relationships that are important to his or her success.

Supervisors' Relationships with Their Employees

A supervisor who is liked and respected by employees will inspire them to work harder and better.[13] But this does not mean the supervisor should be friends with employees. Instead, the supervisor should consistently treat them in a way that reflects his or her role as a part of management. Today's supervisor empowers rather than commands employees, seeking consensus and spending time with employees to learn what they need for job success and career development.

Some of the most inspiring stories of leadership describe leaders who genuinely care about employees and value their ability to contribute to the organization. For example, in the case of employees who are returning military veterans, civilian supervisors sometimes discover that these employees need extra support: a listening ear plus coaching in such civilian expectations as taking initiative, seeking mentors, and getting excited about issues that aren't matters of life or death. However, lending a hand to these employees is practical as well as patriotic. Among other key experiences, veterans typically have overcome difficult challenges, developed strong discipline, and fulfilled important leadership roles.[14] IBM's former president, chairman,

SUPERVISION AND ETHICS

HOW TO BE A GOOD ROLE MODEL

One of the desired behaviors for a leader in any business is for him or her to make a conscious decision to act as a role model. A role model is someone who shows us how to behave properly. Organizations depend on supervisors to act as role models for ethical behavior. But what does this mean exactly? What specific behaviors are desired?

Supervisors should think about the kinds of behavior they expect from their employees, and then be sure to engage in the same kind of behavior themselves. Leaders should be self-aware, accept feedback and constructive criticism, strive to continually grow and improve, and embrace the corporation's cultural values.

Here are some suggestions for being a good role model:

- Give employees a respectful hearing. If an employee's performance is poor, listen to the employee's side of the story before taking action.
- Give rewards based on objective measures. This shows that you are fair.
- Make time for worthy causes. Volunteer for charitable work during your personal time.

- Call daily meetings before work gets started. Give employees a chance to communicate their questions and concerns. Listen respectfully, and make positive changes when you can.
- Assign reasonable amounts of work to each employee. Give all qualified employees a chance at the tasks they enjoy, and spread unpopular tasks around fairly, too.
- Promote opportunities for employees to learn new skills or advance in the organization.
- In terms of priorities, put your employees ahead of your ego. When employees are successful or creative, make sure they get the credit. Trust that when they look good, you will look good too.
- Apply ethical standards to all decisions. Never lie, cheat, or steal, even on small matters.

Sources: Kevin Sharer, "How Should Your Leaders Behave?," *Harvard Business Review*, October 2013, http://hbr.org/2013/10/how-should-your-leaders-behave/ar/1, accessed April 22, 2014; T. L. Stanley, "Be a Good Role Model for Your Employees," *Supervision*, January 2004, downloaded from InfoTrac, http://web5.infotrac.galegroup.com; Edward E. Lawler III, *Treat People Right: How Organizations and Individuals Can Propel Each Other into a Virtuous Spiral of Success* (San Francisco: Jossey-Bass, 2003), pp. 205–209.

and chief executive officer, Sam Palmisano, says experience has showed him that leadership based on concern for employees is not merely idealistic; it gets results:

> I've noticed that some of the most effective leaders don't make themselves the center of attention. They are respectful. They listen. . . . Their selflessness makes the people around them comfortable. People open up, speak up, contribute. They give those leaders their very best.[15]

Supervisors as Role Models

For employees, the supervisor is the person who most directly represents management and the organization. Thus, when employees evaluate the organization, they look at the supervisor's behavior. They also use the supervisor's behavior as a guide for how they should act. If a supervisor takes long lunch breaks, employees will either think that the use of the supervisor's time is unimportant or believe that the company unfairly lets managers get away with violating rules.

To set a good example for employees, the supervisor should follow all the rules and regulations that cover employees. The supervisor should be impartial in the treatment of employees—for example, assigning unpopular tasks to everyone, not just to certain employees. Supervisors also should be ethical, that is, honest and fair. (Chapter 4 discusses ethics in greater detail.) For more ideas on being a positive role model, see the "Supervision and Ethics" box.

Developing Trust

In leading employees, a supervisor is asking them to go somewhere new, to strive for a more challenging goal. Employees will be reluctant to take a chance on pursuing the supervisor's vision unless they feel they can trust the supervisor. Therefore, building trust is an essential part of leadership.

Trust comes from being trustworthy. Supervisors have opportunities every day to show that they act on their convictions, mean what they say, and uphold high ethical standards. Employees notice this behavior. A global survey of more than 7,500 workers found that three-quarters trust their immediate supervisor. Fewer expressed trust in their company's top executives, whom most employees can't observe day to day.[16]

Paul Taffinder, quoted on leadership at the beginning of this chapter, emphasizes that conviction is important for establishing trust because seeing conviction in a leader energizes the followers. Taffinder notes that people who have had to overcome difficult experiences in their past often make good leaders because the hard times inspired them to reflect on what they believe in and where they are headed. This process develops the leaders' conviction about great ideas, so when these leaders express their conviction, others believe in and trust them.[17] Even if you have been fortunate not to have experienced great suffering, you can develop your ability to lead by thinking about your values and objectives and practicing how to express them with conviction.

Building trust takes time and effort, yet the supervisor can lose it with a single unreasonable act. The most important way to build trust is to engage in fair, predictable behavior. The supervisor should fulfill promises and give employees credit when they do something well. Keeping the lines of communication open also builds trust. When the supervisor listens carefully and shares information, employees will not think that he or she is hiding something from them.

Supervisors' Relationships with Their Managers

No matter how good you are at planning, organizing, and leading, your ability to get along with your manager can determine the course of your career at a particular organization. That may not always seem fair, but your manager is the person who usually decides whether you will be promoted, get a juicy assignment or a raise, or even have a job next week. A manager who likes to work with you is more likely to take a favorable (or at least tolerant) view of your performance.

Expectations

Although every manager is different, most expect certain kinds of behavior from the people they manage. As summarized in Figure 8.6 on the following page, a supervisor can reasonably assume that the manager expects loyalty, cooperation, communication, and results.

FIGURE 8.6 | What Managers Expect of Supervisors

While supervisors have certain expectations of those working for them, certain things are also expected of a supervisor.

- *Loyalty* means the supervisor says only positive things about company policies and about his or her manager. If the supervisor cannot think of anything positive to say, silence is better than criticism.
- *Cooperation* means the supervisor works with others in the organization to achieve organizational goals. If the manager offers criticism, the supervisor should listen and try to make improvements. If the criticism seems unreasonable, the supervisor should first make sure that there was no misunderstanding and then try to find constructive aspects of the criticism.
- *Communication* means the manager expects the supervisor to keep him or her informed about the department's performance.
- *Results* means the supervisor should see that the department meets or exceeds its objectives. The best way to look good to the manager is to have a high-performing department.

Learning about Your Manager

You can better meet your manager's expectations if you understand him or her as an individual. Observe how your

Employees may at times wind up feeling unhappy at work. If you are frustrated or dissatisfied, you should take action: consider the source of the problem and talk with your supervisor.

manager handles various situations, try to determine his or her leadership style, and notice what issues are of most importance to your manager. As much as possible, adapt your own style to match your manager's when you are with this person. Also, ask what your manager's expectations are for you and how your performance will be measured.

These efforts to learn about and match the style of your manager are often called "managing up." According to Rosanne Badowski, who worked for more than 14 years as executive assistant to General Electric chief executive Jack Welch, managing up is important because it is about being useful and delivering value: "Doing what you can to make your manager's job easier will not only help them do their job, but you will be considered a valuable asset to your manager and to your organization."[18] For example, if you listen carefully to your manager and learn to read his or her cues, you can sense opportunities to help out with new projects and problems that can develop your career prospects while you contribute. And managers, just like your employees, will appreciate working with someone who keeps the focus on results, not politics, and maintains a positive attitude.

If You Are Dissatisfied

Despite your best efforts, you may find that you are dissatisfied with your manager. It happens to many people at some point in their career. If you are unhappy, begin by considering the source of the problem. Most interpersonal problems arise from the behavior and attitudes of two people, so determine what changes you can make to improve the situation.

If you cannot improve the situation enough by changing your own behavior, talk to your manager, stating the types of actions you are dissatisfied with and how those actions are affecting you. If you cannot resolve the problem, your best bet is probably to hunt for another job. But try to keep your present job while you look for a new one. Prospective employers look more favorably on job candidates who are already employed.

Supervisors' Relationships with Their Peers

If you get along well with your peers in the same and other departments, they will help you look good and get your job done. Their resentment or dislike for you can cause an endless stream of problems. Therefore, supervisors need to cultivate good relations with their peers.

Competition

Sometimes your peers will be competing with you for raises, bonuses, or promotions. Remember that the more you can cooperate, the better you will all look. This means that your competition should be fair and as friendly as possible. If you try to sabotage a co-worker, you probably will be the one who ultimately ends up looking bad.

Criticism

Because you are trying to maintain a positive attitude, you should not go looking for things to criticize about your peers or anyone else. However, if you know that a co-worker has done something that works against the organization's best interests, you should go directly to that person and point out the problem. It usually helps to be polite and diplomatic and to assume that the problem was unintended—an error or an oversight.

If the co-worker resists listening to your criticism and the problem will harm the company, its employees, or its customers, then you should go to your manager to discuss the problem. Focus on the problem and its consequences to the organization, not on the personalities involved. Gossip is not the behavior of a leader; overcoming problems is.

Skills Module

PART ONE: CONCEPTS

Summary

8.1 Discuss the possible link between personal traits and leadership ability.

To find which people will succeed as leaders, researchers have looked for traits that successful leaders hold in common. Traits that may be significant include a sense of responsibility, self-confidence, high energy level, empathy, an internal locus of control, and a sense of humor. However, research results have been inconsistent, leading to the conclusion that traits alone do not predict success as a leader.

8.2 Explain democratic vs. authoritarian leadership.

Depending on how much authority they retain, supervisors can be authoritarian (retaining much authority) or democratic (sharing authority). Most supervisors are neither completely authoritarian nor completely democratic. It is more common for supervisors to make departmental decisions and also allow employees some freedom in the way that they conduct their work.

8.3 Explain major leadership theories.

Fiedler's contingency model says that whether people- or task-oriented leaders perform better depends on leader–member relations, task structure, and the leader's position power. Fiedler recommends that if the leader's preferred leadership style does not fit the situation, the characteristics of the situation should be changed. In contrast, Hersey and Blanchard's life cycle theory maintains that the leader should modify his or her behavior to fit the situation.

As followers mature, leaders should use varying levels of task and relationship behavior. House's path–goal theory of leadership suggests that the primary activities of a leader are to make desirable and achievable rewards available to organization members who attain organizational goals and to clarify the kinds of behavior that must be performed to earn those rewards. According to the path–goal leadership model, a leader should exhibit directive

behavior, supportive behavior, participative behavior, and achievement behavior. The servant leadership model proposes that leaders should put other people's needs, aspirations, and interests above their own. In other words, a servant leader deliberately chooses to serve those around him/her. The entrepreneurial leadership model is based on the attitude that the leader is self-employed. Thus, an entrepreneurial leader acts as if losing money will result in personal financial loss, and making money will result in additional financial income.

8.4 Identify criteria for choosing a leadership style.

The supervisor should select a leadership style that suits his or her own characteristics, as well as those of the employees and the situation. Criteria for evaluating the characteristics of the leader are his or her values, level of confidence in employees, leadership strengths, and tolerance for ambiguity. Criteria for evaluating the characteristics of employees include their need for independence, readiness to assume responsibility, tolerance for ambiguity, interest in the problem, expectations, understanding of and identification with goals, and knowledge and experience. Criteria for evaluating the characteristics of the situation include the type of organization, effectiveness of the group, the nature of the problem or task, and the time available.

8.5 Explain how supervisors can develop and maintain good relations with their employees, managers, and peers.

The supervisor should project a positive attitude, take an interest in others, and help out as needed. With employees, the supervisor should set a good example, be ethical, and develop trust. The supervisor should give his or her manager loyalty, cooperation, communication, and results and adapt to the manager's style. The supervisor should keep competition with peers as fair and friendly as possible and offer any necessary criticism in a constructive way.

Key Terms

leading, *p.* 203
internal locus of control, *p.* 204

authoritarian leadership, *p.* 206
democratic leadership, *p.* 206

laissez-faire leadership, *p.* 206

Review and Discussion Questions

1. Describe the six traits that researchers believe may indicate a good leader. However, research has *not* established a clear link between personality traits and leadership success. What other factors do you think might contribute to success or failure?

2. Claire Callahan supervises the camping department of a large outdoor equipment store. The store manager (Callahan's boss) has given her the objective of increasing sales by 10 percent during the next quarter. Choose one of the three leadership styles (authoritarian, democratic, or laissez faire). Then state three or more steps that Callahan might take to influence her employees to meet the new sales objective.

3. Ann Wong is the accounts payable supervisor at an insurance company. During a time of layoffs, she decides to adopt a more people-oriented leadership style than the style she normally uses. What does this change mean?

4. Do you think it is more realistic to expect supervisors to adjust the situation to meet their preferred leadership style, as suggested by Fiedler's contingency model of leadership, or to adjust their leadership style to fit the situation, as suggested by the life cycle theory of leadership? Explain your reasoning.

5. Do you think it would be more satisfying to be a path–goal leader, a servant leader, or an entrepreneurial leader? Explain your thoughts.

6. In which of the following situations would you recommend that the supervisor use an authoritarian style of leadership? In which situations would you recommend a democratic style? Explain your choices.
   a. The supervisor's manager says, "Top management wants us to find ways to reduce the environmental impact of all our activities." Each department is given wide latitude in how to accomplish this.
   b. A supervisor is uncomfortable in meetings and likes to be left alone to figure out solutions to problems. The supervisor's employees believe that a good supervisor is able to tell them exactly what to do.
   c. A shipment of hazardous materials is on its way to a warehouse. The supervisor is responsible for instructing employees how to handle the materials when they arrive later that day.

7. Identify the leader relationships error in each of the following situations. Suggest a better way to handle each.
   a. Carole Fields's boss compliments her on the report she submitted yesterday. She says, "It was no big deal."
   b. When Rich Peaslee was promoted to supervisor, he told the other employees, "Now, remember, I was one of the gang before this promotion, and I'll still be one of the gang."
   c. The second-shift supervisor observes that the first-shift employees have not left their work areas clean for the last three days. He complains to his manager about the lax supervision on the first shift.

8. Carla Santos doesn't get along with her new manager; the two have disliked each other since the day they met. Santos was transferred to a new department when the previous supervisor left the company, so neither she nor her manager actually chose to work together. Santos doesn't want her job as a supervisor to be jeopardized by an unpleasant relationship. What steps might she take to improve the situation?

Notes

1. Becky Bright, "Leading through Uncertainty," *The Wall Street Journal*, July 10, 2006, http://online.wsj.com; Deborah Gavello, "Leading versus Managing in the 21st Century," *Western Banking*, March 2003, accessed at the Web site of Western Independent Bankers, www.wib.org; Small Business Administration, "Leading vs. Managing: They're Two Different Animals," *Managing Your Business* pages of the SBAWeb site, www.sba.gov, accessed August 9, 2006. Herb Greenberg and Patrick Sweeney, "Managing or Leading?" *Talent Management*, August 2011, pp. 26–29.

2. Rodd Wagner and James K. Harter, "The Heart of Great Managing," *Gallup Management Journal*, June 12, 2008, downloaded from Business & Company Resource Center, http://galenet.galegroup.com.

3. R. J. House and R. R. Mitchell, 1974, "Path–goal theory of leadership," *Journal of Contemporary Business*, 3, 81–97.

4. R. K. Greenleaf, 1977, *Servant Leadership: A Journey into the Nature of Legitimate Power and Greatness*, Mahwah, NJ: Paulist Press.

5. R. K. Greenleaf, 2003, *The Servant-leader Within: A Transformative Path*, Paulist Press.

6. See L. W. Fernald, G. T. Solomon, and A. El Tarabishy, 2005, "A New Paradigm: Entrepreneurial

Leadership," *Southern Business Review*, 30, 2, pp. 1–10.

7. Robert D. Ramsey, "Doing the 'Little Things' Right," *Supervision*, April 2006, downloaded from Business & Company Resource Center, http://galenet.galegroup.com.

8. Jeff Hansel, "Expert Care: Sherry Looker, RN Supervisor," *Post-Bulletin* (Rochester, MN), November 15, 2010, Business & Company Resource Center, http://galenet.galegroup.com.

9. Alice H. Eagly and Blair T. Johnson, "Gender and Leadership Style: A Meta-Analysis," *Psychological Bulletin*, September 1990, 108 (2), pp. 233–256.

10. Scott Powers, "Disney Executive Lee Cockerell Has a Legacy of Leadership," *Orlando Sentinel*, July 27, 2006, http://articles.orlandosentinel.com/2006-07-27/business/COCKERELL27_1_walt-disney-operators-world, accessed April 22, 2014.

11. Vincent Ryan, "Small Business, Big Problems," *CFO*, January 2008, pp. 50–54.

12. Jeffrey Scott, "Give Employees Ownership Thinking," *Landscape Management*, October 2011, pp. 90–94, http://editiondigital.net/article/Give_Employees_Ownership_Thinking/

13. 1155195/123872/article.html, accessed April 22, 2014.

13. For more information on the importance of the supervisor-employee relationship, see L. Stringer, 2006, "The link between the quality of supervisor-employee relationship and the level of the employee's job satisfaction," *Public Organization Review*, 6, 125–142.

14. Emily King, "From Boots to Briefcase: Conquering the 18-Month Churn," *T+D*, April 2011, pp. 36–41.

15. Sam Palmisano, "The Best Advice I Ever Got," *Fortune*, April 30, 2008, http://money.cnn.com/galleries/2008/fortune/0804/gallery.bestadvice.fortune/8.html, accessed April 22, 2014.

16. "Employees Trust Managers More than Top Brass," *HRMagazine*, October 2008, downloaded from Business & Company Resource Center, http://galenet.galegroup.com.

17. Bright, "Leading through Uncertainty."

18. Elizabeth Garone, "What It Means to 'Manage Up,'" *The Wall Street Journal*, October 30, 2008, http://online.wsj.com/news/articles/SB122511931313072047, accessed April 22, 2014.

PART TWO: SKILL-BUILDING

Meeting the Challenge

Reflecting back on page 203, consider how the leadership theories and principles from this chapter might help supervisors lead employees through a difficult period such as a corporate merger, acquisition, or other major change. What leadership behaviors and actions should the supervisor model in order to set a good example for employees to follow? What leadership behaviors and actions should the supervisor model in order to set a good example for employees to follow and to create a positive work environment?

Problem-Solving Case: Leadership Training on the Program at Insight Communications

Insight Communications (made a part of Time Warner in 2012, who subsequently merged with Comcast in 2014) offered cable television and Internet service to more than 750,000 customers in Indiana, Kentucky, and Ohio. One reason Insight was such an attractive investment for Time Warner was that the company had developed a good reputation for customer service. That reputation rested significantly on the hard work of the company's customer care teams, including call center employees, service technicians, and sales representatives.

The supervisors of these teams did not always know how to ensure that their employees delivered excellent service. Insight tended to select people for the supervisory jobs based on excellent technical skills—choosing people who performed well as customer service representatives or service technicians. Once in their new positions, these supervisors had to figure out for themselves how to lead others. And of course, they were not always sure how to do that.

Insight therefore put together a leadership training program for its supervisors. By exploring the idea with professional organizations, the company found that no existing training program targeted supervisory-level employees in cable companies. So Insight hired one of the organizations, the Cable Center, to develop a program for the company's needs. The Cable Center created a two-and-a-half-day class, and Insight tried it out on five supervisors as a test.

The program's content included information about how to set goals, measure results, and develop employees, as well as about leadership skills. The supervisors who participated in this pilot program were pleased with what they learned about leading others. Matt Stephens, a technical operations supervisor in Ohio, found the assessment of his personality to be especially helpful. With greater self-knowledge plus ideas for task-oriented management and ideas for coaching, Stephens reported feeling he was much better prepared to serve as a leader.

Higher-level managers agreed that the leadership training was helpful. Gregg Graff, Insight's senior vice president of field operations, says that when he monitored customer-service phone calls of employees whose supervisors had been trained, he noticed that the quality of assistance had improved.

He attributes that improvement to better coaching by the supervisors. The company credited better customer service for increases in Insight's number of customers and level of earnings.

1. Insight Communications promoted employees with good technical skills into supervisory positions and then taught them leadership skills. Is this the best way to get supervisors to lead well? Why or why not?

2. Identify three principles of leadership from this chapter that you think would be most important to include in the training for supervisors. Briefly explain why you selected these principles.

3. Supervisor Matt Stephens felt that he knew more about leading, and managers see improved performance in the trained supervisors' teams. If you were one of the supervisors, how else would you be able to tell if you were leading effectively?

Source: Kent Gibbons, "Better Service through Coaching," *Multichannel News*, June 21, 2010, p. 28.

Assessing Yourself

Could You Be a CEO?

Every year, *Inc.* magazine surveys the fastest growing firms in the country and reports on their success. The magazine, as well as other studies, examines the personal and professional characteristics of the top company CEOs.

What do you think?

Answer the following questions with what you think studies of successful CEOs find to be true.

1. What percentage of the CEOs in the survey were married with a stable home life?
   - **a.** 40 percent
   - **b.** 60 percent
   - **c.** 80 percent
   - **d.** 100 percent

2. How many of the CEOs were graduates of four-year colleges?
   - **a.** about a fourth
   - **b.** nearly half
   - **c.** about three fourths
   - **d.** all of them

3. How many of the CEOs were 40 or younger?
   - **a.** about a fourth
   - **b.** nearly half
   - **c.** about three fourths
   - **d.** all of them

4. What business sector were most of the fastest growing firms in?
   - **a.** the service sector
   - **b.** manufacturing
   - **c.** selling
   - **d.** distribution

5. Which industry had grown the most dramatically?
   - **a.** computers
   - **b.** telecommunications
   - **c.** business services
   - **d.** both a and b

6. Which of the following was true?
   - **a.** Most of the company founders borrowed their start-up costs.
   - **b.** None of the firms started with less than $5,000 in capital.
   - **c.** Most of the company founders never borrowed their start-up costs.
   - **d.** All of the firms started with substantially more than $5,000 in capital.

7. Which of the following was true?

a. Technology skills or the rights to some intellectual property drove the success of most of the top firms.

b. Highly efficient production processes drove the success of most of the top firms.

c. Technology skills and intellectual property rights had little to do with the success of most of the top firms.

d. Smart people who were willing to work without pay for a period of time lead to the success of the top firms.

8. What was the average annual growth rate of the companies in the survey whose selling was conducted by an in-house sales staff compensated with traditional salary-plus-bonus structure?

a. 25 percent

b. 50 percent

c. 75 percent

d. 100 percent

Answers: 1. c; 2. b; 3. c; 4. a; 5. d; 6. c; 7. a; 8. c

What do studies tell us about successful CEOs?

For many years, *Inc.'s* annual survey as well as countless other studies, have explored various areas of the lives of successful CEOs. They have found that a majority of successful CEOs are married with a stable home life. Education also appears to be tied closely to success, with most CEOs being graduates of four-year colleges.

While wisdom can come with age, advanced age does not seem to be a requirement for being a CEO of a successful company. Many CEOs are under 40 with a sizeable portion of them having founded their first business in their early 20s or earlier.

The growth of the service sector, at the expense of manufacturing, selling, and distribution is a trend that was noticed in the late 1990s and which has continued. The percentages of computer-related and telecommunications businesses that are among the top companies in the United States has grown dramatically.

Another interesting commonality of successful CEOs is that many founded their companies with very little capital and without borrowing any money for start-up costs. They often started small, providing their own start-up funding, capitalizing on specific technology skills or the rights to some intellectual property.

Pause and Reflect

1. Some of the characteristics identified in the questionnaire above do not describe leadership ability. Why do you think marital status, education level, and age are related to CEO status?

2. Do you aim to lead as a CEO someday, or would you prefer to exercise leadership in another capacity?

3. Compare yourself against the characteristics of the CEOs in the questionnaire above. Do you think you have suitable characteristics to be a successful CEO?

Class Skills Exercise

Practicing Leader Relations Principles

Divide the class into groups of four or five students. Each group is assigned one of the four sections in Figure 8.7 on the following page, which is a checklist of ways that employees, including supervisors, can demonstrate competence in developing relationships with organization members.

Each group discusses the principles in its section of the checklist. Based on jobs they have held or situations they have observed, group members describe good or bad practices for developing positive relationships with people. In particular, consider how you have seen supervisors practice or fail to practice these principles.

After the groups have discussed these principles among themselves, they take turns making presentations. Each group selects one principle to present to the class. One representative (or more) from the group gives a brief illustration of that principle.

Source: This exercise was suggested by Corinne R. Livesay, Bryan College, Chatanooga, Tennessee.

FIGURE 8.7 | Human Relations Competencies Checklist

1. Consistently communicate the following attitudes to co-workers, superiors, customers, or patients:

❑ Send out positive verbal and nonverbal signals in all contacts, including telephone.
❑ Remain positive while working with those who are negative.
❑ Be positive and sensitive when those you are dealing with are not.
❑ Deal with all people in an honest, ethical, and moral way.
❑ Avoid ethnic or sexual remarks that could be misinterpreted.
❑ Maintain a sense of humor.
❑ Recognize when you begin to become negative, and start an attitude renewal project.
❑ Develop and maintain a good service attitude.

2. Demonstrate the following human relations skills in dealing with co-workers:

❑ Build and maintain equally effective horizontal working relationships with everyone in your department. Refuse to play favorites.
❑ Build a productive, no-conflict relationship with those who may have a different set of personal values.
❑ Build relationships based on mutual rewards.
❑ Develop productive, healthy relationships with those who may be substantially older or younger.
❑ Maintain a productive relationship even with individuals who irritate you at times.
❑ Treat everyone, regardless of ethnic or socioeconomic differences, with respect.
❑ Work effectively with others regardless of their sexual orientation.
❑ Do not take human relations slights or mistakes from others personally; do not become defensive or attempt to retaliate in kind.
❑ Repair an injured relationship as soon as possible.
❑ Even if you are not responsible for the damage to a working relationship, protect your career by taking the initiative to restore it.
❑ Permit others to restore a relationship with you.
❑ Release your frustrations harmlessly without damaging relationships.
❑ Handle teasing and testing without becoming upset.

3. Demonstrate the following human relations skills in dealing with your superiors:

❑ Build a strong vertical relationship with your supervisor without alienating co-workers.
❑ Be a high producer yourself and contribute to the productivity of co-workers.
❑ Survive, with a positive attitude, under a difficult supervisor until changes occur.
❑ Establish relationships that are mutually rewarding.
❑ Show you can live up to your productivity potential without alienating co-workers who do not live up to theirs.
❑ Live close to your productivity potential without extreme highs or lows regardless of difficult changes in the work environment.
❑ Do not underestimate or overestimate a superior.
❑ Report mistakes or misjudgments rather than trying to hide them.
❑ Show that you can turn any change into an opportunity, including accepting a new supervisor with a different style.
❑ Refuse to nurse small gripes into major upsets.

4. Demonstrate the following professional attitudes and human relations skills:

❑ Be an excellent listener.
❑ Establish a good attendance record.
❑ Keep a good balance between home and career so neither suffers.
❑ Demonstrate that you are self-motivated.
❑ Communicate freely and thoroughly.
❑ Prepare yourself for a promotion in such a manner that others will be happy when you succeed.
❑ Share only positive, nonconfidential data about your organization with outsiders.
❑ Pass only reliable data on to others.
❑ Keep your business and personal relationships sufficiently separated.
❑ Concentrate on the positive aspects of your job while trying to improve the negative.
❑ Make only positive comments about a third party not present.
❑ Leave a job or company in a positive manner; train your replacement so that productivity is not disturbed.
❑ If you prefer to be a stabilizer, develop patience; if you prefer to be a zigzagger, don't stomp on other people's feet, hands, or heads while climbing the success ladder.
❑ Always have a Plan B (a contingency plan for your career).
❑ Avoid self-victimization.

Source: From *Your Attitude Is Sharing*, by Elwood N. Chapman. Copyright © 1995 Pearson Education, Inc. Reprinted by permission of Pearson Education, Inc. Upper Saddle River, NJ.

Building Supervision Skills

Leading a Team

Divide the class into teams of four to six. Either appoint a supervisor for each team, or ask for volunteers. The teams have the following objective: to determine whether the campus library is as user-friendly as it could be and to come up with suggestions for improvement if necessary.

Each supervisor should privately choose a leadership style (task oriented or people oriented) and practice this style during the exercise. Team members should decide on their own characteristics, such as a need for independence, readiness to assume responsibility, and so forth.

At the end of the exercise, each team should discuss with the rest of the class how effective its leader and team members were. Also, they should present their results: Did they come up with some good suggestions for the library?

chapter nine | Problem Solving, Decision Making, and Creativity

learning objectives

After you have studied this chapter, you should be able to:

9.1 Identify the steps in the rational model of decision making.

9.2 Discuss ways people make compromises in following the decision-making model.

9.3 Describe guidelines for making decisions.

9.4 Explain how probability theory, decision trees, and computer software can help in making decisions.

9.5 Discuss advantages and disadvantages of making decisions in groups.

9.6 Describe guidelines for group decision making.

9.7 Describe guidelines for thinking creatively.

9.8 Discuss how supervisors can establish and maintain a creative work climate.

9.9 Identify ways to overcome barriers to creativity.

A Supervision Challenge

RETAINING EMERGENCY DISPATCHERS

In city and county offices nationwide, dispatchers receive calls from worried people who dial 911 for help in an emergency. As you might imagine, the job is extremely stressful. The result? Dispatchers, who often earn low wages and work extra-long shifts, become burned out and call it quits. Turnover is high. This makes for a big staffing headache for supervisors.

Consider the Shawnee County's Emergency Communications Center, which dispatches about 251,000 calls per year. The optimum staff to cover the three shifts of 24/7 service is 45 employees. But for the five-month period from January 1 to May 1, 2013, only 27 dispatchers were employed at the Kansas center.

A primary factor is that, given their resources, supervisors cannot solve the problem of finding candidates who are qualified to be emergency staffers. A short staff means extra stress for overworked dispatchers. In addition, supervisors must request—even demand—that employees work overtime to fill the gaps. "Staffing and overtime [are] a concern in not only our center but others" across the country, confirms a Shawnee Country supervisor. "We are trying to get some people in here," he says. But "emergency dispatcher" is not a position that can be filled by anyone who walks in off the street. An experienced supervisor reports that the job requires about six months of training, so the many vacancies cannot be filled overnight.

Once trained dispatchers are on the job, why is it so difficult for supervisors to retain them? The reason so many employees give is the inherent stress. In addition to the crises that dispatchers must respond to calmly, knowledgeably, and immediately, overwork adds to the strain. In Shawnee County, dispatcher shifts are eight hours, but the workers must work 12 hours straight in

many cases. Considering family to care for and other obligations, that can mean only a few hours' sleep at night. Tired dispatchers can make mistakes.

Then there is the issue of life–work balance. Less control over one's personal time can add to the already emotionally charged nature of the typical dispatcher's work time. Lacking a creative alternative, one emergency call center supervisor in Dallas made the decision to deny employees the earned days off they wanted to take for such important events as family graduations. The practice backfired. Absenteeism rose, leaving those at work under even more stress.

Another problem in many areas is pay. In Shawnee County, a new dispatcher's initial salary was around $13.50 an hour in 2013. Supervisors must try to invent creative ways to retain dispatchers when there are less stressful jobs offering comparable or greater pay.

If you supervised an emergency call center, what steps would you take to try to solve the problem of dispatcher retention? How would you apply your decision-making skills to approach the problem creatively?

Sources: Ann Marie Bush, "911 dispatchers call for help amid long hours, high stress," *The Capital-Journal,* May 25, 2013; Scott Goldstein and Tanya Eiserer, "Dallas 911 call takers say they're overworked, understaffed," *The Dallas Morning News,* September 8, 2012.

No matter how carefully a supervisor plans or how effectively he or she leads, he or she is bound to encounter problems. Human imperfections, new challenges from the environment in which the department operates, and the desire to achieve higher quality are only three sources of problems for a supervisor to solve creatively. Being successful does not mean not having any problems. In fact, it has been said that success simply means solving the right problems. The best managers, including supervisors, are those who know what issues to focus on and respond to problems in a positive way. By solving the right problems—the ones that can improve the quality of work—effective supervisors improve their department's activities and the service they deliver to their customers.

Take the case of Bob Olberding, the former director of plant operations for Mercy Medical Center, a hospital in Cedar Rapids, Iowa. Although Olberding had plans for handling many kinds of problems, they did not include flooding, because the seven-building medical center is located outside the area's 500-year floodplain. However, with major rains in a recent June, the Cedar River was rising fast, and word began to spread that the downtown area might flood. Olberding began to prepare for the possibility of a problem. He verified the site's elevation, learning that it was almost four feet above the river's predicted crest. Even so, he decided he needed to be ready for flooding, just in case. When the electric power shut down, Mercy switched to its backup generators. Then water began to back up in the basement, and Olberding called in more than three dozen plumbers. He decided that the top priority was to keep the electrical system dry. Hospital employees and volunteers surrounded the facility with sandbags. When the water crested eight feet above the original forecast, the targeted efforts of Olberding and his people had kept the damage to a minimum, with only four inches of water in the basement. Still, the problem solving was far from over. Olberding immediately began lining up contractors to replace damaged drywall and doors, knowing that after a major flood, there would be a labor shortage. Within a week, the hospital was again able to receive patients.[1]

decision
A choice from among available alternatives

A decision is a choice from among available alternatives. Solving problems involves making a series of decisions: deciding that something is wrong, deciding what the problem is, deciding how to solve it. Successful problem solving depends on good decisions. This chapter describes how supervisors make decisions and offers some guidelines for doing so effectively. The chapter includes a discussion of decision making in groups and suggestions for thinking creatively.

The Process of Decision Making

Much of a supervisor's job consists of making decisions that cover all the functions of management. What should the supervisor or the department accomplish today or this week? Who should handle a particular project or machine? What should a supervisor tell his or her manager about the customer who complained yesterday? Do employees need better training or just more inspiration? How can a supervisor end the ongoing dispute between two staff members? These are only a few of the issues on which a typical supervisor must act.

In many cases, supervisors make decisions like these without giving any thought to the process of deciding. A supervisor automatically does something because it feels right or because he or she always has handled that problem that way. When a decision seems more complex, a supervisor is more likely to give thought to the decision-making process. For example, in deciding whether to purchase an expensive piece of machinery or fire an employee, a supervisor might make a careful list of pluses and minuses, trying to include all the relevant economic, practical, or ethical concerns. (Making ethical decisions is discussed in Chapter 4.) Even though making many decisions seems automatic, supervisors can improve the way they make them by understanding how the decision-making process works in theory and in practice.

LO9.1 ▶ Identify the steps in the rational model of decision making.

The Rational Model

If you could know everything, you could make perfect decisions. How would an all-knowing person make a decision? This person would probably follow the rational model of decision making, illustrated in Figure 9.1 on the following page.

1. Identify the Problem

According to this model, a decision maker first identifies the problem. See box #1 in Figure 9.1. Recall from Chapter 6 that it is important to distinguish the symptoms of

FIGURE 9.1 | The Rational Model of Decision Making

In a perfect world, the steps to making a decision are very clear-cut.

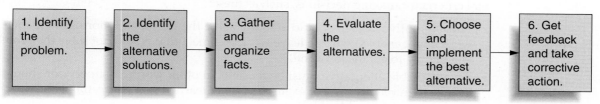

a problem from the problem itself. Usually a supervisor notices the symptoms first, so he or she has to look for the underlying problem.

For example, let's say that a supervisor—we can call him Dave Frantz—finds that he has to work 60 hours a week to do his job as the supervisor of a group of janitorial service workers. Frantz works hard and spends little time socializing, so his effort is not the problem. He observes that he spends approximately half his time doing paperwork required by higher-level management. He decides that the major problem is that too much of his time is spent on paperwork. (Along the way, Frantz also may find and resolve minor problems.)

2. Identify Alternative Solutions

The next step is to identify the alternative solutions. See box #2 in Figure 9.1. In our example, Frantz thinks of several possibilities. He might delegate the paperwork to other employees, hire a secretary, buy software that will automate some of the work, or persuade management to eliminate the required paperwork.

3. Gather and Organize Facts

Next, a decision maker gathers and organizes facts (box #3 in Figure 9.1). Frantz asks his manager if he really has to do all the paperwork; the manager says yes. From the human resources office, Frantz gets information about pay scales for secretaries. He evaluates which aspects of his work could be delegated, and he collects advertisements and magazine articles about various personal computers and software.

4. Evaluate Alternatives

A supervisor then evaluates the alternatives from the information gathered (box #4 in Figure 9.1). This process should be as objective as possible. For a supervisor, relevant criteria include the time required, the money involved, the ethical and legal acceptability of each alternative, and human considerations, such as the likely impact on employees and customers. Ideally, the alternative chosen should have a positive impact in these areas—for instance, lower costs, higher sales, better quality, and more satisfied customers and employees.[2] In the example of Dave Frantz, he determines that he cannot eliminate or delegate the paperwork. He knows that software will cost much less than a secretary, though a secretary would save more of his time. He predicts that his manager will be more open to buying the software than to hiring a secretary.

5. Choose and Implement the Best Alternative

A supervisor next chooses and implements the best alternative (box #5 in Figure 9.1). In our example, Frantz decides he wants to buy the software and prepares a report showing the costs and benefits of doing so. He emphasizes how the company will benefit when he is more efficient and can devote more time to leading and controlling. He selects the program he thinks will best meet his needs at a reasonable cost.

When evaluating and selecting alternatives, how can a supervisor decide which is best? Sometimes the choice is obvious, but at other times, a supervisor needs formal criteria for making decisions, such as these:

- The alternative chosen should actually solve the problem. Ignoring the paperwork might enable Frantz to leave work on time, but it would not solve the problem of how to get the job done.
- An acceptable alternative must be feasible. In other words, a supervisor should be able to implement it. For example, Frantz learned that requesting less paperwork was not a feasible solution.
- The cost of the alternative should be reasonable in light of the benefits it will deliver. Frantz's employer might consider a software program to be a reasonable expense but believe the cost of a full-time secretary is high compared with the benefits of making his job easier.

Getting feedback on changes is a key final step to appropriately utilizing the rational model.

LO9.2 ▶ Discuss ways people make compromises in following the decision-making model.

6. Get Feedback

The last step is to get feedback and take corrective action (box #6 in Figure 9.1). Supervisors cannot simply implement a change and expect that their work is done; they need to follow up to ensure that said change is proving effective. In the example, Frantz takes his proposal to his manager, who suggests some additions and changes, perhaps including helping others in the company to work with the new kind of reports Frantz will be generating. Frantz orders the software, and when it arrives, he automates some of his work, using his experiences to improve on his original ideas.

When a decision will affect the course of someone's career or the expenditure of a lot of money, a supervisor will want to make the best decision possible. One way of doing so is to try to complete each of the steps in the rational model. In general, supervisors can benefit from using this model when they are making complex, formal decisions or when the consequences of a decision are great.

Human Compromises

The example of the rational model of decision making may appear far removed from the daily experiences of most supervisors. Often supervisors have neither the time nor the desire to follow all these steps to a decision. Even when supervisors try to follow these steps, they often have trouble thinking of all the alternatives or gathering all the facts they need. Sometimes no alternative emerges as clearly the best.

Given these human and organizational limitations, supervisors—like all decision makers—make compromises most of the time, as illustrated in Figure 9.2 on the following page and described in the following sections. The resulting decision may be less than perfect, but it is typically one with which the decision maker is willing to live. A supervisor who is aware of the kinds of compromises people make is more apt to be aware of when he or she is using them. In addition, a supervisor may find that though some kinds of compromises are useful in some situations, others are to be avoided as much as possible.

Simplicity

Although we often think we have approached a problem with a fresh perspective and analyzed all the options, most people take a simpler approach. Usually we simply mull over our experiences and consider ways we have handled similar problems in the past. If we consider a few possibilities, we conclude we have covered them all. People tend to select an alternative that they have tried before and

FIGURE 9.2 | Human Compromises in Decision Making

In the real world, decision making is often a less than perfect process that involves a number of compromises.

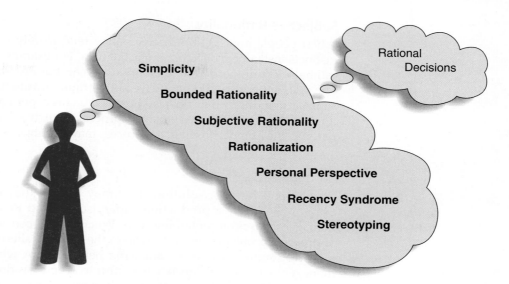

Simplicity

Bounded Rationality

Subjective Rationality

Rationalization

Personal Perspective

Recency Syndrome

Stereotyping

Rational Decisions

that has delivered acceptable results. The downside of this attempt at simplicity is that it tends to bypass innovative solutions, even though they sometimes deliver the best results.

Bounded Rationality

bounded rationality
Choosing an alternative that meets minimum standards of acceptability

When time, cost, or other limitations, such as the tendency to simplify, make finding the best alternative impossible or unreasonable, decision makers settle for an alternative they consider good enough. Choosing an alternative that meets minimum standards of acceptability is a form of **bounded rationality;** that is, a decision maker places limits, or *bounds,* on the *rational* model of decision making. Figure 9.3 shows how bounded rationality works. The decision maker considers alternatives only until one is found that meets his or her minimum criteria for acceptability.

For example, a supervisor who is fed up with tardiness might first be inclined to fire everyone who was late in a particular week. But she knows that choice will be demoralizing, create a sudden and large need for hiring and training, and probably not impress her manager. She therefore rejects that alternative. Then she remembers that she gave "timeliness awards" last year, but that did not stop tardiness, so she rejects that alternative. Finally, she remembers reading an article that recommends spelling out the consequences of the undesirable behavior and then letting the employee experience those consequences. She decides to try that approach. There probably are other ways to solve the problem—maybe even better ways—but the supervisor does not spend any more time trying to think of them.

FIGURE 9.3 | The Process of Bounded Rationality

Sometimes supervisors face limitations in their decision making. This bounded rationality may restrict supervisors from implementing some alternatives, but it does provide an ultimate solution.

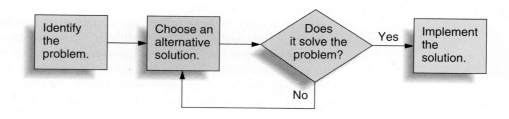

Identify the problem. → Choose an alternative solution. → Does it solve the problem? → Yes → Implement the solution.

No

Subjective Rationality

When people analyze alternatives, they tend to rely on their intuition and gut instincts instead of collecting impartial data. For example, a sales supervisor might estimate, "I think orders will be up next year, but just slightly, say, two percent." The sales supervisor did not arrive at that figure through marketing research or an analysis of industry data; instead he relied on his experience with trends in demand for the product. Thus, even when the process for arriving at the decision is otherwise rational, the numbers used in the process may be subjective and thus not completely accurate.

Rationalization

People tend to favor solutions that they believe they can justify to others. For example, let's say a production supervisor named Renata King knows that her manager focuses on containing costs. When King is considering alternative ways to approach a problem, she tends to favor the low-cost alternative. Another alternative might be more successful, but King believes that whatever the outcome, her manager is likely to appreciate her effort to keep costs down.

Rationalization also interferes with good decisions when the decision maker focuses more on justifying an alternative than on weighing alternatives against previously defined criteria. For example, in considering how to spend the organization's money, a supervisor or manager should think about the impact on achieving company goals. Unfortunately, a decision maker at a Pennsylvania manufacturer of unfinished furniture made an important decision based on justifying a previous decision. In this case, the company had recently expanded and bought extra land for future increases. However, business slowed. The manager had to decide whether to build on the newly acquired land, even though the present facilities were adequate. Spending more on expansion would leave the company with less money to weather a slowdown, but the manager went ahead so that the earlier investment in extra land would not seem like a waste.[3]

To combat problems related to rationalization, supervisors should set clear goals, communicate them to employees, and focus on meeting them. When supervisors focus on what is most important, their employees are likely to do the same. The "Supervision and Ethics" feature describes problems that rationalization causes when applied to ethical matters.

Personal Perspective

Imagine a computer programmer supervisor named Abraham Wassad. As a supervisor, one of his responsibilities is to review computer programmers' documentation and the instructions they write for using their programs. Wassad pointed out to one programmer that some portions of his instructions needed clarification. "It's OK the way it is," insisted the programmer. "*I* understand it."

People often make this programmer's mistake: assuming everyone sees things the way they do. The programmer thinks the instructions must be clear to any (reasonable) person. Such assumptions can lead to incorrect decisions in many areas, including how much information to convey, what working conditions are most important to employees, or what product characteristics customers want. To avoid this problem, decision makers must find out what other people are thinking and then consider those views.

At a company that manufactures coated steel, operators were careless about measuring the coating thickness, although it was an important aspect of product quality. When the thickness was uneven or improper, customers would experience problems with their products. However, the problems might take years to become apparent, and the operators were more focused on what they could see each day, such as the amount of material leaving the plant. The company

SUPERVISION AND ETHICS

WHAT DECISIONS CAN YOU JUSTIFY?

Examples of people behaving unethically can be found weekly in newscasts, newspapers, and other national reports. Examples include chief financial officers manipulating their company's financial reports so that investors will see the company as a sound investment when they really are not or someone using "insider trading" information for their own financial gain. Most people point to these examples and say "How could they do that?" or "Who would be so dishonest?" The truth is, however, that while it is easy to point out the unethical behavior in others, we spend very little time considering our own ethical indiscretions.

As Dan Areily, the author of *The (Honest) Truth About Dishonesty*, points out: "Most of us think of ourselves as honest, but, in fact, we all cheat. From Washington to Wall Street, the classroom to the workplace, unethical behaviour is everywhere. None of us is immune, whether it's the white lie to head off trouble or padding our expense reports." In most cases, we justify our unethical behavior with excuses and rationalizations and we often separate ethical behavior in our personal lives from ethical behavior in the workplace. As the Holistic Education Network Tasmania, Australia states, "Conscientious people sometimes separate ethics into two areas: private and public. Fundamentally decent people thereby feel justified doing things at work that they know to be wrong in other contexts." Some of the justifications listed include:

- It doesn't hurt anyone.
- Everyone is doing it.
- I'm just fighting fire with fire.
- It's OK if I don't gain personally.
- I deserve it.

Do you find yourself saying any of these things or things similar to them? Instead of criticizing the people making the headlines, consider taking a closer look at your own actions and justifications for those actions. Are you a person that can be relied on and taken at your word? If you tell someone you will do something, do you do it? Do you arrive at the time you say you will arrive? Do you send the e-mail with requested information when you say you will? Are you honest when filing your expense report? In your personal life, do you demonstrate ethical behavior? If you notice a cashier missed charging you for an item, do you point it out? If you see someone drop money out of their pocket, do you pick it up and give it back to them? If you find a way to get cable or satellite television or to obtain movies or music without paying for them, do you use it?

Behaving ethically is not something that can be separated between your personal and professional lives. How you behave in either situation impacts how you are viewed by others and how you view yourself. As Alicia Morga, author of *20 Things I've Learned As An Entrepreneur*, says ". . . every time you fail to follow through, no matter how small the commitment or how invisible the consequences, you are chipping away at who you claim to be."

Sources: Giselle Hudson, "Justifying Unethical Behavior WILL Hurt Your Business," *Trinidad and Tobago Newsday*, September 27, 2012, http://www.newsday.co.tt/businessday/0,166829.html, accessed April 27, 2014; Dan Areily, *The (Honest) Truth About Dishonesty: How We Lie to Everyone—Especially Ourselves*, June 2013, Harper Perennial; Alicia Morga, *20 Things I've Learned As An Entrepreneur*, January 2014, No. 8 Media, Inc.; "Justifying Un-ethical Behaviour," Holistic Education Network Tasmania, http://www.hent.org/world/rss/files/ethics/ethics_justify.htm, accessed April 27, 2014.

decided that the solution was to address workers' limited point of view. The workers participated in discussions with product designers, salespeople, and customers. They visited the testing facility where problems were uncovered and installations where the faulty product was in use. This effort helped workers envision why coating thickness was important, and they quickly began improving quality.[4]

Recency Syndrome

recency syndrome
The tendency to remember more easily those events that have occurred recently

People more readily remember events that have occurred recently than those that took place sometime in the past. This tendency is known as the **recency syndrome**. For example, a supervisor might remember that the last time she gave a negative performance appraisal, the employee became hostile but will not recall that a negative appraisal two years earlier led an employee to improve his performance. Clearly, in most situations, an event should not carry more weight simply because it is more recent. This is one reason decision makers need to consider alternatives as fully as is reasonable.

Stereotyping

stereotypes
Rigid opinions about categories of people

Rigid opinions about categories of people are called **stereotypes.** Stereotyping interferes with rational decision making because it limits a decision maker's understanding of the people involved. Stereotypes distort the truth that people offer a rich variety of individual strengths and viewpoints. For example, the stereotype that African-American people are athletic may seem flattering at face value but is insulting and misleading when applied to a particular African-American employee whose strengths are reliability and a gift for public speaking. No doubt, this employee would prefer to be recognized on the basis of his or her unique talents rather than on some stereotypical ones, and a supervisor who can do that will be best able to lead this employee.

The cure for stereotyping is to *not* assume that everyone is alike. Not only does this assumption oversimplify the situation, but it is also, in effect, an insult to other people. It ignores the strengths and values people receive from their culture. Rather, a supervisor should make a conscious, ongoing effort to learn about the various groups of people represented in the workplace. The purpose is to acquire information that serves as a starting point for understanding others while recognizing that individuals within any group are unique.

In addition, a supervisor needs to be aware of his or her own stereotypes about people and situations. In making a decision, a supervisor should consider whether those stereotypes truly describe the situation at hand.

---

connect SELF-ASSESSMENT 9.1

Your Preferred Decision-Making Style

There are a number of different methods for decision making. This assessment will help you identify your preferred style.

LO9.3 ▶ Describe guidelines for making decisions.

Guidelines for Decision Making

Should a supervisor always avoid human compromises in making decisions? Not necessarily. In some situations, seeking to match the rational model would be too costly and time consuming. Sometimes supervisors minimize human compromises by using computer technology to automate part of the decision-making process. For an example, see the "Supervisory Skills" feature. With or without modern technology, a supervisor has a variety of ways to make decisions more rationally. The following paragraphs provide further guidelines for making decisions in the workplace.

Consider the Consequences

A supervisor should be aware of the possible consequences of a decision. For example, hiring and firing decisions can have great consequences for the performance of the department. Purchases of inexpensive items are less critical than purchases of major equipment and computer systems. Some decisions affect the safety of workers, while others make only a slight difference in their comfort.

When the consequences of a decision are great, a supervisor should spend more time on the decision, following the rational model of decision making and seeking to include as many alternatives as possible. When the consequences of the decision are slight, a supervisor should limit the time and money spent in identifying and evaluating alternatives. A supervisor may choose to accept some of the human compromises described previously.

SUPERVISORY SKILLS

MAKING DECISIONS AND SOLVING PROBLEMS

Being a decisive person as well as one who solves problems with those decisions are key skills for a supervisor. The last thing that a supervisor wants to be labeled as is "indecisive." But how do you proceed when you are up against a problem that seems overwhelming or which has many factors and variables?

Working through the steps of the rational model or the scientific method of problem solving that are discussed in this chapter can be a great help in tackling difficult problems. Another option is to apply the Osborne-Parnes Creative Problem solving process. This process breaks down the activity into six stages:

- Objective finding: identify goal, wish, or challenge
- Fact finding: gather data
- Problem finding: clarify the problem
- Idea finding: generate ideas
- Solution finding: select and strengthen solutions
- Acceptance finding: plan for action

As you can see by comparing the various models and processes outlined in this chapter, there are a number of ways to approach making decisions and solving problems. The key is to try different techniques and see what works for you—as well as what works for particular situations. After you make a decision and see the outcome, ask yourself:

- What worked well?
- What did not work?
- If you were to face the same or a similar problem again, what would you do differently?
- What is your take-away from the experience?

Sources: Fiona Ash, "Decision Making and Problem Solving," KnowHow NonProfit: Helping Civil Society Flourish, April 10, 2014, http://knowhownonprofit.org/people/your-development/professional/problemsolving, accessed April 27, 2014; "What Is Creative Problem Solving?," Creative Education Foundation: Where Brainstorming Began, http://www.creativeeducationfoundation.org/our-process/what-is-cps, accessed April 27, 2014.

Respond Quickly in a Crisis

When a nuclear reactor is overheating, the supervisor has no time to weigh each employee's qualifications and select the best employee for each task in handling the crisis. When a store's customer is shouting about poor service, the supervisor has no time to list all the possible responses. Both cases require fast action.

In a crisis, a supervisor should quickly select the course of action that seems best. This is an appropriate application of bounded rationality. Instead of waiting to evaluate other alternatives, the supervisor should begin implementing the solution and interpreting feedback to see whether it is working. On the basis of the feedback, the supervisor may modify his or her choice of a solution.

Reflecting on his career, Jackson Tai, the former chief executive of the financial services company DBS Group Holdings and now on the board of directors of Eli Lilly and Company, is most proud of a decision in which he acted quickly to meet high ethical standards. A few years ago, a Hong Kong branch was being renovated, and dozens of safe deposit boxes were destroyed in an accident. The company immediately assumed full responsibility, apologized publicly, and offered compensation to the customers whose items were damaged or destroyed. Tai says the company was admired "for the fact that we were decisive and took seriously our accountability to customers."[5]

Inform the Manager

A supervisor's manager does not want to hear about every minor decision the supervisor makes each day. However, the manager does need to know what is happening in the department, so the supervisor should inform the manager about major decisions, including those that affect meeting departmental objectives, responses to a crisis, and any controversial decision.

When the manager needs to know about a decision, it is usually smart for a supervisor to discuss the problem before reaching and announcing the decision. The manager may see an aspect of the problem that has escaped the supervisor's attention or have different priorities that lead to a veto or modification of the supervisor's solution. For example, when a supervisor wanted to create a new position for a valued employee, her director gave approval on the condition that the supervisor would not increase her total budget. Knowing and adjusting for such information while weighing the alternatives is less embarrassing to the supervisor and avoids annoying the manager. Of course, in a crisis, the supervisor may not have time to consult with the manager and will have to settle for discussing the decision as soon as possible afterward.

Be Decisive Yet Flexible

Sometimes it is difficult to say which alternative solution is most likely to succeed or will bring the best results. Two alternatives may look equally good, or perhaps none of the choices look good enough. In such cases, a supervisor may find it hard to move beyond studying the alternatives to selecting and implementing one of them. However, avoiding a decision is merely another way of deciding to do nothing, and doing nothing is usually not the best choice. Furthermore, employees and peers find it frustrating to work with someone who never seems to make up his or her mind or get back to them with answers to their questions. Therefore, supervisors need to be decisive.

Being decisive means reaching a decision within a reasonable amount of time. What is reasonable depends on the nature of the decision. For example, a supervisor should not spend hours deciding what assignments to give technicians each morning, but he or she would probably spend several days selecting a candidate to fill a job opening because this decision is more complex and its consequences are greater. The supervisor should pick the alternative that looks best (or at least acceptable) within the appropriate timeframe for the decision, and then focus on implementing it.

Certain kinds of behavior are typical of a decisive supervisor. A decisive supervisor quickly clears his or her desk of routine matters, promptly referring them to the proper people, and keeps work moving. A decisive supervisor assumes complete responsibility for getting the facts needed when he or she must solve a problem. Finally, a decisive supervisor keeps his or her employees informed of what they are expected to do and how they are progressing relative to their objectives.

Being decisive does not mean a supervisor is blind to signs that he or she has made a mistake. When implementing a solution, a supervisor needs to seek feedback that indicates whether the solution is working. If the first attempt at solving a problem fails, a supervisor must be flexible and try another approach. After the supervisor in a Carmel, California, post office removed posters by a popular local cartoonist to comply with a U.S. Postal Service policy to standardize the appearance of its offices, he had to contend with protesters who gathered more than 1,000 signatures on petitions objecting to the action. The protesters even involved their congressman, Sam Farr, who persuaded postal authorities to bend the regulations in favor of local tastes. With its supervisor freed to give his patrons what they wanted, the Carmel post office planned a celebration ceremony to accompany the rehanging of the cartoons.[6]

Avoid Decision-Making Traps

Some supervisors seem to delight in emergency deadlines and crises, and they act as though each decision is a life-or-death issue—one of the decision-making traps illustrated in Figure 9.4 on the following page. But good planning can avert many crises; life-or-death issues are not the usual stuff of a supervisor's job. Making a major issue out of each decision does not make the supervisor more important, but it does interfere with clear thinking. A supervisor must be able to put each issue

FIGURE 9.4 | **Decision-Making Traps**

There are a number of pitfalls and traps that can be hazards to good decision making. Supervisors must attempt to avoid these.

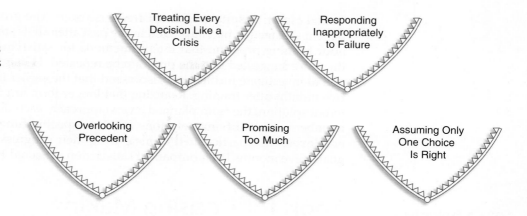

into perspective so that he or she can calmly evaluate the alternatives and devote an appropriate amount of time to finding a solution.

Another trap for decision makers is responding inappropriately to failure. When a supervisor makes a wrong decision, the supervisor will look best if he or she acknowledges the mistake. Finding someone to blame only makes the supervisor seem irresponsible. At the same time, supervisors need not agonize over their mistakes. The constructive approach is to learn whatever lesson the mistake can teach and then move on.

By trying to save time or work independently, some supervisors fail to draw on easily available information. One important source of information is precedent. Have some of the alternatives been tried before? If so, what was the outcome? Answering these questions can help a supervisor evaluate alternatives more realistically. For problems and decisions that are likely to recur, supervisors can set up a system for collecting information to use in future decisions. By consulting with other members of the organization or outside experts, a supervisor often can find readily available data that will improve his or her decision. The supervisor may need to ensure that employees are sharing information effectively. It might be easier to assume all the employees know what they need to know, but that assumption must be tested occasionally. For example, a manufacturer was trying to solve a problem involving a power generator it had been using for more than five years. Because the machinery had been around so long, management doubted that employees needed technical training to solve the problem. However, a group of operators, electricians, engineers, and others scheduled a few hours to review how the generator worked. A few minutes into the presentation, it became apparent that members of each group used different terms for the parts and had different views about the generator's processes. Before they could communicate well enough to solve the original problem, the group members had to establish a common understanding.[7]

Sometimes supervisors are tempted to promise too much. This mistake traps many supervisors because the promises keep people happy—at least until they are broken. For example, a supervisor may promise an angry employee a raise before being sure the budget can handle it. This promise may solve the immediate problem of the employee's anger, but it will backfire if the supervisor cannot deliver the raise. Similarly, a supervisor may tell her manager that she can continue meeting existing deadlines even while a new computer system is being installed. She is not sure of this, but making the promise is a way of avoiding a confrontation with her manager (until the department misses a deadline). Ultimately, everyone will be more pleased if supervisors make realistic promises. Then it is possible to arrive at solutions that will work as expected.

Another trap is to assume there is one "right" decision. That trap at first snagged a group of employees investigating why satisfaction fell among outpatients at

Sacred Heart Hospital in Eau Claire, Wisconsin. The group members knew that patient satisfaction had improved in the past after all its staff participated in a two-hour training program that taught methods for satisfying customers. The group therefore suggested that the program be repeated. However, the group was prodded to investigate further and discovered that the earlier improvement lasted only two months after training. Realizing that longer-term improvement required a different solution, the team planned a new approach: each department involved staff members in identifying solutions for their specific functions and patients. The employees also participated in measuring their progress toward the satisfaction goals. Five months later, outpatient satisfaction at Sacred Heart had soared.[8]

LO9.4 ▶ Explain how probability theory, decision trees, and computer software can help in making decisions.

Tools for Decision Making

Suppose that in preparing a budget for next year, LaTanya Jones, manager of a store's appliance department, needed to determine how many sales associates should work each day of the week. At a factory that produces air conditioners, imagine that a production supervisor named Pete Yakimoto had to determine why the rate of defects was rising and what to do to correct the problem. Yakimoto's employees complained that they were making mistakes because they had to work too fast, and he wondered if hiring more workers could be justified economically.

Problems such as these are difficult to solve mentally. Usually a supervisor facing such complex decisions needs tools and techniques for analyzing the alternatives. Some widely used tools include probability theory, decision trees, and computer software.

Probability Theory

Sometimes a supervisor needs to choose which action will have the greatest benefit (or least cost), but a supervisor cannot completely control the outcome. Therefore, a supervisor cannot be 100 percent sure what the outcome will be. For example, a sales supervisor can tell salespeople whom to call on but cannot control the behavior of the customers. Pete Yakimoto in the previous example can recommend that new workers be hired, but he has only limited control over how the workers will perform. In statistical terms, situations with uncertain outcomes involve risk.

probability theory
A body of techniques for comparing the consequences of possible decisions in a risk situation

To make decisions about risk situations, a supervisor can compare the consequences of several decisions by using probability theory. To use this theory, a supervisor needs to know or be able to estimate the value of each possible outcome and the likelihood (probability) that this outcome will occur. For example, a production supervisor is comparing two stamping presses. The supervisor wants to use a press to produce $1 million in parts per year. Press A costs $900,000, and Press B costs $800,000. Based on the suppliers' claims and track record, the supervisor believes there is a 90 percent chance that Press A will last 10 years (thus producing $10 million in parts) and only a 10 percent chance that it will fail after 5 years (thus producing $5 million in parts). The supervisor believes there is a 30 percent chance that Press B will fail after 5 years.

To use probability theory to make decisions about risk situations, the supervisor can begin by putting the possible outcomes into table format. Table 9.1 shows the

TABLE 9.1 | Possible Outcomes for a Risk Situation

	Five Years of Production	Ten Years of Production
Press A	$5 million — $900,000 = $4.1 million	$10 million — $900,000 = $9.1 million
Press B	$5 million — $800,000 = $4.2 million	$10 million — $800,000 = $9.2 million

Note: Outcomes are computed as the value of production minus the cost of the press.

TABLE 9.2 | Expected
Value of Possibilities

	Five Years of Production	Ten Years of Production
Press A	$4.1 million × 10% = $410,000	$9.1 million × 90% = $8.2 million
Press B	$4.2 million × 30% = $1.3 million	$9.2 million × 70% = $6.4 million

Note: Values are computed as possible outcomes (from Table 9.1) times the probability of those outcomes.

possible outcomes for the stamping presses. In this case, for each press (A or B) and each time period (5 or 10 years), the supervisor subtracted the cost of the press from the value of what the press could produce during that time. Notice that because Press B is cheaper ($800,000), the possible outcomes for that press are greater. Remember, however, that Press B is also more likely to fail after 5 years. The greater probability of failure makes Press B less valuable, so we adjust for that fact by computing the *expected value* (EV) of each possible outcome. To do this for each alternative in Table 9.1, multiply the possible outcome (O) from the table by the probability of that outcome (P). Stated as a formula, $EV = O \times P$. Table 9.2 shows the results of this computation. The supervisor should select the alternative with the highest expected value, which in this case is Press A for 10 years of production, with an expected value of $8.2 million.

Decision Trees

In the real world, most decisions involving probability are at least as complex as the preceding example of purchasing machinery. Sorting out the relative value of the choices can be easier with the use of a graph. Thus, a supervisor may find it helpful to use a decision tree for making decisions in risk situations. A **decision tree** is a graph that helps decision making by showing the expected values of decisions in varying circumstances.[9]

As depicted in Figure 9.5 on the following page, a decision tree shows the available alternatives, which stem from decision points. For each alternative, one of several chance events may occur. As before, the decision maker estimates the probability (or likelihood) of each chance event occurring. To find the expected value of each outcome, the decision maker multiplies the probability by the value of the outcome ($EV = O \times P$). The decision maker should select the alternative for which the expected value is greatest.

For example, a sales supervisor is trying to decide whether to hire a new salesperson at a salary of $40,000. The supervisor estimates that with the new salesperson on board, there is a 60 percent chance that the department's sales will increase from $200,000 to $250,000. Without the new salesperson, the chance for the sales increase is only 50 percent. The supervisor assumes that, at worst, the department will hold steady in either case. The dollar value of each possible outcome is the amount of sales minus the cost of the choice (hiring or not hiring). To find the expected value of each choice, the supervisor multiplies the probability of each outcome by the value of that outcome. Assuming there is a 60 percent chance of sales increasing if the supervisor hires a salesperson (and a 40 percent chance of sales remaining steady), the expected value of hiring is .60($210,000) + .40($160,000), or $190,000. The expected value of not hiring is $225,000. According to the greater expected value for not hiring, the supervisor should decide that it makes more economic sense not to hire a salesperson at this time.

Computer Software

Some computer programs have been developed to help people make decisions. This **decision-making software** leads the user through the steps of the formal decision-making process, shown in Figure 9.1. In addition to having the user identify alternatives, the programs ask the user about his or her values and priorities.[10]

decision tree
A graph that helps decision makers use probability theory by showing the expected values of decisions in varying circumstances

decision-making software
A computer program that leads the user through the steps of the formal decision-making process

FIGURE 9.5 | A Simple Decision Tree

The probability (*P*) of different chance events occurring provide the various possible outcomes in a decision tree.

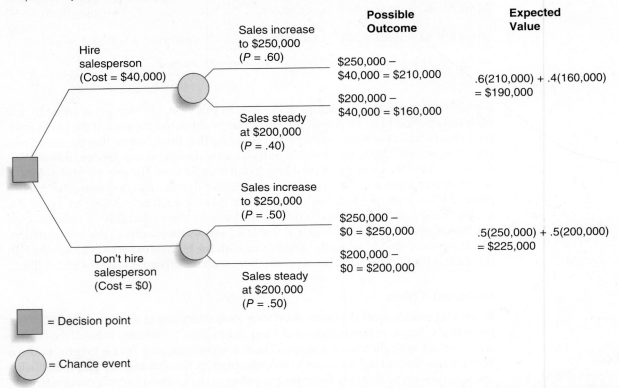

For help in sorting out information, a supervisor might also use spreadsheet or database management software. Spreadsheet software, such as Excel, helps the user organize numbers into rows and columns; it can automatically perform computations such as adding a column of numbers. A database management program, such as Access, IBM DB2, or Oracle Database, systematically stores large amounts of data and makes it easy for the user to request and retrieve specific categories of data. A computerized index of periodicals at your library is an example of this kind of software.

Commerce Bank turned to database management software when it found that some administrators were spending more than two-thirds of their time answering employees' questions. Sometimes branch employees had to wait weeks to receive the information they needed to make decisions. Commerce Bank set up a computer system it named the Wow Answer Guide, which contains details about all the processes involved in bank transactions. When customers have questions or want an employee to help them with an unfamiliar transaction, the employee can find the necessary information in this database.[11]

These kinds of computer software do not make decisions for supervisors, but they can make it easier for supervisors to organize their thoughts and gather information. A supervisor still must creatively identify alternatives and use his or her judgment to select the best solution.

Group Decision Making

Some organizations allow or expect supervisors to work with a team or other group to arrive at a decision. For example, a supervisor might seek input from a team of employees to decide how to meet production targets or encourage them to come up with a solution among themselves. The supervisor also might call on peers in other departments to share their expertise.

LO9.5 ▶ Discuss advantages and disadvantages of making decisions in groups.

Advantages and Disadvantages

Group decision making has some advantages over going it alone. Group members can contribute more ideas for alternatives than an individual could think of alone. Because people tend to draw on their own experiences when generating and evaluating alternatives, a group will look at a problem from a broader perspective.

Also, people who are involved in coming up with a solution are more likely to support the implementation of that solution. They will better understand why the solution was selected and how it is supposed to work, and they will tend to think of it as *their* solution. Chapter 3 elaborates on ways organizations are enjoying these benefits by establishing self-managing work teams and transforming the supervisor's role from commander to coach.

Of course, group decision making also has disadvantages. First, an individual usually can settle on a decision faster than a group can. Second, there is a cost to the organization when employees spend their time in meetings instead of producing or selling. Third, the group can reach an inferior decision by letting one person or a small subgroup dominate the process. Fourth, groups sometimes fall victim to groupthink, or the failure to think independently and realistically that results when group members prefer to enjoy consensus and closeness.[12,13] Here are some symptoms of groupthink:

groupthink
The failure to think independently and realistically as a group because of the desire to enjoy consensus and closeness

- An illusion of being invulnerable.
- Defending the group's position against any objections.
- A view that the group is clearly moral, "the good guys."
- Stereotyped views of opponents.
- Pressure against group members who disagree.
- Self-censorship, that is, not allowing oneself to disagree.
- An illusion that everyone agrees (because no one states an opposing view).
- Self-appointed "mindguards," or people who urge other group members to go along with the group.

In the experience of Johanna Rothman, a consultant specializing in software and information technology (IT) projects, IT experts tend to be eager to reach decisions. When many such people are on a team, that team is vulnerable to groupthink because the group readily latches on to the first idea without searching for different views. Successful IT project managers try to put together teams with more diverse outlooks, including people who are known for questioning ideas and arguing unpopular viewpoints.[14]

When a supervisor notices that his or her group is showing the symptoms of groupthink, it is time to question whether the group is really looking for solutions. A supervisor who also is the group leader should draw forth a variety of viewpoints by inviting suggestions and encouraging group members to listen with an open mind. Another way to overcome groupthink is to appoint one group member to act as devil's advocate, challenging the position of the majority. When the group has reached a decision, the leader also can suggest that everyone sleep on it and settle on a final decision at a follow-up meeting.

LO9.6 ▶ Describe guidelines for group decision making.

Using Group Decision Making

Given the advantages and disadvantages of group decision making, a supervisor would be wise to involve employees in some but not all decisions. When a decision must be made quickly, as in an emergency, a supervisor should make it alone. Individual decisions also are appropriate when the potential benefit of a decision is so small that the cost of working as a group to make the decision is not justified. But when a supervisor needs to build support for a solution, such as measures to cut costs or improve productivity, the group process is useful. Group decision making also can be beneficial when the consequences of a poor decision are great; the benefits of a group's collective wisdom are worth the time and expense of gathering the input.

A supervisor can have a group actually make the decision, or a group may simply provide input, leaving more decision-making responsibility to the supervisor. For example, a supervisor might ask a group only to generate alternatives. If a group is to make the decision, a supervisor may let group members select any alternative, or a supervisor may give the group a few alternatives from which to choose. Whenever supervisors ask for input, they should be sure they intend to use the information. Employees are quickly wise to—and offended by—a supervisor who only pretends to be interested in their ideas.

Encouraging Participation

Because a main benefit of making decisions as a group is the variety of opinions and expertise available, a supervisor leading a decision-making meeting should be sure that everyone participates. One basic way of encouraging participation is for a supervisor to avoid monopolizing the discussion. The supervisor should focus on hearing participants' opinions. Also, some group members will find it easier than others to speak up. The supervisor should notice which participants are quiet and ask their opinions about specific topics being discussed. Finally, a supervisor can encourage participation by reacting positively when people contribute ideas. A barrage of criticism or ridicule will quickly discourage group members from speaking.

Learning to listen takes commitment and practice. Brax Wright runs the family business, Associated Supply Company. He wanted to be seen as involved in the day-to-day operations, so he overwhelmed employees with directions and criticism. When he and his family members learned that this kind of "micromanaging" was hurting the company's performance, they decided to give employees more control. In one situation, Wright learned that employees can outperform management at problem solving. After a problem surfaced involving errors in an inventory count, Wright complained and called a meeting. The employees resisted the owners' focus

Supervisors can encourage participation by not monopolizing discussions, asking questions directly, and reacting positively to contributors.

on assigning blame and successfully turned the discussion to planning improvements in the company's inventory process.[15]

Another barrier to participation is an "us–them" mentality that can pit team members against one another instead of letting them work together to solve a problem. When Harry Jansen Kraemer was a manager at Baxter, he learned that a symptom of this problem is small groups of two or three employees gathering after meetings to carry out whispered side conversations. A main reason why employees do this is that they doubt that their concerns will be taken seriously when the entire team assembles for a discussion. Supervisors can address this problem by inviting quiet individuals to speak up in meetings and by ensuring that people feel free to question or challenge ideas—as long as they do so respectfully. In addition, supervisors need to communicate a clear goal for the entire group, so employees share a sense of common purpose, rather than dividing into factions.[16]

Brainstorming

brainstorming
An idea-generating process in which group members state their ideas, a member of the group records them, and no one may comment on the ideas until the process is complete

Another way to generate ideas in a group is to use brainstorming. **Brainstorming** is an idea-generating process, as shown in Figure 9.6, in which group members state their ideas, no matter how far-fetched they may seem. A member of the group records all the ideas, and no one may criticize or even comment on them until the end of the process.[17]

Another way to obtain a list of ideas that ensures the participation of everyone without criticism is to do brain-writing. When brain-writing, everyone writes down their ideas for solving a problem. No names are listed on the paper. The papers are then exchanged with others who build upon and expand the idea. Exchanging continues until everyone has had the opportunity to read and comment on all the other ideas. All the ideas, which have now become the work of the group as a whole, are then shared and discussed.

Hearing other people's ideas often stimulates the thinking of group members. The supervisor can further open people's thought processes through such mind-expanding tactics as meeting in the work area rather than the usual conference room, asking people outside the group to identify problems, or requesting employees prepare for the meeting by individually listing problems to name at the meeting. Once all the ideas have been listed, the group can evaluate those that hold the most promise.

Brainstorming does have some pitfalls. People who are naturally talkative may dominate the conversation or be more willing to put forth ideas, while others remain silent. And hearing one or two ideas may send the group off down the wrong track. One way to forestall these problems is to ask everyone ahead of time to think about the situation and bring at least one or two ideas. Another option is to take the emphasis off talking by asking everyone to draw, diagram, or build models of their ideas. Supervisors should model trust for the group by listening carefully

FIGURE 9.6 | The Brainstorming Process

Brainstorming is a useful tool for generating new ideas and approaches to solving problems.

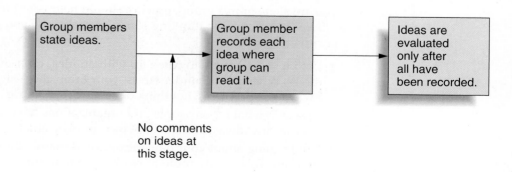

and respectfully to the ideas of others, even if they are outside the supervisor's expectations. Finally, a supervisor can develop employees' idea-generating skills by making idea generation something the group practices regularly, whether or not there is a particular problem to solve. In routine meetings, employees can investigate something they already do well—say, a successful product, process, or solution to a customer problem. The group can talk about why it works and what can be applied to other products, processes, or solutions.[18]

---

connect SELF-ASSESSMENT 9.2

How Creative are You

In the next section, you will learn about the importance of creativity in organizations. Take a few minutes to assess your own creativity using this assessment.

Creativity

Rebecca Liss, a branch operations manager with Kemper Securities, had to be creative when she hired Gail as a new employee. With Gail on board, Liss's group was larger than it ever had been, but there was no money in the budget for additional office space or a computer terminal for Gail. That meant two employees would somehow have to share a terminal. Working with her staff, Liss developed the idea to arrange the desks into an island formation with a computer terminal between the two employees who were to share it.

creativity
The ability to bring about something imaginative or new

This example shows how creative thinking can lead to excellent solutions. Creativity is the ability to bring about something imaginative or new. With decision making, it means being able to generate innovative or different alternatives from those used in the past. When a problem seems unsolvable, the supervisor especially needs creativity to find a fresh approach.[19]

A common notion is that some people are creative, whereas the rest of us are stuck with following routine and ordinary courses of action. Taking the Assessing Yourself quiz on page 254 will provide you with a measure of the state of your own creative skills. If you do not score as high as you would like, take heart—the evidence suggests that people can develop their ability to be creative.

LO9.7 ▶ Describe guidelines for thinking creatively.

Thinking More Creatively

A fundamental way to become more creative is to be open to your own ideas. When trying to solve a problem, think of as many alternatives as you can. Jot them all down without rejecting any; evaluate them only when you are done. This is like the group process of brainstorming. When you can, brainstorming with a group can help stimulate the creativity of the other participants as well as your own. Whether you are alone or in a group, practice should help your ideas flow more easily.

Experts in creative thinking share several steps you can take when you need creative ideas:[20]

- Before you even try to come up with an idea, clear away any major sources of stress. When you're under stress, your brain chemistry is preparing you to run away from problems, not think of new ways to tackle them.
- Research what other people and organizations have done in similar situations. Borrow any ideas you can adapt to your own situation.
- While going about your day, introduce as many new situations and changes as you can. Take a new route to work; try a new cuisine for lunch; rearrange your

workspace. Learning something new can help you make an unexpected connection or get you energized to think in a fresh new way.

- If you're generating ideas on your own, set up some meetings to talk out the issue with others. If you're part of a group project, allow time for individual reflection.
- Bring in new faces, especially if your usual group is stuck in a rut. Of course you'll meet with your manager and your direct reports, but you can also swap ideas with customers, suppliers, people in other departments or functions, and even (as long as you protect confidential information) with people in other companies. Cultivate a wide circle of friends, and strike up conversations with the people you meet. You never know whose stories and experiences will shed light on the issues you care about.

Creative thinking is not always a conscious process. Sometimes creative ideas come from dreaming or daydreaming or come to you while you are doing something else. If you are stuck on a problem, leave it for a while. Walk the dog, take a shower, work on a different task. Above all, do not neglect time for resting and daydreaming. If you are trying to solve the problem as a group and the discussion is not going anywhere, adjourn or at least take a break, and then continue the discussion later.

Dr. Keith Sawyer, a professor of education at the University of North Carolina in Chapel Hill and author of *Group Genius: The Creative Power of Collaboration*, notes that in the modern organization, important innovations are rarely the result of one person's brilliant insight. Instead, they more often come from small changes introduced by many different people. Many of those ideas come about because someone is frustrated with the current way of doing things or sees an analogy to a completely

SUPERVISION: NEW TRENDS

SOCIAL MEDIA APPLICATIONS ARE FERTILE GROUND FOR IDEA GENERATION

Even though employees who deal with problems and processes are often in the best position to submit practical ideas, companies often don't hear them. Employees can go years before they see a suggestion put into practice, and that can discourage them from making suggestions in the future.

One tool that is helping companies correct the problem is social media. The same kinds of computer applications that let individuals post opinions about last night's game and comment on friends' vacation photos can bring employees' innovative ideas out into the open. Organizations are using business-friendly programs such as BrainBank, InnoCentive, and Spigit to collect ideas and make them available within the organization for comments and votes.

For example, PricewaterhouseCoopers (PwC) has set up a Web site called iPlace. Employees of the accounting and consulting firm can visit the Web site to submit ideas for increasing revenues, reducing costs, and improving customer service. Then employees can comment on the ideas submitted and vote on the ideas they like best. PwC promises employees that a team of senior managers will review each idea within 30 days and let the employee know whether it will be tried. More than half of the firm's employees have participated in

iPlace by submitting, commenting about, and voting on thousands of ideas.

The office setting of PwC is far from the only environment in which employees can use this type of application. Bruce Power, a nuclear energy company in Ontario, Canada, set up kiosks around its plant. Employees can stop at one of the kiosks, which resemble ATMs, and submit or read ideas. At Bruce Power, as at PwC, employees are invited to vote on the suggestions. According to the company's chief executive, Duncan Hawthorne, employees have submitted roughly 11,000 ideas, which together have saved the company millions of dollars.

Besides networking within a company, there are social media sites devoted to providing a chance for professionals to interact with each other. One extremely popular professional network is LinkedIn, with over 250 million members. In addition to being able to post your own profile in which you can list current employment as well as the projects you are working on, you can also participate in message boards, share interests, connect with others in your field, connect to people that your associates know, and search for jobs. You can also start conversations on topics of your choosing by sharing images, presentations, and documents.

Sources: Based on Rachel Emma Silverman, "For Bright Ideas, Ask the Staff," *The Wall Street Journal*, October 17, 2011, http://online. wsj.com; LinkedIn, www.linkedin.com, accessed April 27, 2014.

Sometimes, taking the perspective of a child can help you to think in a new, creative way.

different situation that may be unfamiliar to many in the organization. That means leaders, including supervisors, need to pay attention to complaints and listen to ideas from other departments and from employees with unfamiliar life experiences. Creative supervisors ask questions wherever they go, and they listen to the answers, asking people to elaborate until their ideas are clear.[21] Today, as described in "Supervision: New Trends," these conversations may occur online as well as face-to-face.

Personal practices can develop the supervisor's creativity. Here are just a few suggestions.[22] Keep an open mind. Do not act so busy that your colleagues and employees hesitate to share their ideas and concerns with you. Employees who tend to be quiet and shy may have great ideas that you will never hear unless you take the time to encourage them. When someone makes a suggestion, think about it carefully before you respond. Sometimes an idea that sounds faulty contains the seeds of an improvement. Keep a file of ideas that you can review later with a fresh mind. Include ideas that pop up in your reading, conversations, and daydreaming. Try making little changes to your daily routine to keep your creative juices flowing. React to new ideas as if they are something to try out and play around with rather than as challenges to the routine. When coming up with ideas, try out different questions:

- "What could we do if we had all the money in the world?"
- "What if we had no deadline for solving the problem?"
- "How might a child solve this problem?"
- "What would the ideal solution look like?"

Establishing and Maintaining a Creative Work Climate

LO9.8 ▶ Discuss how supervisors can establish and maintain a creative work climate.

A well-led group of creative employees can generate far more good ideas than one creative supervisor trying to come up with all the ideas. To benefit from the entire group's creativity, the supervisor should establish a work climate that encourages creative thinking. The most important step a supervisor can take in this regard is to show that he or she values creativity. When employees offer suggestions, a supervisor should listen attentively and look for the positive aspects of the suggestions. A supervisor also should attempt to implement employees' ideas and should give them credit.

When ideas fail, a supervisor should acknowledge that failure is a sign that people are trying. A supervisor should help employees see what can be learned from the failure. At a Glenview, Illinois, payroll services company called SurePayroll, an employee testing new functions in its computer system once made a truly embarrassing mistake. The employee decided to run the test on data for a fictional company. She made up a company name, Product Kate Test (the employee's first name is Kate), gave the employees obviously fictional names like Salaried Employee One, and entered fictional data for each of them. Then she successfully ran the data through the system. All seemed well for several days, until a government official called to ask about each one of the newly "hired" employees. The employee had forgotten that one of the system's functions was reporting data to the government. When the employee told her supervisor about drawing the wrath of the official, he saw the humor in the situation—and ensured that employees knew not to use fictional data in any future tests. The company also awarded the employee its "Best New Mistake" award, because SurePayroll's managers believe that trying, failing, and learning can be the source of innovation.[23]

The aim is to avoid discouraging employees from making more suggestions in the future. At Google, for example, constant innovation is expected, but management realizes that not every innovation can possibly succeed. Instead, the company focuses on establishing which qualities are most important: that any new product deliver the expected results and do it fast, and that decisions be based on facts, not emotions. Bret Taylor, who helped to create Google Maps, recalls hearing Google cofounder Larry Page assert the goal of speed by saying, "It's OK if you fail, I just want you to fail quickly."[24] A supervisor can apply this approach by ensuring that his or her employees focus on important goals such as customer satisfaction or zero defects. If an employee tries an idea aimed at one of those goals but fails, the supervisor can emphasize the employee's commitment to the goal, rather than the particular failure.

Overcoming Barriers to Creativity

LO9.9 ▶ Identify ways to overcome barriers to creativity.

Often supervisors and employees have difficulty being creative because they are afraid their ideas will fail. A supervisor can overcome this barrier by accepting that employee failures will occur. Overcoming your own fear of failure is more challenging; indeed, the organization may not always reward creativity. The best the supervisor can do is to keep in mind that a lack of creativity will probably prevent big successes as well as big failures.

If an idea does fail, the supervisor should acknowledge the problem and not try to pass the blame on to someone else. The emphasis should be on finding a solution, not on placing blame. Most managers admire supervisors who try ideas after careful thought and who focus on learning from mistakes rather than passing blame. A supervisor who prepares contingency plans (see Chapter 6) and is prepared to focus on solutions is likely to impress his or her superiors, even when the specific idea does not work out as hoped.

Another barrier to creativity is being overly busy. As described previously, creative thinking requires time for quiet and rest. If a supervisor cannot get these breaks at the workplace, he or she needs to allow time for thinking elsewhere—at home, while walking in the woods, while driving. For example, the supervisor can turn off the television for a while each evening. In addition to reflection, another good substitute for television watching is reading. The imagination required to read a book actually helps people develop their ability to think, but the average U.S. adult reads only minutes a day.

Isolation also interferes with creativity. Supervisors need to talk to co-workers in other departments of the organization. They need to talk and listen to their employees. Colleagues in other organizations can be a good source of ideas, as can friends and family members. However, the supervisor must be careful about spending a great deal of time with the same few people. They are less likely to be sources of fresh ideas than are new or less familiar acquaintances.

The Scientific Method in Decision Making

Another approach to decision making is to employ the scientific method. Like the rational model, this approach is systematic and logical and allows the decision maker to be as unbiased as possible while working within the parameters of the information that is known at the time. The steps in this process are:

1. Watch for any signs or symptoms of problems or issues.
2. Define the problem as best as possible given the information known.
3. Collect as much information as possible about the problem and, if necessary, redefine the problem.
4. Search for possible solutions and alternatives.
5. Collect information about all the alternatives identified and organize it in a logical way.
6. Weigh the pros and cons of each alternative.
7. Choose, plan, and then put into action the best alternative.
8. After the solution is implemented, follow up to determine if it is having the desired effect.

Skills Module

PART ONE: CONCEPTS

Summary

9.1 Identify the steps in the rational model of decision making.

According to the rational model, the decision maker first identifies the problem and then identifies the alternative solutions. Next, he or she gathers and organizes facts. The decision maker evaluates alternatives and then chooses and implements the best alternative. Finally, he or she gets feedback and takes corrective action.

9.2 Discuss ways people make compromises in following the decision-making model.

People usually simplify the rational approach to decision making, selecting an alternative that they have tried before and that has delivered acceptable results. Choosing an alternative that meets minimum standards of acceptability is a form of bounded rationality. People tend to analyze alternatives subjectively, relying on intuition and instinct, and favor solutions they can justify. People's analyses also tend to be clouded by the adoption of a personal perspective, the tendency to remember recent events best, and the use of stereotypes.

9.3 Describe guidelines for making decisions.

Supervisors should be aware of the possible consequences of their decisions. In a crisis, a supervisor should respond quickly. With regard to crises and other situations that influence the department's performance, a supervisor should inform his or her manager about the decision, if possible, before making it. Supervisors should be decisive but flexible. They should avoid decision-making traps such as treating all problems as crises, responding inappropriately to failure, failing to draw on available information, and promising too much.

9.4 Explain how probability theory, decision trees, and computer software can help in making decisions.

Probability theory defines the expected value of an outcome in a risk situation as the value of the possible outcome times the probability of that outcome. A decision maker using this theory selects the outcome with the greatest expected value. A decision tree is a graph that shows the expected values of decisions in varying circumstances. Thus, it helps the decision maker use probability theory. Decision-making software leads the user through the rational decision-making process, and spreadsheet and database management software helps users organize their information. The software does not make the decision, but it helps the user think through the problem more logically.

9.5 Discuss advantages and disadvantages of making decisions in groups.

Group members can contribute more ideas for alternatives than an individual could alone. Also, people who are involved in coming up with a solution are more likely to support its implementation. Disadvantages include that groups make decisions more slowly than individuals, the process is more costly, and groups may fall victim to groupthink, actually suppressing different viewpoints.

9.6 Describe guidelines for group decision making.

A supervisor can benefit from group decision making when time permits and when the consequences of a poor decision justify the cost of group decision making. Group decision making is also useful when a supervisor needs to build support for the alternative selected. The group may actually make the decision, or it may provide input such as suggested alternatives, letting the supervisor make the final decision. A supervisor leading a decision-making meeting should make sure that everyone is participating and should react

positively when they do so. Brainstorming, in which members state their ideas no matter how far-fetched they may seem, often helps stimulate the thinking of group members.

9.7 Describe guidelines for thinking creatively.

A fundamental way to become more creative is to be open to your own ideas. When trying to solve a problem, think of as many alternatives as you can, without rejecting any. Creative thinking is not always conscious; dreaming, daydreaming, and engaging in distracting activities actually can help generate ideas.

9.8 Discuss how supervisors can establish and maintain a creative work climate.

Supervisors should show that they value creativity. They should listen to and encourage suggestions. When ideas fail, supervisors should acknowledge that failure is a sign that people are trying. Instead of focusing on blame, the supervisor should see what lessons can be learned from the failure.

9.9 Identify ways to overcome barriers to creativity.

Some barriers to creativity are fear of failure, excessive busyness, and isolation. To overcome these barriers, supervisors need to remember that failing inevitably accompanies trying, to set aside time for thinking and resting, and to communicate with co-workers and peers in other organizations.

Key Terms

Review and Discussion Questions

1. Andrea is in charge of scheduling the work for the service department of a car dealership. Lately, people in the sales department have been taking telephone calls from customers and promising that service work can be completed on a certain day or by a certain time. Consequently, everyone is unhappy—mechanics, salespeople, customers, and Andrea—because the work schedule is disrupted and the service department can't keep up with the promises made to customers. Using the rational model of decision making, what steps might Andrea take to correct the situation?

2. Define *bounded rationality*. Describe a situation in which you resorted to bounded rationality

   as a method of decision making. What were the results of your decision? Do you think this was the best way to make a decision under the circumstances? Why or why not?

3. Franklin Jones, a supervisor in the buying department for a department store, says, "I think these men's jackets are going to be hot this fall. Let's place a big order." What kind of compromises to rational decision making is he using in making his decision? Using the decision-making model, what would be a more rational approach?

4. In each of the following situations, what is interfering with the supervisor's ability to make the best decision? Suggest how the supervisors can improve their decision making.

a. "I think this new smart phone model should be blue," said the design supervisor. "I like blue."

b. "Let's conduct training at three o'clock on Fridays," said the customer service supervisor. "After all, it's been slow the last couple of Friday afternoons."

c. "I'll bet we could boost sales by attracting more women," said the sales manager at an auto dealership. "To generate some traffic, we could hold a little fashion show or a makeup demonstration or something like that every week or so."

5. This chapter presents several guidelines for decision making: Consider the consequences, respond quickly in a crisis, inform the manager, be decisive but not inflexible, and avoid decision-making traps. How would such guidelines influence the way a nursing supervisor handles the following two situations?

a. The supervisor is scheduling nurses for the next month.

b. One of the nurses calls on Friday afternoon to say her father just died, so she will be out next week.

6. Philip is a supervisor who likes to work independently. Whenever he faces a new situation, he prefers to analyze it and make his decision without consulting other sources. How might this method of decision making impact the results of his decision? What might be a better way for Philip to proceed?

7. Rita McCormick is the supervisor of the state office that processes sales tax payments. She has noticed that workers are falling behind and wants to get authorization either to hire two more employees or to schedule overtime until the work gets caught up. McCormick estimates there is an 80 percent chance the workload will continue to be this high and a 20 percent chance that work will fall back to previous levels, which the current employees can handle during regular working hours. (She assumes there is no chance of less work in the future.) Because she will have to pay time and a half for overtime, she assumes that the annual cost of overtime will be $150,000, whereas a workforce with two more employees will cost only $140,000.

a. Construct a decision tree for this problem.

b. Which alternative should the supervisor choose?

8. What are some advantages of making decisions as a group? What are some disadvantages?

9. What are the symptoms of groupthink? What can a supervisor do to overcome groupthink in a team meeting?

10. Roberto Gonzalez wants to make his solutions more creative. When he has a problem to solve, he sits down at his desk and tries to generate as many alternative solutions as he can. Unfortunately, he usually gets frustrated before he comes up with an alternative that satisfies him, so he just picks an acceptable solution and tries to implement it. How can Gonzalez modify his decision-making process to come up with more creative ideas?

11. How can supervisors foster creativity in their department or work group?

Notes

1. Jana J. Madsen, "Mercy Medical Center," *Buildings*, November 1, 2008, http://www.buildings.com/article-details/articleid/6692/title/flood-of-2008-mercy-medical-center.aspx, accessed May 4, 2014.

2. Ted Pollock, "Mind Your Own Business," *Supervision*, December 2005, downloaded from Business & Company Resource Center, http://galenet.galegroup.com.

3. Judd H. Michael and Charles D. Ray, "Management Decisions in the Forest Products Industry: Where Good Companies Go Astray," *Forest Products Journal*, October 2008, pp. 6–14.

4. Craig Sutton, "Get the Most out of Six Sigma," *Quality*, March 18, 2006, http://www.qualitymag.com/articles/84707-quality-management-get-the-most-out-of-six-sigma, accessed May 4, 2014.

5. Kevin Lim, "Turning His Life's Lessons into Corporate Successes," *The Wall Street Journal*, July 24, 2006, http://online.wsj.com/news/articles/SB115369267073614792, accessed May 4, 2014.

6. Laith Agha, "Bates Cartoons Return to Walls," *Monterey County [Calif.] Herald*, July 30, 2006; Laith Agha, "Bringing Back Bill Bates," *Monterey County [Calif.] Herald*, July 6, 2006, both downloaded from Business & Company Resource Center, http://galenet.galegroup.com.

7. Sutton, "Get the Most Out of Six Sigma."

8. Tom Hanson, "On the Line," *Inside Healthcare*, June 2011, pp. 40–42, http://www.inside-healthcare.com/index.php/sections/management/1507-on-the-line, accessed May 4, 2014.

9. For more information on decision trees, see C. Kingsford & S. Salzberg, 2008, "What are decision trees?" *Nature Biotechnology*, 26, p. 1011.

10. For a recent review of software related to decision-making in the military, see C. Wagner, 2006, "Software for stressful decision making," *The Futurist*, 40, p. 8.

11. Deena Amato-McCoy, "Commerce Bank Manages Knowledge Profitably," *Bank Systems + Technology*, January 2003, http://www.banktech.com/architecture-infrastructure/commerce-bank-manages-knowledge-profitab/14700554, accessed May 4, 2014.

12. Further information on groupthink in the context of management decisions can be found in the following article: Rookmim Maharaj, "Corporate governance, groupthink and bullies in the boardroom," *International Journal of Disclosure and Governance*, February 2008, 5, pp. 68–92.

13. See Irving L. Janis, *Groupthink: Psychological Studies of Policy Decisions and Fiascoes*, 2nd ed. (Boston: Houghton Mifflin, 1982).

14. Kathleen Melymuka, "How to Pick a Project Team: Tech Skills Are Only the Beginning," *Computerworld*, April 12, 2004, http://www.computerworld.com/s/article/92031/How_to_Pick_a_Project_Team, accessed May 4, 2014.

15. Timothy G. Habbershon, "A Little Too Hands-On," *BusinessWeek*, July 4, 2004, http://www.businessweek.com/stories/2004-07-04/a-little-too-hands-on, accessed May 4, 2014.

16. Harry M. Jansen Kraemer, "A Clear, Elevating Goal," *T+D*, April 2011, pp. 102–104.

17. For practical tips on how to implement brainstorming sessions, see Chauncey Wilson, "Brainstorming pitfalls and best practices," *Interactions*, September–October 2006, 13, p. 50.

18. Liz Massey, "Five Traits of Successful Creative Teams," *Office Solutions*, October 2008, pp. 38–40, http://creativeliberty.files.wordpress.com/2008/06/osoct08_creativeteam1.pdf, accessed May 4, 2014; and Janet Rae-Dupree, "For Innovators, There is Brainpower in Numbers," *New York Times*, December 5, 2008, http://www.nytimes.com/2008/12/07/business/07unbox.html?_r=2&scp=1&sq=rae-dupree&st=cse&, accessed May 4, 2014.

19. For more on the importance of creativity in the workplace, see T. Suh and H. Shin, 2008, "When working hard pays off: Testing creativity hypotheses," *Corporate Communications*, 13, p. 407.

20. Jeff Haden, "The Easiest—and Hardest—Way to Be More Creative," *Inc.*, November 8, 2011, http://www.inc.com/jeff-haden/easiest-and-hardest-way-to-be-more-creative.html, accessed May 4, 2014; Meryl Davids Landau, "4 Ways to Unleash Your Creative Genius," *U.S. News & World Report*, December 2, 2010, http://health.usnews.com/health-news/family-health/living-well/articles/2010/12/02/4-ways-to-unleash-your-creative-genius, accessed May 4, 2014; Marina Krakovsky, "Eccentric's Corner: Father of Invention," *Psychology Today*, November/December 2010, http://www.psychologytoday.com/articles/201012/eccentrics-corner-father-invention, accessed May 4, 2014.

21. Massey, "Five Traits of Successful Creative Teams"; Rae-Dupree, "For Innovators, There is Brainpower in Numbers"; and Michael Stanleigh, "Guide to Innovation," *Industrial Engineer*, June 2008, pp. 38–41.

22. W. H. Weiss, "Coming Up with Good Ideas," *Supervision*, December 2005, InfoTrac, http://web2.infotrac.galegroup.com; These suggestions are adapted from Weiss, "Coming Up with Good Ideas"; and Pollock, "Mind Your Own Business."

23. Sue Shellenbarger, "Better Ideas through Failure," *The Wall Street Journal*, September 27, 2011, http://online.wsj.com/news/articles/SB10001424052970204010604576594671572584158, accessed May 4, 2014.

24. Dan Fost, "Keeping It All in the Google Family," *New York Times*, November 12, 2008, http://www.nytimes.com/2008/11/13/business/smallbusiness/13tree.html?pagewanted=all, accessed May 4, 2014.

PART TWO: SKILL-BUILDING

Meeting the Challenge

Reflect back on page 227. As a group, discuss the staffing issue faced by dispatcher supervisors, and write a few sentences that define the problem. Is the number of vacant positions a problem or a symptom of the problem?

Next, brainstorm some ideas for solving the problem. Finally, when everyone has had a chance to suggest solutions, have each person rate each idea as either 2 (likely to help), 1 (might help), or 0 (unlikely to help). Find the average rating for each idea.

Did any of your group's ideas receive an average rating near a 2 (likely to help)? If you were a call center supervisor, where would you turn for creative ideas to solve the retention problem? Would getting ideas from actual dispatchers improve the quality of the ideas? How would you use sound decision-making techniques to implement the ideas?

Problem-Solving Case: Improvement Ideas from a Costco Cashier

Steve Heller, an assistant manager at Costco Wholesale Corp.'s store in Carlsbad, California, had a problem to solve. The store's cashiers were not productive enough. Specifically, they were processing customers through checkout stations more slowly than Costco's standards. Heller wanted to find ways to help the cashiers work more efficiently.

To solve this problem, Heller called a meeting with the other store managers. Together, he and the other managers listed possible solutions and discussed the merits of each.

As Heller left the meeting, he passed a bulletin board featuring the store's top-performing employees. He noticed that a cashier named Pam LaBlanc had earned a spot on the board for the first time since she had been hired. Heller walked over to the register where LaBlanc was working and thanked her for her contribution to the store's performance. Then he asked how she had done so well.

Heller learned more than he had expected from such a simple question. LaBlanc explained that she needed to work as a team with the assistants, so she made it a habit to ask them for suggestions. She also gave assistants suggestions for how to help her. From day to day, she worked with different people, so the process became a kind of network of idea sharing.

Heller asked LaBlanc for specific examples, and she offered many. Heller discovered more ideas for productivity improvement from this quarter-hour conversation than he and his management colleagues had thought of in their hours of brainstorming and discussion.

Heller decided the best way to improve productivity would be to have LaBlanc teach what she had learned. She passed her ideas on to the other cashiers. After that, more than half the cashiers in the Carlsbad store were surpassing the company's productivity standards. Heller believes that listening to and acting on a cashier's ideas has also improved the attitudes and work relationships of his employees.

1. How did Steve Heller define the problem described in this case? How did Pam LaBlanc define the problem? How did the problem definition affect the way these two people initially solved the problem?

2. What advantages and disadvantages of group decision making does this case illustrate?

3. Working alone or in groups of three or four students, list ways that Heller can apply what he learned from this experience to continue improving cashier performance. In other words, how can Heller continue enabling employees to improve productivity and quality of service? How might he continue to include them in problem solving?

Source: Bob Nelson, "Good Listeners Make Good Leaders," *Bank Marketing*, March 2004, downloaded from Business & Company Resource Center, http://galenet.galegroup.com.

Assessing Yourself

How Creative Are You?

How many of the following statements apply to you? The more that apply to you, the more likely it is that you can think creatively.

1. I ask a lot of questions.
2. I enjoy word games and puzzles.
3. I write down all my ideas.
4. I know what time of day I am most likely to think of something new.
5. I read and listen to ideas that are contrary to my own beliefs.
6. I often wonder, "What if . . . ?"
7. I enjoy finding out how things work.
8. I make time every day to be alone in a quiet place.
9. I don't make assumptions about people or situations.
10. I read about my own field of work.

11. I read about areas outside my field of work.
12. I can think of more than one way to do most everyday activities.
13. I can laugh at my own mistakes.
14. I speak (or would enjoy learning) a second language.
15. I am willing to take risks.

Pause and Reflect

1. Did more than half the statements apply to you? If a statement does *not* apply to you, does it describe something you can change about yourself?
2. Before you read this chapter and took this quiz, did you think of yourself as a creative thinker? How did the chapter and quiz affect your opinion?

Class Skills Exercise

Solving Problems Individually and in Teams

Divide the class into teams of five or six students. You will do part of this problem-solving exercise on your own and part of it with your team. Then you will compare the two ways of working.

The problem you will consider is that your school is spending more money than it should on energy bills. The school wants to find ways to operate more efficiently by using less energy. Working on your own, think about this problem, and list some ideas for reducing energy use. After several minutes of this, your instructor will direct you to work on this problem as a team. With your team, compile a list of ideas. You can start with the ideas you listed individually; see if you can add further ideas. Use any strategies you learned for creative thinking and generating ideas in a group.

Next, return to individual problem solving. Review the team's list of ideas, and choose one to be the idea you recommend to your school. Write down your reasons for selecting that solution. After several minutes, your instructor will direct you to return to working with your team. As a team, discuss which recommendation to present and why. See if you can agree on a recommendation before time runs out on this exercise.

Finally, as a class, discuss these two approaches to problem solving (individual thought and teamwork). Did you generate more ideas individually or as a team? Which way generated the best ideas? What methods helped you think most creatively? How did you select an idea to recommend when you worked independently and with a team? What criteria did you use for making the decision each way? What principles from the chapter could have helped you improve your problem-solving process?

Building Supervision Skills

Learning from Mistakes

Everyone who makes decisions makes some mistakes; the trick is to learn from them. Divide the class into teams and let each team member present one mistake he or she has made at work or in school, such as missing a deadline or appointment or misunderstanding some instructions. Discuss what the team can learn from each mistake, and choose the one mistake from which every member agrees he or she learned the most. Let each team present the winning mistake and list the lessons they drew from it.

chapter ten | Communication: Theory and Modern Media

learning objectives

After you have studied this chapter, you should be able to:

10.1 Describe the process of communication.

10.2 Distinguish between hearing and listening.

10.3 Describe techniques for communicating effectively.

10.4 Identify barriers to communication and suggest ways to avoid them.

10.5 Distinguish between verbal and nonverbal messages, and name types of verbal messages.

10.6 Identify the directions in which communication can flow in an organization.

10.7 Distinguish between formal and informal communication in an organization.

10.8 Describe the role of the grapevine in organizations.

A Supervision Challenge

BRINGING INFORMATION TO WHERE YOU NEED IT

Business communication has come a long way from hand-typed memos and even productivity applications on desktop computers. Supervisors can now access information on key business systems in real time, from anywhere—and interact with that information directly. Information technology can be very effective in improving efficiency in this way, particularly when supervisors use it to collaborate more closely with other supervisors and their teams. But supervisors should beware of technology being used as a blanket cure-all for communication problems.

Consider the case of Hadronics, a Cincinnati, Ohio company that manufactures cylinders and rollers for the offset printing industry. Communication was breaking down at Hadronics because supervisors had to leave the shop floor to look up information on the desktop computer in their offices. The absence of supervisors, in turn, caused further problems because communication between departments broke down. In short, the information supervisors needed to do their jobs, keep on top of the current status of production and make adjustments, was not where they needed it to be.

Manufacturing components for offset printing is a complex process, requiring supervisors to make frequent adjustments along the way and respond to updated customer requirements. Communication between machining, plating, grinding and thermal spraying departments is extremely important, because each step affects what the other departments should do when they perform their steps in the manufacturing process.

The communication breakdown became too serious to ignore in August 2010. The shop was very busy, but little was being shipped. Work kept stalling and having to be redone, and there was no overall coordination or plan being followed by everyone. The situation had become a full-blown crisis.

Ms. Tina Lopreato, then vice president of operations was tasked with fixing the problem. She asked all staff to come in one Saturday to help work through the problem and identify solutions. It soon became clear that a root cause of the problem was supervisors having to leave the production line to get information from their office computers or try to coordinate with other departments. Hadronics was using industry-standard manufacturing process control software, and everyone

agreed that it was working well. But the information it contained was not at everyone's fingertips and supervisors could not update it easily with what was happening on the shop floor.

Technology is not always the solution to communication problems. The manufacturing process control software vendor did offer an app for handheld devices like smartphones or Blackberries, but it proved unsuitable and ineffective. Supervisors could not use it because it did not provide all of the information on the small screen and it was too hard to make updates. In short, the technology was not suited to the environment or those using it.

Ms. Lopreato was familiar with the Apple iPad and thought that if it could access the desktop software, it would be large enough and durable enough to work for Hadronics staff. She decided to contact an IT services company to see if there was a way that they could access the full manufacturing process control software on a larger tablet device like an Apple iPad. The IT services company worked on the problem and determined that it was possible to access the desktop software on an iPad and use its full functionality, and set up one iPad to test.

Lopreato introduced the iPad to the shop floor gradually, being sensitive to the fact that some employees are resistant to change, and this could be seen as technology for technology's sake. But early results from the initial users were encouraging. More iPads were purchased and set up, and the new system rolled out company-wide.

As you study this chapter, think about how technology affects communication in an organization beyond simple email. How can information technology best support the business and enable timely communication between employees working on a shared task? Was the iPad the right solution for this environment? How should success in addressing a communication problem be measured?

Sources: Based on Emily Probst, "iPads Keep Supervisors on the Shop Floor," *Modern Machine Shop*, April 18, 2011, http://www.mmsonline.com; Natalie Burg, "How Technology Has Changed Workplace Communication," *Forbes*, December 10, 2013, http://www.forbes.com.

communication
The process by which people send and receive information

High-quality work requires effective communication by supervisors and their employees. Communication is the process by which people send and receive information. The information may be about opinions, facts, or feelings. Even hard-nosed businesspeople need information about feelings; for example, a supervisor should know when his or her boss is angry or when employees are discouraged.

Communication is at the heart of the supervisor's job. To work with their managers, their employees, and supervisors in other departments, supervisors send and receive ideas, instructions, progress reports, and many other kinds of information. These and other communications can occupy three-quarters of a supervisor's workday. Thus, supervisors need to know how to communicate and how to do so effectively. This chapter describes basic communication skills and the types of communication that commonly occur in organizations.

LO10.1 ▶ Describe the process of communication.

How Communication Works

"Stop talking and get back to work." Have you ever heard a supervisor deliver these words? Of course, talking—and listening—can also be part of one's work. That's obvious in the case of a salesperson or a call center operator. We could also make the case that a technician in a hospital who chats with a patient before drawing blood or taking an X-ray is performing an important service by putting the patient at ease. But what about employees who are trading gossip beside the elevators or at the water cooler? Many people would conclude that such conversations are interfering with the company's goals.

Two researchers at the Massachusetts Institute of Technology decided to test this assumption, and in their report, they also provide good examples of what goes on when people are communicating. The researchers, Alex Pentland and Benjamin Waber, outfitted employees with badges containing microphones and motion sensors to learn about their communication patterns. Pentland and Waber followed the workers' activities and determined that the workers who interacted the most with their co-workers were the most productive, whether or not they were talking about work-related topics. One reason was that the communications involved a lot more than just trading facts. Workers noticed each other's facial expressions and level of enthusiasm, and they gathered information about each other's values and moods. They interpreted this information and then used it for building relationships and deciding which ideas and actions are likely to succeed in their organization. When it came time to make important work-related decisions, these communicators had already done much of the preparation.[1]

As Pentland and Waber's research suggests, effective communication is about more than simply talking or writing. Rather, communication includes the response of the listener or reader, as well as the way the communicator interprets that response.

The Communication Process

To describe and explain issues such as these, social scientists have attempted to diagram the communication process. As a result, we have a widely accepted model of how communication works. Figure 10.1, on the following page, illustrates one version of this model.

Communication begins when the sender of a message encodes the message. This means the sender translates his or her thoughts and feelings into words, gestures, facial expressions, and so on. The sender then transmits the encoded message by writing, speaking, or other personal contact. If communication works properly, the intended audience receives the message and is able to decode, or interpret, it correctly. Of course, mistakes do occur. Communication breakdowns may occur because of noise, that is, anything that can distort a message by interfering with the communication process. Examples of noise are

noise
Anything that can distort a message by interfering with the communication process

FIGURE 10.1 | The Communication Process

When the communication process works properly, the sender of the message encodes a message, which is then decoded by the receiver of the message. The receiver's feedback to that message is then encoded and transmitted for the original message sender to decode.

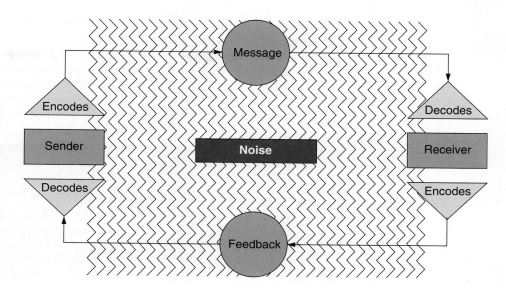

distractions, ambiguous words, and incompatible electronic equipment used to transmit the message.

The sender of the message can recognize and resolve communication problems by paying attention to feedback. **Feedback,** in this sense, is the way the receiver responds—or fails to respond—to the message. Feedback may take the form of words or behavior. For example, research by Liberty Mutual found that when employees are injured at work, supervisor feedback plays an important role in their return to work. When employees discuss the injury, they are sensitive to whether the supervisor seems to be blaming them and whether the supervisor demonstrates concern by following up with them. When supervisors were trained to be more effective in how they respond to employees and communicate with them about the injury, the cost of disability claims declined dramatically.[2] Feedback that demonstrates concern for injured workers would include words, facial expressions, and tone of voice that express interest in the employees' well-being, show that the supervisor listened carefully, and turn the conversation to problem solving, rather than blame.

feedback
The way the receiver of a message responds or fails to respond to the message

LO10.2 ▶ Distinguish between hearing and listening.

Often when others are saying something that we do not like, we might choose to not listen even if we can still hear them.

Hearing versus Listening

Notice in Figure 10.1 that the receiver must decode the message, meaning that the receiver as well as the sender has an active role to play in communication. If the receiver is not playing that role, communication is not occurring.

In many cases, this means the receiver of a message must *listen* to it rather than just *hear* it. Hearing means the brain is registering sounds. Most of us have at some point heard a parent nagging us to clean our rooms or a co-worker complaining about working conditions, but we may not be listening. Listening means paying attention to what is being said and trying to understand the full message. This is the meaning of "decoding" a message. When parents nag or co-workers complain, we often choose not to listen to them.

Thus, as the model of the communication process shows, when we want communication to work, we need to make sure that people are decoding messages as well as sending them. Because communication is an essential part of a supervisor's job, a supervisor must practice good listening skills as well as good writing and speaking skills. The next section discusses listening in greater detail.

connect SELF-ASSESSMENT 10.1

Active Listening Skills Inventory

Because communication is such an important part of a supervisor's job, it is essential to develop excellent skills in this area. One of the best ways to improve your communication skills is to improve your listening skills. This assessment will help you identify your strengths and weaknesses in order to improve your skill at active listening.

LO10.3 ▶ Describe techniques for communicating effectively.

Communicating Effectively

Supervisors need to understand the requests that cross their desks and the questions that employees raise. They need to know when the boss is angry or impressed. They need to ensure that employees understand their instructions. When supervisors succeed in these responsibilities, they are communicating effectively.[3] Figure 10.2 demonstrates that effective communication is most likely to occur when the parties communicate from the receiver's viewpoint, learn from feedback, use strategies for effective listening, and overcome barriers to communication.

Communicate from the Receiver's Viewpoint

Even though we know that other people do not share all our experiences, views, priorities, and interests, we find it is easy to forget this when we are communicating. But such differences make the intended audience more likely to ignore or misunderstand the messages we send. For example, a business owner may find it fascinating and noteworthy that the company has been in the family for four generations. Skilled sales personnel, on the other hand, know that customers would rather hear how the company's services will benefit them. The salespeople therefore communicate with the audience's viewpoint in mind; they focus on what the company can offer customers.

This sales principle applies to all kinds of communication. Simply put, if you want the receiver's attention, interest, and understanding, you must communicate from his or her viewpoint. Applying this principle includes tactics such as using understandable vocabulary, referring to shared experiences, and addressing the receiver's interests. Thus, in explaining to employees that the department will be reorganized, a supervisor should focus on topics such as job security and job design, not on how the changes will make the company more profitable or more like its nearest competitor. After all, employees naturally

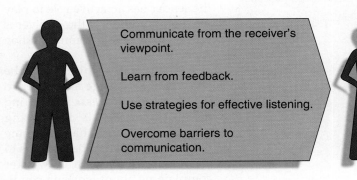

- Communicate from the receiver's viewpoint.
- Learn from feedback.
- Use strategies for effective listening.
- Overcome barriers to communication.

FIGURE 10.2 | Techniques for Effective Communication

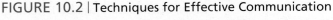

Being able to communicate effectively involves a lot more than just being a good speaker.

are most concerned about their own jobs. For more advice on communicating from the receiver's viewpoint, see "Practical Advice for Supervisors."

Learn from Feedback

Feedback can help supervisors communicate effectively. When a supervisor sends a message, he or she generally expects a certain kind of response. Suppose a supervisor explains a policy requiring that all employees take their lunch breaks sometime between 11:00 a.m. and 1:00 p.m. One type of feedback would be the expressions on employees' faces—do they seem to understand, or do they look confused? Employees also might respond verbally; one might ask whether employees are to take a two-hour lunch break. Another type of response comes from the employees' subsequent behavior. If the employees understood the message, no one will be having lunch after 1:00 p.m. By evaluating the words, facial expressions, and behavior

PRACTICAL ADVICE FOR SUPERVISORS

RECEIVING FEEDBACK FROM EMPLOYEES

Today's supervisors are so busy that they may focus more on giving directions and advice than on listening to what employees are saying. That's too bad, because often employees' ideas and concerns are what spell the difference between the group excelling or falling short. Here are some ideas for ensuring that you really hear what is on an employee's mind:

- When an employee is talking, don't immediately think of a response. Instead, first ask for more details (for example, "Please tell me more about that"), and then verify what the employee is saying (for example, "If I understand, you feel . . . about the situation—is that right?"). Think of yourself as a detective, gathering clues to solve a case.

- When an employee comes up with an idea, make a conscious effort to be open to possibilities, even if the idea is in an area where you have more experience. Employees appreciate the respect you show by listening, and they see that thinking about how to do better is something the organization values.

- Pay attention to employees' emotions, not just their words. If an employee's voice is tense, for example, find out if the person is afraid or angry, and why. In the end, it is usually a relief to name the feelings.

- If the employee seems critical of something you did, try to avoid reacting defensively. Model polite behavior, and focus on the message. You may or may not need to act, but be sure not to miss whatever truth that might be in the message. If you can learn something that helps you be a better supervisor, the message will benefit both of you.

- Remember this simple but easy-to-forget definition: Listening is about being silent. You can even pause to keep thinking when the employee is done speaking. Perhaps he or she just needed to think out loud and doesn't even require a response.

In addition to listening when employees are providing feedback, sometimes it is necessary to encourage employees to provide the much needed feedback—and not just the positive feedback that we all like to hear, but also the constructive criticisms that are necessary for growth. Some ideas for encouraging employees to share their feedback are:

- Have an "open-door" policy—meaning that you are approachable and interested in the criticisms or ideas of others. Be sure to thank employees for their suggestions.

- Keep asking for feedback. This should not be a one-time thing. Rather, you should seek out information from your employees on a regular basis. It is your job to support your team; to provide that support, you need to know what they need.

- Host team or company meals. While eating, mingle with employees and talk about both work-related and non-work related topics. People relax in a more social setting and will feel more at ease.

- Be genuine. If employees know that the leadership team really cares what they have to say, are willing to listen, and will take action if appropriate, then they will be more likely to share their insight.

- Follow up. Even if you decide to not act on a suggestion, always get back with employees who make suggestions so that they know you have considered what they said. If a positive change comes from an employee suggestion, make sure you give credit to the employee.

Sources: Ken Blanchard Companies, "Take the Time to Listen and Provide Feedback," *Ignite,* September 2010, http://www.kenblanchard.com; John Boe, "Feedback: Some People Can't Handle the Truth," *American Salesman,* October 2010, RIS Media, http://rismedia.com/2012-10-17/feedback-some-people-cant-handle-the-truth-2/; Patrick Proctor, "5 Steps to Getting Better Employee Feedback (Even If You Hate It)," *Entrepreneur,* March 28, 2014, http://www.entrepreneur.com/article/232596.

of the people who received the message, the supervisor can determine whether they understood it.

When feedback indicates that a message was not received fully and correctly, the supervisor can try modifying it so that it is better adapted to the receiver. The supervisor may have to eliminate sources of noise, for example, by talking in a location with fewer distractions or choosing clearer words.

A supervisor also can use feedback when he or she is receiving a message. In particular, when a supervisor is uncertain about the meaning of a message, he or she can ask the sender to clarify it. Asking questions is usually a smarter tactic than guessing.

One company that appreciates the importance of feedback is C. R. Bard, which makes products for diagnosing and treating a variety of medical problems. To meet its goals for product innovation and cost reduction, the company needs a flow of ideas from employees at all levels. Bard has communicated this need by posting on its Web site an invitation for suggestions. At some companies, ideas from employees seem to disappear; employees make a suggestion but receive no response. At Bard, however, teams are in place to review each idea and give employees timely feedback. Within a month, each employee who submits a suggestion receives a report of whether the idea has passed the company's screening process. If the idea has value, the employee also receives a reward with this feedback. The quick responses and rewards send employees a message that the company really does care about the ideas submitted. Consequently, in the first 20 months of the idea-generation program, Bard had received more than 1,000 ideas.[4]

Use Strategies for Effective Listening

"Things just aren't done like they used to be," grumbled Tom Wiggins to Allen Pincham, his supervisor at the construction site. "Oh, boy," thought Pincham, "here we go again with the complaining." Pincham began studying some blueprints, ignoring Wiggins until he had blown off some steam and returned to work. Later that week, the general contractor confronted Pincham with a report he had received from Wiggins that some work was not being done according to code. Wiggins had complained that he had tried to inform Pincham but that his attempts were ignored.

Better listening could have saved the construction project much expense and saved Allen Pincham considerable embarrassment. Listening is a key part of communication, and most supervisors could be better listeners. (Test your own listening skills by taking the Assessing Yourself quiz on page 286.) Figure 10.3 lists ten rules for being a good listener.

FIGURE 10.3 | Ten Rules for Good Listening

Listening involves your whole body and mind and can take some practice to be effective at it.

1. Remove distractions and give the speaker your full attention.

2. Look at the speaker most of the time.

3. When the speaker hesitates, give a sign of encouragement such as a smile or nod.

4. Try to hear the main point and supporting points.

5. Distinguish between opinions and facts.

6. Control your emotions.

7. Be patient; do not interrupt.

8. Take notes.

9. At appropriate times, ask questions to clarify your understanding.

10. Restate what you think the speaker's point is, and ask whether you heard correctly.

Effective listening begins with a commitment to listen carefully. A supervisor should not assume that a message will be boring or irrelevant and should instead decide to listen carefully and try to identify important information. For example, when an employee complains frequently about seemingly petty matters, the complaints may hide a broader concern that the employee is not stating directly. Sometimes a supervisor does not have time to listen when someone wants to talk. When that happens, the supervisor should schedule another time to continue the conversation. Supervisors also should keep in mind that some employees are by nature more vocal than others. Quiet employees may have excellent ideas but need encouragement to share them. Employees should not only look for ideas in meetings but also encourage one-on-one conversations to give quieter employees a chance to offer ideas.[5]

A supervisor should also concentrate on the message and tune out distractions. A major type of distraction is planning one's own responses; another is assuming that the listener has nothing interesting to say. When tuning out distractions proves difficult, it may help to take brief notes of what the person is saying, focusing on the key points.

If the speaker uses words or phrases that evoke an emotional reaction, a supervisor must try to control those emotions so that they do not interfere with understanding. One way to respond is to consider whether the speaker is merely trying to vent emotions. In that case, the best response is to listen and acknowledge the emotions without agreeing or disagreeing. Wait until the employee is calm before trying to solve a problem. Then ask questions that seek out the facts underlying an emotional statement: "Stan, you say you are treated unfairly. Would you give me some examples?"

active listening
Hearing what the speaker is saying, seeking to understand the facts and feelings the speaker is trying to convey, and stating what you understand that message to be

In many situations, a supervisor can benefit from using a technique called active listening, pioneered by psychologist Carl R. Rogers. Active listening is not only hearing what the speaker is saying but also seeking to understand the facts and feelings the speaker is trying to convey and then stating what you understand the message to be.[6] The sample dialogues in Table 10.1, on the following page, illustrate two types of listening. In Example 1, the supervisor is simply hearing the employee's words; in Example 2, the supervisor is using active listening. According to Rogers, active listening is a way that supervisors can help employees understand their situation, take responsibility, and cooperate. However, active listening is used effectively only when a supervisor demonstrates a genuine respect for employees and a belief in their ability to direct their own activities.

Be Prepared for Cultural Differences

Supervisors today, more often than in the past, encounter employees or customers from cultures other than their own. Preparation for cultural differences can help supervisors communicate clearly with these people. To be prepared, supervisors can acquaint themselves with basic guidelines for cross-cultural communication.[7]

Stick to simple, basic words: "use" not "utilize," and "before" not "prior to." Use the literal meanings of words. Every culture has its own slang and idioms, such as "over the hill" and "in the ballpark." People from other cultures, especially those who speak another language, may be unfamiliar with these terms. In addition, avoid using the jargon of your industry. When communicating goals and expectations, the supervisor should be literal about what behaviors are desired.

When speaking, talk slowly and pronounce words carefully. You do not need to speak loudly; a common error is to assume that a loud tone of voice is the only way to get the message across. Limited knowledge of English does *not* mean a person is hard of hearing, slow to learn, or even uninterested in learning English. Rather, the person may simply need time to learn the language. Supplement your words with

TABLE 10.1 | Hearing versus Active Listening

Example 1: Hearing	**Word-Processing Operator:** Hey, Wanda, is Finchburg kidding? He wants the whole report ready by the end of the day? That's impossible!
	Supervisor: But that's the job. You'll have to work as fast as you can. We're under tremendous pressure this week.
	Operator: Doesn't he realize we're behind schedule already because of the quarterly reports?
	Supervisor: Look, Don, I don't decide what the managers want. I just have to see that the work gets done, and that's what I'm trying to do.
	Operator: How can I tell my wife I'll be working late *again?*
	Supervisor: You'll have to handle that with her, not me.
Example 2: Active Listening	**Word-Processing Operator:** Hey, Wanda, is Finchburg kidding? He wants the whole report ready by the end of the day? That's impossible!
	Supervisor: Sounds like you're pretty upset about it, Phyllis.
	Operator: I sure am. I was just about caught up after doing all these quarterly reports. And now this!
	Supervisor: As if you didn't have enough work to do, huh?
	Operator: Yeah. I don't know how I'm gonna meet this deadline.
	Supervisor: Hate to work late again, is that it?
	Operator: That's for sure. I made other plans two weeks ago. Seems like everything we do around here is a big rush.
	Supervisor: I guess you feel like your work cuts into your personal time.
	Operator: Well, yeah. I know Finchburg needs this report to land a big customer. I guess that means that this job really *is* important. Maybe if Joel will help me by doing the tables, I can get out of here at a reasonable hour.

Source: Based on "Active Listening" by Carl R. Rogers and Richard E. Farson.

gestures, illustrations, and facial expressions. Suppose the first employee of a gourmet-food business was a Mexican immigrant who spoke mostly Spanish. The supervisor, we will call him David Hodges, might initially need to rely on hand gestures to demonstrate tasks and responsibilities of this new employee. But he and his employee were open to learning each other's languages, and Hodges considers the effort worthwhile: He was rewarded with a loyal and innovative employee.

With written information, the same guidelines about simple rules apply. Also, you may be able to provide a translated version of the information. However, employees may wish to receive an English version as well. ShawCor Pipe Protection has mainly Hispanic employees, and they often take home English versions of work-related information as a way to practice their English skills. In some situations, supervisors cannot assume that employees can read even in their native language. Illustrations are especially important when reading skills are in doubt.

Seek feedback by asking your listener what he or she has heard, but do not ask, "Do you understand?" Many people are too embarrassed to respond that they do not understand the message. Instead, they might remain silent or try to change the subject. In general, yes-or-no questions stimulate too little feedback. For example, instead of asking, "Do you work tomorrow?" (the answer will not guarantee that the person understood), ask, "When are you off this week?" (the person must have some understanding to give a reasonable answer).

Make sure you understand what the other person is saying. Ask for clarification when you need it. Help the speaker relax, and invite him or her to speak more slowly. If you are having trouble understanding a word pronounced by a non-native speaker of English, try asking the person to spell it or show you what he or she means. Most important, assume you can understand, and then try. A supervisor can also signal respect for the employees and their culture by learning some statements of praise in the employees' native language.

Learn about the communication styles used by people from different cultures, and try to match them when appropriate.[8] For example, Asian Americans tend to have a less assertive conversational style than other Americans. Some have complained that they are frequently interrupted. Employees from some Hispanic cultures consider it inappropriate to talk about their accomplishments, so a careless supervisor may underestimate what they have contributed. Also, Hispanic workers may assume that the boss's role is to tell them what to do, so they may consider it wrong to bring up ideas and suggestions. Immigrants from some countries may even have experiences that cause them to distrust people in authority, so they will be unlikely to speak up about safety concerns or other problems at work. Of course, these are only general patterns; a wise supervisor will avoid jumping to conclusions about an individual's character on the basis of cultural preferences.

Generalizing about individuals based on their culture can be a form of stereotyping. Recent research has found that both negative stereotypes (for example, "these type of people are bad at this activity or hold this view") and positive stereotypes (for example, "these type of people are good at this activity or hold this view") hurt the quality of relationships between individuals.[9] Both negative and positive stereotypes depersonalize individuals and result in negative emotions, such as anger and sadness. For example, in a workgroup at an information technology company, a supervisor once singled out an Asian man to handle the quantitative portion of the group's work. When assigning the task, the supervisor engaged in a stereotype that all Asian-Americans are good at math. Although the employee effectively managed the task, he was upset and hurt to be singled out in this way. This kind of experience highlights the point that supervisors need to invest the time to understand their subordinates as individuals, and not classify them on the basis of cultural affiliations.

Supervisors also can help their employees communicate by stressing the importance of keeping communication simple. Share what you learn about communication styles. Compliment employees as they make progress in cross-cultural communication. Thomas Chen, founder of Crystal Window & Door Systems Ltd. in Flushing, New York, offers free English classes to his 200 employees, about three-quarters of whom are Chinese Americans. Bilingual staff members conduct the classes on evenings and weekends and use multimedia and personal instruction to cover everything from conversational English to the technical vocabulary of the industry. On "English-only Fridays," everyone, including the company's growing population of Hispanic workers, gets to practice what has been learned in class. And since everyone is doing it, no one feels uncomfortable.[10]

LO10.4 ▶ Identify barriers to communication and suggest ways to avoid them.

Barriers to Communication

The model of the communication process suggests where barriers to communication can arise. In general, the sender may fail to encode the message clearly, the message may be lost in transmission, or the receiver may misinterpret the message. In practice, these categories of problems often overlap. The resulting barriers may take the form of information overload, misunderstandings, and biases related to perception.

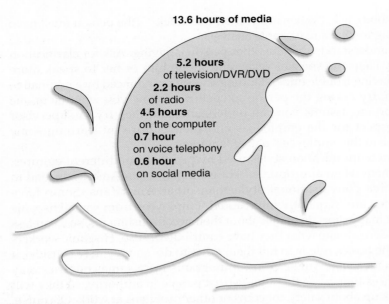

13.6 hours of media

5.2 hours
of television/DVR/DVD
2.2 hours
of radio
4.5 hours
on the computer
0.7 hour
on voice telephony
0.6 hour
on social media

FIGURE 10.4 | A Tidal Wave: Daily Information Consumed by Individuals in the United States

Americans are inundated on a daily basis with information from a wide variety of sources.

Source: Data from James E. Short, "How Much Media? 2013 Report on American Consumers" (Institute for Communications Technology Management, Marshall School of Business, University of Southern California, October 2013.)

Information Overload

Today's world is often called the information age. People are bombarded with information daily, as illustrated in Figure 10.4. On the way to work, radio ads and billboards suggest which brand of automobile or soft drink to buy. At the workplace, memos, magazines, and managers report on trends, policies, and responsibilities. During the course of a day, many employees get information from colleagues, computer screens, printed pages, and telephone calls. In the evening, family members and television announcers recount the day's news. People cope with this barrage of information by tuning out a lot of what they see and hear.

How can a supervisor respond to this barrier to communication? An important way is to give employees only information that will be useful to them. For example, when employees need instructions, a supervisor should think the instructions through carefully, so that new instructions don't have to be provided later. Also, a supervisor should be sure that employees are paying attention. The way to do this is to observe the people receiving the information and look for feedback. A supervisor can say to an employee, "Do you understand what I want you to do? Try putting it in your own words." To his or her manager, a supervisor might say, "Do you think this idea supports your goals for the department?"

Misunderstandings

In decoding a message, the receiver of a message may make errors that lead to misunderstandings. This barrier can arise when a message is needlessly complicated. Imagine a supervisor's memo that reads, "The deterioration of maintenance practices will inevitably lead to conditions that will be injurious to our hitherto admirable safety record." The person who receives this memo is likely to misunderstand it because so much effort is required to figure out what the words mean. Instead, the supervisor could write, "Because the maintenance workers are no longer tuning up the machines each month, the machines are going to wear out and cause injuries."

When the supervisor is the receiver of a message, he or she needs to be careful to understand its true meaning. The supervisor should not hesitate to ask questions about unclear points. It is also helpful to check on the meaning with such responses as, "So you'd like me to . . . " or "Are you saying that . . . ?" A supervisor also needs to recognize when people are intentionally vague or misleading. On those occasions, the supervisor should interpret messages with particular care.

Indra Nooyi, who rose to chief executive of PepsiCo, says careful listening is one of the most important lessons she has learned along the way. She says her father taught her to listen for the speaker's "positive intent." In other words, she starts with the assumption that the speaker is trying to communicate as a way of arriving at something positive. When Nooyi is the receiver of a message, that assumption keeps her from becoming angry and defensive, because she is instead focused on trying to figure out the speaker's positive intention. For example, a comment that sounds hurtful may actually be the person's effort to say that he or she is hurt or confused.[11]

Criticism that is poorly worded and poorly delivered can lead to an employee feeling defensive.

Word Choices

To avoid misunderstandings, a supervisor should be careful to make appropriate word choices when encoding the message. In addition to choosing simple words, this means avoiding ambiguous words. If an employee asks, "Should I use the solvent in the bottle on the left?" the supervisor should not say, "Right."

Problems also can arise from using words that attribute characteristics to another person. Saying "You're so irresponsible!" leads an employee to tune out a message. Instead, a supervisor could describe specific behaviors and his or her own feelings: "That's the second time this week you've made that mistake. I get annoyed when I have to explain the same procedure more than once or twice." This approach is called using "I statements" instead of "you statements." Table 10.2 gives examples of the differences between the two types.

Choosing words carefully is especially important in addressing others. A careful supervisor uses the name of a co-worker or customer instead of "dear" or "honey" unless the supervisor is certain that the receiver in a business setting likes being called by such endearments.

Word choice is also an important element of clarity. Supervisors should avoid using language that obscures their meaning, such as technical jargon that will be unfamiliar to the receiver of the message. One good way to check your written communication for clarity is to read it out loud before sending it. Speakers have the advantage of being able to observe their listeners to look for clues that the listeners understand and are interested in their words. That helped financial adviser Charles Lowenhaupt learn to choose the right words when he meets with clients. When he

TABLE 10.2 | Two Ways to Address Comments to Others

	You Statements	I Statements
Examples	"You're so irresponsible!"	"I'm upset that you've missed the deadline for the third time. When someone in the department misses a deadline, the whole department looks bad. What can we do?"
	"At the next department meeting, you'd better be prepared and be on time, or you're going to be sorry when we review your salary."	"I was not pleased that you were late to the meeting and unprepared. I expect a higher standard of performance."
	"You're bugging the women with those dirty jokes, so just knock it off before we get in trouble."	"I have received complaints from two of the employees in the department that you are embarrassing them by telling dirty jokes. Our company policy and the law both forbid that type of behavior."
Likely response	Defensiveness, ignoring speaker.	Listening, collaborating on a solution.

was starting out in his field, Lowenhaupt met with an elderly client and launched into a lecture on "governance structures, fiduciary responsibility, stewardship, and the obligations of wealth holders to preserve their wealth." He noticed that the client seemed not to be listening, so he asked the client what he would have said to Lowenhaupt's grandfather if they could have discussed this meeting. The client answered, "I would have told your grandfather he was nuts to talk about governance structures, fiduciary nonsense, and obligation. My money would be used to allow freedom, self-actualization, and happiness." From this feedback, Lowenhaupt learned to focus his word choices on what clients care about. He now routinely starts client relationships by asking, "What is your wealth for?" The answers help him communicate and solve problems from the clients' perspective.[12]

Cultural Differences

Another concern involves misunderstandings that result from cultural differences. For example, the mainstream culture in the United States places relatively great emphasis on expressing one's personal opinion. A supervisor from this culture thus could expect that employees would feel free to share ideas and express disagreements. In contrast, people from a culture that places a high value on harmony (for example, Japan) might agree with the speaker out of politeness rather than a shared opinion. People from a culture that values demonstrating respect according to one's place in the hierarchy (for example, Mexico, the Middle East) might be reluctant to express disagreement to a manager or other high-ranking person. A U.S. manager who was unfamiliar with such values might assume mistakenly that employees from these cultures were unable or unwilling to contribute their ideas.

To avoid misinterpreting the words and behavior of others, a supervisor must be familiar with the communication styles of the various cultures of people with whom he or she works. Table 10.3, on the following page, identifies some aspects of communication affected by culture and provides examples of cultural differences. Information about the values and customs of different cultures, of course, does not apply to every member of any culture, but it can sensitize a supervisor to areas in which extra care may be needed to promote understanding.

Inferences versus Facts

Misunderstandings also can arise when the listener confuses inferences with facts. An **inference** is a conclusion drawn from the facts available. A supervisor may observe that an employee is not meeting performance standards. That would be a fact. If a supervisor says, "You're lazy!" to an employee, the supervisor is making an inference based on the fact of the below-par performance. The inference may or may not be true.

Statements using the words *never* and *always* are inferences. A supervisor may claim, "You're always late"—knowing for certain that the employee has been late to work six days straight. However, the supervisor cannot know for certain what the employee *always* does.

Researchers into human behavior have found that many inferences aren't even made consciously. For example, selections for corporate jobs tend to favor people who are taller, and people are less likely to believe statements made by someone with a different accent.[13] If you ask whether taller people make better decisions or whether honesty depends on a person's accent, most people would disagree. But the world is so complex that the human brain finds ways to simplify by making hosts of inferences without our conscious effort. Those inferences are a part of how human beings avoid danger and find help. Where people run into trouble is in assuming they do not have any biases, so they fail to check the accuracy of their assumptions.

To overcome mistakes caused by treating inferences as facts, a supervisor should be aware of them. When sending a message, a supervisor should avoid statements that phrase inferences as facts. When listening to a message, a supervisor should be

inference
A conclusion drawn from the facts available

TABLE 10.3 | Cultural Differences in Communication

Aspect of Communication	Example
Language	Canada has two official languages, English and French. China has many dialects but one standard language, so written communication is widely understood.
Word choices	In Australia, lavish praise sounds insincere, and boasting violates the cultural value placed on equality. Germans do not think jokes are appropriate in a business context; they save humor for social occasions. In India, to avoid making others uncomfortable by saying no, people say, "I'll try."
Gestures	In China, it is difficult to say no, but speakers will indicate there is a problem with an idea by shaking the head or noisily sucking in air. Indians signify "yes" by moving the head from side to side in a kind of figure eight. In Japan, sitting erect in a chair with both feet on the floor signals good manners and interest.
Facial expressions	Chinese people rarely express emotions with facial expressions or smile during introductions. In Mexico, facial expressions are lively and convey much of the message.
Eye contact	Brazilians maintain eye contact during conversations, but when people have different status, the lower-status person shows respect by looking down. French people make frequent and intense eye contact to a degree that would be rude by U.S. standards.
Distance between speaker and listener	People in the United States stand about an arm's length away from each other when speaking. In Israel, people stand close together, and stepping back is rude.
Context (situation in which message is sent and received)	In Brazil, developing relationships is very important, so it is rude to jump into business topics at the beginning of a meal or to rush away at the end of a meeting. At business meetings in India, participants of lower rank will not offer their opinions, and all participants will avoid confrontations. Meetings in India are for presenting conclusions, not for debating and arriving at conclusions.
Conversational rituals (phrases and behaviors that are customs, not meant to be interpreted literally)	In the United States, people greet one another with "How are you?" as a ritual, not really looking for information. The person with higher status should greet first, to avoid seeming unfriendly. In China, a common ritual greeting is "Have you eaten?" The correct response is always "yes."

Sources: Examples from Jeanette S. Martin and Lillian H. Chaney, *Passport to Success* (Westport, CT: Praeger, 2009).

explicit with his or her inferences. For example, a supervisor in a bakery could say, "When you tell me the test of the recipe was a failure, I assume you mean the quality of the bread is poor. Is that correct?"

Biases in Perception

On the basis of their experiences and values, the sender and receiver of a message make assumptions about each other and the message. The ways people see and interpret reality are known as **perceptions.** Look at the picture in Figure 10.5 on the following page. What do you see? You may perceive either an old woman or a young woman.

When perceptions about others are false, messages might get distorted. Imagine that supervisor Al Trejo has decided his employees would like him to pay more

perceptions
The ways people see and interpret reality

FIGURE 10.5 | A Drawing That May Be Perceived in More Than One Way

Everyone brings some biases in perception to the way they view the world. As in this drawing, it is difficult to perceive things in two different ways at the same time.

Source: Edwin G. Boring, "A New Ambiguous Figure," *American Journal of Psychology*, July 1930, p. 444. See also Robert Leeper, "A Study of the Neglected Portion of the Field of Learning—The Development of Sensory Organization," *Journal of Genetic Psychology*, March 1935, p. 62. Originally drawn by cartoonist W. E. Hill and published in *Puck*, November 8, 1915.

prejudices
Negative conclusions about a category of people based on stereotypes

attention to their day-to-day problems and successes. So Al stops by the desk of one of his employees, Kim Coleman, and asks, "What are you doing?" Based on her experiences, Coleman believes that supervisors are quick to criticize, so she perceives that Trejo's question is intended to determine whether she is goofing off. Feeling defensive, Coleman snaps, "My work, of course." Trejo then perceives that Coleman does not want to discuss her work with him.

Prejudices

Broad generalizations about a category of people—stereotypes—can lead to negative conclusions about them. These negative conclusions are called **prejudices,** and they can distort perceptions. In U.S. culture, it is common to attribute certain characteristics to women, African Americans, Asian Americans, blue-collar workers, and many other groups. Of course, these characteristics often do not apply to a particular person. Imagine that a male manager assumes women are irrational and highly emotional and that a female supervisor who reports to him discusses her desire for a raise. Even if she outlines a series of logical points supporting her request, he may perceive her request as irrational and may respond by telling her to "take it easy, things will work out OK." If such poor communication continues, the supervisor might eventually quit in frustration.

The way to overcome communication barriers resulting from prejudices is to be aware of the assumptions we make. Are we responding to what a person is saying or to what he or she is wearing? Are we responding to the message or to the speaker's accent? To the words or to our beliefs about the person's race? Awareness enables the sender and the receiver of a message to focus on understanding rather than assuming.

Biases in Paying Attention

Perception begins when people pay attention to a message or other stimulus. However, biases occur even at this early stage of the perception process. People tend to pay more attention to a message that seems to serve their own self-interests. They also are more apt to hear messages that fit their existing viewpoints and discount messages that contradict those viewpoints. Imagine that an employee suggests a new procedure, to which the supervisor responds, "Your idea will never work." The employee is more likely to think the supervisor is opposed to change than that the idea is unworkable.

The supervisor can combat biases in attention by phrasing messages carefully to appeal to the receiver. In the case of the new idea from an employee, the supervisor might say, "Thank you for your suggestion. I estimate that it will save us about $50 a month. Can you think of a way we can modify it so that implementing it will cost less than $1,500?" This response shows the supervisor was paying attention to the suggestion and recognized at least some of its merit.

LO10.5 ▶ Distinguish between verbal and nonverbal messages, and name types of verbal messages.

Types of Messages

When Sandy walked into her cubicle at the insurance company where she worked, a note signed by her supervisor was on her desk: "See me," it read. "Uh-oh," thought Sandy nervously, "what did I do?"

Sandy walked into her supervisor's office and saw that he was smiling. "Congratulations," he said, "you got the raise we requested."

In this example, Sandy's supervisor communicated with her through a note, a facial expression, and spoken words. Two of the messages were verbal messages; that is, they consisted of words. The third—the smiling face—was a nonverbal message; that is, it was conveyed without words.

Nonverbal Messages

How can anyone get a point across without using words? Although the idea of non-verbal messages might seem surprising or unimportant at first, we continuously send and receive messages through our facial expressions, posture, and other non-verbal cues.[14] In the example of Sandy, the message conveyed by the supervisor's facial expression was as important as the verbal message, "See me." The smile, unlike the note, conveyed to Sandy that her supervisor had good news.

Major types of nonverbal messages are gestures, posture, tone of voice, facial expression, and even silence. We learn the meaning of many such messages simply by participating in our culture. From experience, we can recognize a friendly hand-shake, a cool silence in response to something we say, and the "proper" distance to stand from the person with whom we are talking, part of a concept known as personal space (see Figure 10.6). Imagine that a supervisor and an employee are dis-cussing a problem concerning the employee's work. The employee drops her eyes, looking away from the supervisor. Based on the usual assumptions in American culture, a supervisor is apt to conclude that the employee is dishonest, uninter-ested, or guilty of something.

Because we learn the meaning of nonverbal messages from our culture, people from different cultures have different nonverbal vocabularies. In the previous example, if the employee is a Cambodian woman, she may be trying to communi-cate respect; according to Cambodian custom, looking her supervisor in the eye would be rude. The meanings of nonverbal cues may vary even among different groups of people born in the United States. Failure to recognize different interpreta-tions of nonverbal signals can be misleading, as in the case of a European-American speaker who concludes, on the basis of eye contact, that an African-American lis-tener is not interested in what he or she is saying.

When a person is sending both verbal and nonverbal messages, the nonverbal message may have more influence on the receiver. Most of us can think of examples from daily life: Someone declares, "I'm not upset!" and then stomps out of the room and slams the door, or someone says, "Nice to see you," with his or her back turned and gaze directed to the screen of an iPhone. In those examples, the words contradict the

verbal message
A message that consists of words

nonverbal message
A message conveyed without using words

FIGURE 10.6 | The Etiquette of Proper Distance: Some Cross-Cultural Examples

How far apart we stand when we are conversing is a function of the culture from which we come.

Source: Based on Sondra Thiederman, *Bridging Cultural Barriers for Corporate Success: How to Manage the Multicultural Work Force* (New York: Lexington Books, 1991), p. 132.

- Americans, on average, stand 2 feet apart when conducting business.
- Middle Eastern males typically stand up to 18 inches apart.
- Asians and many African cultures leave a space of 3 feet or more.

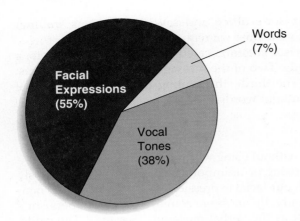

FIGURE 10.7 | Relative Contributions of Several Factors to Total Impact of a Message

When a message is both verbal and nonverbal, the nonverbal message may have more impact on the receiver than the words themselves. This pie chart shows the relative impact, expressed as a percentage, of words, vocal tones (tone of voice), and facial expressions.

Source: Data from Albert Mehrabian, "Communication without Words," *Psychology Today*, September 1968, pp. 53–55.

nonverbal messages. Most people would believe the nonverbal messages that the first person *is* upset and the second person is *not* seeing you or thinking your arrival is nice. Figure 10.7 shows the weight that different components of a message may carry. If the relative importance of nonverbal communication seems surprising, imagine that someone is saying, "You're in trouble!" in an angry tone of voice. Now imagine the same person saying that while laughing. Are the messages identical?

Given the significance of nonverbal messages, supervisors need to be aware of the messages they send. For example, supervisors' nonverbal messages, such as conservative clothing and a firm handshake, should communicate a professional, businesslike attitude. In addition, employees often consider the physical presence of the supervisor as a nonverbal message that the supervisor is interested in what the employees are doing. Employees at an aerospace manufacturer told a consultant that they wanted workplace visits from managers as a sign that the managers cared enough to listen to the employees. This nonverbal message is especially powerful if the supervisor makes eye contact, listens to employees, and asks employees what *they* want to discuss.[15] The nonverbal message of caring sent by the supervisor's physical presence is what Bill Zollars is referring to when he says, "Visibility is incredibly important. It's very hard to lead through e-mails." Zollars, chief executive officer of trucking firm YRC Worldwide Inc. (formerly Yellow Roadway), took on that job when the company was experiencing problems, so his top priority as a leader was to visit and talk with employees.[16]

Verbal Messages

Most nonverbal communication supplements verbal messages. People send verbal messages by speaking (oral communication) or writing (written communication).

Oral Communication

To communicate with employees, supervisors usually depend on oral communication. Every day they talk to employees to explain work duties, answer questions, assign tasks, check progress, and solve problems. This type of communication gives the supervisor an opportunity to send and receive many nonverbal cues along with the verbal ones. Thus, a supervisor can benefit from applying nonverbal communication skills when talking to employees. For example, the supervisor should use a well-modulated tone of voice and allow plenty of time for questions.

Most oral communication occurs face-to-face—in conversations, interviews, meetings, and formal presentations. (Meetings were discussed in Chapter 3.) Technology offers an increasing selection of oral communication channels for people in different locations. We take telephone calls for granted; newer technologies include voice mail, teleconferencing, and videoconferencing.

Speaking before a group makes many supervisors nervous, but nervousness can be positive if it inspires supervisors to be well prepared. Following these steps can help you give a successful presentation:[17]

1. Research your subject matter thoroughly. If you are well informed about the topic, the audience will sense your confidence and will respect you if you answer some questions by saying, "I don't know, but I will find out" (and then do it). Your knowledge should include reasons why the material is important. If you don't see the relevance of the topic, neither will your audience members, and they will tune you out.

2. Research your audience. If you are speaking to people you already know, give some thought to their interests, goals, and learning styles. If you are speaking to people within the organization, use the organization's resources, including your colleagues, manager, and information systems, to learn more about them. If you are speaking to people outside the organization, go online to visit the organization's Web site, look up news articles, and visit social and professional networking sites. If you can, contact some audience members ahead of time to learn about their questions, interests, and problems. Tailor your presentation to what you know about the audience.

3. Write a presentation that starts out with a focus on the benefits you are offering—for example, the solution to a problem or the skills that will help employees meet their goals. The closing portion of the presentation should remind the audience of those benefits.

4. Besides planning what you will *tell* your audience, plan what you will *ask* your audience. Think of ways to get audience members engaged and involved. Remember that the communication process flows in two directions.

5. If you are using presentation software, such as PowerPoint, to display slides, plan your slide presentation as thoroughly as your oral presentation. Proofread it carefully, and test it well before you head to the presentation. When you arrive, make sure your computer is working, and test the slide presentation again.

6. Practice your presentation. Practice frequently, rather than memorizing it, for a more natural delivery style. If you are using slide presentation software, include the slides in the practices. Practice turning each slide to black while you are speaking about something other than what is on the screen, so the slides don't become a distraction.

7. Arrive at the presentation site early. Look around to see where you will be sitting before your presentation and standing to speak. Also notice how far away the audience will be, so you can think about how to build rapport. Walking around on the stage before the audience arrives will increase your comfort in that space during your presentation. As participants arrive, greet them personally to create goodwill with your audience. They will listen more carefully if they start off liking you.

If you want more formal, in-depth help with speaking before a group, your organization may be willing to send you to one of the many training seminars available or to a speech class at a community college. Many people have benefited from participating in meetings of the Toastmasters organization, a nonprofit educational organization that operates clubs worldwide for the purpose of helping members improve their communication, public speaking, and leadership skills. Practice not only can improve your public speaking skills but also diminish your anxiety.

The ability to speak confidently in any public setting is an important attribute for a supervisory or management career. Consultant Pam Lassiter says public speaking can give you a reputation as an expert in your field, which makes your work more satisfying at the same time it builds a network of contacts that can open up career possibilities. However, supervisors need to be careful not to say anything that will embarrass them personally or embarrass their employer. In today's world of e-mail and blogs, one slipup can quickly become infamous. One way supervisors can protect themselves and avoid ethical problems is to let their employer know about their public speaking activities. Supervisors may find that management supports these efforts and will back them up with information and coaching—especially once the supervisors show that they approach speaking opportunities carefully and honestly.[18]

Written Communication

Many situations call for a record of what people tell one another. Therefore, much of the verbal communication that occurs in organizations is in writing. Common forms of written communication include memos, letters, reports, electronic messages, bulletin board notices, and posters.

Memos (short for *memoranda*) are an informal way to send a written message. At the top of the page, the sender types the date, receiver's name, sender's name, and subject matter. Because of their informality, memos lend themselves to communication within an organization.

People writing to someone outside the organization usually send a letter, which is more formal than a memo but has basically the same advantages and disadvantages. Both provide a written document for the receiver to review, and both take a relatively long time to prepare and deliver.

An analysis of how to meet a need or solve a problem takes the form of a report. A report describes the need or problem, and then proposes a solution. Many reports contain charts and graphs to make the message easy to understand. Another helpful technique for a long report (more than two pages) is to start with a paragraph that summarizes the contents. Busy managers can review what the report is about, even if they cannot read the full report right away.

Written messages also can be sent electronically by fax machine or e-mail. In recent years, e-mail has become a popular channel as computer use has spread into almost every organization. The Bureau of Labor Statistics recently determined that more than half of employees use a computer at work. The most common computer activity at work is accessing e-mail and the Internet, performed by about two out of five employees.[19]

E-mail makes communication easier in many ways, but it has its complications, which often arise precisely because of how easy it is to send an e-mail. Whereas preparing a letter or report takes time, offering a chance for reflection and change, an e-mail message is informal. Writers may dash off a message and click "Send" before considering whether it will be misunderstood. The situation is even riskier with the ease of the "Reply to All" feature, which sends the message to anyone who was copied on the original message, not just the original sender. A comment meant for one colleague's eyes suddenly becomes public information for several people, perhaps including one's boss, customers, or vendors. Most common today is the unthinking use of "Reply to All" to send a message that is irrelevant to most of the recipients. When Ben Swett's company, Windowbox.com, lets some employees of a customer know that a product is out of stock, Swett often gets meaningless feedback in the form of politically motivated comments along the lines of "Someone's got to do something about this," copying everyone so the co-workers can see how dedicated the sender is. Likewise, a big customer of Windowbox periodically sends out messages to Windowbox and other suppliers, and one or two suppliers will reply to all with messages such as, "We enjoyed your recent visit to our facility."[20] Rather than becoming a nuisance, e-mail users should send messages only to those who will be interested in the contents.

To communicate a single message to many people, the organization may use posters and electronic or printed bulletin board notices. These are efficient but impersonal ways to send messages, so they usually supplement more personal types of communication. For example, if a factory's managers want to promote quality, they can use posters that say "Quality First." For the message to be effective, however, managers and supervisors also should praise individuals for doing quality work, discuss quality when evaluating performance, and set an example in the quality of their own work. For more advice on this type of written communication, see the "Supervisory Skills" feature.

Modern Media and Message Types

Developments in technology have provided more ways to deliver messages. Modern media used in today's business environment include videoconferencing, text messages, microblogging (for example, on Twitter), status updates on social media, wikis (software for shared creation and editing of Web content), and reports posted online for collaboration. These message types provide exciting options but make selecting a communications channel more difficult. Messages sent via text or Twitter can become so simple that they strip out important social cues. Conversely, computers allow messages shared over distances to be enriched with visual information such as body language and graphics. These communications can take place in real time, without waiting for a report to be mailed or even e-mailed or faxed. Videoconferencing and computer audio/video services such as Skype and GoToMeeting make it possible to hold a meeting whenever ideas or problems arise, even if employees are widely scattered. A company that manufactures consumer packaged goods set up video collaboration systems on its factory floors. It allows production employees to get troubleshooting help from engineers, whether or not

SUPERVISORY SKILLS

COMMUNICATING VISUALLY

Graphs Keep Employees on Target

Supervisors help employees meet high standards by setting challenging goals and then building employee commitment to meet those goals. Supervisors may help their employees meet goals for scrap rates, sales volume, inventory levels, reduction of product defects, absenteeism, injuries, on-time shipments, completion of steps in a project, or other measures. Employees who know what the goals are will be motivated toward meeting each goal, particularly if they can see their progress.

To communicate this information dramatically, many supervisors prepare graphs. On well-designed graphs, employees can easily see what they are striving toward and how far they have come. The following suggestions will help supervisors make their graphs more effective:

- Choose one to three measures that define your group's success. Create one graph for each of these measures.

- Show performance improvement in a consistent and obvious way. For example, a line trending upward generally looks like an improvement.

- Keep graphs simple, using just a few bars or lines per graph. You might show progress toward a goal or the current period's performance versus last period's. In some cases, you might show a longer-term trend, such as falling costs or rising sales.

- Update the graphs regularly, perhaps once a week or once a month. Do not wait several months to update a graph; employees will lose interest in an unchanging graph.

- Post the graph where it is easy for employees to notice. Make it large enough and the colors bold enough that it can be read easily wherever it is posted.

- Explain the graphs you are using, and seek feedback to make sure the employees understand what each graph means.

- When you discuss performance with employees informally and in meetings, mention the results shown in the graphs. The emphasis you place on those results sends a message that the information in the graphs is important.

- Limit any presentations to employees to 20 minutes or less.

- Be clear about exactly what you expect employees to do with or about the information you have provided. There needs to be a "call to action." What can or should employees do to make the graph change in the direction desired?

In some settings today, much of the communication about performance takes place on computers. If you lack skills in preparing computer graphics, many community colleges offer courses that can bring you up to speed. Popular programs like Excel and PowerPoint offer tools for making easy-to-read graphs. Likewise, many organizations, including manufacturing facilities, expect their employees to use graphs so that they can monitor their own performance. Seek training resources for employees who would benefit from extra help in that skill.

Sources: Ed Lisoski, "Checking Your Business Gauges," *Supervision*, January 2005; Ed Lisoski, "Rising from the Ranks to Management: How to Thrive versus Survive," *Supervision*, July 2006; Bob Trebilcock, "Manufacturing Goes Back to School," *Modern Materials Handling*, July 1, 2006, all downloaded from Business & Company Resource Center, http://galenet.galegroup.com; Steven Costello, "5 Ways to Improve Your Employee Presentations," The CBG Benefits Blog, January 7, 2013, http://cbgbenefits.com/5-ways-to-improve-your-employee-presentations, accessed April 30, 2014.

they are in the building, and test new equipment while equipment suppliers observe and coach them. The system saves money by reducing equipment downtime and travel expenses.[21]

In addition to all the social networking sites, there are also business-oriented networking sites such as LinkedIn and Ryze. These tools can be extremely useful in building your professional identity and staying connected to colleagues you get to know as you or they change positions or companies over the span of your career. They can be an avenue for staying abreast of current information and changes in your industry. In addition, you can use them to learn of professional opportunities and new ventures.

You must be cautious while at work, however, to only use these as tools to enhance or improve your work. As with all social media, while on the job their use should be limited to activity that directly benefits the company for which you work. Whether you are looking for another job through a business networking site or want to share a fun photograph with a friend, that should be done on your personal time. It also bears repeating that you should consider carefully before posting comments or images to a social networking site. Negative or sarcastic comments, particularly about your work, can also lead to disastrous results, including being fired. While that snapshot of you and your friends getting wild at a party last weekend might bring back some fond memories, your boss, your employees, or a future employer might see it a little differently—and see you a little differently because of it.

Furthermore, the ability to send and receive information not only at work but also in one's home, car, and airplane seat can contribute to the information overload described earlier in this chapter. Some employees may feel as if they are never able to leave their workplaces fully because their supervisor and co-workers text them at all hours. Electronic media can also become an enormous distraction at work. By one measure, office workers typically interrupt their work 50 times a day to check e-mail and 77 times to send and receive instant messages.[22] After each such interruption, the brain needs time to refocus on the work at hand—as long as half an hour to return to peak productivity. Although many people believe they "multitask," evidence shows that the brain instead is switching back and forth between tasks, and the effort is slowing down the work and increasing the error rate.

One way to minimize the intrusiveness of modern media is to limit the use of phone calls, instant messages, and texting to situations where an immediate reply is essential. When the goal is to provide quick updates or a means to share ideas as they come to mind, less intrusive media include wikis, document-sharing software, and business-related Web pages where employees can use social-media tools such as status updates. Supervisors and their organizations may also be able to help with the problem of constant interruptions. They may be able to set aside time when instant messaging, e-mail, and cell phones are turned off so everyone can concentrate. Supervisors can set—and communicate—expectations that employees need not reply to messages right away outside of working hours. Perhaps most fundamentally, as more and more research shows that multitasking is not real, supervisors need to be realistic about interruptions and avoid praising or rewarding people for trying to direct their attention to several messages at the same time.

Choosing the Most Effective Message Type

With so many ways to send a message, which medium is the best for a supervisor to use? Although face-to-face communication conveys the most information (words *plus* tone of voice *plus* body language *plus* immediate feedback), the most effective and efficient method for a message depends on the situation. Table 10.4, on the following page, gives criteria for choosing written or oral communication. When

TABLE 10.4 | Put It in Writing?

When Written Communication Is Best	When Oral Communication Is Best
Message includes complex information.	Immediate feedback is necessary.
Information is more factual than sensitive.	Message is sensitive.
Okay if others read the message.	Building a relationship with the receiver is important.
A record of the communication is necessary.	Nonverbal cues needed for interpreting the message or feedback.
The receiver can read the language and use the technology (software, printer, etc.).	Receiver might have difficulty reading.

deciding whether to call, meet with, or e-mail or fax a message to someone, the supervisor should consider time and cost limits, the complexity and sensitivity of the issue, the need for a record of the communication, the need for feedback, and the capabilities of the audience.

Time and Cost Limits

Video conferencing is a convenient way for meetings to take place regardless of geographic limitations.

When the supervisor needs to reach someone in a hurry, a letter or memo may be too time-consuming. An employee might be easy to find at his or her desk or on the shop floor. Often, the fastest way to reach someone in the organization is to make a telephone call.

Modern technology shortens the time required to send messages. Fax transmissions, e-mail, and voice mail allow a supervisor to contact people who are away from the telephone much of the day or who are taking other calls. However, these technologies do not ensure that messages will be *received* quickly, because it is the receiver who decides when to pick up the fax or retrieve messages from voice mail or e-mail.

Like time, costs place some limits on the choice of communications media. When people who need to discuss an issue are located far apart, the costs of a videoconference may be less than the costs of bringing everyone together. Midway Games, for example, has its headquarters in Chicago and operates studios in Austin, Texas; Los Angeles; San Diego; Seattle; and Newcastle, England, as well as a sales office in Europe. Videoconferencing is a practical way for the video game company to arrange for employees to share information. In fact, Midway uses its videoconferencing system almost daily.[23]

Complexity and Sensitivity of the Issue

A complex message is clearer if written. For example, the results of a survey or the analysis of a work group's performance are easier to understand in a written report. In a meeting, an oral report will be clearer if supplemented with written handouts, PowerPoint slides, posters, or overhead transparencies. When speed is critical in communicating complex information to someone outside the organization, it may be cost effective to use a fax machine or computer modem.

For emotionally charged issues or when the state of mind of employees is at issue, communicators need the information that comes from tone of voice, gestures, and facial expressions. Such information is also essential for assessing how well employees (especially new ones) are doing. Written communications such as e-mail are thus best suited for objective messages. Sarcasm, humor, and emotion-laden messages are likely to be misinterpreted by receivers of e-mail. Max Messmer, chairman of Accountemps, advises, "Face-to-face meetings reduce the potential for miscommunications." However, a survey commissioned by his company found that most managers preferred to send e-mail because it is so convenient.[24]

The more sensitive a message or situation, the more opportunity there should be for nonverbal communication. Telephone calls, voice mail, and audio e-mail messages provide information through vocal tones. Most information, of course, comes from communicating face to face. Holding a one-on-one or group meeting allows the message sender to defuse anger and dispel misconceptions. It gives the receivers a chance to air their feelings and ask questions. For example, a supervisor who needs to discipline an employee must ensure that the employee understands the problem and has a chance to present his or her point of view. Similarly, an announcement of layoffs or restructuring should be made in person.

Need for a Record

As you will learn in Chapter 12, disciplinary action calls for a written record as well as a face-to-face meeting. A supervisor needs to combine a written message with oral communication. Other actions that call for written records include placing an order and establishing goals for an employee or department.

Need for Feedback

The easiest way to get feedback is to send an oral message. The listeners at the meeting or on the telephone can respond immediately with comments and questions. If feedback is critical, face-to-face communication is more effective than a telephone conversation because the person delivering the message can watch facial expressions as well as hear reactions. Do people look confused, excited, angry, satisfied? If a supervisor explaining a new procedure says, "Do you understand?" and the employee responds with a doubtful "I guess so," the supervisor knows that an example or some other clarification is needed.

Capabilities of the Receiver

People will receive a message only if it comes through a channel they feel comfortable using. In many settings, for example, some employees lack reading skills. If a supervisor believes that an employee cannot read the message, he or she will need to find ways to deliver it through the spoken word, pictures, gestures, or some other means of communication. This situation arises when an employee cannot read at all or reads too poorly to understand a particular message. Some employees may read well in other languages but not in English; in such a case, the supervisor may want to make written messages available in other languages.

The issue of illiteracy is a sensitive one. Supervisors must be tactful and look carefully for signs that employees have trouble reading. Employees with reading difficulties are typically embarrassed about this problem and try to hide it. At ShawCor Limited, Angela Molis handled this sensitive issue by communicating through more than one channel to ensure understanding. Molis prepared training materials that were written in both Spanish and English and contained many diagrams. In addition, during training sessions, she took time to read the materials out loud. Furthermore, Molis trained employees to serve as "zone leaders." These employees share safety lessons with co-workers, who tend to respond better to training from a peer than from a supervisor.[25]

A potentially more widespread concern is people's comfort and skill in using modern technology. Some people feel frustrated or angry when a voice mail system answers the telephone. Supervisors can help by recording an answering message that offers information such as when to expect a return call and how to reach an operator or secretary. Likewise, information offered online will seem convenient to some and inaccessible to others.

Communicating in Organizations

In business, government, and other organizations, communication tends to follow certain patterns. Understanding these patterns can help the supervisor make the best use of them.

LO10.6 ▶ Identify the directions in which communication can flow in an organization.

Direction of Communication

One way to understand patterns of communication is to think in terms of the direction in which the messages flow in an organization. For example, a supervisor might have different challenges when making a message clear to a supervisor in another department than when making it clear to the employees on the supervisor's own team. Figure 10.8 uses the format of an organization chart like those in Chapter 7 to show the basic directions of communication in an organization: upward, downward, and lateral.

Why should a supervisor need to know about the directions of communication? One way a supervisor can use this information is to be sure that he or she is communicating in all directions: downward so employees know what is expected of them and the supervisor understands what is happening in the organization; upward so his or her manager is aware of the supervisor's accomplishments and employees feel encouraged to offer ideas; and laterally so the work of the supervisor's department is well coordinated with the work of other departments.

Downward Communication

downward communication
Organizational communication in which a message is sent to someone at a lower level

When someone sends a message to a person at a lower level, **downward communication** is occurring. A supervisor is receiving a downward communication when listening to instructions or an evaluation from his or her manager or when reading a memo from top management describing a new company policy. The supervisor is sending a downward communication when he or she discusses a problem with an employee or tells an employee how to perform a task. Employees expect to receive enough downward communication to understand how to do their jobs, and they typically like to know enough so that they understand what is going on.

Upward Communication

upward communication
Organizational communication in which a message is sent to someone at a higher level

When someone sends a message to a person at a higher level, **upward communication** is occurring. A supervisor is receiving an upward communication when an employee asks a question or reports a problem. A supervisor is sending an upward communication when he or she tells the manager how work is progressing or asks for a raise. Managers especially want to receive upward communications about controversial matters or matters affecting their own performance.

To be well informed and benefit from employees' creativity, a supervisor should encourage upward communication. Despite the importance of upward

FIGURE 10.8 | Directions of Communication in an Organization

Communication within an organization flows in different directions and it is the supervisors job to make sure that he or she is communicating in all of these directions.

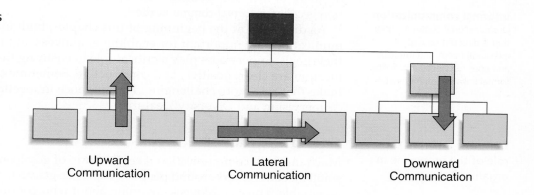

Upward Communication   Lateral Communication   Downward Communication

communication, research indicates that on at least one occasion, 85 percent of surveyed employees did not feel comfortable raising an issue with their supervisor, even though they felt it was very important.[26] In fact, much of the literature around critical communication only addresses how supervisors can confront their employees. Another important communication channel involves how employees can discuss their concerns with their supervisor. Therefore, it is especially important for supervisors to create a safe environment for their employees to express whatever concerns or issues are affecting their overall level of job satisfaction.

A supervisor can enhance upward communication by applying the strategies for effective listening. A supervisor should respond to employees so they know their messages have been received. Another means of encouraging upward communication is to establish a formal way, such as a suggestion box, for employees to provide comments and suggestions. When a Midwestern telecommunications company redesigned its suggestion program, it learned what kinds of programs are most successful. Supervisors can apply some of the lessons this company learned. For example, the supervisor should require that each suggestion be related to company goals. The supervisor might specifically ask for suggestions that decrease scrap or error rates or shorten response times. Some of the best suggestions come from asking employees to identify improvements to their own jobs. Finally, supervisors can request that the people making the suggestion support their ideas with facts and evidence showing the idea's benefits. When the supervisor states the requirement positively, employees become more involved in and excited about their ideas. Of course, the supervisor should implement the well-supported, goal-related ideas—and give credit to those whose ideas help the company.[27]

Lateral Communication

lateral communication
Organizational communication in which a message is sent to a person at the same level

A message sent to a person at the same level is **lateral communication**. Supervisors send and receive lateral communications when they discuss their needs with co-workers in other departments, coordinate their group's work with that of other supervisors, and socialize with their peers at the company.

Formal and Informal Communication

formal communication
Organizational communication that is work related and follows the lines of the organization chart

The communication that follows the lines of the organization chart is known as **formal communication**, which is directed toward accomplishing the goals of the organization. For example, when a supervisor discusses an employee's performance with that employee, the supervisor is helping the employee perform high-quality work. When a supervisor gives the manager a report of the department's weekly activities, the supervisor is helping the manager perform his or her responsibilities for controlling.

LO10.7 ▶ Distinguish between formal and informal communication in an organization.

However, much of the communication that occurs in an organization is directed toward meeting people's individual needs. For example, managers and employees alike may spend time discussing the performance of their favorite sports teams, the behavior of their children, and good places to eat lunch. This type of communication is called **informal communication**.

informal communication
Organizational communication that is directed toward individual needs and interests and does not necessarily follow formal lines of communication

As discussed at the beginning of this chapter, both formal and informal communications are important for enabling employees and the organization to meet their goals. Supervisors play a critical role in ensuring that both types of communication are clear, positive, and constructive. Sometimes, employee diversity can make that role more challenging. For guidance in meeting the challenge, see the "Supervision and Diversity" feature.

LO10.8 ▶ Describe the role of the grapevine in organizations.

Gossip and Rumors

Much informal communication takes the form of gossip and rumors. Gossip is like small talk but centers around people. People use gossip to indicate what behavior is acceptable. Thus, employees gossiping about who got promoted or who is dating

SUPERVISION AND DIVERSITY

WHEN EMPLOYEES FEEL EXCLUDED

A recent report from Catalyst shows that an employee feeling as if they are different from their co-workers, for whatever reasons, make the employee feel alone. These feelings may influence that employee's goals and their chances at advancement. This is clearly a negative for the employee, but it is also a loss of potential talent for the company.

The reasons for feeling like an "other" can vary greatly. It could be because of gender, race/ethnicity, or nationality. For example, a male working in a field that is predominantly women or an African-American woman in an office of white males. Or it might be something less obvious such as a person having grown up in a different part of the country, gone to a different school, or having different political opinions.

The Catalyst study, however, suggests that how differences impact an employee can be determined by the actions of the company and co-workers. Feeling different does not have to mean feeling excluded if the company recognizes differences as an asset. A sense of belonging can be created if a company values differences and makes sure that all employees have equal access to engaging tasks and promotions.

The President and CEO of Catalyst, Deborah Gillis, claims it is best for both the employees and the company when "'otherness' is seen as a strength, rather than a challenge." According to Gillis, "By ensuring that everyone feels included and valued at work, companies are positioned to celebrate and leverage the unique talents and perspectives that each employee brings to the table, creating a workplace where everyone can thrive."

Another problem arises when some employees exclude others by not communicating. That situation began to occur at Xplane, a design and consulting business, after the Portland, Oregon, company acquired a small firm in Madrid, Spain. Sometimes U.S. employees would send e-mails to their co-workers in the United States but leave their Spanish colleagues off the list. That behavior told the Spanish workers, "You're not one of us." Management stepped in with some technology fixes but also realized the importance of face-to-face communication in establishing relationships. Xplane rented apartments in Madrid and Portland and began sending employees from one city to the other to work for a week at a time.

Supervisors may not have employees in different continents, but the principle of bringing workers together still applies. Supervisors can establish better lateral communication by assigning diverse workers to tasks and projects with shared goals and rewards.

Sources: Based on "Companies Lose When Employees Feel Excluded," Catalyst, January 16, 2014, http://www.catalyst.org/media/companies-lose-when-employees-feel-excluded, accessed April 30, 2014; "Feeling Different: Being the "Other" in U.S. Workplaces," Catalyst, January 16, 2014, http://www.catalyst.org/knowledge/feeling-different-being-other-us-workplaces, accessed April 30, 2014; and Nadine Heintz, "In Spanish, It's *un Equipo*, in English, It's a Team: Either Way, It's Tough to Build," *Inc.*, April 2008, pp. 41–42.

---

the new supervisor in the payroll department are typically airing and refining their views about promotion policies and love affairs between co-workers.

Rumors are explanations, sometimes unfounded, for what is going on around us. For example, if a factory gets a visit from the company's board of directors, employees at the factory may spread rumors that the factory is to be sold or the operations moved to South Korea. When people are afraid, they spread rumors to ease their fear while trying to get at the facts. Thus, rumors tend to circulate chiefly during crises and conflicts—and they are often false.

Although rumors and gossip are a fact of life in the workplace, it does not look good for a supervisor to participate in spreading either. As a member of management, a supervisor is expected to know and report the facts about company business. When a supervisor spreads gossip or rumors, word eventually will get around that he or she is responsible for the message.

Although supervisors should distance themselves from rumors and gossip, a supervisor may occasionally hear a story that requires action. For example, team members may be unable to cooperate, or an employee may have violated a work rule. If the story suggests there is a problem requiring the supervisor's involvement, the supervisor must start by trying to learn the facts. Rumors and gossip rarely tell a complete or unbiased version of the truth. People tend to embellish the stories to make them more interesting, and even well-intentioned people perceive situations in a distorted way. For example, we recall the aspects of a situation that are most unusual and interpret them according to our own way of thinking. Therefore, the supervisor needs an open mind and should get the facts from those who are directly involved, not those spreading the rumor. Questions about the situation should focus on the main work-related issue that concerns the supervisor, and the supervisor should avoid words that imply a judgment. The supervisor should ask about observable actions, not opinions and hunches.[28] If the situation is complicated or involves legal issues, the supervisor should seek help from the company's human resource personnel. (Appendix B explores a number of legal areas involving supervisors.)

The Grapevine

grapevine
The path along which informal communication travels

The path along which informal communication travels is known as the **grapevine.** The grapevine is important to supervisors because employees use it as a source of information. Thus, a supervisor must expect that employees sometimes have information before the supervisor has delivered it. Supervisors also must realize that employees may be getting incorrect information through the grapevine, especially in times of crisis or conflict.

Situations that worry employees will cause them to turn to the grapevine when they are not satisfied with the amount of information they receive from management. Troubles in the economy will worry many people, and they will want management to provide information, even if it is bad news. Some managers may notice employees spending more time searching the Internet or making personal phone calls. At the same time, surveyed employees might say their managers are not talking to them about how an economic downturn will affect them. Reporter Carmine Gallo uncovered an example of this behavior. She was talking to a construction contractor who said he was pleased his company had recently obtained a five-year loan that would keep his company going. When she remarked that his employees must be glad, the contractor said he had not gotten around to telling them. When times are bad, supervisors and higher-level managers may feel they are too busy dealing with the hard times to call an employee meeting, but employees who are consumed with worry will not be doing their best work.[29]

Managers are generally unable to control the grapevine of information as it generally springs up on its own. However, knowing about the grapevine can help the supervisor seek out and correct misinformation. The supervisor also can take some steps to see that at least some of the messages in the grapevine are positive and in line with the organization's objectives:[30]

- Be realistic about who communicates through informal channels. In spite of whatever stereotypes you might hear about women gossiping, men as well as women swap stories and try to figure out what is really happening behind the scenes. Also, the grapevine today is not just conversations at the coffee station or drinking fountain. Rumors and gossip are as likely to spread online.

- Listen attentively to employees, and show genuine interest in their concerns. Employees will be more willing to share what they are hearing, and you will be better equipped to quell any false rumors.

- When times are hard and employees are nervous, emphasize communication face-to-face. A group e-mail won't adequately express concern for employees' fears or provide enough opportunity to answer questions. Negative rumors are likely to follow.

- Plant authentic positive messages. Spend time talking with employees and answering their questions. The more you communicate, the more likely your positive messages are to be dispersed through the grapevine.

- Be a trustworthy leader. Employees who see their supervisor as a person of integrity are more likely to believe their supervisor's official messages. Unofficial messages spread through the grapevine will be less important.

Furthermore, if supervisors and other managers are exercising their leadership skills to create an environment in which employees can and want to make positive contributions, both formal and informal communication are important. Supervisors will want to encourage communication among employees so they can improve the ways they work together.

At Southern Company, an electric utility based in Atlanta, Chris Womack says effective communication is an essential part of leadership. According to Womack, Southern's managers are expected to ensure that frontline employees know and understand the company's objectives. He considers open communication a necessary ingredient for retaining and motivating employees. Says Womack, "Honesty fosters a positive work relationship and makes people want to actually work [harder] for a company."[31]

Skills Module

PART ONE: CONCEPTS

Summary

10.1 Describe the process of communication.

The communication process occurs when people send and receive information. It begins when someone encodes a message by putting it into words or nonverbal cues. The sender of the message transmits it by speaking or writing. Then the receiver of the message decodes, or interprets, it. Usually the receiver gives the sender feedback.

10.2 Distinguish between hearing and listening.

Hearing occurs when the brain registers sounds. Listening occurs when the person who hears sounds also pays attention and tries to understand the message.

10.3 Describe techniques for communicating effectively.

Effective communication is most likely to occur when the parties communicate from the receiver's viewpoint, learn from feedback, use strategies for effective listening, and overcome barriers to communication. To listen effectively, the listener should make a commitment to listen, set aside time for listening, and then concentrate on the message. The listener also should try to control his or her emotions, not letting an emotional reaction interfere with understanding. Active listening involves hearing what the speaker is saying, seeking to understand the facts and feelings the speaker is trying to convey, and stating what one understands the message to be. Supervisors also should be prepared for cultural differences in order to communicate effectively. They should stick to simple words, avoid jargon, speak slowly, give the listener time to ask questions, ask for clarification, and learn about the communication styles of different cultures.

10.4 Identify barriers to communication and suggest ways to avoid them.

Barriers to communication include information overload, misunderstandings, perceptions and prejudices, and biases related to perception. Ways to avoid these barriers include giving employees only the information they need, encoding messages carefully and simply, observing feedback, avoiding name-calling, being aware of inferences and prejudices, and phrasing messages to appeal to the receiver.

10.5 Distinguish between verbal and nonverbal messages, and name types of verbal messages.

Verbal messages consist of words. Nonverbal messages are messages encoded without words, such as facial expressions, gestures, or tone of voice. Types of verbal messages include face-to-face discussions, telephone calls, memos, letters, reports, e-mail messages, faxes, and videoconferences.

10.6 Identify the directions in which communication can flow in an organization.

Organizational communication may flow upward, downward, or laterally. Upward communication travels to the sender's superior. Downward communication travels from managers to employees. Lateral communication flows between people at the same level.

10.7 Distinguish between formal and informal communication in an organization.

Formal communication travels along the lines of the organizational chart and is related to accomplishing the goals of the organization. Informal communication may travel in any direction among any members of the organization. It tends to be aimed at achieving personal, rather than organizational, objectives.

10.8 Describe the role of the grapevine in organizations.

The grapevine is the path of much of the organization's informal communications. Much of the information that travels through the grapevine is gossip and rumors. The supervisor generally cannot control this flow of information but should be aware that it exists and that he or she may have to correct misinformation. In addition, by encouraging communication with his or her employees, a supervisor may be able to ensure that some of the messages in the grapevine are positive.

Key Terms

communication, *p.* 256
noise, *p.* 256
feedback, *p.* 257
active listening, *p.* 261
inference, *p.* 266

perceptions, *p.* 267
prejudices, *p.* 268
verbal messages, *p.* 269
nonverbal messages, *p.* 269
downward communication, *p.* 277

upward communication, *p.* 277
lateral communication, *p.* 278
formal communication, *p.* 278
informal communication, *p.* 278
grapevine, *p.* 280

Review and Discussion Questions

1. Phyllis Priestley, a supervisor, wants to tell her boss what she plans to accomplish at a leadership seminar she will be attending next week. She decides to do so in the form of a memo. Briefly describe how this communication will follow the model shown in Figure 10.1.

2. Can a person be hearing but not listening well? Can a person be listening but not hearing well? Explain.

3. Every Monday morning, Ron Yamamoto, a supervisor, must attend a divisional meeting to discuss progress and make plans. Yamamoto finds that most people at the meetings are long-winded and that the meetings as a whole are boring. However, he needs to know what is going on in the division. How can he listen effectively, even though he is bored?

4. Sheila James owns a catering business employing four workers. She just got a contract to cater a wedding reception for a Chinese couple who speak very little English. What steps can James take to make sure her communication with the couple is successful? As a supervisor, what steps might she take with her employees to make sure they understand the couple's wishes as well?

5. In a staff meeting held to introduce new software that will provide office employees with information about the company's financial status, sales figures, and marketing plans, you notice that one of your employees is alternately staring out the window and doodling in his notebook. You are certain he is not paying attention. What barrier to communication might be occurring here? What steps might you take as a supervisor to overcome it?

6. The following examples describe some ways to send messages. Indicate whether each is verbal or nonverbal. For each verbal message, indicate whether it is oral or written.
   a. A long silence accompanied by an icy stare.
   b. A letter delivered by fax machine.
   c. Voice mail.
   d. Laughter.

7. As mail room supervisor, you need to report to your manager that a sack of mail has been misplaced (you are not sure how it happened). Would you want to send this message through written or oral communication? Would you want to deliver it face-to-face? Describe the form of communication you would choose and why you would choose it.

8. Nina Goldberg has been asked by her manager to give a presentation to employees about changes the company is going to make in health care benefits. Using the seven steps described in this chapter (in the Verbal Messages section), how should Goldberg prepare her presentation?

9. Face-to-face communication conveys the most information because the people communicating can learn from each other's body language and tone of voice as well as from the words themselves. However, why shouldn't a supervisor always choose face-to-face communication over other ways?

10. Lee Hamel is a busy supervisor. He rarely hears from his employees except when there is a production snag or scheduling problem. Hamel figures that as long as things run smoothly, his employees are happy. Why might his attitude be counterproductive in the long run? What steps could he take to improve upward communication from his employees?

11. Which of the following organizational communications are formal? Informal?

a. A memo providing information about the company picnic.

b. A meeting at which employees discuss the department's goals for the month.

c. A rumor about a new vacation policy.

d. A discussion between a supervisor and an employee about who will win the World Series.

12. Should a supervisor participate in informal communication? If so, when? If not, why not?

Notes

1. "Workplace Socializing Is Productive," *Gallup Business Journal*, November 13, 2008, http://businessjournal.gallup.com/content/111766/news-flash-workplace-socializing-productive.aspx, accessed April 29, 2014.

2. "One: Worker Health and Bottom Line," *Credit Union Journal*, June 30, 2008, downloaded from Business & Company Resource Center, http://galenet.galegroup.com.

3. For more information on how to communicate effectively, see S. Wu and B. Keysar, 2007, "The effect of information overlap on communication effectiveness," *Cognitive Science*, 31, p. 169.

4. Bruce Vernyi, "Product Development: An Avenue for Ideas," *Industry Week*, August 24, 2005, http://www.industryweek.com/articles/product_development_an_avenue_for_ideas_10671.aspx, accessed April 29, 2014; C. R. Bard, "About Bard," www.crbard.com/About_Bard/About_Bard.html, accessed April 29, 2014.

5. T. L. Stanley, "What Would Buzz Lightyear Do?" *Supervision*, March 2006, downloaded from Business & Company Resource Center, http://galenet.galegroup.com.

6. For more information on the importance of active listening in the context of negotiation, see T. Royce, 2005, "The negotiator and the bomber: Analyzing the critical role of active listening in crisis negotiations," *Negotiation Journal*, 21, p. 5.

7. This section is based on Donna M. Owens, "Multilingual Workforces," *HRMagazine*, September 2005, 50 (9), http://www.shrm.org/Publications/hrmagazine/EditorialContent/Pages/0905owens.aspx, accessed April 29, 2014; Bob Miodonski, "Foreign-Born Workers Deserve Respect," *Contractor*, April 1, 2005, http://contractormag.com/plumbing/cm_newsarticle_623, accessed April 29, 2014; Ed Rosheim, "Bridging Language Gap Leads to More Productive Staff," Workplace Languages, March 6, 2013, http://www.workplacelanguages.com/bridging-language-gap-leads-to-more-productive-staff/, accessed April 29, 2014; Josh Cable, "The Multicultural Work Force: The Melting Pot Heats Up," EHS Today, March 13, 2006, http://ehstoday.com/training/ehs_imp_38115, accessed April 29, 2014.

8. For further information on the role of culture in the process of communication, see N. Buchan, E. Johnson, and R. Croson, 2006, "Let's get personal: An international examination of the influence of communication, culture and social distance on other regarding preferences," *Journal of Economic Behavior & Organization*, 60, p. 373.

9. John Oliver Siy and Sapna Cheryan, "When Compliments Fail to Flatter: American Individualism and Responses to Positive Stereotypes," *Journal of Personality and Social Psychology*, January 2013, 104(1), pp. 87–102, http://depts.washington.edu/sibl/Publications/Siy%20&%20Cheryan%202013.pdf, accessed April 30, 2014.

10. Leigh Buchanan, "The English Impatient," *Inc.*, May 2001, p. 68, http://www.inc.com/magazine/20010501/22498.html, accessed April 30, 2014.

11. Indra Nooyi, "The Best Advice I Ever Got," *Fortune*, April 30, 2008, http://money.cnn.com/galleries/2008/fortune/0804/gallery.bestadvice.fortune/7.html, accessed April 29, 2014.

12. Charles Lowenhaupt, "Giving Clients What They Want," *Accounting Technology*, October 2008, downloaded from Business & Company Resource Center, http://galenet.galegroup.com.

13. Howard J. Ross, "Beware Preconceived Notions," *Chief Learning Officer*, September 2011, pp. 26–29, http://www.clomedia.com/articles/beware-preconceived-notions, accessed April 30, 2014.

14. For more information about the important role of nonverbal messages, see W. Gentry and K. Kuhnert, 2007, "Sending signals: Nonverbal communication can speak volumes," *Leadership in Action*, 27, p. 3.

15. Linda Dulye, "Management Tools: Get Out of Your Office," *HRMagazine*, July 2006, downloaded from Business & Company Resource Center, http://galenet.galegroup.com.

16. Bill Zollars, quoted in "Follow These Leaders: Ten Top Executives Tell Their Secrets," *Fortune*,

December 12, 2005, http://money.cnn.com/2005/12/05/news/newsmakers/leaders_fortune_121205/, accessed April 30, 2014.

17. Patricia Fripp, "Nine Timely Tips for Pre-Presentation Preparation," Fripp & Associates, http://www.fripp.com/blog/9-timely-tips-for-pre-presentation-preparation/, accessed April 30, 2014; Chris Brogan, "Power Presenter," *Entrepreneur*, January 24, 2011, p. 58, http://www.entrepreneur.com/article/217900#, accessed April 30, 2014; Forrest Wall, "Ten Tips for Better Presentations," *T+D*, December 2010, pp. 30–32; Sarah Kessler, "How to Improve Your Presentation Skills," *Inc.*, February 22, 2010, http://www.inc.com/guides/how-to-improve-your-presentation-skills.html, accessed April 30, 2014.

18. Mary K. Pratt, "How to Raise Your Profile without Raising a Ruckus," *Computerworld*, September 29, 2008, http://www.computerworld.com/s/article/326206/How_to_Raise_Your_Profile_Without_Raising_a_Ruckus, accessed April 30, 2014.

19. Bureau of Labor Statistics, "Computer and Internet Use at Work in 2003," news release, August 2, 2005, http://www.bls.gov/news.release/pdf/ciuaw.pdf, accessed April 30, 2014.

20. Jared Sandberg, "Never a Safe Feature, 'Reply to All' Falls into the Wrong Hands," *The Wall Street Journal*, October 25, 2005, http://online.wsj.com/news/articles/SB113019182149778080, accessed April 29, 2014.

21. Marieke Wijtkamp, "Advances in Video Collaboration," Ceramic *Industry*, April 1, 2011, http://www.ceramicindustry.com/articles/91573-special-report-resource-management—advances-in-video-collaboration, accessed April 30, 2014.

22. Joe Robinson, "Tame the E-mail Beast," *Entrepreneur*, February 11, 2010, http://www.entrepreneur.com/article/204980, accessed April 30, 2014; Craig Mindrum, "The Twitching Organization," *Chief Learning Officer*, March 2011, pp. 20–25, http://www.clomedia.com/articles/the-twitching-organization, accessed April 30, 2014.

23. Eric Benderoff and Mike Hughlett, "Teleconferencing Has Reduced Business Travel for Many Companies," *Chicago Tribune*, August 10, 2006, downloaded from Business & Company Resource Center, http://galenet.galegroup.com.

24. "E-mail Preferred to In-Person Meetings," *USA Today*, December 2003, www.findarticles.com.

25. Cable, "The Multicultural Work Force."

26. Further discussion can be found in: D. Tourish and P. Robson, 2006, "Sensemaking and the distortions of critical upward communication in organizations," *The Journal of Management Studies*, 43, p. 711.

27. Peggy Darragh-Jeromos, "A Suggestion System That Works for You," *Supervision*, August 2003, downloaded from InfoTrac, http://web7.infotrac.galegroup.com.

28. Janet R. Waddell, "You'll Never Believe What I Heard," *Supervision*, February 2004, downloaded from Business & Company Resource Center, http://galenet.galegroup.com.

29. Sarah E. Needleman, "Allaying Workers' Fears during Uncertain Times," *The Wall Street Journal*, October 6, 2008, http://online.wsj.com/news/articles/SB122324185911805771, accessed April 30, 2014; Kelsey Hubbard, "In Crisis, Leaders Must Communicate," *The Wall Street Journal*, October 24, 2008, http://online.wsj.com; and Carmine Gallo, "Financial Crisis: Communicating with Employees," *BusinessWeek Online*, October 21, 2008, http://www.businessweek.com/stories/2008-10-21/financial-crisis-communicating-with-employees businessweek-business-news-stock-market-and-financial-advice, accessed April 30, 2014.

30. Grant Michelson, "Make Office Gossip Work for You," *Forbes*, May 19, 2011, http://www.forbes.com/2011/05/19/make-office-gossip-work-for-you.html, accessed April 30, 2014; Bill Conaty, "Cutbacks: Don't Neglect the Survivors," *BusinessWeek*, December 29, 2009, http://www.businessweek.com/stories/2009-12-29/cutbacks-dont-neglect-the-survivors, accessed April 30, 2014; Jon Gordon, "Why Your Company Needs Motivation More than Ever . . . and Six Ways You Can Share It," *Receivables Report*, December 2010, pp. 7–9.

31. Siobhan Benet, "Corporate Cues," *Black Enterprise*, March 2004, www.findarticles.com.

PART TWO: SKILL-BUILDING

Meeting the Challenge

Reflecting back on page 255, consider how important it is to have the right information at the right time to do your job effectively. Supervising a team requires coordinating complex and changeable work between departments. Hadronics had high-quality manufacturing process control software but it was not available to those who needed it, where they needed it. Making it available on an iPad enabled supervisors to see the current status of jobs while on the shop floor, make adjustments to their team's work, and communicate critical information about jobs with other departments. Hadronics reduced rework by more than 25 percent, and improved on-time delivery by 33 percent. Why did this technology work where other approaches had not? What kind of communication problems are being addressed here?

Problem-Solving Case: Billing Department Supervisor Gets a Handle on Open-Door Policy

When she took the position in charge of a hospital's billing department, a supervisor we'll call Jeannie wanted to promote upward communication from her employees. So Jeannie instituted a policy that her "door is always open." Employees were invited to stop in her office to check with her whenever they ran into a problem, thought of a question, or simply wanted encouragement.

To her surprise, Jeannie quickly discovered that at least for her, there *is* such a thing as too much communication. She would settle down to work on a report, and the interruptions would begin almost immediately. During one 20-minute period, four different people stopped in with questions. Her days began to feel chaotic, and Jeannie wanted to put some limits on her open-door policy.

Jeannie decided to be strict about refusing to become engaged in conversations she considers "time wasters." For example, when employees try to share their horror stories about how difficult a client or insurer is being, Jeannie says she doesn't have time to hear it. In her opinion, swapping these stories does not serve a useful purpose.

When Jeannie thought further about how to reduce the number of interruptions, she realized that some of her employees were using her knowledge as a substitute for thinking through problems themselves. She decided that she could help her staff develop if she made it harder for them to simply "delegate problems upward" to her. She set aside afternoon hours for employee questions and began to require that whenever employees come to her seeking help with a problem, they must be prepared to suggest at least one possible solution. She developed a set of questions to ask whenever an employee tells her about a problem:

- Do you have examples of this issue—descriptions of when a similar situation arose and how it was handled then?
- Do you have all of the information about the account in question?
- In your notes about the question, have you included a summary of the issue?
- Have you drafted at least one solution?

Until the answer to all the questions is "yes," Jeannie asks the employees not to come to her. She explained that she wanted them to prepare fully before they bring the problem to her.

When employees are prepared and Jeannie helps them with problems, she makes sure to play a supporting role, rather than taking over a case. For example, if an employee has difficulty collecting an amount and has run through all the options identified, Jeannie might set up meetings with insurers and employees in other departments. She shares these plans with the employees handling the accounts, and she keeps track of all the deadlines she has set for action. She regularly reviews these plans and uses them as a basis for keeping in touch with employees about their progress.

With these limits in place, Jeannie finds that she has fewer interruptions, but she doesn't want to lose touch with her employees. So, following the example of doctors, who go on daily rounds to visit their hospitalized patients, Jeannie goes on rounds through the office to see her employees each day. During her rounds, Jeannie asks employees how they are, how their work is coming along, and whether they have all the resources they need. She also compliments employees who have excelled in some way, and she asks what she can do better as their supervisor. She keeps notes of employee requests, promises to do her best to help, and later reviews her notes to make sure she is following through on promises.

1. What strategies for communicating effectively does Jeannie use? What other strategies would help her communicate more effectively?

2. Discuss whether you think Jeannie is communicating adequately in all directions and whether she is effectively using both formal and informal communication. How could she improve?

3. How could Jeannie apply modern technology to help her manage communication with employees?

Source: Based on Judy I. Veazie, "Open Door or Controlled Chaos," *Health Care Collector*, August 2011, pp. 8–11.

Assessing Yourself

Are You an Effective Listener?

On the line before each statement, score yourself on a scale of 1 (seldom) to 10 (usually) to indicate how often that statement is true about you. Be as truthful as you can in light of your behavior in the last few meetings or gatherings you have attended.

_____ 1. I listen to one conversation at a time.

_____ 2. I like to hear people's impressions and feelings as well as the facts of a situation.

_____ 3. I really pay attention to people; I don't just pretend.

_____ 4. I consider myself a good judge of nonverbal communications.

_____ 5. I don't assume I know what another person is going to say before he or she says it.

_____ 6. I look for what is important in a person's message, rather than assuming it is uninteresting and ending the conversation.

_____ 7. I frequently nod, make eye contact, or whatever to let the speaker know I am listening.

_____ 8. When someone has finished talking, I consider the meaning of his or her message before responding.

_____ 9. I let the other person finish before reaching conclusions about the message.

_____ 10. I wait to formulate a response until the other person has finished talking.

_____ 11. I listen for content, regardless of the speaker's "delivery" style.

_____ 12. I usually ask people to clarify what they have said, rather than guess at the meaning.

_____ 13. I make a concerted effort to understand other people's points of view.

_____ 14. I listen for what the person really is saying, not what I expect to hear.

_____ 15. When I disagree with someone, the person feels that I have understood his or her point of view.

Total Score

Add your total points. According to communication theory, if you scored 131–150 points, you strongly approve of your own listening habits, and you are on the right track to becoming an effective listener. If you scored 111–130, you have uncovered some doubts about your listening effectiveness, and your knowledge of how to listen has some gaps. If you scored 110 or less, you probably are not satisfied with the way you listen, and your friends and co-workers may not feel you are a good listener either. Work on improving your listening skills.

Pause and Reflect

1. Think of a situation in which you believe someone listened to you carefully and a situation in which you believe someone was not paying close attention to what you wanted to say. What was different about the way in which you were treated in those two situations?

2. Identify something you can and will do now to improve the way you listen to others. (If you need ideas, consider the behaviors listed in this quiz.)

Source: From *Management Solutions*, January 1989. Copyright © 1989 by American Management Association. Reproduced with permission of American Management Association via Copyright Clearance Center.

Class Skills Exercise

Communicating Effectively

You learned many principles in this chapter to help you improve your communication skills. This exercise reviews six of those principles and gives you a chance to see how you can use them to improve supervisory communications.

Instructions

1. Review the following list of communication principles:
   a. Use feedback to verify that your message has been received accurately.
   b. Practice active listening.
   c. Select an appropriate method for sending your message.
   d. Be tuned in to nonverbal messages.
   e. Be well prepared when speaking before a group.
   f. Understand the important role of informal communication in the workplace, particularly rumors, gossip, and the grapevine.

2. Read the scenarios and determine which of the communication principles the supervisor violated. In each blank provided, write the letter of that principle from the list in Step 1. The principle you choose should indicate the one that the supervisor could have used to achieve a more positive outcome. (*Hint:* Each principle will be used only once; there is one *most* correct answer for each.)

Scenario	Principle
On Tuesday afternoon, the plant manager gave each of the twelve supervisors throughout the plant a five-page document that spelled out some changes in the employee handbook that would be effective the following month. The plant manager instructed the supervisors to call departmental meetings sometime within the next three days to present the changes to their own staff. Jeff sent out a notice to his employees to be at a 45-minute meeting on Thursday afternoon. Several unexpected events occurred that demanded most of Jeff's time during the next two days. Jeff did manage to make it to the meeting; however, he had only a few minutes beforehand to skim the document. He ended up mostly reading aloud from the document at the meeting.	1. _____
Pete went to talk to his supervisor about a personal problem. He left the meeting feeling that he hadn't gotten through to his supervisor, who seemed preoccupied and distracted throughout their entire conversation.	2. _____
Sid was on his way out the door to meet a customer for a business lunch at a local restaurant. He stopped long enough to give about 90 seconds of hurried instructions about a task he needed one of his employees to do for an afternoon deadline that same day. Sid finished his instructions by glancing at his watch and saying, "I'm going to be late for my luncheon appointment. You got everything OK, didn't you?" The employee mumbled, "Yeah, I guess so," and Sid was out the door.	3. _____

Krista overheard one of the employees in her department telling someone on the phone that he had heard from a reliable source that the company was going to pink-slip 10 percent of the employees on Friday. Krista shook her head in disgust and thought to herself, "Another ridiculous rumor.

With all the rumors floating around this place, I could spend all my time dispelling rumors. I'll let this one die a natural death on Friday; I don't have time to deal with it right now."

Shannon had a long "to do" list for the day and decided to dispense with as many items as she could first thing in the morning by using the e-mail system. She had gotten rid of six tasks by sending messages to the appropriate people. She sent a seventh message that contained confidential information about one of her employees. The next day Shannon's manager spoke with her about a negative situation that had arisen as a result of her seventh message being accessed by some people who should not have seen it. He told her to consider more carefully the messages she chose to send via e-mail.

Michael had decided to delegate an important project to Susan, his most capable employee. He called Susan to go over some of the specifics of the project—one that he saw as a great opportunity for her to show higher management what she was capable of doing. Susan, however, did not share Michael's enthusiasm about her new work assignment. Michael ignored her expressionless face and chose to respond to her verbal responses. For example, when he asked her whether she agreed this was an exciting project, she responded after a few seconds of silence with a mere "yes."

4. _____

5. _____

6. _____

Source: This class exercise was prepared by Corinne Livesay, Bryan College, Chattanooga, Tennessee.

Building Supervision Skills

Interpreting Communications

Divide the class into groups of at least three people. In each group, decide on a scenario that includes three sentences as follows:

1. The words, "I don't think that's right."
2. The sentence that came before it.
3. The sentence that came after it.

Also determine the physical setting and situation in which the sentences were spoken.

Let each group act out its scenario for the class. When all the scenarios have been presented, discuss the following:

- How did the context or situation change the meaning of "I don't think that's right"?

- How did the nonverbal behavior and setting differ in each scene?
- How could each group's "I don't think that's right" be paraphrased into a different sentence?
- Which component communicated the most information about the meaning of the scene—the words, the nonverbal behavior, or the situation?

Source: Adapted from Isa N. Engelberg and Dianna R. Wyann, *Working in Groups: Communication Strategies and Principles* (Boston: Houghton Mifflin, 1997).

chapter eleven | Motivating Employees

learning objectives

After you have studied this chapter, you should be able to:

11.1 Identify the relationship between motivation and performance.

11.2 Describe content theories of motivation.

11.3 Describe process theories of motivation.

11.4 Explain when financial incentives are likely to motivate employees.

11.5 Describe pay plans using financial incentives.

11.6 Discuss the pros and cons of keeping pay information secret.

11.7 Identify ways supervisors can motivate their employees.

A Supervision Challenge

YOU WIN!

Terrific! Awesome! You win! Bells ring, lights flash, and the crowd goes wild! When you play a game, you are rewarded frequently. Play a few minutes of any videogame and look for the ways it keeps players engaged. For meeting an objective, players are rewarded with congratulations and electronic badges, and they advance to a new level. Cheers and whistles!

No wonder playing is more fun than working. No one cheers when the cashier checks out his tenth customer that hour or the technical support guru solves a customer's software glitch. What if working was more fun, like a game, with rewards and levels?

Target wanted to find out if gamification could benefit its stores. It added game elements for cashiers, a key position that is very visible to its customers. In the past, cashiers received no feedback unless a supervisor needed to correct or review the cashier's performance. Now, cashiers see a red or green icon when they check out customers, indicating the time used to scan the customer's items. If scans occurred quickly enough, the icon is green. If the cashier was slow to scan items, the icon is red. A score is displayed on the screen, providing immediate feedback. A slow cashier can see the need to improve checkout times and work faster without receiving negative feedback from a supervisor. It is a game where everybody wins, even those who are not playing! The cashier is happier because the supervisor does not need to issue any corrections or warnings. The supervisor is happier because the interaction with the cashiers is more positive. The customer is happier because the whole shopping experience is faster and more pleasant.

Gamification is the application of game elements to other activities. When work is more fun, employees do a better job, have higher morale, and stay longer with the employer. This benefits everyone. Customers, employees, and employers are happy. The key is positive feedback, virtual crowds cheering or real interaction with supervisors, for the specific actions an employee does well that benefit the company. Supervisors should recognize the behavior and give positive feedback recognizing the employee's success at completing a difficult task. "Great job on fixing Mr. Smith's e-mail problem!"

Gamification includes fast feedback. If employees receive immediate praise for an action, they are likely to repeat it quickly. Setting goals and awarding badges for achieving those goals are additional ways of encouraging and rewarding good work. After a set of goals is reached, employees can "level up," advancing to a new set of tasks, goals, and rewards. Levels can be recognized by badges or titles. Badges can be worn on uniforms where they are recognized by co-workers and customers. Five stars on a uniform reassure customers that they are being served by a knowledgeable professional.

Even with gamification, supervisors still have a vital role to play—workers still need coaching and guidance in achieving goals. Gamification just offers supervisors more options. For example, supervisors can become the point person for identifying problems and creating ways that gamification can overcome those problems. Additionally, supervisors can be certified in gamification design. Many businesses will add career opportunities for gamification experts in the coming years and supervisors at all levels will use gamification elements in their day-to-day coaching activities. Although the crowd might not really roar when an employee meets or exceeds goals, everyone involved—employees, supervisors, and customers—will definitely be happier. Game on!

1. As a supervisor, can you think of any negative aspects of gamification?

2. Would most supervisors be in favor of gamification at their companies? Why or why not?

Sources: Erin Rigik, "Motivating Employees Through Gamification," Convenience Store Decisions, April 12, 2013, http://www.csdecisions.com/2013/04/12/motivating-employees-through-gamification/; Rich Hein, "How to Use Gamification to Engage Employees," CIO, June 6, 2013, http://www.cio.com/article/734521/How_to_Use_Gamification_to_Engage_Employees?page=1&taxonomyId=3123.

FIGURE 11.1 | The Effect of Motivation on Performance

Ultimately, how well as person performs is a combination of his or her abilities and how motivated he or she is.

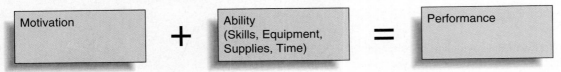

motivation
Giving people incentives that cause them to act in desired ways

Giving people incentives that cause them to act in desired ways is known as **motivation.** Among other things, supervisors must motivate their employees to do good work, complete assignments on time, and have good attendance. Gamification is just one of the ways to do that.

When employees are motivated and also have the ability—the necessary skills, equipment, supplies, and time—they are able to perform well, as illustrated in Figure 11.1. Thus, the objective of motivating employees is to lead them to perform in ways that meet the goals of the department and the organization. Because supervisors are evaluated largely on the basis of how well their group performs, motivation is an important skill for supervisors to acquire.

How the supervisor can make good use of the link between employees' objectives and their performance is discussed in this chapter. Theories of what motivates employees and how the motivation process works are described, legal issues are identified, and the role of money as a motivator is discussed. Finally, practical ways that supervisors can motivate employees are suggested.

LO11.1 ▶ Identify the relationship between motivation and performance.

How Does Motivation Work?

"What's wrong with these people?" exclaimed Martha Wong about the sales clerks she supervises in the shoe department. "We pay them good wages, but when we hit a busy season like this, nobody is willing to put forth the extra effort we need—giving up a break once in a while or even just moving a little faster." Wong needs to figure out what to do so that employees will *want* to keep customers happy during busy periods. Perhaps they expect more money, or perhaps they want something else, such as a feeling of being part of a team.

Imagine that supervisors such as Wong could know exactly what motivates employees. For example, imagine that all salespeople were motivated solely by the money they earn and that social scientists have devised an accurate formula to determine how much money the company must pay to get a given amount of selling. Suppose all administrative assistants were motivated by flexible work hours and all production workers were motivated by recognition from the plant manager. A company that knew this would be in a position to devise the kinds of rewards that employees want. The supervisor could hand out the rewards and know that if employees had the necessary skills, they would do good work.

Of course, no such simple knowledge about motivation exists. Instead, supervisors have to rely on a variety of theories that social scientists have developed. None of the theories is a perfect, proven explanation of how to get employees to behave in a certain way, but all give supervisors some guidance. Familiarity with the best-known theories can help supervisors think of ways to motivate their employees.

LO11.2 ▶ Describe content theories of motivation.

Content Theories

Some theories of motivation have focused on what things motivate workers. These are called *content theories* because they focus on the content of the motivators. Although money is the motivator that comes most readily to mind, some people respond more to other sources of satisfaction. To help you think about what motivates *you*, try the Assessing Yourself quiz on page 316 at the end of this chapter.

Three researchers whose content theories of motivation are widely used are Abraham Maslow, David McClelland, and Frederick Herzberg.

Maslow's Hierarchy of Needs

Psychologist Abraham Maslow assumed that people are motivated by unmet needs. When a person's need for something is not met, the person feels driven, or motivated, to meet that need. To give a basic example, a person who needs food feels hungry and therefore eats something.

According to Maslow's theory, the needs that motivate people fall into five basic categories:

1. Physiological needs are required for survival: food, water, sex, and shelter.
2. Security needs keep you free from harm. In modern society, these might include insurance, medical checkups, and a home in a safe neighborhood.
3. Social needs include the desire for love, friendship, and companionship. People seek to satisfy these needs through the time they spend with family, friends, and co-workers.
4. Esteem needs are the needs for self-esteem and the respect of others. Acceptance and praise are two ways these needs are met.
5. Self-actualization needs describe the desire to live up to your full potential. People on the path to meeting these needs will not only be doing their best at work and at home but also be developing mentally, spiritually, and physically.

Maslow argues that these needs are organized into a hierarchy, illustrated in Figure 11.2. The most basic needs are at the bottom of the hierarchy. People try to satisfy these needs first. At the top of the hierarchy are the needs people try to satisfy only when they have met most of their other needs.

According to this view, people tend to rely on their jobs to meet most of their physiological and security needs through paychecks and benefits such as health insurance. Needs higher on the hierarchy can be satisfied in many places. For example, people satisfy some of their social needs through their relationships with family and friends outside work, and they may seek to meet their self-actualization needs through volunteer work or membership in a religious organization. Nevertheless, people can also satisfy higher-level needs in the workplace. An employee who is applauded for solving a difficult problem or who takes pride in skillfully performing a craft such as carpentry is meeting some higher-level needs at work.

Greater interest in corporate social responsibility at many organizations, coupled with many employees' enthusiasm for serving the community, has led some firms to meet employees' higher-level needs with organized opportunities to do good. For instance, Boston Consulting Group lets employees spend up to a year working for a nonprofit organization, with their pay subsidized by BCG. Today's young workers have a reputation for being especially motivated to serve. Applications to AmeriCorps, which arranges for young people to serve nonprofits around the United States, have been soaring over the past few years. Of course, meaningful work can also take place within businesses, and companies also see young employees' desire to make a difference. Marriott International motivates by offering a management training program in which employees tackle assignments in all facets of hotel

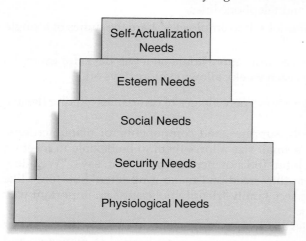

FIGURE 11.2 | Maslow's Hierarchy of Needs
According to Maslow, people only seek to meet higher-level needs as lower-level needs are met.

operations. When Claire Pignataro graduated from college, she was delighted to take a job with Marriott, not so much for the pay, but because the company would let her do something she loves: planning social and corporate events at one of its hotels.[1]

Maslow's hierarchy is a widely cited view of motivation, but it has shortcomings. Critics (including Maslow himself) have noted that the theory is based on clinical work with neurotic patients and was not tested much for relevance to the work setting.[2] Are the needs identified by Maslow really all-inclusive? Do they describe people of many cultures, or just the majority of U.S. workers? The lack of studies investigating the hierarchy of needs makes it impossible to answer such questions with certainty. However, the popularity of Maslow's theory implies that it can be helpful in offering suggestions about what motivates people.

Applied to a work situation, Maslow's theory means the supervisor must be aware of the current needs of particular employees. During a serious recession, a factory supervisor may find that many employees are highly motivated just to keep their jobs so they can pay their bills. In contrast, employees who are less worried about keeping a job may respond well to efforts to meet social needs. At Wyndham International, when David Mussa became vice president, employees rarely stayed long, so he took the time to discuss work with small groups of employees. Mussa had thought that the problem would be money to meet physiological needs. Instead, he learned that the problem was esteem needs. Many of the employees felt the company did not value them, mainly because they rarely received feedback or coaching to help them do their job better. They wanted their supervisors to be more involved and show that they cared. So Mussa hired more supervisors, giving each one more time to spend coaching employees—in fact, supervisors were required to do so.[3]

In this era of increasing numbers of single parents and two-income families in the workforce, a practical concern of many employees is their need for flexibility in their work hours to balance the demands of home and work. Some organizations have responded with "family-friendly" policies, which typically include flexible work arrangements such as the following:

flextime
A policy that grants employees some leeway in choosing which 8 hours a day or which 40 hours a week to work

- Flextime—This policy grants employees some leeway in choosing which 8 hours a day or which 40 hours a week to work.
- *Part-time work*—For employees who can afford to work less than full time, this option frees them to spend more time meeting other needs. It is economically appealing to organizations because few offer a full range of benefits to part-time employees.
- *Telecommuting*—Some employees can and want to work from home, keeping in touch by means of computer and telephone lines.
- Job sharing—To create part-time jobs, two employees share the duties of a single position.
- *Compressed workweek*—Employees work more hours on fewer days (for example, nine hours a day for four days each week), allowing more days off.

job sharing
An arrangement in which two part-time employees share the duties of one full-time job

Figure 11.3, on the following page, shows percentages of companies offering flexible work arrangements.

At IBS, which distributes tools, supplies, and components for manufacturers, managers believe the company's small size allows them to be flexible in meeting employees' needs. Michelle St. John, IBS's owner and president, says, "We allow employees to take time for what they need and make it up later."[4] St. John, like many human resources experts, sees family-friendly policies as an important way to get and keep the best workers.

Recent surveys have found flexible work arrangements at roughly three-fourths of companies.[5] However, these arrangements are often limited to managers and professionals. As Figure 11.3 shows, about half of companies offer flextime to hourly workers, and fewer companies offer them other flexible work arrangements. Companies that do extend this flexibility, however, are enjoying practical benefits. Solix, which processes documents for employee benefits, lets all of its employees set

FIGURE 11.3 | Percent of Companies Offering Flexible Work Options to Hourly/Non-Exempt Workers

Companies can offer flexibility in a variety of ways—all of which lead to more satisfied and motivated employees.

Source: Culpepper, "Flexible Work Arrangements: Popular Alternatives to Enhance Benefits Programs," *Culpepper eBulletin*, June 2009, http://www.culpepper.com.

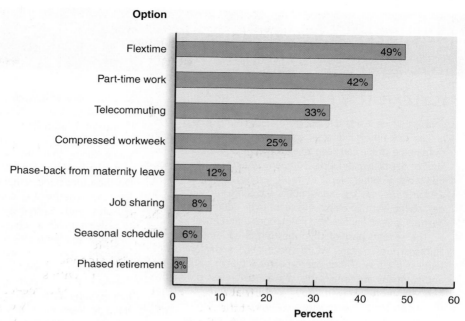

their own work hours. Since it began offering flextime, employee turnover and absences have fallen. Johnson Storage & Moving lets call center employees work from home and allows moving and warehouse workers to adjust their hours for personal needs. The company found that workers' attendance was more reliable when they could choose schedules that fit with their other needs.

When efforts at flexibility result in some employees working at different times and in different locations, some employees may think others are getting a better deal. As described in the "Supervision and Ethics" feature on the following page, it is important to make sure that employees see any policy as fair.

McClelland's Achievement-Power-Affiliation Theory

In the 1960s, David McClelland developed a theory of motivation based on the assumption that through their life experiences, people develop various needs. His theory focuses on three such needs:

1. *The need for achievement*—the desire to do something better than it has been done before.
2. *The need for power*—the desire to control, influence, or be responsible for other people.
3. *The need for affiliation*—the desire to maintain close and friendly personal relationships.

According to McClelland, people have all these needs to some extent. However, the intensity of the needs varies from one individual to the next. The nature of a person's early life experiences may cause one of these needs to be particularly strong.

The relative strength of the needs influences what will motivate a person. A person with a strong need for achievement is more motivated by success than by money. This person tends to set challenging but achievable goals and to assess risk carefully. Someone with a strong need for power tries to influence others and seeks out advancement and responsibility. A person with a strong need for affiliation gives ambition a back seat in exchange for approval and acceptance.

This theory offers a way to understand what motivates the employees of Zappos. com, an online shoe retailer known for its great customer service.[6] What keeps Zappos employees enthusiastic and creative about delighting customers in spite of

SUPERVISION AND ETHICS

IS FLEXIBILITY FAIR?

One employee wants to work from 4:30 a.m. to 1:30 p.m. so he can pick up his kids after school. Another wants to work from home so she can keep an eye on her elderly mother. This kind of flexibility can help a company retain valued workers, but what if others look at those arrangements and feel envious? They work standard hours and come into work every day, so the first two employees seem to be getting something "extra." Is flexibility fair, and if not, does that matter?

The second part of this question is easier to answer. Fairness *does* matter. More specifically, a perception of fairness matters. If employees perceive that the supervisor and company are unfair, they are apt to be less productive and are more likely to quit. When they perceive that the supervisor and company are fair, they tend to be more satisfied and are more likely to stay with the company.

Whether flexibility is fair is a more delicate issue. People measure fairness in different ways. For example, in a recent study, researchers found that the type of reward given by a manager influences the way people think about its fairness. In situations where a manager rewarded employees with money, people thought the rewards were most fair when they directly related to the quality of performance. But when a manager gave out other kinds of rewards, such as boxes of chocolate or extra time off, people thought it was just fine to give every employee the same reward, regardless of performance. This result suggests that managers have some latitude in their use of flexible work arrangements.

Employees generally judge flexibility to be fair when the supervisor or company is treating everyone in exactly the same way—offering those arrangements to all employees. On the other hand, employees might consider fairness in terms of whether the company takes into account each person's needs. By that standard, they might think it is fairer to be lenient with an employee who is experiencing a family crisis than to offer the same amount of flexibility to everyone, regardless of circumstances.

Those different ways of thinking about flexibility show that "fairness" is not something that can be measured objectively. Rather, supervisors need to talk to employees and listen to them to learn more about what they think is important. Involving employees in making decisions such as scheduling provides a good way to hold these conversations. Also, when explaining policies and decisions, supervisors can emphasize the efforts that have been made to ensure fairness.

Sources: National Business Research Institute, "Employer of Choice: Fairness," Employee Survey White Papers, http://www.nbrii.com/employee-survey-white-papers/employer-of-choice-fairness/, accessed May 1, 2014; "Fair Dues," *The Economist,* February 11, 2010, http://www.economist.com/node/15502819, accessed May 1, 2014.

holding mostly low-paying jobs? One motivator is the wide latitude employees have to make decisions, doing anything it takes to please the customer (satisfying needs for power or achievement). Say a customer calls the company with a question or problem. Call center operators can talk as long as it takes to make the customer happy; they can offer coupons, send flowers to the customer, or send the customer to a competitor who has a pair of shoes that are out of stock at Zappos. In addition, at its new headquarters in Las Vegas, the company is engaging employees in helping to brainstorm ways to make the firm's community more livable—for example, cultivating the arts and starting up farmers' markets. This is the broad understanding of sustainability you saw defined in Chapter 4. Working toward building a sustainable relationship with the community gives employees a chance to fulfill needs for achievement and affiliation.

McClelland's theory differs from Maslow's in that it assumes different people have different patterns of needs, whereas Maslow's theory assumes the same pattern of needs for all people. Thus, McClelland considers individual differences. Both theories, however, imply that supervisors must remember that employees are motivated by a variety of possibilities.

Herzberg's Two-Factor Theory

Frederick Herzberg's research led to the conclusion that employee satisfaction and dissatisfaction stem from different sources. According to this two-factor theory, dissatisfaction results from the absence of what Herzberg calls *hygiene factors,* which include salary and relationships with others. For example, someone whose pay is

TABLE 11.1 |
Two-Factor Theory:
Hygiene Factors and
Motivating Factors

Hygiene Factors	Motivating Factors
Company policy and administration	Opportunity for achievement
Supervision	Opportunity for recognition
Relationship with supervisor	Work itself
Relationship with peers	Responsibility
Working conditions	Advancement
Salary and benefits	Personal growth
Relationship with subordinates	

poor (e.g., a physical therapist earning $5,000 less than the average pay for the position) is going to be dissatisfied with the job. In contrast, satisfaction results from the presence of what Herzberg calls *motivating factors,* which include opportunities offered by the job. Thus, an employee who sees a chance for promotion is likely to be more satisfied with the current job than one who does not. Table 11.1 lists the items that make up hygiene and motivating factors.

Herzberg found that employees are most productive when the organization provides a combination of desirable hygiene factors and motivating factors. According to this theory, an organization cannot ensure that its employees will be satisfied and productive simply by giving them a big pay raise every year. Employees also need motivating factors such as the ability to learn new skills and assume responsibility. Like the other content theories, Herzberg's theory tells supervisors that they need to consider a variety of ways to motivate employees.

LO11.3 ▶ Describe process theories of motivation.

Process Theories

Another way to explain how motivation works is to look at the process of motivation instead of specific motivators. Theories that pertain to the motivation process are known as process theories. Two major process theories are Vroom's expectancy–valence theory and Skinner's reinforcement theory.

Vroom's Expectancy–Valence Theory

Assuming that people act as they do to satisfy their needs, Victor Vroom set out to explain what determines the intensity of motivation. He decided that the degree to which people are motivated to act in a certain way depends on three things:

1. *Valence*—the value a person places on the outcome of a particular behavior. For example, a person may highly value the prestige and the bonus that result from submitting a winning suggestion in a contest for improving quality.
2. *Expectancy*—the perceived likelihood that the behavior will lead to the outcome. A person in the example may believe that his or her idea has a 50–50 chance of winning the quality improvement contest.
3. *Instrumentality*—the perceived probability that the promised reward will actually be received. In order for an employee to submit a winning suggestion, he or she should be fairly certain that the behavior will be rewarded as promised.

Vroom's expectancy–valence theory says that the strength of motivation equals the perceived value of the outcome times the perceived probability that the behavior will result in the outcome, as illustrated in Figure 11.4 on the following page. In other words, people are most motivated to seek results they value highly and think they can achieve.

FIGURE 11.4 | Vroom's Expectancy–Valence Theory

According to Vroom's expectancy–valence theory, people are motivated to seek results they value and that they think they can achieve.

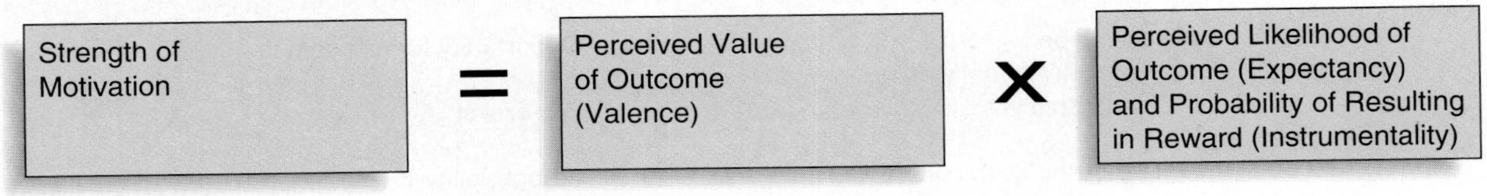

| Strength of Motivation | **=** | Perceived Value of Outcome (Valence) | **X** | Perceived Likelihood of Outcome (Expectancy) and Probability of Resulting in Reward (Instrumentality) |

This theory is based on employees' *perceptions* of rewards and whether they are able to achieve them. Employees may place different values on rewards than a supervisor, and they may have different opinions about their abilities. If a supervisor believes that a good system of rewards is in place but that employees are not motivated, the supervisor might investigate whether employees think they are expected to do the impossible. To learn this, supervisors must be able to communicate well (see Chapter 10).

At Lee County Fleet Management, located in Fort Myers, Florida, fleet manager Marilyn Rawlings applied these principles by repeatedly showing employees they could meet high standards. She works with each employee to prepare a plan for personal growth, including goal setting. Rawlings encourages each employee to set one goal that is a stretch, and then she helps that employee achieve those goals. Rawlings says, "I want people to see that they can accomplish things that they don't think they can do." That experience may change their perceptions so that they will see themselves as able to accomplish more. When Rawlings wanted her organization to obtain the Automotive Service Excellence (ASE) Blue Seal of Excellence, she needed to have two additional technicians become certified by the ASE. The only two who were not yet certified had chosen not to try because they didn't believe they could pass the test. Rawlings raised the value of the outcome by telling each employee that obtaining the certification would make them a hero to the group—and that she would hold a celebration for everyone when the group won the award. The two technicians both tried the exam, and both passed.[7]

Skinner's Reinforcement Theory

From the field of psychology comes reinforcement theory, pioneered by B. F. Skinner. Reinforcement theory maintains that people's behavior is influenced largely by the consequences of their past behavior. Generally, people keep doing things that have led to consequences they like, and people avoid doing things that have had undesirable consequences. For example, praise feels good to receive, so people tend to do things that, in their experience, result in praise.

reinforcement
A desired consequence or the ending of a negative consequence, either of which is given in response to a desirable behavior

punishment
An unpleasant consequence given in response to undesirable behavior

behavior modification
The use of reinforcement theory to motivate people to behave in a certain way

Reinforcement theory implies that supervisors can encourage or discourage a particular kind of behavior by the way they respond to the behavior. They can administer **reinforcement**, which can involve either giving a desired consequence or ending a negative consequence in response to behavior the supervisor wants. Or the supervisor can administer **punishment**, which is an unpleasant consequence of the behavior the supervisor wants to end. Using reinforcement theory to motivate people to behave in a certain way is known as **behavior modification**. In everyday language, we call it "using the carrot and the stick."

For long-term results, reinforcement is more effective than punishment. Psychologists have found that repeated punishment (or failure) can lead to an unhappy consequence called "learned helplessness." This means that if employees are punished repeatedly for failing in some aspect of their work, these employees will eventually believe that they are unable to succeed at the job.

These employees begin to approach the job passively, believing that they will fail no matter what.

Research has indicated that behavior modification programs can be successfully applied in organizational settings.[8] In order to implement these programs, a supervisor should consider the following ideas. First, offer different types of rewards for employees according to the quality of their performance. Second, clearly communicate any feedback to employees by telling them what they are doing right and wrong. Third, if an employee requires punishment of some sort, be sure to deliver this punishment in the absence of other employees. Finally, supervisors should provide rewards and punishments that are substantial and communicate that they are taking the behavior modification program seriously.

Together, Vroom's and Skinner's process theories support the idea that supervisors motivate most effectively when they place less emphasis on punishing infractions and more on giving employees a desirable goal and the resources that enable them to achieve that goal. An example of a supervisor focused on correcting negative behavior involves employee safety. An employee cut his head one day when he forgot to take off his baseball cap and put on a hard hat. Management responded by forbidding all employees from wearing baseball caps to work. Annoyed by the directive, employees showed up for work the next day wearing all kinds of headgear other than baseball caps: cowboy hats, sombreros, and even "Cat in the Hat" style hats. They applied their creativity to a power struggle with management, rather than to safety.[9] In contrast, when Union Square Hospitality Group wanted the chefs at its various restaurants to focus more on cutting costs, it gave them information and tools for better decision making. Whenever more than one chef is working with the same supplier, Union Square negotiates a quantity discount and then distributes information about the deal to all the chefs so that they can decide whether to participate in the arrangement. Chefs first signed on to deals for basics like paper towels and bottled water. Eventually, as they saw costs falling with no compromise in quality, they began to experiment with food suppliers, too.[10] As in this second example, supervisors can empower workers to focus on meeting the organization's goals, rather than simply piling on rules, which workers may resist. For examples of ways in which supervisors can motivate employees and help them prepare for advancement, see "Supervisory Skills" on the following page.

Motivation Theories and the Law

Most of these motivation theories have one element in common: Supervisors must consider individual differences in designing rewards. What motivates one person may not motivate another, so supervisors need to offer a variety of rewards. At the same time, to avoid discrimination, employers must distribute benefits fairly.

The types of rewards a supervisor may use are not entirely under his or her control. Not only does a supervisor have to follow the organization's policies, but he or she must also obey a variety of laws requiring that employers provide certain types of benefits. For example, federal laws set requirements for overtime pay, rest breaks, health insurance for retirees, and many other areas. Most organizations have a human resources professional or department responsible for helping the organization comply with laws related to benefits. The details of these laws are beyond the scope of this book.

However, the requirements of the Family and Medical Leave Act of 1993 are worth noting because they affect the supervisor's role in scheduling work and staffing the department. Under this law, organizations with 50 or more employees within a 75-mile radius must give employees up to 12 weeks of unpaid leave to care for a newborn, adopted, or foster child within one year of the child's arrival. These employers also must offer this time off if employees need to care for a seriously ill child, parent, or spouse or if they themselves have medical conditions that prevent them from doing their jobs. During the time off, the employer must continue to pay the

SUPERVISORY SKILLS

DEVELOPING EMPLOYEES: ABILITY TO PROMOTE

In order for a company to be successful, they need to motivate and retain talented and dedicated workers. One of the ways that can be accomplished is by preparing and then challenging these employees to take on higher-level positions within the company. It is often the case, however, that employees do not get enough feedback from their supervisors and, hence, do not know what it takes to get promoted to the next level. As a supervisor, it is your responsibility to make sure that every employee knows what characteristics and skill sets are desired and to coach your employees so that they can meet these expectations.

The things that managers look for when promoting are:

- *Someone who can prioritize work:* The ability to prioritize work is one of the most important skills that managers are looking for when deciding which employees to promote.
- *A team player:* Employees who are team players, share credit, and can figure out how to support their teammates are highly desirable in a company.
- *An intrapreneur:* Employees that look for ways to help the company and to make internal improvements.

- *Face time:* Employees should take the time to talk, in person, with others at work, including supervisors and managers.
- *A patient employee:* While many motivated employees, particularly younger ones, are anxious to be promoted, they need to realize that they are not prepared for those roles until they have more experience. This can be a key role for a supervisor as coach—to keep them challenged in their current position while they build the experience and skill set required for the next level.
- *Someone who has cross-functional experience:* Experience working in different departments prepares an employee for future management positions.
- *Soft skills over hard skills:* The soft skill of being a good communicator is an extremely important skill that managers look for when promoting. It is easy to find people who can do a hard skill task, but not so easy to find people who are good communicators.

A good supervisor works with employees to develop these skills and, in so doing, prepare to continue to be an asset to the company for years to come.

Source: Based on Dan Schawbel, "7 Things Managers Look for When Promoting," The Fast Track, Intuit QuickBase, August 28, 2013, http://quickbase.intuit.com/blog/2013/08/28/7-things-managers-look-for-when-promoting/, accessed May 1, 2014.

employee's health insurance premiums. The employer also must guarantee that the employee will be able to return to his or her job or an equivalent one. If the need for the leave is foreseeable, the employee must give the organization 30 days' notice.

In some organizations, the supervisor faces a significant challenge in planning and scheduling because of employees' leave. A survey by the Society for Human Resource Management found that about one-third of the workforces of the surveyed companies had requested medical leave during the preceding year, and one-sixth had requested family leave. A leave can make it challenging to motivate the employees who shoulder the extra work. About one-third of the companies in the same survey reported employees had complained that co-workers took leave for reasons the complainers found questionable.[11]

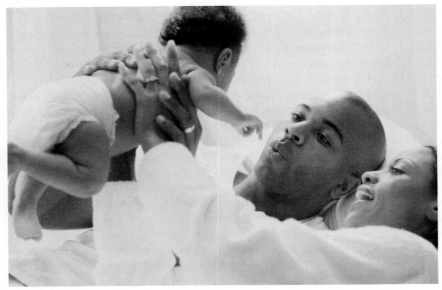

FMLA time off is unpaid, but it allows new parents to spend time with their family knowing that their job will be held for them.

Money as a Motivator

Some supervisors and other managers assume that the main thing employees want out of a job is money. Most people work to earn at least enough to get by. Although money is only one of many available ways to motivate employees, it is an important one. In a study of low-wage, low-skill hospital workers, researchers found that workers were more likely to feel they were being treated with dignity when they had access to training, staffing levels were adequate, and their pay was relatively high for their type of job.[12] This finding suggests that money is important not only as a means to pay the bills but also as a signal of one's value to the organization.

Money is an example of an extrinsic reward, which is defined as a reward that is extraneous to the task accomplished. Another example of an extrinsic reward is an Olympic gold medal. When Olympic athletes win a competition, they are rewarded extrinsically with a medal to wear. Another type of reward is an intrinsic reward, which is defined as a reward that comes directly from performing a task. For example, a manager who spends time helping an employee sort out a personal problem will receive an intrinsic reward in the form of personal satisfaction for helping out another person. Another example of an intrinsic reward would be a sense of increased self-esteem after accomplishing a challenging task.

extrinsic reward
Recognition or compensation that is extraneous to the task accomplished

intrinsic reward
Personal satisfaction that comes directly from performing a task

LO11.4 ▶ Explain when financial incentives are likely to motivate employees.

When Money Motivates

The content theories of motivation imply that money motivates people when it meets their needs. The federal minimum wage is $7.25 per hour, although raising this rate is being debated. For a worker supporting a family of four, this rate of pay would not keep the household above the poverty level, so a minimum-wage job might motivate such employees to work overtime whenever possible, look for a second job, or seek training, promotions, or some other route to better pay.[13] In contrast, a high school student rarely has a family to support. Even with a lower minimum wage for teens and full-time students, a teenage worker might welcome the steady income stream from a minimum-wage job. The opportunity to earn more can be very important to a college student, considering the high cost of college tuition and the potentially great impact of a college degree on the student's future lifestyle. A retired person or a married person whose spouse earns a comfortable income might work primarily for nonfinancial rewards such as a sense of accomplishment or the satisfaction derived from performing a needed service.

If money is to work as a motivator, employees must believe they are able to achieve the financial rewards the organization offers. Thus, if a theater company offers its staff a bonus for selling a given number of season ticket subscriptions over the telephone, the bonus will motivate the employees only if they believe they can sell that many tickets. Or if an organization pays a bonus for employee suggestions that improve quality, the bonus will motivate employees only if they believe they are capable of coming up with ideas.

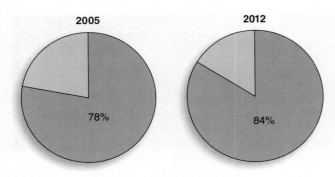

2005   **2012**

78%   84%

FIGURE 11.5 | Companies That Link Pay to Performance, 2005 and 2012

An increasing number of companies are linking financial incentives to performance.

Source: Data from WorldatWork, "Compensation Programs and Practices 2012: A report by WorldatWork," news release, October 2012, http://www.worldatwork.org/waw/adimLink?id=65522.

financial incentives
Payments for meeting or exceeding objectives

LO11.5 ▶ Describe pay plans using financial incentives.

piecework system
Payment according to the quantity produced

Pay Plans Using Financial Incentives

The way a pay plan is structured can influence the degree to which employees are motivated to perform well. Some pay plans offer bonuses, commissions, or other kinds of pay for meeting or exceeding objectives. For instance, a growing number of organizations tie raises and bonuses to accomplishments such as retaining existing customers and meeting established quality goals illustrated in Figure 11.5. Others pay employees a higher rate for learning additional skills, including how to operate lift trucks and computer-controlled machinery or how to develop computer applications to do business globally. Such pay plans are said to use **financial incentives**.[14] A recent survey found that more than 10 cents out of every payroll dollar went to some form of variable pay.[15]

Supervisors rarely have much say in the type of pay plan an organization uses. However, they can motivate better if they understand the kinds of pay plans that offer a financial incentive. Knowing whether the organization's pay system is designed to motivate gives a supervisor clues about the needs of employees for nonfinancial incentives. If the organization's pay plan includes financial incentives but the employees remain unmotivated, a supervisor might look for other kinds of motivators. On the other hand, if the organization's pay plan contains no financial incentives, a supervisor might seek permission to include money for bonuses in the department's budget.

Piecework System

The **piecework system** pays people according to how much they produce. This method is often used to pay independent contractors, that is, people who are self-employed and perform work for the organization. For example, a magazine might pay a writer a fixed rate for each word, or a clothing manufacturer might pay a seamstress a set amount for each shirt sewed. Farm workers may be paid according to how much they harvest. Unlike independent contractors, however, few employees are paid under this system.

Production Bonus System

Production department employees may receive a basic wage or salary plus a bonus that consists of a payment for each unit produced. Thus, an employee might earn $8.50 or more an hour plus $0.20 for each unit produced. This is called a production bonus system. If employees do not appear to be motivated by a production bonus system, the bonus may not be large enough to be worth the extra effort. Employees who work faster earn more money under such a system, but the pay system does not necessarily encourage high-quality work.

There are other types of bonus as well, such as bonuses paid for recommending new employees, delivering exceptional service, or meeting performance targets. Ireland's Ryanair is famous for charging rock-bottom ticket prices but making up some of the low ticket revenue in fees, including a fee for checked baggage. At the John Lennon Airport in Liverpool, England, Ryanair began paying baggage handlers a bonus of five British pounds (equivalent to about $7.85) for every ten passengers they catch trying to carry on luggage that exceeds the weight limit for carry-on bags.[16]

commissions
Payment linked to the amount of sales completed

Commissions

In a sales department, employees may earn **commissions**, or payment linked to the amount of sales completed. For example, a real estate agent listed a house for a brokerage. Upon the sale of the house, the agent might receive a commission of 2 percent of the sale price. The selling agent and the brokerage also would get commissions.

Real estate agents make their money through commission. This means that they will be especially committed to selling a piece of property since they will not make an income otherwise.

Although commissions are most commonly paid to salespeople, companies have applied this type of pay to other positions where the company charges a client for the work the employee completes. At Pinard's Small Engine Repair, a shop located in Manchester, New Hampshire, service technicians receive a commission based on the amount billed for their work. The technicians keep track of the time they spend on billable work. Employees who spend at least half of their time doing billable repairs earn a commission of at least 4 percent of the amount billed for their work. Technicians can earn higher percentages for spending more of their time on billable work. A technician who spends at least 80 percent of his or her time on billable hours will earn a commission of 7 percent—a much larger commission, considering that the amount billed is also likely to be greater. Thus, the pay system encourages technicians at Pinard's to work more efficiently. The shop supports this arrangement by setting up work arrangements so that technicians are free to concentrate on repairs, rather than helping out in the store or answering phones.[17]

Most organizations that pay commissions also pay a basic wage or salary. Otherwise, the financial uncertainty can worry employees to the point that it interferes with motivation. Some people, however, like the unlimited earnings potential of a commission-only job.

Payments for Suggestions

To build employee participation and communication, many companies pay employees for making suggestions on how to cut costs or improve quality. Typically, the suggestion must be adopted or save some minimum amount of money before the employee receives payment. The size of the payment may be linked to the size of the benefit to the organization. In other words, an idea with a bigger impact results in a bigger payment.

Group Incentive Plans

Organizations today are focusing increasingly on ways to get employees and their supervisors to work together as teams. A financial incentive to get people to work this way is the **group incentive plan,** which pays a bonus when the group as a whole exceeds some objective.[18] An organization measures the performance of a work unit against its objectives, and then pays a bonus if the group exceeds the objectives. Google pays its employees an annual bonus. In recent years, it has been struggling to develop a hit product in social media, so it has tied a portion of all employees' bonus to whether the company achieves its goals for social media, including Google+.[19] The idea is that all Google employees are creative thinkers, so everyone potentially can—and must, for the company's long-term success—contribute to success in the social realm.

A frequently used type of group incentive is the **profit-sharing plan.** Under this kind of plan, the company sets aside a share of its profits earned during a given period, such as a year, and divides these profits among the employees.[20] The assumption is that the better the work done, the more the company will earn and, therefore, the bigger the bonuses. In the past, profit sharing was limited chiefly to executives, but more companies today are sharing profits among all employees. InterDyn Cargas, which sells business software and consulting services, uses a

group incentive plan
A financial incentive plan that rewards a team of workers for meeting or exceeding an objective

profit-sharing plan
A group incentive plan under which the company sets aside a share of its profits and divides it among employees

profit-sharing plan as a way to keep employees focused on team success rather than individual performance alone. One-fifth of InterDyn's profits are set aside and divided among employees every six months, with somewhat more allocated to employees who have been at the company longer.[21]

An increasing number of companies are adopting a gainsharing program, under which the company encourages employees to participate in making suggestions and decisions about improving the way the company or work group operates. As performance improves, employees receive a share of the greater earnings. Thus, gainsharing seeks to motivate not only by giving financial rewards but also by making employees feel they have an important role as part of a team.

gainsharing
A group incentive plan in which the organization encourages employees to participate in making suggestions and decisions, then rewards the group with a share of improved earnings

LO11.6 ► Discuss the pros and cons of keeping pay information secret.

Secrecy of Wage and Salary Information

In our society, money is considered a private matter, and most people do not like to talk about what they earn. Thus, in private (nongovernment) organizations, employees generally do not know one another's earnings, though supervisors know what their subordinates earn. In contrast, government employees' earnings are public information, often published in local papers, because taxpayers ultimately pay their wages and salaries.

Does secrecy help or hurt the usefulness of money as a motivator? Certainly, it does not make sense to disclose information if it only embarrasses employees. Most employees overestimate what others earn. This overestimation can result in dissatisfaction because employees believe they are underpaid in comparison.

To motivate employees with the possibility of a raise and a belief that pay rates are fair, the organization must let them know what they can hope to earn. A typical compromise between maintaining privacy and sharing information is for the organization to publish pay ranges. These show the lowest and highest wage or salary the organization will pay an employee in a particular position. Employees do not know how much specific individuals earn, but the ranges show what they can expect to earn if they get a raise, promotion, or transfer to another position.

connect SELF-ASSESSMENT 11.2

What Motivates You

As a supervisor, you will be responsible for motivating your workers. You have learned a great deal in the chapter about motivation theory; but have you ever stopped and thought about what really motivates you? This assessment will encourage you to think about just what makes you want to work hard and do a good job.

LO11.7 ► Identify ways supervisors can motivate their employees.

How Supervisors Can Motivate

The first part of this chapter addressed the theories of motivating. These theories suggest some practical ways supervisors can motivate. Several possibilities are summarized in Figure 11.6, on the following page, and discussed in this section.

Moving Toward Theories Y and Z

In observing the behavior of managers, Douglas McGregor noted that many tend to have a group of attitudes that reflect their beliefs about workers and the workplace. He termed this set of attitudes Theory X. To summarize, a Theory X manager assumes that people dislike work and try to avoid it, that they therefore must be coerced to perform, that they wish to avoid responsibility and would prefer to be directed, and that their primary need is for security. Not surprisingly, these beliefs influence how supervisors

Theory X
A set of management attitudes based on the view that people dislike work and must be coerced to perform

FIGURE 11.6 | Ways Supervisors Can Motivate Employees

The theories of motivation suggest some practical ways that supervisors can motivate employees.

Making Work Interesting
- Job rotation
- Job enlargement
- Job enrichment
- Customer contact

Having High Expectations

Providing Valued Rewards

Relating Rewards to Performance

Treating Employees as Individuals

Encouraging Participation

Providing Feedback

and other managers behave. Theory X supervisor would adopt an autocratic leadership role, keeping a close eye on employees and looking for occasions when they need to be disciplined to keep them performing adequately.[22]

McGregor advises that managers can benefit from adopting a much different set of attitudes, which he terms **Theory Y**. According to Theory Y, working is as natural an activity as resting or playing, and people will work hard to achieve objectives to which they are committed. They can learn to seek responsibility and to be creative in solving organizational problems. Supervisors and other managers who adhere to Theory Y focus on developing the potential of their employees. Their style of leadership tends to be democratic (see Chapter 8). Table 11.2 summarizes these two sets of assumptions.

Today, a common view among people studying management is that Theory Y is appropriate for many situations. To see what a Theory Y manager looks like, consider Don T. Davis, a former branch manager of Smith Barney, now Morgan Stanley Smith Barney. Davis focused on providing the office's eighty-five financial consultants with the resources they needed to serve their clients. Explains Davis, "I've been around here a long time. I'm able to call someone and say, 'I need you to help me out here.'" Every day, Davis took several walks around the brokerage offices, making himself available to the financial consultants in case they had problems or needed encouragement. He often accompanied them on calls to prospects so he could better coach them in sales and teamwork. He also identified situations in which he could help employees by pairing them with those who had expertise

Theory Y

A set of management attitudes based on the view that work is a natural activity and that people will work hard and creatively to achieve objectives to which they are committed

TABLE 11.2 | Contrasting Leader Attitudes

Theory X	Theory Y
People dislike work and try to avoid it.	Working is as natural an activity as resting or playing.
People must be coerced to perform.	People will work hard to achieve objectives to which they are committed.
People wish to avoid responsibility and prefer to be directed.	People can learn to seek responsibility.
People's primary need is for security.	Many people are able to be creative in solving organizational problems.

Source: Based on Douglas McGregor, *The Human Side of Enterprise* (New York: McGraw-Hill, 1960).

in products the client needs. In one situation, a financial consultant was having difficulty getting a new client set up, so Davis arranged for this major prospect to travel to New York and meet experts. The trip smoothed the process for the financial consultant, who was then able to set up services for that client.[23]

In the 1980s, management experts extended their view of managing and leading to include **Theory Z**, developed by William Ouchi. Theory Z supervisors seek to involve employees in making decisions, consider long-term goals when making plans, and give employees relatively great freedom in carrying out their duties. This theory is based on comparisons of management styles in the United States and Japan. It assumes that whereas Japanese workers are more productive than their U.S. counterparts, the difference stems in part from different management styles. Thus, Theory Z was developed in an attempt to adapt some Japanese management practices to the U.S. workplace. The Japanese practices include employee involvement and lifetime employment.

Theory Z
A set of management attitudes that emphasizes employee participation in all aspects of decision making

Making Work Interesting

When employees find their work interesting, they are more likely to give it their full attention and enthusiasm. In general, work is interesting when it has variety and allows employees some control over what they do. Work can be made more interesting through job rotation, job enlargement, job enrichment, and increased customer contact.

Job rotation involves moving employees from job to job to give them more variety. For example, the employees in a production department may take turns operating all the machines in the factory. Job rotation requires that employees have relatively broad skills. As a result, the supervisor or company must provide for **cross-training**, or training in the skills required to perform more than one job. The opportunity to learn new skills through cross-training can in itself motivate employees.[24]

job rotation
Moving employees from job to job to give them more variety

cross-training
Training in the skills required to perform more than one job

Job enlargement is an effort to make a job more interesting by adding more duties to it. Thus, a machine operator might be responsible not only for running a particular machine but also for performing maintenance on the machine and inspecting the quality of the parts produced with the machine. As with job rotation, this approach assumes that variety in a job makes it more satisfying, with the result that employees are more motivated.

job enlargement
An effort to make a job more interesting by adding more duties to it

Job enrichment is the incorporation of motivating factors into a job. Herzberg called the factors that enrich a job "motivators." Generally, an enriched job gives employees more responsibility to make decisions and more recognition for good performance. Thus, enriched jobs are more challenging and, presumably, more rewarding. For example, instead of requiring salespeople in a department store to call a supervisor whenever a customer has a complaint, the store might authorize them to handle complaints as they see fit. They would have to call a supervisor only if solving the problem would cost the store more than some set amount, say, $500.

job enrichment
The incorporation of motivating factors into a job—in particular, giving the employee more responsibility and recognition

When modifying jobs to make them more interesting, the organization and supervisor must remember that not all employees are motivated by the same things at the same time. Thus, while some employees may eagerly accept the new variety in their jobs, others are likely to be less enthusiastic. Some workers may think jobs are being redesigned simply to get more work out of people for the same amount of money. A supervisor must be careful to emphasize the advantages of the new arrangement and listen to employee reactions.

Work also can be made more meaningful by giving employees some contact with the people who receive and use their products (goods or services). Nurses and salespeople are routinely in contact with the people they serve, but production workers and accounting personnel have less customer contact. Sometimes a supervisor can arrange to have workers visit the users of the products. For example, a group of production workers might be sent to visit a customer who is having trouble operating a machine the company manufactures. The workers not only would be able to help the customer but might also get some ideas for making the machine better. Accounting personnel might meet the people in the company who use their reports to make sure they understand and are satisfied with the reports.

Having High Expectations

Effective motivation can lead to performance beyond employees' own expectations of themselves. When someone expects a lot of us, we often find that we can do a lot. When little is expected, we tend to provide little. In either case, the expectations are self-fulfilling.

Pygmalion effect
The direct relationship between expectations and performance; high expectations lead to high performance

The direct relationship between expectations and performance is known as the **Pygmalion effect.** The name comes from the Greek myth of Pygmalion, a king of Cyprus who carved a statue of a beautiful maiden and then fell in love with her. He so wished she were real that she became real.

According to the Pygmalion effect, a supervisor who says to an employee, "You're so dense, you never get the procedures right," will not motivate effectively. Instead, the employee will decide that understanding procedures is beyond his or her capacity. Therefore, a supervisor who wishes employees to set high standards for themselves must think and speak with the assumption that the employees are capable of meeting high standards. A supervisor might say, "These procedures are complicated, but I'm sure that if you study them regularly and ask questions, you can learn to follow them."

An individual who recognizes the value of high expectations is major-league baseball player Alex Gordon. When the Kansas City Royals selected him in 2005, he became the number two pick in that year's draft, and expectations for his baseball career soared. Gordon's reaction? As he prepared for the start of a game, playing with the Wichita Wranglers Class AA team, he told a reporter, "I actually liked the expectations. It gives me that little bit more motivation to do well."[25]

Providing Rewards That Are Valued

The content theories of motivation indicate that a variety of rewards may motivate but that not all employees will value the same rewards at the same time. The supervisor's challenge is to determine what rewards will work for particular employees at particular times. This means appreciating the needs people are trying to meet and the variety of ways a supervisor can provide rewards.

An attractive award motivates employees in and of itself, but supervisors and other managers can add to the attraction by making the experience of receiving the award pleasant, too. At Hormel Foods in Rochester, Minnesota, receiving annual profit-sharing checks is part of a late-year celebration. The company serves milk and cookies and passes out the checks in what plant manager Mark Coffey calls a "fun and festive day." Production supervisor Bill Hacker agrees that the check distribution time in November is "always a

Some employees might be more motivated to make sales if they know that a portion of the profits will come back to them.

happy day around here."[26] Supervisors at any company that distributes group incentives could add to their motivational value by contributing to a positive mood at those times.

Of course, there are some limits to a supervisor's discretion in giving rewards. Company policy or a union contract may dictate the size of raises employees get and the degree to which raises are linked to performance as opposed to seniority or some other measure. However, supervisors can use the theories of motivation, coupled with their own experience, to identify the kinds of rewards over which they have some control. For example, a supervisor has great freedom in administering rewards such as praise and recognition. Many supervisors have some discretion in job assignments. Employees who have a high need for achievement (McClelland's theory) or are trying to meet esteem or self-actualization needs (Maslow's theory) may appreciate opportunities for additional training. Employees who have a high need for affiliation or are seeking to meet social needs may appreciate being assigned to jobs in which they work with other people.

Relating Rewards to Performance

The rewards a supervisor uses should be linked to employee performance. Unfortunately, employees seldom see a clear link between good job performance and higher pay. If there is a connection, employees should be aware of it and understand it. Another means of connecting rewards to performance is in the way supervisors express praise. "Practical Advice for Supervisors" suggests a way to offer performance-related praise. Linking rewards to the achievement of realistic objectives is a way to help employees believe they can attain desired rewards.

PRACTICAL ADVICE FOR SUPERVISORS

GIVING CREDIT WHERE CREDIT IS DUE

Johanna Rothman helps project teams of information technology experts learn to work together effectively. As team leader and consultant, she has found that it is a common misconception that people do not need or desire credit for their work. This is not true. Rothman recommends always keeping the following in mind:

- *Give credit to the people that did the work.* When you are the supervisor, it is critical to make sure you know who did the work and to make sure that the "higher ups" in the company know as well. Your employees need to know that you appreciate the work they perform and that you are not the sort of person who will take credit for their work.

- *When miscommunications occur, fix them.* Sometimes people say things they do not intend. At other times, people hear things that were not actually said. When these communication errors occur, it is important to fix them as quickly as possible. A written communication, such as an e-mail or memo, will allow you the time to choose your words carefully. Reiterate how much you appreciate your employees and the work that they do.

- *It is not possible to appreciate employees too much.* Expressing sincere appreciation to a team can boost morale and encourage them to continue to perform at a high level. For individual employees, a hand-written, personalized note of thanks can have an amazing impact. When you are writing a note or thanking an employee in person, Rothman recommends using the following format:

  <First name>, I appreciate you for <specific thing the person did>. It gave me <specific benefit to me>.

- *Giving credit makes you look like a star.* Giving credit to employees for the work they have performed makes you look like a star to your employees as well as to the rest of the organization. Even if not everyone you hired is doing an outstanding job, you are managing them in such a way that they are functioning well as part of a team. As Rothman says, "The more the people who work for you are doing great work, the better you look. And the more you look like you don't have to work hard to manage them, the better you are as a manager—and the better you look."

Source: Based on Johanna Rothman, "Management Myth 24: People Don't Need External Credit," Rothman Consulting Group, December 17, 2013, http://www.jrothman.com/2013/12/management-myth-24-people-dont-need-external-credit/, accessed May 1, 2014.

As Vroom's expectancy–valence theory described, rewards are most likely to motivate employees when the employees view them as achievable.

At Great Scott Broadcasting, an independent broadcasting company in Pottstown, Pennsylvania, sales reps for the company's eight radio stations in Maryland and Delaware must be knowledgeable about audience demographics, marketing protocol, and other key information about selling radio spots. With a game called Trivia Feud, general manager Cathy Deighan ensures that the reps have the information they need to answer clients' questions quickly and accurately. The competitive 15-minute game is played at every weekly sales meeting—"It can get pretty crazy," says Deighan—and each person on the winning team gets a prize, such as a gift certificate for dinner, a free car wash, or cash.[27]

The use of objectives is a basic way to link rewards to performance (see Chapter 6). For example, the management by objectives (MBO) system provides rewards when employees meet or exceed the objectives they have helped set for themselves. Thus, if a museum's cafeteria workers are supposed to leave their work areas spotless at the end of each shift, they know whether they have done what is necessary to receive their rewards, such as regular pay raises or extra time off.

Using clear objectives to help motivate employees is an important way to make sure that when employees try hard, they are trying to do the right things. As discussed in Chapter 7, Rackspace, the founder of OpenStack®, links rewards to its goal of delivering "fanatical" customer support. The company is divided into teams that bring together employees from various functions, including account management and tech support. Each team is responsible for meeting its own set of financial and service goals, including customer turnover, growth in existing customers' business with Rackspace, and number of referrals from customers. Each month, if teams meet their goals, team members receive bonuses in amounts up to 20 percent of their salaries. Customer praise gets posted on the walls, and individuals receive recognition through the monthly Straitjacket Award; employees grant this award by voting for the employee whose customer support was most fanatical.[28] (For a discussion of communicating goals and other information to employees, see Chapter 10.)

Treating Employees as Individuals

Most of the theories of motivation emphasize that different things motivate individuals to different degrees. Table 11.3 lists the top reasons that workers in a global survey gave for taking a job with a company. Notice that employers' expectations for what the workers would value most did not always match employees' opinions in the survey.

A supervisor who wishes to succeed at motivating has to remember that employees will respond in varying ways. A supervisor cannot expect that everyone

TABLE 11.3 | Top Reasons for Taking a Job with a Company

Source: Information from Phaedra Brotherton, "Improving Economy Boosts Talent Management Efforts," *T+D*, January 2011, pp. 16–17.

Rank	Employees' Top Reasons	Employers' Beliefs about Employees
1	Competitive base pay	Competitive base pay
2	Challenging work	Reputation as a great place to work
3	Convenient work location	Challenging work
4	Opportunities for career advancement	Business/industry of organization
5	Vacation, holidays, paid time off	Opportunities to learn new skills
6	Reputation as a great place to work	Opportunities for career advancement
7	Flexible schedule	Organization's financial health

will be excited equally about cross-training or overtime pay. Some employees might prefer an easy job or short hours, so that they have time and energy for outside activities. Even employees in a particular group, such as part-time workers, can have different preferences For example, some part-timers may prefer the shorter hours, while others took part-time jobs hoping they would be a steppingstone to a full-time position. Among those who prefer part-time, some may see the job as a way to pay the bills while freeing time for other roles, such as artist, actor, or parent. In contrast, students working part-time may be eager to apply lessons from school on the job and begin developing a career through the part-time work. Effective supervisors not only respect these differences but also find ways these diverse employees can contribute—say, giving students challenging assignments to develop their skills, noticing when the artist's unique perspective contributes important ideas, and recognizing that parenting responsibilities change so that these part-timers may be looking for greater responsibility at work in the future.[29]

Another aspect of treating employees as individuals is recognizing their diversity. This includes differences in race and gender as well as age, religion, physical abilities, and culture as well as differences in personal qualities. It is the supervisor's responsibility to make sure that everyone in the workplace feels like they belong, that no one feels threatened in any way, and that each employee performs to the fullest potential. How is that accomplished? Team-building activities will help to build a sense of cohesion and belonging. Enforcing a zero tolerance policy on workplace bullying ensures that no one feels threatened or intimidated in any way. Last, understanding how to motivate a diverse workforce requires the supervisor to understand how to manage diversity itself. Start by recognizing that each employee has his or her own background, beliefs, attitudes, values, and way of thinking. Rather than treat everyone the same or apply broad assumptions, supervisors need to understand what makes each employee unique and build on those strengths.[30]

As much as possible, a supervisor should respond to individual differences. When a particular type of motivation does not seem to work with an employee, a supervisor should try some other motivator to see if it better matches the employee's needs.

Encouraging Employee Participation

One way to learn about employees' needs and benefit from their ideas is to encourage employees to participate in planning and decision making. As you read in Chapter 9, employees tend to feel more committed when they can contribute to decisions and solutions. They also are likely to cooperate better when they feel like part of a team.

Whole Foods Market gives teams of employees great decision-making authority. The supermarket chain extended this practice to a recent decision about health insurance benefits. The company had a self-insured plan, but claims overwhelmed the plan's funds, so Whole Foods developed a plan using medical savings accounts. The company deposits money into employee accounts, and the employees, who pay no premiums, pick up the first $500 of prescription costs and $1,000 of other medical bills. After that, bills are paid from the savings accounts. After a one-year trial, Whole Foods had its employees evaluate whether to continue the new savings account approach or opt for traditional insurance coverage. By an overwhelming margin, the employees voted to keep the medical savings accounts. Part of the appeal is likely that Whole Foods workers tend to be relatively young and healthy; in a recent year, only 10 percent of employees spent all the money in their accounts, and the remaining dollars rolled over into the next year's account. Because the employees don't have to pay insurance premiums, more of them elect the insurance coverage as part of their benefits package. And Whole Foods is delighted, because the arrangement is helping it control health coverage expenses.[31]

Providing Feedback

People want and need to know how well they are doing. Part of a supervisor's job is to give employees feedback about their performance. When the supervisor tells employees that they are meeting or exceeding objectives, the employees know they are doing something right. When a supervisor tells employees that they are falling short of objectives, the employees know they need to improve. Most people will try to improve when given a chance to do so.

Praise is an important kind of feedback. In monitoring employees, a supervisor should look for signs of excellent performance and let the employees know, in specific terms, that the good work is appreciated and that it benefits the organization.

There are many ways to deliver praise. For example, a nursing supervisor might write a memo to a nurse, in which the supervisor comments on the nurse's courteous manner with patients and how it gives patients a good impression of the hospital. Or, a police force supervisor might remark to an officer that the officer's paperwork is always complete and legible. When Dave Marin was a bank manager, he invented a simple method of praise that surprised him with its impact. While preparing for a sales meeting, he bought a bag of stones and marked each one with a large U. The message: "You rock." Marin gave one out to each employee he praised at the meeting. Thinking the rocks were a little silly, Marin was surprised when employees started asking him if he would be giving them out at the next meeting. He was even more surprised when, years later, he began hearing that employees had kept their rewards as a valued possession.[32] Their value did not, of course, come from the worth of the rocks themselves, but from the treasure of public praise.

A supervisor does not have to use a dramatic approach to praising a behavior. Praise is so easy to give and its potential rewards are so great that the supervisor can and should use it routinely, as long as it is sincere.

Even if acknowledgment is just a quick note of appreciation, it is important that employees know their hard work is noticed and appreciated.

Skills Module

PART ONE: CONCEPTS

Summary

11.1 Identify the relationship between motivation and performance.

To perform well, employees must be motivated. Motivation is giving people incentives to act in certain ways. For motivation to work, a supervisor needs to know what rewards employees value.

11.2 Describe content theories of motivation.

Content theories of motivation attempt to identify what motivates people. According to Maslow's theory, people are motivated by unmet needs. These needs fall into a hierarchy: physiological, security, social, esteem, and self-actualization. People attempt to satisfy lower-level needs before they focus on higher-level needs. According to McClelland, people have achievement,

power, and affiliation needs. The intensity of each kind of need varies from person to person. Herzberg's two-factor theory says that employees are dissatisfied when hygiene factors are absent and satisfied when motivating factors are present.

11.3 Describe process theories of motivation.

Process theories explain how motivation works through its process. According to Vroom's theory, the intensity of a person's motivation depends on the value the person places on the outcome of a behavior, the perceived likelihood that the behavior will actually lead to the outcome, and the perceived probability that the outcome will actually occur. People are most motivated to seek results they value highly and think they can achieve. Reinforcement theory, pioneered by B. F. Skinner, says people behave as they do because of the kind of consequences they experience as a result of their behavior. The supervisor can therefore influence behavior by administering the consequences (in the form of reinforcement or punishment).

11.4 Explain when financial incentives are likely to motivate employees.

Money motivates people when it meets their needs. The employees must believe they are able to achieve the financial rewards the organization offers.

11.5 Describe pay plans using financial incentives.

Under a piecework system, employees are paid according to how much they produce. A production bonus system pays a basic wage or salary plus a bonus based on performance; for example, an amount per unit assembled. Commissions are payments tied to the amount of sales completed. Some organizations pay employees for making useful suggestions about cutting costs or improving quality. Group incentive plans pay a bonus when the group as a whole exceeds an

objective. Profit-sharing and gainsharing plans are types of group incentives.

11.6 Discuss the pros and cons of keeping pay information secret.

Keeping pay secret respects employees' desire for privacy. However, to be motivated by the possibility of greater earnings and a sense that pay rates are fair, employees must know what they can hope to earn. Typically, an organization balances these needs by publishing pay ranges that show the least and most the organization will pay an employee in a particular job.

11.7 Identify ways supervisors can motivate their employees.

Supervisors can motivate employees by moving toward Theory Y and Theory Z styles of management, making work interesting through job rotation, job enlargement, job enrichment, and contact with users of the product or service. Other ways to motivate include having high expectations of employees, providing rewards that are valued, relating rewards to performance, treating employees as individuals, encouraging employee participation, and providing feedback, including praise.

Key Terms

motivation, *p.* 292
flextime, *p.* 294
job sharing, *p.* 294
reinforcement, *p.* 298
punishment, *p.* 298
behavior modification, *p.* 298
extrinsic reward, *p.* 301
intrinsic reward, *p.* 301

financial incentives, *p.* 302
piecework system, *p.* 302
commissions, *p.* 302
group incentive plan, *p.* 303
profit-sharing plan, *p.* 303
gainsharing, *p.* 304
Theory X, *p.* 304
Theory Y, *p.* 305

Theory Z, *p.* 306
job rotation, *p.* 306
cross-training, *p.* 306
job enlargement, *p.* 306
job enrichment, *p.* 306
Pygmalion effect, *p.* 307

Review and Discussion Questions

1. Name and rank the five basic needs, from lowest to highest, that Maslow described in his hierarchy of needs. If a supervisor applies this hierarchy to his or her employees, what are some specific ways that employees' needs could be met?

2. What are some family-friendly policies that companies now have in place so that employees can balance home and work? What other family-friendly policies might help employees to meet the demands in their lives and thus motivate them at work?

3. What are the three categories of needs that McClelland identified in his theory? Which category of needs do you think is strongest for you?

4. What are the hygiene factors and motivating factors described by Herzberg? Consider

your current job or one you held most recently. Which factors are(were) present at that job? How would you say they affect(ed) your level of satisfaction? Your level of motivation?

5. John Lightfoot believes he has a 75 percent chance of earning a bonus of $100. John believes there is only a 50 percent chance that his company will pay him the bonus even if he rightfully deserves it. Mary Yu believes she has a 75 percent chance of qualifying for a raise of $1,000 a year. Mary believes that there is only a 50 percent chance that her company will pay her the bonus even if she rightfully deserves it. According to Vroom's theory, is it correct to conclude that Mary will be more intensely motivated by her potential reward than John will be by his? Explain.

6. Andre Jones supervises computer programmers. He expects each programmer to turn in a progress report by quitting time each Friday.

   a. Name at least one way Jones can use reinforcement to motivate employees to turn in their reports on time.

   b. Name at least one way Jones can use punishment to motivate employees to turn in their reports on time.

   c. Which of these approaches do you think would be most successful? Why?

7. Pete Polito supervises a cross-functional team whose task is to evaluate whether the in-line skates his company manufactures are safe and up-to-date in design and style. Using Theory Y, what steps might Polito take to lead his team to its goal?

8. In which of the following situations do you think money would be an effective motivator? Explain.

   a. The economy is slow, and even though the salespeople think they are doing their best, sales are down. Sales supervisor Rita Blount tells the sales force that anyone whose weekly sales are up by 10 percent next week will receive a $5,000 bonus.

   b. A retailer such as Best Buy announces that the top performer in the store will be a prime candidate for a management job in a store the company is opening in another state. Whoever takes the job will receive a raise of at least 9 percent.

   c. A respiratory therapist who is the parent of two high school–aged children can earn an extra $500 this month by accepting a schedule that involves working on weekends.

9. Which type or types of pay plan (piecework, production bonus, commission, payment for suggestions, group incentive) would work best in each of the following situations? Why?

   a. A company wants to motivate employees in the manufacturing department to fulfill increased orders for wooden toys as the company tries to expand from a regional market to a national market.

   b. A car dealership wants to emphasize teamwork in its service department.

10. Antonio Delgado supervises the police officers of the Fourth Precinct. Name some ways in which he can make their work more interesting.

11. A supervisor at an online jewelry retailer reads a report stating that 15 percent of all orders subsequently are returned, but this figure is considered better than the industry average. How can she use the Pygmalion effect to motivate employees to reduce the number of returns even further?

12. What is wrong with each of the following attempts at motivation?

   a. A sales supervisor for an insurance company believes that employees appreciate an opportunity to broaden their experiences, so she rewards the top performer each year with an all expenses–paid leadership seminar. The seminar lasts a week and is conducted at a hotel in a city 200 miles away.

   b. The supervisor of a hospital cafeteria awards one employee a $50 bonus each month. To give everyone an equal chance at receiving the bonus, the supervisor draws names written on slips of paper from a jar.

   c. A maintenance supervisor in a pickle factory believes that qualified employees should be able to tell whether they are doing a good job. Therefore, the supervisor focuses motivation efforts on thinking up clever rewards to give out each year to the best performers.

Notes

1. Lindsey Gerdes, "The Best Places to Launch a Career," *BusinessWeek*, September 13, 2007, www.businessweek.com/stories/2007-09-13/the-best-places-to-launch-a-careerbusinessweek-business-news-stock-market-and-financial-advice, accessed May 1, 2014.

2. See, for example, Abraham Maslow, *Eupsychian Management* (Homewood, IL: Irwin, 1965);

C. P. Alderfer, "An Empirical Test of a New Theory of Human Needs," *Organization Behavior and Human Performance* 4 (1969), pp. 142–175.

3. Jennifer O'Herron, "Don't Miss the Mark: Motivation That Works," EE Times, June 1, 2005, http://www.eetimes.com/document.asp?doc_id=1197812.

4. Kimberly Griffiths, "How to Find 'Em and How to Hold 'Em," *Industrial Distribution*, April 1, 2006,

downloaded from Business & Company Resource Center, http://galenet.galegroup.com.

5. Culpepper, "Flexible Work Arrangements: Popular Alternatives to Enhance Benefits Programs," *Culpepper eBulletin*, June 2009, http://www.culpepper.com; Grant Thornton, "Want a Flex Work Schedule? Global Survey Says Look for a Job in Finland, Sweden or Australia; Avoid Japan, Greece or Armenia," news release, June 6, 2011, http://www.grantthornton.com. Examples from Katherine Reynolds Lewis, "Flexible Jobs = Happy Worker Bees?" *Fortune Management*, April 20, 2011, http://management.fortune.cnn.com; Rachel Emma Silverman, "For Hourly Jobs, White-Collar Perks," *The Wall Street Journal*, October 3, 2011, http://online.wsj.com.

6. Christopher Palmeri, "Now for Sale, the Zappos Culture," *BusinessWeek*, January 11, 2010, EBSCO-host, http://web.ebscohost.com; Michael Bartlett, "What Motivates Employees? Not What You Think," *Credit Union Journal*, July 4, 2011, p. 18; "Got Talent? Companies' Concerns," *The Economist*, September 10, 2011, Business & Company Resource Center, http://galenet.galegroup.com.

7. Larry Stewart, "Rewarding Teamwork Turns a Shop Around," *Construction Equipment*, January 1, 2006, http://www.constructionequipment.com/rewarding-teamwork-turns-shop-around, accessed May 1, 2014.

8. S. Certo and S. Certo, 2009. *Modern Management: Concepts and Skills* (Prentice Hall: Upper Saddle River, NJ) 2009, 11th ed., pp. 404–406.

9. Josh Williams, "Improving Management Support for Safety to Optimize Safety Culture," *Occupational Hazards*, June 2008, https://www.safetyperformance.com/ImprovingManagementSupportforSafetytoOptimizeSafetyCulture.pdf, accessed May 1, 2014.

10. Hannah Clark Steiman, "Let's Get Together: How to Persuade Workers to Cut Costs," *Inc.*, October 2008, pp. 46, 48 (interview with Danny Meryer).

11. Society for Human Resource Management, "11-Year-Old FMLA in Need of Medical Treatment," news release, February 17, 2004, www.shrm.org.

12. Peter Berg and Ann C. Frost, "Dignity at Work for Low Wage, Low Skill Service Workers," *Industrial Relations*, Autumn 2005, downloaded from Business & Company Resource Center, http://galenet.galegroup.com.

13. U.S. Department of Labor, Wage and Hour Division, "Questions and Answers about the Minimum Wage," http://www.dol.gov, accessed May 1, 2014; Chris Isidore, "Not Getting By on Minimum Wage," *CNN Money*, September 27, 2011, http://money.cnn.com/2011/09/27/news/economy/minimum_wage_jobs/.

14. For more information on financial incentives, see K. Kubo and T. Saito, 2008, "The relationship between financial incentives for company presidents and firm performance in Japan," *Japanese Economic Review*, 59, p. 401.

15. Julia Chang, "Spread the Wealth: Letting Your Salespeople Profit When Your Company Does," *Sales & Marketing Management*, June 2006, downloaded from Business & Company Resource Center, http://galenet.galegroup.com.

16. Valentina Jovanovski, "Staff Rewarded 50p for Spotting Ryanair Fliers with Excess Bags," *Daily Mail*, November 15, 2011, http://www.dailymail.co.uk/travel/article-2061769/Ryanair-charges-Incentives-given-Liverpool-airport-workers-spotting-oversized-handluggage.html; "Airport Staff Offered Scheme to Help Catch Ryanair Passengers with Excess Baggage," *Daily Telegraph*, November 15, 2011, http://www.telegraph.co.uk/finance/newsbysector/transport/8890300/Airport-staff-offered-scheme-to-help-catch-Ryanair-passengers-with-excess-baggage.html, accessed May 1, 2014.

17. "Leading Dealers Share Tips on Technician Compensation Plans, Managing Cash Flow, Product Line Selection, Marketing the Dealer Advantage, Serving Commercial Customers, and More," *Yard & Garden*, March 2006, downloaded from Business & Company Resource Center, http://galenet.galegroup.com.

18. For a closer look at group incentive plans, see M. Singer, P. Donoso, and C. Rodriguez-Sickert, 2008, "A static model of cooperation for group-based incentive plans," *International Journal of Production Economics*, 115, p. 492.

19. Austin Carr, "Report: Google Ties 25% of Employee Bonuses to Success in Social," *Fast Company*, April 7, 2011, http://www.fastcompany.com/1745514/report-google-ties-25-employee-bonuses-success-social; Murad Ahmed, "Google Finally Takes On Facebook by Invitation Only," *Times (London)*, July 13, 2011, http://www.thetimes.co.uk/tto/business/industries/technology/article3092161.ece, accessed May 1, 2014; "Google Execs Talk Reorganization, Strategy after Brief Larry Page Appearance," *PC Magazine Online*, http://www.pcmag.com/article2/0,2817,2383612,00.asp, accessed May 1, 2014.

20. For information on how to successfully implement profit-sharing plans, see M. Magnan, S. St-Onge, and D. Cormier, 2005, "The adoption and success of profit-sharing plans in strategic business units: Opportunism or contingency?", *International Journal of Productivity and Performance Management* 54, p. 355.

21. Antoinette Alexander, "The Lure: Smart Compensation Plans Can Keep Staff in a Tight Market," *Accounting Technology*, July 2006, downloaded from Business & Company Resource Center, http://galenet.galegroup.com.

22. Douglas McGregor, *The Human Side of Enterprise* (New York: McGraw-Hill, 1960).

23. Jane Wollman Rusoff, "Portrait of a Branch Manager," *Research*, July 2004, downloaded from

Business & Company Resource Center, http://galenet.galegroup.com.

24. For a recent article on cross-training, see K. Yang, 2007, "A comparison of cross-training policies in different job shops," *International Journal of Production Research*, 45, p. 1279.

25. David Boyce, "Expectations Part of Deal for Gordon," *Kansas City Star*, April 12, 2006, downloaded from Business & Company Resource Center, http://galenet.galegroup.com.

26. Karen Colbenson, "Hormel Delivers Bonus Checks," *Post-Bulletin (Rochester, Minn.)*, November 26, 2008, downloaded from Business & Company Resource Center, http://galenet.galegroup.com.

27. Erika Germer, "Tell Them What They've Won!" *Inc.*, April 2001, p. 70.

28. Alison Overholt, "Cuckoo for Customers," *Fast Company*, June 2004, http://www.fastcompany.

com/48967/cuckoo-customers, accessed May 1, 2014.

29. Mark Rowh, "Managing Part-Time Employees," *Office Solutions*, May 13, 2008, http://www.redorbit.com/news/health/1382506/managing_parttime_employees/.

30. Scott Morgan, "How to Motivate a Diverse Workplace," Everyday Life by Demand Media, http://everydaylife.globalpost.com/motivate-diverse-workplace-6891.html, accessed May 1, 2014.

31. Ron Lieber, "New Way to Curb Medical Costs: Make Employees Feel the Sting," *The Wall Street Journal*, June 23, 2004, http://online.wsj.com/news/articles/SB108793995630244509, accessed May 1, 2014.

32. Dave Marin, "Viewpoint: Rock-Solid Results from Simple Praise," *American Banker*, April 7, 2006, downloaded from Business & Company Resource Center, http://galenet.galegroup.com.

PART TWO: SKILL-BUILDING

Meeting the Challenge

Reflecting back on page 291, consider the challenges faced by a business you have worked for or visited frequently. Identify a weakness in the company's processes or service. If you were a supervisor at the company, what game elements would you suggest to reduce or eliminate the weakness?

Problem-Solving Case: Motivating Employees at Nucor Corporation

Today Nucor Corporation is the largest producer of steel in the United States, so it is hard to believe it was once an underdog in a struggling industry. What has set the company apart is a focus on motivating and empowering employees. The employee focus is illustrated by the custom of printing each individual's name on the cover of Nucor's annual report. But the concern for employees is much more practical and goes far beyond symbols.

Nucor's pay system is remarkable. At all levels of the company, the largest share of employees' income is tied to their performance. Base pay for a Nucor steelworker is near $10 per hour, far below the industry range of $16 to $21. But on top of that, steelworkers can earn a bonus based on the amount of defect-free steel produced during their shift. Those bonuses can triple the workers' pay, taking it far above the industry average. Tying the bonus to the entire shift's performance also motivates employees to cooperate to get the job done. In addition, the company pays out profit sharing, encouraging employees to care about the entire company's performance. The company computes the bonus on every order of steel and pays it weekly, so employees have plenty of reinforcement. In 2005, a typical Nucor steelworker earned $79,000 plus $2,000 from a special bonus celebrating record earnings for the company plus nearly $18,000 in profit sharing. Managers receive similarly large amounts of their pay in the form of bonuses and profit sharing.

For employees new to Nucor, often used to relying on base pay, the compensation arrangement seems alarming at first. Once they get a taste of bonuses, however, they become highly motivated. When Nucor acquired a steel plant in Auburn, New York, workers wanted to keep their old pay system, so management simply continued paying them the old way but announcing what they would have made under Nucor's system. Eventually employees began to see that a new way of thinking could fill up their pocketbooks. David Hutchins, a Nucor supervisor in

Auburn, says that before Nucor acquired his plant, workers in his group tended to relax whenever an earlier stage of operations slowed down. But with a bonus riding on their shift's output, the employees no longer think of themselves as separate groups: "Wherever the bottleneck is," explains Hutchins, "we go there, and everyone works on it." Before long, output in Auburn was up, and so were paycheck totals.

Motivation at Nucor is about more than pay, however. The company encourages employees to share ideas and empowers them to make decisions and solve problems. Supervisors, for example, make decisions more typical of a plant manager. Once, following the failure of an electrical grid at the Hickman, Arkansas, plant, a group of electricians at Nucor facilities in Decatur, Alabama, and Hertford County, North Carolina, traveled to Hickman to work on the problem. They did not need to get a supervisor's approval; they just needed to do what they determined was most important.

Along with cooperation, Nucor fosters friendly competition in order to stimulate creative thinking. For example, plants often hold contests among the shifts to see which one can meet a goal related to output, safety, or efficiency.

1. How does performance-based pay motivate Nucor employees? Would this pay system be effective if Nucor did not also empower employees to make decisions? Why or why not?
2. Supervisors do not set up the pay system for a large company like Nucor. How can Nucor's supervisors contribute to employee motivation?
3. Does this description of Nucor sound like an organization in which you would feel motivated? Why or why not? Which theory of motivation would best explain your feelings?

Source: Nanette Byrnes, "The Art of Motivation," *BusinessWeek*, May 1, 2006, http://www.businessweek.com/stories/2006-04-30/the-art-of-motivation, accessed May 1, 2014.

Assessing Yourself

What Motivates You?

What makes a job appealing to you? Rank the following job factors from 1 to 12. Assign 1 to the factor you consider most important and 12 to the factor you consider least important.

_____ 1. Work that is interesting and meaningful.
_____ 2. Good wages or salary.
_____ 3. Authority to make important decisions.
_____ 4. Comfortable work environment, such as a clean, modern laboratory, fancy store, or attractive office.
_____ 5. Likable co-workers.
_____ 6. Good relationship with supervisor.
_____ 7. Clear understanding of the department's and company's goals and performance requirements.
_____ 8. Appreciation and recognition for doing a good job.
_____ 9. Opportunities to learn new skills.
_____ 10. Prestigious title or occupation.
_____ 11. Chance for advancement.
_____ 12. Job security.

Pause and Reflect

1. Which of these motivators can you expect from working as a supervisor?
2. Can you modify your own job so that it includes more of these factors?
3. How can you as a supervisor make these motivators available to employees?

Class Skills Exercise

Learning What Motivates Workers

If you have not already done so, answer the Assessing Yourself questions. Then, by a show of hands, determine how many class members selected each response as most important and how many as least important. The instructor might tally the responses on the chalkboard or overhead projector or fill in the table below:

	Number of Students Rating the Item	
Self-Assessment Item	**Most Important**	**Least Important**
1.	_____	_____
2.	_____	_____
3.	_____	_____
4.	_____	_____
5.	_____	_____
6.	_____	_____
7.	_____	_____
8.	_____	_____
9.	_____	_____
10.	_____	_____
11.	_____	_____
12.	_____	_____

Discuss the following questions:

- Which response or responses did most class members choose as most important?
- Which response or responses did most class members choose as least important?
- Do you think these choices are typical of most employees today? Why or why not?
- How could a supervisor use this information to motivate employees?

Building Supervision Skills

Developing Motivational Methods

This chapter deals with one of the most challenging areas for supervisors: motivating employees. This exercise will help you develop a comprehensive list of motivating methods on which to draw when faced with employees whom you feel are not performing to their full potential.

1. Figure 11.6 on page 305 shows several motivational methods. Drawing on what you have learned about motivation in this class and elsewhere, list methods, techniques, and strategies that can serve as a source of ideas on how to motivate people.

2. For the purposes of this exercise, do not be concerned about the economic impact of your ideas or a plan for carrying them out. For example, if you suggest a bonus to reward your employees for good performance, there is no need to provide a formula for computing the bonus. At the same time, however, do not make ridiculous suggestions that would not make good business sense, such as suggesting that you reward all employees and their families with a two-week all-expenses-paid vacation to Bermuda.

3. Divide the class into groups. Then develop a group list that can be copied for each group member. There will undoubtedly be many days in your management career when you will be able to use this list to help you generate some ideas about how to motivate an unmotivated employee. Also, the list can be improved over time as you develop greater experience as a motivational leader.

Things I can do to be a motivational leader	Characteristics of a motivating work environment	Ways to reward my employees for good performance	Strategies I can use to improve the way work is done	Organizational policies or benefits
Help employees set challenging yet achievable goals	Goods and services employees believe in	Publish achievements in company newsletter	Communicate clear performance standards	Flexible work schedule to accommodate personal and family needs

chapter twelve | Problem Employees: Counseling and Discipline

learning objectives

After you have studied this chapter, you should be able to:

12.1 Identify common types of problem behavior among employees.

12.2 Explain why and when supervisors should counsel employees.

12.3 Describe counseling techniques.

12.4 Discuss effective ways of administering discipline.

12.5 Describe the principles of positive discipline and self-discipline.

12.6 Explain how supervisors can detect and confront troubled employees.

12.7 Specify how supervisors can direct troubled employees in getting help and then follow up on the recovery efforts.

12.8 Discuss the role of the supervisor's manager and the human resources department in helping the supervisor with problem employees.

A Supervision Challenge

A TROUBLESOME WORKER TAKES CHEVRON TO COURT

Todd Ion had worked at a Chevron refinery for several years without incident before he was labeled a "problem employee." His behavior became erratic. His performance started to slide. He took days off without his supervisor's OK. He even had an outburst on the job. Within weeks, Ion was fired. What caused his downfall, and how did his supervisor handle it?

Ion was clearly under a mountain of stress. His wife had recently taken their son and moved out of state. Adding to the strain, the boy was having great difficulty adapting to the new arrangement. As a possible solution, Ion was awarded custody for six months. Spending more time with his son meant spending less time at work. Ion asked his supervisor for the company leave policy so he could review his options.

Soon after, Ion took it upon himself to disclose his personal circumstances to a more senior supervisor. He would need to take longer lunch periods to be with his son, he explained. He also asked the supervisor to sit down with him in the next few days to discuss a leave of absence so that he could focus on his son full time. Whether the supervisor never received the request, forgot it, or chose to ignore it, the meeting was never held.

More than a month later, Ion's supervisors suspended him for five days. They said that he was not working up to company standards and that he was taking overly long lunches. They placed him on a performance agreement and an attendance improvement plan. All of this compounded his level of stress.

Ion sought counseling from Chevron's employee assistance program (EAP). He learned that he might qualify for time away from work under the Family and Medical Leave Act (FMLA). An EAP counselor sent him to a doctor, and promised that his medical information would be kept confidential. The doctor diagnosed Ion with debilitating stress. That would help him receive the leave he clearly needed.

The counselor also told Ion to take sick days after the suspension. He did so, but did not get advance clearance from his supervisor. As such, he assumed that Ion was deliberately avoiding work and no longer committed to his job. The supervisor sent an e-mail to the general manager, outlining the employee's troublesome behavior, and reporting the disciplinary steps he had taken.

Meanwhile, Ion visited the Chevron clinic to file FMLA paperwork. When he arrived, he was already in an agitated state. When asked to sign a form that would release his medical records, he blew up and was led from the clinic by security.

That was the final straw: Ion was dismissed a few days later. The letter of termination stated that the cause was "abuse of management constituting insubordination." Ion sued Chevron, citing interference and retaliation claims under FMLA.

In district court, the company said that it would have fired Ion regardless of his seeking FMLA leave. Chevron won the case, at least for a time.

On appeal in the Fifth Circuit Court, judgment was reversed. Ion's attorneys pointed out that his supervisor did not inform him that he could receive further discipline—including firing—after the performance agreement and attendance improvement plan were put into place. Also, Ion was not terminated until after he filed for leave under FMLA. The court was convinced that his leave request might have influenced the decision to discharge Ion. Otherwise, he might never have been let go.

Do you think that the Chevron supervisor explained his disciplinary actions to Ion sufficiently? Was it the supervisor's responsibility to help Ion meet the goals of the performance agreement and attendance improvement plan? How could Ion and his supervisor each have communicated more effectively?

Sources: Wolters Kluwer Law & Business, "Employer Failed To Show It Would Have Fired Employee For Work Issues and Faking Need For FMLA Leave," October 11, 2013, http://news.wolterskluwerlb.com/news/employer-failed-to-show-it-would-have-fired-employee-for-work-issues-and-faking-need-for-fmla-leave/; Christian Schappel, "Abusive, underperforming employee fights his way to FMLA victory in court," October 31, 2013, http://www.hrbenefitsalert.com/abusive-underperforming-employee-fights-his-way-to-fmla-victory-in-court/.

When a supervisor does a good job of leading, problem solving, communicating, and motivating, most employees will perform well. Even so, a supervisor occasionally faces the challenge of a "problem" employee, one who is persistently unwilling or unable to follow the rules or meet performance standards. In general, problem employees fall into two categories: (1) employees *causing* problems—for example, by starting fights or leaving early—and (2) employees *with* problems, such as an employee whose money worries or home life issues are a distraction from work. By handling these troubled employees appropriately, a supervisor can help resolve the problem without hurting the morale or performance of other employees.

This chapter provides guidelines for supervising problem employees. It describes some common problems requiring special action on the part of a supervisor and explains two basic courses of action to take: counseling and discipline. The chapter also discusses how to help a troubled employee. Finally, the chapter describes the kinds of support a supervisor can expect from superiors, the human resources department, and other experts.

Problems Requiring Special Action

LO12.1 ▶ Identify common types of problem behavior among employees.

For the third straight Monday, Peter Dunbar had called in sick. Other employees were grumbling about having to do extra work to make up for his absences, and rumors were flying about the nature of Dunbar's problem. His supervisor knew she would have to take action, beginning with some investigation into what the problem was.

When supervisors observe poor performance, they tend to blame the employee for lacking ability or effort. But when supervisors or employees need to explain their own poor performance, they may blame the organization or another person for not providing enough support. This inconsistency suggests that some digging is needed to uncover the true source of a performance problem. For example, the supervisor might consider the following questions:

- Has the employee performed better in the past?
- Has the employee received proper training?
- Does the employee know and understand the objectives he or she is to accomplish?
- Is the supervisor providing enough feedback and support?
- Has the supervisor encouraged and rewarded high performance?
- Are other employees with similar abilities performing well? Are they experiencing similar difficulties?

These questions and the discussions they lead to can be viewed as part of an ongoing cycle of improvement between a supervisor and an employee, as shown in Figure 12.1.

Although persistent failure to perform up to standards may result from many problems, the problems that supervisors most commonly encounter among employees are absenteeism and tardiness, insubordination and uncooperativeness, alcohol and drug abuse, workplace violence, and theft.

FIGURE 12.1 | Improving Performance

Continuous communication between an employee and a supervisor can lead to improved performance.

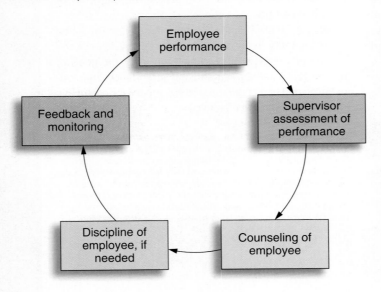

Absenteeism and Tardiness

An employee who misses work, even part of a day, is expensive for an employer. The company frequently must pay for those unproductive hours—for example, by providing sick pay to an employee who calls in sick. In addition, the other employees may be less productive when they have to cover for someone who is absent or tardy. A recent survey found that unscheduled absenteeism cost employers as much as $765,000 per year.[1]

Of course, employees who really are sick should take time off. As discussed in "Supervision and Ethics," the company provides sick days for good reasons: to allow employees to rest and recover and to prevent them from infecting the rest of the workforce. Recent research indicates that absenteeism is associated with physical health stressors, including being diagnosed with a heart condition, being diagnosed with a chronic condition, and being hospitalized.[2] It is important to note that psychological health stressors (e.g., depression, anxiety) were not significantly associated with absenteeism. Rather, employees seeking mental health treatment for psychological health stressors were more likely to show up for work even when a sickness absence was justified. In other words, employees seeking mental health treatment were more likely to work under suboptimal conditions. Whatever the cause of absenteeism, problems arise when absences are unexcused or recur with suspicious regularity. In addition, missing work is often a sign of a deeper problem, such as a family crisis, anger about something at work, or plans to leave the organization.

Effective action against tardiness and absenteeism targets the cause of this problem behavior. Unscheduled absences are more frequent at organizations where morale is poor. As shown in Figure 12.2 on the following page, the most common reasons given for taking unscheduled time off are personal illness and family issues. Employers can help employees manage these needs through programs such as paid time-off banks,

SUPERVISION AND ETHICS

THE ETHICS OF ABSENCES

As a supervisor, you count on all the employees in your group to be at work, contributing to your group's goals. You also want to set a good example of dedication and responsibility. But what about those days when you wake up with a sore throat, cough, or other sign that you are coming down with a nasty cold? Should you push through your illness and make the trip to work?

Probably not, says ethicist Bruce Weinstein, although a recent survey by CareerBuilder says that 30 percent of employees do. According to Weinstein, staying home from work is an ethical decision. He says it comes down to matters of fairness in four areas:

1. You cannot serve your clients, customers, or employees well when you feel wretched.

2. Infecting your co-workers with your germs is unkind. You do not appreciate catching a cold or flu from someone, and it is not fair to pass your illness on to others. Furthermore, the next person you infect could have a chronic illness or impaired immune system; for them, your illness could be serious.

3. Surprisingly, you may be costing your employer money by going to work. A study by researchers at Cornell University found that ill employees add to employers' health costs.

4. When you are sick, you need to take care of yourself. Ethics calls for you to treat everyone with kindness; it would be unfair to yourself to work when you need rest.

For supervisors, this ethical question has another angle: What is the ethical way to treat your workers when they are the ones who are coughing, sneezing, and feeling miserable? One of the reasons that employees give for going to work when they are sick is workplace pressure and guilt from their boss. Following Weinstein's reasoning, however, the answer is clear: encourage workers to stay home and get better. In the end, it will be easier for your group to meet its goals if everyone is feeling healthy.

Sources: Based on Bruce Weinstein, "Should You Go to Work When You're Sick?" *BusinessWeek*, February 28, 2008, www.businessweek.com/stories/2008-02-28/should-you-go-to-work-when-youre-sick-businessweek-business-news-stock-market-and-financial-advice, accessed May 5, 2014; "CareerBuilder's Annual Study Reveals Most Outrageous Excuses Workers Have Given When Calling in Sick," CareerBuilder, October 24, 2013, http://www.careerbuilder.com/share/aboutus/pressreleasesdetail.aspx?sd=10%2F24%2F2013&id=pr786&ed=12%2F31%2F2013, accessed May 6, 2014.

FIGURE 12.2 | Why Employees Had Unscheduled Absences

The reasons for unscheduled absences are varied; while the largest percentage are for illness, there are clearly many other factors at play.

Source: "2007 CCH Unscheduled Absence Survey," https://www.cch.com/Absenteeism2007/, accessed May 4, 2014.

insubordination
Deliberate refusal to do what the supervisor or other superior asks

meaning employees are allowed a given number of paid days off, which they can use when they are sick, have family needs, or want to take a vacation. If an employee takes days off for doctors' appointments or family crises, fewer days remain for vacationing. Wisco Industries offers positive reinforcement for good attendance: cash incentives to employees who work at least a minimum number of hours during each period.[3] In addition, supervisors can reduce absenteeism by creating a positive work environment in which morale is high.

Insubordination and Uncooperativeness

When poor performance results from not understanding how to do a job, the solution is relatively simple. A supervisor must make sure that instructions are communicated clearly and that the employee is receiving the proper training. But sometimes an employee performs poorly or breaks rules because he or she chooses to do so. Such an employee may simply be uncooperative, or the employee may engage in insubordination, the deliberate refusal to do what a supervisor or other superior asks.

Many kinds of negative behavior fall into these categories. An employee may have a generally poor attitude—criticizing, complaining, and showing a dislike for a supervisor and the organization. He or she might get into arguments over many kinds of issues. An employee may make an art form out of doing as little as possible. The employee might spend most of the day socializing, joking around, or just moving slowly. Another employee might regularly fail to follow rules—"forgetting" to wear safety equipment or sign out at lunchtime. Some employees even blame the supervisor or organization when reprimanded. When the supervisor objects to a problem behavior ("Please don't use your cell phone to make personal calls during work hours"), the employee twists the situation into something the *supervisor* is supposed to fix ("Well, how am I supposed to manage my kitchen renovation if I can't take contractors' calls at work?"). This type of behavior can go on endlessly unless the supervisor defines specific limits and requires the employee to figure out a way to stay within those limits or be disciplined.[4]

Although these problems are serious, it is important for supervisors to see the difference between employees who do not do their work properly because they choose not to and employees who do not do their work because they need help. One manager who has this skill is Mike Speckman, vice president of sales for inSilica, a company that sells semiconductors. Speckman once had a salesperson who was disorganized and spent almost every minute on existing customers, rather than cultivating the new ones that could help the company grow. Where some supervisors might have seen a lost cause, Speckman saw an employee with a desire to learn. He decided to travel with the salesperson on calls to prospective customers. On the first call, Speckman led the conversation to show how the work was to be done. On the second call, he and the salesperson worked as a team.

Supervisors need to define expectations for employees. This can help to prevent employees from prioritizing personal affairs over their work responsibilities.

On the third call, the salesperson took the lead, and Speckman was there just to watch and provide support. The coaching gave the salesperson the necessary confidence to become successful.[5]

Alcohol and Drug Abuse

The abuse of alcohol and drugs by workers is costly in several ways. According to the National Institute on Drug Abuse, employees who use drugs are three times as likely to be tardy and more than three times as likely to be involved in an accident at work. Absences and medical costs also are much greater among drug abusers. And employees who abuse alcohol and drugs are far less productive than their co-workers who stay sober.[6]

Unfortunately, substance abuse is not uncommon at work. A study by the Department of Labor found that one-third of employees say drugs are illegally sold in their workplace, and one in five young employees say they have used marijuana while on the job. According to the federal government's Substance Abuse and Mental Health Services Administration, about one out of ten full-time and part-time workers abuse or are dependent on alcohol or drugs. The problem is much greater at companies that are small or medium-sized (under 500 employees), perhaps because these companies are less likely to have formal procedures for maintaining a drug-free workplace. In a study of seven companies in various industries, the cost of substance abuse by employees came to more than $5,000 for extra health insurance benefits and lost productivity.[7]

The Americans with Disabilities Act (ADA), which prohibits discrimination on the basis of physical or mental disability, treats substance abuse arising from an addiction as a disability. Therefore, substance abuse may not be legal grounds for firing an employee. The supervisor should encourage the employee to get help, even if doing so requires adjusting the employee's work schedule or permitting the employee to take a disability leave to get treatment. In addition, actions taken with regard to the employee should focus on work performance, not on the substance abuse itself. For example, a supervisor might warn, "If I catch you picking fights with your co-workers again, I will have to suspend you." This warning addresses the employee's job-related behavior. (For more on the ADA and other laws against employment discrimination, see Chapter 15.)

Although a supervisor must treat each employee fairly and avoid discrimination, he or she also has a responsibility to help ensure that the workplace is safe for employees and others. If an employee's suspected substance abuse is creating a hazard, a supervisor must act. Again, the key is to address job-related behavior and job requirements, including safety. (The section on troubled employees, pages 337–340, provides guidelines for handling employees who abuse drugs or alcohol.) In addition to expecting supervisors to spot problem behavior, some companies for which safety is critical conduct random drug testing of employees. One of those companies is Ercole Electric, located in Fredericksburg, Maryland. Ercole's president, Greg Semuskie, said, "My employees thanked me for starting a drug [testing] program. They all knew who was taking drugs, and they didn't want to work with them. They told me they felt safer with this program."[8]

Workplace Violence

Security managers at *Fortune* 1000 companies recently responded to a Securitas USA survey by ranking workplace violence as the number two security threat facing their organizations. After almost a decade in the top slot, workplace violence is now just slightly less of a concern than cyber security.[9] An estimated 2 million incidents of workplace violence occur each year, and according to the Bureau of Labor Statistics, homicide causes almost 500 deaths on the job every year.[10]

Several factors contribute to workplace violence. Workers who abuse alcohol or drugs or who have psychological problems may be more likely to engage in violence at work. Employees who are under stress, either at work or away, may explode in violence. While other employees handle stress without becoming violent, problems are particularly likely if employees feel they are treated unfairly, fail to communicate their problems effectively, and feel frustrated and unable to do anything about their situation. Together, these circumstances suggest that supervisors may sometimes be able to head off or at least prepare to handle violence by paying close attention to their employees, fostering good communication (see Chapter 10), and treating employees fairly (see Chapters 4 and 8).[11]

Another factor associated with workplace violence is domestic violence. If an employee is being abused by a spouse, parent, or other third party, the abuser may carry violent behavior to the workplace. The employee might receive threatening phone calls or even disruptive visits from the abuser. Domestic violence is behind millions of days of absences each year, and millions more in lost productivity. The problem is widespread, with over one-fourth of women saying they are or have been victims of domestic violence.[12] To address these business losses and out of concern for abused workers and their colleagues, some companies, including Macy's and State Farm Insurance, offer information and help for employees who are victimized at work or at home. These efforts may include secure parking spaces, flexible hours, and referrals to employee assistance programs for counseling.[13]

Whatever the cause, supervisors should be prepared for the possibility of workplace violence.[14] They should be aware of warning signs such as an employee who appears to be under the influence of drugs or alcohol, does not control angry outbursts, has a history of intimidating others, talks about or shows off weapons, and jokes about workplace violence. If an employee complains of feeling threatened by another employee or an outsider, the supervisor should take these concerns seriously. The supervisor also should work with the organization's human resource department to develop and practice plans for moving to safety in the event of a violent incident. The supervisor should turn to the human resource department for assistance if a problem employee seems threatening and does not respond to the basic measures described in this chapter. In that case, or if an employee is coping with domestic violence, the necessary measures may require efforts beyond what the supervisor can provide.

In the aftermath of workplace violence, heightened fear, anger, and other emotions may continue to affect employees' ability to cope with their jobs and lives. Supervisors can help the group by providing opportunities to talk over the experience but not pressuring anyone to speak up. If members of the supervisor's staff were injured or killed in a workplace incident, it may be helpful for the supervisor to express concern with a visit or note to the injured workers or the workers' survivors. The supervisor should help the group return gradually to a normal routine. As much as possible, the supervisor should try to project a calm image and allow breaks at times when employees seem overwhelmed. Of course, the supervisor also may feel affected by a violent incident. If so, the supervisor should allow time for resting and talking over the situation with a counselor or other trusted person.[15]

Theft of Money, Goods, Time, and Information

Statistics indicate that stealing by employees is a huge problem. Although stores have to keep an eye out for shoplifters, a national study found that the largest share of merchandise losses at retailers resulted from employee theft. Of the $44 billion worth of merchandise that U.S. retailers lost in a recent year, employee theft accounted for more than $18.1 billion, or 41 percent, of that loss (see Figure 12.3 on the following page).[16] Shoplifting, by contrast, is a significant ($14.6 billion) but noticeably smaller problem.

Stealing by employees happens in all kinds of businesses. For example, Multi-Point Communications, which provides online conferencing services, was the victim

FIGURE 12.3 | Merchandise Losses at Retailers

Theft from a company's own employees is a larger issue than shoplifting for retailers.

Source: Data from Richard C. Hollinger, "Academic Viewpoint: National Retail Security Survey Executive Summary," *LP Magazine*, March 24, 2014, http://www.lpportal.com/academic-viewpoint/item/2966-2012-nrss-executive-summary.html.

of theft by a finance employee. The fifty-person company had been enjoying strong performance, so no one noticed for years that small sums were disappearing off the company's books and into the employee's pockets. Eventually, when the employee was on vacation, the company's owner noticed bookkeeping entries for some strange-looking expenses. A forensic accountant came in to examine the books and determined that the vacationing employee had stolen $250,000 over a seven-year period.[17]

Not all thefts involve money or tangible goods. Employees can also "steal time" by giving the employer less work than they are paid for, taking extra sick leave, or altering their time cards. Lost time is also more and more often spent surfing the Internet or posting status updates on social media. Just a few years ago, employees carried out these activities on their company-supplied computers. Many employers have handled the problem by blocking the Web sites where the most time is wasted. Some employers also install software on their computer systems to monitor employees' keystrokes or the Web sites they visit. The software analyzes the data to identify where nonwork-related computer activity is occurring. Today, however, these practices are more difficult because so many employees bring their own mobile devices to work. One recent survey found that over three-fourths of employees with Facebook accounts visited the site during their workday, and another survey found that 40 percent of Web surfing during work hours is for personal reasons.[18] For ideas on how to address the problem of wasted time in the age of mobile technology, see "Supervisory Skills."

SUPERVISORY SKILLS

CONTROLLING

Minimizing Losses from Modern Technology

Today's modern gadgets and information systems are helping businesses build strong customer relationships and operate at amazing levels of efficiency. But misuse of the technology can do the opposite: hurting the company's reputation and introducing malware into sophisticated computer systems. Supervisors are responsible for ensuring that their employees are following the company's rules for on-the-job computer use. Also, beyond those rules, several guidelines can help to ensure that employees stay efficient and safe when they have Internet access.

Mobile devices with a whole array of applications and features are simply irresistible today. Just a few years ago, employers could hope to ban employees from using their own devices to log into company computer networks. Today, more and more companies are giving up on the bans. The simple fact is that employees *will* buy their own smart phones and tablets, bring them to work, and sneak peeks online. Some supervisors work in situations where they can ensure that all employees store their personal gadgets in a locker before starting work. Other supervisors must be realistic and set enforceable rules, such as turning off and pocketing mobile devices while serving customers or participating in meetings. Also, when employees are working with corporate

data on mobile devices, it is essential that they use passwords to protect access to the data and keep their devices safely locked up when not in use.

Another issue is the use of social media while at work. Clearly, time spent reviewing scenes of friends' weekend adventures is time not spent working. Many companies handle this problem behavior by blocking access to sites like Facebook and YouTube. A growing number are treating these unofficial breaks as reasonable—the equivalent of a quick trip to the coffee pot or water cooler. Some even find that time spent networking online can be work related or can refresh employees' creative thinking and concentration. In cases where employees have access to social media at work, supervisors need to set clear goals, so they have a measure of whether employees are spending enough time on work. If employees are missing targets, the supervisor would work with them to diagnose the problem and perhaps identify use of social media as something that has to change.

Sources: "IT's Arab Spring," *The Economist*, October 8, 2011, http://www.economist.com/node/21531112, accessed May 5, 2014; Tamara E. Russell, "Employment Law Meets Social Media: Advice for Employers," *HR Focus*, October 2011, pp. 4–7; James Surowiecki, "In Praise of Distraction," *New Yorker*, April 11, 2011, http://www.newyorker.com/talk/financial/2011/04/11/110411ta_talk_surowiecki, accessed May 5, 2014.

The theft of information also is a serious and growing problem, made even easier by new communications technology. Several years ago, an administrative assistant at the Coca-Cola Company was charged with offering to sell trade secrets to PepsiCo. Pepsi tipped off executives of its rival, who notified the FBI. In other cases, employees did not adequately protect data on computers, and the computers were stolen by outsiders. An employee of PSA HealthCare, based in Norcross, Georgia, downloaded data about patients into a laptop computer, which the employee then carried out of the office. Later the computer was stolen from the employee's car. This incident occurred even though PSA has policies forbidding employees from removing data from the company's offices.[19]

The widespread nature of employee theft indicates that supervisors must be on guard against it. In addition to following the broad guidelines in this chapter for handling employee problems, supervisors should take measures to prevent and react to theft. Each organization has its own procedures, varying according to type of industry. In addition, supervisors should carefully check the background of anyone they plan to hire (part of the selection process described in Chapter 15).

To prevent information theft, the monitoring of employees may need to focus on access to and retrieval of data. For example, a financial services employee used his access to request credit reports for many customers. The employee then sold the data to companies that created fake identities for fraudulent purposes. Detecting exactly when and how employees are using data is extremely difficult, so employers are increasingly using high-tech tools. For example, access cards that employees swipe through a scanner provide a trail of electronic information about each employee's use of the company's information system.[20]

Supervisors should make sure that employees follow all procedures for record keeping. They should take advantage of ways to build employee morale and involvement; employees who feel like a part of the organization are less likely to steal from it. Supervisors also should make sure employees understand the costs and consequences of theft. Perhaps most important, supervisors should set a good example by demonstrating ethical behavior.

The Small Business Administration advises supervisors who suspect an employee is stealing not to investigate the crime themselves. Instead, they should report their suspicions to their manager and to the police or professional security consultants.[21]

Social Media Behavior

Employees represent the organization with their actions, even when not on the job. As such, it is important for employees to understand that their online communications, including social media posts, may negatively reflect on themselves. For example, a college graduate recently received a job offer from Cisco. Using her Twitter account, the graduate posted, "Cisco just offered me a job! Now I have to weigh the utility of a fatty paycheck against the daily commute to San Jose and hating the work." A Cisco employee read the tweet and referred it to the hiring manager, who ultimately rescinded the job offer. Additional stories abound of employees being terminated for posting inappropriate pictures or comments to the Web. These examples highlight the importance of closely monitoring online communication to ensure that workers represent themselves and their employers well.[22]

Counseling

LO12.2 ▶ Explain why and when supervisors should counsel employees.

If a supervisor responds to problem behavior immediately, he or she will sometimes be able to bring the problem to a quick end without complex proceedings. For example, a supervisor can respond to each complaint from an employee who constantly complains about the way things are done by calmly asking the employee to suggest some alternatives. Not only does this discourage complaining, but it also may uncover some good, new ways of operating. In many cases, however, the supervisor must take further steps to demonstrate the seriousness of the problem behavior.

Often the most constructive way a supervisor can address problem behavior is through counseling. **Counseling** refers to the process of learning about an individual's personal problem and helping the employee resolve it. Employees themselves should be able to resolve a relatively simple problem, such as tardiness caused by staying up too late watching television, without the supervisor's help. For more complex problems, such as those stemming from financial difficulties or substance abuse, the solution will require getting help from an expert. Because counseling is a cooperative process between supervisor and employee, employees are likely to respond more positively to it than to a simple order that they "shape up or ship out."

counseling
The process of learning about an individual's personal problem and helping him or her resolve it

Benefits of Counseling

Counseling benefits employees in several ways. It can ease their worries or help them solve their problems. Working cooperatively with a supervisor to resolve a problem gives employees a sense that the supervisor and organization are interested in their welfare. This belief in turn can improve job satisfaction and motivation. The resulting improvements in productivity benefit the employee through performance rewards.

The organization benefits too. Employees who receive needed counseling are well motivated and more likely to meet performance standards. The changes in an employee's attitudes also carry over to the work of other employees. When personal problems affect one employee's work, the others suffer consequences such as working harder to make up for the problem employee's lapses. Also, being around someone with a negative attitude tends to drag down the spirits of others in the group. After counseling improves the problem employee's performance and attitude, the whole group tends to do better.

Appropriate Times to Counsel

A supervisor should counsel employees when they need help determining how to resolve a problem that is affecting their work. Sometimes an employee will approach a supervisor with a problem, such as marriage worries or concern about doing a good job. At other times, a supervisor may observe that an employee seems to have a problem when, for example, the quality of the employee's work is declining.

It is essential for supervisors to remember that they lack training to help with many kinds of problems. They are not in a position to save a marriage, resolve an employee's financial difficulties, or handle an alcoholic family member. A supervisor should help an employee solve a problem only when qualified to do so. In other cases, a supervisor should simply listen, express concern, and refer the employee to a trained professional. The human resources department may be able to suggest sources of help.

Counseling Techniques

LO12.3 ▶ Describe counseling techniques.

directive counseling
An approach to counseling in which the supervisor asks the employee questions about the specific problem; when the supervisor understands the problem, he or she suggests ways to handle it

Counseling involves one or more discussions between the supervisor and the employee. These sessions should take place where there will be privacy and freedom from interruptions. The sessions may be directive or nondirective (see Figure 12.4 on the following page).

Directive versus Nondirective Counseling

The most focused approach to counseling is **directive counseling**, in which a supervisor asks an employee questions about a specific problem. The supervisor listens

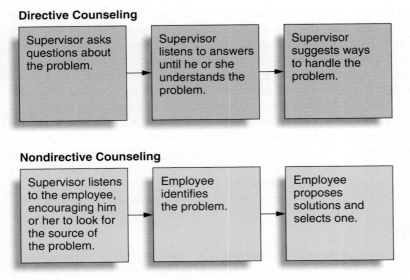

Directive Counseling

Supervisor asks questions about the problem. → Supervisor listens to answers until he or she understands the problem. → Supervisor suggests ways to handle the problem.

Nondirective Counseling

Supervisor listens to the employee, encouraging him or her to look for the source of the problem. → Employee identifies the problem. → Employee proposes solutions and selects one.

FIGURE 12.4 | Directive versus Nondirective Counseling

Both directive and nondirective counseling produce solutions, but nondirective counseling may have more lasting results since it requires the employees to be more involved in identifying and resolving the problem.

until he or she understands the source of the problem. Then the supervisor suggests ways to handle the problem.

For example, assume that Bill Wisniewski, a computer programmer, has been absent a number of times during the past month. The supervisor might ask, "Why have you been missing so many days?" Wisniewski replies, "Because my wife has been sick, and someone needs to look after my kids." The supervisor would follow up with questions about the condition of Wisniewski's wife (for example, to learn whether the problem is likely to continue), the ages and needs of their children, and so on. Then the supervisor might suggest finding alternative sources of care, perhaps referring Wisniewski to a company program designed to help with such problems.

In most cases, a supervisor and employee will receive the greatest benefit when the supervisor helps the employee develop and change instead of merely looking for a solution to a specific problem. To accomplish this, the supervisor can use nondirective counseling. With this approach, a supervisor should primarily listen, encouraging the employee to look for the source of the problem and propose possible solutions. In the preceding example, a supervisor would ask open-ended questions such as "Would you tell me more about that?" Ideally, by working out his own solution, Wisniewski would find that he has the ability to resolve many family problems without missing a lot of work.

nondirective counseling
An approach to counseling in which the supervisor primarily listens, encouraging the employee to look for the source of the problem and propose possible solutions

The Counseling Interview

The counseling interview starts with a discussion of what the problem is (see Figure 12.5). It then moves to a consideration of possible solutions and the selection of one solution to try. The interview ends with the supervisor scheduling a follow-up meeting.

The person who requested the counseling begins by describing the problem. If the employee requested help, the employee should begin. If the supervisor set up the interview because something seemed wrong, the supervisor should begin. The supervisor should focus on behavior and performance—what people do, not who they are—and encourage the employee to do the same. For example, if the employee says, "The other employees are prejudiced against me," the supervisor should ask the employee to describe what actions led to that conclusion. In addition, the supervisor should use the principles of active listening, described in Chapter 10.

Because counseling often occurs as a result of an employee's personal problems, the employee may be emotional during counseling sessions. The supervisor needs

FIGURE 12.5 | The Counseling Interview

The basic outline of a counseling interview allows time to accurately identify the problem, develop solutions, and select a viable solution. Follow-up after the interview is also key to assure success.

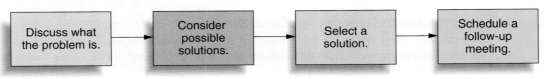

Discuss what the problem is. → Consider possible solutions. → Select a solution. → Schedule a follow-up meeting.

to be prepared for crying, angry outbursts, and other signs of emotion. He or she should be calm and reassure the employee that these signs of emotion are neither good nor bad. Of course, there are appropriate and inappropriate ways to express emotions. Suppose a salesperson in a hardware store has a 10-year-old son with behavior problems. It would not be appropriate for the salesperson to express his worry and frustration by snapping at customers.

Next, the supervisor and employee should consider ways to solve the problem. Instead of simply prescribing a solution, the supervisor usually can be more helpful by asking the employee questions that will help the employee come up with ideas. Employees are more likely to cooperate in a solution they helped develop. Asking an employee to suggest solutions can be an especially effective way to end constant whining and complaining by that employee. When the supervisor and employee agree on a particular solution, the supervisor should restate it to make sure the employee understands. (Chapter 9 provides more detailed guidelines for mutual problem solving.)

Finally, the supervisor should schedule a follow-up meeting, which should take place just after the employee begins to see some results. At the follow-up meeting, the employee and the supervisor review their plans and discuss whether the problem has been or is being resolved. For example, in the case of the salesperson in the hardware store, the supervisor might say, "I've noticed that we haven't received any more customer complaints about your service. In fact, one woman told me you went out of your way to help her." Notice that the supervisor is focusing on work performance, which the supervisor is qualified to discuss, rather than on the employee's family problems. If the employee replies, "Yes, I've been so much calmer ever since I started talking to that counselor about my son," the supervisor has a good indication that the employee is resolving the problem.

Discipline

> **discipline**
> Action taken by the supervisor to prevent employees from breaking rules

"I can't stand Marcia's surly attitude any longer!" fumed Don Koh, Marcia's supervisor. "If she doesn't cut it out, she's going to be sorry." This supervisor is eager for the employee to experience the consequences of her behavior. However, despite the anger and frustration that can be generated by supervising a problem employee, a supervisor needs to apply discipline in constructive ways. Discipline is action taken by a supervisor to prevent employees from breaking rules. In many cases, effective discipline can quickly bring about a change in an employee's behavior.

LO12.4 ▶ Discuss effective ways of administering discipline.

Administering Discipline

In administering discipline, a supervisor should distinguish between discipline and punishment. (See the Assessing Yourself quiz on pages 345–346 to help you determine the difference.) As described in Chapter 11, punishment is an unpleasant consequence given in response to undesirable behavior. Discipline, in contrast, is broader; it is a teaching process. The supervisor explains the significance and consequences of the employee's behavior and then, if necessary, lets the employee experience those consequences.

The specific ways in which a supervisor applies these steps may be dictated by company policies or the union contract, if any. Thus, a supervisor must be familiar with all applicable policies and rules. These should include respecting the rights of employees in the discipline process. Employees' rights include the following:[23]

- The right to know job expectations and the consequences of not fulfilling those expectations.
- The right to receive consistent and predictable management action in response to violations of the rules.

- The right to receive fair discipline based on facts.
- The right to question management's statement of the facts and to present a defense.
- The right to receive progressive discipline (described in the next section).
- The right to appeal a disciplinary action.

The Discipline Process

Before administering discipline in response to problem behavior, supervisors need to have a clear picture of the situation. They may observe the problem themselves, or someone may tell them about the problem. In either case, supervisors need to collect the facts before taking further action.

As soon as possible, a supervisor should meet with the employees involved and ask for each employee's version of what happened. For example, a supervisor who believes that one of his or her employees is using the office telephone for excessive personal calls should not make hasty accusations or issue a general memo stating company policy about phone use. Rather, the supervisor should ask the employee directly and in private what his or her telephone conversations were about. In getting the employee's version of a problem, a supervisor should use good listening practices and resist the temptation to get angry.

When a supervisor observes and understands the facts behind problem behavior, disciplining an employee occurs in as many as four steps: warnings, suspension, demotion, and dismissal (see Figure 12.6). This pattern of discipline is "progressive" in the sense that the steps progress from the least to the most severe action a supervisor can take. A warning is unpleasant to hear but fulfills the important purpose of informing employees about the consequences of their behavior before more punitive measures are taken. Suspension, demotion, and discharge are more upsetting to an employee because they hurt the employee in the pocketbook.

Warning

A warning may be either written or oral. Some organizations have a policy that calls for an oral warning followed by a written warning if performance does not improve. Both types of warning are designed to make sure that the employee understands the problem. A warning should contain the following information:

- What the problem behavior is.
- How the behavior affects the organization.
- How and when the employee's behavior is expected to change.
- What actions will be taken if the employee's behavior does not change.

Thus, a supervisor might say, "I have noticed that in the last two staff meetings, you have made hostile remarks. Not only have these disrupted the meetings, but they lead your co-workers to take you less seriously. I expect that you will refrain

FIGURE 12.6 | Possible Steps in the Discipline Process

This progressive pattern of discipline assures that employees are aware of the potential consequences of their behavior so that they can correct their behavior before being dismissed.

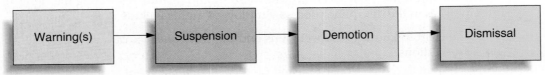

from such remarks in future meetings, or I will have to give you a suspension." As in this example, the warning should be brief and to the point.

In the case of a written warning, it is wise practice to ask the employee to sign the warning, which documents that the first step in the discipline process took place. If the employee refuses to sign the warning, even with minor changes, the supervisor should note the employee's refusal or call in someone (such as the supervisor's manager) to witness the refusal.

Suspension

suspension
Requirement that an employee not come to work for a set period of time; the employee is not paid for the time off

A **suspension** is the requirement that an employee not come to work for a set period of time, during which the employee is not paid. The length of the suspension might run from one day to one month, depending on the seriousness of the problem. Suspensions are useful when the employee has been accused of something serious, such as stealing, and the supervisor needs time to investigate.

Demotion

demotion
Transfer of an employee to a job involving less responsibility and usually lower pay

A **demotion** is the transfer of an employee to a job with less responsibility and usually lower pay. Sometimes a demotion is actually a relief for an employee, especially if the employee has been goofing off or performing poorly because the job was more than he or she could handle. In such a case, the employee might welcome returning to a job where he or she is competent. More often, however, a demotion leads to negative feelings—a punishment that continues for as long as the employee holds the lower-level job.[24]

Dismissal

dismissal
Relieving an employee of his or her job

The permanent removal of an employee from a job is called **dismissal,** termination, or discharge. The organization cannot really regard dismissal as a success because it then has to recruit, hire, and train a new employee. Nevertheless, a supervisor sometimes must dismiss an employee who commits a serious offense or who will not respond to other forms of discipline. Occasionally an employee or supervisor may decide that correcting a problem is impossible, or at least too difficult or expensive. In addition to continued failure to correct problem behavior, dismissal may occur because an employee deliberately damages the organization's property, fights on the job, or engages in dangerous practices (for example., a railroad engineer who drinks on the job).

Dismissing an employee is never easy, but it is sometimes a necessary part of the job to ensure a positive work environment for the remaining employees. At Wire One Technologies, Ric Robbins had a sales representative who continuously sacrificed teamwork for personal gain. According to Robbins, a regional vice president, that employee would visit his colleagues' offices and glance around, looking for clues to sales leads. The employee's co-workers spent so much energy protecting themselves from the unethical employee that they couldn't work effectively. Robbins had to fire the sales rep to preserve the team's morale and performance.[25]

Supervisors can only make so many efforts to resolve an employee's problematic behavior before termination is necessary.

Many organizations have policies requiring a supervisor to involve higher-level management before dismissing an employee. Supervisors should be familiar with any such policy and follow it.

In following the steps in the discipline process, a supervisor should remember that the objective is to end the problem behavior. A supervisor takes only as many steps as are necessary to bring about a change in behavior: The ultimate goal is to solve the problem without dismissing the employee.

Guidelines for Effective Discipline

When an employee is causing a problem—from tardiness to theft to lack of cooperation—the supervisor needs to act immediately. That is not always easy to do. Pointing out poor behavior and administering negative consequences are unpleasant tasks. However, by ignoring the situation, a supervisor is signaling that the problem is not serious. As a result, the problem gets worse. Seeing that the problem behavior leads to no consequences, an employee may increase it, and other employees may follow this example.

In contrast, when Kathleen R. Tibbs was an in-flight supervisor with Eastern Airlines, she faced up to the unpleasant task of disciplining an employee with unacceptable attendance. Tibbs had the employee suspended for seven days. Her action inspired the employee to address the personal problems that led to her poor attendance.

When discussing the problem with an employee, a supervisor should focus on learning about and resolving the issue at hand. This meeting is no time for name-calling

PRACTICAL ADVICE FOR SUPERVISORS

CRITICIZING CONSTRUCTIVELY

When employees engage in problem behavior, supervisors need to be able to discuss the situation in a way that leads to a solution. Generally, that includes some constructive criticism so the employee knows exactly what the supervisor is dissatisfied about. Under any circumstances, this can be a difficult task. If the employee is someone that you struggle to like on a personal level or with whom you are frustrated, this can be even more difficult. Here are some ideas for keeping your criticism constructive regardless of who the employee is or your personal feelings toward them:

- *Pretend the person is a highly-respected colleague.* When you are dealing with colleague you respect, you choose your words carefully. When you are frustrated with someone who is not performing to the level you expect, it is difficult to not come off sounding impatient or extremely critical—without the constructive part. If, however, you imagine that the person is a respected colleague you will be more concerned about how they will receive your feedback and suggestions for improvement and will, therefore, be more civil in your tone and fairer in your assessment.
- *Illustrate your point.* Anytime you have to provide feedback or criticism, it can be difficult for the other person to hear. To make the conversation easier, think of examples to illustrate the point you need to make or the situation you need to talk about before the meeting. If you can come up with "generic" examples that are not specifically or only linked to the employee you are meeting with, the employee can imagine the situation from a third person point of view which makes the message easier to hear. This leads to the employee feeling less defensive.

- *Put the employee in control.* Everyone likes to be in control of their situation, so give the employee that chance. After illustrating your point, allow the employee the opportunity to express how he or she would deal with the situation. Ask: "What would you do if you were me?" The employee can then find their own solution to a challenging situation and will likely be more motivated to act on that solution.

- *Give the employee a chance.* After having taken the time to identify the issue and develop a solution, the employee needs a chance to make the changes that plan requires. You can also ask the employee to identify and resolve other issues like the one being discussed going forward. This gives the employee ownership of resolving the problem and of their career.

Source: Based on Jennifer Winter, "Giving Constructive Criticism—That Won't Make Anyone Cringe," *Forbes*, June 5, 2012, http://www.forbes.com/sites/dailymuse/2012/06/05/giving-constructive-criticism-that-wont-make-anyone-cringe/, accessed May 6, 2014.

1. Act immediately.

2. Focus on solving the problem at hand.

3. Keep emotions in check.

4. Administer discipline in private.

5. Be consistent.

FIGURE 12.7 | Guidelines for Effective Discipline
The guidelines for effective discipline seem logical but may take practice to follow in the workplace.

or dredging up instances of past misbehavior. Nor is it generally useful for a supervisor to dwell on how patient or compassionate he or she has been. Instead, a supervisor should listen until he or she understands the problem and then begin discussing how to correct it in the future. Talking about behaviors instead of personalities helps the employee understand what is expected. For ideas on how to discuss problem behavior constructively, see the "Practical Advice for Supervisors" feature.

A supervisor should keep emotions in check. Although it is appropriate to convey sincere concern about the problem, a supervisor's other feelings are largely irrelevant and can even stand in the way of a constructive discussion. When an employee breaks the rules or seems unwilling to do a good job, it is only natural for a supervisor to feel angry. The supervisor should get control over this anger before confronting the employee in order to be objective rather than hostile. Being calm and relaxed when administering discipline tells an employee that the supervisor is confident of what he or she is doing.

Discipline should be a private matter. The supervisor should not humiliate an employee by reprimanding the employee in front of other employees. Humiliation only breeds resentment and may actually increase problem behavior in the future.

A supervisor also should be consistent in administering discipline. One way to do this is to follow the four steps of the discipline process outlined previously. Also, a supervisor should respond to *all* instances of misbehavior rather than, for example, ignore a long-standing employee's misdeeds while punishing a newcomer. At the same time, the seriousness of the response should be related to the seriousness of the problem. The policy for workplace violence or drug use would likely be cause for immediate dismissal because of the danger involved. Likewise, Stater Bros. Markets, a grocery store chain, has a policy of immediately dismissing any employee who engages in theft or sells liquor to a minor lacking proper identification.[26] The response to an occasion of tardiness would be less severe. The point is to have and follow a consistent policy for serious and minor problems. Even better, consistency should extend to praising and rewarding positive performance. The guidelines for effective discipline are summarized in Figure 12.7.

Documentation of Disciplinary Action

Employees who receive discipline sometimes respond by filing a grievance or suing the employer. To be able to justify his or her actions, a supervisor must have a record of the disciplinary actions taken and the basis for the discipline. These records may be needed to show that the actions were not discriminatory or against company policy. As noted previously, one type of disciplinary record is a signed copy of any written warning. In addition, other disciplinary actions should be recorded in the employee's personnel file, as directed by the human resources department.

Supervisors often use past performance appraisals as documentation of the need for disciplinary action. However, this approach often backfires because many supervisors are reluctant to give negative evaluations. A performance appraisal that has an employee's work recorded as average, adequate, or meeting only minimal standards does not support dismissal of that employee. This is why it is essential for the supervisor to give accurate performance appraisals (see Chapter 17).

Documentation is especially important when a supervisor must terminate an employee. Because the experience is so emotional, some former employees respond with a lawsuit. The employee's file should show the steps the supervisor took leading up to the termination and a record of the specific behaviors that led the supervisor to dismiss the employee.

Careful documentation also is essential for organizations, which have many disciplinary rules and policies aimed at protecting employees from arbitrary or politically based actions by supervisors. These rules may have the unintended consequence of protecting problem employees from well-deserved discipline, unless the supervisor can fully document the problem behavior, preferably with witnesses. An example of just how challenging this process can be involves alleged abuses of residents at the Communities of Oakwood, a state-run home for mentally disabled persons. Of 15 employees charged with abuse in recent years, about half had previously received reprimands or suspensions for various misdeeds as severe as being intoxicated at work and changing patients' prescriptions. Administrators at Oakwood must win the approval of a personnel board before they can dismiss such employees. This requirement protects the employees from being fired based on politics, but it also places a burden on supervisors to provide specific, supportable documentation of any problem behavior.[27]

Documentation of employee counseling and discipline provides the organization with information it can use to ensure employees are treated fairly. Such documentation also helps insulate the organization from the threat of employment liability, or claims of harm. For example, upset employees may sometimes pursue legal recourse, or lawsuits, as a response against perceived injustice or equity. By documenting exchanges between management and employees, organizations can defend themselves against such claims by showing how employees were treated fairly.

LO12.5 ▶ Describe the principles of positive discipline and self-discipline.

positive discipline
Discipline designed to prevent problem behavior from beginning

Positive Discipline

Ideally, discipline should not only end problem behavior, it should also prevent problems from occurring. Discipline designed to prevent problem behavior from beginning is known as **positive discipline**, or preventive discipline. An important part of positive discipline is making sure employees know and understand the rules they must follow. A supervisor also should explain the consequences of violating rules. For example, a production supervisor might explain that company policy calls for the dismissal of any employee caught operating machinery while under the influence of drugs or alcohol.

A supervisor also can administer positive discipline by working to create the conditions under which employees are least likely to cause problems. Employees may engage in problem behavior when they feel frustrated. For example, if the organization sets a sales quota higher than salespeople think they can achieve, they may give up and goof off instead of trying their best. If computer operators complain that they need more frequent rest breaks to prevent health problems, and no changes are made, they may adopt a negative attitude toward the company's apparent lack of concern for their well-being. This reaction is related to another source of problem behavior: feeling as if one is not an important part of the organization. If employees conclude that they and management are at odds, some may turn their energy toward seeing what they can get away with.

To combat such problems, a supervisor needs to be aware of and responsive to employees' needs and ideas. A supervisor should encourage upward communication, promote teamwork, and encourage employees to participate in decision making and problem solving. The effective use of motivation techniques also helps prevent the frustration and alienation that can lead to problem behavior. Finally, through good hiring and training practices, a supervisor can help ensure that employee values, interests, and abilities are a good match with the job and the organization.

decision-making leave
A day off during which a problem employee is supposed to decide whether to return to work and meet standards or to stay away for good

At some companies, positive discipline includes a day off with pay for employees who fail to respond to efforts to educate them about following the rules and meeting performance standards. During this suspension, known as a **decision-making leave**, the employees are supposed to decide whether to return to work and meet standards or to stay away for good. If the employees choose to come back, they work with a supervisor to develop objectives and action plans for improvement.

FIGURE 12.8 | Improving Performance

If a supervisor is effective, employees are engaged, highly motivated, and performing to the best of their abilities.

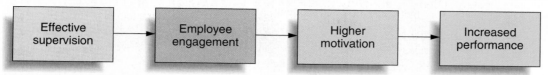

Finally, a supervisor should not only punish problem behavior but also reward desirable kinds of behavior, such as contributing to the department's performance. For example, a supervisor should recognize those who make suggestions for improvements or resolve sticky problems. (See Chapter 11 for specific ideas.)

Self-Discipline

An effective program of positive discipline results in self-discipline, in which employees voluntarily follow the rules and try to meet performance standards. Most people get satisfaction from doing a job well, so self-discipline should result when employees understand what is expected. Supervisors can help encourage self-discipline by communicating not only the rules and performance standards but also the reasons for those rules and standards.

In an ideal setting, an effective supervisor can engage employees to the point that they are self-disciplined, motivated, and performing at a high level, as shown in Figure 12.8.

Also keep in mind, a supervisor who takes long lunch breaks or spends hours chatting with friends on the telephone or the Internet is in no position to insist that employees put in a full workday. If supervisors expect employees to follow the rules, they must set a good example by exercising self-discipline.

---

connect SELF-ASSESSMENT 12.1

Can You Distinguish Between Discipline and Punishment

In your job as a supervisor, you will need to apply discipline at some time. Ignoring problems because you do not want to discipline a worker is not effective supervisory behavior. There is a difference, though, between positive discipline and punishment. This assessment will help you differentiate between them.

Troubled Employees

So far, this chapter has emphasized problems that can be solved by giving employees more information or helping them change their behavior. However, some employees have problems that make them unable to respond to a simple process of discipline or counseling. That may be the case when one employee routinely bullies others. In addition to bullies, troubled employees may include people who are substance abusers or have psychological problems.

LO12.6 ▶ Explain how supervisors can detect and confront troubled employees.

Detection of the Troubled Employee

The first signs that a supervisor has a troubled employee tend to be the kinds of discipline problems described previously in this chapter. A supervisor may notice that an employee is frequently late or that the quality of an employee's work has been slipping. If disciplinary action or counseling seems ineffective in resolving the problem, a supervisor may have a troubled employee.

TABLE 12.1 | Possible Signs of Alcohol or Drug Use

Slurred speech.
Clumsy movements and increased accidents.
Personality changes.
Decreased ability to work as part of a team.
Smell of alcohol on the employee's breath.
Growing carelessness about personal appearance and the details of the job.
Increase in absenteeism or tardiness, along with unbelievable excuses.
Daydreaming.
Leaving the work area; making frequent visits to the restroom.
Violence in the workplace.

In the case of substance abuse, the supervisor might notice signs that the employee has been using alcohol or drugs. The examples listed in Table 12.1 are among the most common behavioral signs. (Note that these are only hints that the employee might be using drugs or alcohol. There may be other explanations for these behaviors.) Perhaps a supervisor will even find the employee in possession of drugs or alcohol. When an employee is suspected of drug use, some organizations have a policy of confirming the suspicion through the use of drug testing.

Because there may be another explanation for symptoms that look like the effects of using alcohol or illicit drugs (for example, taking prescription medications), a supervisor should avoid making accusations about what he or she believes is going on. Thus, a supervisor should not say, "I see you've been drinking on the job." Instead, the supervisor should focus on job performance: "I see something is hurting the quality of your work this week. Let's talk about what the problem is and how to solve it."

Confrontation of the Troubled Employee

Ignoring a problem does not make it go away. Thus, hoping an alcoholic employee will seek help rarely works. It only helps the employee maintain the illusion that the substance abuse is not causing significant problems. After all, if the boss does not complain, how bad can the work be? Therefore, when a supervisor suspects a problem, he or she needs to confront the employee.

The first step is to document the problem. A supervisor should keep notes of instances in which an employee's performance is not acceptable. When collecting this information, a supervisor should be sure to keep notes on all employees whose performance is slipping, not just the one person targeted.

When a supervisor has gathered enough supporting evidence, he or she should confront the employee. The supervisor should go over the employee's performance, describing the evidence of a problem. Then the supervisor should refer the employee to a source of counseling or other help by saying something like, "I think something is troubling you, and I want you to see an employee assistance counselor." Finally, the supervisor should explain the consequences of not changing. In some cases, accepting help may be a requirement for keeping the job. Thus, the supervisor might say, "There's no shame in getting help, and we'll keep it private. But you

After a supervisor has organized the necessary materials and evidence, he or she should sit down with the employee to discuss the issues.

are responsible for doing your job safely and up to standards. If you don't, I'll have to follow our disciplinary procedures for unacceptable performance." Experts agree that this type of warning from a supervisor can be one of the most effective ways to motivate a substance-abusing employee to get help.

During the confrontation, the employee may become angry or defensive. This reaction is common in such situations, so the supervisor should not take it personally or overreact. The employee also may come up with excuses that sound particularly sad and compelling. In any case, the supervisor must continue to focus on the employee's behavior on the job and the way the employee's behavior affects the organization. No matter how outraged the employee or how impressive or creative the excuse, the employee's behavior must improve.

Some caution is advisable, however. Supervisors should avoid taking on the role of doctor, counselor, or police officer. That means the supervisor must not try to diagnose what may be medical or psychological problems. Supervisors also should protect their employees' privacy and give employees a fair chance to respond to any complaints. Also, if the workplace is governed by a union contract, the supervisor must follow its requirements. By focusing on objective measures of job requirements and performance, the supervisor can avoid falling into traps such as pitying employees, covering up for them, or allowing the workplace to become unfair or unsafe because the supervisor is reluctant to confront problems.[28]

LO12.7 ▶ Specify how supervisors can direct troubled employees in getting help and then follow up on the recovery efforts.

Aid in and Evaluation of Recovery

Most organizations have developed procedures for providing help to troubled employees. When a supervisor believes that problems are occurring because an employee is troubled, the organization's procedures need to be investigated. In most cases, the place to start is with the human resources department.

The type of treatment program tends to depend on the size of the organization. Many small organizations refer troubled employees to a counseling service. Another policy is simply to tell the employee to get help or lose the job. A supervisor should be careful in pursuing the latter approach. If possible, the ultimate objective should be the employee's rehabilitation, not dismissal. Not only is rehabilitation more compassionate, but it also tends to be less costly than hiring and training a new employee, and it is less likely to violate laws prohibiting employment discrimination.

employee assistance program (EAP)
A company-based program for providing counseling and related help to employees whose personal problems are affecting their performance

Other organizations, especially large ones, offer an **employee assistance program (EAP).** An EAP is a company-based program for providing counseling and related help to employees whose personal problems affect their performance.[29] It may be simply a referral service, or it may be fully staffed with social workers, psychologists, nurses, career counselors, financial advisers, and other professionals. These programs are voluntary (employees do not have to participate unless they want to)

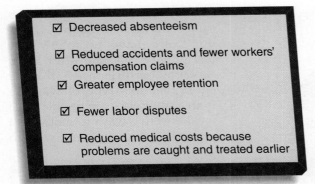

☑ Decreased absenteeism

☑ Reduced accidents and fewer workers' compensation claims

☑ Greater employee retention

☑ Fewer labor disputes

☑ Reduced medical costs because problems are caught and treated earlier

FIGURE 12.9 | Benefits of an Employee Assistance Program

Employee assistance programs benefit both the employees and the employers.

Source: Office of Disability Employment Policy, U.S. Department of Labor, "Employee Assistance Programs for a New Generation of Employees," January 2009, http://www.dol.gov/odep/documents/employeeassistance.pdf, accessed May 5, 2014.

and confidential (participation is a private matter). Services of EAPs include recovery from substance abuse, financial and career counseling, referrals for child care and elder care, AIDS education and counseling, and helping employees work with others of a different cultural background. Figure 12.9 identifies benefits that organizations have experienced as a result of using EAPs. A supervisor who is concerned about troubled employees might investigate such benefits and encourage the organization to consider offering an EAP. Some employees would be unlikely to seek out help without the push of a referral from their supervisor.[30]

The reason for providing EAPs and other sources of counseling is to improve the employee's performance. It is up to the supervisor to see that the treatment plan is producing the desired results at the workplace. Any signs of improvement not related to performance (for example, abstinence from alcohol) are irrelevant from the supervisor's point of view.

Sources of Support

LO12.8 ▶ Discuss the role of the supervisor's manager and the human resources department in helping the supervisor with problem employees.

Supervising problem employees is a delicate matter. Supervisors must be careful to motivate and correct rather than to generate hostility and resentment. At the same time, supervisors must be careful to follow organizational procedures, union requirements, and laws regarding fair employment practices. Fortunately, supervisors can get support from their superiors, the organization's human resources department, and outside experts.

When an employee fails to respond to initial counseling attempts, a supervisor should try discussing the problem with his or her manager. The manager may be able to offer insights into how to handle the problem. In addition, some steps, such as suspension or dismissal, may require that the supervisor get authorization from a higher-level manager.

It is also wise to consult with the human resources department, which has information about company policies on discipline and how to document it. Human resources personnel can advise a supervisor on how to proceed without breaking laws, violating a contract with the union, or putting the organization at risk in case of a lawsuit. In addition, personnel specialists have expertise that can make them good sources of ideas on what to say or what corrective measures to propose. Sometimes just talking about a strategy helps a supervisor to think of new ways to approach the problem.

In small organizations with no human resource staff, a supervisor and his or her manager may agree that the problem requires the help of outside experts. They may contract with a consultant, a labor attorney, or a human relations specialist who provides services on a temporary basis. The fee paid to such an expert may seem high but can be far less than the cost of defending a wrongful-termination lawsuit. The local office of the Small Business Administration (SBA) also may be able to provide help. The SBA assistance may include a referral to an executive in one of its programs for providing small businesses with free advice.

In summary, when an employee's problems or problem behavior threatens to disrupt the workplace, a supervisor should not despair. The effective use of counseling and discipline can solve many of these problems. When they do not, a variety of people inside and outside the organization stand ready to help.

Skills Module

PART ONE: CONCEPTS

Summary

12.1 Identify common types of problem behavior among employees.

The problems that supervisors most often encounter are absenteeism and tardiness, insubordination and uncooperativeness, alcohol and drug abuse, workplace violence, and employee theft of money, goods, time, and information.

12.2 Explain why and when supervisors should counsel employees.

Counseling helps employees solve their problems, which enables them to perform better at work. It therefore improves productivity as well as the attitudes and job satisfaction of employees. Supervisors should counsel employees when they need help determining how to resolve a problem that is affecting their work. When an employee has a problem with which the supervisor is unqualified to help, the supervisor should refer the employee to a professional.

12.3 Describe counseling techniques.

Counseling consists of one or more discussions between the supervisor and the employee. These discussions may involve directive counseling, in which the supervisor asks the employee questions to identify the problem and then suggests solutions. Or the discussions may be nondirective, with the supervisor primarily listening and encouraging the employee to look for the source of the problem and identify possible solutions. At the beginning of the interview, the person who identified the problem describes it, focusing on behavior and performance. Next, the supervisor and employee consider ways to solve the problem. Finally, the supervisor schedules a follow-up meeting to review the planned solution and determine whether the problem is being resolved.

12.4 Discuss effective ways of administering discipline.

After collecting the facts of the situation, the supervisor should meet with the employee or employees involved and ask for their version of what has happened. The supervisor should use good listening techniques. Then the supervisor issues a warning. If necessary, the supervisor lets the employee experience the consequences of unsatisfactory behavior through suspension, demotion, and ultimately dismissal. The supervisor takes as many steps as are necessary to resolve the problem behavior. The supervisor should administer discipline promptly, privately, impartially, and unemotionally. The supervisor should document all disciplinary actions.

12.5 Describe the principles of positive discipline and self-discipline.

Positive discipline focuses on preventing problem behavior from ever beginning. It can include making sure employees know and understand the rules, creating conditions under which employees are least likely to cause problems, using decision-making leaves when problems occur, and rewarding desirable behavior. Effective positive discipline results in self-discipline among employees; that is, employees voluntarily follow the rules and try to meet performance standards. Supervisors who expect self-discipline from their employees must practice it themselves.

12.6 Explain how supervisors can detect and confront troubled employees.

The supervisor can look for discipline problems and investigate whether they are symptoms of personal problems. With substance abuse, the supervisor might notice signs that the employee is using alcohol or drugs. When the supervisor suspects that an employee is troubled, he or she should document the problem and then meet with the employee and describe the evidence of a problem, focusing on the employee's performance at work. The supervisor should refer the employee to a source of help and explain the consequences of not getting help. The supervisor should be careful not to overreact to an employee's emotional response or creative excuses.

12.7 Specify how supervisors can direct troubled employees in getting help and then follow up on the recovery efforts.

Supervisors should learn their organization's procedures for helping troubled employees and then follow those procedures. This may involve referring employees to help outside the organization or to the organization's employee assistance program. The supervisor is responsible for seeing that the employee's performance is improving, not for evaluating evidence of improvement unrelated to work.

12.8 Discuss the role of the supervisor's manager and the human resources department in helping the supervisor with problem employees.

The supervisor's manager and the human resources department can help the supervisor handle problem employees in ways that follow organizational guidelines, legal requirements, or union contracts.

A supervisor should discuss the problem with his or her manager and the human resources department to get information about the organization's policies for handling problem employees and suggestions for addressing the specific problem. The organization may offer an employee assistance program whose ultimate goal is the employee's rehabilitation.

Key Terms

insubordination, *p. 324*
counseling, *p. 329*
directive
counseling, *p. 329*
nondirective
counseling, *p. 330*

discipline, *p. 331*
suspension, *p. 333*
demotion, *p. 333*
dismissal, *p. 333*
positive
discipline, *p. 336*

decision-making
leave, *p. 336*
employee assistance
program (EAP), *p. 339*

Review and Discussion Questions

1. Dennis McCutcheon supervises the employees who work in the building supplies department of a large discount hardware store. One of his employees, Kelly Sims, has been late to work every Tuesday and Thursday for the last three weeks. Sometimes she disappears for more than an hour at lunch. Although Sims had a positive attitude when she started the job, recently McCutcheon has overheard her complaining to co-workers and being less than friendly to customers. Using the questions listed in the section "Problems Requiring Special Action" (pp. 322–328), how might he uncover the true source of Sims's performance problem?

2. What is the difference between directive and nondirective counseling? Give an example of each in the form of a brief dialogue.

3. An employee explains to her supervisor that her performance has been slipping because she has been distracted and frightened by threats from her former husband.

   a. Should the supervisor counsel the employee about her job performance? Explain.

   b. Should the supervisor counsel the employee about the threats from her former husband? Explain.

4. While counseling an employee, a supervisor made the following statements. What is wrong with each statement? What would be a better alternative for each?

   a. "Your laziness is becoming a real problem."

   b. "Knock off the shouting! The way your performance has been lately, you have no right to be angry."

   c. "What you need to do is to take this job more seriously. Just focus on getting your work done, and then we won't have a problem."

5. What are the steps in the discipline process? In what kinds of situations would a supervisor take all these steps?

6. What additional type of information should be included in the following warning to an employee?

   "I noticed that you returned late from lunch yesterday and three days last week. This upsets the other employees because they get back promptly in order to give others a chance to take their breaks. Beginning tomorrow, I expect you to be back on time."

7. Describe four guidelines for disciplining employees effectively.

8. Jackie Weissman supervises a group of technicians in a laboratory that conducts medical tests. It is extremely important that the technicians follow lab procedures to obtain accurate test results. What steps can Weissman take to apply positive discipline with her group?

9. a. What are some signs that an employee has been abusing alcohol or drugs?

b. Why should a supervisor avoid making a statement such as, "You've been coming to work high lately"?

10. What steps should a supervisor take in confronting an apparently troubled employee?

11. Rick Mayhew's nine-year-old son was recently diagnosed with a chronic illness that is difficult and expensive to treat. In addition, Mayhew's elderly mother-in-law is going to be moving in to live with his family. His supervisor has noticed that his performance has been suffering lately; he is often late to work, leaves early, and has trouble concentrating on his work. The supervisor does not want to lose Mayhew as an employee. Would an employee assistance program help Rick? Why or why not?

12. Tom Chandra has a problem with one of the production workers he supervises. The worker has been ignoring instructions about the new procedures for operating a lathe, preferring instead to follow the old procedures. What kind of help can Chandra get from his manager and the human resources department in handling this problem?

Notes

1. Bob Moulesong, "Unscheduled Absences: Find Effective Ways to Manage Employees' Attendance," *Missoulian*, July 8, 2012, http://missoulian.com/business/local/unscheduled-absences-find-effective-ways-to-manage-employees-attendance/article_1d53353c-ca02-11e1-901c-0019bb2963f4.html, accessed May 5, 2014.

2. For a recent description of factors associated with absenteeism, see J. MacGregor, J. Cunningham, and N. Caverley, 2008, "Factors in absenteeism and presenteeism: Life events and health events," *Management Research New*s, 31, p. 607.

3. "Strategies That Can Help You Deal with Excessive Absences," *HR Focus*, December 2003, downloaded from Business & Company Resource Center, http://galenet.galegroup.com.

4. Barbara Nefer, "How to Deal with Verbal Manipulators," *Supervision*, June 2008, downloaded from Business & Company Resource Center, http://galenet.galegroup.com.

5. Michele Marchetti, "When Salespeople Struggle," *Sales & Marketing Management*, April 2006, downloaded from InfoTrac, http://web4.infotrac.galegroup.com.

6. Judy Swartley, "Coming Clean," *EC&M, Electrical Construction & Maintenance*, April 1, 2006, http://ecmweb.com/archive/coming-clean, accessed May 4, 2014.

7. Ibid.; "2012 National Survey on Drug Use and Health: Summary of National Findings and Detailed Tables," Substance Abuse and Mental Health Services Administration, http://www.samhsa.gov/data/NSDUH/2012SummNatFindDetTables/Index.aspx, accessed May 5, 2014; "Alcohol and Other Substance Abuse: Prevalence, Cost and Impact on Productivity," *Employee Benefit News*, September 1, 2004, downloaded from Business & Company Resource Center, http://galenet.galegroup.com.

8. Swartley, "Coming Clean."

9. Securitas Security Services USA, "Top Security Threats and Management Issues Facing Corporate America," 2012, http://www.securitasinc.com/Global/United States/2012 Top Security Threats.pdf, accessed May 4, 2014.

10. Bureau of Labor Statistics, "National Census of Fatal Occupational Injuries in 2012," news release, August 22, 2013, www.bls.govnews.release/pdf/cfoi.pdf, accessed May 4, 2014. For more information about the legal issues associated with workplace violence, see R. Paetzold, A. O'Leary-Kelly, and R. Griffin, 2007, "Workplace violence, employer liability, and implications for organizational research," *Journal of Management Inquiry*, 16, p. 362.

11. Jennifer L. Parent, "Preventing Disruptive Behavior in the Workplace," *New Hampshire Business Review*, November 7, 2008; and Diane Stafford, "Head Off Flashpoints Where Stressed Workers Can Explode," *Kansas City Star*, October 7, 2008, both downloaded from Business & Company Resource Center, http://galenet.galegroup.com.

12. Jared Shelly, "Violently Ill," *Human Resource Executive*, September 1, 2008, http://www.hreonline.com/HRE/view/story.jhtml?id=123894582, accessed May 5, 2014.

13. Ibid.; and "Blue Shield Against Violence," Blue Shield of California Foundation, www.blueshieldcafoundation.org/programs/program-area/blue-shield-against-violence, accessed May 5, 2014.

14. Parent, "Preventing Disruptive Behavior in the Workplace"; Shelly, "Violently Ill"; and Brian Haas, "Watch Out for Warning Signs of Workplace Violence," *Sun Sentinel (Fort Lauderdale, Fla.)*, October 11, 2008, downloaded from Business & Company Resource Center, http://galenet.galegroup.com.

15. Center for the Study of Traumatic Stress, "Recovery in the Aftermath of Workplace Violence: Guidance for Supervisors," fact sheet, Uniformed Services University of the Health Sciences, http://www.cstsonline.org/wp-content/resources/CSTS_aftermath_workplace_violence_supervisors.pdf, accessed May 5, 2014.

16. Richard C. Hollinger, "Academic Viewpoint: National Retail Security Survey Executive Summary," *LP Magazine*, December 1, 2011, http://www.lpportal.com/academic-viewpoint/item/2966-2012-nrss-executive-summary.html, accessed May 5, 2014.

17. Sarah E. Needleman, "Business Owners Get Burned by Sticky Fingers," *The Wall Street Journal*, March 11, 2010, http://online.wsj.com/news/articles/SB10001424052748703862704575099661793568310, accessed May 5, 2014.

18. Joan Goodchild, "Not Safe for Work: What's acceptable computer use in today's office?," *CSO*, June 16, 2010, http://www.csoonline.com/article/2125247/compliance/not-safe-for-work–what-s-acceptable-computer-use-in-today-s-office-.html, accessed May 5, 2014.

19. Caroline Wilbert, "Coke Employee Faces Charges of Wire Fraud, Stealing Trade Secrets," *Atlanta Journal-Constitution*, July 6, 2006, downloaded from Business & Company Resource Center, http://galenet.galegroup.com; David Gulliver, "Health Care Firm Loses Data," *Sarasota Herald Tribune*, August 17, 2006, http://www.heraldtribune.com/article/20060817/BUSINESS/608170745, accessed May 5, 2014.

20. Karen Krebsbach, "The Enemy Within," American Banker: Bank Technology News, June 1, 2004, http://www.americanbanker.com/btn/17_6/-223091-1.html, accessed May 5, 2014.

21. For information on factors associated with employee theft, see L. McClurg and D. Butler, 2006, "Workplace theft: A proposed model and research agenda," *Southern Business Review*, 31, p. 25.

22. Dylan Love, "13 People Who Got Fired For Tweeting," Business Insider, May 16, 2011, http://www.businessinsider.com/twitter-fired-2011-5?op=1, accessed May 6, 2014.

23. List of rights provided by Corinne R. Livesay, Bryan College, Chattanooga, TN.

24. For more information on the effects of demotion, see C. Belzil and M. Bognanno, 2008, "Promotions, demotions, halo effects, and the earnings dynamics of American executives," *Journal of Labor Economics*, 26, p. 287.

25. Christopher Stewart, "Desperate Measures," *Sales & Marketing Management*, September 2003, downloaded from InfoTrac, http://web5.infotrac.galegroup.com.

26. Rick McLaughlin, "More Than Punishment Involved in Correcting Employee's Poor Performance," *Knight Ridder/Tribune Business News*, August 22, 2003, downloaded from Business & Company Resource Center, http://galenet.galegroup.com.

27. Beth Musgrave, "Some Workers Had Past Problems: Seven Charged Had Been Disciplined Before," *Lexington Herald-Leader*, July 21, 2006, downloaded from Business & Company Resource Center, http://galenet.galegroup.com.

28. U.S. Department of Labor, "Drug-Free Workplace Advisor: Supervisor Training," eLaws Drug-Free Workplace Advisor, www.dol.gov/elaws/asp/drugfree/supervisor/screen45.asp, accessed May 5, 2014.

29. For a recent review of the effectiveness of EAP's, see K. Elliott and K. Shelley, 2005, "Impact of employee assistance programs on substance abusers and workplace safety," *Journal of Employment Counseling*, 42, p. 125.

30. See Tamara Cagney, "Why Don't Supervisors Refer?" *Journal of Employee Assistance*, January–March 2006, downloaded from Business & Company Resource Center, http://galenet.galegroup.com.

PART TWO: SKILL-BUILDING

Meeting the Challenge

Review "A Supervision Challenge" on page 321, to prepare for your group work. Together, list all of the disciplinary actions administered. Which do you think were communicated effectively? Why or why not? How would you confront a problem employee?

Next, discuss what you, as supervisors, would do first after identifying an employee who could benefit from counseling. How might you help with and evaluate the employee's progress?

Problem-Solving Case: Suspensions of Lexington, Kentucky, Police Officers

A police officer in Lexington, Kentucky, was troubled by content some other officers had posted on the MySpace.com networking Web site. These officers discussed their work, including arrests they had made. Their postings included put-downs such as slurs about gays and mentally disabled people and comments that they worked for Lexington's "snobby people" and the "Lexington Fayette Urban Communist [instead of County] Government." Photos on these officers' MySpace pages showed them in uniform.

The officer who was disturbed by the content reported the sites to a supervisor. The supervisor pursued the complaints, and the police department sought guidance from Urban County's law department, so that the officers' First Amendment rights to free speech would be respected. A board of police and law officials met privately to review the officers' conduct and recommend appropriate discipline. The board recommended to Lexington's police chief, Anthony Beatty, that five officers be charged with conduct unbecoming an officer, be suspended for 80 hours without pay, and receive additional sensitivity training beyond the training routinely given to all Lexington's police officers. Police Chief Beatty accepted the recommendations and presented the plan for discipline to each of the officers.

The officers accepted their discipline. After completing their suspension, they were to return to full-duty status. Beatty told a reporter, "In my discussions [with the officers] we certainly have talked about getting this behind us, moving on and making us an even better agency and enhancing our relationship with the community that we serve. And all of the officers are committed to doing just that and are very remorseful for what happened."

1. Was it appropriate for the police department to discipline the officers for behavior that took place outside their jobs? Why or why not?

2. If you had been the supervisor who received the complaint about the officers' MySpace postings, how would you have reacted? Whom would you talk to, and what would you ask?

3. Overall, as described here, does this case provide an example of effective discipline? Can you suggest a few ways a police department supervisor could add to the effectiveness of the discipline in this situation? (Keep in mind that government agencies, such as this police department, often have to follow strict procedures for documentation and decision making.)

Sources: Cassondra Kirby and Michelle Ku, "Two Officers Suspended for MySpace Postings: City Council Accepts Recommendation," *Lexington Herald-Leader*, June 23, 2006; Cassondra Kirby, "Three Police Officers Suspended for Web Postings," *Lexington Herald-Leader*, July 7, 2006, both downloaded from Business & Company Resource Center, http://galenet.galegroup.com.

Assessing Yourself

Can You Distinguish between Discipline and Punishment?

Write True or False on the line before each of the following statements.

_____ 1. If an employee failed to do something I requested, I would immediately dock his or her pay.

_____ 2. If I noticed that an employee was leaving work early on a regular basis, I would revoke his or her lunch privileges.

_____ 3. If I saw two employees arguing, I would ask each separately for his or her version of the story.

_____ 4. If I had to issue a warning to an employee, I would make certain that he or she understood exactly what behavior the warning referred to.

_____ 5. If an employee insults me personally, I will insult the employee in return, so that he or she understands how I feel.

_____ 6. No matter how angry I feel inside at an employee, I will not act hostilely.

_____ 7. If an employee is doing poorly, I will note that in the performance appraisal.

_____ 8. If an employee were late to work the day of the company picnic, I would force him or her to stay on the job rather than leave early with everyone else to attend the picnic.

_____ 9. If I smelled alcohol on the breath of an employee after lunch, I would immediately fire the person.

_____ 10. If I caught an employee violating a company policy, I would immediately discuss the behavior and its consequences with the person.

Scoring True responses to statements 1, 2, 5, 8, and 9 illustrate punishment; True responses to statements 3, 4, 6, 7, and 10 illustrate discipline.

Pause and Reflect

1. For statements 1, 2, 5, 8, and 9, try to think of a way to use positive discipline in place of punishment to prevent or correct the problem behavior.

2. Is punishment ever necessary or desirable in the workplace? If so, when might it be appropriate? If not, why not?

3. Can you think of a work situation in which you experienced punishment? If so, did it benefit you (for example, by teaching you a valuable lesson)?

Class Skills Exercise

Evaluating Disciplinary Action

The postal service has adopted a disciplinary code that substitutes a letter of reprimand for the 7- to 14-day suspension without pay that repeated infractions once drew. As an extreme penalty, workers may be given one payless "day of reflection."

The post office feels the new policy treats "adults like adults." But the president of the National Rural Letter Carriers Association fears employees may see the new discipline as a mere "slap on the wrist."

Debate these two views.

Source: "World Week," *The Wall Street Journal*, November 3, 1998, p. 1.

Building Supervision Skills

Handling Performance Problems

This is a role-playing exercise. One class member volunteers to take on the role of supervisor. Another classmate volunteers to be the problem employee. The scenario:

> Chris Johnson has been a teller in the main branch of a bank for five years. Lately, Chris has been making a lot of mistakes. Chris often counts out money wrong and has had to redo many receipts that contain errors. Customers have begun complaining about the mistakes Chris makes and the detached, distracted manner in which Chris provides service. But at Chris's most recent performance appraisal, just two months ago, Chris's overall rating was excellent, leading to a generous wage increase. Chris's supervisor, Pat Smith, must decide how to respond to the decline in Chris's performance.

Before the role-play begins, the class discusses what the supervisor should do. Based on the information given, should Pat use counseling, discipline, both, or neither? Once the class agrees on a general strategy, the two volunteers act it out.

Then the class discusses what happened:

- Did the supervisor do a good job of applying the techniques selected? What did the supervisor do well? What could the supervisor have done better?
- Did the employee and supervisor arrive at a workable solution? Explain.
- How can the supervisor follow up to see whether the employee is improving?

chapter thirteen | Managing Time and Stress

learning objectives

After you have studied this chapter, you should be able to:

13.1 Discuss how supervisors can evaluate their use of time.

13.2 Describe ways to plan the use of time.

13.3 Identify some time wasters and how to control them.

13.4 List factors that contribute to stress among employees.

13.5 Summarize consequences of stress.

13.6 Explain how supervisors can manage their own stress.

13.7 Identify ways organizations, including supervisors, can help employees manage stress.

A Supervision Challenge

OH NO!

Connie Larson was stressed—the jittery stomach, trembling fingers, what-am-I-going-to-do kind of stress—every day. Yet, despite the stress, Connie Larson went to work every day, appearing pleasant to customers and supportive to her sales team. This was a part of her responsibility as supervisor.

The stress came from the high sales goals set by her employer, White House Black Market. As a supervisor, Larson was in charge of tracking sales and ensuring that sales associates met their sales goals. These goals were set by the company, not the sales associate or the supervisor. Intensifying the pressure was the fact that the company was constantly increasing sales goals and the pressure to meet those goals. Instead of two items per sale, the goal became three items per sale. Instead of a small bonus for a $300 sale, a very small bonus was awarded for a sale of at least $400. This is not uncommon in the retail industry; sales associates are generally given a commission on sales only if they exceed the previous year's sales. If they do not exceed last year's sales, they are paid only minimum wage. All of this, however, added up to stress. Stress for the sales associates and stress for Larson, their supervisor. Furthermore, as a supervisor, Larson was expected to stifle her stress and present herself as being always confident and level-headed.

To enforce the company's sales goals, Larson tracked sales, encouraged competition, and offered incentives. For the sales associates, she created bar charts that were updated after each sale to show progress toward sales goals. The charts were posted in the employees' area to foster competition among the sales associates. For incentives, she bought Starbucks gift cards for the sales associate with the most sales. Even these small rewards encouraged sales associates to perform better.

To help associates meet their sales goals, Larson conducted training and worked with the associates on taking advantage of opportunities for add-on sales. Even product returns became opportunities for additional sales. Of course, the threat of earning only minimum wage instead of commissions also "encouraged" sales associates to perform better—but increased the stress level of all the sales associates and Larson.

To ease the pressure, Larson emphasized the positive and fun side of the job. Larson enjoyed working with her sales team, regardless of her roles as sales goal enforcer. Working with the latest fashion trends and making their clients happy were definite pluses for the sales associates. Additional training improved their skills and made them more confident about meeting sales goals. The sales team began to enjoy their time working together. The sales team would also socialize together after work, which helped them create a better balance between life and career.

Today, in her work as a life coach, Larson focuses on helping her clients relieve stress and make smart life choices.

1. What method of relieving stress would you recommend to the sales associates at White House Black Market?

2. How did Larson's job as a supervisor prepare her to become a life coach?

Source: Alizah Salario, "Retail Manager Stressed by 'Never Enough' Sales Strategy," WeNews, July 15, 2013, http://womensenews.org/story/she-works-hard-the-money/130714/retail-manager-stressed-never-enough-sales-strategy.

A supervisor who has a bad day may feel as though everything is out of control. Instead of working on what he or she wants, the supervisor attempts to solve unexpected problems and soothe upset employees and customers. Although workdays like this affect employees and managers at all levels, they are a particular problem for supervisors because a supervisor's people-oriented job means solving many needs and conflicts. To minimize and cope with these difficulties, supervisors must manage their time and stress.

This chapter describes basic techniques of time and stress management. It identifies ways supervisors can control how they use time. Then it defines stress and describes its consequences. Finally, the chapter suggests ways supervisors themselves can cope with stress and also help employees do so.

Time Management

Sean Mulligan's typical day is hectic. Just when he gets on the telephone, someone is at the door with a problem; he almost never finds the time to sit down and ponder the problem. By the end of the day, Mulligan is exhausted, but he would be hard-pressed to say what he accomplished. Lisa Ng's days are also busy, but when someone interrupts her, she pulls out her calendar and makes an appointment for later. She starts out each day knowing what tasks are essential, and she always manages to complete them.

Which kind of supervisor would you rather have working for you? Which kind would you rather be? Time is the only resource we all have in equal shares: Everyone gets 24-hour days. To evaluate your own responses to time pressures, take the Assessing Yourself quiz on pages 376–377.

Supervisors who are in control of their time find that their jobs are easier and that they can get more done. Getting a lot done is a good way to impress higher-level management. The practice of controlling the way you use time is known as time management.[1]

time management
The practice of controlling the way you use time

Time management techniques can be as simple as putting things away as soon as you are done with them, using an appointment calendar to keep track of your schedule, and getting all the information you need *before* you start on a project. Whereas this chapter provides broad guidelines for time management, each supervisor must work out the details. A look at the many different varieties of calendars, planners, and scheduling tools available in your nearest office supply or app store, whether in paper form or as software, will convince you that no two people get organized in quite the same way.

---

connect SELF-ASSESSMENT 13.1

How Well Do You Use Technology To Manage Time

You probably already spend a great deal of your day on your computer, your tablet, or your smartphone. But how much of that time is actually productive? It is very easy to get sidetracked by an interesting post on social media or message from a friend. Use this assessment to start brainstorming ways to be more effective in using technology to save time rather than waste it.

LO13.1 ▶ Discuss how supervisors can evaluate their use of time.

time log
A record of what activities a person is doing hour by hour throughout the day

Understanding How You Use Time

Before you can take control over the way you use time, you have to understand what you already are doing. A practical way to learn about your use of time is to keep a time log, a record of what activities you are doing hour by hour throughout the workday. Figure 13.1, on the following page, provides an example. Each half-hour during the day, write down what you did during the previous half-hour. Do not wait until the end of the day; this level of detail is too difficult to remember.

After you have kept a time log for at least one typical week, review your log. Ask yourself the following questions:

- How much time did I spend on important activities?
- How much time did I spend on activities that did not need to get done?
- How much time did I spend on activities that someone else could have done (perhaps with some training)?
- What important jobs did I not get around to finishing?

FIGURE 13.1 | Format for a Time Log

Keeping a daily time log allows you to evaluate what you spend your time doing and whether it is the best use of your time.

Date _____

Time	Activity	Others Involved	Location
7:30–8:00			
8:00–8:30			
8:30–9:00			
9:00–9:30			
9:30–10:00			
10:00–10:30			
10:30–11:00			
11:00–11:30			
11:30–12:00			
12:00–12:30			
12:30–1:00			
1:00–1:30			
1:30–2:00			
2:00–2:30			
2:30–3:00			
3:00–3:30			
3:30–4:00			
4:00–4:30			
4:30–5:00			
5:00–5:30			

From your review, you may see some patterns. Do you reserve a certain time of day for telephone calls or meetings? Do you frequently interrupt what you are doing to solve a problem or move on to something more interesting? Do you tackle the most important jobs first or the easiest ones? Do you get caught up in behaviors that waste time? One business writer describes common time wasters that plague supervisors: working without a plan, working with fuzzy goals or too many goals, supervising every detail of employees' work, worrying, excessive socializing, pursuing perfectionism, putting off tasks, beating around the bush when delivering bad news, correcting your own mistakes or those of others (instead of doing it right the first time), filling out paperwork, waiting around without any plan to pass the time productively, attending meaningless meetings, dealing with those who do not put in a full day's work, and getting angry.[2] Another waste of time is trying to cope with a flood of electronic messages by multitasking. For example, more than half of workers have 100 or more e-mails in their in-box, and for them, it is easy to think that answering messages while trying to listen to a meeting or write a report

SUPERVISORY SKILLS

TIME MANAGEMENT

Rest for Success

Some ambitious people believe their success depends on constant hard work with no time to rest. They may even brag that they do fine on four hours of sleep each night. However, research supports the idea that getting enough rest is not a sign of weakness but a practice that promotes high achievement.

Successful supervisors have to:

- be creative and energetic
- exercise good judgment
- be in tune with how they affect other people
- react calmly to surprises and problems

All of these requirements are much easier to meet when well rested. When people are exhausted, feelings are more apt to get hurt, and judgment becomes impaired. Memory and concentration suffer. Worse, if this happens to you, you might not even notice. A study at the University of Pennsylvania's Wharton School found that subjects who were allowed to sleep only four hours at night suffered losses in thinking ability but claimed they were not impaired.

Sleep is especially important during difficult times or when handling big challenges, because it helps the body cope with stress. Ironically, when work is stressful, sleeping may be more difficult.

When arranging your time to meet work goals, you can also engage in practices that will help you get enough rest.

- Try to schedule activities in such a way that you go to bed and get up at about the same time each day.
- Early in your day is the best time for stressful activities and caffeine consumption; avoid them near bedtime.
- Fit in time for meditation and exercise.
- Do not take your stress to bed with you.

A recent study by PewResearch found that 58 percent of American adults have smartphones and 44 percent of them sleep with their smartphones by their bed. Except in a really dire situation, calls and text messages should wait until you are done sleeping.

Sources: Anne Fisher, "Make Sleep Work for You," *Fortune Small Business*, August 25, 2008, http://cnn.money.com; Leslie Garcia, "How Getting a Good Night's Sleep Helps during the Day," *Dallas Morning News*, August 19, 2008, http://www.rep-am.com/articles/2008/09/05/lifestyle/360766.txt?p=9; and Bharat Savur, "Too Stimulated to Sleep?" *Business Line*, August 15, 2008, http://www.thehindubusinessline.in/life/2008/08/15/stories/2008081550090400.htm; "Mobile Technology Fact Sheet," PewResearch Internet Project, updated January 2014, http://www.pewinternet.org/fact-sheets/mobile-technology-fact-sheet/.

will save time. In fact, that approach actually slows down the brain as it tries to jump back and forth between activities.[3]

The answers to these and similar questions will help you see where you need to change. After you have tried applying the principles in this chapter for a while, you might want to try keeping a time log again to see how you have improved.

Keeping a time log is also helpful for people who feel out of control of their personal time. For example, if you are frustrated at how little time you spend with loved ones or if you cannot find the time for charitable work, keep a log of how you use your hours outside work. You may find that you are spending a lot of time on an unimportant activity that you can cut back on so you free up time for something else. As described in the "Supervisory Skills" feature, one important goal for success might be ensuring you get enough sleep to think clearly and handle the challenges of supervision.

LO13.2 ▶ Describe ways to plan the use of time.

Planning Your Use of Time

On the basis of what you learned from keeping a time log, you can plan how to use your time better. You need to make sure that the most important things get done each day before you move on to less important activities. You must set priorities. Thus, your planning consists of deciding what you need to do and which activities are most important.

Planning your use of time begins with the planning process described in Chapter 6. If you follow the guidelines in that chapter, you will routinely establish objectives for the year, specifying when each must be completed. With these yearly objectives in mind, you can figure out what you need to accomplish in shorter time periods—each quarter, month, and week. Review your objectives regularly, and use them to plan what you will need to accomplish each week and day. For ideas on how to use mobile devices to make this process easier, see "Practical Advice for Supervisors."

PRACTICAL ADVICE FOR SUPERVISORS

USING MOBILE APPS TO MANAGE YOUR TIME

A lot of supervisors today carry smartphones or tablet computers to keep up with people and information on the go. These devices can run software applications (apps) developed to help a supervisor carry out time management routines without the need to juggle notebooks, index cards, and paper calendars. Apps tend to be inexpensive, so a supervisor trying to get organized should research a few and try downloading a highly rated app to see if staying organized is easier with a mobile device.

The selection of apps is constantly growing, so this list is just an introduction to some of the possibilities that have been created:

- ToodleDo offers a to do list that the user can customize by sticking to the basics or adding features such as a tracker of progress toward goals. It also can send e-mail and text reminders to the user's smartphone.

- An app called simply Things uses the format of an e-mail program to let users organize to do lists for work and personal projects. Users can create to do lists for projects, set up regularly scheduled activities (say, a staff meeting every Thursday morning), and generate lists of tasks according to dates or priorities.

- Do It (Tomorrow) addresses one basic problem of time management: deciding what has to be done today and what can be postponed. This app displays a two-page date book for the current date and the next day. The user can enter the day's to do list. Then the user checks off tasks as they are completed, moves them around on the list as priorities shift, and moves them to the next day if necessary. This app is primarily beneficial for those who need help staying focused on the day's priorities and want an easy-to-use system.

- RememberTheMilk.com is an online program that saves users from having to remember to carry around lists. Users can have lists texted or e-mailed to their smartphone or other mobile device. The program can also sync information to Google Calendar, which is a useful tool for sharing schedules online. RememberTheMilk also has a location feature that can identify what other errands the user needs to run while he or she is in a detected location.

- Microsoft OneNote, which is part of the Microsoft Office suite, is a digital notebook that lets you take notes, store images, save links to news articles and URLs, and even draw ideas in freehand. These items can be sorted, stored, and then searched later. The app version and the desktop version can be synched through SkyDrive.

Sources: Liz Magill, "Top 10 Time Management iPad and iPhone Apps," *Intuit Small Business,* May 9, 2011, http://blog.intuit.com; Lisa Caplan, "Time Management for the Organizationally Challenged with Do It (Tomorrow) HD," *AppAdvice,* February 23, 2011, http://appadvice.com; Maureen Sullivan, "Make It Easier on Yourself," *Women in Business,* Fall 2011, EBSCOhost, http://web.ebscohost.com; "The Taskmasters," *Entrepreneur,* May 2011, p. 45; Rich Hein, "9 Top iPhone and iPad Productivity and Time Management Apps," *CIO,* April 18, 2013, http://www.cio.com/slideshow/detail/96495#slide3.

Keeping a "To Do" list is a great way to stay organized and ensure that you complete all required tasks.

Making a "To Do" List

Many people find it helpful to spend a few minutes at the end of each week writing a list of things to do—what they must accomplish during the next week. When you have made your list, write an *A* next to all the activities that must be completed that week; they are your top priorities. Then write a *B* next to all the activities that are important but can be postponed if necessary. Label everything else *C;* these activities are your lowest priorities for the week. Schedule times for doing your A-level and B-level activities. If you have more time, work on your C-level activities. As you complete each activity on the "to do" list, check it off.

How do you know when is the best time to do the activities on your list? Here are some guidelines to follow for creating weekly and daily schedules:

- First, record all the activities that must occur at a set time. For example, you do not have any choice about when to schedule your regular Monday morning staff meeting or the appointment you made with your manager for 3:00 p.m on Thursday.

- Next, find times for your remaining A-level activities. Try to avoid scheduling them at the end of the day (on a daily plan) or week (on a weekly plan). If a crisis comes up, you will need another chance to finish these activities. Schedule your B-level activities next.

- Schedule the most challenging and most important activities for the times of day when you are at your best. If you are sleepy after lunch or get off to a slow start in the morning, schedule top-priority activities for times when you are more alert.
- Learn to use the calendar or scheduling tools built into your computer operating system. For instance, Microsoft Works Calendar and Microsoft Office Outlook Calendar allow you to record upcoming events, meetings, appointments, and holidays, and it will also send you customized reminders of each (with audio signals, if you like). Other programs, such as IBM Notes and shared Google Calendars, allow you to schedule a team meeting and post the day, time, and location on the calendars of all the team's members.
- Schedule time for thinking, not solely for doing. Remember that the creative process requires time for reflection (see Chapter 9).
- Do not fill up every hour of the day and week. Leave some time free to handle unexpected problems and questions from your employees and others. If problems do not occur, so much the better. You will have time for the C-level activities.

Be careful that your "to do" list serves its purpose and does not become a goal in itself. Some time management consultants say writing lists can become a substitute for getting started on the list items. Certainly, list writing can become time-consuming. Communications consultant Ilya Welfeld maintains lists of lists, including a priority list that supplements the "to do" list she keeps in Microsoft Outlook's Tasks. Deanna Brown, publisher of a magazine called *Breathe,* spends a half-hour each day composing a list of things to do. "Call mother" was on the list for a month, which Brown rationalized by saying that including the task was a sign "I'm thinking about her."[4]

LO13.3 ▶ Identify some time wasters and how to control them.

Controlling Time Wasters

Many supervisors find that certain activities and attitudes are what most often lead them to waste time. Figure 13.2 identifies the most common time wasters: meetings, telephone calls, e-mail, paperwork, unscheduled visitors, procrastination, perfectionism, failure to delegate, and inability to say no. Some of the activities are necessary, but a supervisor does not always manage the time spent on them wisely.

Meetings

The main reason many supervisors hate meetings is that meetings often waste time. People slowly drift into the room, then devote time to chatting while waiting for latecomers. When the formal meeting finally gets under way, the discussion may drift off onto tangents, and the group may never complete the task that it gathered to address. Meetings like these are understandably a source of frustration.

When you attend a meeting chaired by someone else, it is hard to control wasted time. You can encourage careful use of time by being prompt. If meetings tend to start late, you might bring along some reading material or other work to do while you wait. If the discussion at the meeting seems irrelevant, you might try tactfully asking the speaker to explain how the current discussion will help in accomplishing the goal of the meeting.

When you call a meeting, you can use time wisely by starting promptly. If the discussion veers off course, politely remind participants about the subject at hand. It is also smart to set an ending time for the meeting.

FIGURE 13.2 | Common Time Wasters

A large part of managing time well is to be alert to and striving to manage the more common time wasters. The better you are at controlling these, the better managed your time will be.

If you cannot solve the problem in the time allotted, schedule a follow-up meeting. (Chapter 3 provides more ideas for holding effective meetings.)

Telephone Calls, Texts, and E-Mail

When other people call or text you, they usually have no way of knowing whether the time is convenient. Consequently, most of us get telephone calls, texts, and instant messages when we are busy with something else. When they interrupt the work flow, all of these are time wasters.

One way to take control of your time is to remember that you are not a slave to the telephone. If you are fortunate enough to have an assistant to screen your calls, have that person answer your telephone when you are working on top-priority jobs. If you answer the telephone while you are in a meeting or doing something important, explain to the caller that you cannot give the call the attention it deserves at that time, and schedule a convenient time to call back. Of course, you have to use this approach carefully. If the person calling is your manager or a customer, the telephone call may be your top priority.

When you are placing calls yourself, think ahead. Schedule time for making calls each day, bearing in mind different time zones when calling long distance. Before you call someone, make sure you have the information you need close at hand; it does not make sense to place a client on hold while you fetch the file containing the answers he or she wanted. Not only does that waste time, but it also annoys the person who has to wait. If the person you are calling is not available, ask when you can reach him or her instead of simply leaving a message. That way, you have control over when the call will be made.

For all its apparent convenience, e-mail can absorb another major block of supervisors' time. Some employees receive 100 or more messages a day. The time required to read and respond to the incoming messages challenges employees to come up with strategies for e-mail management. At the offices of *The Wall Street Journal*, one employee reads each message when it arrives, ignoring only the ones that are obviously spam, deletes about half as unimportant, and then saves the rest. Another employee periodically reviews her messages in the preview pane, deletes unimportant messages, reads the important ones, and then sorts the messages into folders so she can refer to them later. If a message requires further action later (for example, when she receives more information), this employee keeps it in her in-box.[5]

In addition to the sheer volume of information, e-mail, texts, and IMs present another challenge that is at least as serious: interruptions. According to studies of worker behavior, an interrupted worker takes 25 minutes to return to the original task. The reason is that the worker usually detours into other activities after the interruption.[6] So every time you stop what you are working on to open a message, you can expect it will take a while before you return to your previous train of thought. Young workers grew up with this challenge and may believe they are well equipped to "multitask," but a recent study found that messages interrupting a task resulted in more errors by 18- to 21-year-olds than by subjects aged 35 to 39.[7]

Some highly productive people have figured out ways to minimize the impact of these interruptions. Some keep a word-processing page open for recording any ideas and reminders as they come to mind. These people can use the program's search feature to locate the ideas later. Others send themselves e-mail reminders because they have a habit of periodically checking their e-mail anyway. Still others follow the principle of fully handling an interruption only if it will take less than two minutes. Longer interruptions go straight to the person's calendar or "to do" list. Then the person tackles the next item on the list (the new item only if it's now the highest priority).[8]

To keep from being overwhelmed, supervisors should learn to prioritize their e-mail, delete junk mail unread, limit the number of messages sent and the number of recipients, and avoid forwarding or responding to chain letters or other kinds of nonbusiness correspondence. Unless you have an extremely time-critical job, you do not need to check e-mail every three minutes.

Paperwork and Reading Material

Supervisors spend a lot of time reading and writing. They receive mail, reports, and magazines to read, and they must prepare reports, letters, and memos to send to others. Reading and writing are not necessarily a waste of time, but many supervisors perform these activities inefficiently.

Most advice on how to manage paperwork is based on the principle of handling each item only once. Set aside specific time to read all the papers that cross your desk. At that time, decide whether each item is something you need to act on. If not, throw it away immediately. If you must act, determine the most efficient response. An efficient way to respond to a memo is to write a brief response across the top and return the memo to the sender. If you have an assistant, you can record voice messages for responses to letters as you read them. Or consider whether you can respond to a letter with a telephone call. If you learn that you must set time aside to do research or prepare a report, schedule that time immediately.

Most supervisors have a multitude of magazines, newsletters, and newspapers from which to choose. Each supervisor will find that some of these are very helpful, others somewhat helpful, and still others not relevant at all. To cut the time spent poring over the unhelpful publications, a supervisor should decide which ones are useful and cancel subscriptions to the rest. It is wise to look at the table of contents in the somewhat helpful publications for relevant information rather than to turn every page. A supervisor who finds that an internal company report he or she receives provides little useful information might ask to be taken off the distribution list.

Unscheduled Visitors

Supervisors are interrupted at times by unscheduled visitors: customers, peers, employees, salespeople, or anyone else who turns up without an appointment. Because seeing these people is an unplanned use of time, the interruptions can interfere with getting the job done. Figure 13.3 shows some broad guidelines for handling this potential problem.

When a supervisor regularly spends time with unscheduled visitors on unimportant matters, a lot of time gets wasted. The key is to know which interruptions are important. For example, when an angry customer demands to see the manager and interrupts a supervisor in a store, an important part of the supervisor's job is to make that customer happy. When a supervisor's manager occasionally drops in to discuss an idea, the supervisor will probably have to work around the manager's schedule. But when a co-worker in another department stops in to report on his vacation or a salesperson shows up unannounced, the interruption does not carry a high priority.

With low-priority interruptions, the supervisor needs to take control of his or her time diplomatically. The supervisor might say to the co-worker back from

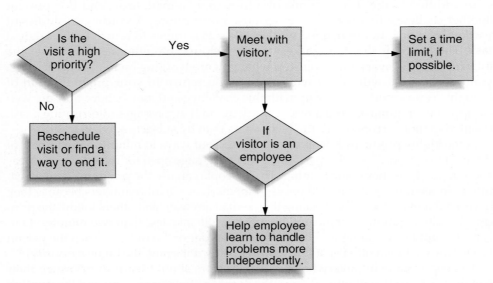

FIGURE 13.3 | Handling Unscheduled Visitors

Unscheduled visits occur for a lot of reasons and are sometimes necessary. How you handle these visits, however, can determine if they become a huge source of "time wasting" for you or not.

vacation, "It's great to hear you had fun last week. Let's have lunch together so you can tell me about it." When salespeople call without an appointment, a supervisor can ask them simply to leave some literature. Another response to unscheduled visitors is to set a time limit. For example, the supervisor might say, "I've got five minutes. What's on your mind?" If the problem is urgent or seems to deserve more time, the supervisor can arrange to meet the visitor later for a specified amount of time.[9]

Standing is a useful signal. If you see an unwanted visitor heading toward your office, stand and meet the visitor at your door, then talk to the visitor there. This sends a message that you expect the conversation to be brief. Meeting with someone else at his or her desk or in a conference room allows you to get up and leave when you have completed your business. If you meet with someone in your office, standing up when you finish sends a signal that the meeting is over.

Interruptions from employees can be tricky to handle because part of a supervisor's job is to listen to employees and help them with work-related problems. At the same time, a constant stream of interruptions could mean that employees have too little training or authority to handle their work. If an employee interrupts with a problem, one approach is to listen and then ask, "What do you suggest we do about that?" This shows that the supervisor expects the employee to participate in finding solutions. With practice, the employee may learn to handle problems more independently.

If the problem is not urgent—for example, if it does not hold up an employee's work—a supervisor may want to schedule a later time when supervisor and employee can meet to work on the problem. At that later time, of course, the supervisor should give priority to the meeting with the employee and discourage interruptions from others. Thus, employees will learn that a supervisor will listen and work with them, although not necessarily on a moment's notice.

Procrastination

Sometimes it is hard to start an activity. Maybe you have to write a proposal to buy a new computer system. You are not quite sure how to write that kind of proposal, so you are grateful when the telephone rings. You talk for a while, and that conversation reminds you to follow up on an order with a supplier. So you make another telephone call. You get up to stretch your legs and decide it is a good time to check on how your employees are doing. Bit by bit, you manage to get through the entire day without doing any work on the proposal. This process of putting off what needs to be done is called **procrastination**.[10]

procrastination
Putting off what needs to be done

Procrastination is a time waster because it leads people to spend their time on low-priority activities while they avoid the higher priorities. The best cure for procrastination is to force yourself to jump in. To do that, focus on one step at a time. Decide what the first step is, then do that step. Then do the next step. You will find that you are building momentum and that the big job no longer seems so overwhelming.

If you need more incentive to get started, give yourself a reward for completing each step. For example, you might decide that as soon as you complete the first step, you will go for a walk in the sunshine, call a customer who loves your product, or take a break to open your mail. If the project seems thoroughly unpleasant, you can concentrate on the rewards. The ultimate reward of course is to finish the job.

Here are a few other tips for conquering procrastination:[11]

- Be clear about what is happening when you procrastinate; do not deceive yourself. Procrastination is trading off long-term goals to feel better for a few minutes while you avoid doing something unpleasant. Is that really such a good trade-off? It also may involve pretending you will be in the mood to tackle the project later. Is that ever really true? Being honest might make it a little easier to force yourself to get going.

- When procrastination is tempting you, focus on the short term. Instead of fretting over how big and unpleasant the whole job is, think about how great it will feel to finish the next short step in the project. One rule of thumb is to divide up your projects into 30-minute segments. The thought that you will be working on something for just a half hour may not stir up as much desire to stall.

- Make specific decisions about what you will do the next time you are tempted to procrastinate. For example, you might decide ahead of time, "When I sit down to write the report, if I feel tempted to check my e-mail first, I'll open my word-processing program instead and type the report title immediately, so I'm starting to think about the report instead of the e-mail."

- As much as you can, turn off distractions. Close your e-mail and instant-messaging programs when you need to concentrate. Turn off your cell phone.

- Prepare for the next temptation to procrastinate by ending an ongoing project in a place where it's easy to get started the next time you work on it. For example, if you are writing a report, end in the middle of a paragraph. Finishing the paragraph will be easier than starting a new thought, so getting started again will be less intimidating.

Perfectionism

One reason people put off doing necessary work is that they are afraid what they do will not live up to their standards. Although high standards can inspire high performance, perfectionism can make people afraid to try at all. **Perfectionism** is the attempt to do things perfectly. It may sound like a noble goal, but human beings are imperfect. Expecting to be perfect therefore dooms a person to failure.

Instead of being a slave to perfectionism, determine the highest standard you realistically can achieve. You may be able to meet a higher standard by drawing on the expertise of employees and peers. When you find yourself avoiding a difficult task, remind yourself that your goals are realistic, and then give the job your best try.

Failure to Delegate

Perfectionism often underlies the failure to delegate work. Even when someone else can do a job more efficiently in terms of that person's cost and availability, supervisors may resist delegating because they believe only they can really do the job right. This attitude stands in the way of appropriate delegating. In terms of time management, the result is that the supervisor has taken on too much work.

Instead, the supervisor should learn to delegate effectively. Supervisors who feel overloaded should set aside some time to list all their tasks and review the list. Are all the activities and associated paperwork still necessary? If not, the supervisor can seek permission to discontinue those. Supervisors also should identify some activities that their employees could be trained to handle and then begin to delegate those activities.

Inability to Say No

To control your use of time, you must be able to say no when appropriate. However, it is easy to let other people and their demands control how we use our time, so we end up overextending ourselves by taking on more tasks than we can possibly do well. How do you react when someone asks you to chair a committee, manage a new project, or take an active role in a local charity? Most people are uncomfortable saying no when the opportunity is for a worthwhile project or they do not want to hurt somebody's feelings. But when we take on too many things, we cannot do our best at any of them.

If someone comes to you with an opportunity that will require a significant commitment of time, learn to tell the person politely that you will consider the offer and reply later at some specific time. Then assess your present commitments and priorities. Decide whether you should take on this new task. You may decide that you

perfectionism
The attempt to do things perfectly

have time for it, but in other instances you will have to decline, claiming that you do not have enough time to do justice to the task. If your life is already busy but the opportunity seems important, try asking yourself, "What activity am I willing to give up in order to make time for this new one?"

If your own supervisor asks you to take on an urgent new task, saying no is not really an option. Still, there are some ways to cope. One is to talk to the manager about priorities: Which other responsibilities can be done later or by someone else so you can take care of the new task? Assure the manager that your concern is to do what will matter most to the department and the organization. Also, you can put these decisions into a larger context by meeting with your supervisor weekly or monthly to review what you are working on and accomplishing. That way, when a new task comes up, the manager will have a clearer picture of how it will fit in with all the other results you are accomplishing, and the two of you will already have a habit of setting priorities.[12]

For those times when you cannot say no, try these tips:

1. Ask the person making the request how the two of you can plan better for the next time.

2. Remind the person that he or she now owes you one and, for example, could cover your shift next time you need time off.

3. Suggest your own timetable. For instance, say, "I can do that by the end of the week."

4. Put a time limit on your participation. For instance, explain that you can only give an hour and no more.[13]

Whatever you decide, a thoughtful approach does both you and the other person a favor. If you do not have the time to complete a task well and on schedule, it is better to give the other person a chance to find somebody else. None of us likes to find out that the person we have been counting on is overcommitted and does not have enough time to do the job well.

Stress Management

Failure to manage time wisely is one reason supervisors find their jobs difficult. It is frustrating to leave the workplace knowing that you did not accomplish anything you really wanted to that day. Supervisors also have difficulty hearing a lot of complaints, working in a dangerous environment, and trying to live up to unrealistic expectations. To cope, supervisors can use the techniques of stress management.

stress
The body's response to coping with environmental demands

Stress refers to the body's response to coping with environmental demands such as change, frustration, uncertainty, danger, or discomfort. Usually when we think of stress, we think of the response to problems—for example, arguments, cold, or long hours of work. Stress also results from the challenges that stimulate us and from the happy changes in our lives. Thus, buying a car is stressful, and so is getting married or promoted. People experiencing stress typically undergo physiological changes such as faster heartbeat, faster breathing, higher blood pressure, greater perspiration, greater muscle strength, and decreased gastric (stomach) functioning, among other changes.

LO13.4 ▶ List factors that contribute to stress among employees.

Causes of Stress

The environmental demands that cause stress may arise in the workplace, in people's personal lives, and in the conflicts that can arise between the two.

Work-Related Causes

Job factors linked to stress involve the organization's policies, structures, physical conditions, and processes (the way work gets done).[14] Examples of each type are

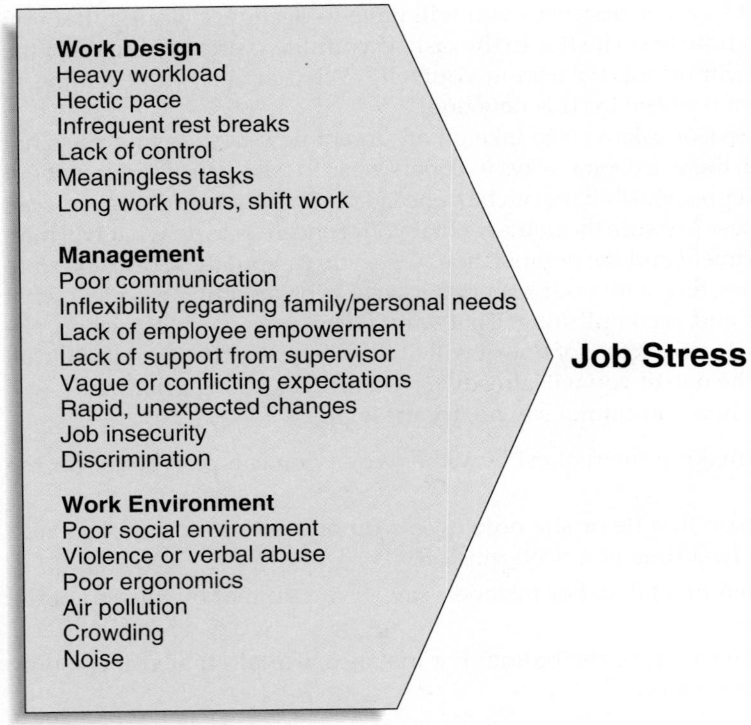

Work Design
Heavy workload
Hectic pace
Infrequent rest breaks
Lack of control
Meaningless tasks
Long work hours, shift work

Management
Poor communication
Inflexibility regarding family/personal needs
Lack of employee empowerment
Lack of support from supervisor
Vague or conflicting expectations
Rapid, unexpected changes
Job insecurity
Discrimination

Work Environment
Poor social environment
Violence or verbal abuse
Poor ergonomics
Air pollution
Crowding
Noise

Job Stress

FIGURE 13.4 | Job Factors Linked to Stress

Many different factors can contribute to work-related stress.

Source: Based on American Institute of Stress, "Stress and Heart Disease, Type A Behavior and Heart Disease, Prevention and Treatment of Heart Disease, Heart Disease and Job Stress," Topics of Interest, http://www.stress.org, accessed December 8, 2011.

identified in Figure 13.4. Employees tend to experience the most stress if policies seem unfair and ambiguous, the structure makes jobs relatively unsatisfying, physical conditions are uncomfortable, and processes interfere with employee understanding of what is happening and how well they are doing.

The recent crisis in the financial industry and the slowdown in the economy have brought stress related to possible job losses, home foreclosures, pay cuts, eroded retirement savings, and general uncertainty about the future. Whether workers are worried about keeping their jobs or about personal losses such as inability to pay for a child's college education, their worries at work tend to spill over and make the work environment tense for everyone.[15] The discussion of troubled employees in Chapter 12 provides guidance for situations such as these.

Recurring efforts at downsizing have contributed to a great deal of employee stress. Many employees see job cuts as a long-term trend that prevails without regard to whether they do their best or the organization earns a profit. A case in point is Pam Cromer, who worked for Westinghouse Electric Corporation in Pittsburgh. She worked up to 80 hours a week when the company was struggling during the early 1990s. One night part of her face went numb, which Cromer learned was caused from clenching her teeth too hard—the result of tension. Despite Cromer's willingness to sacrifice, she was laid off in cutbacks that occurred after she had been with Westinghouse 22 years. At a going away party, her co-workers observed, "The winners get to leave, and the losers get to stay."[16]

A supervisor's own behavior also can be a source of stress for employees. A supervisor who communicates poorly, stirs up conflict, and metes out discipline arbitrarily is creating stressful working conditions. Other supervisory behaviors that can contribute to employee stress are demonstrating a lack of concern for employee well-being and checking up on every detail of an employee's work. If you've ever typed while someone peered over your shoulder, you know that you can almost feel your blood pressure rise. Supervisors also contribute to stress when they make the employees' job more difficult—for example, by giving vague directions or interrupting them with matters than can wait.

Michael Gelman is the executive producer of *Live! with Kelly and Michael*, a free-wheeling morning television show filmed in New York. Over the two-and-a-half decades he has held the job, Gelman has found his own way of coping with the particular stress of working with on-air personalities. "There are absolutely no second chances on live television," comments Gelman. "When things go awry and Regis [a former host] grumbles and complains, I don't take it personally. It's all part of his shtick. We just move on . . . there is that 5 percent of the time when my feelings are indeed hurt and I want to blurt out, 'Wait a minute.' But that would be out of character."[17]

Personal Factors

Even when faced with similar job factors and supervisory behavior, some employees will have a greater stress response than others. General feelings of negativism,

TABLE 13.1 | Behavior Patterns Associated with Type A and Type B Personalities

Source: Adapted from Meyer Friedman and Ray H. Rosenman, *Type A Behavior and Your Heart* (New York: Fawcett Crest, 1974), pp. 100–101, summarized in Jane Whitney Gibson, *The Supervisory Challenge: Principles and Practices* (Columbus, OH: Merrill Publishing, 1990), p. 309.

Type A	Type B
Moving, walking, eating rapidly	Having varied interests
Feeling impatient with people who move slower than you	Taking a relaxed but active approach to life
Feeling impatient when others talk about something that is not of interest to you	
Doing two or three things at the same time	
Feeling unable to relax or stop working	
Trying to get more and more done in less and less time	

Type A personality
A pattern of behavior that involves constantly trying to accomplish a lot in a hurry

Type B personality
A pattern of behavior that focuses on a relaxed but active approach to life

helplessness, and low self-esteem can contribute to stress. In addition, some medical researchers have observed that the people who are more likely to have heart disease (presumably a sign of stress) tend to share a similar pattern of behavior, which the researchers have named the Type A personality. A **Type A personality** refers to the behavior pattern of constantly trying to get a lot done in a hurry. It includes the behaviors listed in the left column of Table 13.1. Research suggests that some Type A people seem to thrive on their approach to life, whereas others—those prone to heart disease—have an excess amount of hostility along with the basic Type A characteristics. To help those at risk, physicians often recommend adopting contrasting behaviors, known collectively as a **Type B personality** (see Table 13.1).

Another source of stress is the sheer inability to leave the job behind when it's appropriate to do so. According to a nationwide survey by Steelcase, which sells office furniture, more than 4 out of 10 workers say they spend some of their vacation time doing work. Technology makes it easy for employees to check e-mail, read messages on their smartphones, or complete a report on their notebook computer. Although rest is necessary for people to refresh themselves so they can do their best, respondents to the survey most often justified working while on vacation as necessary for finishing an assignment or catching up on tasks.[18]

Work–Family Conflict

Stress also can be increased for people who experience conflict between the demands of work and home. Women have traditionally borne the primary responsibility for homemaking and the family's well-being, so as a group they are particularly vulnerable to this source of stress. However, balance can be an issue for employees of either sex and any age. A study by Jennifer Deal of the Center for Creative Leadership (CCL) found that at different life stages, work–family balance may involve commitments to pursue personal interests, raise children, care for elderly parents, and prepare for retirement, among other possibilities. Interestingly, other researchers at CCL have found that managers who are actively engaged in balancing their own work–family conflicts tend to get higher leadership ratings from bosses, peers, and employees who report to them.[19] Managers who have successfully tackled this type of stress have had to develop skills at prioritizing, negotiating, and resolving conflicts—valued skills in any organization.

LO13.5 ▶ Summarize consequences of stress.

Consequences of Stress

Stress is a fact of life. Life would be boring without some sources of stress, and most people seek out some degree of stress. Some people even are attracted to jobs billed as

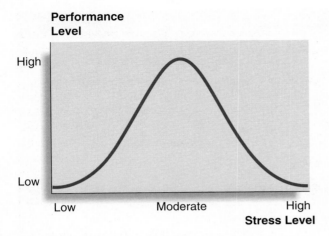

Performance Level

High

Low

Low · Moderate · High

Stress Level

FIGURE 13.5 | Stress Levels and Performance

Too little or too much stress results in a low performance level. A moderate amount of stress, however, seems to cause workers to perform at a high level.

challenging or exciting—those likely to be most stressful. On the job, employees tend to perform best when they are experiencing a moderate degree of stress (see Figure 13.5).

However, too much stress brings problems, especially when the sources of stress are negative (for example, a critical manager or unsafe working conditions). As Figure 13.5 indicates, performance falls when the amount of stress moves from moderate to high. In a highly stressful environment, people are more apt to develop heart disease, high blood pressure, ulcers, and possibly other diseases. Because of illness and unhappiness, they take more time off from work. The National Institute for Occupational Safety and Health reported that the number of lost work days from anxiety, stress, and neurotic disorders was four times greater (an average of 26 days lost) than those lost for all nonfatal injuries or illnesses (an average of six days lost), even though the psychological disorders occurred less frequently overall.[20] When employees are at work, the sources of stress may also distract them from doing their best and make them prone to accidents.

In addition to hurting the organization through poor performance and attendance, excess stress can hurt employees as individuals. People experiencing stress tend to feel anxious, aggressive, frustrated, tense, and moody. They may be overly sensitive to criticism, have trouble making decisions, and be more likely to have trouble maintaining mutually satisfying relationships with loved ones. They may be unable to get enough sleep. People under stress are also at risk for abusing drugs and alcohol.

Because of these potential negative consequences of stress, supervisors should notice when employees seem to be experiencing more stress than they can handle effectively. Table 13.2 lists some signs that indicate when employees may be experiencing excess stress. If some of these signs exist, a supervisor should try to reduce the stress employees are experiencing and recommend some coping techniques. (Approaches to stress management are described in the next section.)

TABLE 13.2 | Possible Signs of Excess Stress

Decline in work performance.
Increase in use of sick days.
Increase in number of errors and accidents.
Moodiness and irritability.
Fatigue.
Loss of enthusiasm.
Aggressive behavior.
Difficulty making decisions.
Family problems.
Apparent loss of concern for others and their feelings.*
Feeling that it's impossible to help other people.*
Feeling of inability to get your job done fully or well.*

*Possible signs of burnout.

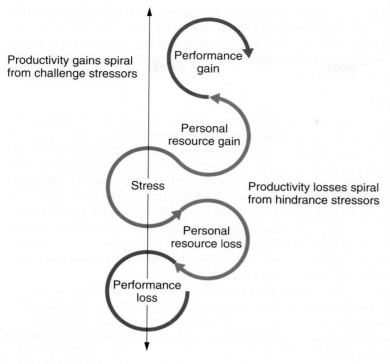

Productivity gains spiral from challenge stressors

Productivity losses spiral from hindrance stressors

FIGURE 13.6 |

Challenge stressors can lead to an overall productivity gain while hindrance stressors can lead productivity loss.

Stress–Performance Relationship

Stress can have a positive or negative influence on an employee's productivity, depending on the type of stressor in question. For example, *challenge stressors* are stressors that are viewed by individuals as opportunities to grow and develop. Analogous to weight-training or running, challenge stressors place employees in new environments where they are stretched and challenged to succeed. As a result, these help employees gain personal resources that enhance their productivity and well-being. However, *hindrance stressors* are stressors that impede an individual's ability to perform. Examples may include ambiguity about supervisor expectations, an excessive workload, organizational politics, or competing demands between different supervisors. Hindrance stressors drain personal resources from employees that hinder their productivity. The interaction between productivity and both challenge and hindrance stressors is illustrated in Figure 13.6.

Hindrance stressors also may arise from non-work sources. For example, divorce, chronic illnesses, and the death of a family member or friend can deeply strain individuals and negatively impact their productivity. It is often impractical for management to control these non-work stressors, but it is critical for supervisors to recognize when their employees are experiencing these stressors. Supportive supervisory interactions can help employees work through these difficult circumstances.

Burnout

burnout
The inability to function effectively as a result of ongoing stress

A person who cannot cope with stress over an extended period of time may experience burnout. **Burnout** is the inability to function effectively as a result of ongoing stress. Employees who are burned out feel drained and lose interest in doing their jobs. Typically, burnout occurs in three stages:

1. The employee feels emotionally exhausted.
2. The employee's perceptions of others become calloused.
3. The employee views his or her effectiveness negatively.

Burnout is worse than just needing a vacation. Therefore, it is important to cope with stress before it leads to burnout.

Some signs of excess stress that may indicate burnout are indicated with an asterisk (*) in Table 13.2. Supervisors who observe these signs in employees should not only seek to reduce stress but also be sure that employees are being rewarded for their efforts. Burnout is especially likely to occur when people feel they are giving of themselves all the time, with little or no return.[21] For that reason, burnout is reported widely among employees in the so-called helping professions, such as health care and teaching.

LO13.6 ▶ Explain how supervisors can manage their own stress.

Personal Stress Management

Because stress arises from both personal and job factors, a full effort at stress management includes actions at both levels. Personal stress management is especially important for people who hold jobs that are by nature highly stressful, such as the supervisor of nurses in a hospital's intensive care unit or the supervisor of a crew of firefighters.

A variety of techniques are available for personal stress management: time management (discussed in the first part of this chapter), positive attitude, exercise, biofeedback, meditation, well-rounded life activities, and psychotherapy. Supervisors can use these techniques to improve their own stress levels, and they also can encourage employees to use them.

Time Management

Making conscious, reasoned decisions about your use of time helps prevent the stress that can result from wasted time or unrealistic goals. Thus, a good start for handling the stress related to balancing work and family responsibilities is to set priorities. Thomas Alby, a project manager in Germany, emphasizes the importance of planning project schedules with enough time to deal with unexpected issues and of setting priorities when those issues arise. Alby notes that project managers often jump right on the urgent issue even if another activity might have a higher priority. Then the end of the workday rolls around, and the high-priority tasks still remain to be done. Alby not only schedules his work carefully, but also sets aside time for activities that strengthen his health and lift his spirit: early-morning runs and twice-weekly practice with a rock band in the evening.[22]

As Alby understands, time management priorities should include time for resting and recharging. Bolstered by research reports showing a link to improved safety and job performance, some managers are even putting naps on their schedules.

Time management principles are also useful for managing the stress of balancing work and home responsibilities. If family activities are on your "to do" list, you have a built-in response when another request conflicts with family time: "I have other commitments at that time." Except in unusual circumstances, avoid taking work home with you. It signals to your family that work is more important to you than your time with them, and concentrating on work at home is difficult anyway. General Colin Powell understood this years ago when he took over a command in Frankfort, Germany. Powell told the officers under his command not to work on weekends unless it was absolutely necessary: "Anyone found logging Saturday or Sunday hours for himself or his troops had better have a good reason."[23]

Being realistic about time is ultimately less frustrating than expecting yourself to handle everything. Instead of criticizing yourself for what you did not do, make an effort to give yourself a pat on the back for all the times you strike a balance between home and work commitments.

Positive Attitude

As mentioned previously, people with a negative outlook tend to be more susceptible to stress. Thus, supervisors can reduce their stress response by cultivating a positive attitude. Ways to do this are to avoid making negative generalizations and look for the positives in any situation. Saying to oneself, "This company doesn't care about us; all it cares about is profits" or "I'll never get the hang of this job," contributes to a negative attitude. A supervisor can consciously replace such thoughts with more positive ones: "The competition is tough these days, but we each can contribute to helping this company please its customers" and "This job is difficult, but I will plan a way to learn how to do it better."

In the positive examples, a supervisor is focusing on the areas over which he or she has control. This helps to defuse the sense of helplessness that can increase stress and contributes to a positive outlook.[24]

Supervisors can cultivate a positive attitude in themselves and others by finding and focusing on what makes their work meaningful. For example, their job and their group's work may satisfy customers (inside or outside the organization). They may help people find opportunities to learn and develop. They may produce useful goods or make people feel more comfortable or healthy. In whatever ways they contribute to society, when people see their work as meaningful, they tend to be less bothered by stress.[25]

Exercise

Experts on stress believe that the human body long ago developed a stress response to help people handle dangerous situations. Early peoples had to face storms or attacks by wild animals and human enemies. The basic responses are either to fight the danger or to run away. For this reason, the physical changes in response to stress are known as the "fight-or-flight syndrome."

Because the body's response to stress is to get ready for physical action, a logical way to respond to workplace stress is to look for an outlet through physical activity. Although it is never appropriate to punch your manager when he or she criticizes you or to run away when clients complain, other forms of exercise can provide a similar release without negative social consequences. Some people enjoy running, walking, or riding a bicycle before or after work—or as a way to get to work. Others prefer to work out at a health club, participate in sports, or dance. Besides letting off steam, exercising strengthens the body's organs so that they can better withstand stress.

Biofeedback

Some people have devoted time to developing an awareness of such automatically controlled bodily functions as pulse rate, blood pressure, body temperature, and muscle tension and have learned to control these functions. Developing an awareness of bodily functions in order to control them is known as **biofeedback**. People use biofeedback to will their bodies into a more relaxed state.

Meditation

While meditation has religious overtones for many people, in its general form, it is simply a practice of focusing one's thoughts on something other than day-to-day concerns. The person meditating focuses on breathing, on a symbol, or on a word or phrase. People who practice regular meditation find that it relaxes them and that the benefits carry beyond the time spent meditating.

Well-Rounded Life Activities

For someone who gets all of his or her satisfaction and rewards from working, job-related stress is more likely to be overwhelming. No job is going to be rewarding all the time, so some of your satisfaction should come from other areas of life. For instance, if your manager is impatient and fails to praise you for completing an important project, you can offset your frustrations by enjoying the love of friends and family members or hearing the cheers of your softball teammates when you make a good play.

In other words, people who lead a well-rounded life are more likely to experience satisfaction in some area of life at any given time. This satisfaction can make stress a lot easier to cope with. Leading a well-rounded life means not only advancing your career but also devoting time to social, family, intellectual, spiritual, and physical pursuits. One person might choose to read biographies, join a volleyball team, and volunteer in a soup kitchen. Another person might take bicycle trips with the kids on weekends and be active in a religious congregation and a professional organization. These varied pursuits not only help people manage stress but also make life more enjoyable.

Psychotherapy

Another coping mechanism that has been demonstrated to be helpful in combating burnout is psychotherapy. Psychotherapy often involves discussing and processing current life stressors in a confidential manner. Participants in psychotherapy report that feeling understood by their psychotherapist helps to ease the hardships that life often brings. In a recent study of school counselors, it was documented that the counselors that participated in psychotherapy had significantly lower levels of burnout than the counselors that did not participate in psychotherapy.[26] Although further research is needed to understand whether these results would

Exercising is a great way to decrease stress.

biofeedback
Developing an awareness of bodily functions in order to control them

generalize to other work populations, an important foundation has been set in which psychotherapy seems to be useful in combating workplace burnout.

Organizational Stress Management

LO13.7 ▶ Identify ways organizations, including supervisors, can help employees manage stress.

Although employees can take many actions to cope with stress, a significant reduction in stress requires attacking it at its source. Many sources of stress may arise from the policies and practices of the organization and its management. Therefore, any serious effort at stress management must include organizational interventions.

Organizational stress management can operate on several levels. Supervisors can adjust their behavior so that they do not contribute unnecessarily to employee stress. Also, many organizations have helped employees manage stress through job redesign, environmental changes, and wellness programs. Although a supervisor rarely can carry out all these measures single-handedly, he or she may be in a position to recommend them to higher-level managers. Also, a supervisor who knows about any stress management measures offered by the organization is in a better position to take advantage of them and recommend them to employees.

Behavior of the Supervisor

Understanding sources of stress can help supervisors behave in a manner that minimizes unnecessary stress and enhances employee confidence. Supervisors should avoid behavior that contributes to raising employee stress levels. For instance, knowing that feelings of helplessness and uncertainty contribute to stress, supervisors can minimize such feelings through clear communication and regular feedback. Where possible, supervisors also can empower employees to make decisions and solve problems, thereby giving them more control. Table 13.3 summarizes some basic approaches to reducing stress in the workplace.

TABLE 13.3 | How Supervisors Can Minimize Organizational Stressors

Source: Based on Center for the Promotion of Health in the New England Workplace, "How Employers Can Reduce Stress," *Stress@Work*, University of Massachusetts–Lowell, http://www.uml.edu/Research/Centers/CPH-NEW/stress-at-work/employers.aspx, accessed May 8, 2014.

Job design	• Chances to use skills and learn new skills
	• Frequent breaks
	• Control over pace of work
	• Predictable schedules
	• Protection from physical stressors
Communication	• Information that reduces uncertainty
	• Clearly defined roles and responsibilities
	• Positive tone of messages
Motivation	• Participation in decision making
	• Work schedules compatible with outside interests and responsibilities
	• Praise for good performance
	• Opportunities for advancement and development
Social climate	• Opportunities to interact with co-workers
	• Zero tolerance of harassment and discrimination
	• Supervision consistent with organization's values

SUPERVISION AND ETHICS

ETHICAL TREATMENT OF RESEARCH ASSISTANTS

Ethics is a key part of the discussion when setting up any research project. Considerations include the ethical collection of data, any possible conflicts of interest or scientific misconduct, and making sure the correct individuals are included as authors. When humans are involved in the study, a good deal of thought is put into assuring that those involved in the study are treated ethically and fairly and not exposed to any unnecessary risks. Additionally, researchers must apply for approval of their studies when human subjects are involved. What is not often considered, however, is the ethical treatment of the research assistants whose work is so vital to the implementation of countless studies.

The typical work of a research assistant includes many long hours for which they receive little or no pay. Also, depending upon the lead researcher and project, they may not receive any credit or appreciation for the work they do. In a nutshell, many research assistants are treated in exactly the opposite manner that this text recommends supervisors (in this case, the lead researcher) treat their employees (the other research assistants).

In addition to how the supervisor treats the research assistants and the work expectations, a recent study identified that research assistants are often at risk of being exposed to physical harm and emotional stress, including harsh judgment from others. These risks are most likely to come from the actual research being done. For example, one study was exploring how people reacted to someone "cutting" in line. The research assistants were assigned the task of being the ones to step in front of other people in line. This put the research assistants at risk for all three types of potential harm.

Employees working in different industries also face harm from unethical and abusive supervision. For example, recent research suggests that supervisors can engage in bullying and verbal abuse of subordinates. These unethical supervisors may also "depersonalize" the subordinates working for them, which happens when a supervisor views a subordinate solely as a means to a desired end. The net results is a difficult work environment for employees who must balance their professional needs against the stresses they encounter while working on the job.

So, what can be done about these risks? Karen Naufel and Denise Beike propose a "Research Assistant's Bill of Rights." This document outlines a possible ethics code for the supervisors of research assistants. Some of these appear to be very basic rights, such as the right to safety or the right counseling, and yet research has shown that many research assistants do not even have these. Other "rights," such as the right to receive feedback and the right to proper training, are opportunities for lead researchers (supervisors) to enable others to grow and improve.

While some components of this "Bill of Rights" are specific to research assistants and their supervisors, most of them can be applied to any industry looking for guidelines to treat employees fairly and ethically. In a larger context, these studies highlight the need to hold supervisors accountable for the ethical treatment of their subordinates.

Sources: Karen Z. Naufel and Denise R. Beike, "The Ethical Treatment of Research Assistants: Are We Forsaking Safety for Science?," Journal of Research Practice, 9 (2), 2013, http://jrp.icaap.org/index.php/jrp/article/view/360/318; Alice G. Walton, "The 'Dark Side' of Leadership: The Impact of a Bad Boss Can go Viral Through the Office," Forbes, February 2, 2013, http://www.forbes.com/sites/alicegwalton/2013/02/07/the-dark-side-of-leadership-the-impact-of-a-bad-boss-can-go-viral-though-the-office/.

Supervisors' behavior can help employees cope with stressful situations. For example, as described in the "Supervision and Ethics" feature, even in stressful situations, supervisors can treat employees ethically. Similarly, research shows that day care employees are more likely to feel satisfied and less likely to quit if their supervisor stresses that they are a valuable part of a team with a common mission and gives them a role in planning their work. Emergency medical services (EMS) workers cope better after traumatic incidents if their supervisors support them with encouraging words and give them some time to "calm down and decompress."[27] Employees understand that their supervisor cannot fix every cause of stress, but the supervisor *can* determine how he or she treats the employees.

As noted previously, employees with low self-esteem tend to be more susceptible to stress than those with high self-esteem. Therefore, supervisors should avoid behavior that can damage self-esteem, such as put-downs and criticism with no clue about how to improve. Better still, supervisors should behave in esteem-enhancing ways, including the generous use of praise (when it can be offered sincerely) and feedback to employees about how their efforts add value to the work group or the organization as a whole.

Changes in the Job

Recall from Figure 13.5 that many characteristics of a job can be sources of stress. Just a few of the job factors linked to stress include unfair policies, ambiguous procedures, lack of opportunities for advancement, and poor communication. A supervisor has at least some control over many of these matters. For example, supervisors can improve their ability to be fair and communicate instructions clearly and precisely.

In general, an important part of stress management involves identifying job factors linked to stress and then modifying those factors when possible. Sometimes a supervisor cannot act alone to make a change; for example, he or she may not be powerful enough to resolve conflicts with another department. In such cases, a supervisor should be sure that higher-level managers know about the stress-related job factors and how they are affecting employees.

An example from the Hospice of Marion County Healthcare Alliance shows the importance of listening and responding to employee concerns. The hospice, located in Ocala, Florida, set up a program it calls Adopt a Senior Manager. Under the program, employees can arrange to "shadow" a senior manager or ask that person to shadow them (that is, accompany them as they carry out their work). When Sandy Parr was an admissions nurse at the hospice, she was concerned about the organization's efforts to increase each day's patient admissions. Parr was concerned that admitting so many patients would be stressful and impossible to do well, so she asked the hospice's chief executive, Alice Privett, to shadow her. Privett not only saw the need to reduce the workload but also increased her appreciation of the excellent work done by the admissions nurses.[28] A supervisor cannot act alone to establish a companywide program such as the one at the Hospice of Marion County. However, a supervisor is in the best position to ask for and investigate employee concerns, as Alice Privett did, and can bring them to the attention of higher-level managers.

When the sources of stress include boring or overly difficult jobs, the organization may be able to change the job requirements to make them less stressful. As described in Chapter 11, a routine job can be made more interesting through job enlargement or job enrichment. An overly difficult job can be made less so by giving employees further training or reassigning some responsibilities so that the work is divided more realistically.

Environmental Changes

Some characteristics of the job environment can add to employee stress. For example, it is a strain on employees to cope with noise, poor lighting, uncomfortable chairs, and extremes of heat and cold. When possible, an organization should reduce stress by fixing some of these problems. A supervisor is frequently in an excellent position to identify needed environmental changes and report them to the managers who can make the changes. That is likely to be the case when employees complain about uncomfortable chairs or dark work areas.

Supervisors also can recognize environmental stressors that are beyond the organization's control. When four hurricanes struck Florida during a six-week period, employees throughout the state experienced stresses—sometimes dramatically. Some managers, including Dick Dobkin of Ernst & Young, helped employees cope by assuring them that family concerns took priority over job responsibilities. At some jobs, however, such assurances were impossible. Safety requirements demanded that air traffic controllers and airline dispatchers stay

Supervisors need to evaluate weather conditions and whether or not it is safe enough for employees to make the commute.

on the job. Hurricane Charley tore off part of the roof of AirTran Airways' headquarters in Orlando, sparing the area directly over the company's systems operations center. According to AirTran's public relations manager Judy Graham-Weaver, "Our dispatch people were actually in the building; they were literally hanging on, with air-conditioning units blowing off the roof and whatnot."[29] Such a crisis calls for leadership, dedication, and genuine appreciation for the employees who endure extraordinary environmental challenges.

Wellness Programs

Most organizations provide their employees with health insurance, and many also take an active role in helping employees stay well. The usual way to do this is to provide a **wellness program,** or organizational activities designed to help employees adopt healthful practices. These activities might include exercise classes, stop smoking clinics, nutrition counseling, and health screening such as cholesterol and blood pressure tests. Some organizations even have constructed exercise facilities for employees. In a recent survey, three-quarters of employers reported offering wellness programs. The most common services reported were flu shots at the workplace, communications about health and safety, weight management programs, onsite exercise facilities, health fairs, health risk assessments, and smoking cessation programs.[30]

wellness program
Organizational activities designed to help employees adopt healthy practices

For example, in Bradenton, Florida, Tropicana operates a fitness center. About one-fifth of its 1,600 employees pay a small fee to participate. Jean Johnson, a customer logistics worker, says exercising there keeps her focused on health, reinforcing her efforts to stop smoking. The company also sponsored a "weight loss challenge," including personal assessments, workout plans, and weekly weigh-ins.[31]

Tropicana and other companies with wellness programs are not just bringing down stress levels. They are also slashing costs related to unhealthy employees. Doctors Hospital in Sarasota, Florida, operates a fitness center, arranges discounts for employees who join the Sarasota YMCA, hosts Weight Watchers meetings, and offers 15-minute massages as stress breaks. These apparent luxuries are justified, says the hospital's director of human resources, Theresa Levering, because healthier employees tend to file fewer health insurance claims.[32] After the city government of Chattanooga, Tennessee, set up in-house clinics and a fitness center for its employees, the city was able to negotiate a health insurance contract with no premium increase. Other nearby governments saw their insurance costs jump higher at the same time. At another Chattanooga employer, UnumProvident, employees can use onsite clinics for routine tests and shots. The arrangement improves productivity and reduces absenteeism because employees do not have to take time off to visit their doctor for these services.[33]

Given the benefits of wellness programs, it makes sense for supervisors to participate in and support them. When possible, supervisors can avoid scheduling activities that conflict with participation in the programs. They can encourage employees to participate, and they can set good examples by their own participation. However, supervisors should focus on encouraging all employees to participate in the program instead of singling out employees and encouraging them to make specific changes such as losing weight or cutting out cigarettes. After all, having a specialist conduct the wellness program frees the supervisor to concentrate on work-related behaviors—and avoid charges that the supervisor has discriminated against an employee with a disability such as obesity or addiction to nicotine.

A Word About Personality

The guidelines given in this chapter for managing time and stress have worked for many people. However, the degree to which a person will succeed at using any particular technique depends in part on that person's personality. This text does not explore psychological theory, but a brief look at one approach to understanding personality types may be helpful. The Myers-Briggs Type Indicator is a test that classifies people into 16 personality types on the basis of the work of psychiatrist Carl Jung.[34] These 16 personality types describe the traits a person has along four dimensions, as illustrated in Figure 13.7. For example, one individual might be an extrovert, an intuitive, a feeler, and a perceiver. Another person will have a different combination of the four traits. These traits are not considered good or bad; each has its own strengths and weaknesses.

Knowing your personality type can suggest suitable techniques for managing your own time and stress. Thus, an introvert may find that meditation is a pleasant

FIGURE 13.7 | A Basis for Categorizing Personality Types

According to the Myers-Briggs Type Indicator, a person's personality traits fall somewhere along each of these four dimensions.

Source: Adapted from Otto Kroeger and Janet M. Thuesen, "It Takes All Types," *Newsweek*, Management Digest advertising section, September 7, 1992.

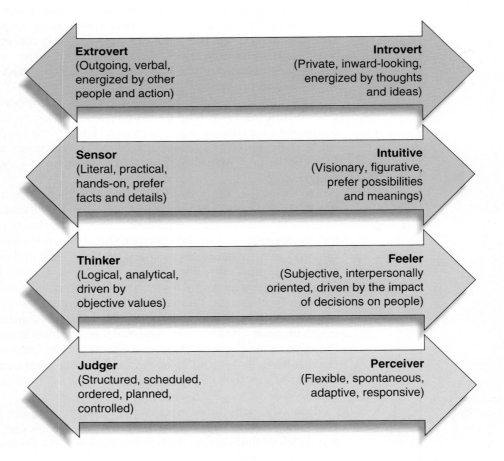

Extrovert
(Outgoing, verbal, energized by other people and action)

Introvert
(Private, inward-looking, energized by thoughts and ideas)

Sensor
(Literal, practical, hands-on, prefer facts and details)

Intuitive
(Visionary, figurative, prefer possibilities and meanings)

Thinker
(Logical, analytical, driven by objective values)

Feeler
(Subjective, interpersonally oriented, driven by the impact of decisions on people)

Judger
(Structured, scheduled, ordered, planned, controlled)

Perceiver
(Flexible, spontaneous, adaptive, responsive)

way to relieve stress, whereas an extrovert may find meditation impossible but dancing with friends refreshing. Judgers have an easy time applying such time management aids as "to do" lists. Perceivers also make those lists, but they lose them and cannot seem to make time to find them. To manage their time, these personality types need heroic amounts of self-discipline—or maybe a job that requires flexibility more than structure.

When you discern that a particular behavior does not fit your personality type, you have a choice. You can make the effort to develop the contrasting trait. For instance, a feeler might list logical criteria for making a decision that must be objective. Or you can avoid situations that require you to behave in ways unsuited to your personality. If the feeler in the previous example really hates making decisions objectively, this person might seek out a job or organization in which highly subjective decisions are valued.

In addition, recognizing different personality types can help you understand the behavior of other people. For example, if you think your manager's head is always in the clouds, perhaps he or she is an intuitive and you are a sensor. Such insights alone can ease a great deal of stress.

Skills Module

PART ONE: CONCEPTS

Summary

13.1 Discuss how supervisors can evaluate their use of time.

A practical way to evaluate time use is to keep a time log. A supervisor enters his or her activities for half-hour periods throughout the workday. After a week or two of keeping the time log, a supervisor reviews the information to see whether his or her time is being used efficiently.

13.2 Describe ways to plan the use of time.

A supervisor can plan his or her use of time by making a list of things to do for the day or week, then rating each item on the list as A (things that must be done), B (things that are important but can be postponed if necessary), or C (everything else). A supervisor then schedules specific times for completing the A- and B-level activities. When time permits, a supervisor works on the C-level activities. A supervisor should not fill up every hour of the day, so that free time is available to handle unexpected problems. A supervisor can plan his or her time with the help of a variety of computer software programs designed specifically for time management. A supervisor also can use programs called desktop organizers.

13.3 Identify some time wasters and how to control them.

Many meetings waste time. A supervisor who calls a meeting can start the meeting on time, keep the discussion on track, and end it on time. A supervisor can control

telephone calls by having someone screen them, returning calls at the same time every day, preparing for calls to be made, and scheduling calls instead of leaving messages. Ways to manage e-mail, texts, and instant messages include choosing times to read and answer messages, using software to keep messages organized in file folders, and adding time-consuming e-mail interruptions to a "to do" list. To handle paperwork and reading material, a supervisor should handle each item only once, decide which items are essential, dictate responses or make telephone calls when possible, and designate a time for reading. With unscheduled visitors, a supervisor can schedule a later meeting, stand to signal that a meeting is ending or will be short, or specify a time limit for the discussion.

The best way to handle procrastination is to tackle the project one step at a time, giving oneself rewards along the way. To combat perfectionism, a supervisor should set high but reasonable standards. Perfectionism is a cause of failure to delegate, so a supervisor must strive to delegate work effectively. Finally, supervisors sometimes find themselves taking on too many projects. The solution is to say no to projects they do not have time to complete properly.

13.4 List factors that contribute to stress among employees.

Certain job factors linked to stress involve the organization's policies, structures, physical conditions, and processes. Notably, when employees feel out of control and the workplace is unsafe or unpredictable, employees will suffer more from the effects of stress. Personal factors also can make a person more vulnerable to stress. Such factors include general feelings of negativism, helplessness, or low self-esteem, as well as a Type A personality—constantly trying to get a lot done in a hurry. Conflicts between work and personal life may be a further source of stress.

13.5 Summarize consequences of stress.

Stress is the body's response to coping with environmental demands. These demands can come from change, frustration, uncertainty, danger, or discomfort. Stress can be stimulating, but an excessive amount of it leads to illness and lowered performance. People under stress feel anxious, aggressive, frustrated, tense, and moody, and they may overreact to criticism. They are also at risk for abusing drugs and alcohol. When a person cannot cope with stress over an extended period of time, the person may experience burnout.

13.6 Explain how supervisors can manage their own stress.

Supervisors and others can manage stress by using time management, having a positive attitude, getting

exercise, using biofeedback, meditating, leading a well-rounded life, and perhaps undergoing psychotherapy. These actions do not reduce the amount of stress the person is under, but they do make a person better able to handle it.

13.7 Identify ways organizations, including supervisors, can help employees manage stress.

Supervisors and other managers can seek to eliminate or minimize the job factors linked to stress. They should communicate clearly, give regular feedback to employees, and empower workers to make decisions and solve problems. When working conditions are stressful, supervisors should make an extra effort to provide support and appreciation and treat employees ethically and with dignity. Supervisors also should behave in ways that enhance employees' self-esteem. In addition, they can make jobs more interesting through job enlargement or job enrichment and can ensure that the work environment is safe and comfortable. Organizations also can offer wellness programs that provide services such as health clinics, instruction in exercise and weight control, and stop smoking programs.

Key Terms

time management, *p.* 350
time log, *p.* 350
procrastination, *p.* 357
perfectionism, *p.* 358

stress, *p.* 359
Type A personality, *p.* 361
Type B personality, *p.* 361
burnout, *p.* 363

biofeedback, *p.* 365
wellness program, *p.* 369

Review and Discussion Questions

1. For one week, keep a time log of your activities at work or at school. Follow the format of Figure 13.1. What does it tell you about your own time management habits?

2. Demetrius Jones prepared the following list of things to do:

Performance appraisal for Angela	A
Clean out files	C
Finish report due Wednesday	A
Prepare a plan for training employees	B
Find out why Kevin has been making more errors lately	B
Read professional journals	C

    a. Which activities should Demetrius consider most important? Least important?

    b. Which activities should Demetrius schedule for times when he is at his best?

    c. If Demetrius fits all these activities onto his weekly schedule and finds he has time left over, what should he do about the "free" time?

3. Assume you are the supervisor of social workers at a hospital. One of your co-workers, a nursing supervisor, asks you to meet with him in his office to discuss a mutual problem. When you arrive at the agreed-upon time, he says, "I'll be right back as soon as I deliver these instructions to one of the nurses and grab a cup of coffee." After you get started 10 minutes later, the supervisor takes several telephone calls, interrupting the meeting for 5 minutes at a time. "Sorry," he says after each call, "but that call was important." An hour into the meeting, you have not made much progress toward solving your problem.

    a. How would you feel in a situation like this? How does your co-worker's behavior affect your performance? How does it affect his performance?

    b. How could you react in this situation to improve your use of time?

4. Imagine that you came to work an hour early so that you could get started on a large proposal that you have due in a week. Fifteen minutes into the project, a co-worker stops by to tell you about her recent vacation. After she leaves, your manager pokes his head into your office and asks if you can spare a minute. Finally, you settle into your proposal. Five minutes after the official start of the workday, one of your employees comes into your office and informs you that she is going to resign. What is the best way to handle each of these unscheduled visitors?

5. You know that you have an important assignment to complete by the end of the week, but you put off starting it on Monday because you want to get everything else out of the way first. In addition, you want a clean slate so that you can concentrate and do a perfect job. Suddenly on Thursday, you realize you can't possibly finish the assignment by the next day. You've procrastinated all week. What steps could you have taken to avoid procrastinating and thus complete the assignment on schedule?

6. Which of the following are sources of stress? Explain.

a. A supervisor who gives you vague and confusing instructions and then criticizes your results.

b. Buying a house.

c. Working at a boring job.

d. Getting a promotion to a supervisory position you have wanted for a year.

7. Sales supervisor Anita Feinstein does not understand all the fuss about stress. She feels stimulated by a job that is exciting and contains many challenges. Does her attitude show that stress is not harmful? Explain.

8. Describe the signs of burnout. Describe the three stages of burnout. What should a supervisor do when he or she observes burnout in an employee?

9. Name five job factors linked to stress over which a supervisor could have some control.

10. How do the following responses help a person cope with stress?

a. Exercising.

b. Using biofeedback.

c. Meditating.

d. Participating in a wellness program.

e. Psychotherapy

Notes

1. For recent empirical findings related to time management, see B. Claessens, W. van Eerde, C. Rutte, and R. Roe, 2007, "A review of the time management literature," *Personnel Review*, 36, p. 255.

2. Robert Ramsey, "15 Time Wasters for Supervisors," *Supervision*, March 2008, downloaded from Business & Company Resource Center, http://galenet.galegroup.com.

3. Eve Tahmincioglu, "It's Time to Deal with That Overflowing In Box," *NBCNEWS.com*, January 24, 2011, http://www.nbcnews.com/id/41135478/ns/business-careers#.U2pTlPldWSo, accessed May 7, 2014; Derek Dean and Caroline Webb, "Recovering from Information Overload," *McKinsey Quarterly*, January 2011, http://www.mckinsey.com/insights/organization/recovering_from_information_overload, accessed May 7, 2014.

4. Jared Sandberg "To-Do Lists Can Take More Time than Doing, but That Isn't the Point," *The Wall Street Journal*, September 8, 2004, http://online.wsj.com/news/articles/SB109460145618411891, accessed May 7, 2014.

5. Jason Fry, "A Tale of Two Emailers," *The Wall Street Journal*, January 30, 2006, http://online.wsj.com/news/articles/SB113830574062457385, accessed May 7, 2014.

6. Clive Thompson, "Meet the Life Hackers," *New York Times Magazine*, October 16, 2005, www.nytimes.com/2005/10/16/magazine/16guru.html?pagewanted=all&_r=0, accessed May 7, 2014.

7. See Maggie Jackson, "Quelling Distraction: Help Employees Overcome 'Information Overload,'" *HRMagazine*, August 2008, downloaded from Business & Company Resource Center, http://galenet.galegroup.com.

8. Thompson, "Meet the Life Hackers"; and "Ask Inc.," *Inc.*, January 2008, p. 60.

9. Pace Productivity, "Time Tips," www.getmore-done.com/category/time-tips/, accessed May 7, 2014.

10. For further reading on procrastination, see T. O'Donoghue and M. Rabin, 2008, "Procrastination on long-term projects," *Journal of Economic Behavior & Organization*, 66, p. 161.

11. Timothy Pychyl, "Procrastination: Oops, Where Did the Day Go?" *Psychology Today*, September 6, 2011, last reviewed April 27, 2014, http://www.psychologytoday.com/articles/201109/procrastination-oops-where-did-the-day-go; John Boe, "Do It Now!" John Boe International, http://johnboe.com/private/do_it_now.html, accessed

May 7, 2014; Teresa Amabile and Steven Kramer, "How to Save an Unproductive Day in 25 Minutes," *The Wall Street Journal*, December 7, 2011, http://online.wsj.com/news/articles/SB10001424052970204770404577082532864410386, accessed May 7, 2014.

12. Elaine Pofeldt, "Tackle Your To-Do List in Record Time," *Money*, August 8, 2011, http://money.cnn.com/2011/08/08/pf/productivity_strategies.moneymag/, accessed May 7, 2014.

13. Pace Productivity, "Time Tips."

14. For more information about different types of workplace stress, see S. Aziz and J. Cunningham, 2008, "Workaholism, work stress, work-life imbalance: Exploring gender's role," *Gender in Management*, 23, p. 553.

15. Elizabeth Bernstein, "When a Co-Worker Is Stressed Out," *The Wall Street Journal*, August 26, 2008, http://online.wsj.com/news/articles/SB121970425860670819, accessed May 7, 2014; and Rob Waters and David Olmos, "Mental-Health Lines Buzz in U.S. Recession Depression," *Bloomberg.com*, September 19, 2008, www.bloomberg.com/apps/news?pid=newsarchive&sid=aEidcDQzs.U4&refer=us, accessed May 7, 2014.

16. Frank Grazian, "Are You Coping with Stress?" *Communication Briefings*, 14, no. 1, p. 3.

17. Michael Gelman, "The Boss: No Second Chances on Live TV," *The New York Times*, February 14, 2001, p. C8, http://www.nytimes.com/2001/02/14/business/14BOSS.html, accessed May 7, 2014.

18. Margarita Bauza, "Study: More Americans Do Work on Their Vacations," *Detroit Free Press*, August 8, 2006, downloaded from Business & Company Resource Center, http://galenet.galegroup.com.

19. Joan Gurvis, "The Balancing Act," *Human Resource Executive*, June 16, 2008, http://www.hreonline.com/HRE/view/story.jhtml?id=101779582, accessed May 7, 2014.

20. Centers for Disease Control and Prevention/National Institute for Occupational Safety and Health, "Work Organization and Stress-Related Disorders" www.cdc.gov/niosh/programs/workorg/, accessed May 7, 2014.

21. For more information on the predictors of workplace burnout, see C. Maslach and M. Leiter, 2008, "Early predictors of job burnout and engagement," *Journal of Applied Psychology*, 93, p. 498.

22. Jenn Danko, "Under the Gun," *PM Network*, November 2010, pp. 54–57.

23. T. L. Stanley, "Balance and Organization," *American Salesman*, August 2004 (quoting Colin Powell's autobiography, *My American Journey*), downloaded from Business & Company Resource Center, http://galenet.galegroup.com.

24. Grazian, "Are You Coping with Stress?"

25. "The Meaning of Work Generates Stress or Well-Being," *CNW Group*, October 29, 2008, downloaded from Business & Company Resource Center, http://galenet.galegroup.com.

26. For more information about this study, see H. Wiseman and S. Egozi, May 1, 2006, "Personal therapy for Israeli school counselors: Prevalence, parameters, and professional difficulties and burnout," *Psychotherapy Research*, 16, pp. 332–347, http://www.edu.haifa.ac.il/personal/hadas_w/files/Wiseman-Egozi2006.pdf, accessed May 7, 2014.

27. Claudia Hale-Jinks, Herman Knopf, and Kristen Kemple, "Tackling Teacher Turnover in Child Care: Understanding Causes and Consequences, Identifying Solutions," *Childhood Education*, Summer 2006, pp. 219–226, downloaded from InfoTrac, http://web2.infotrac.galegroup.com; "Peer and Supervisor Support May Be Critical Coping Strategies for Emergency Medical Services Personnel, Research Indicates," *CNW Group*, January 25, 2006, downloaded from Business & Company Resource Center, http://galenet.galegroup.com.

28. Ann Pomeroy, "Great Places, Inspired Employees," *HRMagazine*, July 2004, 49 (7), http://www.shrm.org/Publications/hrmagazine/EditorialContent/Pages/0704great.aspx, accessed May 7, 2014.

29. Dave Simanoff, "Workers' Needs Should Be First in Stress Times, Experts Say," *Knight Ridder/Tribune Business News*, September 18, 2004, downloaded from Business & Company Resource Center, http://galenet.galegroup.com; Sara Kennedy, "Airline's Dispatchers Weather a Storm," *The New York Times*, September 26, 2004, http://query.nytimes.com/gst/fullpage.html?res=9901EEDC1339F935A1575AC0A9629C8B63, accessed May 7, 2014; Jeff Zeleny, "Fourth Hurricane, Jeanne, Slashes into Weary Florida," *Knight Ridder/Tribune Business News*, September 26, 2004, downloaded from Business & Company Resource Center, http://galenet.galegroup.com.

30. "Employers Increase Wellness Push with New Programs, Incentives," *Employee Benefit News*, July 1, 2006, downloaded from Business & Company Resource Center, http://galenet.galegroup.com.

31. Sara Kennedy, "Physically, Fiscally Fit: Wellness Strategy Can Prove to Be Good Business," *Bradenton (Fla.) Herald*, July 2, 2006, downloaded from Business & Company Resource Center, http://galenet.galegroup.com.

32. Ibid.

33. Emily Berry and Herman Wang, "Wellness Programs Aim to Hold Down Health Costs," *Chattanooga (Tenn.) Times/Free Press*, July 21, 2006, http://www.carehere.com/includes/downloads/072106_tfp.pdf, accessed May 7, 2014.

34. Seth A. Berr, Allan H. Church, and Janine Waclawski, "The Right Relationship Is Everything: Linking Personality Preferences to Managerial Behaviors," *Human Resource Development Quarterly* 11 (2), Summer 2000, pp. 133–157.

PART TWO: SKILL-BUILDING

Meeting the Challenge

Reflecting back on "A Supervision Challenge" on page 349, consider the challenges faced by supervisors in a career or local business that interests you. How could those supervisors relieve stress and help their co-workers handle stress? With your group, come up with additional ways that you, as a supervisor, could offer support and encouragement to your team.

Problem-Solving Case: Do Supervisors Need "Freedom" to Manage Their Time?

Information scientist Fred Stutzman noticed that whenever he went online, he was just a click or two away from a treasure trove of information, entertainment, and social connections. Just one little click, and he could find some tidbit that would be more engaging than whatever project he had sat at the computer to tackle. As he told a reporter recently, being on the Internet provides a "sense that at any point in time, you can dip into this stream." Consequently, Stutzman, like other computer users, finds that he doesn't give 100 percent of his attention to what he is supposedly doing at his computer.

So Stutzman used his computer expertise to create a new piece of software he named Freedom. Freedom basically provides a means of escape from online distractions by making it hard for computer users to go online when they have set aside time for other work. When a user launches Freedom, it asks how long it should disable the computer's Internet access—any period of time within a range from one minute to eight hours. Next, it asks the user whether it should allow access to the local network, which might include printers or other computers to which the user is connected locally. After the user answers the questions and provides a password, Freedom delivers freedom from distractions by shutting off connections as specified.

What if you try Freedom but then realize that your plan was a mistake because you need to look up critical information online or print a document a customer is waiting for? Freedom offers an out that is intentionally annoying: you have to reboot the computer (shut it down and restart it). The process is not complicated but is troublesome enough that users would bother with it only if they really need the local-network or Internet connection. Writer and radio show host Peter Sagal appreciates using Freedom as a way to stay focused when writing books and screenplays. He relearned to work without distractions by setting Freedom first for short time periods and then gradually increasing the duration of the uninterrupted time day by day.

Supervisors might agree with Stutzman and Sagal that concentrating at the computer has become more difficult as the Internet has introduced more and more ways for users to distract themselves—social media, news feeds, funny or heartwarming videos, e-mail from customers and co-workers, and instant messages from colleagues, to name just a few. But is Freedom the best solution for supervisors? Perhaps they would be better off to follow the advice of Linda Stone, an expert in the impact of computers on thinking. Stone says running software that makes us use computers appropriately is only a first step toward what is the real and meaningful change: learning to control ourselves at our computers.

1. Imagine you are a sales supervisor who works primarily in an office at headquarters, staying in touch with traveling sales representatives to coach them and oversee their performance. Why might you need Internet access? Would you need to have that access all day long, every minute of the day? Why or why not?

2. Continuing with the example in question 1, how do you think it would change your support of the sales reps if you used a program like Freedom to stay offline for an hour or two every day? How do you think it would change your ability to complete other kinds of work, such as writing reports, thinking of new ways to motivate workers, and planning for future goals and budgets?

3. Discuss your opinion of Linda Stone's view that individuals should learn to police themselves online, rather than relying on software to help them manage their computer use. For a supervisor, is getting control over time by any means more important, or is learning self-control more important?

Source: Based on "Stay on Target," *The Economist*, June 12, 2010, http://www.economist.com/node/16295664, accessed May 6, 2014.

Assessing Yourself

How Well Do You Use Technology to Manage Time?

Complete this simple quiz to find out how well you use technology to save and manage time. Each of the following statements represents a simple yet tried-and-true method of time-saving technology. Rate yourself on each: If you practice the method regularly, give yourself a "3." Practice it sometimes, give yourself a "2." Practice it rarely, you get a "1." And if you never practice it, you receive a "0." Now, take a moment to complete the quiz.

1. I skim professional journals via the Web. — 3 2 1 0
2. I send agendas, meeting minutes, assignment summaries, and other notices to co-workers and employees using e-mail. — 3 2 1 0
3. I maintain working files in a single, readily accessible directory, enabling me to work on current projects whenever I have spare moments. — 3 2 1 0
4. Using planning or spreadsheet software, I list and monitor objectives, strategies, and tasks necessary for the completion of my goals. — 3 2 1 0
5. I group tasks related to each software package together and complete each group of related tasks at the same time. — 3 2 1 0
6. I organize documents with an intuitive file structure. — 3 2 1 0
7. I maintain a perpetual "to do" list on a computerized task manager or in a special file, checking off items as they are completed. — 3 2 1 0
8. Using numerical rankings in a spreadsheet, I analyze and identify priorities. — 3 2 1 0
9. I maintain my calendar and other key information using portable digital technology. — 3 2 1 0
10. I have software that maintains my key organizational resources, such as contacts, tasks, events, and crucial records. — 3 2 1 0
11. I maintain "idea files" into which I post thoughts, jottings, and potential tasks. — 3 2 1 0
12. I use e-mail to forward documents to co-workers. — 3 2 1 0
13. I associate related files to each other with HTML links. — 3 2 1 0
14. I consolidate Web searches into a specific time of the day or week. — 3 2 1 0
15. I conduct "offline" Web searches to save time. — 3 2 1 0
16. Through e-mail, discussion lists, and team software, I participate in virtual meetings. — 3 2 1 0
17. Using shared directories, I post public files containing policies, forms, and other information regularly used by the people around me. — 3 2 1 0
18. I transfer files from my office computer to my home or laptop, and vice versa. — 3 2 1 0
19. I have begun using voice input to save keyboarding or personal dictating time. — 3 2 1 0
20. I append the names of files with dates for easy retrieval. — 3 2 1 0
21. I use my computer to send broadcast faxes and e-mails when appropriate. — 3 2 1 0
22. I maintain a directory and bookmarks of commonly used reference materials. — 3 2 1 0
23. I use shortcuts, such as templates and macros, to speed up my work. — 3 2 1 0

24. I handle business transactions online.   3 2 1 0

25. I maintain financial data in a simple accounting program or,   3 2 1 0
if appropriate, using spreadsheet or database software.

26. I maintain files for every person I work with, detailing meeting   3 2 1 0
summaries, assignments, and other notes.

27. I automatically create multiple drafts of a document, noting   3 2 1 0
relevant changes with each successive draft.

28. I automate correspondence and mailing functions using mail   3 2 1 0
merge features.

29. I use spreadsheet software to prepare budgets, expense reports,   3 2 1 0
statistical analyses, and other numerical data.

Now, total your score and figure out where you stand. If you rated between 75 and 90, congratulations! You are developing some outstanding time-saving technology skills. A rating between 50 and 74 means that you have learned a number of practical skills, and you are probably aware of the many ways technology can help you master time. Maintain your commitment to learn more. A rating below 50 means that you may have some catching up to do. If you find yourself in this category (and even if you do not) review the principles noted in this time quiz. Read up on the latest technology. Take a course or seminar to learn how you can better use these remarkable tools in your daily life.

Pause and Reflect

1. Does technology help you manage your time? Why or why not?
2. Can some of these techniques, if misused, become time *wasters*?
3. Identify one of the technologies on this list that you have not used but plan to try (or one you would like to use more, or differently).

Source: From Richard G. Ensman, "Technology and Time Management: How Do You Rate?" *Manage,* November 1, 2001. Reprinted with permission.

Class Skills Exercise

Using Time Wisely

Each student, in turn, tells the class how he or she wastes time. The instructor lists the ways on the chalkboard or overhead projector. Then the class discusses the list.

- Which time wasters are most common?
- Are they really just time wasters, or are they also stress reducers?

Source: The idea for this exercise was provided by Sylvia Ong, Scottsdale Community College, Scottsdale, Arizona.

Building Supervision Skills

Managing Time and Stress

Divide the class into teams of four or five students. Assign each team an imaginary project with a completion date (or have the teams come up with one on their own). Suggested projects are cleaning up one of the common areas used by students at the school, recruiting classmates to participate in a fund-raising activity, or developing publicity for an upcoming arts event. Then have the teams (1) make a "to do" list outlining how they plan to set priorities for the project and use their time, (2) note how they plan to control time wasters, and (3) describe how they plan to manage any stress associated with trying to complete the project properly and on schedule.

At the end of the exercise, have students identify themselves as Type A or Type B personalities and discuss how this contributes to the way they approach getting things done as team members.

chapter fourteen | Managing Conflict and Change

learning objectives

After you have studied this chapter, you should be able to:

14.1 List positive and negative aspects of conflict.

14.2 Define types of conflict.

14.3 Describe strategies for managing conflict.

14.4 Explain how supervisors can initiate conflict resolution, respond to a conflict, and mediate conflict resolution.

14.5 Identify sources of change and explain why employees and supervisors resist it.

14.6 Discuss how supervisors can overcome resistance and implement change.

14.7 Describe the types of power supervisors can have.

14.8 Identify common strategies for organizational politics.

A Supervision Challenge

ACCEPTING CHANGE AT BEST BUY

Business changes can affect anyone in an organization, from front-line employees right up to the CEO. Even when supervisors are being impacted, they must lead by example, model professional conduct for their teams, and guide their staff through tough changes. But that is easier said than done.

Consider the case of Best Buy, a multinational consumer electronics retailer, facing major organizational changes in early 2014. Headquartered in Richfield, Minnesota, the company has over 1,400 stores and locations in the United States and employs over 140,000 people worldwide. After a disappointing Christmas season, which saw their stock fall 30 percent, the company announced that it was planning to cut some 2,000 managers from its staff. Cutting district, regional, and store managers is a somewhat unusual move, although in-store staff levels have also been affected in other rounds of layoffs.

Whenever a business loses staff, it is trying to respond to factors that threaten the profitability and viability of the enterprise, and to instill confidence in its investors and stakeholders. Market forces and economic pressures are major external sources of the changes that a business may undergo. Best Buy had been facing declining revenues for some time and had been implementing several strategies for achieving profitability, including closing stores and cutting back non-essential services, among other tactics. There have even been layoffs at headquarters. The company is clearly struggling to right itself.

This is a challenging environment to work in for everyone, whether you are a supervisor who is remaining, a supervisor who is leaving, or front-line staff dealing with customers. For supervisors it may be particularly challenging to keep up-to-date on the company's latest plans, and to communicate objectives and expectations to staff in as calm and professional a manner as possible. A supervisor who is leaving may have to deal with upset employees and team members. Supervisors who are staying may have employees turning to them for guidance.

Industry analysts are not confident that this latest strategy will work for Best Buy. This does not help supervisors because their staff follow the news just as much as anyone, and may put more credence in what they are hearing on the news than what they hear from their own management.

It may be tempting to tell your team how you are really feeling at this point, especially if you have a friendly relationship with them. But that is a very bad idea. If you bad-mouth senior management or express a lack of confidence in the company's ability to navigate these changes successfully, you are undermining your position, not to mention the company. First-level supervisors represent the company to their staff, so you have a duty to do your best to manage the changes and overcome resistance. Supervisors may be friendly with their staff but their first duty is to the company—failure to perform in this manner may result in a supervisor's termination.

As you study this chapter, think about how this kind of change affects supervisors and their teams, the company's rank-and-file foot soldiers. How can you propose and implement change, even when you may be the victim of it? How can you overcome resistance from your team? How can you be true to yourself and your feelings while still fulfilling your obligations to the company as its representative?

Sources: Based on Anshel Sag, "Massive Layoffs at Best Buy, Huge Management Reshuffling," *Bright Side of News*, March 4, 2014, http://www.brightsideofnews.com; James Covert, "Best Buy Cutting 2000 Managers," *New York Post*, February 26, 2014, http://nypost.com.

Conflicts and changes are bound to occur in any organization. Whether they are constructive or destructive depends significantly on the supervisor's ability to manage them.

This chapter addresses conflict management by examining the nature of conflict and ways to respond to conflict constructively. The chapter also discusses the role of change in the workplace and how supervisors can implement it. Finally, the chapter considers an aspect of organizational behavior that often affects the management of both conflict and change—organization politics—and describes how supervisors can use politics ethically and effectively.

Conflict

conflict
The struggle that results from incompatible or opposing needs, feelings, thoughts, or demands within a person or between two or more people

In the context of this book, **conflict** refers to the struggle that results from incompatible or opposing needs, feelings, thoughts, or demands within a person or between two or more people. If supervisor Janet Speers sees that an employee she likes is taking home office supplies, her feelings for the employee come in conflict with her belief that stealing is wrong. If her feelings and belief are both strong, she will have difficulty resolving the issue. Likewise, if two employees disagree over how to fill out time sheets for sick days, there is a conflict between the employees. In this case, the organization should have a clear procedure to make the conflict easy to resolve.

LO14.1 ▶ List positive and negative aspects of conflict.

Positive and Negative Aspects of Conflict

Sometimes conflict is a positive force that can bring about necessary changes. Imagine that a business that develops computerized information systems has hired a new systems analyst, Jordan Walsh. Walsh gets all the boring and routine jobs— filing, running errands, proofreading documentation. If he acts cheerful, the other employees will assume there is no conflict (although he may feel one internally). Of course, this situation is not good for Walsh; he feels insulted, is bored every day, and is missing out on the experience he needs to develop his career. This arrangement is also bad for the employer, who is paying for a systems analyst but not benefiting from his talents. Furthermore, if Walsh quits, the company will have to bear the expense of repeating the hiring process. However, if Walsh complains to his supervisor about his limited role, the conflict will surface, and the resolution may leave everyone, including Walsh, better off. Thus, when conflict serves as a signal that a problem exists, it can stimulate a creative response.

Ongoing conflict also has negative consequences. People who are engaged in disputes are under stress, which takes a physical toll. In addition, people who are busy arguing and trying to persuade others to take their sides are not involved in more productive activities. Finally, depending on the source of the conflict, the people involved may be angry at management or the organization, so they may vent their anger in ways that are destructive to the organization, such as taking extra time off or sabotaging equipment.

The consequences of conflict may depend partly on the way that it is resolved. If people treat a conflict as an opportunity for constructive problem solving and change, the outcomes may well be positive. If people routinely see conflict as a need for someone to win at someone else's expense, or for a manager to impose control, the conflict is more likely to have negative consequences.[1]

frustration
Defeat in the effort to achieve desired goals

Most notably, when conflict is viewed as a win–lose proposition, the loser will experience **frustration**; that is, defeat in the effort to achieve desired goals. An employee who has her request for a flextime arrangement turned down experiences frustration. So does an employee who can't convince a prospective customer to return his phone calls. Most of us can handle a little frustration philosophically, with words such as, "Oh, well, I can't always have my own way" or "No one can have it all." However, repeated frustration tends to generate anger. A frustrated employee may engage in destructive behavior such as sabotage, aggression, insubordination, and absenteeism. (Chapter 12 covers the supervision of employees who engage in such behaviors.) To help supervisors head off problems arising from frustration, this chapter emphasizes forms of conflict resolution aimed at finding a solution that is satisfactory to all parties.

FIGURE 14.1 | Types of Conflict

There are several different types of conflict that can come into play in the workplace.

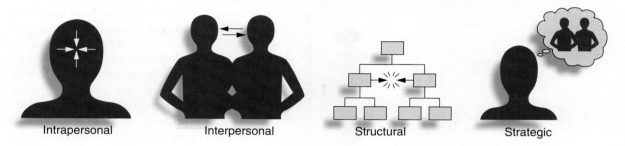

Intrapersonal   Interpersonal   Structural   Strategic

LO14.2 ▶ Define types of conflict.

Types of Conflict

Before a supervisor can respond effectively to a conflict, he or she needs to understand the real nature of that conflict. Who is involved? What is the source of the conflict? A supervisor is likely to respond differently to a conflict that results from a clash of opinions than one stemming from frustration over limited resources.

As defined, conflict may arise within an individual (intrapersonal) or between individuals or groups. The basic types of conflict involving more than one person are called interpersonal, structural, and strategic, as illustrated in Figure 14.1.

Intrapersonal Conflict

An intrapersonal conflict arises when a person has trouble selecting from among goals. Choosing one of two possible goals is easy if one is good and the other bad. For example, would you rather earn $1 a year as a drug dealer or $1 million a year as the microbiologist who discovered a cure for cancer? Of course, we rarely are faced with such unrealistically easy choices. Most choices fall into three categories:

1. A choice between two good possibilities (for example, having a child or taking an exciting job that requires travel year-round).

2. A choice between two mixed possibilities (for example, accepting a promotion that involves moving away from your family or keeping your current, but monotonous, job to be near your family).

3. A choice between two bad possibilities (for example, reorganizing your department in a way that requires either laying off two employees or eliminating your own position).

Because these choices are not obvious, they result in conflict.

Supervisors should consider whether they or their organization are contributing unnecessarily to intrapersonal conflicts. For example, do they reward unethical behavior or pressure employees to behave unethically? If so, they are setting up conflicts between employees' values and their desire to be rewarded.

Listening to others with an open mind can help supervisors correct actions that add to conflict. Michael Feiner saw this principle when he was a PepsiCo executive. Feiner learned that one of his employees had bypassed the chain of command to ask higher-level management to increase salaries in the employee's group. Feiner was upset at what he perceived to be an action that undermined him as the supervisor, so he angrily confronted his employee. The employee explained that he went to higher-level managers because he had repeatedly brought his proposal to Feiner and Feiner had repeatedly rejected the salary increases without listening to the employee's arguments in favor of them. Feiner recognized that by neglecting to listen to the proposal, he had allowed the conflict to persist.[2] Listening to others and admitting one's mistakes can be difficult, requiring self-discipline and maturity. In Feiner's example, however, the effort made him a more effective manager.

Supervisors are often willing to work with their employees' schedules so that these employees can feel that they are living a more unified life between work and home.

Listening and talking to others can also help supervisors resolve their own intrapersonal conflicts. Sometimes conflicts persist because a person has not fully explored the alternatives. An example is conflict in balancing one's roles at work and at home. Management professor Stewart Friedman advises his students to look at work and family as aspects of one unified life and consider how to improve results overall, rather than trading off one area of life against the other. One of Friedman's assignments is for students to talk to their co-workers and family members about what is expected of them and then think creatively about how to meet those requirements. The students have found the assignment difficult at first but ultimately helpful in improving their work and family lives. For example, one married student discovered that his pregnant wife wanted him to go along on appointments with the doctor. He was surprised but negotiated an adjustment in his hours and discovered that he appreciated the morning family time. Speaking directly about the situation to his wife and boss helped him avoid the kind of conflict that might have arisen if he had arranged his time on the basis of his guesses about what they wanted from him.[3]

In many cases, a supervisor lacks the expertise to resolve an intrapersonal conflict. When supervisors notice that an employee is struggling with an intrapersonal conflict, they should consider who might be able to help. People with skills in handling various types of intrapersonal conflicts include psychologists, religious advisers, and career counselors.

Interpersonal Conflict

Conflict between individuals is called *interpersonal conflict*. Supervisors may be involved in interpersonal conflicts with their manager, an employee, a peer, or even a customer. In addition, they may have to manage conflicts between two or more of their employees. Interpersonal conflicts may arise from differing opinions, misunderstandings of a situation, or differences in values or beliefs. Sometimes two people just rub each other the wrong way. Differences are especially likely to arise in a diverse workforce, where there may be more variety in employees' values and opinions. Supervisors should take a lead role in managing these differences so they do not become a source of negative conflict. For example, the "Supervision and Diversity" feature describes some ways to manage conflict between age groups at work. (For more ideas, see the discussion of diversity in Chapter 5, the ideas for leading employees in Chapter 8, and the section on managing interpersonal conflict later in this chapter.)

Interpersonal conflicts are especially difficult when one or more people lack "emotional intelligence," or the ability to manage emotions and interpersonal relationships. People with emotional intelligence have a combination of self-awareness (recognizing their emotions and how they affect others), self-regulation (ability to control emotions and maintain integrity), self-motivation (striving to meet goals and improve themselves), social awareness (empathy, concern for others, and understanding of how people operate in groups), and social skills such as leadership, cooperation, and communication.[4] Consider the team that designed Nissan's GT-R luxury sports car to compete for the first time against Porsche and Ferrari.

SUPERVISION AND DIVERSITY

WHEN GENERATIONS COLLIDE

A supervisor's team may consist of employees from two, three, or even four different generations. Although many differences certainly exist within each generation, it is often the variations from generation to generation that can result in misunderstandings and conflict. For example, older employees tend to bring a strong work ethic and a cautious approach to risk taking, while baby-boomers will put in long hours to make a difference. Young workers are at ease with Internet technologies and expect employers to give them wide latitude in using the technology and to support them in their efforts to find work–life balance. Thus, a conflict might arise when young workers expect to have access to social media, at least during breaks, while an older manager sees social media primarily as a source of risk to the organization.

One way supervisors can prevent intergenerational differences from becoming a source of negative conflict is to first educate themselves about the people in their group. What generations are represented? Learn about the life experiences and values of these age groups. That knowledge can help supervisors be aware of possible issues to explore when employees are having difficulty getting along with one another. For example, if younger workers are less formal, older workers may interpret their behavior as disrespect. By having a proactive dialogue about this, however, employees can learn from one another what kinds of behavior are interpreted as respectful, so they can avoid unintentionally offending each other.

Another tactic is to redefine differences as a source of strength for the group. Look for ways that employees in one generation can use their strengths to contribute to the group's overall performance. Young employees tend to like a lot of feedback, so supervisors might pair them up with older employees serving as mentors. This has the added advantage of acknowledging the value of the older employees' work and life experience. Conversely, if the department is introducing Internet tools, younger employees might be able—and eager—to be "reverse mentors" to older employees. This approach is especially effective if the older employees see the change as a chance to expand their skill sets.

Finally, supervisors can establish ground rules for appropriate behavior. For example, employees of all generations should treat one another with respect. That includes listening to one another and stating one's own opinions without negativity or insulting others or their opinions. Being young or old is not an excuse for failure to get along or meet goals. When there are generational differences, it is the supervisor's job to understand those differences and find a way to use those differences as assets that benefit the organization.

Sources: Larry Johnson and Meagan Johnson, "Resolving Intergenerational Workplace Conflict," *Baseline*, November/December 2010, p. 17; Denise Zaporzan, "Four Generations, One Workplace: Watch Us Work," *CMA Management*, October 2010, pp. 12–13, http://www.nxtbook.com/nxtbooks/naylor/cmamanagement_201010/index.php#/12, accessed May 12, 2014; and Leigh Elmore, "Generation Gaps," *Women in Business*, June 2010, http://www.nxtbook.com/nxtbooks/abwa/inbusiness_201006/index.php?startid=8, accessed May 12, 2014.

Company spokesman Simon Sproule told a reporter, "The process was not all sweetness and light. There were arguments and disagreements. It was very intense but more so because everyone was interested in the car."[5] Team leaders and team members alike had to recognize that emotions were riding high so that they could channel their energy into communicating, solving problems, and meeting shared goals—hallmarks of an emotionally intelligent team—rather than blaming and complaining.[6]

Structural Conflict

Conflict that results from the way the organization is structured is called *structural conflict*. Conflict often arises between line and staff personnel, and production and marketing departments are often at odds. In the latter example, marketing wants to give customers whatever they ask for, and production wants to make what it can easily and well.

Structural conflict often arises when various groups in the organization share resources, such as the services of a word-processing or maintenance department. Each group wants its jobs handled first, but the support department obviously cannot help everyone first. Some of the most unpleasant structural conflict occurs when the "shared resource" is one employee who reports to two different managers.

Some organizations are structured so that employees report to a functional manager and a project manager, or perhaps a supervisor's manager ignores the chain of command and gives directions to the supervisor's employees. An extreme example made work impossible for Eric Knudsen. At the software company where he was selected to lead the development of a new product, he was expected to deliver results to a sales director and marketing director from one business group, as well as to a marketing director and a business operations manager from a different group. If that weren't hard enough, a vice president began directing Knudsen's efforts as well. Knudsen complained, "It was difficult to know who was holding the purse strings, who to support and who to ignore." Eventually, the structural conflict became unbearable, and Knudsen quit his job.[7]

When structural conflict arises between two groups of employees reporting to a supervisor or between a supervisor's group and another group, the supervisor may be able to help minimize or resolve it by providing opportunities for the two groups to communicate and get to know each others' viewpoints, having them collaborate on achieving a mutually desirable goal, and giving each group training or experience in what the other group does.

If some employees involved in a structural conflict report to another supervisor, managing the conflict requires the cooperation of the two supervisors. Engaging that cooperation may require the appropriate use of political tactics, discussed in the last section of this chapter.

Because supervisors do not establish an organization's structure, they have limited impact on the sources of structural conflict. However, they do need to be able to recognize it. Knowing that a conflict is structural frees a supervisor from taking the issue personally and alerts him or her to situations that require extra diplomacy. A supervisor also may be able to understand the other party's point of view and communicate it to his or her employees.

Strategic Conflict

Most of the conflicts described so far arise unintentionally when people and groups try to work together. However, sometimes management or an individual intentionally will bring about a conflict to achieve an objective. This is referred to as a strategic conflict. For instance, a sales department might hold a contest for the highest sales volume and the most impressive example of delighting a customer. Or a manager might tell two employees that they are both in the running for a retiring supervisor's job. In both examples, the intent is to use competition to motivate employees to do exceptional work.

Managing Interpersonal Conflict

Restaurant manager Phyllis Jensen schedules the hours each server will work during the upcoming week. She has noticed that one of the servers, Rich Yakima, scowls when he gets his assignments and does so for hours afterward. She asked Yakima about it, and he replied, "You know just what the problem is. You know I've been wanting an evening off every weekend so I can go out with my girlfriend, but every week you have me working Friday and Saturday nights. And I've noticed that Rita and Pat always get the hours they want." Responding to problems such as this is known as conflict management.[8]

conflict management
Responding to problems stemming from conflict

LO14.3 ▶ Describe strategies for managing conflict.

Strategies

How can Jensen manage the conflict involving Yakima? She can begin by recognizing the various strategies available for conflict management shown, on the following page, Figure 14.2: compromising, avoiding, forcing a solution, and resolving.

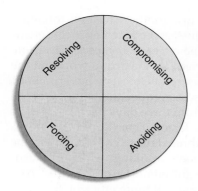

FIGURE 14.2 | Strategies for Conflict Management

There are four different primary approaches to managing a conflict, each of which has advantages and disadvantages in different situations.

compromise
Settling on a solution that gives each person part of what he or she wants; no one gets everything, and no one loses completely

On the basis of her understanding of these strategies, Jensen can choose the most appropriate one for the circumstances. To see which conflict management strategy you tend to select most frequently, take the Assessing Yourself quiz on pages 407–408.

Compromising

One conflict management strategy is to reach a **compromise,** which means the parties to the conflict settle on a solution that gives both of them part of what they wanted. No party gets exactly what it wanted, but neither loses entirely either. Both parties presumably experience a degree of frustration—but at a level they are willing to live with.

People who choose to compromise are assuming they cannot reach a solution completely acceptable to everyone, but they would rather not force someone to accept a completely disagreeable choice. In that sense, compromise does not really solve the underlying problem; it works best when the problem is relatively minor and time is limited.

Avoiding

Conflict is unpleasant, so people sometimes try to manage conflict by avoiding it. For example, if sales supervisor Jeanette Delacroix finds the people in the human resources department stuffy and inflexible, she can avoid dealing with that department. When contact with human resources is absolutely necessary, she can delegate the responsibility to a member of the sales force.

This strategy makes sense if you assume that all conflict is bad. If you successfully avoid all conflicts, life looks serene on the surface. However, people do disagree, and sometimes people with opposing viewpoints have important ideas to share. Avoiding those conflicts does not make them go away, nor does it make opposing points of view any less valid or significant. Therefore, it is important to be selective in avoiding conflicts. These strategies are most useful for conflicts that are not serious and for which a solution would be more difficult than the problem justifies.

This point is especially important with regard to today's diverse workforce. A person's point of view often seems puzzling, irritating, or downright incorrect to someone of another race, age, or sex. It takes extra work to understand people who are different from us. However, a supervisor must give equal attention to the views of all employees, not only those the supervisor understands best. Pretending that everyone is looking at a situation the same way does not make it so. It can even foster a belief among some employees that the supervisor is discriminating against them.

At the same time, people in many non-Western cultures believe it is best to avoid conflicts, placing a higher value on harmony than on "telling it like it is."[9] People with these values are less likely than employees from Western cultures to complain to their supervisor or to deliver bad news. Thus, a supervisor may not realize there is a problem, such as a dispute between employees or a possibility that a task will be completed late. A supervisor must tactfully ensure that employees know that the supervisor wants to be aware of any problems in order to help resolve them.

Forcing

Because ignoring or avoiding a problem does not make it go away, a supervisor may want to try a more direct approach to ending a conflict. One possibility is to force a solution. This means that a person or group with power decides what the outcome will be. For example, if machinist Pete Desai complains to his supervisor that he never gets overtime assignments, the supervisor can respond, "I make the assignments, and your job is to do what you're told. This weekend it's going to be Sue and Chuck, so make the best of it." Or if two supervisors present conflicting proposals for allocating space among their departments, a committee of higher-level managers could select one proposal, allowing no room for discussion.

In an organization with self-managed work teams, another twist on forcing a solution is more likely. The team may decide that instead of reaching a consensus on some issue, it will simply vote on what to do. The majority makes the decision. Or the team leader may make the overall decision and let the group work out the details. During Timothy Riordan's management career in Ohio city governments, he once was trying to lead his employees in a project to reduce the time needed to process payments of citizens' taxes and water bills from three days to two days. The team was stuck on how to make employees work faster. Then Riordan forced a decision: The processing time would shrink from three days to completion on the day received. The forced decision shifted everyone's thinking. One supervisor exclaimed, "Well, we're going to have to do things differently around here." And the team began to restructure the whole process to make it more efficient.[10]

Forcing a solution is a relatively fast way to manage a conflict, and it may be the best approach in an emergency. Reaching consensus, for example, tends to be difficult and time-consuming, whereas a team can vote on an issue quickly. However, forcing a solution can cause frustration. In organizations seeking teamwork and employee empowerment, forcing a solution works against those objectives by shutting off input from employees with a minority viewpoint. The bad feelings that accompany frustration and exclusion from decision making may lead to future conflict.

Resolving

conflict resolution
Managing a conflict by confronting the problem and solving it

The most direct—and sometimes the most difficult—way to manage conflict is to confront the problem and solve it. This is the conflict management strategy called **conflict resolution**. Confronting the problem requires listening to both sides and attempting to understand rather than to place blame. Next, the parties should identify the areas on which they agree and the ways they can both benefit from possible solutions. Both parties should examine their own feelings and take their time at reaching a solution. (Chapter 9 provides further guidelines for problem solving.)

Confronting and solving a problem makes a different assumption about the conflict than other strategies for conflict management, which tend to assume that the parties have a *win–lose conflict*. In other words, the outcome of the conflict will be that one person wins (that is, achieves the desired outcome), and the other person must lose. In contrast, conflict resolution assumes that many conflicts are *win–win conflicts*, in which the resolution can leave both parties better off. Frustration is avoided, and both sides feel like winners.

---

connect SELF-ASSESSMENT 14.1

What Is Your Conflict Handling Style?

As you are probably realizing by now, different situations call for different methods of handling them. The same is true with conflict. This assessment will help you identify the conflict handling style with which you are most comfortable. Remember though, it may not be the most appropriate style in all situations.

LO14.4 ▶ Explain how supervisors can initiate conflict resolution, respond to a conflict, and mediate conflict resolution.

Initiating Conflict Resolution

When a supervisor has a conflict with another person, he or she needs to resolve that conflict constructively. Otherwise, the conflict is unlikely to go away on its own. When initiating conflict resolution, a supervisor should act as soon as he or she is aware of the problem. As the problem continues, a supervisor is likely to get increasingly emotional about it, which only makes resolution more difficult.

FIGURE 14.3 | Initiating Conflict Resolution

Conflict resolution is a process, not just taking a single action. It takes work and practice to become proficient at conflict resolution.

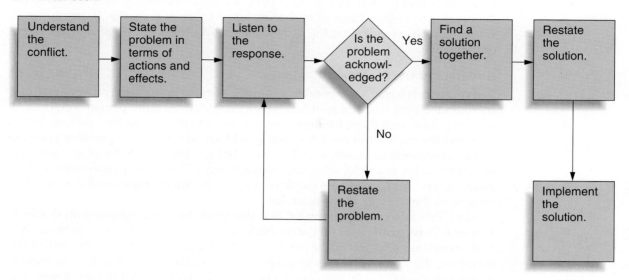

You cannot control the other person's response, so occasionally conflict resolution might not go much beyond your statement of the problem. Helene Dublisky once had reason to believe a colleague had given their supervisor false information that Dublisky had violated a policy of her employer, a utility company. Dublisky phoned her co-worker and described the situation as objectively as she could. According to Dublisky, the co-worker was silent for a moment, said, "I have to go now," and hung up the phone. Although the two employees did not discuss a solution, Dublisky had no further problems with backstabbing. Carl Robinson, a career coach, agrees that this kind of effort to resolve conflict is worthwhile, because it alerts the other employee that you will take action when conflicts arise. Similarly, management psychologist Nina Christopher suggests asking if there are any problems you should be aware of. If that does not generate a response, Christopher recommends adding, "I understand from others in the department that you have some issues you're unhappy about with me, and I'd like for us to discuss them directly."[11]

Prepare for conflict resolution by understanding what the conflict is (the first step in Figure 14.3). Focus on behavior, which people can change, not on personalities, which they cannot change. What is the action that is causing the problem, and how does that action affect you and others? For example, you might tell a supervisor in another department, "I haven't been getting the weekly sales figures until late Friday afternoon. That means I have to give up precious family time to review them over the weekend, or else I embarrass myself by being unprepared at the Monday morning staff meetings."

When used politely, this type of approach even works with one's manager. You might say, "I haven't heard from you concerning the suggestions I made last week and three weeks ago. That worries me, because I think maybe I'm giving you too many ideas or not the right kind."

After you have stated the problem, listen to how the other person responds. If the other person does not acknowledge there is a problem, restate your concern until the other person understands or until it is clear that you cannot make any progress on your own. Often a conflict exists simply because the other person has not understood your point of view or your situation. When you have begun communicating about the problem, the two of you can work together to find a solution. Restate your solution to be sure that both of you agree on what you are going to do (the final steps in Figure 14.3).

Responding to a Conflict

Sometimes a supervisor is party to a conflict that is bothering someone else. When the other person makes the supervisor aware of the conflict, it is up to the supervisor to respond in a way that makes a solution possible. If an employee says, "You always give me the dirty assignments," it is not helpful to get angry or defensive.

Understand the Problem

The constructive way to respond to a conflict is first to listen to the other person and try to understand what the problem is really about. If the other person is emotional, let that person vent those feelings, then get down to discussing the problem. Try to interpret the problem in the terms you would use to express the problem yourself. Avoid statements of blame, and find out what specific actions the other person is referring to. For example, when an employee says, "You always give me the dirty assignments," you can ask the employee to give specific examples and then describe how he or she feels about the behavior.

Mark Preiser took this important first step when he was a partner with Walter F. Cameron Advertising in Hauppauge, New York. An account manager at his agency had committed to delivering a job by a particular deadline, but on the day of the deadline, the artist who was to prepare the visuals called in sick. The furious account manager was on the phone, shouting. He doubted that the artist was sick. Instead, he suspected the weather: The day was snowy, and the artist often missed work on snowy days. Preiser joined the conversation and learned that the artist was afraid. He had been in a serious car accident on a snowy day, and ever since, driving in the snow had terrified him. Preiser worked with the account manager and artist to arrange for the artist to be able to take work home whenever a snowstorm was in the weather forecast.[12]

Understanding the problem can be complicated if one of the people involved has a "hidden agenda"—a central concern that is left unstated. Typically, a person with a hidden agenda is angry or upset about something but directs those feelings toward some other issue. For example, a colleague in another department explodes, "What's wrong with you? The numbers in your report are off by a mile!" Your colleague is not really angry because you made a mistake. He is nervous because he has to make a presentation to the board of directors, and he wonders if the incorrect numbers are your way to mislead him so that he looks uninformed and you get the promotion he wants. Or maybe your colleague simply has had a frustrating day, and your mistake is the last straw.

If another person's feelings seem to be out of proportion to the problem he or she is describing, look for a hidden agenda. Finding one can save you from trying to resolve the wrong conflict. In addition, when you are upset about something yourself, it is usually more constructive to describe the problem directly than to leave others guessing at your hidden agenda.

Work on a Solution

When you understand the problem, build an environment of working together on a solution. To do this, agree with some aspect of what the other person has said. In the previous example, you might say, "You've really disliked your last three assignments." Then you and the other person should be ready to begin identifying possible solutions. The final step is to agree on what the solution will be and how you will carry it out. Figure 14.4 summarizes this approach on the following page.

Mediating Conflict Resolution

Sometimes a supervisor is not personally involved in a conflict, but the parties ask the supervisor to help resolve it. If the parties to the conflict are peers of the

FIGURE 14.4 | Responding to a Conflict

Responding to and resolving a conflict requires both good listening and communication skills as well as a willingness to work together towards a resolution.

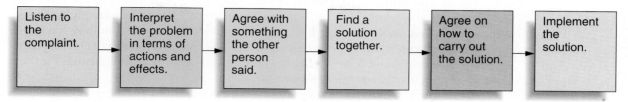

| Listen to the complaint. | → | Interpret the problem in terms of actions and effects. | → | Agree with something the other person said. | → | Find a solution together. | → | Agree on how to carry out the solution. | → | Implement the solution. |

supervisor, getting involved can be risky, and the supervisor might be wiser to tactfully refer the peers to a higher-level manager. If the parties to the conflict are the supervisor's employees, then mediating the conflict is part of the supervisor's job and an important way to keep the department functioning as it should.

To mediate a conflict, a supervisor should follow these steps:

1. Begin by establishing a constructive environment. If the employees are calling one another names, have them focus on the issue instead of such destructive behavior.
2. Ask each person to explain what the problem is. Get each person to be specific and to respond to the others' charges.
3. When all parties understand what the problem is, have them state individually what they want to accomplish or what will satisfy them.
4. Restate in your own words what each person's position is. Ask the employees if you have understood them correctly.
5. Have all participants suggest as many solutions as they can. Begin to focus on the future.
6. Encourage the employees to select a solution that benefits all of them. They may want to combine or modify some of the ideas suggested.
7. Summarize what has been discussed and agreed on. Make sure all participants know what they are supposed to do in carrying out the solution and ask for their cooperation.

Throughout this process, continue your efforts to maintain a constructive environment. Keep the emphasis off personalities and blame; keep it on your mutual desire to find a solution.

L. Randolph Lowry, an expert in dispute resolution, emphasizes that people tend to handle the emotions of a conflict better if they can see there is a process in place so they can have a voice in the matter.[13] Even if the process is as simple as the meeting where the supervisor has each person state his or her concerns and plan a solution together, the participants will be likely to respond to the fairness of the opportunity to air both sides of the conflict. People want to be treated with respect, and they want to be heard. Meeting those desires sometimes dispels the emotions behind a conflict even if the parties to the conflict cannot have everything they want.

Change in the Workplace

Conflict is both a cause and a consequence of change. When people experience a conflict, they manage it by making changes to the situation or their attitudes. For instance, faced with conflicts between the demands of work and family, employees increasingly have tried to balance the two rather than choose one over the other. Their efforts have forced organizations to consider the adoption of policies and values that are more family friendly. When change occurs—in the workplace and elsewhere—conflict accompanies the need to let go of familiar behaviors and attitudes.

The greater desire to balance work and home life is only one of many sources of change in the workplace today.[14] External sources of change include higher expectations for quality and stiffer foreign competition. Modern technology has made communication faster and more flexible and has changed job requirements. Especially for workers in high-tech fields, training and retraining are essential for them to keep up with industry developments.

With stiff international competition, supervisors and higher-level managers endure continuing pressure to cut costs. As the price of health insurance rises year after year, some companies are trying to cut costs by persuading employees to make changes even outside work. At Weyco, a medical-benefits company in Michigan, employees who smoke but do not participate in the company's stop-smoking program get fired, and employees who do not get a set of required medical tests and physical checkups must pay a higher share of their insurance premiums. And at Blue Cross/Blue Shield of North Carolina, employees who are obese must pay higher insurance premiums unless they participate in wellness programs. The plan's executive medical director, Dr. Don Bradley, explains that the wellness programs are offered as a way to pay the lower rate: "The secret here is to keep this as an incentive rather than a punishment."[15]

Because of these and many other changes, an organization's success (its profitability, in the case of a business) depends on how well it adapts to changes in its environment. For example, an organization must respond when a new competitor enters the marketplace or a new law limits how it may operate.

Change is a fact of organizational life, so supervisors do not decide *whether* organizations should change but *how* to make the changes work. They can do this better if they recognize the various factors that can affect the success of a change:

- *The change agent*—The person trying to bring about the change should have skills in implementing change and solving the related problems, as well as expertise in the area affected.
- *Determination of what to change*—Any changes should make the organization more effective in delivering high quality.
- *The kind of change to be made*—The change can involve process and equipment; policies, procedures, and job structure; and people-related variables such as attitudes and communication skills.
- *Individuals affected*—Some people are more open to change than others. Also, people will see some changes as beneficial to them but other changes as harmful.
- *Evaluation of change*—An evaluation can indicate whether it is necessary to modify the change process or make further changes.

Supervisors are the organization's primary link to operative employees, so they must understand how employees are likely to respond to changes, be able to communicate information about the changes to employees, and help employees respond positively.

LO14.5 ▶ Identify sources of change and explain why employees and supervisors resist it.

Sources of Change

As shown in Figure 14.5 on the following page, changes can originate with management, employees, or external forces. Organizations change when management sees an opportunity or a need to do things better. Examples of an opportunity are a new computer system that is more efficient or a new procedure that can lead to higher-quality service. A need may also arise because performance is inadequate. When Zipcar, a car-sharing service, brought in a new chief executive, Scott Griffith, the start-up company was losing money. After more careful analysis of what the company

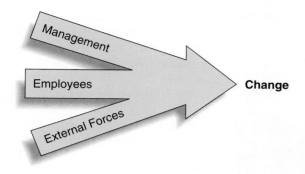

FIGURE 14.5 | Sources of Change

Change in an organization can come from a variety of sources, and supervisors do not always decide whether the change should occur—they must just determine how to make the changes work.

was doing and where its money was coming from and going, Griffith saw a need for a variety of changes. He put managers of each city in charge of their city's profits and losses and gave them wide latitude to succeed. That gave the city managers the responsibility and authority to start making changes of their own for profitability.[16]

Not only managers but also an organization's employees may bring about changes. Forming a union could lead to changes in the way management reaches agreements with employees and the conditions under which employees work. Many organizations actively respond to employee suggestions on how to improve quality and cut costs.

As the U.S. workforce becomes increasingly diverse in terms of age, race, and sex, the forces for change from employees are likely to strengthen. People of diverse backgrounds can offer a greater variety of creative solutions. In addition, the challenge of working harmoniously with different kinds of people can itself lead to a push for changes, such as provisions for different religious holidays or guidelines on how to treat people fairly.

Other changes are imposed from outside. New laws and regulations often lead to changes within organizations. A local government organization might have to make changes in response to voters' refusal to approve a tax increase. A series of lawsuits might cause an organization to reexamine how it makes a product. The size and composition of the workforce may affect whom the organization hires and how much training it provides.

Understanding the workforce is an important part of being able to effectively lead employees. Each generation is marked by a set of shared experiences that help define the professional aspirations and expectations of its members. If supervisors are aware of these characteristics, they may be able to better adapt their strategies in order to best connect with employees (while also understanding that not all employees within a generation can be grouped together or assumed to be alike). As Table 14.1 shows, Americans born between the mid-1940s and the mid-1960s are known as "Baby Boomers." These people were born and grew up in a time of significant socioeconomic and political change, and now largely comprise the leadership positions of most organizations. Conversely, Americans born between the early 1980s and early 2000s are known as the "Millennials."[17] Also sometimes called "Generation Y," these individuals grew up with heavy exposure to technology that Baby Boomers lacked, and experienced comparatively less change than some prior generations. Research suggests that there are significant differences in how people in these different generations view the world and interpret information, which can sometimes precipitate conflict at work.

Economic trends also are important. For example, businesses usually are able to seek growth more aggressively when the economy is expanding. But during

TABLE 14.1 | American Generations of the Last Century

Generation Name	Approximate Years of Birth
G.I./Greatest Generation	1901–1924
Silent Generation	1925–1942
Baby Boomers	1943–1960
Generation X	1960–1981
Generation Y/Millenials	1982–2004

In the wake of economic changes, securing customer loyalty has become an emphasis. Companies like Hyundai have made efforts to create more appealing products for customers. These include warranties and quick-delivery for parts.

downturns, change is also common and can be especially difficult. Following the recent drop in the housing market and crisis in the financial industry, many consumers and businesses found themselves short on cash and unable to make purchases. As a result, many businesses had to make changes to stay afloat. Vail Resorts saw a fall-off in business and responded by laying off workers and suspending raises for others. Other companies have saved money by cutting schedules for workers earning an hourly wage. Companies that laid off workers included Walgreens, Cigna, and Logitech.[18] Layoffs and cutbacks in hours impose financial hardships on workers, and layoffs often add to the workloads of employees who remain.

Another economic change hitting manufacturers is that they are finding that selling their products is often less profitable than providing related services, such as repairs and maintenance of their products. This knowledge is driving change in some companies' strategy. Some manufacturers are responding to the information by developing the staff, facilities, and know-how to add services to their product lines. For instance, Caterpillar set up systems to deliver spare parts anywhere within 24 hours, and Hyundai Motor Company offers extended warranties, delivering service to individual customers as needed. These changes affect a company's values, its staffing needs, and its focus on serving customers.[19]

LO14.6 ▶ Discuss how supervisors can overcome resistance and implement change.

Resistance to Change

Any change, such as the adoption of a new procedure in the workplace or the completion of a major training program, requires work. People are fearful because change carries the risk of making them worse off. For example, when a company announces a "restructuring," employees start worrying about layoffs and a dramatic increase in employee workloads.

People's resistance to change is greatest when they are not sure what to expect or why the change is necessary. Change stirs up fear of the unknown, another normal human response. Furthermore, when people do not understand the reasons for change, the effort to change does not seem worthwhile.

Sometimes even when change is positive, it meets resistance. When Jeff Koeze took over from his father as the head of the family business, Koeze Company, which sells nuts in stores and as mail-order gifts, he wanted to empower employees to make the company run smoothly. But one of his first discoveries was that employees were uninterested in pursuing his ideas for change. Investigating, he learned that his father had tended to bring up ideas but forget about them by the time employees had researched them, so employees had learned not to take new ideas seriously. Koeze brought in a psychologist to coach employees in new ways of communicating. However, they were suspicious of the process and the trouble it might cause—that it might generate criticism and conflict. Resistance was less intense when Koeze brought in another expert to help improve service at the company's stores. This consultant gathered store workers every other week to discuss specific

SUPERVISORY SKILLS

IMPLEMENTING CHANGE: UNFREEZING

Supervisors are in a position to make changes within their own work group. Even small changes can motivate employees and contribute to significant performance improvements. Supervisors can unfreeze their employees by encouraging a process of change that allows employees to think of themselves and their group as innovators and to see that they are part of moving the company forward as a whole.

This encouragement for change can come from the very top of the organization. In a recent interview, IBM's chief executive Virginia Rometty said that her message to the company's more than 400,000 employees is to "embrace the future, and quickly, rather than resist it." She is sending a clear message to all within the company, at every level, to "unfreeze."

Why is this message necessary? Analysts say that IBM was too slow to understand and act on the significance that "the cloud" brought to the computing world. Instead of treating cloud computing as a new product line, as it should have been, they treated it as an extension of an existing product line. Consequently, instead of being one of the leaders in cloud computing, IBM is now threatened with the loss of a large part of their business. They have, however, started a

new strategy by buying a cloud computer start-up company, selling off less profitable business units, and shifting their way of thinking. Rometty recognizes that the company has some catching up to do and that in order for this to happen, all of IBM's employees need to work together to make the changes necessary for the company to be successful into the future. "We are making progress, and we just need to keep moving with speed," said Rometty.

One way that a supervisor can aid in implementing change is to regularly ask, "How can we do our work better?" This encourages employees to get in the habit of thinking about change as part of their responsibility. To stimulate innovation, make improvements part of the group's regular routine. Taking an active role gets employees more involved in the change process, increasing their commitment to the success of each innovation. Change is a given in the modern workplace. Supervisors who develop their employees' ability to welcome and create change are building a valuable asset for their organization.

Sources: Steve Lohr, "IBM Chief Says Better Times Lie Ahead," *The New York Times*, May 11, 2014, http://www.nytimes.com/2014/05/12/technology/ibm-poised-for-growth-chief-says.html?_r=2, accessed May 13, 2014; Charlie Campbell, "IBM Chief Says Better Times Lie Ahead," *Time*, May 12, 2014, http://time.com/95667/ibm-ceo-growth/, accessed May 13, 2014.

problems and ideas. Initially, workers felt intimidated to be working with a professor, but they came to see that the company really cared about helping them succeed. Focusing on practical issues, they developed new policies and procedures that made satisfying customers easier and less stressful.[20]

Implementing Change

To implement change, a supervisor must overcome resistance to it, ensure that the change is made, and create the conditions in which the change is likely to last. Noted behavioral scientist Kurt Lewin has set forth a model for this process.[21] Lewin's model, which is illustrated in Figure 14.6, indicates that a successful change has three phases:

1. *Unfreezing*—People recognize a need for change.
2. *Changing*—People begin trying to behave differently.
3. *Refreezing*—The new behavior becomes part of employees' regular processes.

FIGURE 14.6 | Lewin's Model of Change

According to Lewin, a supervisor needs to overcome resistance to change, make sure that the change is made, and make sure that the conditions are right for the change to last.

This model makes two assumptions about the change process. First, before a change can occur, employees must see the status quo as less than ideal. Second, when employees begin changing, the organization must provide a way for the new behavior to become established practice. As described in the "Supervisory Skills" feature supervisors can help create this kind of openness to change in their work groups.

Unfreezing

In the unfreezing phase, the supervisor or other person responsible for implementing the change must spell out clearly why a change is needed. When former NFL commissioner Paul Tagliabue wanted football team owners to agree to adopt free agency and a salary cap for players, most owners worried that they could not succeed under the new arrangement because the teams in the biggest markets would take all the best players. Tagliabue focused on showing owners why the change was actually in their best interests. Eventually, he convinced enough of them that a majority voted to accept the change.[22] In essence, then, unfreezing means overcoming resistance to change.

Many changes require not only performing new tasks but also adopting new attitudes, such as a willingness to assume decision-making responsibility and a strong commitment to sustainability. Employees may have difficulty changing their attitudes, especially if they are unsure about management's sincerity. Therefore, supervisors leading a change may need to adjust their own attitudes first—finding something in the change to be enthusiastic about—so that they can be genuinely enthusiastic with their employees.[23] Also, management needs to address employee resistance arising from fears about the change. The organization relies heavily on supervisors—as management's link to operative employees—to carry out this responsibility, for which they need good communication skills (see Chapter 10). The following guidelines may help as well:[24]

- Find out as much as you can about the reasons for the change, and explain those reasons to employees. Especially describe benefits of the change that employees will appreciate—say, reduced strain on the planet's resources, happier customers to deal with, a sizable bonus at the end of the quarter, or a safer, healthier workforce.

- If you can, roll out the change gradually. Identify the people who are most open-minded about the change, and have them be the pioneers. Praise their successes, and enable them to help you promote the benefits of the change to their co-workers.

- Be honest with employees. If you do not know the answers to any questions or concerns, promise to investigate and share what you learn. People tend to be less fearful when they believe they will be treated fairly and with honesty.

- If the change will involve layoffs, do not try to hide that or any other bad news. Employees will guess it anyway. Rather than being reassured by the absence of bad news, they will lose trust and become more fearful and resistant.

- Listen to employees' questions and ideas about the change. Nervous employees will pepper you with questions and concerns, but these could actually lead to better ways of communicating and implementing the change. When possible, involve employees in making decisions about how to implement the change.

In listening to and answering questions, remember that some employees will not think of questions until some time has passed. Therefore, provide opportunities for employees to ask questions on an ongoing basis, not just at the time a change is announced.

Changing

When employees appreciate the need for a change and have received any necessary training, they are ready to begin altering their behavior. The key to implementing change is to build on successes. A supervisor should determine those aspects of the change over which he or she has control, then seek to carry them out successfully. A supervisor should point out each success the group achieves along the way. As employees see the change achieving desirable results, they are more likely to go along with it and even embrace it.

Demonstrating practical success was important when Fokker Aerotron began applying the tools of lean manufacturing to its administrative departments. The company, which maintains and repairs parts for the aerospace industry, already could show that in its operations, lean methods had halved turnaround time and dramatically boosted on-time delivery rates. But some employees were skeptical about whether lean process improvement would be relevant for office work. Fokker Aerotron began by targeting the invoicing process (preparing bills and submitting them to customers for payment). A team of employees and managers met to review the existing process to identify where waste was occurring, what was causing the waste, and how the process could be improved. At first, few employees spoke up, but as they began to see how they poured effort into unproductive activities, they became more enthusiastic and creative. The purchasing supervisor, for example, was surprised when she realized that the invoicing process took more than three days and involved 80 steps, requiring 1,080 feet of travel for the invoice, including 12 trips to the printer. Applying lean principles shrank this effort to a one-day process with half as many steps. No one was sorry to cut out the 30 percent of paperwork identified as unnecessary. Measuring the dramatically reduced waste of this one process showed employees that lean makes business sense and inspired them to apply lean in other administrative areas.[25]

Fokker Aerotron started its program to eliminate waste in administrative processes without waiting to fully convince its people the program was worthwhile. As in this example, building on successes generally entails starting with basic changes in behavior, rather than beginning with an effort to change values. Values, by their nature, are more resistant to change. To induce changes in behavior, the change effort should include tangible or intangible rewards for the desired behavior. As employees experience positive outcomes, their attitudes become more positive, and their values may shift as well.

A supervisor who has control over scheduling a change should establish reasonable deadlines. As employees meet each deadline, the supervisor can point out their on-time achievements. For example, imagine that an accounting department is installing a new computer system. Instead of focusing simply on whether everyone is using the system properly, a supervisor can establish dates for setting up various pieces of equipment and learning to operate different parts of the system. Then the supervisor can note that the terminals arrived on time, that everyone learned how to log on and enter their password in a single training session, and so on.

A supervisor also might have control over which people are directly involved in the change or the order in which people get involved. The supervisor of the accounting department might recognize that some employees are already enthusiastic about the new system or are flexible and open to change. These people should learn the system first; then they can spread their enthusiasm around and help other employees when it is their turn to learn.

Similarly, if a group of employees works well together and enjoys one another's company, a sensible approach is to keep these employees together. For example, the change of adding another shift might proceed more smoothly if informal groups are not split into different shifts. In contrast, when a change involves bringing together two groups of employees from different organizations, locations, or shifts, a supervisor might build cooperation by teaming up employees from each group.

Refreezing

The change process is complete only when employees make the new behavior part of their routine. However, because new procedures are less comfortable than the old and familiar ones, employees may revert to their old practices when the initial pressure for change eases. In organizations that do not manage change effectively, managers may assume a change effort has succeeded simply because employees modified their behavior according to instructions. But if employees merely fulfill the basic requirements of a change without adjusting their attitudes, and if the organization has not arranged to reinforce and reward the change, backsliding is likely.

That is just what happened to a hospital unit's attempt to start a self-directed work team. The employees of the hospital unit at first seemed to embrace that change when they said good-bye to a 15-year supervisor who had controlled with a strong hand. They agreed to operate as a team and chose a leader with a more low-key personality. Team members quickly stepped in and handled the administrative work their former supervisor had performed, and their new supervisor had no problem delegating. But as time passed, the team members began expecting their leader to handle more and more of the administrative duties, and the team leader allowed the old ways to return.[26]

Backsliding is a natural response among employees, but it can become a problem unless a supervisor acts to get everyone back on track. A supervisor should remind employees about what they have achieved so far and what is expected of them in the future (see the principles of motivation described in Chapter 11). An important part of refreezing is for employees to be rewarded for behavior that shows they have made the desired change.

Proposing Change

In many situations, a supervisor wants to make a change but needs to ask higher-level management for authority to implement it. A supervisor also is wise to ask his or her manager about changes that are controversial, difficult to implement, or of major importance. These situations require a supervisor to make a proposal to higher-level management.

To propose a change effectively, the supervisor should begin by analyzing it. How will it help the organization better achieve its goals? Will it improve quality or productivity? What steps are required to carry it out? How much will it cost? Who will carry it out? What training will be required? Only when the answers to these questions confirm that the change is beneficial and feasible is the supervisor in a valid position to continue with the proposal.

Recall that the change process begins with convincing others of the need for a change (unfreezing, in Lewin's model). Some organizations actively cultivate suggestions for improvement, making it relatively easy for a supervisor to sell a change. In other organizations, management may view change more cautiously. Thus, it is often important for a supervisor to begin by helping management see the situation that gives rise to the need for a change. A supervisor may have to do this before he or she even mentions changing something.

Once a supervisor's groundwork has prepared management for the proposal, a supervisor should have one ready to submit. Except for simple changes, a supervisor should make proposals in writing. The beginning of a proposal should contain a brief summary of what the change is and why it is desirable. Then the supervisor can provide details about the procedure for change and the costs and benefits involved. (For more suggestions about upward communication and reports, see Chapter 10; for guidelines on maintaining good relations with your manager, see Chapter 8.)

Organizational Politics and Power

Implementing change and resolving conflicts are easier for a person who has a relatively strong position in the organization. Thus, supervisors can most effectively manage conflict and change if they are able to improve their positions within an organization. Together, the activities through which people do this are

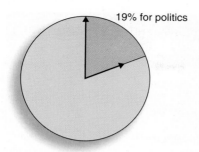

19% for politics

FIGURE 14.7 | Share of Time Spent by Managers on Organizational Politics

A study found that managers spend almost one full day out of every five dealing with organizational politics.

Source: "Reducing Conflict in the Office," *USA TODAY Magazine*, July 2003, downloaded from LookSmart's Find Articles, www.findarticles.com.

organizational politics
Intentional acts of influence to enhance or protect the self-interest of individuals or groups

power
The ability to influence people to behave in a certain way

position power
Power that comes from a person's formal role in an organization

personal power
Power that arises from an individual's personal characteristics

LO14.7 ▶ Describe the types of power supervisors can have.

called **organizational politics.**[27] Improving one's position is not in itself good or bad; therefore, politics also is not innately good or bad. Political skills *are* important, however. They help a supervisor obtain the cooperation and support of others in the organization. As illustrated in Figure 14.7, one survey found that managers spend almost a full day out of every five-day workweek on matters related to organizational politics, including the politically motivated activities of their employees. More about organizational politics is available in the Appendix that follows this chapter.

The usual way that people use politics to improve their positions is by gaining power. **Power** is the ability to influence people to behave in a certain way. For instance, one supervisor says, "I wish everyone would be at work on time," yet employees continue to come in late. Another supervisor gets employees so excited about their contribution to the company that they consistently arrive at work on time and perform above what is required of them. The second supervisor has more power than the first.

Sources of Power

Editorial supervisor Stan Bakker has a decade-long track record of turning manuscripts into bestsellers. When he tells one of the editors on his staff how to handle a particular author or manuscript, the editor invariably follows Bakker's directions. Why? Partly because he is the boss, and partly because the editors respect his expertise. Thus, Bakker's power comes both from his position in the company and from his personal characteristics.

Power that comes from a person's formal role in an organization is known as **position power.** Every supervisor has some position power with the employees he or she supervises. Higher-level managers, in turn, have a greater degree of position power.[28]

In contrast, **personal power** is power that arises from an individual's personal characteristics.[29] Because a person does not need to be a manager in an organization to have personal power there, employees sometimes view a co-worker as an informal leader of their group. If a supervisor announces a reorganization, one employee may successfully urge everyone to rally around the new plan—or may undermine morale by making fun of the changes. The informal leader in a group could be someone that other employees see as having expertise or being fun to work with.

Supervisors cannot eliminate personal power in subordinates, but they should be aware of it so they can use it to their advantage. A supervisor can watch for problems that might arise when the supervisor and an informal leader have conflicting goals. Perhaps more important, a supervisor can seek ways to get an informal leader on his or her side; for example, a supervisor might announce a decision to the informal leader first or discuss plans with that person.

Types of Power

Because power comes from their personal characteristics as well as their position in the organization, supervisors can have a variety of types of power. A supervisor who has less position power than he or she would like might consider the following types of power to see whether some can be developed. These types are summarized in Table 14.2 on the following page.

Legitimate power comes from the position a person holds. Thus, a supervisor has legitimate power to delegate tasks to employees. To exercise legitimate power effectively, a supervisor needs to be sure employees understand what they are directed to do and are able to do it.

Referent power comes from the emotions a person inspires. Some supervisors seem to light up the room when they enter; they have a winning personality that includes enthusiasm, energy, and genuine enjoyment of the job. People like working for such

TABLE 14.2 | Types of Power

Power Type	Arises From
Legitimate	The position a person holds
Referent	The emotions a person inspires
Expert	A person's knowledge or skills
Coercive	Fear related to the use of force
Reward	Giving people something they want
Connection	A person's relationship to someone powerful
Information	Possession of valuable information

a supervisor and often perform beyond the call of duty because they want the supervisor to like them. A person with referent power is often called "charismatic."

Expert power arises from a person's knowledge or skills. Employees respect a supervisor who knows the employees' jobs better than they do. Their respect leads them to follow the supervisor's instructions. For example, the head of a company's research and development team might be a scientist who is well regarded in the field. Researchers could be expected to ask for and rely on this supervisor's advice.

Coercive power arises from fear related to the use of force. A supervisor who says, "Be on time tomorrow, or you're fired!" is using coercive power. This type of power

Two supervisors who are also golfing buddies may create a situation of connection power, where their relationship outside the workplace could lead to advantages within the workplace.

may get results in the short run, but in the long run, employees come to resent and may try to get around this supervisor. A supervisor who often relies on coercive power should consider whether he or she is doing so at the expense of developing other, more appropriate types of power.

Reward power arises from giving people something they want. The reward given by a supervisor might be a raise, recognition, or assignment to a desired shift. A supervisor who plans to rely on reward power to lead employees had better be sure that he or she is able to give out rewards consistently. Often supervisors are limited in this regard. Company policy may put a ceiling on the size of raises to be granted, or there may be only a few assignments that really thrill employees.

Connection power is power that stems from a person's relationship to someone powerful. Imagine that two supervisors are golfing buddies. One of them gets promoted to the job of manager of purchasing. The other supervisor has connection power stemming from his relationship to the new manager.

Similarly, if one of the organization's employees is the daughter of a vice president, she has connection power as a result of that family relationship. Connection power can be a problem for the organization and its managers when the people who have it place the interests of their relationship ahead of the interests of the organization. Nevertheless, it is a fact of organizational life.

Information power is power that arises from possessing valuable information. Someone who knows which employees are targeted in the next round of layoffs or when the department manager will be out of town has information power. The secretaries of top managers have information power as well as connection power.

LO14.8 ▶ Identify common strategies for organizational politics.

Political Strategies

A person's political strategies are the methods the person uses to acquire and keep power within the organization. Depending on the particular strategies a person chooses and how he or she uses those strategies, they may be ethical or unethical. The following strategies commonly are used in organizations:[30]

- *Building relationships*—Politically skillful supervisors build positive, appropriate relationships with people at their level of the organization, above their level, and below. They socialize, listen, and learn about the interests and goals of the people around them.

- *Making a good impression*—Not only the supervisor but also his or her organization can benefit when the supervisor's desire and ability to contribute are well known. Therefore, political behavior includes communications that help a person be known in a positive way. Examples include offering ideas, sharing progress reports, announcing accomplishments, and asking to take on more responsibility. Gaining a good reputation from the start is far easier than trying to salvage a reputation if others try to damage it.

- *Helping others*—Acts that go beyond job responsibilities to make other people's work easier or more rewarding will cement relationships and contribute to a positive reputation. People want to be associated with a supervisor who is known for being helpful. For example, a supervisor can pay attention to employees' ambitions and be quick to recommend them for promotions and special assignments.

- *Signaling confidence*—People are more likely to accept that someone is acquiring and using power if the person seems confident in his or her role. Ways to project confidence include speaking firmly and carrying one's body erect, with good posture. Of course, it is essential to stay educated about the company's goals and culture and the supervisor's own area of work, so statements made assertively are also accurate and insightful.

For examples of using political strategies ethically, see "Supervision and Ethics."

SUPERVISION AND ETHICS

MAKING A GOOD IMPRESSION ETHICALLY

Successful supervisors not only lead their employees well but also know how to make a good impression on their own boss, so that this person trusts them and gives them the responsibility and resources they need. How is this achieved? Following are some guidelines for ethical political strategies for making a good impression on your manager:

- *Assume that your boss is as committed to good practices and good results as you are.* If you are disappointed in something your boss does (or does not do), assume that your boss would prefer to be more effective but is not aware of the problem or does not know how to solve it. With that viewpoint as a start, try to imagine the situation from your boss's perspective, and then offer solutions in a tone that shows you appreciate the boss's situation and are trying to help. With most managers, this will get you further than the extremes of either constant criticism or mindless compliments and agreement.

- *Learn how your boss operates.* Does he or she like to be involved in every decision? If so, offer plenty of information so that the boss will feel informed. Does the boss prefer short e-mails or long conversations? Adapting your communication style to the boss's will increase the

chances that your ideas and accomplishments will be noticed.

- *Let your boss know what you are doing and achieving.* Using whatever communication practices work best, establish a habit of keeping the boss up-to-date. Be prepared to give specifics about the status of your group's projects. Be honest and do not exaggerate, but do not just assume your manager knows what you have accomplished or how hard you're working.

- *Share credit with your employees.* Supervisors may be tempted to use every success in their department as an opportunity for individual glory. But if you take all the credit, not only will you alienate your employees, you will also signal that you do not know how to delegate, motivate, and lead others—key responsibilities of a supervisor.

Sources: Based on Patrick Lencioni, "How to Manage Your Boss," *The Wall Street Journal,* January 2, 2009, http://online.wsj.com/news/articles/SB123090863169649129, accessed May 13, 2014; Kimberly Alyn, "Cultural Power vs. Real Leadership: Whose Side Are You On?" *Firehouse,* July 2008, downloaded from Business & Company Resource Center, http://galenet.galegroup.com; and Mark Opperman, "Getting Through to the Boss," *Veterinary Economics,* June 2008, http://veterinarybusiness.dvm360.com/vetec/Veterinary+business/Getting-through-to-the-boss/ArticleStandard/Article/detail/520551, accessed May 13, 2014.

Building a Power Base

At the heart of organizational politics is building a base of power. The particular approach used varies with the kinds of power an employee or manager might acquire. Figure 14.8 summarizes some possible approaches. Some people take on more responsibility in an effort to become needed in the organization. Others seek control over resources; the supervisor with more employees or a bigger budget is considered to be more powerful.

FIGURE 14.8 |
Approaches to Building a Power Base

There are a number of different ways to build a power base—all of which are part of organizational politics.

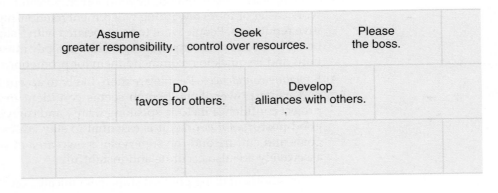

Assume greater responsibility.	Seek control over resources.	Please the boss.
Do favors for others.	Develop alliances with others.	

An important way supervisors can build their power bases is to please their managers. Peers and subordinates who recognize that a supervisor has a close relationship with the manager tend to treat the supervisor carefully to avoid antagonizing the manager.

To do favors so that others will be in one's debt is yet another approach. Bribery of course is unethical, but there are many ethical ways to do favors for others. A supervisor might offer to stay late to help a co-worker finish a project or jump-start the co-worker's car on a cold day. When the supervisor needs help or a favorable word from someone, the co-worker probably will be happy to return the favor.

Doing favors can help a supervisor with one of the other techniques for building a power base: developing alliances with others in the organization. A supervisor who has many people on his or her side is able to get more done and build a good reputation. This does not mean supervisors have to hang around with greedy, pushy, or unethical co-workers. Instead, they should identify people they admire as potential allies. Alliances can be built with these people by earning their trust, keeping them informed, and developing comfortable relationships through common interests.

Establishing a Competitive Edge

On the assumption that there are limits to the number of promotions and other goodies available, organization members seek to gain a competitive edge. They try to stand out so that when raises, promotions, and choice assignments are handed out, they will be the recipients. Ethical efforts to establish a competitive edge generally are based on trying to do an exceptional job.

Some unethical approaches to establishing a competitive edge are spreading lies and rumors about peers and taking credit for the ideas and work of subordinates. Trying to look good at the expense of someone else may be effective at first, but when the truth comes out, the person who uses this tactic winds up the biggest loser. Other people learn to distrust such a person. In the long run, the most successful way to look exceptional is to produce exceptional results.

Socializing

At many organizations, part of the game of getting ahead includes socializing with co-workers. Perhaps the people who get promoted the fastest are those who on occasion play golf with the boss or go out for a drink after work. Depending on a supervisor's behavior in these situations, socializing can be helpful, or it can put an end to an employee's career growth.

Common sense can help the supervisor handle socializing appropriately. For example, a supervisor who gets drunk at a party is likely to behave foolishly. Likewise, dating a subordinate is an invitation to trouble. If the relationship lasts, other employees are likely to be jealous of the subordinate and doubt the supervisor's ability to be fair. If the relationship does not work out, the supervisor could be set up—justly or unjustly—for charges of sexual harassment by an angry subordinate. (For an explanation of sexual harassment, see Appendix B.)

In general, the wisest course is to be sensible but natural. For example, a supervisor should not push to become a buddy of the manager or of subordinates. Nor should a supervisor use social occasions as an opportunity to make a big impression; showing off is hardly an effective way to build relationships.

Skills Module

PART ONE: CONCEPTS

Summary

14.1 List positive and negative aspects of conflict.

When it leads to necessary changes, conflict is a positive force because it signals that a problem exists. However, ongoing conflict puts people under stress and takes up time that could be spent more productively. When conflict involves anger at management or the organization, it may lead to destructive behavior.

14.2 Define types of conflict.

Conflict may be intrapersonal, taking place within one person. Conflict between individuals is called interpersonal. Structural conflict results from the way the organization is structured. Strategic conflict is brought about intentionally to achieve some goal, such as motivating employees.

14.3 Describe strategies for managing conflict.

One strategy is to compromise, or agree to a solution that meets only part of each party's demands. Another approach is to avoid the conflict or pretend it does not exist. Forcing a solution occurs when a person with power selects and imposes the outcome. None of these strategies tries to solve the underlying problem, and all assume that the situation is a win–lose for those involved. Confronting and resolving the problem, called conflict resolution, assumes that a conflict can be a win–win situation.

14.4 Explain how supervisors can initiate conflict resolution, respond to a conflict, and mediate conflict resolution.

To initiate conflict resolution, a supervisor must begin by understanding what the conflict is. The supervisor then states the problem and listens to the response; when the parties are communicating, they can find a solution and agree upon what each person will do.

To respond to a conflict, a supervisor should listen to the other person and try to understand the problem. Then the supervisor can build cooperation by agreeing with part of the statement and working with the other person to reach a solution.

To mediate conflict resolution, a supervisor begins by establishing a constructive environment, then asks each person to explain what the problem is and state what he or she wants. Next the supervisor restates each position, asks for suggested solutions, and encourages the parties to select a mutually beneficial solution. Finally, the supervisor summarizes what course of action has been agreed upon.

14.5 Identify sources of change and explain why employees and supervisors resist it.

Change can come from management in response to an opportunity or need to do things better. It can come from employees in the form of unionizing or making suggestions. Change can be imposed by external forces such as the government. Employees and supervisors resist change because it typically requires extra effort and sometimes leaves people worse off. Other reasons for resisting change are fear of the unknown and worry that one is incapable of making the change.

14.6 Discuss how supervisors can overcome resistance and implement change.

To overcome resistance to change, supervisors can recognize and respond to employees' feelings. They also can keep employees informed about the change, being realistic but emphasizing any benefits. The supervisor should give employees opportunities to ask questions about the change. To implement change, the supervisor should build on successes. This includes communicating successes as they occur, setting reasonable deadlines for the steps that must be taken, and involving first the people who are most likely to be enthusiastic about the change.

14.7 Describe the types of power supervisors can have.

Supervisors can have legitimate power, which comes from their position in the organization; referent power, which comes from the emotions they inspire in others; expert power, which comes from their knowledge or skills; coercive power, which comes from fear related to their use of force; reward power, which comes from giving people something they want; connection power, which comes from their relationships to people in power; and information power, which comes from the possession of valuable information.

14.8 Identify common strategies for organizational politics.

Political strategies involve building a power base, establishing a competitive edge, and socializing. The ways that individuals carry out those strategies in organizations include building relationships, making a good impression, helping others, and signaling confidence.

Key Terms

conflict, *p.* 380
frustration, *p.* 380
conflict management, *p.* 384

compromise, *p.* 385
conflict resolution, *p.* 386
organizational politics, *p.* 397

power, *p.* 397
position power, *p.* 397
personal power, *p.* 397

Review and Discussion Questions

1. On her first day on the job, Jenna's supervisor introduces her incorrectly to her co-workers, mispronouncing her name. For several weeks after that, Jenna's co-workers, intending to be friendly, pronounce her name incorrectly. Jenna goes along with it, not wanting to jeopardize her new relationships. Finally, feeling uncomfortable about the situation, Jenna approaches her supervisor about the mistake. Is this a positive or negative conflict? Why?

2. Imagine that you are a production supervisor at a hand-tool manufacturer such as Snap-On Tools. Your manager says, "I know you were looking forward to your trip to Hawaii next month, but we will be stepping up production, and three new employees will be joining your group. I wish you would consider staying to make sure everything goes smoothly."

   a. What is the nature of the conflict in this situation? In other words, what two goals is it impossible for you to achieve at the same time?

   b. List as many possible solutions as you can think of to resolve this conflict.

   c. Which solution do you prefer? How could you present it to your manager?

3. Identify each of the following conflicts as interpersonal, structural, or strategic.

   a. The production department's goal is to make parts faster, and the quality control department wants slower production to reduce the rate of defects.

   b. The new salesperson in a company's sales force wanted to learn his job quickly, so he identified the region's top performer and frequently sends text messages to the veteran salesperson. However, that salesperson sees the texts as an annoying interruption that could hurt her own performance, so she ignores most of the texts.

   c. One cashier at a supermarket is much older than the others, and he does not spend much time talking to them. The other cashiers criticize him for not being a team player.

4. Why does compromise generally leave both parties feeling frustrated?

5. Rachel Gonzalez supervises servers at a restaurant. She knows that many of them are upset about the hours she has scheduled for them, but she believes that people should not argue. So she avoids discussing the subject, and she posts the following week's schedule just before leaving for the day. What is wrong with this approach to conflict management? What would be a better way to manage this conflict?

6. Ron Herbst is a supervisor in a clinical laboratory. He has noticed that one employee regularly comes to work in a surly mood. The employee is getting his work done on time, but his attitude seems to be affecting other employees.

   a. How can Ron initiate conflict resolution with this employee? How should he describe the problem?

   b. If the employee responds to Ron's statement of the problem by saying, "I'm fine. Don't worry about me," what should the supervisor do and say?

7. The managers of a soft drink bottling company decide that production workers will each learn several jobs and rotate among those jobs. They have read that this technique improves productivity, and they believe that workers will be happier because their jobs will be more interesting. However, many of the employees and their supervisors are reluctant to make the change. What could explain their resistance?

8. What are the factors that can affect the success of a change?

9. How can a supervisor overcome resistance to change?

10. What is the primary reason that efforts for change within an organization fail? What can a supervisor do to avoid this failure and ensure that change will be successful?

11. What are the two basic sources of power available to a supervisor? Which do you think is more important to the supervisor's effectiveness? Why?

12. Which type or types of power is the supervisor exerting in each of the following situations?

   a. A sales supervisor promises a $50 bonus to the first salesperson to close a sale this week.

   b. One day a month, a supervisor orders in pizza and joins her employees for lunch. The employees look forward to these gatherings because the supervisor joins them in recounting funny stories, and she usually is able to fill them in on some management plans.

   c. A supervisor in the bookkeeping department got his job thanks to a referral from his father, who regularly plays racquetball with the company's president. Since the supervisor was hired, the president has visited the bookkeeping department a couple of times to see how he is doing. The manager of the department is very diplomatic in his criticism of the supervisor.

   d. When the employees in a word-processing department make many errors per page or a particularly glaring error, their supervisor posts the offending pages on the department bulletin board to shame the employees into performing better.

13. A sales supervisor believes she could be more effective if she had more cooperation from the company's credit department. If the credit of potential customers could be approved faster, her salespeople could close more sales. What political tactics would you recommend that the sales supervisor consider to get more cooperation from the credit department?

Notes

1. For more information on the effects of conflict, see O. Ayoko and A. Pekerti, 2008, "The mediating and moderating effects of conflict and communication openness on workplace trust," *International Journal of Conflict Management*, 19, p. 297.

2. Cheryl Dahle, "Deflecting the Knife of a Backstabber," *The New York Times*, August 8, 2004, http://www.nytimes.com/2004/08/08/business/career-couch-deflecting-the-knife-of-a-backstabber.html, accessed May 12, 2014.

3. Tatsha Robertson, "Between Work and Life There's Balance," *Boston Globe*, June 19, 2005, www.boston.com.

4. Sandi Redman, "Increasing Emotional Intelligence in the Workplace," *The Exchange*, August–September 2008, downloaded from Business & Company Resource Center, http://galenet.galegroup.com.

5. Coco Masters, "Revving Up Nissan," *Time*, March 13, 2008, p. Global 8.

6. Marcia Hughes and James Bradford Terrell, "The Emotionally Intelligent Team," *Industrial Engineer*, April 2008, pp. 34–38.

7. Jared Sandberg, "Office Democracies: How Many Bosses Can One Person Have?" *The Wall Street Journal*, November 22, 2005, http://online.wsj.com/news/articles/SB113260914591203402, accessed May 12, 2014.

8. For a review of the conflict management literature, see Z. Ma, Y. Lee, and K. Yu, 2008, "Ten years of conflict management studies: Themes, concepts and relationships," *Journal of Conflict Management*, 19, p. 234.

9. For an interesting related study, see Catherine H. Tinsley and Jeanne M. Brett, "Managing Workplace Conflict in the United States and Hong Kong," *Organizational Behavior and Human Decision Processes* 85, no. 2 (2001), pp. 360–381.

10. Anne Spray Kinney, "Financial Leadership for the Twenty-First Century: An Interview with Five Public Sector Leaders," *Government Finance Review*, February 2005, downloaded from Business & Company Resource Center, http://galenet.galegroup.com.

11. Dahle, "Deflecting the Knife of a Backstabber."

12. Patricia Kitchen, "Ways to Defuse Conflict at Work," *(Melville, N.Y.) Newsday*, July 2, 2006, downloaded from Business & Company Resource Center, http://galenet.galegroup.com.

13. Karen E. Klein, "Better Ways to Handle Business Conflict," *Bloomberg Businessweek*, February 4, 2011, http://www.businessweek.com/smallbiz/content/feb2011/sb2011024_744270.htm, accessed May 12, 2014.

14. See, for example, Dianne Jacobs, "Sharing Knowledge: How to Thrive in Times of Change," *Ivey Business Journal Online*, July–August 2005, http://iveybusinessjournal.com/topics/the-workplace/sharing-knowledge-how-to-thrive-in-times-of-change#.U3D2UvldWSo, accessed May 12, 2014; Marvin J. Cetron and Owen Davies, "Trends Now Shaping the Future," *The Futurist*, May–June 2005, pp. 37–50.

15. Randy Dotinga, "Can Boss Insist on Healthy Habits?" *Christian Science Monitor*, January 11, 2006, www.csmonitor.com/2006/0111/p15s01-ussc.html, accessed May 12, 2014.

16. Stephanie Clifford, "How Fast Can This Thing Go Anyway?" *Inc.*, March 2008, pp. 94–101, http://www.inc.com/magazine/20080301/how-fast-can-this-thing-go-anyway.html, accessed May 12, 2014.

17. "American Generations Through the Years," *CNN Living*, May 5, 2011, http://www.cnn.com/interactive/2011/05/living/infographic.boomer/, accessed May 13, 2014; William Strauss and Neil Howe, *Generations: The History of America's Future, 1584 to 2069*, Quill, 1992; "Millennials: A Portrait of Generation Next," Pew Research Center, February 24, 2010, http://www.pewresearch.org/millennials/, accessed May 13, 2014.

18. "Vail Resorts Feels Effect of Slump in Economy," *Rocky Mountain News (Denver, Colo.)*, January 9, 2009, http://www.therocky.com/news/2009/jan/09/skier-visits-revenue-fall-vail-resorts/, accessed May 12, 2014; and Jeannine Aversa, "More Jobs Melt Away; Unemployment Hits 7.2%," *Seattle Times*, January 10, 2009, http://seattletimes.com/html/businesstechnology/2008611830_jobs10.html, accessed May 12, 2014.

19. Richard McCormack, "Service Is an Overlooked Ingredient for Success in Manufacturing," *Manufacturing and Technology News*, March 3, 2006, http://customerservicezone.com/cgi-bin/db/jump.cgi?ID=1237, accessed May 12, 2014.

20. Jeff Bailey, "The Education of an Educated CEO," *Inc.*, December 2008, www.inc.com/magazine/20081201/the-education-of-an-educated-ceo.html, accessed May 12, 2014.

21. Kurt Lewin, "Frontiers in Group Dynamics: Concept, Method, and Reality of Social Sciences—Social Equilibrium and Social Change," *Human Relations*, June 1947, pp. 5–14.

22. Matthew Boyle and Christopher Tkaczyk, "Follow These Leaders," *Fortune*, December 12, 2005, http://money.cnn.com/2005/12/05/news/newsmakers/leaders_fortune_121205/, accessed May 12, 2014.

23. David Bolchover, "Why Mood Matters," *Management Today*, November 1, 2008, http://www.managementtoday.co.uk/news/857772, accessed May 12, 2014.

24. Jennifer Robison, "Overcoming the Fear of Change," *Gallup Management Journal*, January 7, 2011, http://gmj.gallup.com; Stephanie Baker, "The Challenge of Change," *Healthcare Registration*, January 2010, pp. 3–5; Pat Zigarmi and Judd Hoekstra, "What's Killing Your Change Initiatives?" *Chief Learning Officer*, June 27, 2011, pp. 20–22, http://www.clomedia.com/articles/what-s-killing-your-change-initiatives, accessed May 12, 2014.

25. Bill Peterson, "Taking Lean beyond the Shop Floor," *Industry Week*, April 2010, pp. 41–42, http://www.industryweek.com/companies-amp-executives/consider-taking-lean-beyond-shop-floor, accessed May 12, 2014.

26. Joseph A. Raelin, "Growing Group Leadership Skills," *Security Management*, June 2004, downloaded from Business & Company Resource Center, http://galenet.galegroup.com.

27. For a study on the prevalence of organizational politics, see D. Buchanan, 2008, "You stab my back, I'll stab yours: Management experience and perceptions of organization political behaviour," *British Journal of Management*, 19, p. 49.

28. For an interesting look at the effects of position power, see T. Schubert, 2005, "Your highness: Vertical positions as perceptual symbols of power," *Journal of Personality and Social Psychology*, 89, p. 1, http://www.igroup.org/schubert/papers/schubert_jpsp05.pdf, accessed May 12, 2014.

29. For more information on why people develop personal power, see M. van Dijke and M. Poppe, 2006, "Striving for personal power as a basis for social power dynamics," *European Journal of Social Psychology*, 36, p. 537.

30. Beth Weissenberger, "How to Win at Office Politics," *Bloomberg Businessweek*, February 23, 2010, http://www.businessweek.com/managing/content/feb2010/ca20100222_142589.htm, accessed May 12, 2014; Jeffrey Pfeffer, "Don't Dismiss Office Politics—Teach It," *The Wall Street Journal*, October 24, 2011, http://online.wsj.com/news/articles/SB10001424053111904060604576570574190457198, accessed May 12, 2014; Careers Guide, "How to Handle Office Politics," *The Wall Street Journal*, May 8, 2009, http://guides.wsj.com/careers/how-to-overcome-career-obstacles/how-to-handle-office-politics/, accessed May 12, 2014.

PART TWO: SKILL-BUILDING

Meeting the Challenge

Reflecting back on page 379, imagine that the employees in a department at a BestBuy store will be losing their department supervisor. Working as a group, list the conflicts you would expect to arise from this situation. Mark each change on the list with *i* for intrapersonal, *I* for interpersonal, *Su* for structural, or *Sa* for strategic. What type of change does this represent? Will there be resistance to the change? Now, consider how this change will be implemented in the workplace, and how stress for the employees can be minimized.

Problem-Solving Case: National Conflict Resolution Center Helps Find Win–Win Solutions

For people embroiled in a conflict, it can be hard to envision a solution that both sides can accept. Anger and hurt feelings may overwhelm their ability to think about the problem and consider everyone's point of view. In those sticky situations, many organizations turn to the National Conflict Resolution Center (NCRC), based in San Diego, California.

The NCRC operates three divisions. Its Business Center offers organizations the services of a panel of experts to mediate disputes among co-workers, employees, and management or between customers and companies. Without choosing sides, the mediator leads a conversation in which the parties to the dispute discuss the problem and develop a solution that all parties agree upon. The Training Institute trains individuals in how to mediate conflict resolution. And the San Diego Mediation Center helps neighborhood and community organizations resolve local disputes. Through these services, the NCRC has taken a lead in resolving thousands of disputes.

Mediation services cost $250 to $400 an hour—a lot of money, but far less than the cost of hiring a lawyer to resolve a conflict in court. Another benefit of mediation in the workplace is that it moves people from thinking of each other as opponents. If an employee has a complaint about a supervisor, both people will be upset at work each day the dispute continues. Productive work relationships become difficult. When the individuals enter mediation, they begin thinking about solving the problem instead of fighting about it. In addition, the NCRC has found that participants gain a feeling of empowerment, because they are contributing to the outcome of the mediation process.

The NCRC's Training Institute has lessons that apply to any supervisor. Most basically, the mediator's job is about listening. Robin Seigle, director of the Business Center, explained, "So often people get into conflicts because of an assumption they make about the other person." When the parties to a conflict sit down with a mediator, they hear each other's description of the situation, and often they learn that their assumptions were not completely correct. Trainer Barbara Filner gives examples of the kinds of questions a mediator asks: "What were you hoping would happen? What were you thinking about?" By understanding what the participants want under ideal circumstances, the mediator can help them work toward a resolution that helps them. According to one of the institute's trainees, Brandon Moreno, effective listening also helps calm people down. Moreno said that since he has received mediation training, people tell him "that I'm able to engage people, and get them to open up and build rapport."

One of the NCRC's clients is the federal Transportation Safety Administration (TSA). Following the attacks of September 11, 2001, anxiety about the safety of air travel rose, and TSA screeners have been under pressure to keep passengers safe. At the same time, screening procedures can feel invasive and inconvenient to passengers. Under these stressful conditions, conflicts can erupt. Training in mediation skills has helped TSA employees deal with stressed-out co-workers, as well as with nervous and impatient travelers.

1. Based on this description of mediators, what kinds of supervisory skills are needed for mediating a conflict? Consider the various skills described in Chapters 1 through 14.

2. When might a supervisor benefit from using trained mediators, such as NCRC mediators, rather than mediating a conflict him- or herself? Why would the experts be important in these situations?

3. Suppose you are a supervisor of TSA screeners in an airport. You notice that a passenger is visibly upset about having her carry-on bag inspected. As you step near the table where the inspection is taking place, you hear her say, "You're going to make me miss my flight." Would you get involved in this situation? If so, how? What, if any, mediation skills from NCRC might help you?

Source: Pat Broderick, "Defusing Disputes: National Conflict Resolution Center Seeks Solutions to Variety of Problems and Issues," *San Diego Business Journal*, March 7, 2005, downloaded from Business & Company Resource Center, http://galenet.galegroup.com; National Conflict Resolution Center, "Frequently Asked Questions," www.ncrconline.com/FAQs/FAQs.php, accessed May 10, 2014.

Assessing Yourself

What Is Your Conflict-Handling Style?

Everyone has a basic style for handling conflicts. To identify the strategies you rely upon most, indicate how often each of the following statements applies to you. Next to each statement, write *5* if the statement applies often, *3* if the statement applies sometimes, and *1* if the statement applies never.

When I differ with someone . . .

_____ **1.** I explore our differences, not backing down, but not imposing my view either.

_____ **2.** I disagree openly, and then invite more discussion about our differences.

_____ **3.** I look for a mutually satisfactory solution.

_____ **4.** Rather than let the other person make a decision without my input, I make sure I am heard and also that I hear the other person out.

_____ **5.** I agree to a middle ground rather than look for a completely satisfying solution.

_____ **6.** I admit I am half wrong rather than explore our differences.

_____ **7.** I have a reputation for meeting a person halfway.

_____ **8.** I expect to say about half of what I really want to say.

_____ **9.** I give in totally rather than try to change another's opinion.

_____ **10.** I put aside any controversial aspects of an issue.

_____ **11.** I agree early on, rather than argue about a point.

_____ **12.** I give in as soon as the other party gets emotional about an issue.

_____ **13.** I try to win the other person over.

_____ **14.** I try to come out victorious, no matter what.

_____ **15.** I never back away from a good argument.

_____ **16.** I would rather win than end up compromising.

To score your responses, add your total score for each of the following sets of statements:

Set A: statements 1–4   Set C: statements 9–12

Set B: statements 5–8   Set D: statements 13–16

A score of 17 or more on any set is considered high. Scores of 12 to 16 are moderately high. Scores of 8 to 11 are moderately low. Scores of 7 or less are considered low. Each set represents a different strategy for conflict management:

- Set A = Collaboration (I win, you win).
- Set B = Compromise (Both win some, both lose some).
- Set C = Accommodation (I lose, you win).
- Set D = Forcing/domination (I win, you lose).

Source: From *Supervision: Managerial Skills for a New Era*, by Von der Embse. Copyright © 1987 Pearson Education, Inc. Reprinted by permission of Pearson Education, Inc., Upper Saddle River, NJ.

Pause and Reflect

1. For which conflict management style is your score highest? Are you surprised?

2. What are some advantages of the style(s) you use most often? Some disadvantages?

3. Do you think you would benefit from becoming more comfortable with conflict management styles for which your score was low?

Class Skills Exercise

Resolving Conflict

This exercise is based on role-playing. One class member takes the role of a supervisor, and two class members act as the employees. The supervisor leaves the room for five minutes as the employees act out the following scenario:

> Pat and Chris work in a communications department, monitoring social media and writing about the company in blogs, Twitter feeds, press releases, and other media channels. Pat trips on the cord to Chris's computer, shutting it off and erasing the project Chris was working on. Chris is upset. If Chris does not finish the job by the end of the day, the failure to meet a deadline will show up on Chris's performance records and hurt Chris's chances for getting a raise. In addition, the manager who requested the work will be upset, because this is an important project.

This is a basic scenario; the employees should be creative in adding details. For example, they can address the following questions:

- Did Pat erase the files on purpose?
- Has Pat ever done something like this before?
- Do these employees otherwise get along?
- Are communications in general and this conflict in particular complicated by some difference between the employees (age, sex, race, and so on)?

After the two class members have acted out the scene, the supervisor returns to the room, and the role-playing continues as the employees bring their conflict to the supervisor. The supervisor should try to manage the conflict.

When the supervisor is satisfied with how the conflict has been handled (or when 10 minutes have elapsed), the class discusses the following questions:

1. Did the supervisor understand the real problem? If not, what was the real problem?
2. Did the supervisor and employees solve the problem? Was the solution a good one?
3. In what ways was the supervisor effective in resolving the conflict? How could the supervisor improve his or her approach?
4. What other possible solutions might the supervisor and employees have considered?

Building Supervision Skills

Exercising Power to Bring about Change

Divide the class into teams of five or more students. Each student receives a card marked with the type of power he or she possesses: legitimate, referent, expert, coercive, reward, connection, or information. (If the group is small, some students may have two types of power.) Students should not show other team members which card they have. Each team has a goal: to convince the rest of the class that changing something (e.g., holding class in the evening instead of the afternoon) is a good idea.

Using the different kinds of power, each team presents its idea to the class. Afterward, the class should discuss how effective each team was, how effective individual team members were, and what type of power was most effective in getting people to respond positively to the idea of change.

Organizational Politics

Most students of supervision find the study of organizational politics intriguing. Perhaps this topic owes its appeal to the antics of Hollywood's corporate villains who get their way by stepping on anyone and everyone. As we will see, however, organizational politics includes, but is not limited to, dirty dealing. Organizational politics is an ever-present and sometimes annoying feature of modern work life. "According to 150 executives from large U.S. companies, office politics wastes an average of 20 percent of their time; that's 10 weeks a year."[1] On the other hand, organizational politics is often a positive force in modern work organizations. Skillful and well-timed politics can help you get your point across, neutralize resistance to a key project, or get a choice job assignment.

Roberta Bhasin, a district manager for US West, put organizational politics into perspective by observing the following:

> Most of us would like to believe that organizations are rationally structured, based on reasonable divisions of labor, a clear hierarchical communication flow, and well-defined lines of authority aimed at meeting universally understood goals and objectives.
>
> But organizations are made up of *people* with personal agendas designed to win power and influence. The agenda—the game—is called corporate politics. It is played by avoiding the rational structure, manipulating the communications hierarchy, and ignoring established lines of authority. The rules are never written down and seldom discussed.
>
> For some, corporate politics are second nature. They instinctively know the unspoken rules of the game. Others must learn. Managers who don't understand the politics of their organizations are at a disadvantage, not only in winning raises and promotions, but even in getting things *done*.[2]

We explore this important and interesting area by (1) defining the term *organizational politics,* (2) identifying three levels of political action, (3) discussing eight specific political tactics, (4) considering a related area called *impression management,* and (5) discussing how to manage organizational politics.

Definition and Domain of Organizational Politics

"*Organizational politics* involves intentional acts of influence to enhance or protect the self-interest of individuals or groups."[3] An emphasis on *self-interest* distinguishes this form of social influence.

Supervisors are endlessly challenged to achieve a workable balance between employees' self-interests and organizational interests. When a proper balance exists, the pursuit of self-interest may serve the organization's interests. Political behavior becomes a negative force when self-interests erode or defeat organizational interests. For example, researchers have documented the political tactic of filtering and distorting information flowing up to the boss. This self-serving practice puts the reporting employees in the best possible light.[4]

Source: Robert Kreitner and Angelo Kinicki, *Organizational Behavior*, 5th edition. Copyright © The McGraw-Hill Companies. Reproduced with permission of The McGraw-Hill Companies.

Uncertainty Triggers Political Behavior

Political maneuvering is triggered primarily by *uncertainty*. Five common sources of uncertainty within organizations are

1. Unclear objectives.
2. Vague performance measures.
3. Ill-defined decision processes.
4. Strong individual or group competition.[5]
5. Any type of change.

Regarding this last source of uncertainty, organization development specialist Anthony Raia noted, "Whatever we attempt to change, the political subsystem becomes active. Vested interests are almost always at stake and the distribution of power is challenged."[6]

Thus, we would expect a field sales representative, striving to achieve an assigned quota, to be less political than a supervisor working on a variety of projects. While some supervisors stake their career success on hard work, competence, and a bit of luck, many do not. These people attempt to gain a competitive edge through some combination of the political tactics discussed below. Meanwhile, the salesperson's performance is measured in actual sales, not in terms of being friends with the boss or taking credit for others' work. Thus, the supervisor would tend to be more political than the field salesperson because of greater uncertainty about management's expectations.

Because employees generally experience greater uncertainty during the earlier stages of their careers, are junior employees more political than more senior ones? The answer is yes, according to a survey of 243 employed adults in upstate New York. In fact, one senior employee nearing retirement told the researcher: "I used to play political games when I was younger. Now I just do my job."[7]

Three Levels of Political Action

Although much political maneuvering occurs at the individual level, it also can involve group or collective action. Figure A illustrates three different levels of political action: the individual level, the coalition level, and the network level.[8] Each level has its distinguishing characteristics. At the individual level, personal self-interests

FIGURE A | Levels of Political Action in Organization

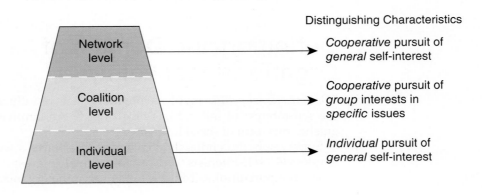

Distinguishing Characteristics

Cooperative pursuit of *general* self-interest

Cooperative pursuit of *group* interests in *specific* issues

Individual pursuit of *general* self-interest

are pursued by the individual. The political aspects of coalitions and networks are not so obvious, however.

People with a common interest can become a political coalition by fitting the following definition. In an organizational context, a *coalition* is an informal group bound together by the *active* pursuit of a *single* issue. Coalitions may or may not coincide with formal group membership. When the target issue is resolved (a sexually harassing supervisor is fired, for example), the coalition disbands. Experts note that political coalitions have "fuzzy boundaries," meaning they are fluid in membership, flexible in structure, and temporary in duration.[9]

Coalitions are a potent political force in organizations. Consider the situation Charles J. Bradshaw faced in a finance committee meeting at Transworld Corporation; Bradshaw, president of the company, opposed the chairman's plan to acquire a $93 million nursing home company:

> [The senior vice president for finance] kicked off the meeting with a battery of facts and figures in support of the deal. "Within two or three minutes, I knew I had lost," Bradshaw concedes. "No one was talking directly to me, but all statements addressed my opposition. I could tell there was a general agreement around the board table. . . ."
> Then the vote was taken. Five hands went up. Only Bradshaw voted "no."[10]

After the meeting, Bradshaw resigned his $530,000-a-year position, without as much as a handshake or good-bye from the chairman. In Bradshaw's case, the finance committee was a formal group that temporarily became a political coalition aimed at sealing his fate at Transworld. Coalitions on the corporate boards of American Express, IBM, and General Motors also ousted the heads of those giant companies.

A third level of political action involves networks.[11] Unlike coalitions, which pivot on specific issues, networks are loose associations of individuals seeking social support for their general self-interests. Politically, networks are people oriented, while coalitions are issue oriented. Networks have broader and longer-term agendas than do coalitions. For instance, Avon's Hispanic employees have built a network to enhance the members' career opportunities.

Political Tactics

Anyone who has worked in an organization has firsthand knowledge of blatant politicking. Blaming someone else for your mistake is an obvious political ploy. But other political tactics are more subtle. Researchers have identified a range of political behavior.

One landmark study, involving in-depth interviews with 87 managers from 30 electronics companies in Southern California, identified eight political tactics. Top, middle, and supervisors were represented about equally in the sample. According to the researchers: "Respondents were asked to describe organizational political tactics and personal characteristics of effective political actors based upon their accumulated experience in all organizations in which they had worked."[12] Listed in descending order of occurrence, the eight political tactics that emerged were

1. Attacking or blaming others.
2. Using information as a political tool.
3. Creating a favorable image. (Also known as impression management.)[13]
4. Developing a base of support.
5. Praising others (ingratiation).
6. Forming power coalitions with strong allies.
7. Associating with influential people.
8. Creating obligations (reciprocity).

TABLE A | Eight Common Political Tactics in Organizations

Political Tactic	Percentage of Managers Mentioning Tactic	Brief Description of Tactic
1. Attacking or blaming others	54%	Used to avoid or minimize association with failure. Reactive when scapegoating is involved. Proactive when goal is to reduce competition for limited resources.
2. Using information as a political tool	54	Involves the purposeful withholding or distortion of information. Obscuring an unfavorable situation by overwhelming superiors with information.
3. Creating a favorable image (impression management)	53	Dressing/grooming for success. Adhering to organizational norms and drawing attention to one's successes and influence. Taking credit for others' accomplishments.
4. Developing a base of support	37	Getting prior support for a decision. Building others' commitment to a decision through participation.
5. Praising others (ingratiation)	25	Making influential people feel good ("apple polishing").
6. Forming power coalitions with strong allies	25	Teaming up with powerful people who can get results.
7. Associating with influential people	24	Building a support network both inside and outside the organization.
8. Creating obligations (reciprocity)	13	Creating social debts ("I did you a favor, so you owe me a favor").

Source: Adapted from R. W. Allen, D. L. Madison, I. W. Porter, P. A. Renwick, and B. T. Mayes, "Organizational Politics: Tactics and Characteristics of Its Actors," *California Management Review*, Fall 1979, pp. 77–83.

Table A describes these political tactics and indicates how often each reportedly was used by the interviewed managers.

The researchers distinguished between reactive and proactive political tactics. Some of the tactics, such as scapegoating, were *reactive* because the intent was to *defend* one's self-interest. Other tactics, such as developing a base of support, were *proactive* because they sought to *promote* the individual's self-interest.

What is your attitude toward organizational politics? How often do you rely on the various tactics in Table A? You can get a general indication of your political tendencies by comparing your behavior with the characteristics in Table B.

TABLE B | Are You Politically Naive, Politically Sensible, or a Political Shark?

Characteristics	Naive	Sensible	Sharks
Underlying attitude	Politics is unpleasant.	Politics is necessary.	Politics is an opportunity.
Intent	Avoid at all costs.	Further departmental goals.	Self-serving and predatory.
Techniques	Tell it like it is.	Network; expand connections: use system to give and receive favors.	Manipulate; use fraud and deceit when necessary.
Favorite tactics	None—the truth will win out.	Negotiate, bargain.	Bully; misuse information: cultivate and use "friends and other contacts."

Source: Reprinted from J. K. Pinto and O. P. Kharbanda, "Lessons for an Accidental Profession," *Business Horizons*, March–April 1995. Copyright © 1995, with permission from Elsevier.

Would you characterize yourself as politically *naive,* politically *sensible,* or a political *shark*? How do you think others view your political actions? What are the career, friendship, and ethical implications of your political tendencies?[14]

Impression Management

Impression management is defined as "the process by which people attempt to control or manipulate the reactions of others to images of themselves or their ideas."[15]

This encompasses how one talks, behaves, and looks. Most impression management attempts are directed at making a good impression on relevant others. But, as we will see, some employees strive to make a bad impression. For purposes of conceptual clarity, we will focus on upward impression management, or trying to impress one's immediate supervisor. Still, it is good to remember that anyone can be the intended target of impression management. Parents, teachers, peers, employees, and customers are all fair game when it comes to managing the impressions of others.

A Conceptual Crossroads

Impression management is an interesting conceptual crossroads involving self-monitoring and organizational politics.[16] Perhaps this explains why impression management has gotten active research attention in recent years. High self-monitoring employees ("chameleons" who adjust to their surroundings) are likely to be more inclined to engage in impression management than would low self-monitors. Impression management also involves the systematic manipulation of attributions. For example, a supervisor will look good if upper management is encouraged to attribute organizational successes to her efforts and attribute problems and failures to factors beyond her control. Impression management definitely fits into the realm of organizational politics because of an overriding focus on furthering one's *self-interests.*

Making a Good Impression

If you "dress for success," project an upbeat attitude at all times, and avoid offending others, you are engaging in favorable impression management—particularly so if your motive is to improve your chances of getting what you want in life.[17] There are questionable ways to create a good impression, as well. For instance, Stewart Friedman, director of the University of Pennsylvania's Leadership Program, recently offered this gem:

> Last year, I was doing some work with a large bank. The people there told me a story that astounded me: After 7 p.m., people would open the door to their office, drape a spare jacket on the back of their chair, lay a set of glasses down on some reading material on their desk—and then go home for the night. The point of this elaborate gesture was to create the illusion that they were just out grabbing dinner and would be returning to burn the midnight oil.[18]

Impression management often strays into unethical territory.

An analysis of the influence attempts reported by a sample of 84 bank employees (including 74 women) identified three categories of favorable upward impression management tactics.[19] Favorable upward impression management tactics can be *job focused* (manipulating information about one's job performance), *supervisor focused* (praising and doing favors for one's supervisor), and *self-focused* (presenting oneself as a polite and nice person). Take a short break from your studying to complete the questionnaire in Table C on the following page. How did you do?

TABLE C | How Much Do You Rely on Upward Impression Management Tactics?

Instructions

Rate yourself on each item according to how you behave on your current (or most recent) job. Add your circled responses to calculate a total score. Compare your score with our arbitrary norms.

	Rarely Very Often
Job-Focused Tactics	
1. I play up the value of my positive work results and make my supervisor aware of them.	1—2—3—4—5
2. I try to make my work appear better than it is.	1—2—3—4—5
3. I try to take responsibility for positive results, even when I'm not solely responsible for achieving them.	1—2—3—4—5
4. I try to make my negative results not as severe as they initially appear to my supervisor.	1—2—3—4—5
5. I arrive at work early and/or work late to show my supervisor I am a hard worker.	1—2—3—4—5
Supervisor-Focused Tactics	
6. I show an interest in my supervisor's personal life.	1—2—3—4—5
7. I praise my supervisor on his/her accomplishments.	1—2—3—4—5
8. I do personal favors for my supervisor that I'm not required to do.	1—2—3—4—5
9. I compliment my supervisor on her or his dress or appearance.	1—2—3—4—5
10. I agree with my supervisor's major suggestions and ideas.	1—2—3—4—5
Self-Focused Tactics	
11. I am very friendly and polite around my supervisor.	1—2—3—4—5
12. I try to act as a model employee around my supervisor.	1—2—3—4—5
13. I work harder when I know my supervisor will see the results.	1—2—3—4—5
	Total score = _____

Arbitrary Norms

13–26 Free agent

27–51 Better safe than sorry

52–65 Hello, Hollywood

Source: Adapted from S. J. Wayne and G. R. Ferris, "Influence Tactics, Affect, and Exchange Quality in Supervisor-Subordinate Interactions: A Laboratory Experiment and Field Study," *Journal of Applied Psychology*, October 1990, pp. 487–499.

A moderate amount of upward impression management is a necessity for the average supervisor today. Too little, and busy managers are liable to overlook some of your valuable contributions when they make job assignment, pay, and promotion decisions. Too much, and you run the risk of being branded a "schmoozer," a "phony," and other unflattering things by your co-workers.[20] Excessive flattery and ingratiation can backfire by embarrassing the target person and damaging one's credibility. Also, the risk of unintended insult is very high when impression management tactics cross gender, racial, ethnic, and cultural lines.[21] International experts warn:

> The impression management tactic is only as effective as its correlation to accepted norms about behavioral presentation. In other words, slapping a Japanese subordinate on the back with a rousing "Good work, Hiro!" will not create the desired impression in Hiro's mind that the expatriate intended. In fact, the behavior will likely create the opposite impression.[22]

Making a Poor Impression

At first glance, the idea of consciously trying to make a bad impression in the workplace seems absurd. But an interesting new line of impression management research has uncovered both motives and tactics for making oneself look bad. In a survey of the work experiences of business students at a large northwestern U.S. university, more than half "reported witnessing a case of someone intentionally looking bad at work."[23] Why? Four motives came out of the study:

> (1) Avoidance: Employee seeks to avoid additional work, stress, burnout, or an unwanted transfer or promotion. (2) Obtain concrete rewards: Employee seeks to obtain a pay raise or a desired transfer, promotion, or demotion. (3) Exit: Employee seeks to get laid off, fired, or suspended, and perhaps also to collect unemployment or worker's compensation. (4) Power: Employee seeks to control, manipulate, or intimidate others, get revenge, or make someone else look bad.[24]

Within the context of these motives, *unfavorable* upward impression management makes sense.

Five unfavorable upward impression management tactics identified by the researchers are as follows:

- *Decreasing performance*—restricting productivity, making more mistakes than usual, lowering quality, neglecting tasks.
- *Not working to potential*—pretending ignorance, having unused capabilities.
- *Withdrawing*—being tardy, taking excessive breaks, faking illness.
- *Displaying a bad attitude*—complaining, getting upset and angry, acting strangely, not getting along with co-workers.
- *Broadcasting limitations*—letting co-workers know about one's physical problems and mistakes (both verbally and nonverbally).[25]

Recommended ways to manage employees who try to make a bad impression can include affording them more challenging work, greater autonomy, better feedback, supportive leadership, clear and reasonable goals, and a less stressful work setting.[26]

Managing Organizational Politics

Organizational politics cannot be eliminated. A supervisor would be naive to expect such an outcome. But political maneuvering can and should be managed to keep it constructive and within reasonable bounds. Harvard's Abraham Zaleznik put the issue this way: "People can focus their attention on only so many things. The more it lands on politics, the less energy—emotional and intellectual—is available to attend to the problems that fall under the heading of real work."[27]

An individual's degree of politicalness is a matter of personal values, ethics, and temperament. People who are either strictly nonpolitical or highly political generally pay a price for their behavior. The former may experience slow promotions and feel left out, while the latter may run the risk of being called self-serving and lose their credibility. People at both ends of the political spectrum may be considered poor team players. A moderate amount of prudent political behavior generally is considered a survival tool in complex organizations. Experts remind us that

> . . . political behavior has earned a bad name only because of its association with politicians. On its own, the use of power and other resources to obtain your objectives is not inherently unethical. It all depends on what the preferred objectives are.[28]

TABLE D | Some Practical Advice on Managing Organizational Politics

To Reduce System Uncertainty
Make clear what are the bases and processes for evaluation.

Differentiate rewards among high and low performers.

Make sure the rewards are as immediately and directly related to performance as possible.

To Reduce Competition
Try to minimize resource competition among managers.

Replace resource competition with externally oriented goals and objectives.

To Break Existing Political Fiefdoms
Where highly cohesive political empires exist, break them apart by removing or splitting the most dysfunctional subgroups.

If you are an executive, be keenly sensitive to managers whose mode of operation is the personalization of political patronage. First, approach these persons with a directive to "stop the political maneuvering." If it continues, remove them from the positions and preferably, the company.

To Prevent Future Fiefdoms
Make one of the most important criteria for promotion an apolitical attitude that puts organizational ends ahead of personal power ends.

Source: Reprinted from D. R. Beeman and T. W. Sharkey, "The Use and Abuse of Corporate Politics," *Business Horizons*, March–April 1987. Copyright © 1987, with permission from Elsevier.

With this perspective in mind, the practical steps in Table D are recommended. Notice the importance of reducing uncertainty through standardized performance evaluations and clear performance–reward linkages.[29] Measurable objectives are the supervisor's first line of defense against negative expressions of organizational politics.[30]

Notes

1. C. Pasternak, "Corporate Politics May Not Be a Waste of Time," *HRMagazine,* September 1994, p. 18.

2. R. Bhasin, "On Playing Corporate Politics," *Pulp & Paper,* October 1985, p. 175. See also N. Gupta and G. D. Jenkins, Jr., "The Politics of Pay," *Compensation & Benefits Review,* March–April 1996, pp. 23–30.

3. R. W. Allen, D. L. Madison, L. W. Porter, P. A. Renwick, and B. T. Mayes, "Organizational Politics: Tactics and Characteristics of Its Actors," *California Management Review,* Fall 1979, p. 77. See also K. M. Kacmar and G. R. Ferris, "Politics at Work: Sharpening the Focus of Political Behavior in Organizations," *Business Horizons,* July–August 1993, pp. 70–74. A comprehensive update can be found in K. M. Kacmar and R. A. Baron, "Organizational Politics: The State of the Field, Links to Related Processes, and an Agenda for Future Research," in *Research in Personnel and Human Resources Management,* Vol. 17, ed. G. R. Ferris (Stamford, CT: JAI Press, 1999), pp. 1–39.

4. See P. M. Fandt and G. R. Ferris, "The Management of Information and Impressions: When Employees Behave Opportunistically," *Organizational Behavior and Human Decision Processes,* February 1990, pp. 140–158.

5. The first four are based on the discussion in D. R. Beeman and T. W. Sharkey, "The Use and Abuse of Corporate Politics," *Business Horizons,* March–April 1987, pp. 26–30.

6. A. Raia, "Power, Politics, and the Human Resource Professional," *Human Resource Planning,* no. 4 (1985), p. 203.

7. A. J. DuBrin, "Career Maturity, Organizational Rank, and Political Behavioral Tendencies: A Correlational Analysis of Organizational Politics and Career Experience," *Psychological Reports,* October 1988, p. 535.

8. This three-level distinction comes from A. T. Cobb, "Political Diagnosis: Applications in Organizational Development," *Academy of Management Review,* July 1986, pp. 482–496.

9. An excellent historical and theoretical perspective of coalitions can be found in W. B. Stevenson, J. L. Pearce, and L. W. Porter, "The Concept of 'Coalition' in Organization Theory and Research," *Academy of Management Review,* April 1985, pp. 256–268.

10. L. Baum, "The Day Charlie Bradshaw Kissed Off Transworld," *BusinessWeek,* September 29, 1986, p. 68.

11. See K. G. Provan and J. G. Sebastian, "Networks within Networks: Service Link Overlap, Organizational Cliques, and Network Effectiveness," *Academy of Management Journal*, August 1998, pp. 453–463.

12. Allen et al., "Organizational Politics," p. 77.

13. See W. L. Gardner III, "Lessons in Organizational Dramaturgy: The Art of Impression Management," *Organizational Dynamics*, Summer 1992, pp. 33–46.

14. For more on political behavior, see A. Nierenberg, "Masterful Networking," *Training & Development*, February 1999, pp. 51–53.

15. A. Rao, S. M. Schmidt, and L. H. Murray, "Upward Impression Management: Goals, Influence Strategies, and Consequences," *Human Relations*, February 1995, p. 147.

16. Fandt and Ferris, "The Management of Information and Impressions" pp. 140–158; W. L. Gardner and B. J. Avolio, "The Charismatic Relationship: A Dramaturgical Perspective," *Academy of Management Review*, January 1998, pp. 32–58; L. Wah, "Managing–Manipulating?—Your Reputation," *Management Review*, October 1998, pp. 46–50; M. C. Bolino, "Citizenship and Impression Management: Good Soldiers or Good Actors?" *Academy of Management Review*, January 1999, pp. 82–98.

17. For related research, see M. G. Pratt and A. Rafaeli, "Organizational Dress as a Symbol of Multilayered Social Identities," *Academy of Management Journal*, August 1997, pp. 862–898.

18. S. Friedman, "What Do You Really Care About? What Are You Most Interested In?" *Fast Company*, March 1999, p. 90. See also B. M. DePaulo and D. A. Kashy, "Everyday Lies in Close and Casual Relationships," *Journal of Personality and Social Psychology*, January 1998, pp. 63–79.

19. See S. J. Wayne and G. R. Ferris, "Influence Tactics, Affect, and Exchange Quality in Supervisor-Subordinate Interactions: A Laboratory Experiment and Field Study," *Journal of Applied Psychology*, October 1990, pp. 487–499. For another version, see Table 1 (p. 246) in S. J. Wayne and R. C. Liden, "Effects of Impression Management on Performance Ratings: A Longitudinal Study," *Academy of Management Journal*, February 1995, pp. 232–260.

20. See R. Vonk, "The Slime Effect: Suspicion and Dislike of Likeable Behavior toward Superiors," *Journal of Personality and Social Psychology*, April 1998, pp. 849–864; M. Wells, "How to Schmooze Like the Best of Them," *USA Today*, May 18, 1999, p. 14E.

21. See P. Rosenfeld, R. A. Giacalone, and C. A. Riordan, "Impression Management Theory and Diversity: Lessons for Organizational Behavior," *American Behavioral Scientist*, March 1994, pp. 601–604; R. A. Giacalone and J. W. Beard, "Impression Management, Diversity, and International Management," *American Behavioral Scientist*, March 1994, pp. 621–636; A. Montagliani and R. A. Giacalone, "Impression Management and Cross-Cultural Adaptation," *The Journal of Social Psychology*, October 1998, pp. 598–608.

22. M. E. Mendenhall and C. Wiley, "Strangers in a Strange Land: The Relationship between Expatriate Adjustment and Impression Management," *American Behavioral Scientist*, March 1994, pp. 605–620.

23. T. E. Becker and S. L. Martin, "Trying to Look Bad at Work: Methods and Motives for Managing Poor Impressions in Organizations," *Academy of Management Journal*, February 1995, p. 191.

24. Ibid., p. 181.

25. Ibid., pp. 180–181.

26. Ibid., pp. 192–193.

27. Data from G. R. Ferris, D. D. Frink, D. P. S. Bhawuk, J. Zhou, and D. C. Gilmore, "Reactions of Diverse Groups to Politics in the Workplace," *Journal of Management*, no. 1 (1996), pp. 23–44. For other findings from the same database, see G. R. Ferris, D. D. Frink, M. C. Galang, J. Zhou, K. M. Kacmar, and J. L. Howard, "Perceptions of Organizational Politics: Prediction, Stress-Related Implications, and Outcomes," *Human Relations*, February 1996, pp. 233–266. Also see M. L. Randall, R. Cropanzano, C. A. Bormann, and A. Birjulin, "Organizational Politics and Organizational Support as Predictors of Work Attitudes, Job Performance, and Organizational Citizenship Behavior," *Journal of Organizational Behavior*, March 1999, pp. 159–174.

28. A. Drory and D. Beaty, "Gender Differences in the Perception of Organizational Influence Tactics," *Journal of Organizational Behavior*, May 1991, pp. 256–257. Also see L. A. Rudman, "Self-Promotion as a Risk Factor for Women: The Costs and Benefits of Counterstereotypical Impression Management," *Journal of Personality and Social Psychology*, March 1998, pp. 629–645; J. Tata, "The Influence of Gender on the Use and Effectiveness of Managerial Accounts," *Group & Organization Management*, September 1998, pp. 267–288.

29. See S. J. Wayne and R. C. Liden, "Effects of Impression Management on Performance Ratings: A Longitudinal Study," *Academy of Management Journal*, February 1995, pp. 232–260.

30. Rao, Schmidt, and Murray, "Upward Impression Management," p. 165.

chapter fifteen | Selecting Employees

learning objectives

After you have studied this chapter, you should be able to:

15.1 Discuss common roles for supervisors in the selection process.

15.2 Distinguish between job descriptions and job specifications and explain how they help in selecting employees.

15.3 List possible sources of employees.

15.4 Identify the steps in the selection process.

15.5 Discuss how a supervisor should go about interviewing candidates for a job.

15.6 Define types of employment tests.

15.7 Summarize the requirements of antidiscrimination laws.

15.8 Explain how hiring decisions are affected by the Americans with Disabilities Act (ADA).

15.9 Describe the requirements of the Immigration Reform and Control Act (IRCA) of 1986.

A Supervision Challenge

FINDING SEASONAL WORKERS FOR AMAZON

When online shoppers post orders at Amazon's Web site, employees go to work in the bricks-and-mortar world of the company's huge warehouses. Much of the inventory is stored and packaged at facilities located in Fernley, Nevada; Campbellsville, Kentucky; and Coffeeville, Kansas. By locating these facilities off the beaten path, Amazon keeps costs low, but it also encounters a challenge in the final two months of each year: how to find enough workers to keep orders flowing when shopping heats up for the holidays. Each fall, Amazon hires thousands of temporary warehouse workers—15,000 in one recent year—to meet the annual surge in demand. But in the small communities where the warehouses are located, the pool of candidates is limited.

Amazon has found a solution in a relatively new kind of migrant workers who call themselves "workampers." These are people, many of them retirees, who enjoy the lifestyle of touring the country in recreational vehicles and finance their activities by taking temporary jobs in various locations. Some of them take the jobs as an adventure, but others work out of necessity. When the recent financial crisis and economic recession put a dent in retirement funds and permanent job prospects, the ranks of this group swelled with people who might otherwise have stayed on the job or relaxed during retirement. By one count, roughly half a million people in the United States consider themselves workampers, and their median age is 53.

To find workampers, Amazon sends representatives to RV shows, where they staff booths and describe work opportunities to RV enthusiasts. The company also advertises jobs in the employment databases of Web sites that cater to the interests of workampers. When the company selects qualified people, it gives them the chance to pick which location they want to work at, and it pays for their camping fees, including utilities, during the time of their employment.

The result of this hiring strategy is a workforce that includes people who might not look like the typical warehouse worker. For example, Ray and Sarann Williams, a married couple in their seventies, traveled from their home in Utah to work in the Kentucky warehouse one year and in the Nevada warehouse the next year. The workdays are grueling, especially in the final weeks before Christmas, but employees are proud of their endurance and enjoy the chance to make new friends among their temporary co-workers. Irene Luft has returned to Amazon's Kansas facility several years in a row, working 10-hour shifts, because she enjoys touring the country, meeting new people, and then seeing many of those same faces when they return each year. Not everyone can keep up with the demands, however. Terry and April McFail became workampers after Terry was laid off from his job with Dow Chemical and they lost their home to foreclosure. They took positions with Amazon, but April, who has diabetes, found she could not lift packages weighing up to 30 pounds for 10 hours a day, four days a week.

Finding qualified people to fill physically demanding temporary jobs is especially difficult in a community with a small pool of labor. Yet a supervisor's success depends largely on the supervisor's people. How can Amazon's warehouse supervisors help to ensure that the company brings in people who can succeed in these jobs at the company's busiest time of the year?

Sources: Stu Woo, "Welcome to Amazon Town," *The Wall Street Journal,* December 20, 2011, http://online.wsj.com; Steve Osunsami, "Americans Turn to the Open Road, Looking for Jobs in Their RVs," *ABC News,* November 30, 2010, http://abcnews.go.com; Lynn Neary, "Amazon's Seasonal 'Workampers' Fill Holiday Orders," National Public Radio, December 22, 2011, http://www.npr.org; Jere Downs, "Workers Hopscotch across USA for Temp Checks," *USA Today,* November 27, 2010, http://www.usatoday.com; Jaimie Hall Bruzenak, "Amazon Workampers in the News—Again," *RV Home Yet?,* December 21, 2011, http://blog.rvlifestyleexperts.com.

Amazon needs to be especially creative in finding seasonal employees because its warehouses are located in small communities with a limited pool of workers. This is an effort worth making, because at Amazon, as at every organization, success depends on finding the right kind of people. Not only is careful hiring necessary for practical business reasons, but it must meet legal requirements. In addition to this practical business reason, careful hiring is important because it must meet several legal requirements. Thus, it is in a supervisor's best interests to do a good job in helping select employees. Enthusiastic, well-qualified people are more likely to deliver high quality than indifferent, unqualified people. This is especially true in today's leaner organizations; when fewer employees are getting the work done, each employee has a greater impact on the organization's overall performance. However, a recent survey found that almost half of newly hired employees lose their job within a year and a half. Often, those employees had the necessary technical skills but didn't fit in well—for instance, because they lacked motivation or couldn't accept feedback.[1]

This chapter addresses the supervisor's role in selecting employees, which often entails working with the organization's human resources (or personnel) department. The chapter explains how supervisors define needed qualities of jobs and employees by preparing job descriptions and job specifications. It describes how organizations can recruit candidates and decide whom to hire. Finally, it addresses some legal issues that supervisors and others in the organization must be aware of when hiring.

Roles in the Selection Process

LO15.1 ▶ Discuss common roles for supervisors in the selection process.

A supervisor's role in the selection process can vary greatly from one organization to another. In small organizations, a supervisor may have great latitude in selecting employees to fill vacant positions. Other organizations have formal procedures that require the human resources department to do most of the work, with the supervisor simply approving the candidates recommended. In most cases, a supervisor works to some extent with a human resources department. In this way, a supervisor benefits from that department's skills in screening and interviewing candidates and from its familiarity with laws regarding hiring practices.

As described in Chapter 3, a growing number of organizations expect employees to work in teams. At the least, the use of teamwork requires the selection of employees who will be effective team members. A supervisor might therefore try to identify candidates who are cooperative and skilled in problem solving or who have helped a team achieve good results in the past. In other cases, the use of teamwork dramatically changes a supervisor's role in the selection process. When teamwork takes the form of self-managing work teams, a team generally interviews candidates and recommends or selects new team members. A supervisor, as team leader, needs to understand the principles of selection so that he or she can coach employees in carrying out the process. The organization's human resources staff supports the team, rather than the individual supervisor.

Selection Criteria

LO15.2 ▶ Distinguish between job descriptions and job specifications and explain how they help in selecting employees.

To select the right employees, the supervisor, team (if applicable), and human resources department have to be clear about what jobs need to be filled and what kind of people can best fill those jobs. A supervisor or self-managed team provides this information by preparing job descriptions and job specifications, as well as consulting with the human resources department as needed. Table 15.1, on the following page, details basic kinds of information to include in job descriptions and job specifications.

job description
A listing of the characteristics of a job, including the job title, duties involved, and working conditions

A **job description** is a listing of the characteristics of the job—that is, the observable activities required to carry out the job. A written job description typically includes the title of the job, a general description, and details of the duties involved.[2] As you will see subsequently in this chapter, it is important for the job description to spell out the essential duties of the job. When appropriate, a job description may also describe working conditions. Figure 15.1, on the following page, shows a sample job description for a maintenance technician.

TABLE 15.1 | Contents of the Job Description and Job Specification

Source: From *Modern Management*, 12th edition, by Samuel C. Certo and S. Trevis Certo. Copyright © 2012 Pearson Education, Inc. Reprinted by permission of Pearson Education, Inc., Upper Saddle River, NJ.

Job Description	Job Specification
Job title	Education
Location	Experience
Job summary	Skills—technical, physical, communication, and interpersonal
Duties	Training
Productivity and quality standards	Judgment and initiative
Machines, tools, and equipment	Emotional characteristics
Materials and forms used	Physical effort
Relationships—supervision and working conditions	Unusual sensory demands (sight, smell, teams, if any)

job specification
A listing of the characteristics desirable in the person performing a given job, including educational and work background, physical characteristics, and personal strengths

A **job specification** is a listing of the characteristics desirable in the person performing the job. These include four types of characteristics:[3]

1. *Knowledge*—Information required to perform the tasks in the job description.
2. *Skills*—Proficiency in carrying out the tasks in the job description.
3. *Abilities*—General enduring capabilities required for carrying out the tasks in the job description.
4. *Other characteristics*—Any additional characteristics related to the successful performance of the essential tasks (e.g., personality characteristics).

FIGURE 15.1 | Sample Job Description: Maintenance Mechanic

A job description typically includes a listing of characteristics of the job as well as details of the duties involved.

Source: From Raymond Noe, John R. Hollenbeck, Barry Gerhart, and Patrick M. Wright, *Human Resource Management: Gaining a Competitive Advantage*, 4th ed., 2003 Copyright © 2003, The McGraw-Hill Companies.

General Description of Job General maintenance and repair of all equipment used in the operations of a particular district. Includes the servicing of company vehicles, shop equipment, and machinery used on job sites.

- *Essential Duty (40%): Maintenance of Equipment*
Tasks: Keep a log of all maintenance performed on equipment. Replace parts and fluids according to maintenance schedule. Regularly check gauges and loads for deviances that may indicate problems with equipment. Perform nonroutine maintenance as required. May involve limited supervision and training of operators performing maintenance.

- *Essential Duty (40%): Repair of Equipment*
Tasks: Requires inspection of equipment and a recommendation that a piece be scrapped or repaired. If equipment is to be repaired, mechanic will take whatever steps are necessary to return the piece to working order. This may include a partial or total rebuilding of the piece using various hand tools and equipment. Will primarily involve the overhaul and troubleshooting of diesel engines and hydraulic equipment.

- *Essential Duty (10%): Testing and Approval*
Tasks: Ensure that all required maintenance and repairs have been performed and that they were performed according to manufacturer specifications. Approve or reject equipment for readiness to use on a job.

- *Essential Duty (10%): Maintain Stock*
Tasks: Maintain inventory of parts needed for the maintenance and repair of equipment. Responsible for ordering satisfactory parts and supplies at the lowest possible cost.

Nonessential Functions
Other duties as assigned

A job specification for the maintenance technician's position therefore would include characteristics such as knowledge about the company's vehicles and shop equipment, skills in repairing these things, broad mechanical abilities, and a commitment to high-quality work.

A supervisor (or team with the supervisor's coaching) should provide the information that applies to a particular job. If a job description and job specification already exist for a position, a supervisor should review them to make sure they reflect current needs. Preparing and using these materials helps a supervisor base hiring decisions on objective criteria—how well each candidate matches the requirements of the job. Without them, a supervisor risks hiring people solely because he or she likes them better than others.

Recruitment

LO15.3 ▶ List possible sources of employees.

recruitment
A process of identifying people interested in holding a particular job or working for the organization

To select employees, the supervisor and human resources department need candidates for the job. Identifying people interested in holding a particular job or working for the organization is known as **recruitment,** which involves looking for candidates from both inside and outside the organization.

Looking Inside the Organization

Many employees are eager to accept a promotion. Less commonly, employees welcome the variety of working in a new department or at a different task even when the transfer does not involve more money or prestige. These changes can be a source of motivation for employees.

Increased motivation is only one way the organization benefits from promotions and transfers. In addition, the promoted or transferred employees start the new job already familiar with the organization's policies and practices. It may be easier to train new people for entry-level jobs than to hire outsiders to fill more complex positions.

To find employees who are interested in and qualified for a vacant position, a supervisor or human resources department recruits within the organization. Internal recruitment is conducted in two basic ways: job postings and employee referrals. A job posting is a list of the positions that are vacant in the organization. Typically, a job posting gives the title of the job, the department, and the salary range. In addition, a supervisor's employees may be able to recommend someone for the job—friends or relatives who do not currently work for the organization or qualified candidates they have met through trade or professional groups. Some organizations pay employees a bonus for referrals if the candidate is hired.

Looking Outside the Organization

A growing organization will especially need to look outside the organization for at least some of its employees. New hires are less familiar with the organization, but they bring fresh ideas and skills that the organization may lack. The basic ways to identify qualified candidates outside the organization are through advertising, employment agencies, online job sites and blogs, and schools. In addition, as described in "Supervision: New Trends," creative companies do not limit themselves to the basic methods.

Help wanted advertisements are a popular way to recruit candidates for a job. Most people at some time or another read the want ads in online and print publications to see what jobs are available. Organizations can advertise in journals and magazines directed toward a specialized audience. For example, a research

SUPERVISION: NEW TRENDS

MARRIOTT GETS PLAYFUL ABOUT RECRUITING

If you want to find employees, you have to go where workers are these days, and increasingly often, that means online, on Facebook, playing games. To find people inspired by the challenge of pleasing guests while making a profit, Marriott International has begun offering Facebook users a chance to play My Marriott Hotel, a game that simulates hotel management.

The first part of the game to launch simulates a hotel kitchen. Players are in charge of managing the kitchen, which starts out with one basic range and one cook. They make decisions to purchase food and equipment, hire workers, assign orders to cooks, inspect the work, and handle quality problems whenever customers return food. They score points when customers are satisfied, lose points when customers complain, and earn rewards for making a profit.

In contrast to other games available for mobile devices, My Marriott Hotel was designed with input from hotel employees to pose realistic challenges. Marriott's intention is that some players will find the challenges exciting and will realize they would enjoy and succeed in hotel work. The company needs to fill about 50,000 positions a year, and many of the jobs and hotel locations draw workers from communities where hotel stays are outside their normal experiences. Therefore, the company needs to acquaint potential workers with the idea that hotel work is something they can imagine doing before it can even begin to receive applications and screen candidates. To this end, the game is playable by diverse workers around the world: it is available in English, Spanish, French, Arabic, and Mandarin versions.

Just one month after it launched, My Marriott Hotel had more than 12,000 active users. Most of them are located in the United States, Egypt, and India. The Indian participation is especially important, because out of the 70 countries where Marriott has operations, India has some of the greatest growth potential. At the same time, much of the Indian population is unfamiliar with Western-style hotels and their culture of service. The game helps these potential employees imagine what might otherwise be unimaginable work.

Cultural differences aside, today's young workers are spending more and more of their time on social media. Getting in touch with them online may become the norm for recruiters in the West as well.

Sources: Alexandra Berzon, "Enough with 'Call of Duty,' Answer the Call in Room 417," *The Wall Street Journal,* June 6, 2011, http://online.wsj.com/news/articles/SB10001424052702304432304 576367493214200856, accessed May 14, 2014; Marriott International, "My Marriott Hotel Opens Its Doors on Facebook," news release, June 7, 2011, http://news.marriott.com/2011/06/my-marriott-hotel-opens-its-doors-on-facebook.html, accessed May 14, 2014; Alexandra Guadagno, "A Foray into Social Recruiting: The Untold Stories behind 'My Marriott Hotel,'" *Human Resources IQ,* August 1, 2011, http://www.humanresourcesiq.com/hr-technology/columns/my-marriott-hotel-the-untold-stories/, accessed May 14, 2014.

laboratory looking for a writer might advertise in *Technical Communications*, and a manufacturer looking for an engineer to develop new products might advertise in *Design News*. Advertising in these kinds of specialized publications limits the recruiting to candidates with a background (or at least an interest) in the relevant field.

Employment agencies seek to match people looking for a job with organizations looking for employees. These agencies may be government run, in which case they do not charge for their services, or private. Many private agencies charge the employer for locating an employee, and some charge the person searching for a job. In either case, the agency collects a fee only when someone is hired. Using an agency makes sense when the organization lacks the time or expertise to carry out an effective recruiting effort. (In addition, organizations are increasingly relying on agencies to recruit all types of temporary employees.) Agencies also help screen candidates, a step in the selection process described in the next section.

Online recruiting has become the most popular way to match candidates to jobs. Posting job openings online is convenient and inexpensive for reaching candidates around the nation. Employers can list information about job openings on their own Web sites or through job-listing services such as Monster,

Most job hunting today takes place online. Even companies that advertise job openings in other ways will still request that some application materials be submitted electronically.

CareerBuilder, and Yahoo HotJobs. Some companies have supplemented this information with podcasts, allowing candidates to download audio files describing opportunities to work at the company, along with other information such as tips for interviewing. Consulting firm Bain & Company tried out podcasting as an efficient way to reach graduates of the Indian Institute of Management for jobs at its new facility in India. Response was so positive that Bain decided to expand its use of podcasts to recruit from additional schools in other countries.[4] Another Internet tool, the blog (Web log or online personal journal), is becoming a resource for online recruiting. Blogs specializing in a particular industry or company sometimes include links to relevant information about employment. Knowing that Internet users may be looking for jobs online, some recruiters are writing their own blogs to attract these job hunters. At Microsoft, recruiter Heather Hamilton writes about careers at the company; in one week, Hamilton's blog had 25,000 page views. Hamilton commented, "I could be on the phone all day every day and not reach that many people."[5] When companies use these tools, they should have systems in place for responding to applicants.

Depending on the requirements of the job, a supervisor might want employees who recently have graduated from high school, a community college, a trade school, a prestigious university, or some other type of school. In such cases, the organization might seek job candidates through schools of the desired type. Large organizations that expect to hire many recent graduates sometimes send recruiters to talk to students at the targeted schools. Many schools also arrange various kinds of listings of employers who are interested in hiring. Recruiting through schools is a way to limit candidates to those with the desired educational background. A growing number of companies are extending these efforts to internships. Hiring a student for a summer is a way to see how that person handles a variety of situations. In a recent survey, employers said they offer full-time jobs to more than half of their interns.[6]

Recently, a slowing economy has meant that many employers do not have to do much recruiting, but there are exceptions. The demand for nurses outstrips the supply, so efforts to recruit nurses can get creative. In Wisconsin, Wheaton Franciscan Healthcare put on a "hiring event," offering experienced nurses $50 gas cards in exchange for coming to the event and interviewing for jobs. In Michigan, Residential Home Health also staged a hiring event. The company, which provides in-home nursing services, conducted a trivia contest with a celebrity host and big prizes, and also poured free champagne for the event's attendees. The recruiters know that keeping good nurses requires good pay and working conditions, but the hiring events and prizes help them get noticed in a job market where the best candidates might not even think to apply.[7]

LO15.4 ▶ Identify the steps in the selection process.

The Selection Process

In recent years, organizations typically have had many more candidates than they have needed to fill their vacant positions. Thus, once an organization has identified candidates for a job, it begins the major work: the selection process. Through this process, the supervisor and human resources department seek the person who is best qualified to fill a particular job. Figure 15.2 shows how the various steps in the selection process narrow the field of candidates. Usually the human resources department does the initial screening, and the supervisor makes the final decision.

In the traditional approach shown in Figure 15.2, the field of candidates narrows as the organization screens applications and résumés, interviews candidates, and conducts tests and background checks. A growing number of organizations have begun using computer technology to make this process more efficient. Often, the technology provides testing and automated interviews before any candidates are invited to in-person interviews.

Screening Employment Applications and Résumés

Candidates for a job respond to recruitment by filling out an employment application or sending in a résumé. On the following pages, Figure 15.3 shows a sample employment

FIGURE 15.2 | The Selection Process

The selection process allows and organization to find the best person for a job from a large pool of candidates.

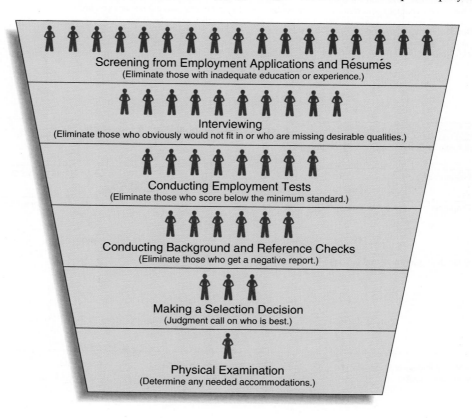

Screening from Employment Applications and Résumés
(Eliminate those with inadequate education or experience.)

Interviewing
(Eliminate those who obviously would not fit in or who are missing desirable qualities.)

Conducting Employment Tests
(Eliminate those who score below the minimum standard.)

Conducting Background and Reference Checks
(Eliminate those who get a negative report.)

Making a Selection Decision
(Judgment call on who is best.)

Physical Examination
(Determine any needed accommodations.)

FIGURE 15.3 | Sample Employment Application

An employment application serves as the first screening tool in the employment selection process.

OPTIONAL APPLICATION FOR FEDERAL EMPLOYMENT – OF 612	Form Approved OMB No. 3206-0219

Section A – Applicant Information

*Use Standard State Postal Codes (abbreviations). If outside the United States of America, and you do not have a military address type or print "OV" in the State field (Block 6c) and fill in the Country field (Block 6e) below, leaving the Zip Code field (Block 6d) blank.

1. Job title in announcement	2. Grade(s) applying for	3. Announcement number
4a. Last name	4b. First and middle names	5. Social Security Number

6a. Mailing address*	7. Phone numbers (include area code if within the United States of America)
	7a. Daytime

6b. City	6c. State	6d. Zip Code	7b. Evening

6e. Country (if not within the United States of America)

8. Email address (if available)

Section B – Work Experience

Describe your paid and nonpaid work experience related to this job for which you are applying. Do not attach job description.

1. Job title (if Federal, include series and grade)

2. From (mm/yyyy)	3. To (mm/yyyy)	4. Salary per $	5. Hours per week

6. Employer's name and address	7. Supervisor's name and phone number
	7a. Name
	7b. Phone

8. May we contact your current supervisor?   Yes ☐   No ☐
If we need to contact your current supervisor before making an offer, we will contact you first.

9. Describe your duties and accomplishments

Section C – Additional Work Experience

1. Job title (if Federal, include series and grade)

2. From (mm/yyyy)	3. To (mm/yyyy)	4. Salary per $	5. Hours per week

6. Employer's name and address	7. Supervisor's name and phone number
	7a. Name
	7b. Phone

8. Describe your duties and accomplishments

U.S. Office of Personnel Management
Previous edition usable

NSN 7540-01-351-9178
50612-101

Page 1 of 2

Optional Form 612
Revised December 2002

FIGURE 15.3 | (*continued*)

Section D – Education

1. Last High School (HS)/GED school. Give the school's name, city, state, ZIP Code (if known), and year diploma or GED received:

2. Mark highest level completed: Some HS ☐   HS/GED ☐   Associate ☐   Bachelor ☐   Master ☐   Doctoral ☐

3. Colleges and universities attended. Do not attach a copy of your transcript unless requested.

			Total Credits Earned		Major(s)	Degree (if any), Year Received
			Semester	Quarter		
3a. Name						
City	State	Zip Code				
3b. Name						
City	State	Zip Code				
3c. Name						
City	State	Zip Code				

Section E – Other Qualifications

Job-related training courses (give title and year). Job-related skills (other languages, computer software/hardware, tools, machinery, typing speed, etc.). Job-related certificates and licenses (current only). Job-related honors, awards, and special accomplishments (publications, memberships in professional/honor societies, leadership activities, public speaking, and performance awards). Give dates, but do **not** send documents unless requested.

Section F – General

1a. Are you a U.S. citizen?   Yes ☐   No ☐   →   1b. If no, give the Country of your citizenship

2a. Do you claim veterans' preference?   No ☐   Yes ☐   →   If yes, mark your claim of 5 or 10 points below.

2b.   5 points ☐   →   Attach your *Report of Separation from Active Duty* (DD 214) or other proof.

2c.   10 points ☐   →   Attach an *Application for 10-Point Veterans' Preference* (SF 15) and proof required.

3. Were you ever a Federal civilian employee?   No ☐   Yes ☐   →   If yes, list highest civilian grade for the following:

3a. Series	3b. Grade	3c. From (mm/yyyy)	3d. To (mm/yyyy)

4. Are you eligible for reinstatement based on career or career-conditional Federal status?   No ☐   Yes ☐
   If requested in the vacancy announcement, attach *Notification of Personnel Action* (SF 50), as proof.

Section G – Applicant Certification

I certify that, to the best of my knowledge and belief, all of the information on and attached to this application is true, correct, complete, and made in good faith. I understand that false or fraudulent information on or attached to this application may be grounds for not hiring me or for firing me after I begin work, and may be punishable by fine or imprisonment. I understand that any information I give may be investigated.

1a. Signature	1b. Date (mm/dd/yyyy)

application. The first stage of the selection process is to review the applications or résumés to screen out candidates who are unqualified or less qualified than others. The objective of screening is to narrow the pool of applicants to the number that the supervisor or human resources department wants to interview for the job.

Usually someone in the human resources department takes care of the screening process, comparing the applications or résumés with the job description prepared by the supervisor and eliminating the candidates who obviously fail to meet the qualifications called for in the job description.

Supervisors seldom participate actively in this process, but sometimes they know of a candidate whom they would like to consider. In such cases, the name of this person is sent to the human resources department with the request that the person be included in the selection process. Rarely does the human resources department screen out a person that a supervisor wants included.

Interviewing Candidates

LO15.5 ▶ Discuss how a supervisor should go about interviewing candidates for a job.

When the human resources department has narrowed the list of candidates to a few people, the next step is to interview them. Objectives of interviewing include narrowing the search for an employee by assessing each candidate's interpersonal and communication skills, seeing whether the supervisor and employee are comfortable with each other, and learning details about the information the candidate has provided on the application or résumé. In addition, each candidate has an opportunity to learn about the organization, which helps him or her make a decision about accepting a job offer.

Learning and carrying out effective interviewing practices sometimes may seem like a lot of trouble to a supervisor. When tempted to look for shortcuts, a supervisor should bear in mind the significance of selection interviews. For any new employee, the organization will spend tens, maybe hundreds, of thousands of dollars on salary, benefits, and training. Thus, collecting the information needed to make the right hiring decision is at least as important as doing the research for making other investments of comparable size. Viewed in this light, carefully preparing for and conducting a selection interview is well worth the time and effort.

Who Should Interview?

The initial interview with a job candidate frequently is conducted by someone in the human resources department. Depending on an organization's policies and practices, a supervisor may participate in later interviews. For this reason, a supervisor can benefit from understanding how to interview effectively.

An organization may support the use of teamwork by having teams (or several team members) interview job candidates. Team interviews provide evidence of how a candidate interacts with a team. Sometimes accounting firms use teams of interviewers to obtain multiple perspectives on job candidates and to give the candidates a better sense of the firm's culture. Some firms include "greeters" in team interviews of candidates who are junior- and senior-year college students. The greeters are recent graduates who work at the firm and try to build rapport with job candidates. The hope is that if candidates are more relaxed, they will receive a better impression of the firm and will be able to express themselves more genuinely.[8] When supervisors are part of team interviews, they need to combine skills in interviewing with skills in facilitating group processes (see Chapters 3 and 9).

Technology also is modifying the supervisor's role as interviewer by automating standard parts of the interview. HarQen, a Milwaukee company, offers employers a service called Voice Advantage. A company using Voice Advantage assigns someone, often a human resources specialist, to prerecord up to 12 interview questions. The company selects candidates to be interviewed and sends them an e-mail inviting them to call in for the automated interview. When the candidate calls, he or

FIGURE 15.4 | The Interviewing Process

Following the interview process outlined here helps to insure that the company will hire the best possible candidate.

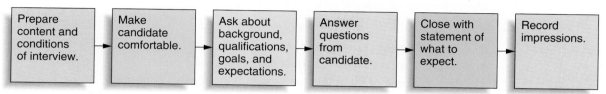

| Prepare content and conditions of interview. | → | Make candidate comfortable. | → | Ask about background, qualifications, goals, and expectations. | → | Answer questions from candidate. | → | Close with statement of what to expect. | → | Record impressions. |

she hears the interview questions and has up to two minutes to answer each question. In this kind of hiring situation, savvy candidates rehearse answers to typical questions ahead of time, so they are ready to speak well about their work experiences and personal qualities within the allotted time.[9]

Preparation for the Interview

As shown in Figure 15.4, the interviewer should begin the interviewing process by preparing. To prepare for an interview, an interviewer should review the job description and develop a realistic way to describe the job to candidates. An interviewer also should review an applicant's résumé or job application and consider whether the information given there suggests some specific questions to ask. Suppose the interviewer wants to know why a candidate chose a particular major in school or switched fields—say, leaving a job as a salesperson to become a mechanic. The interviewer also will want to inquire about any time gaps between jobs. Finally, the interviewer should arrange for an interview location that meets the conditions described in the next section.

Interview Conditions

Most job candidates feel at least a little nervous. This can make it hard for an interviewer to tell what a person would be like on the job. Therefore, it is important for an interviewer to conduct the interview under conditions that put a candidate at ease. Good interview conditions include privacy and freedom from interruptions. Seating should be comfortable. Some interviewers sit next to the candidate at a small table, rather than behind a desk, to create a less formal, more equal setting. Candidates also can be put at ease by offering them a cup of coffee and taking a minute or two for comments on a general, noncontroversial topic such as the weather.

Privacy is sometimes difficult for a supervisor to arrange. Many supervisors do not have an office with a door to close. If possible, a supervisor should arrange to use a conference room or someone else's office. At the very least, a supervisor interviewing in a cubicle should hang a "Do Not Disturb" sign outside.

Supervisors trend toward interpersonal or professional interview styles. An interpersonal interview style is informal in nature, and signals that the supervisor is interested in getting to know the candidate both as a prospective employee and an individual. Conversely, a professional interview style tends to be formal in nature. A professional interview style focuses primarily on the information pertinent to the job itself. Typically, candidates prefer an interpersonal style that builds rapport with the interviewer, and there are not significant differences between these two styles in terms of the information gained through the interview.[10]

Creating a comfortable setting for interviews can enable a supervisor to set job candidates at ease so that they can present the best version of themselves.

Content of the Interview

After making the candidate comfortable, an interviewer should begin by asking general questions about the candidate's background and qualifications. An interviewer also should ask a candidate about his or her goals and expectations concerning the job. The following questions are among those most commonly asked:[11]

- Why do you want to work for our company?
- What kind of career do you have planned?
- What have you learned in school to prepare for a career?
- What are some of the things you are looking for in a company?
- How has your previous job experience prepared you for a career?
- What are your strengths? Weaknesses?
- Why did you attend this school?
- What do you consider to be one of your most worthwhile achievements?
- Are you a leader? Explain.
- How do you plan to continue developing yourself?
- Why did you select your major?
- What can I tell you about my company?

When the interviewer has asked enough questions to gauge the candidate's suitability for the position, he or she should give the candidate a chance to ask questions. Not only can this opportunity help the candidate learn more, but it also can give the interviewer insight into the candidate's understanding and areas of concern. For more guidance on preparing and using interview questions, see the "Practical Advice for Supervisors" feature.

The interviewer should close the session by telling the candidate what to expect regarding the organization's decision about the job, such as a telephone call in a week or a letter by the end of the month. As soon as the candidate has left, the interviewer should jot down notes of his or her impressions about the candidate. Memories fade fast, especially when the interviewer meets many candidates.

The questions an interviewer asks must be relevant to performance of the job. This means that an interviewer may not ask questions about the candidate's age, sex, race, marital status, children, religion, or arrest (as opposed to conviction) record.[12] For example, an interviewer may not ask, "So, are you planning to have any children?" or "What nationality is that name?" Such questions violate antidiscrimination laws, described subsequently in this chapter. Table 15.2 on the following pages identifies many permissible and impermissible questions. A supervisor who is in doubt about whether a particular question is allowable should check with the human resources department before asking it.

Interviewing Techniques

The person who conducts the interview may choose to make it structured, unstructured, or a combination of the two. A **structured interview** is one based on questions an interviewer has prepared in advance. By referring to the list of questions, the interviewer covers the same material with each candidate.[13] In an **unstructured interview,** an interviewer has no list of questions prepared in advance but thinks of questions on the basis of an applicant's responses. An unstructured interview gives an interviewer more flexibility but makes it harder to be sure that each interview covers the same material.

A practical way to combine these two approaches is to prepare a list of questions that must be covered with each candidate. Then, an interviewer who wants the candidate to clarify a response to a particular question asks a follow-up question such as, "Please tell me about your reasons for handling the problem that way." An interviewer need not ask the questions in the order written so long as all of them are covered eventually. On the basis of a candidate's

structured interview
An interview based on questions the interviewer has prepared in advance

unstructured interview
An interview in which the interviewer has no list of questions prepared in advance but asks questions on the basis of the applicant's responses

PRACTICAL ADVICE FOR SUPERVISORS

INTERVIEWING JOB CANDIDATES

Duane Lakin, a psychologist in Wheaton, Illinois, says there's a reason most supervisors struggle with interviewing job candidates: "Most people are not very good at interviewing because it is not their primary job." Besides getting some training in how to interview, use the following suggestions to improve your interview technique with applicants:

- Identify the skills and behaviors you want in an employee. If you already have successful employees holding similar positions in your group, think about what qualities and behaviors make them successful.

- Based on the preceding step, ask each candidate to give examples of using those skills or behaviors. For example, if you need someone who is a team player, you might ask, "In your last job, how did you handle disagreements with other members of your team?"

- When applicants give examples, especially when they are vague, use follow-up questions to probe for details. In the previous example of handling disagreements, you might follow up with, "What happened when you tried that? What did you learn from that experience?" If someone says their greatest weakness is "perfectionism," ask how perfectionism caused problems in a previous job.

- When candidates talk in generalities (for instance, "I'm a people person" or "I'm quality focused"), ask what they mean. Ask them to give an example. That will help you determine whether the candidate's words mean what you hope they do.

- Keep your probing pleasant, and encourage candidates to relax. The idea is to encourage them to be frank and honest about themselves, not defensive.

- Discuss the position with the candidate and give them as much information as you can about their potential duties and job responsibilities. This could lead to a more informative conversation for both you and the candidate.

- Compare candidates against the job description and job specification, not against one another. Choose one who meets or exceeds your requirements, not just the best of an unsatisfactory group. If no one meets your requirements, keep looking.

One company that applies these tips is the Golden Corral restaurant chain. The company has established interview questions based on behaviors that are desirable for its jobs. Golden Corral provides interviewers with follow-up questions that help them compare candidates' work experiences with the core skills the company has identified for each position. On the basis of information provided by the candidates, the company scores them on various traits, including their education level and the restaurant volume they have worked with in the past. According to Golden Corral's senior vice president of operations, Lance Trenary, "We . . . insist that we don't hire anyone below [a preset] level."

Sources: Kathryn Tyler, "Train for Smarter Hiring," *HRMagazine,* May 2005, http://www.shrm.org/publications/hrmagazine/editorialcontent/pages/0505tyler.aspx, accessed May 14, 2014; Steve Weinberg, "Determining the Formula for Hiring the Best People," *Kitchen & Bath Design News,* June 2006, http://www.forresidentialpros.com/article/10425527/determining-the-formula-for-hiring-the-best-people, accessed May 14, 2014; Cord Cooper, "Deal with People Effectively: Snare a Top-Notch Team," *Investor's Business Daily,* October 6, 2005, http://news.investors.com/management-leaders-in-success/100605-412452-deal-with-people-effectively-snare-a-top-notch-team.htm, accessed May 14, 2014.

TABLE 15.2 | Permissible and Impermissible Questions for Selection Interviews

Category	Interviewer May Ask	Interviewer May Not Ask
Name	Current legal name; whether candidate has ever worked under another name	Maiden name; whether candidate has ever changed his or her name; preferred courtesy title (e.g., Ms., Miss, Mrs.)
Address	Current residence; length of residence	Whether candidate owns or rents home, unless it is a bona fide occupational qualification (BFOQ) for the job; name and relationship of person with whom applicant resides
Age	Whether the candidate meets a minimum age requirement set by law (e.g., being 21 to serve alcoholic beverages)	Candidate's age; to see a birth certificate; how much longer candidate plans to work before retiring; dates of attending elementary or high school; how applicant feels about working for a younger (or older) boss

(continued)

TABLE 15.2 | Permissible and Impermissible Questions for Selection Interviews (*continued*)

Category	Interviewer May Ask	Interviewer May Not Ask
Sex	Candidate's sex if it is a BFOQ (e.g., a model or restroom attendant)	Candidate's sex if it is not a BFOQ
Marital and family status	Whether the candidate can comply with the work schedule (must be asked of both sexes if at all)	Candidate's marital status; whether the candidate has or plans to have children; other family matters; information about child care arrangements; questions about who handles household responsibilities; whether candidate is seeking work just to supplement the household income
National origin, citizenship, race, color	Whether the candidate is legally eligible to work in the United States; whether the candidate can prove this, if hired	Candidate's national origin, citizenship, race, or color (or that of relatives); how candidate feels about working with or for people of other races
Language	List of languages the candidate speaks or writes fluently; whether the candidate speaks or writes a specific language if it is a BFOQ	Language the candidate speaks off the job; how the candidate learned a language
Arrests and convictions	Whether the candidate has been convicted of a felony; other information if the felony is job related	Whether the candidate has ever been arrested; information about a conviction that is not job related
Height and weight	No questions	Candidate's height or weight
Health history and disabilities	Whether the candidate is able to perform the essential functions of the job; how (with or without accommodation) the candidate can perform essential job functions	Whether the candidate is disabled or handicapped; how candidate became disabled; health history; whether the candidate smokes; whether the candidate has AIDS or is HIV positive
Religion	Whether the candidate is a member of a specific religious group when it is a BFOQ; whether the candidate can comply with the work schedules	Religious preference, affiliations, or denomination; name of applicant's priest, pastor, rabbi, or other religious leader
Personal finances	Credit rating if it is a BFOQ	Candidate's credit rating; other information about personal finances, including assets, charge accounts; whether candidate owns a car
Education and work experience	Job-related education and experience	Education and experience that are not job related
References	Names of people willing to provide references; names of people who suggested that the candidate apply for the job	Reference from a religious leader
Military service	Information about job-related education and experience; whether candidate was dishonorably discharged	Dates and conditions of discharge; eligibility for military service; experience in foreign armed services
Organizations	List of memberships in job-related organizations such as unions or professional or trade associations	Memberships in any organizations that are not job related and would indicate race, religion, or other protected group; candidate's political affiliation

Sources: Richard D. Irwin, Inc., "Management Guidelines," Appendix 2, December 1, 1991; Robert N. Lussier, *Supervision: A Skill-Building Approach* (Homewood, IL: Irwin, 1989), pp. 254–255; Janine S. Pouliot, "Topics to Avoid with Applicants," *Nation's Business*, July 1992, pp. 57–58; Gary Dessler, *Human Resource Management* (Upper Saddle River, NJ: Prentice Hall, 2000), p. 234.

comments, an interviewer may want to move to a question further down the list. Even though the format varies somewhat from candidate to candidate, this approach ensures that an interviewer does not omit important topics from some interviews.

Within either a structured or an unstructured interview, an interviewer may ask questions that are open-ended or closed-ended. An **open-ended question** is one that gives the person responding broad control over the response. A **closed-ended question** is one that requires a simple answer, such as yes or no. An example of an open-ended question is, "What experiences in your past job will help you carry out this one?" Examples of closed-ended questions are, "Did you use an iPad on your last job?" and "Which shift do you prefer to work?"

Open-ended questions tend to be more useful in interviewing, because they lead a candidate to provide more information. For example, to learn how thoroughly a candidate has researched the job—an indication of how serious he or she is about the position—an interviewer might ask, "What would you look for if you were hiring a person for this position?" Many supervisors rely heavily on the use of open-ended questions when interviewing job candidates. For example, a shift supervisor might pose this question to a candidate for a nursing position:

> A high, drug-using pregnant woman comes into the office, wanting immediate help. She has missed two previously scheduled appointments. The case manager is busy with another client and has a second client arriving in 20 minutes. How do you handle such competing demands?

Sometimes there is no single correct answer. Rather, supervisors who utilize this approach will look for candidates who show an ability to set priorities and justify the course of action selected.

Because the candidate decides how to answer an open-ended question, the answer sometimes is not clear enough or specific enough. Then, the interviewer will want to probe for more details, possibly saying, "Can you give me an example of that?" or "What do you mean when you say your last job was 'too stressful'?"

Problems to Avoid

When conducting an interview, a supervisor needs to avoid some common errors in judgment. One of these is making decisions based on personal biases. For example, a supervisor may dislike earrings on men or certain hairstyles worn by women. However, these characteristics are unlikely to indicate how well a candidate would carry out a job. Likewise, being a friend or relative of a supervisor is not a good predictor of job performance. Making a hiring decision on the basis of these and other biases can lead an interviewer to exclude the person who is best qualified.

Another source of errors is the **halo effect,** which means forming an overall opinion on the basis of one outstanding characteristic. For example, many people will evaluate someone's personality on the basis of the person's handshake. "She has a firm grasp," an interviewer might think with regard to a candidate. "I can tell that she's energetic, decisive, and gets along well with people," when the candidate might not have any of those desirable traits. An interviewer needs to look for evidence of each trait, not just lump them all together.

A supervisor also needs to avoid giving candidates a misleading picture of the organization. If a candidate seems desirable, the supervisor may be tempted to describe the organization in glowing terms so that the candidate will want to work there. But if the reality is not so wonderful, the new employee is bound to be disappointed and angry. He or she may even quit. On the other hand, within the

open-ended question
A question that gives the person responding broad control over the response

closed-ended question
A question that requires a simple answer, such as yes or no

halo effect
The practice of forming an overall opinion on the basis of one outstanding characteristic

Some employers will require that job candidates take an aptitude test to ensure that they have the experience and capability to perform the job's responsibilities.

bounds of realism, a supervisor should give a good impression of the organization and its people. Even a candidate who is not the best person for the job may someday be a customer or be in a position to influence other people's views about the organization.

Administering Employment Tests

From a résumé or employment application, it is relatively easy to see where a candidate worked and went to school, but how can you tell whether a candidate really has the skills to do the job? Just because Pete Wong works for the marketing division at a candy company does not mean he knows how to sell candy (maybe that is why he wants to leave). Just because Ruth Petersen got a college degree in engineering does not mean she can apply her knowledge to working with a team to prepare the layout of an actual plant.

One way to see whether employees have the necessary skills is to administer an employment test. A variety of employment tests are available:

LO15.6 ▶ Define types of employment tests.

- A test that measures an applicant's ability to learn skills related to the job is known as an **aptitude test.**[14]
- An applicant may take a **proficiency test** to determine whether he or she has the skills needed to perform a job. An example is a word-processing test for a secretarial position.
- For jobs that require physical skills, such as assembling, an applicant may take a **psychomotor test,** which measures a person's strength, dexterity, and coordination.
- Some organizations also use personality tests, which identify various personality traits. Kurt Swogger used personality tests to hire and reassign employees in the research and development group at Dow Chemical's plastics division. By sorting out employees who are inclined to dream up big new ideas, those who see opportunities to modify existing products, and those who are more in tune with customers and markets, Swogger transformed a plodding division into a team of innovators. The focus on personality has resulted in more new ideas from the division as well as a faster pace of development.[15]
- Many organizations, especially large companies, test for drug use. In general, drug testing is legal at nonunion companies and is allowed at unionized companies if the parties agree to it during contract negotiations. At some organizations, all employees are subject to drug testing; other organizations limit tests to positions where drug use would pose a serious safety risk, as in the case of machine operators or pilots.[16]

aptitude test
A test that measures a person's ability to learn skills related to the job

proficiency test
A test that measures whether the person has the skills needed to perform a job

psychomotor test
A test that measures a person's strength, dexterity, and coordination

Usually the human resources department handles the testing of applicants.

Some tests contain language or other biases that make them easier for employees of one ethnic group than another. Using these tests could violate antidiscrimination laws, described subsequently in this chapter. Similarly, personality tests can pose a problem if they identify candidates with mental or emotional disabilities.[17] Discrimination laws cover individuals with a disability if they are able to perform the job's required functions. Therefore, if a supervisor wants to use employment tests, the tests should be reviewed by the human resources department or an outside expert to ensure that they are not discriminatory.

Despite these restrictions, employers can be creative in devising employment tests that focus on job requirements. Candidates for fire-fighting jobs with Central Pierce Fire & Rescue, near Tacoma, Washington, participate in role-play simulations to see how well they handle citizens who are upset. The organization's human resources manager, Karen Johnson, says some candidates handle the role-players beautifully, but "We've had a couple candidates throw [a role-player] out the door"—figuratively speaking, it is hoped.[18] The Chrysler Group has candidates for assembly jobs undergo tests of how quickly and accurately they assemble parts. Candidates for professional and management jobs are given tests in which they must react to memos and phone calls. They may also engage in role-playing where they coach someone playing the role of an employee with a job-related problem.[19]

Conducting Background and Reference Checks

Many résumés and job applications contain false information. For example, according to a recent study by Kroll, Inc., about one-fifth of job candidates exaggerated their educational achievements. In a survey of human resource professionals, a majority said that when they investigate, they find inaccuracies in résumés "often" or "sometimes." Similarly, some Internet users have posted tips on how to guess the "right" answers to personality tests, possibly enabling applicants to lie about themselves, if necessary, to get an interview. By some accounts, the recent economic downturn has increased the likelihood of false information, as job seekers facing greater competition do whatever it takes to land a position.[20]

A basic way to verify that the information on a job application or résumé is correct is to check references. Not only can checking an employee's background save the organization from hiring an unqualified person, but it also can protect the organization from lawsuits. The courts have held employers responsible for crimes committed by an employee whose background at the time of hire was not investigated reasonably, with the result that the organization hired someone with a history of misdeeds for a position where he or she could do harm.[21, 22]

A supervisor or a member of the human resources department may call or write to schools and former employers, or the organization may pay an employee screening company to do a background check. The relatively small fee to use one of these companies can be money well spent by an organization that is too small for a human resources staff. In recent years, heightened security concerns and the easy availability of personal data on the Internet have increased the use of background checks. However, supervisors should be aware that various state and federal laws protect individuals' privacy and limit the types of information employers may use and the way they gather information. For some examples, see Figure 15.5 on the following page. When there is any doubt, the supervisor should get advice from a qualified expert before initiating a background check.

Applicants may give several kinds of references:

- *Personal references*—people who will vouch for the applicant's character.
- *Academic references*—teachers or professors who can describe the applicant's performance in school.
- *Employment references*—former employers who can verify the applicant's work history.

FIGURE 15.5 | Examples of Restrictions on Background Checks

Background checks do not give a potential employer unlimited access to a candidate's personal information—some laws limit the types of information available to potential employers.

Source: Privacy Rights Clearinghouse, "Employment Background Checks," Fact Sheet 16, rev. June 2004, March 2014, www.privacyrights.org.

Do not request:
Bankruptcies after 10 years
Arrest and civil lawsuit records
  after 7 years
Accounts placed for collection
  (7 years old or older)

Do not consider in hiring decisions:
Bankruptcies
Workers' compensation
Medical history

Get permission first:
Education records
Certain military
  service information

Most people can think of a friend or teacher who can say something nice about them, so the main use of personal and academic references is to screen out the few cases of people who cannot do so.

Previous employers are in the best position to discuss how an applicant performed in the past. However, to avoid lawsuits from former employees, many organizations have a policy of giving out very little information about past employees. Often a background check will yield only that the applicant did in fact hold the stated position during the dates indicated. Some employers may be willing to discuss the applicant's performance, salary, promotions, and demotions. Because previous employers are cautious about what they disclose, a telephone call to a former supervisor may be more fruitful than a written request for information. People are sometimes willing to make off-the-record statements over the telephone that they will not commit to in writing.

Making the Selection Decision

The final decision of whom to hire is usually up to the supervisor. Typically, more than one person will survive all the preceding steps of the screening process. As a result, the final decision is usually a judgment call.

A supervisor can handle the dilemma of several well-qualified people being considered for a position by looking for additional relevant selection criteria. In practice, hiring decisions often reflect a variety of issues, including the supervisor's comfort level. Supervisors sometimes choose an employee like themselves so that they will feel comfortable; they also might select a person whose strengths differ from and thus balance their own strengths. Entrepreneur and writer Mike Michalowicz recommends emphasizing personal qualities—for example, attitude, work ethic, and values. When one of Michalowicz's companies needed to hire a computer forensic examiner (someone who studies computer hard drives to identify evidence for use in court), Michalowicz picked a man with little computer background but high energy, a positive attitude, and a history of making intelligent decisions. Michalowicz concluded that this person could be trained in the technical skills. Within months, the new hire was working independently, and within a year, he was handling the company's most complicated jobs.[23] A supervisor can improve his or her selections by applying the principles of effective decision making covered in Chapter 9.

When a supervisor has selected the candidate to hire, the human resources department or supervisor offers the job to the candidate. The person who offers the job is responsible for negotiating pay and fringe benefits and settling on a starting date. If none of the candidates a supervisor has identified seem satisfactory, no candidate has to be picked and the recruiting process can be repeated. Perhaps the organization can look in new places or try to attract better candidates by offering more money.

Requesting a Physical Examination

In the past, many organizations have required that job candidates pass a physical examination. However, since Congress passed the Americans with Disabilities Act (described later in this chapter), experts have advised that employers request a physical exam only after a job offer is made.[24] A physical examination after the job offer helps the organization determine whether the person is physically able to fulfill job requirements, yet the timing of the exam reduces the risk that someone will sue the company for refusing to hire him or her because of a disability. Another use of the physical exam is to determine whether the person is eligible for any life, health, and disability insurance that the company offers as benefits.

An illness, disability, or pregnancy may not be used as the basis for denying a person a job unless it makes the person unable to perform the essential functions of the job. If a physical examination suggests a condition that may interfere with the person's ability to perform these essential functions, the company—very likely someone in the human resources department—should ask the candidate how it can adapt the equipment or job to accommodate that person. Because of these limitations on the use of information from physical examinations, most organizations will want the human resources department to handle the exams and the issue of how to accommodate employees with disabilities. A supervisor can then focus on a candidate's experience and talents.

Legal Issues

Congress has passed laws that restrict employment decisions. Most of these laws are designed to give people fair and equal access to jobs based on their skills, not on their personal traits such as race or physical disabilities. Whatever a supervisor's role in selecting employees, he or she must be aware of the laws affecting hiring to help ensure that the organization's actions are legal. While a number of these issues were discussed previously in Chapter 5, they are revisited here in a more comprehensive fashion for the purpose of enriched knowledge.

LO15.7 ▶ Summarize the requirements of antidiscrimination laws.

Antidiscrimination Laws

Certain federal laws prohibit various types of employment discrimination.

- Under Title VII of the Civil Rights Act of 1964 (commonly known as Title VII), employers may not discriminate on the basis of race, color, religion, sex, or national origin in recruiting, hiring, paying, firing, or laying off employees, or in any other employment practices. The government agency charged with enforcing this law is the **Equal Employment Opportunity Commission (EEOC)**. The EEOC investigates charges of discrimination and may pursue a remedy in court or arrange for mediation (which means an impartial third party hears both sides and decides how to resolve the dispute).

- The Age Discrimination in Employment Act of 1967, as amended in 1978 and 1986, prohibits employers from discriminating on the basis of age against people over 40 years old.

- The Rehabilitation Act of 1973 makes it illegal for the federal government to refuse a job to a disabled person because of the disability, if the disability does not interfere with the person's ability to do the job.

Equal Employment Opportunity Commission (EEOC)
The federal government agency charged with enforcing Title VII of the Civil Rights Act

- The Americans with Disabilities Act of 1990 prohibits employers in state and local governments and the private sector from discriminating against a qualified person with a disability. The next section, on workplace accessibility, describes the extent to which employers are required to accommodate persons with disabilities.

- The Pregnancy Discrimination Act of 1978 makes it unlawful to discriminate on the basis of pregnancy, childbirth, or related medical conditions. Recently, the EEOC filed suit on behalf of three women who said they had been discriminated against by the Bloomberg business news group. Then dozens of other female employees said they, like the first three, had seen their responsibilities shrink or promotions dry up after they became pregnant while employed by Bloomberg.[25] Supervisors should be aware that while such cases are quite rare, they should never assume that a pregnant employee is not committed to her job or career. If an employee or job candidate requests any pregnancy-related accommodations, the supervisor should work with the human resource department to ensure these requests are addressed in a manner that avoids discrimination.

- Disabled veterans and veterans of the Vietnam War receive protection under the Vietnam Era Veterans Readjustment Act of 1974, which requires federal contractors to make special efforts to recruit these people. (This is a type of affirmative action, described shortly.) In deciding whether a veteran is qualified, an employer may consider the military record only to the extent it is directly related to the specific qualifications of the job.

- Under the Genetic Information Nondiscrimination Act of 2008, it is illegal to discriminate against a qualified person because of genetic information, such as the results of a genetic test or a family history of diseases.

Figure 15.6 illustrates the categories of workers protected by the antidiscrimination laws.

Although some people criticize these laws as a burden on employers, organizations should benefit from making employment decisions on the basis of people's knowledge, skills, and abilities instead of incidental personal traits such as race, age, or sex.

As the managers of many organizations have observed the growing diversity of the workforce and their customers, they have decided that simply avoiding discrimination is too limited a policy. They have adopted policies called "managing diversity." At an organization that effectively manages diversity, managers and employees create a climate in which all employees feel respected and able to participate. Valuing diversity is a view that extends beyond legally protected differences to fair treatment of employees who differ

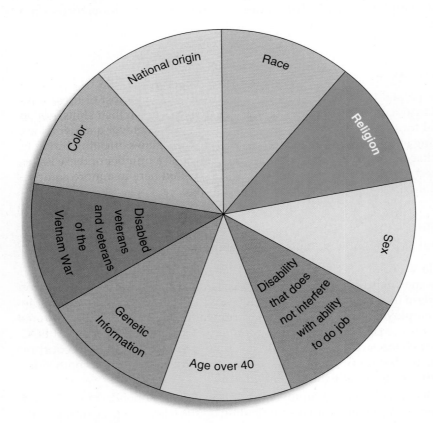

FIGURE 15.6 | Categories of Workers Protected by Antidiscrimination Laws

Many different groups of people are protected by the country's antidiscrimination laws.

SUPERVISION AND DIVERSITY

SMALL BUSINESS DIVERSITY

While it is not all that difficult for large, multi-national companies to employ a diverse workforce, establishing diversity in a small business can be much more difficult. All businesses, however, regardless of their size, should be aware of the different cultures within their organization as well as of the advantages that differing points of view and perspective could bring to the inter-office dynamics.

Some recommendations for acknowledging and promoting diversity in a small business include:

- Familiarize yourself with the Americans with Disabilities Act (ADA). Determine what is required by law and make sure those policies are in place. Then, consider what accommodations or changes can be made that go beyond the bare minimum. Are there things that could be easily implemented that would make the workplace more inviting to all?

- Ensure that all employees have a way to convey any concerns or issues they may have in a safe environment where they will not fear reprisal or other forms of intimidation. Employees should feel comfortable presenting problems as well as new ideas, suggestions for improvements, and innovations. This is key to a dynamic and productive work environment.

- Hold team-building events that are inclusive of people of all abilities. These give employees a chance to get to know one another better, to learn about each other's cultures, and to become more comfortable in their work environment.

These simple steps can be completed whether you have 10 employees or 10,000 employees. Being a small company does not mean that you can ignore the call to creating a diverse workforce. Nor should you want to as a diverse workforce can be critical to keeping a small company from becoming stagnant.

Source: Based on Megan Totka, "Embracing Cultural Diversity in a Small Business Environment," Business2Community, September 11, 2012, http://www.business2community.com/startups/embracing-cultural-diversity-in-a-small-business-environment-0277532#!NCaKT, accessed May 14, 2014.

in other ways as well, such as military service, sexual orientation, and age differences not protected by law (employees younger than 40). A recent report by the Society for Human Resource Management found that three-fourths of the organizations surveyed said they make diversity a consideration in all of their policies and business initiatives.[26]

Managing diversity implies that the organization is hiring and promoting a variety of people. For this and other purposes, many organizations have established affirmative action programs. **Affirmative action** refers to plans designed to increase opportunities for groups that traditionally have been discriminated against. In effect, these plans are an active attempt to promote diversity in the organization, not just treat everyone the same way. For examples of ways to promote diversity in the workplace, see the "Supervision and Diversity" feature.

affirmative action
Plans designed to increase opportunities for groups that traditionally have been discriminated against

Some people mistakenly think that affirmative action means setting up artificial quotas that favor some groups at the expense of others. However, organizations can increase opportunities in other ways. In addition to using training to create a pool of qualified applicants, some companies recruit at schools where many students are members of racial minorities.

Ballot initiatives in California and Washington were aimed at curtailing affirmative action programs in hiring by state and local governments. People who favor affirmative action policies argue that because several candidates often have the qualifications to fill any given job, intentionally giving some jobs to people from disadvantaged groups not only is ethical but also supports the achievement of the benefits related to diversity. Whatever your opinion of affirmative action, it is important to note that—except for employers that have federal contracts or

TABLE 15.3 | Disability Status under the Americans with Disabilities Act

"Disability" Includes	"Disability" Does Not Include
Substantial limitation preventing a person from conducting a major life activity	Cultural and economic disadvantages
Physical and mental impairments	Common personality traits, such as impatience Pregnancy
Severe obesity (weight in excess of 100 percent of the norm or that arises from a medical disorder)	Normal deviations in weight, height, or strength
History of using drugs as the result of an addiction	Temporary or short-term problems Illegal drug users disciplined for current abuse
	Illegal drug use that is casual (not related to addiction)

Source: From "What Constitutes a Disability?" *Nation's Business,* June 1995, U.S. Chamber of Commerce.

Note: People with disabilities are protected from employment discrimination only to the extent that their disability does not prevent them from performing the essential functions of the job.

subcontracts—organizations are not required by law to set up these programs. Rather, affirmative action programs are one possible response to laws against discrimination.

LO15.8 ▶ Explain how hiring decisions are affected by the Americans with Disabilities Act (ADA).

Workplace Accessibility

In 1990, when Congress passed the Americans with Disabilities Act, state governments and private-sector employers with more than 15 employees joined the federal government in being prohibited from discriminating on the basis of mental or physical disability. A person who can perform the essential functions of a job may not be prevented from doing so simply because the person has a mental or physical disability. Table 15.3 summarizes criteria for disability status under the ADA. Organizations also must avoid discrimination in public accommodations, transportation, government services, and telecommunications.

One benefit to organizations that comply with the ADA is that it encourages employers to take advantage of a large pool of potential workers whose talents are often ignored. Cornell University's Rehabilitation Research and Training Center estimates that roughly 8 percent of the working-age U.S. population is disabled and only about 16 percent of people with disabilities are employed. The rate of employment for disabled persons has actually declined over the past two decades.[27] But companies that do make the effort to recruit and hire qualified workers with disabilities are often rewarded with dedicated employees. Forest Pharmaceuticals, for example, hired Richard Nero, a disabled veteran of the war in Iraq, as a computer engineer. Nero—who suffered a traumatic brain injury and post-traumatic stress disorder after a jet carrying him was shot down—needed some accommodations, such as scheduling flexibility and a windowless private office to minimize distractions. However, Nero's skill in testing and implementing software is not easy to find, and he is deeply appreciative of the chance to work following his military service.[28] As wounded veterans continue to return home from Iraq and Afghanistan, this story represents the kind of hiring opportunity that U.S. employers and their supervisors need to explore if they want employees who have demonstrated courage and loyalty.

Accommodations for Employees with Disabilities

To comply with the ADA, employers must make accommodations for employees with disabilities if the necessary accommodations are "readily achievable," that is, easy to carry out and possible to accomplish without much difficulty or expense. Businesses may receive a tax credit of up to $15,000 to help offset the cost of making their establishments accessible.

This law extends beyond wheelchair accessibility to require accommodations for any eligible disabled employee, including those with impaired sight and hearing, arthritis, high blood pressure, and heart disease. Thus, accommodations might include door handles that are easy to manipulate and TDD telephones for hearing-impaired employees. For employees with mental disabilities, appropriate accommodations may include speaking more slowly, allowing extra time, if possible, for someone to read application materials, demonstrating (rather than merely describing) application and job procedures, and replacing a written test with an "expanded interview," at which an employee who has difficulty describing abilities may demonstrate them instead.[29] In addition, organizations can head off many problems related to mental disabilities by making extra coaching and counseling available to employees as needed. Grace Louie, who manages a San Francisco Safeway store, says about one-tenth of her 150 employees are disabled. She says some people need to have a supervisor demonstrate the job because they have difficulty reading, but "Once they get going, they're usually fine."[30]

Offering wheelchair accessible work spaces is a way that employers can accommodate employees and meet the requirements established by the ADA.

What Supervisors Can Do

Supervisors can take several steps to comply with the ADA. One is to review and revise job descriptions. Because an organization cannot discriminate against those who can perform the essential functions of the job, each job description should indicate what is essential. It should focus on the results the employee must achieve instead of the process for achieving those results. For example, a job description for a telephone line worker might say "Repair telephone lines located at the top of a pole" but not "Climb telephone poles." In addition, supervisors should make sure that production standards are reasonable; current employees should meet those standards.

When interviewing candidates, a supervisor should be careful not to ask whether they have a physical or mental condition that would prevent them from performing the job. Rather, after making a job offer, the organization will seek to accommodate any impairments the person may have. Similarly, the supervisor should not ask for candidates' health history, including any on-the-job injuries that candidates have suffered.

LO15.9 ▸ Describe the requirements of the Immigration Reform and Control Act (IRCA) of 1986.

Immigration Reform and Control Act

By passing the Immigration Reform and Control Act (IRCA) of 1986, Congress gave employers responsibility for helping discourage illegal immigration. IRCA forbids employers to hire illegal immigrants and requires them to screen candidates to make sure they are authorized to work in the United States. At the same time, however, employers may not use these requirements as a rationale for discriminating against candidates because they look or sound "foreign."

This means the employer must verify the identity and work authorization of *every* new employee. To do this, the employer can ask each new employee to show such documentation as a valid U.S. passport, unexpired Immigration Authorization Service document, unexpired work permit, birth certificate, driver's license, or social security card.[31] Employers may also use an online program called E-Verify, which lets them check the data provided by employees against government databases to confirm that the information is accurate. Federal contractors are required to use E-Verify, and several states require some or all employers in the state to use the system. In large organizations, the IRCA primarily affects the human resources department, giving it an extra task in the hiring process. In small organizations, however, a supervisor may be responsible for verifying that all his or her new employees are authorized to work in the United States.

Purpose of Employee Selection Laws

It is important to remember that the aforementioned employee selection laws are designed in order to ensure that all persons have equal opportunities to all jobs. Regardless of certain characteristics, including religion, race, veteran status, age, gender, and disability, everyone should have the chance to succeed at any job for which they are qualified. By adhering to the selection laws outlined in this chapter, supervisors are upholding the very principles upon which the United States was founded, including equality for all.

Skills Module

PART ONE: CONCEPTS

Summary

15.1 Discuss common roles for supervisors in the selection process.

In most cases, a supervisor works with a human resources department in the selection process. If the organization depends on teams, a supervisor might try to identify candidates who are cooperative and skilled in problem solving or who have helped a team achieve good results in the past. If a team is making the selection, the supervisor as team leader needs to understand the principles of selection so that he or she can coach employees in carrying out the selection process. A supervisor also prepares job descriptions and job specifications, consulting with the human resources department as needed.

15.2 Distinguish between job descriptions and job specifications and explain how they help in selecting employees.

A job description is a listing of the characteristics of the job—observable activities required to carry out the job. A job specification is a listing of characteristics desirable in the person performing the job. The two forms help show how well each candidate matches the job requirements.

15.3 List possible sources of employees.

An organization may recruit inside and outside the organization. Current employees may be promoted or transferred to fill job openings, or they may recommend people for jobs at the organization. Outside the organization, employees can be recruited through help wanted advertisements, employment agencies, online job sites or blogs, and schools.

15.4 Identify the steps in the selection process.

On the basis of employment applications or résumés, the staff of the human resources department screens out unqualified candidates. Next, the human resources department or the supervisor interviews candidates. An organization may administer employment tests. Background and reference checks are conducted on candidates in whom the organization is still interested. A supervisor makes a selection decision, after which a candidate may be asked to take a physical examination.

15.5 Discuss how a supervisor should go about interviewing candidates for a job.

First, a supervisor should prepare for the interview by reviewing the job description and each applicant's

...r job application, planning questions, and ...ing for a place to conduct the interview that ...rs privacy and freedom from interruptions. When a candidate arrives, a supervisor should make him or her comfortable and then ask about the candidate's goals and expectations for the job. Questions must be relevant to the performance of the job and should include both open-ended and closed-ended questions. The interviewer should avoid making common errors in judgment, such as personal biases, or offering misleading information about the organization. Then a candidate should have a chance to ask questions. A supervisor should close the interview by telling a candidate what to expect. As soon as the candidate leaves, the supervisor should make notes of his or her impressions.

15.6 Define types of employment tests.

Aptitude tests measure a person's ability to learn job-related skills. Proficiency tests measure whether a person has the skills needed to perform a job. Psychomotor tests measure strength, dexterity, and coordination. Personality tests identify personality traits. Many organizations also test for drug use. Physical examinations may be required after a job offer is made.

15.7 Summarize the requirements of antidiscrimination laws.

The organization, including the supervisor, must avoid actions that discriminate on the basis of race, color, religion, sex, national origin, age over 40 years, genetic information, or physical or mental disability, including pregnancy-related disabilities. These laws apply to recruiting, hiring, paying, firing, and laying off employees and to any other employment practice. In addition, federal contractors and subcontractors must use affirmative action to encourage the employment of minorities and veterans of the Vietnam War. When evaluating veterans' qualifications, an employer may use only the portions of the military record that are related to job requirements.

15.8 Explain how hiring decisions are affected by the Americans with Disabilities Act (ADA).

The ADA prohibits discrimination on the basis of mental or physical disability against people who can perform the essential functions of a job. Instead, employers must make accommodations for employees with disabilities if the necessary accommodations are readily achievable. To comply with the law, supervisors should review and revise job descriptions to make sure they indicate what functions of the job are essential. When interviewing candidates, a supervisor should avoid asking about disabilities and a candidate's health history.

15.9 Describe the requirements of the Immigration Reform and Control Act (IRCA) of 1986.

Under IRCA, employers are responsible for helping discourage illegal immigration. They may not hire people who are not authorized to work in the United States, yet they may not discriminate against people who simply appear to be foreigners. Thus, employers must verify the identity and work authorization of every new employee.

Key Terms

job description, *p.* 420
job specification, *p.* 421
recruitment, *p.* 422
structured interview, *p.* 430
unstructured interview, *p.* 430

open-ended question, *p.* 433
closed-ended question, *p.* 433
halo effect, *p.* 433
aptitude test, *p.* 434
proficiency test, *p.* 434

psychomotor test, *p.* 434
Equal Employment
Opportunity Commission
(EEOC), *p.* 437
affirmative action, *p.* 439

Review and Discussion Questions

1. Think of your current job or a job you recently held. Write a job description and a job specification for the job. How well do (or did) you match the requirements of the job?

2. A business executive said that people tend to make the mistake of hiring in their own image. What does this mean? How does this tendency make it more difficult for an organization to build a diverse workforce?

3. In recruiting for each of the following positions, what source or sources of candidates would you recommend using? Explain your choices.

   a. A receptionist for a city government office.
   b. A lathe operator.
   c. A graphic artist for an advertising agency.
   d. A nurse for an adult day care facility.

4. Describe what happens during the screening process. What does the human resources department look for when reading employment applications and résumés?

5. Supervisor Lisa Kitzinger is interviewing candidates to add a social-media expert to her sales team. Kitzinger works in a cubicle, and she has an assistant who could help during

the interview process. What can she do to put candidates at ease?

6. Which of the following questions is (are) appropriate for a job interview for the position of office manager for an automobile dealership?

   a. Do you attend church regularly?

   b. Do you know how to use our computer and telecommunications systems?

   c. Are you familiar with our line of cars?

   d. Are you married?

   e. Aren't you close to retirement age?

   f. What skills did you develop at your previous job that you feel would be helpful in this job?

7. How can an interviewer combine the techniques of structured and unstructured interviews?

8. Donald Menck, the supervisor on a boatbuilding line, interviews a male job candidate who comes to the interview dressed in a jacket and tie. Menck is surprised by the candidate's clothing, which is more formal than what is needed on the job; he is also impressed. He assumes that the candidate is intelligent and motivated. What common error in judgment is Menck making? What steps should he take during the interview to overcome it?

9. An airline has a policy that all its employees must receive a physical examination before they start working for the company. At what point in the selection process should the company request the examination? How may the airline use this information?

10. Which of the following actions would be considered discriminatory under federal laws? Explain your answers.

    a. A company creates a policy that all employees must retire by age 65.

    b. A supervisor gives the biggest raises to men, because they have families to support.

    c. A company that recruits at colleges and universities makes at least 20 percent of its visits to schools that are historically black.

    d. In a department where employees must do a lot of overtime work on Saturdays, a supervisor avoids hiring Jews because Saturday is their day of rest and worship.

11. Joel Trueheart supervises customer service representatives for a toy company. The employees handle complaints and questions from customers calling the company's toll-free telephone number. To fill a vacancy in the department, Trueheart has reviewed many résumés and is in the process of interviewing a few candidates. One of the most impressive résumés is that of Sophia Ahmad, but when Trueheart meets her, he is startled to observe that she is blind. What should he do to make sure he is complying with the Americans with Disabilities Act?

12. What steps must employers take to ensure that they are complying with the Immigration Reform and Control Act?

Notes

1. Michael Kinsman, "Job No. 1 for Supervisors: Hiring the Right Person," Employment Crossing: Law Crossing, Career Corner, http://www.lawcrossing.com/article/1127/Job-No-1-for-supervisors-hiring-the-right-person/#, accessed May 14, 2014.

2. For more information on the contents of a job description, see M. Gan and B. Kleiner, 2005, "How to write job descriptions effectively," Management Research News, 28, p. 48.

3. Raymond A. Noe, John R. Hollenbeck, Barry Gerhart, and Patrick M. Wright, Human Resource Management: Gaining a Competitive Advantage, 6th ed. (New York: McGraw-Hill/Irwin, 2008), p. 160.

4. Aman Singh, "Podcasts Extend Recruiters' Reach," The Wall Street Journal, April 24, 2006, http://online.wsj.com/news/articles/SB114583384995933630, accessed May 14, 2014.

5. Kris Maher, "Blogs Catch On as Online Tool for Job Seekers and Recruiters," The Wall Street Journal, September 28, 2004, http://online.wsj.com/news/articles/SB109633136599429648, accessed May 14, 2014.

6. Margarita Bauza, "A Change in Recruiting: The Long Interview," Detroit Free Press, June 5, 2006, http://www.freep.com/article/20060605/BUSINESS06/606050347/A-CHANGE-RECRUITING-long-interview, accessed May 14, 2014.

7. Dinesh Ramde, "Job-Cut Blues? Not for Nurses," Roanoke (Va.) Times, January 6, 2009, downloaded from Business & Company Resource Center, http://galenet.galegroup.com.

8. Sharon L. Kimmell, Pamela K. Keltyka, and Emeka Ofobike, "Recruiting the Best Accounting Students in a Tight Market: Some Guidance," CPA Journal, October 2008, pp. 68–71.

9. Joyce Lain Kennedy, "Hello There, Automated Phone Interviews," Telegram & Gazette (Worcester, MA), January 31, 2011, http://www.telegram.com/article/20110131/NEWS/101310330/1237/mobile&TEMPLATE=MOBILE, accessed May 14, 2014.

10. Ramon Henson, Charles F. Cannell, and Sally Lawson, "Effects of Interviewer Style on Quality of Reporting in a Survey Interview," *Journal of Psychology*, 1976, 93, pp. 221–227.

11. John M. Ivancevich, *Human Resource Management*, 11th ed. (New York: Irwin/McGraw-Hill, 2010), p. 590.

12. For more information on appropriate and inappropriate interview questions, see B. Neuson, 2007, "Avoid discrimination claims when interviewing job candidates," *Nursing Management*, 38, p. 16.

13. For more on structured interviews, see T. Maurer, J. Solamon, and M. Lippstreu, 2008, "How does coaching interviewees affect the validity of a structured interview?" *Journal of Organizational Behavior*, 29, p. 355.

14. An example of an aptitude test related to firefighting can be found in the following article: A. Harley and C. James, 2006, "Fire-fighters' perspectives of the accuracy of the Physical Aptitude Test (PAT) as a pre-employment assessment," *Work*, 26, p. 29.

15. Alison Overholt, "Are You a Polyolefin Optimizer? Take This Quiz!" *Fast Company*, April 2004, http://www.fastcompany.com/48901/are-you-polyolefin-optimizer-take-quiz, accessed May 14, 2014.

16. Bill Leonard, "SHRM Poll: Drug Testing Applicants Favored by More than Half of Employers," *HR News*, September 16, 2011, http://www.shrm.org/publications/hrnews/pages/drugtestingfavored.aspx, accessed May 14, 2014; U.S. Department of Labor, "Drug-Free Workplace Policy Builder," section 7, *eLaws: DrugFree Workplace Advisor*, http://www.dol.gov/elaws/asp/drugfree/drugs/screen1.asp, accessed May 14, 2014.

17. Rosemary Winters, "Some Companies Use Tests in Criteria for Personnel Decisions," *Salt Lake Tribune*, November 14, 2005, downloaded from Business & Company Resource Center, http://galenet.galegroup.com.

18. Shirleen Holt, "Job Hunters, Simulate This," *The Standard Times*, February 15, 2005, downloaded from South Coast Today, http://www.southcoasttoday.com/apps/pbcs.dll/article?AID=/20050215/NEWS/302159939, accessed May 14, 2014.

19. Erin White, "Employers Gauge Candidates' Skills at 'Real-World' Tasks," *The Wall Street Journal*, January 16, 2006, http://online.wsj.com/news/articles/SB113736773174447186, accessed May 14, 2014.

20. Cari Tuna and Keith J. Winstein, "Economy Promises to Fuel Résumé Fraud," *The Wall Street Journal*, November 17, 2008, http://online.wsj.com/news/articles/SB122671047127630135, accessed May 14, 2014; and Vanessa O'Connell, "Test for Dwindling Retail Jobs Spawns a Culture of Cheating," *The Wall Street Journal*, January 7, 2009, http://online.wsj.com/news/articles/SB123129220146959621, accessed May 14, 2014.

21. Gary Dessler, *Human Resource Management*, 8th ed. (Upper Saddle River, NJ: Prentice Hall, 2000), p. 173.

22. For an opposing view to this argument, see P. Harris and K. Keller, 2005, "Ex-offenders need not apply: The criminal background check in hiring decisions," *Journal of Contemporary Criminal Justice*, 21, p. 6.

23. Mike Michalowicz, "The Best Recruits May Not Be Who You Think," *The Wall Street Journal*, October 4, 2011, http://online.wsj.com/news/articles/SB10001424052970204524604576610961317004204, accessed May 14, 2014.

24. Dessler, Human Resource Management, pp. 49–52.

25. Tom Bawden, "Bloomberg Faces 58 Claims of Bias over Pregnancy," *Times (London)*, May 2, 2008, downloaded from Business & Company Resource Center, http://galenet.galegroup.com.

26. Robert Rodriguez, "Diversity Finds Its Place," *HRMagazine*, August 2006, http://www.shrm.org/publications/hrmagazine/editorialcontent/pages/0806rodriguez.aspx, accessed May 14, 2014.

27. Melissa J. Bjelland, Richard V. Burkhauser, Sarah von Schrader, and Andrew J. Houtenville, *2010 Progress Report on the Economic Well-Being of Working-Age People with Disabilities* (Cornell University: Rehabilitation Research and Training Center on Employment Policy for Persons with Disabilities), http://digitalcommons.ilr.cornell.edu/cgi/viewcontent.cgi?article=1284&context=edicollect, accessed May 14, 2014.

28. U.S. Department of Labor, "America's Heroes at Work Success Story: Richard Nero," *America's Heroes at Work*, http://www.americasheroesatwork.gov, accessed May 14, 2014.

29. Equal Employment Opportunity Commission, "Questions and Answers about Persons with Intellectual Disabilities in the Workplace and the Americans with Disabilities Act," www.eeoc.gov/laws/types/intellectual_disabilities.cfm, accessed May 14, 2014.

30. David Armstrong, "Building Bridges at Work," *San Francisco Chronicle*, May 4, 2006, http://www.sfgate.com/business/article/Building-bridges-at-work-Students-with-2498253.php, accessed May 14, 2014.

31. Dawn D. Bennett-Alexander and Laura B. Pincus, *Employment Law for Business*, 6th ed. (New York: Irwin/McGraw-Hill, 2009), p. 327; Miriam Jordan, "Feds Target Illegal Hires," *The Wall Street Journal*, February 17, 2011, http://onlines.wsj.com; National Conference of State Legislatures, "E-Verify," Issues and Research: Immigration, revised December 18, 2012, http://www.ncsl.org/research/immigration/everify-faq.aspx, accessed May 14, 2014.

PART TWO: SKILL-BUILDING

Meeting the Challenge

Reflecting back on page 419, discuss with your group the kinds of job candidates you would expect to get from recruiting "workampers" and your expectations for how well these people would perform as warehouse workers during the busy holiday season.

Working together and sharing any experiences group members might have of warehouse and retailing jobs, list all the duties and standards you can think of for Amazon's warehouse employees. Depending on the time limits and resources available to your class, your instructor may also direct you to gather information by looking up job listings online or visiting the Bureau of Labor Statistics *Occupational Outlook Handbook* (http://www.bls.gov/oco/). Then list the qualities you think are important in holding these types of jobs.

Use your lists and any additional research to develop a job description and job specifications for this job. What can Amazon do to ensure that it fills these positions without illegal discrimination?

Problem-Solving Case: Wanted by Honda: Engineers Who Love Small-Town Living

Although the U.S.-based Big Three automakers General Motors, Ford, and Chrysler have announced cutbacks and layoffs recently, some auto companies are still hiring. Toyota, Nissan, Honda, and other companies have set up operations in the United States. While they employ far fewer in the United States than the Big Three, their ranks are growing. Nearly one out of four jobs with auto companies in the United States are with companies other than the Big Three. Honda R&D Americas recently told a reporter that it was adding about 100 employees a year and had 50 positions it was trying to fill with engineers.

To staff those positions, Honda faces a challenge: its location. The Honda research and development facility is located in an out-of-the-way spot in Ohio, the town of Raymond, located about 60 miles northwest of Columbus. Most automotive research facilities in the United States are located near Detroit, because so much of the industry talent lives and works in that area. The Honda plant sits on an 8,000-acre plot of land along with the company's Transportation Research Center, and Honda operates two assembly plants in nearby Marysville and East Liberty. Surrounding this complex are cornfields.

Because of its location, Honda does not seek most of its recruits from other auto companies. It hires local residents to fill manufacturing jobs, and for engineers, it turns to schools in the region to find recent graduates. Carol Hadden, who manages human resources, says one good source of engineering recruits has been Ohio State University.

Knowing that small-town life does not appeal to many recent grads, Honda requires applicants to visit the Raymond site for their first interview. Allen explains, "We make them come here to make sure they know where we are." Those who look around and like the location have a better chance of being enthusiastic about a career at Honda R&D.

1. Suggest three ways Honda R&D Americas could recruit engineers to fill jobs at its research and development facility in Raymond, Ohio.

2. If you were interviewing a candidate for a job at this facility, what would you ask to determine whether the candidate would be satisfied to stay at Honda?

3. How would Honda R&D's emphasis on recruiting recent graduates, rather than experienced automotive engineers, affect your job if you were the supervisor of these employees? Would you want Honda to change its recruiting strategy? Why or why not?

Sources: Lindsay Chappell, "Honda's U.S. R&D Center Looks Locally for Talent," *Automotive News*, March 20, 2006; Lillie Guyer, "Cutbacks Aside, Industry Still Needs Engineers," *Automotive News*, March 27, 2006; Gail Kachadourian, "Auto Jobs: A Big Tilt Away from the Big Three," *Automotive News*, April 25, 2005, all downloaded from Business & Company Resource Center, http://galenet.galegroup.com.

Assessing Yourself

Would You Hire You?

One of the criteria supervisors look for in a job candidate is a good fit with the company culture. Use this quiz to determine what you value in your own work environment, and you will have a better idea what kind of firm might want to hire you.

The 54 items below cover the full range of personal and institutional values you would be likely to encounter at any company. Divide the list of items into the 27 choices that would be evident in your ideal workplace, and the 27 that would be least evident. Keep dividing the groups in half until you can rank-order them, and then fill in the numbers of your top and bottom 10 choices in the space provided. Test your fit in a hiring situation by seeing whether the company's values match your top and bottom 10.

Your top 10 choices:

——— ——— ——— ——— ——— ——— ——— ——— ——— ———

Your bottom 10 choices:

——— ——— ——— ——— ——— ——— ——— ——— ——— ———

The Choice Menu

You are:

1. Flexible
2. Adaptable
3. Innovative
4. Able to seize opportunities
5. Willing to experiment
6. Risk taker
7. Careful
8. Autonomy seeker
9. Comfortable with rules
10. Analytical
11. Attentive to detail
12. Precise
13. Team oriented
14. Ready to share information
15. People oriented
16. Easygoing
17. Calm
18. Supportive
19. Aggressive
20. Decisive
21. Action oriented
22. Eager to take initiative
23. Reflective
24. Achievement oriented
25. Demanding
26. Comfortable with individual responsibility
27. Comfortable with conflict
28. Competitive
29. Highly organized
30. Results oriented
31. Interested in making friends at work
32. Collaborative
33. Eager to fit in with colleagues
34. Enthusiastic about job

Your company offers:

35. Stability
36. Predictability
37. High expectations of performance
38. Opportunities for professional growth
39. High pay for good performance
40. Job security
41. Praise for good performance
42. A clear guiding philosophy
43. A low level of conflict
44. An emphasis on quality
45. A good reputation
46. Respect for the individual's rights
47. Tolerance
48. Informality
49. Fairness
50. A unitary culture throughout the organization
51. A sense of social responsibility
52. Long hours
53. Relative freedom from rules
54. The opportunity to be distinctive, or different from others

Pause and Reflect

1. Considering your current job or your most recent job, do you think you are (were) a good fit with your organization's culture?
2. Putting yourself in your supervisor's shoes, if you could make the choice again, would you (as your supervisor) hire you?

Source: From Matt Siegel, "The Perils of Culture Conflict," *Fortune*, November 9, 1998. Copyright ©1998 Time, Inc. All rights reserved.

Class Skills Exercise

Preparing to Interview Job Candidates

This chapter has covered the steps involved in making sound employee selection decisions. Finding employees who have the necessary skills to meet today's workplace challenges is not an easy task. Most organizations are facing similar challenges: adapting to technological changes, improving quality, dealing with workforce diversity, reorganizing work around teams, and empowering employees at all levels to improve customer service. This exercise focuses on the skills employers are looking for in today's job candidates, and it provides practice in developing interview questions that will help you in your evaluation of prospective employees.

Instructions

1. Study Table A.
2. Match the letter of each specific skill from Table A with the appropriate descriptor in Table B on the following pages. (Each answer will be used only once. The first two answers have been done for you in the left-hand column.)
3. In the space after each descriptor in Table B, write an interview question to ask job candidates that will give you insight into their abilities in each area; assume you are interviewing job candidates to fill a job as bank teller. (The first two are already filled in to give you an idea of some sample questions.)

Source: The class exercise was prepared by Corinne Livesay, Bryan College, Chattanooga, Tennessee.

TABLE A | 16 Job Skills Crucial to Success

Category of Skill	Specific Skills in Each Category	
Foundation Competence	a Knowing how to learn	
	b Reading	
	c Writing	
	d Computation	
Communication	e Listening	
	f Oral communication	
Adaptability	g Creative thinking	
	h Problem solving	
Personal management	i Self-esteem	
	j Goal setting and motivation	
	k Personal/career development	
Group effectiveness	l Interpersonal skills	
	m Negotiation	
	n Teamwork	
Influence	o Organizational effectiveness	
	p Leadership	

Source: Adapted from Anthony P. Carnevale, *America and the New Economy* (San Francisco: Jossey-Bass, 1991).

TABLE B | Descriptors of Specific Skills

Answer	Descriptor and Interview Question
i	1. Employers want employees who have pride in themselves and their potential to be successful. *Question: Can you describe a task or project you completed in your last job that you were particularly proud of?*
h	2. Employers want employees who can think on their feet when faced with a dilemma. *Question: If you had a customer return to your teller window and claim, in a rather loud and irritated voice, that you had made a mistake, how would you handle the situation?*
	3. Employers want employees who can assume responsibility and motivate co-workers when necessary. *Question:*
	4. Employers want employees who will hear the key points that make up a customer's concerns. *Question:*
	5. Employers want employees who can learn the particular skills of an available job. *Question:*
	6. Employers want employees who can resolve conflicts to the satisfaction of those involved. *Question:*
	7. Employers want employees who have some sense of the skills needed to perform well in their current jobs and who are working to develop skills to qualify themselves for other jobs. *Question:*
	8. Employers want employees with good mathematics skills. *Question:*
	9. Employers want employees who can work with others to achieve a goal. *Question:*
	10. Employers want employees who can convey an adequate response when responding to a customer's concerns. *Question:*
	11. Employers want employees who have some sense of where the organization is headed and what they must do to make a contribution. *Question:*
	12. Employers want employees who can come up with innovative solutions when needed. *Question:*
	13. Employers want employees who can clearly and succinctly articulate ideas in writing. *Question:*
	14. Employers want employees who know how to get things done and have the desire to complete tasks. *Question:*

(continued)

TABLE B | Descriptors of Specific Skills (*continued*)

Answer	Descriptor and Interview Question
	15. Employers want employees who can get along with customers, suppliers, and co-workers. *Question:*
	16. Employers want employees to be analytical, to summarize information, and to monitor their own comprehension of the reading task. *Question:*

Building Supervision Skills

Interviewing and Selecting New Employees

This exercise simulates an abbreviated version of the selection process. Imagine that the manager of a family-style restaurant such as Denny's needs to hire a server. Working together, the class develops a job description and job specification. The instructor records them on the chalkboard or overhead projector. When in doubt about the details, class members should use their imaginations. The objective is for the class to agree that these two lists are reasonable and complete.

When the job description and job specification are complete, the class develops a list of interview questions that would indicate whether a candidate is appropriate for this job. Besides creating questions to ask, the class also might consider other ways to determine this information during an interview (for example, observing some aspects of the candidates' behavior).

Next, four class members take on the following parts for a role play:

1. Restaurant manager.
2. Candidate 1: a college student with eagerness but no restaurant experience.
3. Candidate 2: a woman who appears to be about 60 years old and who had eight years' experience as a server during the 1960s.
4. Candidate 3: a man with four years' experience as a server in five different restaurants.

The class members taking these roles should feel free to add details to these descriptions of "themselves." The person acting as the restaurant manager interviews each candidate for no more than five minutes each. (A real interview would probably last much longer.)

The role-playing interviews could be videotaped and then played back during the discussion.

Finally, the class discusses one or both of these topics:

1. *Selecting a candidate:* By a show of hands, the class votes for which candidate they would recommend hiring. What are your reasons for choosing that particular candidate?

2. *Interviewing techniques:*
   - Did the restaurant manager interview objectively, based on the criteria determined at the beginning of the exercise?
   - Did the interview cover all the important points?
   - Did the manager use open-ended or closed-ended questions?
   - How did the manager's style of questioning help or hurt the information gathering process?
   - Did the candidates have a chance to ask questions?
   - Did the manager obey the antidiscrimination laws?
   - How did the interviewing experience feel to the candidates? To the manager?

chapter sixteen | Providing Orientation and Training

learning objectives

After you have studied this chapter, you should be able to:

16.1 Summarize reasons for conducting an orientation for new employees.

16.2 Discuss how a supervisor and the human resources department can work together to conduct an orientation.

16.3 Identify methods for conducting an orientation.

16.4 Describe the training cycle.

16.5 Explain how supervisors can decide when employees need training.

16.6 Define major types of training.

16.7 Describe how a supervisor can use coaching and mentoring to support training.

16.8 Discuss how a supervisor can evaluate the effectiveness of training.

A Supervision Challenge

SUPERVISOR TRAINING AT PETCO

Great supervisors are not born with all of the skills they need to supervise successfully, but they can learn many of the skills they lack. Successful supervisors make companies successful. Therefore, businesses that want to succeed train their supervisors.

Petco is a large company with more than 1,200 stores serving pet owners by selling merchandise and pet services such as grooming and training. Petco, however, does not stop at training pets; Petco also trains its supervisors. Petco saw a direct link from trained supervisors to effective sales associates to satisfied customers. Satisfied customers lead to business success and profitability.

How was Petco's management training developed? Stiff competition from specialty stores and large superstores challenged Petco's business model and initial success. Petco began to search for solutions that would help it compete successfully in the changing business environment. Petco began working with a consulting company known as Root. Root determined that improving supervisors' skills would affect Petco's success. Root created a training program that would teach Petco's supervisors the role of supervisors in Petco's organization and improve their basic skills as supervisors.

The initial training was presented to corporate executives and managers. After thorough training, these corporate managers presented workshops to managers below them in the organization chart, who trained the supervisors reporting to them. Supervisors trained the workers. Rolling out the training in this fashion demonstrated both that corporate managers, managers, and supervisors understood the concepts well enough to teach them to others and that they were committed to teaching and using the new skills at every level of the organization. Over time, all Petco personnel in the entire organization were educated on the company's business direction and their roles in the company's success.

General managers and supervisors in Petco stores received training specific to their roles in Petco's organization. Their abilities to lead and manage sales associates, who interact with customers on a daily basis, were considered to be among the most important components in Petco's business strategy. Training focused on coaching, expectations, and follow-up.

Rather than watching sales associates to correct inappropriate behavior, supervisors began coaching employees on appropriate behavior. This improved supervisors' relationships with their sales associates because they were teaching associates new skills instead of waiting for them to fail and then correct their behavior. It also improved the associates' attitude to Petco and their skills.

Setting expectations also improved sales associates' attitude. They learned the skills they needed to perform and how to perform them. Associates were given the authority to perform the tasks that were their responsibility and supervisors were able to perform their tasks and delegate responsibilities to associates when necessary with the confidence that the sales associates would perform the tasks as well as the supervisors could.

At every level, managers and supervisors learned to follow up on the training they received and the training they presented to others. They learned to reinforce positive behaviors and mentor fellow staff members. Consequently, Petco became a more positive enjoyable place to work.

By 2013, most of the stores had participated in the training program. How has this training led to success for Petco? Managers, supervisors, and associates have become more confident in their skills. Employees are staying with Petco longer. Additionally, customers are more satisfied and more loyal.

Training is critical to success at all levels of an organization.

1. How does training create customer loyalty?

2. Why were store managers and supervisors important in Petco's training?

Sources: Charlie Piscitello, "Petco Maps Out a New Leadership Strategy," *Chief Learning Officer*, January 2013; "Fact Sheet—General," About Petco, http://about.petco.com/press-room/fact-sheet/, accessed May 20, 2014; "Manager Development Program," Root Solutions, http://www.rootinc.com/solutions/manager-development-program/, accessed May 20, 2014.

Supervisors are responsible for making sure their employees know what to do and how to do it. Good selection practices ensure that employees are capable of learning their jobs and perhaps already know how to carry out many of the tasks they were hired to perform. However, especially in view of the intense changes faced by most organizations, even the best employees need some degree of training. In this context, **training** refers to increasing the skills that will enable employees to better meet the organization's goals.[1]

training
Increasing the skills that will enable employees to better meet the organization's goals

Training is a major expense. Businesses in the United States invested over $164 billion in employee learning in 2012, representing hundreds of dollars per employee.[2] And these formal programs may be only a small part of all the training that goes on in organizations. Army nurse Rose A. Hazlett attributes much of her success in the military to informal coaching provided by her supervising officers. During her first duty station, when she was an enlisted Navy seaman, her Navy supervisor recommended that Hazlett go to college and consider health care as a field. Hazlett started with courses at a community college and eventually

FIGURE 16.1 | Training Provided by U.S. Companies

According to *Training* magazine's 32nd annual comprehensive analysis of employee-sponsored training, these are the types of training products and services that U.S. companies intend to purchase in 2014.

Learning management systems	38%
Online learning tools and systems	37%
Content development	30%
Authoring tools/systems	29%
Classroom tools and systems	29%
Presentation software and tools	24%
Audio and web conferencing products and systems	23%
Certification	23%
Consulting	23%
Mobile learning	20%
Courseware design	19%
Assessment and analysis testing	18%
Business skills	18%
Games and simulations	18%
Knowledge management tools/systems	14%
Support/on-demand learning tools and systems	14%
Talent management tools and systems	14%
Training management administration	11%
Customer relationship management	9%
Audience response systems	7%
Enterprise learning systems	7%
Translation and localization	6%
Web 2.0	5%

Source: 2013 Training Industry Report, *Training,* November/December 2003, http://www.trainingmag.com/sites/default/files//2013_Training_Industry_Report.pdf.

earned a bachelor's degree (later adding a master's degree and admission to a doctorate program). As a nurse and a young lieutenant following her transfer to the Army, Hazlett reported to the chief nurse. That officer taught Hazlett lessons she would take to heart: "As an officer, people would have to respect the bars on my shoulders, but respect as a person was something I would have to earn . . . the result of my respecting those under my guidance and command." Hazlett credits the informal training of these conversations with more experienced people with helping her become "who I am today—a proud, Hispanic American nurse, patriot, and leader."[3]

Employee training, however it is conducted, meets important needs. New employees need a chance to learn the specific ways things are done in the organization. In addition, employees are best equipped to contribute to a changing workplace when they have an opportunity to learn new skills and improve their existing ones through a variety of training programs. Well-trained employees can deliver higher quality than poorly trained people. Training can improve productivity by holding down a variety of costs: overtime pay for employees unfamiliar with their jobs, workers' compensation and lost time of employees injured when they fail to follow safe practices, lawsuits arising from misconduct such as sexual harassment (discussed in Appendix B), and much more. Finally, well-trained employees are likely to be more satisfied because they know what they are doing and how it contributes to achieving the organization's goals. Figure 16.1 shows the types of training that U.S. companies were planning on conducting or purchasing in 2014, according to a recent survey.

This chapter describes types of training for employees and ways supervisors can participate. It begins by laying out the supervisor's role in orientation, the employee's first learning experience. Next, the chapter discusses types of training available once employees are on board and explains how supervisors can assess when training is needed. The chapter also addresses the growing expectation that supervisors supplement formal training with coaching or mentoring. Finally, the chapter describes why and how to evaluate training efforts.

Orientation of New Employees

Do you remember your first day at your current or most recent job? When you arrived, you might not have known where you would be working or where the restrooms were. You probably did not know your co-workers or how they spent their lunch hour. You might not have known the details of how to carry out your job, including where and how to get the supplies or materials you would need.

The uncertainty you felt is common to new employees in all kinds of organizations. For that reason, supervisors should assume that all employees need some form of orientation. In this context, orientation refers to the process of giving new employees the information they need to do their work comfortably, effectively, and efficiently. Most companies offer employees a formal orientation program. Even in organizations in which someone else is responsible for carrying out a formal orientation program, supervisors must ensure that their employees begin their jobs with all the information they need.[4]

orientation
The process of giving new employees the information they need to do their work comfortably, effectively, and efficiently

LO16.1 ▶ Summarize reasons for conducting an orientation for new employees.

Benefits of Orientation

An employee who spends the day hunting for the photocopier, trying to figure out how to operate a cash register, or looking for someone to explain how to fill out a purchase order is not working efficiently. The primary reason organizations have orientation programs is that the sooner employees know basic information related to doing their jobs, the sooner they can become productive. They can work faster and with fewer errors, and their co-workers and supervisor can spend less time helping them.

Not only does orientation give new employees the knowledge they need to carry out their work, but it also reduces their nervousness and uncertainty. This frees new employees to focus on their jobs rather than their worries, which boosts employee efficiency and reduces the likelihood they will quit.

Another reason for conducting orientation is to encourage employees to develop a positive attitude. The time spent on an orientation session shows that the organization values the new employees. This will almost certainly add to employees' feelings of satisfaction and desire to cooperate as part of the organization. It can make new employees feel more confident that joining the organization was a good idea. In addition, work is more satisfying when we know how to do it well. The organization benefits because employees with positive attitudes tend to be more highly motivated, so they are more likely to do good work.

Positive attitudes and commitment arise partly from healthy, supportive work relationships. When an orientation shows a new employee that the supervisor and co-workers want him or her to succeed, the new employee has more ability and desire to meet expectations. Nancy Ahlrichs suggests some ways to strengthen positive work relationships during orientation. According to Ahlrichs, the supervisor should be physically nearby on the first day, signaling that the supervisor is glad to have the new employee on board and wants to make the transition smooth. Tours and introductions help the new employee get acquainted with others. A welcoming e-mail message from top management or the supervisor adds a positive touch that shows the company cares. Assigning the new employee to a buddy or mentor (discussed subsequently in this chapter) who can provide information and encouragement gives the new employee a valuable resource. These interpersonal aspects of orientation are important to include along with any written or computerized orientation materials.[5]

One approach to orientation that applies all of these principles takes place at Saint Francis Hospital in Memphis. There, an 18-week orientation program for newly hired nurses is aimed at preparing them to meet the day-to-day challenges of their demanding jobs. In school, nurses develop extensive technical skills, but working in a hospital also involves coping with anxious patients, impatient doctors, and vast amounts of paperwork. To prepare the new nurses, orientation at Saint Francis includes assignments to learn techniques from a more experienced colleague, as well as meetings with a mentor (a role described later in this chapter), who helps the nurse with professional development. In addition, when nurses encounter difficult experiences, such as the death of a patient, they may meet with a debriefer, who helps the nurse make sense of the experience. Experienced nurses who are new to Saint Francis undergo a shorter version of the orientation program. Since the hospital began using the orientation program, its turnover among new nurses has been cut in half.[6]

The Supervisor's Role

LO16.2 ▶ Discuss how a supervisor and the human resources department can work together to conduct an orientation.

In a small organization, supervisors often are responsible for conducting the orientation. If you are one of those supervisors, look for ways to adapt the principles in this chapter to your group's particular needs.

Large organizations generally have a formal orientation program conducted by the human resources department. Even so, supervisors have a role in orientation. Whereas the formal orientation program focuses on information pertaining to the organization as a whole, supervisors still must convey information about the specifics of holding a particular job in a particular department. If you are a supervisor in these circumstances, learn which of the topics and methods your human resources department already covers, and then consider ways you and your employees can handle any remaining ones. See the "Supervisory Skills" feature for some specific ways to manage the "honeymoon" period.

Orientation Topics

When the human resources department and supervisor share responsibility for conducting an orientation, the human resources department typically covers topics related to the organization's policies and procedures, including hours of work and breaks; location of company facilities such as the lunchroom and exercise facilities; procedures for filling out time sheets; and policies regarding performance appraisals, pay increases, and time off. The human resources department also handles the task of having new employees fill out the necessary paperwork, such as enrollment forms for insurance policies and withholding forms for tax purposes. The person conducting the orientation should explain each of these forms to new employees.

A supervisor is responsible for orientation topics related to performing a particular job in a particular department. A supervisor explains what the department does and how these activities contribute to the organization's goals. A supervisor

SUPERVISORY SKILLS

PROVIDING ORIENTATION

Orientation Ideas from the Pros

There are a variety of successful approaches to new employee orientation. There is no one "right" way to do it. Having some orientation plan in place and following it, however, is very important to successfully getting a new employee up to speed quickly. In the following examples, experienced managers share their thoughts about what has helped them prepare new employees to deliver results.

- At Sawhill Custom Kitchens and Design, located in Minneapolis, Minnesota, new employees receive a handbook spelling out the company's philosophy and policies, as well as a job description detailing the requirements of the position. A new employee also is assigned to a senior designer and "shadows" the veteran, accompanying him or her to see how an experienced person works with customers. Because employees must be familiar with the products they sell, Sawhill also sends employees on tours of manufacturers' facilities, where they learn about the product lines.
- Training at Belgrade TrueValue, a hardware store in Belgrade, Montana, starts even before individuals are hired. During job interviews, owner Steve Bachmeier asks candidates to describe their best and worst experiences with customer service. This launches a conversation about Belgrade TrueValue's standards for customer service. After the candidate is hired, that emphasis continues through mentoring and hands-on training. In addition, pamphlets and classroom training provide new employees with information about the store's products. New employees in the store spend their first two days working with a trainer in the checkout area. Because the store has a goal that no customer will stand in a line waiting for a cashier, all employees learn to handle checkout. Following that initial training, employees receive one page of information each week for four weeks and are encouraged to seek out the managers listed on the information sheets, as a way to show initiative and become acquainted with the store's management. The first week's material covers topics such as how to read shelf tags and stock shelves. The following three weeks cover specific departments in the store. The program is designed to build employees' know-how and confidence to ask for help in resolving customers' questions.

- At another TrueValue store, Wabash TrueValue, located in Wabash, Indiana, employees spend their first few hours on the job working alongside owner Brian Howenstine. That coaching from the top gives Howenstine a chance to talk about his expectations as well as company policies. Then, so that the new hire doesn't feel overwhelmed, Howenstine has the person spend the rest of the day just wandering around the store and becoming familiar with what is on the shelves.

Sources: "What Do You Find to Be the Most Important Aspects of Effectively Training Employees?" *Kitchen and Bath Design*, June 2006; Darci Valentine, "New-Hire Training Tips: A Guide to Teaching Them the Ropes," *Do-It-Yourself Retailing*, February 2006, both downloaded from Business & Company Resource Center, http://galenet.galegroup.com.

FIGURE 16.2 | Sample Checklist for Orientation

A checklist of topics to cover can help a supervisor stay on track with a new employee's orientation and make sure that all the important information is conveyed.

SUPERVISORS' CHECKLIST
The Right Start for New Hourly Paid Employees

A. Explain (before employee starts the job):
1. Rate of pay, including overtime.
2. Pay day.
3. Initial job or assignment.
4. Hours—call out—holiday pay—no tardiness.
5. Starting and quitting time.
6. Lunch period—relief periods.
7. Whom to call if unable to come to work (give name and phone number on card).
8. Work clothes arrangement—laundry.
9. No smoking areas.
10. Safety rules—no running—mesh gloves—reporting all accidents, etc.
11. Sanitation—this is a food factory.
12. Name benefits (will explain later).
13. Possible job difficulties—sore muscles or hands, dizziness, nausea, etc. (encourage to stick it out).
14. Buying of company products.
15. Nothing from plant without order.
16. Importance of quality product.

B. Show:
1. Locker—restrooms.
2. Lunchroom.
3. Where employee will work—introduce to supervisor and immediate co-workers.
4. Explain the job—use JIT.
C. Talk to new employee (to encourage):
1. Twice first day.
2. Once each day the next four days.
D. After one week, explain:
1. Vacation.
2. Hospitalization.
3. EBA—Group.
4. Pension.
5. Suggestion plan.
6. Union contract, if organized plant (probationary period).

Source: Adapted from a Swift and Company document.

who covered this information in the selection interview should repeat it during the orientation process. As described subsequently, the supervisor's orientation should point out the locations of facilities the employee will need to use and explain any of the department's own policies and procedures.

A supervisor's orientation also should provide instructions on how to perform the job. A supervisor may be able to explain a simple job at one time, but most jobs are more complex and will require a supervisor to first give an overview of the job's responsibilities and then, over the course of days or weeks, show the employee how to perform different aspects of the job. To build morale while training, a supervisor also can explain why the employee's job is important—that is, how it contributes to meeting department and organizational objectives.

A supervisor should prepare and follow a checklist of the topics to cover during the orientation of new employees. Figure 16.2 is adapted from a checklist distributed to supervisors at Swift and Company; it is printed on a two-by-three-inch card so supervisors can easily refer to it. In preparing a checklist, a supervisor should include items that fit his or her particular situation.

LO16.3 ▶ Identify methods for conducting an orientation.

Orientation Methods

The methods a supervisor uses will depend on the organization's policies and resources. For example, a large organization with a human resources department may provide a handbook of information for new employees and spell out orientation procedures to follow. A small organization may expect individual supervisors to develop their own orientation methods. Some common methods include using an employee handbook, conducting a tour of the facilities, and encouraging the involvement of co-workers.

Employee Handbook

employee handbook
A document that describes an organization's conditions of employment, policies regarding employees, administrative procedures, and related matters

If the organization publishes an employee handbook, a new employee should be introduced to this document during the orientation. An **employee handbook** describes an organization's conditions of employment (e.g., attendance, behavior on the job, performance of duties), policies regarding employees (e.g., time off, hours of work, benefits), administrative procedures (e.g., filling out time sheets and travel expense reports), and related matters. A supervisor should show a new employee what topics are covered in the handbook and explain how to use it to find answers to questions. For example, an employee might use the handbook to learn how long he or she must work to qualify for three weeks' vacation.

Tour of Facilities

Another important orientation method is to give the employee a tour. The tour might start with the employee's own work area, which should already be prepared with the supplies, tools, or equipment the employee will need. The supervisor then shows the employee the locations of physical facilities he or she will need to know about, including restrooms, water fountain, coffee station, fax, and photocopier, and where to get supplies, parts, or other materials needed to do the job.

During the tour, the supervisor should introduce the new employee to the people with whom he or she will be working. Friendly, positive words during introductions can help make the new employee part of the team. In introducing a new nurse to her colleagues in the hospital, a supervisor might say, "This is Janet Strahn. She's one of the top graduates from Northern, and I know we're all going to appreciate her help." In introducing a new maintenance mechanic to a machine operator in the department, a supervisor might say, "Pedro is the guy you'll need if your machine goes down." In both examples, the supervisor is emphasizing the importance of the new employee to the department.

Involvement of Co-Workers

A new employee's co-workers have an important role to play in orientation. Their behavior goes a long way toward making the new employee feel either welcome or like an outsider. Therefore, a supervisor should ask all employees to help welcome newcomers. If the organization tries to build team spirit through activities such as clubs and sports teams, a supervisor should see that they are well publicized so that new employees can participate easily. A supervisor may encourage co-workers to invite a new employee to join them on breaks and at lunch. On the employee's first day, a supervisor can help a new employee feel welcome by inviting him or her to lunch.

Follow-Up

In addition to the initial information provision, an orientation should involve follow-up. A supervisor should check with new employees at the end of the first day and the first week to make sure they understand what they are supposed to be doing and know where to get what they need. At all times, a supervisor should encourage employees to ask questions.

Of course, a supervisor should not stop following up after one week. Regularly checking on the performance and progress of employees is part of a supervisor's control responsibilities.

LO16.4 ▶ Describe the training cycle.

Training

As mentioned previously, employees need continued training even after they have worked for the organization for years. Training shows employees how to do the basics of their jobs and then helps them improve their skills. It also helps employees

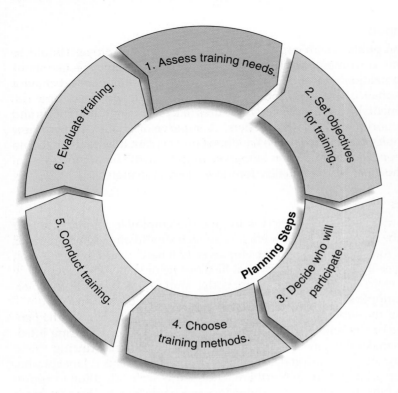

FIGURE 16.3 | The Training Cycle

Training is not something that happens just once and then is not thought of again. It is a process that occurs in an ongoing cycle.

adapt to changes in the workplace. Because change occurs in every organization, the need for training continues (see Chapter 14).

The Training Cycle

The process of providing training occurs in a cycle of steps (see Figure 16.3). The first step is to assess needs for training. As described in the next section, assessment of training needs is part of a supervisor's job. In addition, higher-level management or the human resources department may identify a need for various kinds of training. The next three steps involve planning the training. Then someone conducts the training as planned. Finally, the training should be evaluated.

Planning Steps

A supervisor or other person proposing the training begins the planning stage by setting objectives for it. These objectives are based on a comparison of the current level and the desired level of performance and skills. In other words, they specify progress from the current level to the desired level. The training objectives should meet the criteria for effective objectives (see Chapter 6). Thus, they should be written, measurable, clear, specific, and challenging but achievable. Training objectives also should support the organization's goals by helping develop the kind of employees who can make the organization more competitive. At United Technologies Corporation (UTC), business challenges have forced the company to focus on reducing its workforce and making the remaining employees more efficient. Despite the difficult climate that follows cutbacks, UTC has to ensure that the remaining employees know they are valued and appreciate the need to apply their skills more productively than ever. To meet that goal, UTC established a training program for its frontline supervisors, comprising more than 10,000 supervisors whose employees make products as diverse as helicopters, elevators, and fuel cells. The training program emphasizes supervisory skills such as constructively discussing performance with employees.[7]

A supervisor also decides who will participate in the training program. For example, training pertaining to how to prevent and avoid sexual harassment applies to all employees, so everyone in the department would participate. But training on how to operate a new piece of equipment would include only those who might use that equipment. This decision may take into account the interests and motivation levels of employees, as well as their skills. For example, an employee who is eager to advance in the organization will want to participate in many training activities to develop a variety of skills. An employee who is interested primarily in job security will probably want just enough training to keep up to date on how to perform the job.

The last step in planning training is to choose the training methods. Some training methods are described subsequently in this chapter. If selecting a training method is part of a supervisor's role, he or she may wish to consult with the human resources department or a training expert to learn which techniques will best meet the objectives of the training.

Implementation

Once the training has been planned, someone must conduct it in a timely manner. In some cases, the trainer may be a supervisor. A department's employees may be qualified to conduct some kinds of training, such as demonstrating how to use a computer system. In other cases, a professional trainer is more appropriate. The choice depends on the expertise of a supervisor or employee, the content and type of training, and the time and money available for training. A supervisor with a big budget and little expertise in a particular area of training is most likely to use an in-house or outside expert. Training topics most often tackled by a supervisor are those about the specific job or department instead of company policies and values, interpreting the company's performance, or working effectively as a team.

When a supervisor is conducting the training, he or she can benefit from applying principles of learning.[8] One of these principles is that adults generally get the most out of training if they are taught a little at a time over a long period, especially if the training is seeking to change behavior rather than merely add to the learner's store of knowledge. Thus, shutting down for a day of training would be less effective than scheduling a half hour every week or so. Another principle is that adults want to see how the training content applies to their everyday problems and needs. Generally, they bring significant experience to the training sessions, and the training program should acknowledge and draw upon what they already know.

Expert trainers also advise that sessions should combine a variety of methods because individuals have different learning styles; they approach a subject and retain information in varying ways. Training methods should include visual and spoken information, as well as a chance to involve employees in trying what they learn, perhaps through role-plays, simulations, or games. At the very least, training should engage employees in asking and answering questions. The methods should be appropriate for presenting the theory and instruction (procedures, methods, rules, and so forth) of the subject matter, as well as for presenting models of how to carry out the new skill and experiences with trying the new skill. At Kimberly-Clark, for example, employees had trouble learning about the company's supply chain (all the steps to get a product to consumers) from slide presentations and meetings. When training expanded to include simulation games and video presentations, employees began to understand the process and why it affected the company's performance.[9] The information shown in Figure 16.4 shows a static picture of the major categories of training methods used by U.S. employers. In recent years, the Training Industry Report has shown a trend toward the increased use of blended learning techniques as well as increased use of all of the technology-based training methods: computer-based and online training methods, Webcast and virtual classrooms, and social networking and mobile device-based training.

Finally, motivation is as important to successful learning as it is to other employee activities. Training will therefore be most effective when it reflects the principles of motivation discussed in Chapter 11.

Evaluation

After the training is over, the supervisor evaluates the results. Did it meet the objectives? The last

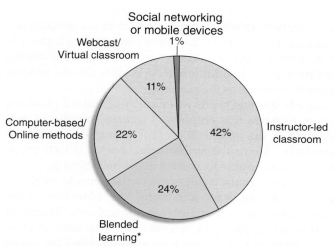

*Any combination of the other methods shown.

FIGURE 16.4 | Use of Various Training Methods

There are many different ways to deliver training to employees. The key is to find the one, or a combination, that works best for the particular training required and the employees who are receiving the training.

Source: Data from "2011 Training Industry Report," *Training*, November/December 2011, pp. 22–35.

section of this chapter discusses the evaluation of training in greater detail. Evaluation completes the training cycle by helping the supervisor identify needs for additional training.

LO16.5 ▶ Explain how supervisors can decide when employees need training.

Assessment of Training Needs

Whether or not supervisors conduct much of their employees' formal training, they are still responsible for recognizing needs for training. With input from the employees, supervisors should determine the areas of training that employees will need and schedule the times for them to receive it.

Needs assessment should be an ongoing, not an occasional, concern of supervisors. Change is such a dominant force today that organizations depend on a workforce that continually learns and develops to give them a competitive edge.

A supervisor has several ways to identify training needs. First, a supervisor can observe problems in the department that suggest a need for training. For example, if a restaurant's customers are complaining about the quality of service, the manager might conclude that some or all of the staff needs training in how to satisfy customers. Or if forms sent from one department to another frequently contain a similar type of error, the department's supervisor should investigate why the people filling out the forms are making this type of mistake. Although frequent questions from employees are not necessarily a "problem," they do indicate that employees may need training in some area.

Certain areas of change also signal a need for training, and a supervisor should pay attention to them and consider what new knowledge and skills employees will need to keep abreast. If an organization encourages employee empowerment and teamwork, employees will need to know how to make decisions, evaluate team efforts, and listen to team members. When new technology (from a competitor, supplier, or elsewhere) affects an organization or the individuals in it, employees will need to learn about that technology and gain skill in applying it. If a department or its customer base is becoming more diverse, employees will need to learn how to respect, communicate with, and achieve objectives with people of different cultures.

Another way to obtain information about training needs is to ask employees. Employees frequently have opinions about what they must learn to do a better job. At a minimum, supervisors and employees should discuss training needs during performance appraisals (see Chapter 17). In addition, a supervisor should encourage employees to communicate their needs as they arise.

Finally, a supervisor can identify training needs when carrying out the planning function. Executing plans often requires that employees receive training in new skills or procedures. For example, if the organization will be introducing a new product, salespeople will have to be able to communicate its benefits to customers, and customer service staff will have to be able to answer questions about it.

In addition to recognizing these signals, a supervisor also should evaluate them. Do they indicate a need for training or for something else? Sometimes poor performance is not a training problem but a motivation problem. Errors or defects may be a symptom that employees lack resources or cooperation from elsewhere in the organization. Frequent questions may signal a need for better communication instead of (or in addition to) training. Before spending money on training, a supervisor should consider whether it is the best response to these signals. A good place to begin may be to ask the relevant employees to help find the underlying issue.

Mandatory Training

A supervisor is not the only one to decide when training is required. Government regulations, union work rules, or company policy may dictate training in certain circumstances. If the state mandates a number of continuing education classes for teachers, if the union requires an apprenticeship of so many months for pipe fitters, or if the company's top managers decide that everyone should take a class in total quality management, the supervisor's job is to make sure that his or her employees get the required training. The supervisor does so primarily through decisions related to scheduling and motivation.

Learning Environment

Along with planning for formal training sessions, supervisors can help organizations meet the need for training by fostering a climate that values learning. This kind of climate has been called a "learning environment." Daniel R. Tobin, a business consultant and coach, has said that if team members "aren't learning from each other or aren't learning together, they're not really part of a team." Rather, they are "just a bunch of people that happen to work for the same boss."[10] Tobin encourages supervisors to create a learning environment by meeting with employees before and after any training program the employees attend. In these meetings the supervisor and employee discuss what lessons from the program will be most important to focus on and how the lessons learned can be applied at work.

Another way to foster a learning environment is to set a good example. Supervisors should develop their own knowledge and skills through a variety of means, from reading to attending seminars. Also, supervisors should share information generously with employees. They can enable employees to learn from one another by encouraging them to exchange what they have learned through their education, training activities, and experience. When employees request time and other resources for training, a supervisor should view the training as an investment to be evaluated, not merely a distraction from the "real work" of the organization.

Retraining Employees

Like one's muscles and memory, work-related skills are subject to atrophy, which is a condition where employees lose the ability to perform work-related functions over time. The loss of employee skills due to atrophy is a potential impediment to the competitiveness of an organization. To combat this, ongoing training in the basic skills required of employees is necessary in many companies. Customers can also provide great insight into training needs of employees. As the needs of customers change, the demands they make of a company and its employees can drive and direct the kinds of training required. Finally, changing technologies may require companies to adapt and invest in additional training for employees. Companies wishing to stay competitive must conduct training needs assessments to help identify areas of deficiency in the existing workforce. These assessments ascertain if there are skills that some employees lack or that they are not as proficient at as they could be. As illustrated in Figure 16.5, the degree of skills atrophy, changing customer needs, changing technologies, and the results of training needs assessment all impact the frequency with which retraining of employees is needed.

The frequency of training will vary according to the utilization of a given skill and the dynamics of the environment

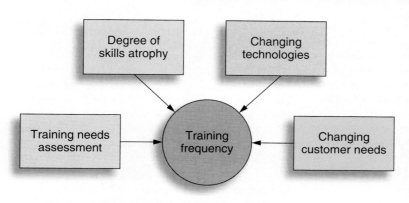

FIGURE 16.5 | The Need to Retrain Employees

A number of factors can impact how frequently employees need to be retrained.

where the skill is being used. For example, a computer programmer or engineer may require training for new software packages when those packages are first published. Likewise, medical practitioners like surgeons should be trained frequently to ensure they maintain the ability to engage in effective surgical procedures. The key is to engage employees in training when a deficiency is identified and they can readily apply any skills gained through training.[11]

Life-Long Learning

Life-long learning refers to the ongoing acquisition and enhancement of knowledge, skills, and abilities by individuals. Compared with episodic learning periods, including college, life-long learning reflects the pursuit of bettering oneself on a consistent basis. There are a number of reasons that individuals engage in life-long learning, but companies can benefit greatly from encouraging the ongoing pursuit of knowledge by their employees. Notably, life-long learning provides employees with additional knowledge, skills, and abilities that can enable them to better connect with customers, engage in creative decision making and problem-solving, and identify ways of improving work. One potential drawback to providing employees with ongoing training and learning opportunities is that employees could take their newly gained knowledge, skills, and abilities and leverage them with other firms. Thus, instead of encouraging training that may cause good employees to leave, it is important that the firm encourage training for roles inside the company. In a broader context, life-long learning makes a labor force more productive, meaning astute local, regional, and national governments should encourage the practice of life-long learning by their citizens.[12]

To keep your mind fit and in condition for life-long learning requires that you exercise your brain. The "Supervision: New Trends" feature outlines one way to exercise your brain—through brain training apps delivered via smartphones.

SUPERVISION: NEW TRENDS

TRAINING YOUR BRAIN

Regardless of your position within a company, to be an asset to the company, you need to keep your mind sharp. The more active and agile your mind is, the better it will be equipped to learn new things and adapt to changing situations.

Fortunately, there are countless apps for tablets, smartphones, and iOS devices that enable you to exercise your brain. A key benefit of these is that they are easily accessible and you can use them whenever you have a couple of minutes between meetings, while relaxing at lunch, while riding mass transit, or when waiting for an appointment. Plus, they are fun!

Different apps are available depending upon if you have an Android phone, iPhone, or Window's phone. But each has at least a couple of apps from which to choose. Some of the more popular apps for sharpening your memory and improving reasoning include:

- Find Differences
- Fit Brains
- Brain Fitness Pro

- Luminosity
- Clockwork Brain
- Memory Trainer
- Training Your Brain
- Eidetic
- Critical Thinking University Think-O-Meter
- Brain Challenge
- Brain Age

Many of these are free or have a nominal cost. Download a couple and see which you find to be the most fun or that interest you most—then begin your brain training.

Sources: Chedna Ngak, "Brain Training Mobile Apps to Sharpen Your Mind," CBS News, March 21, 2014, http://www.cbsnews.com/news/eye-on-apps-brain-training-mobile-apps/, accessed May 22, 2014; "Round-Up of the 5 Best Brain Training Apps This Year," Spreeder, http://www.spreeder.com/blog/round-up-of-the-5-best-brain-training-apps-this-year/, accessed May 22, 2014; Kristin Ambrosino, "Seven Brain Games for Your Smartphone," Men's Fitness, http://www.mensfitness.com/life/gearandtech/seven-brain-games-your-smartphone, accessed May 22, 2014.

FIGURE 16.6 | Types of Training

There are many different types of training available. When choosing the type of training to be used, a supervisor should take into account the expense versus the benefits, what resources are available, and what the employee's needs are.

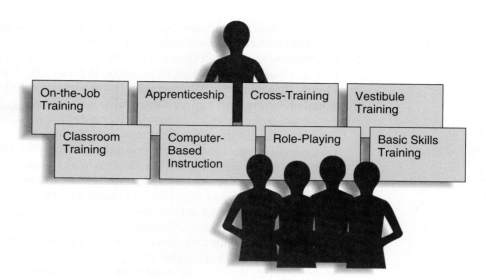

On-the-Job Training

Apprenticeship

Cross-Training

Vestibule Training

Classroom Training

Computer-Based Instruction

Role-Playing

Basic Skills Training

LO16.6 ▶ Define major types of training.

Types of Training

A variety of types of training are available for employees (see Figure 16.6). Most organizations use a variety of training methods. At Regions Financial, a banking company based in Birmingham, Alabama, candidates for management jobs rotate through a variety of banking positions and participate in classroom training, computer-based instruction, and on-the-job training guided by a mentor. Verizon Wireless gives each of its customer service representatives 96 hours of training, including simulations, classroom instruction, and on-the-job learning.[13]

In selecting or recommending a type of training, a supervisor should consider the expense relative to the benefits, the resources available, and trainees' needs for practice and individualized attention. No matter what type of training is used, a supervisor should be sure that the trainer understands the objectives of the training and the ways to carry them out. A supervisor also should counsel employees who seem discouraged and praise them when they show progress.

On-the-Job Training

on-the-job training
Teaching a job while trainer and trainee perform the job at the work site

In many cases, the easiest way to learn how to perform a job is to try it. Teaching a job while trainer and trainee do the job at the work site is called **on-the-job training**. The trainer—typically a co-worker or supervisor—shows the employee how to do the job, and then the employee tries it.[14]

An employee who learns in this way benefits from being able to try the skills and techniques being taught. The results tell immediately whether the employee understands what the trainer is trying to teach. However, on-the-job training carries the risk that an inexperienced employee will make costly and even dangerous mistakes. Thus, this type of training is most suitable when the tasks to be learned are relatively simple or the costs of an error are low. For more complex or risky tasks, it may be wiser to use other forms of training before or instead of on-the-job training.

Apprenticeship

apprenticeship
Training that involves working alongside an experienced person, who shows the apprentice how to do the various tasks involved in a job or trade

Many tradespeople learn their trades through an **apprenticeship**. This involves working alongside an experienced person, who shows the apprentice how to do the various tasks involved in the trade. Thus, an apprenticeship is a long-term form of on-the-job training. (Many apprenticeship programs also require that apprentices complete classroom training.) Most apprenticeships are in the building trades, such as carpentry and pipe fitting.

In the electric utility industry, effective apprenticeship programs are needed to prepare new employees to take over as lineworkers. The older generation of baby-boomers is creating many vacancies as these experienced lineworkers retire. Choctawhatchee Electric Cooperative (CHELCO), a utility serving northwest Florida, has met this challenge with its own apprenticeship program. Unlike traditional show-and-tell approaches, CHELCO's apprenticeship program emphasizes hands-on experiences in the workplace under the guidance of expert workers who have been taught training techniques and learning styles. Apprentices in CHELCO's program undergo 15 weeks of external training in the theory behind the jobs, and then they begin three-month rotations in which they work in underground, over-head, maintenance, and service crews. As the apprentices demonstrate competency and meet performance standards, the trainer increases their responsibilities and the risk level of their tasks. At the same time, the apprentices continue to take courses at the Northwest Lineman College.[15]

An apprenticeship program is more complicated to set up than simple on-the-job training for individual tasks. However, it is one way to help a supervisor meet training needs that require months or years of learning.

Cross-Training

As you learned in Chapter 11, an increasing number of organizations are using job rotation, meaning that employees take turns performing various jobs. Job rotation requires that employees learn to perform more than one job. Teaching employees another job so that they can fill in as needed is known as cross-training. Employees who have completed cross-training can enjoy more variety in their work, and their supervisor has more flexibility in making assignments. The resulting flexibility also makes cross-training necessary for many forms of teamwork.

Vanamatic Company, a machine shop in Delphos, Ohio, uses cross-training to enable its employees to work in teams. Each team carries out production tasks for a manufacturing cell, in which various machine tools are used to make a particular product. Through cross-training, each member of a team learns to perform all the jobs in the manufacturing cell, such as operating a screw machine and a machining center. Employees also are tested to identify their strengths and work preferences. Teams allocate the work among their members, trying to assign each worker to a preferred area of operation. But when special needs arise, everyone can jump in and help as needed. According to Adam Wiltsie, the company's manufacturing engineer, "The operators enjoy the change of pace provided by doing different jobs in the cell," and efficiency is much greater than it was under the traditional arrangement of each employee specializing in just one process or machine.[16]

In planning cross-training, a supervisor should make sure that employees spend enough time practicing each job to learn it well. Some jobs are more complex than others and will require more training time. Also, some employees will learn a given job faster than others.

Vestibule Training

vestibule training
Training that takes place on equipment set up in a special area off the job site

While on-the-job training is effective, it is not appropriate as initial training for jobs that have no room for errors, such as piloting or nursing. In those cases, people learn principles or techniques before doing the actual job. A type of training that allows employees to practice using equipment off the job is called **vestibule training**. Employees undergoing vestibule training use procedures and equipment set up in a special vestibule school. For example, a large retail store might set up a training room containing cash registers, or an airline might use a simulated cabin for training flight attendants.

Vestibule training is appropriate when the organization hires people who do not already know how to use its equipment. Employees learn to operate the equipment without the pressure of accidents occurring, customers getting impatient, or other employees depending on a minimum amount of output. The expense of vestibule training or other off-the-job training is higher because employees are not producing goods or services for the organization while they undergo the training. However, if the organization hired only people who already had all the necessary skills, it would probably have to pay more and might have difficulty finding enough qualified candidates.

Vestibule training is appropriate for the complex jobs carried out by workers at the Mears Group, an engineering and construction company that specializes in excavating for, installing, maintaining, and repairing pipelines. The company built a training and research facility at its Rosebush, Michigan, headquarters. The training setup includes 1,800 feet of pipe in several diameters, laid out in a space that can be flooded to represent conditions in the field. Trainees encounter various surface conditions, such as gravel and concrete, as well as damaged pipes and coatings for them to inspect. The pipes are wired to simulate electrical problems as well. The aim is for employees to see what problems look like in the test facility so that they can identify and handle the same problems safely outside this controlled environment. New employees complete several days of safety training and then undergo training in their specific job requirements. Later, as their job requirements expand, employees may receive additional training on the job or back at the training facility.[17]

Classroom Training

As shown earlier in Figure 16.4, the largest share of training time is devoted to classroom instruction. More than 43 percent of training hours are instructor-led classes, not counting blended learning activities (which may include classroom training) and classroom-style instruction delivered via Webcasts.[18] Classroom training takes place in a class or seminar where one or more speakers lecture on a specific topic. Seminars are available from a variety of sources on many topics, so a supervisor who is considering attending or sending employees to a seminar should first make sure the topic will be relevant to job performance. Classroom training also can occur at the workplace, even if the organization lacks the time or facilities for formal classes.

The main advantage of classroom training is that the person conducting it can deliver a large quantity of information to more than one person in a relatively short time. Depending on the format and trainer, it can be a relatively inexpensive way to convey information. A disadvantage is that most of the communication travels in one direction—from the lecturer to the audience. One-way communication is less engaging and memorable. In addition, classroom training rarely allows the learners to practice what they are learning.

Classroom training therefore benefits from the trainer's ability to maintain a high level of interest, such as by including computer-based instruction and role-playing. Randstad North America, a temporary-employment agency, sent its 250 branch managers to a five-day course exploring some of the basics of supervision. The emphasis was on applying the course's lessons, so to learn about coaching, participants were asked to bring in an example: the most difficult employee they needed to coach. Each manager then paired up with another participant for role-playing. In each participant's role-play, the branch manager played him- or herself, and the partner played the problem employee.[19]

Classroom training can be an effective way to provide important information all at once to a large number of people.

Computer-Based Instruction

At a growing number of organizations, computer software is taking the place of classroom-based trainers. In fact, according to *Training* magazine, almost

26 percent of training courses are delivered via computer-based training with no live instructor involved, and another 5.2 percent of training is delivered via social networking or mobile devices.[20] Computer-based instruction typically uses a computer to present information, generate and score test questions, keep track of the trainee's performance, and tell the trainee what activities to do next. This type of training is a common way of learning to use a new computer program; the software comes with a series of lessons that give the user a chance to try using it. Computer-based training that employs the Internet is commonly referred to as e-learning. Table 16.1 lists 10 major advantages that e-learning offers organizations. E-learning is particularly useful when trainees are spread over a wide geographic area. In that case, the organization may use *distance learning*, in which computers and communications technology deliver the course content to participants who are located far away from the provider of the training.

Some firms have already put themselves on the leading edge of integrating technology into workforce training. One innovation is to use the technology of video games to make learning more interesting and enjoyable. Cold Stone Creamery has a custom online game that simulates one of its stores. Players learn portion control by scooping ice cream as the timer runs out; when it does, they see whether they served too much. Almost three out of every ten Cold Stone employees

TABLE 16.1 | E-Learning Offers 10 Major Advantages

Source: Used with permission from Iowa State University; Dean of Students Office. http://www.dso.iastate.edu/asc/academic/elearner/advantage.html.

1. **Schedule:** Work can be scheduled around work and family.

2. **Time/Cost:** E-learning reduces travel time and travel costs for off-campus students.

3. **Selection:** Learners may have the option to select learning materials that meet their level of knowledge and interest.

4. **Mobility:** Learners can study anywhere they have access to a computer and Internet connection.

5. **Pace:** Self-paced learning modules allow learners to work at their own pace.

6. **Flexibility:** Learners can join discussions in the bulletin board threaded discussion areas at any hour, or visit with classmates and instructors remotely in chat rooms.

7. **Interaction:** Instructors and learners both report that e-learning fosters more interaction among learners and instructors than in large lecture courses.

8. **Accommodation:** E-learning can accommodate different learning styles and facilitate learning through a variety of activities.

9. **Knowledge:** E-learning develops knowledge of the Internet and computers skills that will help learners throughout their lives and careers.

10. **Self-Confidence:** Successfully completing online or computer-based courses builds self-knowledge and self-confidence and encourages learners to take responsibility for their learning.

downloaded this learning game voluntarily because they find it so entertaining. Canon trains repair personnel with a game in which they drag and drop parts onto an image of a copier. If they send the part to the wrong place, a light flashes and a buzzer goes off. Canon compared the performance of trainees using the game with performance of trainees who learned from manuals; the gamers' scores were noticeably higher.[21]

interactive multimedia
Computer software that brings together sound, video, graphics, animation, and text and adjusts content on the basis of user responses

Computer-based instruction is becoming more engaging and widespread because of the growing affordability of **interactive multimedia.** This software brings together sound, video, graphics, animation, and text. The best interactive multimedia programs adjust the course content on the basis of the student's responses to questions. Interactive multimedia typically is delivered online or on DVD. Accenture, a management consulting and technology service company, uses interactive multimedia to create simulations in which trainees practice answering questions and otherwise interacting with digitized images of clients. Likewise, retailer JCPenney uses interactive multimedia to train customer service representatives in its credit card division. The computer simulates phone calls from customers, so the reps can practice handling irate (and reasonable) customers.

Some computer-based training uses simulations, as in the previous example of Cold Stone Creamery. The computer displays conditions that an employee might have to face. For example, a flight simulator would show pilot trainees the cockpit and the view from the window. Another simulation might be of dials and other readouts monitoring the performance of machinery. A trainee uses the computer's keyboard or some other device to respond to the situation displayed by a computer, and the simulator responds by showing the consequences of the trainee's actions. This enables the trainee to practice responding to conditions without suffering the real consequences of a mistake, such as a plane crashing or a boiler exploding.

Computer-based instruction has a significant cost advantage over other methods when there are many trainees. An organization may not have to pay a trainer. In addition, trainees can work at their own pace, eliminating the frustration that arises from a class moving too fast for them to understand the material or too slow to maintain their interest. A good training program can help trainees learn faster or better than they might through another training technique. At JCPenney, customer service representatives trained with interactive multimedia reach peak proficiency in one-third less time than employees who had more traditional training. Accenture also credits interactive multimedia for its employees having "deeper competencies, more skill and knowledge."[22] The lower cost of computer-based training is a likely reason the use of such training has increased even as companies cut their overall training budgets.[23]

Even small companies can benefit from computer-based training. Thumbtack. com, an Internet business that links consumers with local service providers, finds online learning especially useful for training its growing staff in the Philippines. Employees at the company's San Francisco headquarters put together an online training program based on a dozen documents plus several videos that show company policies and operations. Newly hired employees at any location can review the documents and visit YouTube to watch the videos on their own. Then supervisors guide the employees as they begin their new jobs. In addition, the company gives all its employees access to databases containing answers to questions frequently asked by employees, so they can continue learning beyond the orientation period.[24]

Some people, however, are nervous about using a computer. A supervisor or other trainer must encourage and help these people. Also, some forms of computer-based instruction do not allow employees to work as a team, ask questions, or exchange ideas. When these training features are important, a supervisor should choose software that offers these capabilities, supplement the computer-based training, or select other training methods. It's also a good idea to keep an eye on how employees are using the computer-based training. For example, do they take advantage of all the features and complete assignments on their own, or do they need guidance or a modified learning method?

Experts offer the following advice for successfully implementing a computer-assisted training program:[25]

- Tell learners what they will be able to do after the training.
- Include rewards, such as money, time off, better working conditions, new tools and equipment, or career opportunities.
- Minimize noise and interruptions in the learning environment and maximize access, speed, and ease of use.
- "Chunk" instruction into segments of 20 minutes or less.
- Vary the media, including a variety of audio, video, and print materials as well as simulations and interactive tools.
- Give legitimate feedback.
- Remember to incorporate the human touch via chat rooms, e-mail, electronic office hours, audio streaming, or online mentoring.
- Reinforce learning with questionnaires or "alumni" chat sessions.

Role-Playing

role-playing
A training method in which roles are assigned to participants, who then act out the way they would handle a specific situation

To teach skills in working with other people, an organization may use **role-playing**. This method involves assigning roles to participants, who then act out the way they would handle a specific situation. Some of the exercises in this book use role-playing. A technique that enhances the usefulness of role-playing is to videotape the session and play it back so participants can see how they looked and sounded.

Role-playing gives people a chance to practice the way they react to others, making it especially useful for training in human relations skills such as communicating, resolving conflicts, and working with people of other races or cultures.[26] People who have acted out a particular role—for example, the role of supervisor—generally have more sympathy for that person's point of view. The major potential drawback of role-playing is that, to be most useful, it requires a trainer with expertise in conducting it.

Role-playing, like other kinds of training, now has online forms. Role-playing on the Internet may use games and simulations. The best ones are designed to closely mimic real-world challenges, and they engage the learner with their sophisticated graphics and plot lines. By training with simulation technologies, employees can practice how they would handle difficult situations, and if they make a mistake, the consequences to the company are minimal. For example, a call center employee can practice handling calls from angry (pretend) customers, and if the employee fails to soothe the customers, no accounts are actually lost. Oil companies use the virtual world of Second Life to create graphical images of oil platforms. Employees visit the virtual oil platforms to practice how they should respond if a fire breaks out.[27]

Basic Skills Training

An often-heard complaint among employers today is that it is increasingly difficult to find enough employees with the basic skills necessary to perform modern jobs. An increasing number of employers are responding to this problem by conducting their own training in basic skills. Organizations that offer such programs not only improve the skills of their workers but also attract and keep employees who are highly motivated. However, basic skills education offers some challenges to the employer. One is that employees may resist attending because they are embarrassed or afraid the organization will punish them if it finds out they do not have basic skills. To address this challenge, an organization should name the program carefully, calling it something like "workplace education" or "skills enhancement." Supervisors and other managers should reassure employees that participating in the program does not place their jobs in danger. In addition, experts recommend rewarding employees for participating in a basic skills program.

Certification Training

Another option for training and development is to outsource it to certifying organizations. In some industries, such as accounting, civil engineering, or securities and investments, individuals must obtain an appropriate license in order to practice, and these licenses are given on a competitive basis. However, an increasing number of organizations offer additional certifications that specify an individual as an expert in a given domain. For example, the Society for Human Resource Management (SHRM) is a global organization that certifies individuals as experts in human resource management practices. Like most of its counterparts, SHRM requires ongoing education to maintain one's certification. However, the possession of these certifications can help companies bolster their expertise in doing work, and also their image in the eyes of customers.

LO16.7 ▶ Describe how a supervisor can use coaching and mentoring to support training.

coaching
Guidance and instruction in how to do a job so that it satisfies performance goals

Coaching to Support Training

After employees have received training, a supervisor should take on the role of coach to help them maintain and use the skills they have acquired. **Coaching** is guidance and instruction in how to do a job so that it satisfies performance goals. The concept comes from sports, where a coach constantly observes team members in action, identifies each player's strengths and weaknesses, and works with each person to help him or her capitalize on strengths and improve on weaknesses. The most respected coaches generally encourage their team members and take a personal interest in them.

Just like sports coaches do with their players, supervisors should provide guidance, leadership, and feedback to their employees.

In a business context, coaching involves similar activities. As coach, a supervisor engages in regular observation, teaching, and encouragement to help employees develop so that they in turn can help the team succeed. Much of this coaching is done informally to back up the more formal training process.

In this role, a supervisor observes employees' performances daily and provides feedback. To encourage employees, a supervisor should praise them when they meet or exceed expectations. A supervisor should consider whether good performance is evidence that the employees can be given key responsibilities or have strengths that should be further developed. When an employee makes a mistake, the supervisor should work with the employee, focusing on the problem rather than any perceived deficiencies in the employee's character.

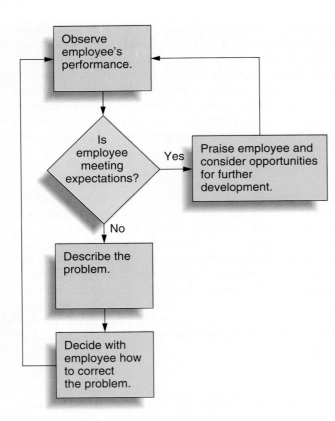

FIGURE 16.7 | The Coaching Process

Coaching is an ongoing process that, if done correctly, should aid in the continual improvement of employees.

mentoring
Providing guidance, advice, and encouragement through an ongoing one-on-one work relationship

Together, the supervisor and employee should decide how to correct the problem—perhaps through more training, a revised assignment, or more reliable access to resources. A supervisor and employee should work on only one problem at a time, with the supervisor continually looking for signs of employee progress. Figure 16.7 summarizes the process of coaching.

The process of coaching is different from simply telling employees what to do. It emphasizes learning about employees, then drawing on and developing their talents. (The Assessing Yourself quiz on page 480 can help you evaluate your coaching potential.) Acting as a coach is especially appropriate for supervisors in organizations that encourage employees to participate in decision making and teamwork.

Mentoring

In some cases, a supervisor may focus coaching efforts on one employee. This practice is called **mentoring,** or providing guidance, advice, and encouragement through an ongoing one-on-one work relationship. Mentoring seems to play an important role in employee retention, as "career mentoring . . . psychologically influences the employer's affection towards employees and their perceived costs of separation."[28] A supervisor should not use a mentoring relationship as an excuse for failure to encourage all employees in the work group. However, mentoring may be an appropriate way to support the training of an employee who has especially great potential, needs extra attention to contribute fully, or has been assigned to the supervisor for that purpose. Some organizations use mentoring of minority and female employees to help them learn to navigate in a setting where communication styles, values, expectations, and so on may differ from those with which they are familiar. As a supervisor, you, too, may have a mentor. For ideas to help you make the most of such a relationship, see the "Practical Advice for Supervisors" feature.

At Plante & Moran, a large accounting and management consulting firm based in Southfield, Michigan, new employees are assigned to two mentors. One is a partner who serves a traditional mentoring role, guiding the new employee in his or her career development. The other mentor, known as a buddy, serves a less formal role. The buddy is closer to the new employee in experience level and can help the new employee navigate day-to-day issues. With the support of these two mentors, new employees can explore their goals and options more fully. For example, when Carol Lamb realized that working as an auditor was unsatisfying, her mentor gave her a chance to try recruiting new employees at college campuses. Lamb eventually became campus recruiting manager for the firm. In general, starting out in an accounting or consulting career is intense and exhausting, but as in Lamb's case, mentors can help new employees stay on track—and, indeed, are keeping turnover of new employees well below the industry average.[29]

Some of the activities that mentors undertake include listening or acting as a sounding board, sharing knowledge and experience, guiding employees to discover the results of their own behavior, and sharing what they know about opportunities in the organization and its future direction. For example, Dan Boehm once saw that a young salesperson at the software company where they

PRACTICAL ADVICE FOR SUPERVISORS

WHAT TO DO WITH YOUR MENTOR

Finding a more experienced manager to act as your mentor can give your career a terrific boost. This person can spot your strengths, help you correct what's holding you back, and connect you to new and valuable opportunities. But to get the most out of a mentoring relationship, you need a positive, goal-oriented approach. The following tips will help you benefit from having a mentor.

- Request—and listen to—feedback. Whenever your mentor can watch you in action, whether in a meeting or on a sales call, ask him or her to evaluate your performance. If you hear something you do not like, avoid getting defensive, and try to understand how you can improve.
- Value your differences. If your mentor differs from you in terms of age, sex, disability status, race, personality, business function, or in other ways, use the difference as a

chance to broaden your horizons. Look for areas of common interest, but also try to appreciate the insights you can receive from a different perspective.

- Learn about your mentor. Invest in your relationship by researching your mentor's educational and professional background. With that information as a starting point, ask thoughtful questions.
- Set goals for your mentoring relationship. Agree how often you will meet, and define the areas of expertise where you are hoping for feedback. Look for ways you can also help your mentor.
- When you make a mistake, admit it. Then work with your mentor to figure out what you can learn from your mistake.

Source: Based on Yoji Cole, "How to Be Coachable and Get the Most from Your Mentor," *DiversityInc*, www.diversityinc.com, accessed May 21, 2008.

worked was having difficulty closing any sales. By observing and listening to the sales rep, Boehm concluded the young salesperson needed to shift the focus away from his own fears and frustrations and begin concentrating on clients' needs. Boehm coached the salesperson on how to explore each prospect's personality, objectives, and problems. He encouraged the salesperson to set achievable short-term goals. Eventually, the salesperson's confidence returned, and his performance improved.[30]

connect SELF-ASSESSMENT 16.1

Could You Coach Someone?

How comfortable will you be as a coach or mentor? This assessment can help you determine the level of your coaching skills and point out areas that you may need to work on.

LO16.8 ▶ Discuss how a supervisor can evaluate the effectiveness of training.

Evaluation of Training

A supervisor is often in the best position to determine whether training is working. The most basic way to evaluate training is to measure whether the training is resolving the problem. Are new employees learning their jobs? Is the defect rate falling? Do employees use the new computer system properly? Are customers now praising the service instead of complaining about it? Looking for answers to such questions is central to the control process, described in Chapter 6.

Other people, including the employees who have participated in the training, also can provide information to help evaluate training. They might fill out a questionnaire (see Figure on the following page), or the organization might set up a team of people to evaluate the organization's training methods and content.

FIGURE 16.8 |
Questionnaire for
Evaluating Training

Training evaluations can be
customized to fit the specific
type of training being
conducted. The results of
these evaluations can be used
to improve the training
program.

Title of Training _____

Date _____ **Trainer** _____

Instructions: Please respond to each question and return this questionnaire at the end of the
training session. Your responses are confidential.

	Strongly Agree	Agree	Neutral	Disagree	Strongly Disagree
1. The objectives of the training were clearly defined.	O	O	O	O	O
2. The training met the stated objectives.	O	O	O	O	O
3 The training met my expectations.					
4. The topics covered were relevant to me.	O	O	O	O	O
5. The training will be useful in my work.	O	O	O	O	O
6. The training facilities were adequate.	O	O	O	O	O
7. The trainer was well prepared.	O	O	O	O	O
8. The trainer was knowledgeable.	O	O	O	O	O
9. The training materials used were helpful.	O	O	O	O	O
10. The content was organized in a way that made it easy to follow.	O	O	O	O	O
11. There were ample opportunities for participation and interaction.	O	O	O	O	O
12. The time provided for this training was adequate.	O	O	O	O	O

13. What did you like most about this training? _____

_____

14. What did you like least about this training? _____

_____

15. How could this program be improved? _____

_____

_____

16. Do you have any other comments or suggestions? _____

_____

If the evaluation suggests that training is not meeting its objectives, the training
may have to be modified or expanded. The type of training may not be appropriate
for the training needs. For example, new employees who are having difficulty
learning job skills may not have enough opportunity to practice what they are being
taught. To identify what kinds of changes to make, the supervisor can ask questions
such as the following:

- Was the trainer well prepared?
- Did the trainer communicate the information clearly and in an interesting way?
- Did the training include visual demonstrations in addition to verbal descriptions
  of how to do the task?
- Were the employees well enough prepared for the training program?
- Did the employees understand how they would benefit from the training?

- Did employees have a chance to ask questions?
- Did the employees receive plenty of praise for their progress?

In contrast, when training is effective, employees and groups should be showing improvement and meeting performance targets. At Verizon Business, training for information technology (IT) employees combines online and classroom learning, with extra help provided to employees who fall behind. The program is a measurable success because the percentage of employees who pass their certification tests is above average for the industry. At the Beryl Companies, training of call center employees is evaluated in terms of participants' reactions, how much they learn, how well they transfer those lessons back to work, and whether their performance improves as a result. In this case, the trainers have measured improved levels of customer service and low employee turnover following regular training sessions.[31]

Whatever the outcome, training represents a cost to the organization. Consequently, it is worth conducting only when it leads to improved performance, as measured by increased quantity, quality, or both. Training that does not produce results should be changed or discontinued. In organizations in which supervisors and others are selective and use only training that meets evaluation criteria, training programs are not an expense but a valuable investment in the organization's human resources.

Skills Module

PART ONE: CONCEPTS

Summary

16.1 Summarize reasons for conducting an orientation for new employees.

The primary reason to conduct an orientation is that the sooner new employees know basic information related to their job, the sooner they can become productive. Orientation also reduces the nervousness and uncertainty of new employees, and it helps them develop a positive attitude by boosting job satisfaction.

16.2 Discuss how a supervisor and the human resources department can work together to conduct an orientation.

In a small organization, a supervisor may conduct most or all of the orientation. In a large organization, the human resources department may handle most of the task. In either case, it is up to the supervisor to convey information about the specifics of holding a particular job in a particular department. This includes explaining what the department does and what the new employee's job entails. Typically, the human resources department covers topics related to the organization's policies and procedures.

16.3 Identify methods for conducting an orientation.

During the orientation, a new employee should be introduced to the organization's employee handbook. A supervisor (or someone else) should give the employee a tour of the workplace, pointing out facilities the employee will need to use. During the tour, the employee should be introduced to the people with whom he or she will be working. A supervisor should instruct other employees in their role of welcoming a new employee. At the end of the first day and the first week, the supervisor should follow up to make sure the new employee understands the new job.

16.4 Describe the training cycle.

First, a supervisor (or someone else) assesses training needs. The next three steps cover planning the training: setting objectives, deciding who will participate, and choosing the training method. Then someone (a supervisor, an employee, or a professional trainer) conducts the training. The last step is to evaluate the success of the training. Evaluation sometimes suggests needs for additional training.

16.5 Explain how supervisors can decide when employees need training.

A supervisor may observe problems in the department that indicate a need for training. Areas of change may signal training needs. A supervisor may ask employees about the kinds of training they need or identify training needs when carrying out the planning function. Some training may be mandated by government regulations, union work rules, or company policy. Finally, retraining may be necessary if a worker's skills have atrophied, if customer needs change, or if an assessment of training needs identifies an area for improvement.

16.6 Define major types of training.

The organization may use on-the-job training, which involves learning while performing a job. Related training methods are apprenticeships and cross-training (that is, training employees in more than one job). The training also may take place off-site through vestibule training or in a classroom. Classroom training can be more effective when it includes computer-aided instruction (particularly interactive multimedia) and role-playing. Some computer-aided instruction involves simulations. In an organization in which employees lack basic skills, such as the ability to read directions or work with numbers, the organization may offer basic skills training. Finally, in some industries, licenses or certifications to attest to the fact that an individual is an expert in a particular field or in performing certain activities.

16.7 Describe how a supervisor can use coaching and mentoring to support training.

To help employees maintain and use the skills they have acquired, a supervisor takes on the role of coach, guiding and instructing employees in how to do a job so that it satisfies performance goals. The supervisor observes employee performance and provides feedback on it. Supervisor and employee work together to devise a solution to any problem. Then the supervisor reviews the employee's performance to make sure the employee understood what to do and is doing it. A supervisor may act as a mentor to an employee, providing guidance, advice, and encouragement through an ongoing one-on-one work relationship. Some organizations use mentoring of minority and female employees as a way to help them learn to navigate unfamiliar work situations.

16.8 Discuss how a supervisor can evaluate the effectiveness of training.

To evaluate training, a supervisor measures whether the problem addressed by the training is being solved. In addition, participants in the training may fill out a questionnaire in which they evaluate their experience. When training is not producing the desired results, a supervisor should attempt to find out why and then correct the problem.

Key Terms

training, *p. 454*
orientation, *p. 455*
employee handbook, *p. 459*
on-the-job training, *p. 465*

apprenticeship, *p. 465*
vestibule training, *p. 466*
interactive multimedia, *p. 469*
role-playing, *p. 470*

coaching, *p. 471*
mentoring, *p. 472*

Review and Discussion Questions

1. Describe a job or activity for which you received training. What was the purpose of this training?

2. Describe a situation in which you received an orientation. What did the orientation consist of? How was the orientation different from training?

3. When Al DeAngelis started his new job as a computer programmer, he arrived in his department at 9:30 a.m., after having spent time in the human resources department filling out forms. Marcia Eizenstadt, his supervisor, shook his hand and said, "Al, I'm so glad you're starting with us today. We need your talents tremendously." Then, explaining that she would be tied up all day in important planning meetings, Eizenstadt showed DeAngelis to his desk and gave him a slip of paper on which she had written the link to the company's online employee handbook. "Read this carefully," said Eizenstadt. "It'll tell you everything you need to know about working here. By tomorrow or the next day, I hope we'll be able to sit down and go over your first assignment." DeAngelis spent the rest of the day reading the manual, wishing for a cup of coffee, and trying to smile pleasantly in response to the quizzical looks he was getting from other employees passing by and glancing into his cubicle.

   a. What aspects of DeAngelis's orientation were helpful?

   b. How could it have been improved?

4. What are the steps in the training cycle?

5. Who determines when training is needed? What are some indications of a need for training?

6. Phil Petrakis supervises the housekeepers at a hotel in a big city. He has found that the easiest and fastest way to train his staff is to give them a memo describing whatever new policy or procedure he wants to teach. When the employees have read the memo, the training is complete—it is as simple as that. What is wrong with this approach?

7. Which type or types of training would you recommend in each of the following situations? Explain your choices.

   a. Teaching air traffic controllers how to help pilots land planes safely.

   b. Improving the decision-making skills of production workers so they can better participate in the company's employee involvement program.

   c. Teaching a plumber how to replace sewer lines.

   d. Teaching a receptionist how to operate the company's new telephone system.

8. At a department meeting, production supervisor Lenore Gibbs announced, "Starting next month, the company will be offering a class for any of you who can't read. It will take place after work in the cafeteria." How do you think employees with reading difficulties would react to Gibbs's announcement? How can she phrase the announcement so that employees will be more likely to attend the class?

9. What is coaching? Why is it especially appropriate in organizations that encourage employee involvement and teamwork?

10. What is a mentor? What steps might a mentor take to help a Japanese employee who has been transferred from the Tokyo office to company headquarters in the United States? How might these actions help the employee and the organization?

11. Think back to the training you described in question 1. Evaluate its effectiveness. In what ways might it have been improved?

Notes

1. For information about the effects of providing training opportunities for employees, see A. Dysvik and B. Kuvaas, 2008, "The relationship between perceived training opportunities, work motivation and employee outcomes," *International Journal of Training and Development*, 12, p. 138.

2. "2013 State of the Industry," Association for Talent Development Research, http://www.astd.org/Publications/Research-Reports/2013/~/link.aspx?_id=AAB5B551916342BCAC0FCE7DBE5D4EF6&_z=z, accessed May 21, 2014.

3. Rose A. Hazlett, "A Military Victory," *Minority Nurse*, www.minoritynurse.com/article/military-victory, accessed may 21, 2014.

4. For an article describing the importance of continued learning after an official orientation, see M. Akdere and S. Schmidt, 2007, "Measuring the effects of employee orientation training on employee perceptions of organizational culture: Implications for organization development," *The Business Review*, 8, p. 234.

5. Nancy S. Ahlrichs, *Manager of Choice: Five Competencies for Cultivating Top Talent* (Palo Alto, CA: Davies-Black Publishing, 2003), pp. 139–141.

6. Daniel Connolly, "Mentors Help Guide Nurses to Help Them Succeed, Stay in Profession," *Commercial Appeal (Memphis, Tenn.)*, October 16, 2008, http://www.commercialappeal.com/news/2008/oct/16/on-the-job-help/?print=1, accessed May 21, 2014.

7. John S. McClenahen, "The Next Crisis: Too Few Workers," *Industry Week*, December 21, 2004, http://www.industryweek.com/global-economy/next-crisis-too-few-workers, accessed May 21, 2014.

8. See, for example, Tiffany Potter and Nancy Heineke, "Professional Training: Adult Learning Theory Meets GIS," *GEO World*, July 2006, downloaded from Business & Company Resource Center, http://galenet.galegroup.com; and Morris Sims, "Keys to Effective Enterprise Learning," *National Underwriter Life & Health*, June 23, 2008, http://www.lifehealthpro.com/2008/06/22/keys-to-effective-enterprise-learning, accessed May 21, 2014.

9. Karl Albrecht, "Take Time for Effective Learning," *Training*, July 2004, http://ip-50-63-221-144.ip.secureserver.net/article/take-time-effective-learning, accessed May 21, 2014; Holly Dolezalek, "Pretending to Learn," *Training*, July–August 2003, http://ip-50-63-221-144.ip.secureserver.net/article/pretending-learn, accessed May 21, 2014.

10. Ladan Nikravan, "The Right Learning Culture Helps a Company Compete," *Chief Learning Officer*, December 14, 2011, http://clomedia.com/articles/the-right-learning-culture-helps-a-company-compete, accessed May 21, 2014.

11. Toby Marshall, "The Training Paradox—Train them and they're more valuable to me and my competitors!," http://ezinearticles.com/?The-Training-Paradox—Train-Them-and-Theyre-More-Valuable-to-Me-and-My-Competitors!&id=1503883, accessed May 21, 2014.

12. D. N. Aspin and J. D. Chapman, "Towards a philosophy of lifelong learning," *Second International Handbook of Lifelong Learning*, Springer Netherlands, 2012, pp. 3–35.

13. "Training Best Practices 2006," *Training*, March 2006, downloaded from Business & Company Resource Center, http://galenet.galegroup.com.

14. For an interesting examination of how on-the-job training affects job satisfaction, see Y. Georgellis and T. Lange, 2007, "Participation in continuous, on-the-job training and the impact on job satisfaction: Longitudinal evidence from the German labour market," *The International Journal of Human Resource Management*, 18, p. 969.

15. Danny Fugate, Dan Paul, and Susan Neumans Van Buren, "Moving beyond Show and Tell: An Improved Method to Train Apprentice Lineworkers," *Management Quarterly*, Fall 2010, pp. 26–35.

16. Chris Koepfer, "Integrating Machining Centers into the Work Flow," *Production Machining*, August 2006, pp. 34–38.

17. Jeff Griffin, "Unique Training Facility Provides Multiple Workforce Solutions," *Underground Construction*, November 2008, pp. 18, 20.

18. "2013 Training Industry Report," *Training*, November/December 2013, pp. 22–35, www.trainingmag.com/sites/default/files//2013_Training_Industry_Report.pdf, accessed May 22, 2014.

19. Jack Gordon, "Movin' 'Em Up, through Effective Training," *Sales & Marketing Management*, June 2006, downloaded from InfoTrac, http://web2.infotrac.galegroup.com.

20. "2013 Training Industry Report," p. 30.

21. Reena Jana, "On-the-Job Video Gaming," *BusinessWeek*, March 27, 2006, http://www.businessweek.com/stories/2006-03-26/on-the-job-video-gaming, accessed May 21, 2014.

22. Tammy Galvin, "2003 Industry Report: *Training Magazine*'s 22nd Annual Comprehensive Analysis of Employer-Sponsored Training in the United States," *Training*, October 2003, InfoTrac, http://web1.infotrac.galegroup.com.

23. See, for example, "Training Best Practices 2006."

24. Gwen Moran, "How to Make Employee Training a Winning Investment," *Entrepreneur*, November 3, 2011, http://www.entrepreneur.com/article/220569#, accessed May 21, 2014.

25. Jim Moshinskie, "Tips for Ensuring Effective E-Learning," *HR Focus*, August 2001, pp. 6–7.

26. For an article discussing the importance of role-playing in the medical industry, see Nikendei C, Zeuch A, Dieckmann P, Roth C, Schäfer S, Völkl M, Schellberg D, Herzog W, Jünger J. 2005, "Role-playing for more realistic technical skills training," *Medical Teacher*, 27, p. 122.

27. Dave Zielinski, "Training Games," *HR Magazine*, March 2010, pp. 64–66.

28. T. Chew and S. Wong, 2008, "Effects of career mentoring experience and perceived organizational support on employee commitment and intentions to leave: A study among hotel workers in Malaysia," *International Journal of Management*, 25, p. 692.

29. Jenny Cromie, "The Golden Rule Works for Plante & Moran," *Incentive*, July 7, 2008, http://www.incentivemag.com/Incentive-Programs/Articles/The-Golden-Rule-Works-for-Plante—Moran/, accessed May 21, 2014.

30. Betsy Cummings, "Coaching Clinic," *Sales & Marketing Management*, December 2003, downloaded from InfoTrac, http://web4.infotrac.galegroup.com.

31. Matt Bolch, "Taming Tech Training," *Training*, September 26, 2008, downloaded from Business & Company Resource Center, http://galenet.galegroup.com.

PART TWO: SKILL-BUILDING

Meeting the Challenge

Reflecting back on page 453 consider the challenges faced by Petco and other specialty stores. What actions did Petco take to overcome those challenges? In many industries, the turnover rate of employees is very high. High employee turnover means that managers must train new employees to fill positions sometimes multiple times a year. Would the same solutions that worked for Petco work at other companies facing stiff competition and high employee turnover rates?

Suppose that your group is a team of consultants who have been asked to create a training program that that will bring down a company's rate of employee turnover. The company might be a restaurant, hospital, airline, or other company facing competition. The company will try your ideas in one location first to see if they work. Review the training ideas in this chapter and then prepare a memo recommending a training program. Indicate why you think the program will improve turnover at the test location.

Problem-Solving Case: Training Call Center Employees

The employees in a call center need to be able to speak to customers politely, but their skill set is more complicated than etiquette. They also need to handle a range of questions and problems about particular products. Whenever their company adds a new line of products or services, the employees have to be prepared to answer a new set of questions. Thus, training is an ongoing concern in call centers. The traditional approach is to present new material in a classroom setting and supplement this learning with other training components.

For efficiency and flexibility, call center training often uses Web-based components. The most common form of these is called asynchronous Web-based training, a set of modules that each agent completes independently at his or her own computer by viewing the course content and then answering questions at his or her own pace. No live instructor is needed. Sometimes, the modules include a simulation in which the trainee handles calls from actors posing as customers with questions or problems related to the course content.

Some organizations can afford to customize their training programs to make them more engaging than reading text and answering multiple-choice questions. One such call center hired a training company called Resource Bridge to develop online training with the flavor of a video game. Modules for teaching courtesy and professionalism show animated videos of three agents taking a phone call. One agent has a stiff manner, another speaks in pleasant, conversational tones, and the third is extremely casual, addressing the caller as "hon." When trainees choose the style they think is most appropriate, the training video shows the customer's reaction, rather than just indicating whether the choice is correct. For example, the customer responds to being called "hon" by becoming annoyed at the familiarity. Trainees quickly realize that the approach is ineffective.

When supervisors monitor agents' calls, they can use the recordings to identify training opportunities. If the supervisor observes that an employee is having difficulty handling a particular type of problem or customer, the supervisor can send the employee a Web-based training module that addresses the situation. Envision Click2Coach is a software tool that lets the supervisor select video demonstrations of how to handle a type of problem. The supervisor can record a voice-over explanation of how the employee could have handled a problem more effectively. These and other training programs allow supervisors to select graphics, documents, and audio clips (including recordings of the calls the employee handled) for insertion into the training modules. This capability lets the supervisor efficiently coach individual employees while both remain at their desks.

Electronic coaching is easy and flexible, so supervisors need to be reminded of the importance of face-to-face communication with employees. Personal communication to offer encouragement is essential as a way to reinforce their use of the desired skills.

New employees or employees who have just learned a new set of skills may begin working in a "nesting area." They are seated together in an area of the call center where one or two supervisors are close at hand to provide assistance and answer questions. Also, experienced agents may be assigned to help employees in the nesting area. Placing them in this coaching role may make employees feel more at ease (it can be more comfortable to seek help from a peer rather than from a supervisor). At the same time, coaching others can reinforce the more experienced employees' knowledge and develops them to become supervisors in the future.

Another popular way to train agents is to assign them to a veteran employee who serves as a mentor. For example, if a supervisor at Georgia Power's call center determines that new agents have a weakness in a particular skill, the supervisor assigns those agents to experienced employees who excel in that skill. The agents and their mentors sit near one another so that the mentors are readily available to help. However, Paula Sacks, a Georgia Power supervisor, notes that mentors must be selected carefully. The mentors must be more than skillful at their jobs; they also must be good communicators who are willing to use part of their time for coaching.

1. Imagine that you are a supervisor in a call center, where you oversee 20 employees who handle questions and problems from people who buy your client's products—furniture that must be assembled using basic hand tools. Your client is preparing the launch of new products: rugs and other accessories. Now your agents must be prepared for a new set of issues, such as questions related to

fabrics and colors. Which of the methods described in this case will you use to prepare the agents for these changes? Why?

2. Prepare a training plan for your agents. Will you train them all at once or in groups? Which methods will you use first? Will you start the training before or during the product launch?

3. What, if anything, will you need to learn to prepare yourself for these changes? How will you develop your own skills?

Sources: Greg Levin, "The End of Agent Training as We Know It," *EE Times*, July 1, 2006, http://www.eetimes.com/document.asp?doc_id=1198048&page_number=2, accessed May 21, 2014; Kelli Gavant, "Resource Bridge Helps Companies Improve Training," (*Arlington Heights, IL.*) *Daily Herald*, April 19, 2006, downloaded from Business & Company Resource Center, http://galenet.galegroup.com.

Assessing Yourself

Could You Coach Someone?

This quiz is designed to evaluate your potential to act as a coach in support of training. Write True or False before each of the following statements.

_____ 1. The best way to get something done is to do it yourself.

_____ 2. If I give someone clear instructions, I know that person will get the job done without my checking on him or her.

_____ 3. I do not mind if someone asks me questions about how to do a job.

_____ 4. If I give someone instructions on how to perform a task, it is that individual's responsibility to complete it.

_____ 5. I like to let people know when they have done something right.

_____ 6. If someone makes a mistake, we focus on solving the problem together.

_____ 7. If someone makes a mistake, I correct the problem myself.

_____ 8. If someone does not follow company procedures, I assume he or she has not read the company handbook.

_____ 9. I think that interactive multimedia software is the best form of training for everyone.

_____ 10. Training a new employee should not last more than a week.

Scoring: True responses to statements 2, 5, and 6 show good potential for coaching. True responses to the other statements show that you need to become aware of the needs of individuals, then work on drawing on and emphasizing their talents.

Pause and Reflect

1. According to this quiz, how strong are your coaching skills?

2. How might you improve your coaching ability?

Class Skills Exercise

Being a Trainer

One or more students volunteer to teach the class a skill. If possible, the volunteers should have time to prepare their "training session" before the class meets. Some "trainers" might like to work as a team. Suggestions for skills to teach follow; use your creativity to add to the list:

- Folding paper hats.
- Doing a card trick.
- Communicating a message in sign language.
- Making punch for a party.

After the training session or sessions, the class discusses the following questions:

1. How can you evaluate whether this training was successful? If possible, try to conduct an evaluation of what the class learned. What do the results of this evaluation indicate?

2. What training techniques were used? Would additional or alternative techniques have made the skill easier to learn? What changes would have helped?

Building Supervision Skills

Orienting a New Team Member

Divide the class into teams of four or five. Select (or ask for a volunteer) one member of each team to play the role of a newcomer to the school (the newcomer might pose as a transfer student, a student from another country, or the like). The rest of the team will do its best to orient the newcomer to the school. Team members might want to take responsibility for different areas of knowledge; for example, one might draw a map of campus and town for the newcomer, pointing out bus routes and important or useful locations; another might volunteer information about study groups or social activities. At the end of the session, the newcomer should evaluate and discuss how effective the orientation was.

chapter seventeen | Appraising Performance

learning objectives

After you have studied this chapter, you should be able to:

17.1 Summarize the benefits of conducting performance appraisals.

17.2 Identify the steps in appraising performance systematically.

17.3 Discuss guidelines for avoiding discrimination in performance appraisals.

17.4 Compare types of appraisals.

17.5 Describe sources of bias in appraising performance.

17.6 Explain the purpose of conducting performance appraisal interviews.

17.7 Tell how supervisors should prepare for a performance appraisal interview.

17.8 Describe guidelines for conducting the interview.

A Supervision Challenge

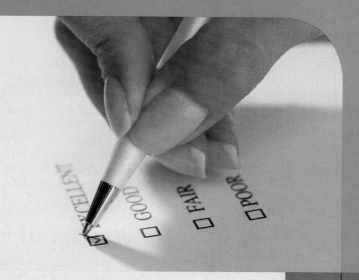

MAKING PERFORMANCE APPRAISALS MATTER AT ROCHESTER YMCA

Many companies have an annual ritual that is as regular as the New Year's Day holiday: Once a year, supervisors fill out a form rating each employee's performance and then invite the employee to a meeting to discuss it. Considering how widespread annual reviews have become, it is amazing how few people appreciate the effort. Recent surveys find that a majority of supervisors see little value in annual performance reviews, and a majority of employees say the effort has no impact on their performance.

Until recently, the situation was the same at the YMCA of Greater Rochester. This New York nonprofit had a rigid, one-sided process for reviewing performance. Fernan Cepero, the vice president of human resources, says people dreaded the reviews. Supervisors doubted that going over the ratings did anything to "help their employees with development and didn't provoke conversation." Employees agreed; in Cepero's words, they saw the reviews as "a check-in-the-box exercise where they felt they had no input." Something needed to change. What good could the reviews have been accomplishing if neither supervisors nor employees could see any benefit in them?

The YMCA's management concluded that the process would be more meaningful if it promoted conversations between supervisors and their employees about how the employees could succeed. If employees felt more involved in the review process, perhaps they would be able to see the benefit and actually value the opportunity to review the past year and look toward the upcoming year. After considering different ways to improve the approach, the organization chose to implement "Self Evaluations" where employees were asked to participate in the process by evaluating their own performance. The self-appraisals provide a chance for employees to describe situations in which they have performed well. Employees are also encouraged to identify areas in which they would like more training.

Under this new arrangement, supervisors do not go into the appraisal interview with ratings completed. Rather, they engage in a dialogue about the employee's accomplishments, areas for improvement, and training

goals. The review became a conversation. In the past, some employees may have felt that annual reviews were the time each year where their performance was simply "graded." Now, the review addresses other important topics beyond simple performance. For example, one YMCA Self Evaluation Form asks employees to explain how their supervisors could help them to obtain goals. Employees also list job responsibilities and whether they match their job descriptions.

Each prompt on the evaluation is a talking point rather than just an answer to submit. Both the employee and the supervisor have the opportunity to discuss strengths and weaknesses, goals, and expectations. This new approach also provides employees with more involvement in the review. They have time to prepare for the meeting and the opportunity to provide examples and explain their rationale.

Of course, this self-evaluation plan is not full-proof. There are instances where employees severely overrate (or underrate) themselves. But even these occurrences can be addressed and potentially remedied through a conversation.

As you study this chapter, think about how this change in performance appraisals at the YMCA might make them more effective. Also consider what new challenges the YMCA's supervisors faced when the appraisal process becomes less one-sided and more of a conversation.

Sources: Based on Adrienne Fox, "Curing What Ails Performance Reviews," *Society for Human Resource Management,* January 2009, http://www.shrm.org/publications/hrmagazine/editorialcontent/pages/0109fox.aspx, accessed May 7, 2014; "Ann Arbor YMCA Self Evaluation Form," *YMCA,* http://www.annarborymca.org/sites/default/files/pdf/staff/selfeval.pdf, accessed May 7, 2014.

performance appraisal
Formal feedback on how well an employee is performing his or her job

Formal feedback on how well an employee is performing on the job is known as a performance appraisal (or a performance review or performance evaluation). Most organizations require that supervisors conduct a performance appraisal of each of their employees regularly, typically once a year. Therefore, supervisors need to know how to appraise performance fairly.

This chapter discusses reasons for conducting performance appraisals and describes a process for appraising performances systematically. It describes various types of appraisals used by organizations today. It also tells how to avoid biases and how to conduct an appraisal interview.

LO17.1 ▶ Summarize the benefits of conducting performance appraisals.

Purposes of Performance Appraisal

Performance appraisals provide the information needed by employees to improve the quality of their work. To improve, employees need to hear how they are doing. As described in Chapters 7 and 10, a supervisor should provide frequent feedback. Performance appraisals supplement this informal information with a more thought-out, formal evaluation. (Employees who get enough informal feedback probably will not be surprised by the results of the appraisal.) A formal performance appraisal ensures that feedback to an employee covers all important aspects of the employee's performance.

On the basis of this information, the employee and supervisor can plan how to improve weak areas. In this way, performance appraisals support the practice of coaching, described in Chapter 16. For instance, Harriet Cohen, a Ventura, California, consultant, advises her clients to include personalized goals that match up with each employee's ambitions. So if a supervisor has an employee who hopes to move into management someday, the appraisal could include progress on goals related to handling greater responsibility. For another employee with different ambitions, the coaching could focus on becoming an expert at a particular activity.[1]

An appraisal also can help motivate employees. Most people appreciate the time their supervisor spends discussing their work, as well as praise for good performance; just hearing the supervisor's viewpoint can be motivating. Steve Miranda, chief human resource and strategic planning officer at the Society for Human Resource Management, says that after an effective appraisal, employees "feel energized that the boss appreciates their strengths, values their contribution, and sees their potential."[2] Employees also tend to put forth the greatest effort in the areas that get appraised. Therefore, by rating employees on the kinds of behavior it considers important, an organization encourages them to try hard in those areas and keeps skilled workers in the firm. At Johnson & Johnson, feedback includes information on how team accomplishments support the division's and company's progress toward overall goals. This approach emphasizes teamwork and develops a feeling among employees that their efforts really matter.[3]

Above all, supervisors should remember that performance appraisals are part of the ongoing control process. Understandably, supervisors feel uncomfortable bringing up their employees' shortcomings, but when they let their discomfort rule, they are missing out on this important opportunity to identify and correct problems. Peter Talibart of the law firm Norton Rose suggests thinking of this responsibility as similar to getting your car's engine tuned up; appraisals are a chance to keep the workplace moving smoothly and efficiently.[4] When McKesson Corporation determined that it wanted its call center employees to develop specific skills, the company had the agents and their mentors complete appraisals rating their skill level in each area. For each area in which an employee needed to improve, the employee created a personal development plan, and the company allowed six months for the employee to reach an acceptable level of skill. Some agents initially resisted, but as they saw that the process was fair and encouraged them to develop, they became motivated.[5]

Finally, performance appraisals provide important records for the organization. They are a useful source of information when deciding on raises, promotions, and discipline, and they provide evidence that these appraisals were administered fairly. A performance appraisal also provides documentation on employees whose behavior or performance is a problem. (For more on supervising problem employees, see Chapter 12.)

LO17.2 ▸ Identify the steps in appraising performance systematically.

A Systematic Approach to Appraising Performance

To deliver their potential benefits, appraisals must be completely fair and accurate. Supervisors therefore should be systematic in appraising performance. They should follow a thorough process, use objective measures when possible, and avoid discrimination.

The Appraisal Process

The appraisal process takes place in four steps, as illustrated in Figure 17.1. A supervisor establishes and communicates expectations for performance and standards for measuring performance. A supervisor also observes individual performance and measures it against the standards. On the basis of this information, the supervisor reinforces performance or provides remedies.

Establish and Communicate Expectations for Performance

During the planning process, a supervisor determines what the department or work group should accomplish (see Chapter 6). Through action plans, a supervisor spells out who is to do what to accomplish those objectives. From this information, it is relatively easy to specify what each employee must do to help the department or work group meet its objectives. One approach is to list the three to five major responsibilities of each position; the appraisal then focuses on these responsibilities.

For example, suppose Francine Bloch supervises the delivery personnel for a chain of appliance stores in Dallas. Each driver is expected to operate the vehicle safely, deliver every appliance without damaging anything, and be polite to customers.

A supervisor must make sure employees know and understand what is expected of them. To do this, the supervisor should make sure that objectives for the employees are clear, and he or she should communicate them effectively (see Chapter 10). Employees are most likely to understand and be committed to objectives when they have a say in developing them. More and more firms now require that supervisors and employees together set mutually acceptable performance goals.

FIGURE 17.1 | The Process of Performance Appraisal

Rather than a single, short-term event, a performance appraisal is actually a series of steps.

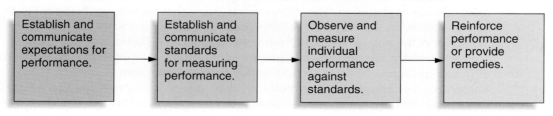

| Establish and communicate expectations for performance. | → | Establish and communicate standards for measuring performance. | → | Observe and measure individual performance against standards. | → | Reinforce performance or provide remedies. |

Establish and Communicate Standards for Measuring Performance

Because expectations for performance are objectives, each expectation should be measurable (see Chapter 6). In appraising performance, a supervisor's task includes deciding how to measure employees' performance and then making sure employees know what will be measured. For instance, if the supervisor is looking for effective teamwork, this performance might be defined in terms of attendance (on time) at team meetings, ideas offered to meet the team's challenges, and communication to the team about the progress the person is making on team assignments.[6] With Bloch's employees, the standards would include delivering all appliances without damage, having zero accidents or traffic tickets, and receiving no complaints from customers about service.

Observe and Measure Individual Performance against Standards

Through the control process, a supervisor should continuously gather information about each employee's performance. This is an ongoing activity, not something the supervisor saves to do when filling out appraisal forms. Ways to gather information include keeping regular performance records (such as a work team's output or the customer calls handled by each employee), saving customer notes of complaint or praise, writing a summary whenever an employee is observed doing something exceptional, and encouraging employees to keep track of their accomplishments. This record keeping may seem time-consuming, but it is essential. Some companies ease the burden by installing performance appraisal software. At New Balance Athletic Shoe, appraisals are automated using software called eAppraisal. Supervisors enter each employee's goals into the system, along with measurement data related to achievement of the goals. Employees can use the software to look up their progress toward their goals at any time. They also can enter information about their own accomplishments, so supervisors can refer to those examples when preparing appraisal reports.[7]

When preparing a performance appraisal, a supervisor compares the performance information with the standards for the employee being appraised. In the example, Bloch would keep records of completed and uncompleted deliveries, damage, accidents, traffic tickets, and customer complaints (and compliments). When appraising a particular employee's performance, she can see how often each type of problem (or success) arose with the employee.

Reinforce Performance or Provide Remedies

To keep employees motivated and informed, a supervisor needs to tell them when they are doing something right, not just when they are making a mistake. Thus, the final step of the appraisal process includes reinforcement for good performance. This can be as simple as pointing out to employees where they have performed well. For example, Bloch might compliment one of the drivers on a letter of praise from a customer. A supervisor might want to comment that this information will be placed in the employee's permanent record with the organization.

Where performance falls short of standards, an employee needs to know how to improve. A supervisor may state a remedy, but asking the employee to help solve the problem is often more effective. In the case of a driver who has received two traffic tickets for illegal left turns, Bloch might point out this situation and ask the driver for an explanation. The driver might reply that he was confused because he was lost. With that information, Bloch and the driver can work together to get the driver better acquainted with finding his way around Dallas.

Bloch and the driver thus are treating the underlying problem (the driver's difficulty in finding his way around) rather than the symptom (the traffic tickets). Therefore, the driver's performance in this area can improve in the future. In general, to move beyond discussing symptoms to uncover the underlying problems, a supervisor and employee can ask which of the following kinds of causes led to the poor performance:

- *Inadequate skills*—If the problem is the employee's lack of certain skills, a supervisor should see that the employee gets the necessary training, as described in the previous chapter.
- *Lack of effort*—If the problem is a lack of effort on the employee's part, a supervisor may need to apply the principles of motivation discussed in Chapter 11.
- *Shortcomings of the process*—If organizational or job-related policies and procedures reward inefficient or less-than-high-quality behavior, the supervisor and employee may be able to change the way work is done.
- *External conditions*—If the problem is something beyond the control of supervisor and employee (for example, a poor economy, lack of cooperation from another department, a strike by suppliers), the appraisal standards and ratings should be adjusted so that they are fair to the employee.
- *Personal problems*—If performance is suffering because the employee has personal problems, a supervisor should handle the situation with counseling and discipline (see Chapter 12).

In investigating the underlying problem, a supervisor may gain important insights by asking what can be done to help the employee reach goals. Before the appraisal is over, an employee should have a clear plan for making necessary changes.

Of course, when performance problems are occurring, supervisors should not wait months or a year to talk to employees about the problems. Many companies require a performance appraisal of each employee once a year, but supervisors should see that requirement as just a starting point. The appraisal process can—and should—be taking place throughout the year with frequent communication about goals and performance. The "Supervision: New Trends" feature describes how social-media applications are making it easier for employees to receive frequent feedback.

What to Measure in an Appraisal

Waitress Kelly O'Hara was furious as she walked out of her performance appraisal interview. "Irresponsible!" she muttered to herself, "Lazy! Who does he think he is, calling me those things? He doesn't know what he's talking about." O'Hara's reaction shows that labeling people with certain characteristics is not a constructive approach to conducting an appraisal. Labels tend to put people on the defensive, and they are difficult, if not impossible, to prove.

Instead, a performance appraisal should focus on *behavior* and *results*. Focusing on behavior means that the appraisal should describe specific actions or patterns of actions. Focusing on results means describing the extent to which an employee has satisfied the objectives for which he or she is responsible. If O'Hara's supervisor had noted that he had received several complaints about slow service, he and O'Hara could have worked on a plan to minimize these complaints. Perhaps the problem was not even O'Hara's behavior but recurrent backlogs in the kitchen. The focus on meeting objectives would be more constructive than simply evaluating O'Hara as "lazy," because it tells an employee exactly what is expected. This focus is also fairer, especially if the employee helped to set the objectives. Figure 17.2 summarizes qualities of performance appraisal measures that motivate employees to meet objectives.

☺ Objective
☺ Job-related
☺ Based on behaviors
☺ Within employee's control
☺ Related to specific tasks
☺ Communicated to employee

FIGURE 17.2 | Qualities of Effective Performance Appraisal Measures

If the performance appraisal measures are effective, they will motivate employees, not discourage them.

Source: Susan M. Heathfield, "Take Those Numeric Ratings and . . .," About.com, http://humanresources.about.com/od/perfmeasurement/a/numericratings.htm, October 14, 2004.

SUPERVISION: NEW TRENDS

PERFORMANCE APPRAISAL, SOCIAL-MEDIA STYLE

More and more adults today are used to sharing their experiences and opinions with their social networks online. Adults routinely turn to social media to declare political opinions and see what their friends did over the weekend, or they post reviews of restaurants they visited or videogames they tried. Seeing how easy these applications make the sharing of views, some companies are applying social-media tools, such as LinkedIn, Twitter, and Facebook, to their performance appraisal processes. Such social-media tools enable organizations to receive employee performance feedback from a broad range of respondents, including peers, customers, supervisors, and subordinates. The key idea behind these tools is that ratings of performance are not always accurate because of organizational politics, relationships, and other social dynamics within a given workplace. Thus, performance appraisal via social media can help provide a forum in which to gain arguably more honest assessments.

Another advantage of social media for performance evaluation is that feedback can be gained on an ongoing basis, allowing employees to recalibrate their efforts if a deficiency is noted. Generally, performance appraisal via social media is less of a structured process with steps and deadlines, and more of an ongoing stream of informal feedback. Employees at all levels of the organization can post a request for feedback on how they are handling an assignment. That feedback can come from anyone who participates in the network, and depending on the system, it may be anonymous. For example, in organizations using an application called Ripple, managers can "like" tasks their employees have performed. Employees and their supervisors also can request and receive feedback by making wall posts or sending private messages.

A third advantage of social-media-style feedback is its speed and relative ease of delivery. It also can be targeted to particular projects or situations. Supervisors—and also an employee's colleagues—can post praise, appreciation, and concerns when they experience notable performance, rather than having to recall examples at review time. When the feedback is anonymous, the reviewers may also be blunter and less polite. Such feedback is more uncomfortable to receive, but it also may uncover important issues that employees might not be aware of otherwise. One way supervisors can encourage helpful feedback is simply to ask, "What specific thing can I do to be more effective?"

Because they are so informal and immediate, social-media applications function well as an add-on to more traditional systems for performance appraisal, and should not be used as a "stand-alone" mechanism for appraising an employee's performance. A supervisor in an organization that uses social media in this way can coach and motivate with social media while gathering information for the more formal process of a scheduled performance appraisal.

Of course, there are downsides to using social media for performance appraisal. First, because anonymity protects appraisers from identification, responses may be less filtered and polite. This can create irreconcilable conflict within the workplace. Furthermore, systems can be used in a malicious way by employees to "get back" at disliked employees or in an effort to sabotage projects. Finally, because of the anonymity inherent in many of these systems, there is no way to follow up with respondents regarding unclear or ambiguous evaluations.

Social media can be a powerful tool for performance appraisal. However, like more traditional mechanisms of evaluation, it must be carefully managed to maximize its positive impact.

Sources: Pat Galagan, "Ready or Not?" *T+D*, May 2010, pp. 29–31; Narendra Patil, "Tell Me about Me," *Talent Management*, August 2011, pp. 16–17, 21; Laurie Chamberlain, "Does Your Performance Management Need a Tune-Up?" *Strategic Finance*, November 2011, pp. 18, 20, 61; Jenny Hill, "Could social media revolutionise the performance appraisal process?," *HRMagazine*, May 22, 2012, http://www.hrmagazine.co.uk/hro/features/1073216/could-social-media-revolutionise-performance-appraisal-process, accessed May 22, 2014.

In many cases, a supervisor uses an appraisal form that requires drawing conclusions about the employee's personal characteristics. For example, a supervisor might need to rate an employee's dependability or attitude. Although such ratings are necessarily subjective, a supervisor can try to base them on observations about behavior and results. One approach is to record at least one specific example for each category rated. A rating on a personal characteristic seems more reasonable when a supervisor has evidence supporting his or her conclusion.

LO17.3 ▶ Discuss guidelines for avoiding discrimination in performance appraisals.

EEOC Guidelines

As described in Chapter 15, the Equal Employment Opportunity Commission (EEOC) is the government agency charged with enforcing federal laws against discrimination. The EEOC published the Uniform Guidelines on Employee Selection Procedures, which include guidelines for designing and implementing performance appraisals. In general, the behaviors or characteristics measured by a performance appraisal should be related to the job and to succeeding on the job. For example, if the appraisal measures "grooming," then good grooming should be important for success in the job. Because of this requirement, a supervisor and others responsible for the content of performance appraisals should make sure that what they measure is still relevant to a particular job.

Just as hiring should be based on a candidate's ability to perform the essential tasks of a particular job, so appraisals should be based on the employee's success in carrying out those tasks. The ratings in a performance appraisal should not be discriminatory; that is, they should not be based on an employee's race, sex, or other protected category but on an employee's ability to meet standards of performance. Furthermore, an employee should know in advance what those standards are, and the organization should have a system in place for employees to ask questions about their ratings.

Performance Appraisals and Pay Reviews

Many organizations review an employee's wage or salary level at the time of the performance appraisal. This reinforces the link the company makes between performance and pay increases. An employee with an excellent rating would be eligible to receive the largest allowable increase, whereas someone rated as a poor worker might not get any raise or only a cost-of-living increase.

However, reviewing pay and performance at the same time presents a potentially serious drawback. Employees may focus on the issue of money, so a supervisor has more difficulty using the performance evaluation as an opportunity for motivating and coaching. A majority of companies (68 percent in a recent study by Development Dimensions International) direct their managers to separate performance appraisals from discussions of pay.[8] In those organizations, a supervisor can more readily keep the appraisal focused on the employee's performance. At other organizations, a supervisor who must review pay rates at the same time as performance should make an extra effort to emphasize performance, and it is especially important to provide coaching and feedback about performance throughout the year.

LO17.4 ▶ Compare types of appraisals.

Types of Appraisals

Many techniques have been developed for appraising performance. The human resources department or higher-level management usually dictates which type the supervisor will use. An organization that has all supervisors use the same approach establishes a way to keep records showing performance over time, especially when an employee reports to more than one supervisor during his or her employment. Although a supervisor has to use the appraisal format selected for the whole organization, he or she may be able to supplement it with other helpful information. A supervisor can use the "Comments" section of a preprinted form or attach additional information to it.

Graphic Rating Scales

graphic rating scale
A performance appraisal that rates the degree to which an employee has achieved various characteristics

The most commonly used type of appraisal is the **graphic rating scale**, which rates the degree to which an employee has achieved various characteristics, such as job knowledge or punctuality. The rating is often scored from 1 to 5, for example, with 5 representing excellent performance and 1 representing poor performance. Some appraisal forms include space for comments, so that a supervisor can provide

FIGURE 17.3 | Typical Graphic Rating Scale

A graphic rating scale is relatively easy to use and provides scores that can measure improvement from year to year.

Name _____	Department _____			Date _____
	Outstanding	**Good**	**Satisfactory**	**Fair**	**Unsatisfactory**
Quantity of work Volume of acceptable work under normal conditions Comments:	☐	☐	☐	☐	☐
Quality of work Thoroughness, neatness, and accuracy of work Comments:	☐	☐	☐	☐	☐
Knowledge of job Clear understanding of the facts or factors pertinent to the job Comments:	☐	☐	☐	☐	☐
Personal qualities Personality, appearance, sociability, leadership, integrity Comments:	☐	☐	☐	☐	☐
Cooperation Ability and willingness to work with associates, supervisors, and subordinates toward common goals Comments:	☐	☐	☐	☐	☐
Dependability Conscientious, thorough, accurate, reliable with respect to attendance, lunch periods, reliefs, etc. Comments:	☐	☐	☐	☐	☐
Initiative Earnestness in seeking increased responsibilities; self-starting, unafraid to proceed alone Comments:	☐	☐	☐	☐	☐

support for his or her ratings. Figure 17.3 is a sample appraisal form using a graphic rating scale.

The main advantage of a graphic rating scale is that it is relatively easy to use. In addition, the scores provide a basis for deciding whether an employee has improved in various areas. However, the ratings themselves are subjective; what one supervisor considers "excellent" may be only "average" to another. Also, many supervisors tend to rate everyone at least a little above average. Some appraisal forms attempt to overcome these problems by containing descriptions of excellent or poor behavior in each area. Other rating scales pose a different problem by labeling performance in terms of how well an employee "meets requirements." Presumably, the supervisor wants *all* employees to meet the requirements of the job, but if the scale rates everyone at the top, it is less useful for coaching and rewarding employees. Microsoft tries to address these problems by requiring that only a small percentage of each supervisor's employees be given a rating of "outstanding" in terms of meeting their goals. This requirement forces the supervisor to rate some employees lower than others. In contrast, the City of Fort Worth Equipment Services Department decided its rankings would be based on the collection of hard data, such as the time an employee takes to complete particular repairs. The information about time spent on each project is compared against industry standards to see whether the employee is more or less productive than those standards. The data show whether the employee should be rated a five or something less on the agency's five-point scale.[9]

Paired-Comparison Approach

paired-comparison approach
A performance appraisal that measures the relative performance of employees in a group

The **paired-comparison approach** measures the relative performance of employees in a group. A supervisor lists the employees in the group and then ranks them. One method is to compare the performance of the first two employees on the list. A supervisor places a check mark next to the name of the employee whose performance is better, then repeats the process, comparing the first employee's performance with that of other employees. Next, the supervisor compares the second employee on the list with all the others, and so on until each pair of employees has been compared. The employee with the most check marks is considered the most valuable.

A supervisor also can compare employees in terms of several criteria, such as work quantity and quality. For each criterion, a supervisor ranks the employees from best to worst, assigning a 1 to the lowest-ranked employee and the highest score to the best employee in that category. Then all the scores for each employee are totaled to see who has the highest total score.

The paired-comparison approach is appropriate when a supervisor needs to find one outstanding employee in a group. It can be used to identify the best candidate for a promotion or special assignment. However, paired comparisons make some employees look good at the expense of others, which can make it ineffective for motivating team performance or coaching employees. In recent years, more companies have used paired comparisons as a way to help them reduce their workforce. These

Ranking employees based on success, much the same way that sports have winners and losers, is an appraisal approach that has been both criticized and applauded.

companies must weigh the advantages of identifying the least productive workers against the possible harm to morale and teamwork among the remaining employees.[10]

In recent years, business experts have debated the benefits of appraisal methods that rank employees. One of the chief advocates is former GE chief executive, Jack Welch. According to Welch, "differentiation is based on the principle that the team with the best players wins."[11] In this view, constantly identifying the team's worst performers—even if they perform better than employees at other organizations—and removing them frees up the company to keep bringing in the best. Rather than being unkind or unfair, Welch insists, this approach motivates workers because it is open and honest. Critics, however, complain that the philosophy behind this kind of ranking runs counter to the teamwork an organization is trying to promote. If the goal is for everyone to work together so the whole organization wins, then it hurts the organization to follow a system in which some people will be losers. That approach, critics argue, will promote conflict and destructive competition within the team.

Forced-Choice Approach

forced-choice approach
A performance appraisal that presents an appraiser with sets of statements describing employee behavior; the appraiser must choose which statement is most characteristic of the employee and which is least characteristic

In the forced-choice approach, the appraisal form gives a supervisor sets of statements describing employee behavior. For each set of statements, a supervisor must choose one that is most characteristic and one that is least characteristic of the employee. Figure 17.4 illustrates part of an appraisal form using the forced-choice approach.

These questionnaires tend to be set up in a way that prevents a supervisor from saying only positive things about employees. Thus, the forced-choice approach is used when an organization determines that supervisors have been rating an unbelievably high proportion of employees as above average.

Essay Appraisal

Sometimes a supervisor must write a description of the employee's performance, answering questions such as "What are the major strengths of this employee?" or "In what areas does this employee need improvement?" Essay appraisals often are used along with other types of appraisals, notably graphic rating scales. They provide an opportunity for a supervisor to describe aspects of performance that are not thoroughly covered by an appraisal questionnaire. The main drawback of essay appraisals is that their quality depends on a supervisor's writing skills.

Behaviorally Anchored Rating Scales (BARS)

behaviorally anchored rating scales (BARS)
A performance appraisal in which an employee is rated on scales containing statements describing performance in several areas

Some organizations pay behavioral scientists or organizational psychologists to create behaviorally anchored rating scales (BARS). These scales rate employee

FIGURE 17.4 | Forced-Choice Items

The forced-choice approach prevents a supervisor from saying only positive things about employees.

Instructions: Rank from 1 to 4 the following sets of statements according to how they describe the manner in which _____

(name of employee)

performs the job. A rank of 1 should be used for the most descriptive statement, and a rank of 4 should be given for the least descriptive. No ties are allowed.

_____	Does not anticipate difficulties
_____	Grasps explanations quickly
_____	Rarely wastes time
_____	Easy to talk to
_____	A leader in group activities
_____	Wastes time on unimportant things
_____	Cool and calm at all times
_____	Hard worker

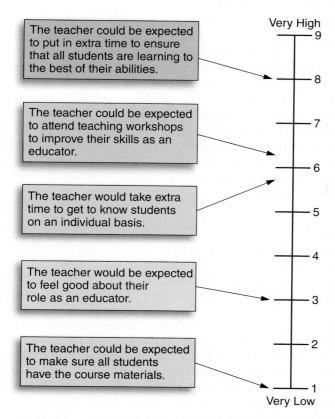

The teacher could be expected to put in extra time to ensure that all students are learning to the best of their abilities.

The teacher could be expected to attend teaching workshops to improve their skills as an educator.

The teacher would take extra time to get to know students on an individual basis.

The teacher would be expected to feel good about their role as an educator.

The teacher could be expected to make sure all students have the course materials.

Very High
9
8
7
6
5
4
3
2
1
Very Low

FIGURE 17.5 | A Behaviorally Anchored Rating Scale for Nurses

Behaviorally anchored rating scales rate employee performance using a series of statements that describe the range of performance from ineffective to effective. The advantage of this performance rating system is that it can be tailored to specific jobs and specific organizations.

performance in several areas, such as work quantity and quality, using a series of statements that describe effective and ineffective performance in each area. In each area, a supervisor selects the statement that best describes how an employee performs.[12] The statements in the rating scales are different for each job title in the organization. Figure 17.5 shows a behaviorally anchored rating scale measuring the performance area of teaching competence.

The major advantage of using BARS is that they can be tailored to the organization's objectives for employees. In addition, the BARS approach is less subjective than some other approaches because it uses statements describing behavior. However, developing the scales is time consuming and therefore relatively expensive.

Checklist Appraisal

A checklist appraisal contains a series of questions about an employee's performance. Figure 17.6 shows the format for this kind of appraisal. A supervisor answers yes or no to the questions. Thus, a checklist is merely a record of performance, not an evaluation by a supervisor. The human resources department has a key for scoring the items on the checklist; the score results in a rating of an employee's performance.

Although the checklist appraisal is easy to complete, it has several disadvantages. The checklist can be difficult to prepare, and each job category will probably require a different set of questions. Also, a supervisor has no way to adjust the answers for any special circumstances that affect performance.

Critical-Incident Appraisal

critical-incident appraisal
A performance appraisal in which a supervisor keeps a written record of incidents that show positive and negative ways an employee has acted; the supervisor uses this record to assess the employee's performance

To conduct a **critical-incident appraisal,** a supervisor keeps a written record of incidents that show positive and negative ways an employee has acted. The record should include dates, people involved, actions taken, and any other relevant details. At the time of the appraisal, a supervisor reviews the record to reach an overall evaluation of an employee's behavior. During the appraisal interview, a supervisor should give an employee a chance to offer his or her views of each incident recorded.

FIGURE 17.6 | Sample Checklist Appraisal

A checklist appraisal allows a supervisor to record performance but does not allow for any evaluation.

	Yes	No
1. Does the employee understand and meet the requirements of their job description?		
2. Did the employee meet his/her goals for the current review period?	___	___
3. Does the employee follow work rules and procedures?	___	___
4. Has the company received any positive feedback from customers concerning this employee?		
5. Has the company received any negative feedback from customers concerning this employee?	___	___
6. Does the employee work well with others when completing projects?	___	___

This technique has the advantage of focusing on actual behaviors. However, keeping records of critical incidents can be time consuming, and even if a supervisor is diligent, important incidents could be overlooked. Also, supervisors tend to record negative events more than positive ones, resulting in an overly harsh appraisal. A diligent supervisor can, however, use critical-incident appraisals as a tool for motivating and developing employees. For example, as an adviser to plumbing and mechanical contractors, Paul Ridilla has found that companies can improve performance by identifying and recording the kinds of behavior that add value to the organization: suggesting innovations, working extra hours, training co-workers, and providing the superior service that leads customers to send thank-you notes. Ridilla advises that supervisors keep track of these and other positive behaviors—and recognize and reward them.[13]

Work-Standards Approach

work-standards approach

A performance appraisal in which an appraiser compares an employee's performance with objective measures of what the employee should do

To use the work-standards approach, a supervisor tries to establish objective measures of performance. A typical work standard would be the quantity produced by an assembly-line worker. This amount should reflect what a person normally could produce. A supervisor then compares an employee's actual performance with the standards.

Although the work-standards approach has been applied largely to production workers, the principle of objectively measuring outcomes makes sense for a variety of jobs. Work standards are one of the tools that Bank of Newport uses to appraise its tellers' performance. The Rhode Island bank uses "mystery shoppers," who visit each branch once a month. The mystery shoppers observe and record specific behaviors, including whether the employees make eye contact, use the customer's name, and thank them for their business. According to Robert E. Maddock, an executive with Bank of Newport, tellers initially disliked having their behavior recorded in this way, but they appreciated the system more when they saw that they would be recognized for meeting the standards.[14]

Management by Objectives (MBO)

Chapter 6 introduced management by objectives (MBO) as a planning tool. In an organization that uses MBO, a supervisor will also use this approach for appraising performance. A supervisor compares each employee's accomplishments with the objectives for that employee. If the employee has met or exceeded his or her objectives, the appraisal will be favorable. The main advantages of this system are that an employee knows what is expected and a supervisor focuses on results rather than more subjective criteria.

Computer systems can readily link a variety of departmental performance measures, such as sales or production levels or customer satisfaction surveys, to performance appraisals. This makes the use of MBO even more practical for today's organizations. In New York, the North Shore–LIJ Health System switched from a paper-based system of performance appraisal to a computer-based system. The older system had required supervisors to fill out 10-page forms asking them to rate each employee on subjective factors such as "leadership" and "respectfulness." The new system ties ratings to achievement of measurable goals. Maria Giraldo, nurse manager in the intensive-care unit of one of the system's hospitals, appreciates the clarity about what is expected of her. Appraisal interviews can move beyond deciding whether she did a good job to more helpful conversations about how to keep improving. Giraldo and other supervisors and employees can get the most out of an MBO-based appraisal system by actively participating when objectives are set and regularly reviewing the objectives with their supervisor to ensure they are still relevant and up-to-date.[15]

Assessments by Someone Other Than the Supervisor

Supervisors cannot know how an employee behaves at all times or in all situations. Nor can supervisors always appreciate the full impact of an employee's behavior on people inside and outside the organization. To supplement what supervisors do know, other people might offer insights into an employee's behavior. For this reason, supervisors may combine their appraisals with self-assessments by the employee or appraisals by peers and customers. Appraisals of supervisors and other managers also may come from their subordinates. Combining several sources of appraisals is called **360-degree feedback**.[16] A recent survey found that about one out of five organizations were using some form of 360-degree feedback, including appraisal information from customers or peers.[17]

Several police departments have improved the performance of their officers by using 360-degree feedback as the basis of coaching.[18] These departments use computer systems into which supervisors, the officers themselves, and others who worked with the officers enter evaluations of how well they handled specific incidents or their jobs over a period of time. The officers' supervisors review the ratings and discuss with the employees how to bring the ratings higher. Knowing that others are watching their performance, the employees focus on the behaviors that will make a difference, and then their ratings generally improve.[19]

To use self-assessments, a supervisor can ask each employee to complete an assessment before the appraisal interview. Then the supervisor and employee compare the employee's evaluation of his or her own behavior with the supervisor's evaluation. This can stimulate discussion and insights in areas where the two are in disagreement. At the IKEA chain of home furnishing stores, self-assessment is not just an appraisal tool but also part of a commitment to helping employees develop and earn promotions. Employees complete a self-assessment process that helps them identify their strengths. With their supervisors, the employees review the results of the self-assessment and prepare a plan for achieving their career goals within the company.[20] Supervisors also can use the concept of a self-appraisal to advance in their own careers. For some suggestions, read the "Supervisory Skills" feature.

Appraisals by peers—often called **peer reviews**—are less common, but their use is growing, especially in organizations that use teamwork. Employees who work in teams usually appraise the performance of their team members. The teams do this in meetings, in which they discuss each team member's strengths and areas that need improvement. Presumably, employees will react more positively to peer reviews in which all employees participate equally than to peer reviews used occasionally for selected employees. A challenge of peer reviews is ensuring that all peers are prepared to give objective feedback. A recent study found that members of a peer group tended to give higher evaluations to group members who had a similar social style (mix of assertiveness and responsiveness).[21] When the organization uses peer reviews, supervisors should prepare group members to apply the principles of objective evaluation described in this chapter. Employees may need training, and the appraisal method should focus on measurable, specific behaviors.

The drive to please customers in a highly competitive market, coupled with a desire for practical information on performance, has encouraged some companies to institute programs in which customers appraise employees' performance. As mentioned previously, one way to obtain objective feedback on customer service is to use "mystery shoppers." Those people contact the organization to make a particular purchase or to ask for help with a predetermined problem. The mystery shopper then records the results of the experience. This type of appraisal is most effective when employees know what specific behaviors are desired and the mystery shopper measures those behaviors. For example, cashiers at Bruster's Real Ice Cream,

360-degree feedback
Performance appraisal that combines assessments from several sources

peer reviews
Performance appraisals conducted by an employee's co-workers

SUPERVISORY SKILLS

APPRAISING AND PLANNING: USING SELF-APPRAISAL FOR CAREER ADVANCEMENT

Taking a position as a supervisor places you on the first rung of the management ladder. This is a significant time to evaluate your abilities and career goals to plan the next phase of your career. A thoughtful self-appraisal is especially important in today's workplace, which rewards creative career planning and life-long learning.

When it is time for your annual performance review, instead of stressing over it, think of it as an opportunity for career development. The self-evaluation or self-appraisal gives you the opportunity to control the performance review process. If you construct your self-appraisal carefully, you can steer the conversation with your manager toward the positives and toward items that will help boost your career.

Managers cannot remember all of your successes, failures, or what you have learned in the past year. It is up to you to create a detailed and thorough appraisal. Following are some suggestions for what elements to include in your self-appraisal:

- *Before you begin writing, ask how your self-appraisal will be used.* Will it be in your HR file? Will it be used for raises and the performance review? Knowing who the audience will be and in what ways it will be used, can guide your writing.
- *Share your successes—and be specific.* List all of the projects you have worked on or completed in the last year. (If you keep a project or performance journal, this task becomes much easier.) Most managers have many evaluations to complete, so if you provide a detailed list that they can work from, the chances are very good that what you list will end up in your performance evaluation.
- *Discuss what you have learned.* Identify anything that has enhanced your skills, any training you attended, or, for example, if new equipment has been installed in the last year, what you have learned from day-to-day activities. Describe any new skills you have acquired and list how they will help in your career development. Detail how these new skills apply to your job as well as how they allow you to be an asset to the organization.
- *Be objective and consider your challenges.* Be honest and objective about the challenges you have faced in the past year. Did you overcome those challenges? Are you still working on overcoming these challenges? Listing specific steps you will take in the coming year to overcome current challenges is an excellent way to show that you are willing to work at the areas where you have weaknesses. If you have an evaluation form that requires rating yourself, be as objective as you can and think about how your manager would likely rate you in each category.
- *Admit to mistakes.* However, couch these in terms of showing that you understand what went wrong and why and discuss what you are doing to avoid these mistakes in the future.
- *Write in terms of long-term employment and career development.* Managers want employees that are looking to expand their capabilities and take on more responsibility. If your manager can see that you are looking at the bigger picture, they will be more likely to consider you in their bigger picture as well.
- *Allow yourself time to write and review.* Take the time to do yourself justice. Trying to summarize an entire year in, for example, one hour of writing is not likely going to result in the best self-appraisal. Schedule time to write a fair and balance self-appraisal. Include time to set the appraisal aside and then come back and review it. Use spell-check and grammar-check and re-read it several times.

If your self-appraisal is used in your performance review, you can then use this as a stepping stone for leading the discussion in the right direction for your career. If there are areas that you have identified as challenges in the previous year, ask for training, mentoring, or coaching. All managers like to have employees who know when to ask for help. Be specific in your request and target working with those who have the experience and knowledge to help advance your skills and career.

Last, end your performance review by looking ahead and planning for the coming year. Ask your manager what additional tasks you could take on or what projects they plan for you to work on. Ask what additional skills they would like to see you acquire. Framed by a candid and well-thought-out self-appraisal, wrapping up with a discussion based on these questions will likely lead to additional career opportunities in the coming year.

Sources: Jeremy Reis, "7 Tips for a Career Boost Through Your Self Evaluation," LearnThat, September 23, 2013, http://learnthat.com/7-tips-for-a-career-boost-through-your-self-evaluation/, accessed May 22, 2014; Dominique Jones, "How to Write a Great Self Appraisal in Six Steps," TalentSpace Blog, December 3, 2013, http://www.halogensoftware.com/blog/how-to-write-a-great-self-appraisal-in-six-steps, accessed May 22, 2014.

located in Columbus, Georgia, are supposed to invite each customer to come back again. Mystery shoppers making purchases at Bruster's note whether the cashier they encounter issues this invitation. Bruster's reinforces the effort by awarding cash prizes to cashiers who earn a perfect score from a mystery shopper.[22]

360-degree feedback allows all employees to provide evaluations of co-workers and supervisors. It's important that these reviews are kept anonymous and that employees are prepared for potentially long, harsh feedback.

At an increasing number of major corporations, subordinates rate how well their bosses manage. Typically, ratings are anonymous, to protect the workers. The purpose of these subordinate appraisals is to give managers information they can use to supervise more effectively and to make their organization more competitive. The appraisals also support the trend toward giving operative employees a greater voice in how an organization is run.

Subordinate appraisals and other 360-degree feedback can correct some of the appraisal biases described in the next section. They also can provide information that is more useful for problem solving and employee development than the typical results of a traditional top-down appraisal. For example, executive coach John Parker Stewart worked with a sales and marketing manager of five employees, all of whom were nearly ready to quit their jobs in frustration. The manager could not see the problem until Stewart showed him the results of upward appraisals. All five employees indicated this manager failed to give them credit for their work; they felt they received no appreciation when they went the extra mile. After the manager recovered from this blow to his pride, he was able to improve the way he rewarded and recognized his team, and the employees repaid him with their loyalty.[23]

For 360-feedback to be effective, the person managing the review process should ensure that the responses are anonymous. Subordinates especially may be afraid to respond honestly if they think that the person being reviewed will retaliate for negative comments. Also, organizations need to prepare employees to understand and apply the feedback from a 360-degree review. Because the feedback comes from many different, typically anonymous sources, it may be long, complex, and at times harsh. Paul Warner, director of consulting services at DecisionWise, a survey creator, recommends coaching to guide each employee through the results, help him or her draw up an action plan, and follow up to help the employee carry out the action plan.[24]

LO17.5 ▶ Describe sources of bias in appraising performance.

Sources of Bias

Ideally, supervisors should be completely objective in their appraisals of employees. Each appraisal should directly reflect an employee's performance, not any biases of a supervisor. Of course, this is impossible to do perfectly. We all make compromises in our decision-making strategies and have biases in evaluating what other people do. Supervisors need to be aware of these biases so that their effect on the appraisals can be limited or eliminated. Figure 17.7, on the following page, shows some sources of bias that commonly influence performance appraisals.

harshness bias
Rating employees more severely than their performances merit

Some supervisors are prone to a **harshness bias,** that is, rating employees more severely than their performance merits. New supervisors are especially susceptible to this error, because they may feel a need to be taken seriously. Unfortunately, the harshness bias also tends to frustrate and discourage workers, who resent the unfair assessments of their performance.

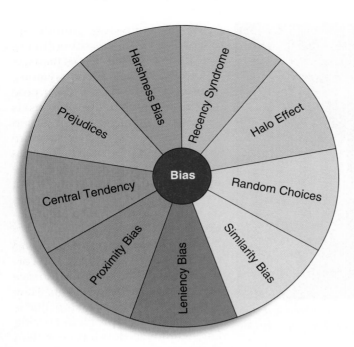

FIGURE 17.7 | Sources of Bias in Performance Appraisals

Performance appraisals can be biased by a number of factors. Supervisors need to be aware of these biases so they can eliminate them or limit their impact.

leniency bias
Rating employees more favorably than their performances merit

central tendency
The tendency to select employee ratings in the middle of a scale

proximity bias
The tendency to assign similar scores to items that are near each other on a questionnaire

similarity bias
The tendency to judge others more positively when they are like yourself

At the other extreme is the **leniency bias.** Supervisors with this bias rate their employees more favorably than their performance merits. A supervisor who does this may want credit for developing a department full of "excellent" workers. Or the supervisor may simply be uncomfortable confronting employees with their shortcomings. The leniency bias may feel like an advantage to the employees who receive the favorable ratings, but it cheats the employees and department of the benefits of truly developing and coaching employees.

A bias that characterizes the responses to many types of questionnaires is **central tendency,** which is the tendency to select ratings in the middle of the scale. People seem more comfortable on middle ground than taking a strong stand at either extreme. This bias causes a supervisor to miss important opportunities to praise or correct employees.

Proximity means nearness. The **proximity bias** refers to the tendency to assign similar scores to items that are near each other on a questionnaire. If a supervisor assigns a score of 8 to one appraisal item, this bias might encourage the supervisor to score the next item as 6 or 7, even though a score of 3 is more accurate. Obviously, this tendency can result in misleading appraisals.

When using a type of appraisal that requires answers to specific questions, a supervisor might succumb to making *random choices.* A supervisor might do this when uncertain how to answer or when the overall scoring on the test looks undesirable. For example, if a supervisor thinks an appraisal is scoring an employee too low, he or she might give favorable ratings in some areas about which the supervisor has no strong feelings. Supervisors who catch themselves making random choices should slow down and try to apply objective criteria.

The **similarity bias** refers to the tendency to judge others more positively when they are like ourselves. Thus, we tend to look more favorably on people who share our interests, tastes, background, or other characteristics. For example, in appraising performance, a supervisor risks viewing a person's performance in a favorable light because the employee shares his or her flair for dressing in the latest fashions. Researchers have recently documented that the existence of demographic similarities between supervisors and subordinates, including age and gender, is often associated with better performance appraisals of the subordinate.[25] Alternatively, a supervisor might interpret negatively the performance of an employee who is much shyer than the supervisor.

As described in Chapter 9, the *recency syndrome* refers to the human tendency to place the most weight on events that have occurred most recently. In a performance appraisal, a supervisor might give particular weight to a problem the employee caused last week or an award the employee just won, but he or she should be careful to consider events and behaviors that occurred throughout the entire period covered by the review. The most accurate way to do this is to keep records throughout the year, as described earlier with conducting a critical-incident appraisal.

The *halo effect,* introduced in Chapter 15, refers to the tendency to generalize one positive or negative aspect of a person to the person's entire performance. Thus, if supervisor Ben Olson thinks that a pleasant telephone manner is what makes a good customer service representative, he is apt to give high marks to a representative with a pleasant voice, no matter what the employee actually says to the customers or how reliable the performance. Possibly more harmful is the impact of a supervisor who develops a broadly negative opinion about an employee.

Finally, the supervisor's *prejudices* about various types of people can unfairly influence a performance appraisal. A supervisor needs to remember that each employee is an individual, not merely a representative of a group. A supervisor who believes that African Americans generally have poor skills in using standard English needs to recognize that this is a prejudice about a group, not a fact to apply to actual employees. Thus, before recommending that a black salesperson needs to improve her speaking skills, a supervisor must consider whether the salesperson really needs improvement in that area or whether the supervisor's prejudices are interfering with an accurate assessment. This is especially important in light of the EEOC guidelines discussed earlier in the chapter.

connect SELF-ASSESSMENT 17.1

How Well Do You Accept Evaluations?

Many supervisors find it difficult to engage in performance appraisal interviews. They do not like telling workers that there are problems with their performance. Supervisors also receive performance appraisals from their managers. Many dread these interviews. How well do you handle performance feedback?

The Performance Appraisal Interview

The last stage of the appraisal process—the stage at which a supervisor reinforces performance or provides remedies—occurs in an interview between supervisor and employee. At this time, a supervisor describes what he or she has observed and discusses this appraisal with the employee. Together they agree on areas for improvement and development.

Supervisors often dread conducting appraisal interviews. Pointing out another person's shortcomings can be unpleasant. To overcome these feelings, it helps to focus on the benefits of appraising employees. Supervisors can cultivate a positive attitude by viewing the appraisal interview as an opportunity to coach and develop employees.[26]

LO17.6 ▶ Explain the purpose of conducting performance appraisal interviews.

Purpose of the Interview

The purpose of holding an appraisal interview is to communicate information about an employee's performance. Once a supervisor has evaluated an employee's performance, the supervisor needs to convey his or her thoughts to the employee. An interview is an appropriate setting for doing so because it sets aside time to focus on and discuss the appraisal in private. The interview is also an opportunity for upward communication from the employee. By contributing his or her viewpoints and ideas, an employee can work with the supervisor on devising ways to improve performance.

The purpose of an appraisal interview is more difficult to achieve when cultural differences between the supervisor and employee cause misunderstandings. The "Supervision and Diversity" feature identifies some cross-cultural challenges of appraisal interviews and suggests ways to meet the challenges.

LO17.7 ▶ Tell how supervisors should prepare for a performance appraisal interview.

Preparing for the Interview

Before the appraisal interview, a supervisor should allow plenty of time for completing the appraisal form. The form should be completed carefully and thoughtfully, not in a rush during the hour before the interview. In addition to filling out the form, the supervisor should think about the employee's likely reactions to the appraisal and plan how to handle them. A supervisor also should be ready with some ideas for correcting problems noted in the appraisal.

SUPERVISION AND DIVERSITY

PERFORMANCE FEEDBACK ACROSS CULTURES

Our cultural background greatly influences how we communicate with and relate to people at work. For example, some cultures, including the dominant U.S. culture, tend to use a low-context style of communication, where we put our message into words that are direct and to the point. Most U.S. managers expect their words to be taken at face value. In cultures with a high-context communication style, people interpret a message in terms of its entire context, including body language and the relationship between the speaker and listener, so the words themselves would be subtler, or else the speaker would be considered harsh. Likewise, cultures differ in terms of the importance placed on a person's position in the organization and the value placed on individual achievement or group success.

Imagine how such differences would play out in an appraisal interview. In the dominant U.S. culture, employees and their supervisors expect the language of the feedback to be specific and direct and to accurately reflect the individual's accomplishments. Employees are expected to present their accomplishments to their supervisor in a similar manner.

But suppose an employee comes from a culture with a high-context communication style. In that case, feedback that the supervisor considers direct and useful might sound like an insult to the employee. In that case, the supervisor might be more effective if the feedback starts with gentler, more general observations leading to a conversation about how the employee might progress. The supervisor should carefully observe the employee's nonverbal signals, rather than taking silence as a sign of agreement.

Or suppose an employee comes from a culture that values group harmony and relationships over personal accomplishments. If the supervisor's company values and measures individual accomplishments, the supervisor should be prepared to explain that these are the measures used by the company and to show how they contribute to the whole group's success. Praise for successes and expectations for improvement can be expressed in terms of how the employee's efforts help the whole group. The supervisor might collect examples of appreciation (or frustration) from other group members as well as examples of individual accomplishments (or shortcomings).

How is a supervisor to identify and prepare for such differences? You cannot be an expert in all cultures, but you can educate yourself. Visit a library to find some of the many books that have been published on cross-cultural management. Also work with your company's human resources department to obtain training and guidance in this area, targeting cultural groups represented by the company's employees and customers.

Source: Based on Nancy R. Lockwood, "Selected Cross-Cultural Factors in Human Resource Management," Society for Human Resource Management, *Research Quarterly*, Third Quarter 2008, http://www.shrm.org/Research/Articles/Documents/September%202008%20Research%20Quarterly%20-%20Selected%20Cross-Cultural%20Factors%20in%20Human%20Resource%20Management.pdf, accessed May 22, 2014.

A supervisor should notify the employee about the appraisal interview ahead of time. Giving a few days' or a week's notice allows the employee to think about his or her performance. Then the employee can contribute ideas during the interview.

In addition, a supervisor should prepare an appropriate meeting place. The interview should occur in an office or other room where supervisor and employee will have privacy. The supervisor should arrange to prevent interruptions such as telephone calls.

LO17.8 ▶ Describe guidelines for conducting the interview.

Conducting the Interview

At the beginning of the interview, a supervisor should try to put an employee at ease. Employees are often uncomfortable at the prospect of discussing their performance. An offer of coffee and a little small talk may help to break the ice.

The supervisor can begin by reviewing the employee's self-appraisal, if one was completed, with the employee, asking him or her to give reasons for the various ratings. Then a supervisor describes his or her rating of the employee and how he or she arrived at it. A supervisor can start by describing overall impressions and then explain the contents of the appraisal form. The supervisor should explain the basis for the ratings, using specific examples of the employee's behavior and results. Most employees are waiting for the "bad news," so it is probably most effective to describe areas for improvement first, followed by the employee's strengths. People need to know what they are doing well so that they will continue on that course, realizing that their efforts are appreciated.

After describing the evaluation of the employee's performance, a supervisor should give the employee time to offer feedback. The employee should be able to agree or disagree with the supervisor's conclusions, as well as ask questions. This is an important time for the supervisor to keep an open mind and apply the listening skills discussed in Chapter 10. Hearing the employee's reactions is the first step toward resolving any problems described in the appraisal.

Problem Solving and Coaching

When the supervisor and employee understand each other's point of view, they should reach a decision on how to solve problems described in the appraisal. Together they can come up with a number of alternatives and select the solutions that seem most promising. Sometimes the best solution is for the employee to make behavioral changes; at other times, the supervisor may need to make changes, such as keeping the employee better informed or improving work processes.

Proponents of quality management have criticized performance appraisals for connecting rewards mainly to individual performance. The problem, they say, is that the quality of employees' performance depends mainly on the organization's systems, which give each employee the necessary information, authority, and materials. Some organizations address this shortcoming by using appraisal interviews as an opportunity to identify organizational factors that are standing in the way of success. For example, WD-40 Company starts with the belief that employees and their supervisors need to cooperate in order for the company to succeed. WD-40 employees contribute to defining their job requirements, and supervisors are expected to coach employees throughout the year. During appraisal interviews, held once every quarter, the supervisor meets with each employee to take note of all the goals the employee has achieved. Where the employee has not met a goal, the supervisor is supposed to ask the employee what is interfering with achievement of the goal. WD-40 expects supervisors to consider that some of the necessary changes may involve the resources and conditions provided by the company. Furthermore, the supervisor's own manager meets with the supervisor to go over the reviews of the supervisor's employees. They discuss how the company can enable the supervisor to help team members meet all their goals.[27]

In addition to problem solving, appraisal interviews often include time for discussion related to coaching the employee and helping the employee develop a career with the organization. Strengths and shortcomings identified in the performance appraisal often provide indications of areas in which the supervisor and employee could work together to develop desirable skills through further training or experience. Discussing employees' potential for growth and improvement is essential. Author and consultant Brayton Bowen calls this effort taking "time to educate and communicate as well as evaluate."[28] For example, the supervisor might help the employee identify ways to succeed personally and as part of the team. However, employees may have difficulty shifting their focus away from pay and past performance, especially when performance appraisals are directly or indirectly tied to pay levels. A supervisor therefore should not use performance appraisal interviews as a substitute for coaching on a continuing basis.

Signatures

At the end of the interview, the supervisor and employee usually are required to sign the appraisal form. By doing so, they acknowledge that the interview

FIGURE 17.8 | The Process of Conducting a Performance Appraisal Interview

Following these steps in the process of conducting a performance appraisal interview will enable a supervisor to have a productive and meaningful discussion with an employee, and should lead to continued employee improvement.

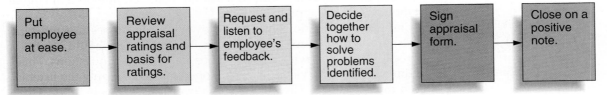

has been conducted and that the employee has read and understood the form. If the employee refuses to sign, the supervisor can explain that this is all the employee's signature means. If that explanation does not persuade the employee to sign, the supervisor can note on the appraisal form that the employee refused to sign and check with the human resources department regarding what procedures to follow next. The employee should receive a copy of the appraisal form.

The supervisor should close the interview on a positive note, with a comment such as, "You've been doing a great job," or, "I think that with the plans we've made, your work will soon be up to standards." Figure 17.8 summarizes the interviewing process.

Follow-Up

Even after the interview is over, a supervisor continues appraising performance. He or she needs to follow up on any actions planned during the interview. Is the employee making the promised changes? Is the supervisor providing the resources, such as training, that are necessary for improvements to occur? This follow-up should be an ongoing process, not an activity left for the next year's performance appraisal.

Skills Module

PART ONE: CONCEPTS

Summary

17.1 Summarize the benefits of conducting performance appraisals.

Performance appraisals provide information necessary for employees to improve the quality of their work. Appraisals can motivate employees by demonstrating the interest of the supervisor and the organization in them, keeping them informed, and indicating the important areas of performance. Performance appraisals also provide important records for the company, which managers use to make decisions about raises, promotions, and discipline.

17.2 Identify the steps in appraising performance systematically.

First, a supervisor establishes and communicates expectations for performance; second, he or she establishes and communicates standards for measuring performance. Third, a supervisor observes each employee's performance, measuring it against the standards. Fourth, a supervisor provides reinforcement for acceptable or excellent performance and works with the employee to develop remedies for inadequate performance.

17.3 Discuss guidelines for avoiding discrimination in performance appraisals.

As much as possible, an appraisal should focus on objective measures of behavior and results—specifically, how well an employee carries out the essential tasks of the job. The behaviors and employee characteristics measured should be related to the job and succeeding on the job.

17.4 Compare types of appraisals.

Graphic rating scales rate the degree to which an employee has achieved various characteristics, such as job knowledge and punctuality. The paired-comparison approach measures the relative performance of employees in a group. The forced-choice approach presents a supervisor with sets of statements describing employee behavior, and the supervisor chooses the statements that are most characteristic of the employee and those that are least. An essay appraisal includes one or more paragraphs describing an employee's performance. Behaviorally anchored rating scales (BARS) rate employee performance in several areas by using a series of statements that describe effective and ineffective performance in each area. A checklist appraisal consists of a series of yes-or-no questions about an employee's performance. A critical-incident appraisal is based on an ongoing record of incidents in which an employee has behaved positively or negatively. The work-standards approach is based on establishing objective measures of performance, against which an employee's performance is compared. Management by objectives is a system of developing goals with employees and comparing their performance to those goals. In addition, a supervisor may combine several sources of appraisal in 360-degree feedback, including having employees prepare self-assessments, obtaining peer assessments and customer assessments, or asking for appraisals (usually anonymous) of the supervisor.

17.5 Describe sources of bias in appraising performance.

Supervisors who want to prove they are tough may succumb to the harshness bias, rating employees too severely. Supervisors who hate to deliver bad news may succumb to the leniency bias, rating employees too favorably. The central tendency leads some supervisors to give their employees rankings in the middle of the scale. The proximity bias refers to the tendency to assign similar scores to items that are near each other on a questionnaire. Random choices sometimes are made when an appraiser is uncertain about answers or uncomfortable with an overall rating. The similarity bias is the tendency of people to judge others more positively when they are like themselves. The recency syndrome may lead a supervisor to give too much weight to events that have occurred recently. The halo effect leads an appraiser to use one positive or negative trait to describe a person's entire performance. Finally, people are influenced by their prejudices about groups.

17.6 Explain the purpose of conducting performance appraisal interviews.

The purpose of conducting an interview is to communicate the supervisor's impressions of an employee's performance to that employee. In addition, it is an opportunity for an employee to present his or her viewpoint and ideas so that supervisor and employee can work together on improving performance.

17.7 Tell how supervisors should prepare for a performance appraisal interview.

A supervisor should take as much time as necessary to complete an appraisal form thoughtfully. Supervisor also should think about how the employee is likely to react and plan how to handle his or her reactions. A supervisor should be ready with ideas for resolving problems noted in the appraisal. Finally, the supervisor should notify the employee about the interview ahead of time and prepare an appropriate place to meet without interruptions.

17.8 Describe guidelines for conducting the interview.

A supervisor first should attempt to put the employee at ease. Then the supervisor and employee should go over the self-appraisal, if any, and the supervisor's appraisal of the employee. The supervisor should focus first on areas for improvement and next on areas of strength. The employee should have time to give feedback; then the supervisor and employee should work together to develop solutions to any problems identified. The supervisor and employee sign the appraisal form, and then the supervisor closes with a positive comment. After the interview, the supervisor needs to follow up to make sure that planned actions are taken.

Key Terms

performance appraisal, *p.* 484
graphic rating scale, *p.* 489
paired-comparison approach, *p.* 491
forced-choice approach, *p.* 492
behaviorally anchored rating scales (BARS), *p.* 492

critical-incident appraisal, *p.* 493
work-standards approach, *p.* 494
360-degree feedback, *p.* 495
peer reviews, *p.* 495

harshness bias, *p.* 497
leniency bias, *p.* 498
central tendency, *p.* 498
proximity bias, *p.* 498
similarity bias, *p.* 498

Review and Discussion Questions

1. What is a performance appraisal? How do organizations benefit from using performance appraisals?

2. June Pearson was just promoted to supervisor of the bookkeeping department at an insurance company. According to the company's schedule for appraising performance, she needs to conduct an appraisal of Ron Yamamoto, one of the employees, only a month after she started the job. Pearson cannot find any records of goals established for Yamamoto, so she asks his peers and others with whom he has contact to describe his performance. On the basis of this information, Pearson completes an appraisal form and conducts an interview.

   a. Which steps of the systematic approach to appraising performance has Pearson omitted?

   b. How do you think Yamamoto will react to this interview?

   c. Can you think of anything else Pearson could have done to improve this particular appraisal? Explain.

3. Name and describe briefly the five kinds of causes of poor performance.

4. Which of the following are appropriate ways to measure an employee's performance?

   a. Day after day, more than three customers are lined up at Janet's cash register, so her supervisor concludes that she is a slow worker.

   b. Jonathan smiles a lot, so his supervisor assumes he is happy.

   c. Wesley is late to work every Wednesday morning, so his supervisor plans to find out the cause.

   d. Nick habitually takes longer to deliver pizzas than his company promises its customers, so his supervisor notes that he is inefficient.

   e. Production in the group that Caitlin oversees has fallen off somewhat in the last two months, so her supervisor discusses with her the possible reasons.

5. How can a supervisor avoid illegal discrimination in performance appraisals?

6. At a manufacturing company in south suburban Chicago, one policy stated that each manager and employee must be appraised at one-year intervals. At the same time, the company conducts a review of the person's wages or salary, usually giving at least a small raise. In recent years, like many manufacturers, this company has become concerned about reducing costs. The policy regarding performance appraisals has been modified: Managers' appraisals now must be conducted *at least* a year after the manager's salary was last reviewed. One supervisor was reviewed in December of one year, then in February (14 months later), and then in May of the third year.

   a. What reasons do you think the supervisor's manager had for delaying the performance appraisals so that they were more than a year apart?

   b. What effects do you think the delays had on the supervisor?

7. What type of performance appraisal is used most frequently? What are advantages and disadvantages of this approach?

8. What type of performance appraisal was (or is) used at your most recent job? How effective do you think it is? Why?

9. At a company that sells X-ray equipment, an important new sales territory is opening up. Patrick O'Day, the supervisor of the company's sales force, wants to assign the territory to the best qualified salesperson. How can he compare the performance of the members of the sales force to select the best candidate for the job?

10. Give an advantage and a disadvantage of using each of the following types of appraisals:

    a. Essay appraisal.

    b. Behaviorally anchored rating scale (BARS).

    c. Checklist.

    d. Critical-incident appraisal.

11. Which type of bias does each of the following situations illustrate?

    a. Anne Compton is a new supervisor. To make sure that her employees and her manager take her judgments seriously, she gives each of her employees a lower rating than the previous supervisor did.

    b. Ron is late in completing Noreen's written performance appraisal. To finish it as quickly as possible, he looks it over and adds some negative ratings to an overall positive review so that it looks balanced.

    c. Renee really likes her new employee, Joan. Recently, Joan and her family moved to the same town in which Renee lives; their children attend the same school; Renee and Joan even enjoy lunchtime shopping together. When it comes time for Joan's performance review, Renee rates Joan high in every category.

12. Reginald DeBeers hates conducting appraisal interviews, so he has the process down to a science. Fifteen minutes before the end of the workday, he meets with the employee who is to be appraised. He gets right down to business, explaining what the employee's ratings are and how he arrived at each number. Then the employee and supervisor sign the form. By then, it is quitting time, and DeBeers rises to shake hands with the employee, saying either "Keep up the good work" or "I'm sure you'll do better next time."

What parts of the interviewing process does DeBeers omit? What are the consequences of leaving out these steps?

Notes

1. "How to Conduct Annual Employee Reviews," *Inc.*, December 2008, www.inc.com/magazine/20081201/how-to-conduct-annual-employee-reviews.html, accessed May 22, 2014.

2. Ibid.

3. Barbara Kiviat, "The Rage to Engage," *Time*, April 28, 2008, p. Global 10.

4. Sarah Campbell, "How to . . . Construct an Appraisals System," *The Times (London)*, December 17, 2008, downloaded from Business & Company Resource Center, http://galenet.galegroup.com.

5. Greg Levin, "Agent Development in Action!" *Call Center*, June 1, 2006, downloaded from Business & Company Resource Center, http://galenet.galegroup.com.

6. Michael M. Grant, "Six Sigma for People? The Heart of Performance Management," *Human Resource Planning*, March 2006, downloaded from Business & Company Resource Center, http://galenet.galegroup.com.

7. Drew Robb, "Appraising Appraisal Software," *HRMagazine*, October 2008, pp. 65–70, http://www.shrm.org/publications/hrmagazine/editorialcontent/pages/1008robb.aspx, accessed May 22, 2014.

8. "Parallels between Performance Management Quality and Organizational Performance," *Supervision*, September 2003, downloaded from InfoTrac, http://web4.infotrac.galegroup.com.

9. Benjamin J. Romano, "Under Pressure, Microsoft Fights to Keep Its Workers," *Seattle Times*, May 19, 2006, http://seattletimes.com/html/microsoft/2003004687_microsoft19.html, accessed May 22, 2014; Larry Stewart, "Fort Worth: Performance Measures Motivate Change," *Construction Equipment*, June 1, 2005, http://www.constructionequipment.com/performance-measures-motivate-change, accessed May 22, 2014.

10. "Parallels between Performance Management Quality and Organizational Performance."

11. Jack Welch and Suzy Welch, "The Case for 20-70-10," *BusinessWeek*, October 2, 2006, http://www.businessweek.com/stories/2006-10-01/the-case-for-20-70-10, accessed May 22, 2014. See also Lisa Vollmer, "Create Candor in the Workplace, Says Jack Welch," *Stanford GSB News*, Stanford Graduate School of Business, April 2005, http://www.gsb.stanford.edu/news/headlines/vftt_welch.shtml, accessed May 22, 2014; Liz Ryan, "Ten Management Practices to Axe," *Bloomberg Businessweek*, February 5, 2010, http://www.businessweek.com/managing/content/feb2010/ca2010024_442061.htm, accessed May 22, 2014.

12. For a closer look at the use of BARS in the workplace, see H. Chung and M. Khan, 2008, "Classification of unethical behaviors in the management of information systems: The use of behaviorally anchored rating scale procedures," *International Journal of Management*, 25, p. 262.

13. Paul Ridilla, "'That's Not My Job' Scorecard: Recognize Extra Effort by Your Employees or It Won't Continue," *Plumbing & Mechanical*, July 2004, http://www.pmmag.com/articles/87386-that-s-not-my-job-scorecard-br-paul-ridilla?v=preview, accessed May 22, 2014.

14. Bill Stoneman, "To Reduce Turnover, Turn the Teller into a Team Player," *American Banker*, July 8, 2003, downloaded from Business & Company Resource Center, http://galenet.galegroup.com.

15. Joe Light, "Performance Reviews by the Numbers," *The Wall Street Journal*, June 29, 2010, http://online.wsj.com/news/articles/SB10001424052748703964104575334832074865058, accessed May 22, 2014.

16. For more information about 360 degree feedback, see M. Millmore, D. Biggs, and L. Morse, 2007, "Gender differences within 360-degree managerial performance appraisals," *Women in Management Review*, 22, p. 536.

17. "Parallels between Performance Management Quality and Organizational Performance."

18. 360-degree feedback has also been implemented in the academic world: K. Sanwong, 2008, "The development of a 360-degree performance appraisal system: A university case study," *International Journal of Management*, 25, p. 16.

19. Roger Seiler, "Getting Results with 360 Assessments: Continuous and Periodic Ratings by Superiors and Peers Helps Employees Grow in Their Positions," *Law Enforcement Technology*, September 2005, downloaded from Business & Company Resource Center, http://galenet.galegroup.com.

20. Julie Forster, "IKEA's Unusual Benefits, Attitude Scores Hit with Workers," *Knight Ridder/Tribune Business News*, July 14, 2004, downloaded from Business & Company Resource Center, http://galenet.galegroup.com.

21. Gary L. May and Lisa E. Gueldenzoph, "The Effect of Social Style on Peer Evaluation Ratings in Project Teams," *Journal of Business Communication* 43, no. 1 (January 2006), downloaded from Business & Company Resource Center, http://galenet.galegroup.com.

22. Danee Attebury, "Mystery Shoppers Keep Employees on Their Toes," *Columbus (Ga.) Ledger-Enquirer*, August 1, 2006, http://www.advancedfeedback.com/content-files/keepemployeesontoes.pdf, accessed May 22, 2014; Barry Himmel, "Customer Service Impact," *Rental Equipment Register*, January 1, 2006, downloaded from Business & Company Resource Center, http://galenet.galegroup.com.

23. Julia Chang, "Feedback Needed," *Sales & Marketing Management*, February 2004, downloaded from InfoTrac, http://web4.infotrac.galegroup.com.

24. Carolyn Heinze, "The Ins and Outs of 360-Degree Assessments," *Systems Contractor News*, May 6, 2010, http://www.systemscontractor.com.

25. M. Schraeder and J. Simpson, 2006, "How similarity and liking affect performance appraisals," *The Journal for Quality and Participation*, 29, p. 34.

26. For more information on successfully presenting critical feedback, see B. Asmub, "Performance appraisal interviews: Preference organization in assessment sequences," *The Journal of Business Communication*, 2008, 45, p. 408.

27. David Witt, "Building a Performance-Based Culture," *Chief Learning Officer*, May 2011, pp. 42–45, 55.

28. R. Brayton Bowen, "Today's Workforce Requires New Age Currency," *HRMagazine*, March 2004, downloaded from InfoTrac, http://web2.infotrac.galegroup.com.

PART TWO: SKILL-BUILDING

Meeting the Challenge

Reflecting back on page 483, in what ways might introducing self-appraisals at the YMCA of Greater Rochester have made the job of performance appraisal easier for supervisors? In what ways might the change have made the task harder? How might a YMCA supervisor need to adapt the appraisal interview for (a) an employee with an inflated view of his or her own performance; (b) an employee who is uncomfortable with "bragging" about his or her accomplishments; and (c) an employee who is vague about his or her career goals?

Have one member of your group play the role of the supervisor and one play the role of the employee. Choose one or more of the employee types from the preceding paragraph, and role-play an appraisal interview.

Afterward, discuss how well the issues were handled in the role-play. What could the supervisor (and employee) have done to address the issues more effectively?

Problem-Solving Case: Appraising Employees in a Dental Office

Jill Strode supervises the office staff in a dental office. One of Strode's accomplishments was to develop a system for appraising the performance of the employees she supervises.

For each employee, Strode spells out the specific areas of responsibility that will be evaluated. The areas she evaluates match the responsibilities stated in the employee's job description. Thus, for the checkout receptionist, Strode indicates that she will evaluate how that person handles five areas of responsibility, including checkout procedures and telephone communications. In evaluating how an employee handles each area, Strode looks for specific traits, such as knowledge, initiative, innovation, and courtesy. The following excerpts from an appraisal of the checkout receptionist illustrate the format of the appraisals:

JOB RESPONSIBILITY: Checkout Procedures and Folder Routing . . .

Accuracy: Very good overall. Attention to details is superb in all areas. Seldom forgets any part of the "checkout" procedure.

Example: Ability to pick up on errors made in charting, double-checking folders for missed steps (insurance, scheduling, etc.), thoroughness.

Innovation: Below average. This area has remained unchanged since we installed the system. Procedural changes have been suggested by the supervisor and implemented by the checkout receptionist. Needs improvement.

Example: Complaints with folder errors and patient flow have been verbalized; however, no suggestions for changes or improvement in procedures have been offered. Space limitations in checkout area still a concern . . . suggestions for improvements?

To review the performance appraisal with the employee, Strode sets up a formal appraisal meeting. She has developed the following agenda list of topics to cover during the meeting:

1. Review specific areas of responsibility that will be evaluated. Make any changes or additions if needed.
2. Appraisal for each specific area.
   a. Set goals for improvement and change (at least two improvements/changes for each).
   b. Set training dates, if needed.
   c. Get feedback from staff on appraisal from supervisor.
3. Overall appraisal of traits as exemplified in daily activities and actions.
4. Review goals and training dates.
5. Questions and answers from list.
6. Open forum for discussion: employee to supervisor.

Strode then follows up to make sure that the employee and supervisor carry through on the goals and plans they established during this interview.

1. Based on the information given, what type of performance appraisal has Strode developed?
2. Based on the agenda Strode uses for appraisal interviews, what principles of effective appraisals does she follow?
3. Consider whether the examples in this case seem to be useful tools for conducting appraisals of the clerical employees in a dental practice. Suggest additions or improvements by answering the following questions:
   a. In the excerpt from the sample appraisal, what additional information would improve this appraisal?
   b. How, if at all, would you revise the agenda for the appraisal interview?
   c. Why do you think your suggestions would improve the appraisal process?

Source: Jill Strode.

Assessing Yourself

How Well Do You Accept Evaluations?

It can be difficult for any of us to accept judgment or criticism, and sometimes we may become emotional and fail to listen. This little quiz should help you find out how well you are prepared to receive feedback, which is just as important for a supervisor as giving it. Ask yourself the following questions.

1. Do I prepare for my performance review by gathering examples of work I've done well and compliments I've received from colleagues?
2. Have I been accomplishing what my job description calls for? Have I accepted and fulfilled my responsibilities on major assignments?
3. Have I improved on the job, learned additional skills, and/or taken on greater responsibilities?
4. Have I created a list of things about my performance that I can improve? Have I prioritized weaknesses and selected three to work on immediately?
5. Do I tell myself during the review, "I need to listen to this. It will help me grow personally and professionally"?

6. Do I stay tuned in to what I am hearing?
7. Can I remain objective and unemotional as far as possible?
8. Do I hold back from interrupting?
9. Do I summarize and restate what I hear to be sure I have heard it correctly?
10. Do I ask for specific and action-oriented feedback?
11. Have I created an action plan for attaining my goals?
12. Do I follow up to assess my own progress?

Pause and Reflect

1. How can accepting criticism help you in your career?
2. In what areas of accepting evaluations do you want to improve?
3. What will you do to improve in the areas you have identified?

Sources: Susan Vaughn, "Rethinking Employee Evaluations," *Los Angeles Times*, April 8, 2001, p. W1; "Give Yourself a Job Review," *American Salesman*, May 2001, pp. 26–27.

Class Skills Exercise

Developing a Performance Evaluation System

Students should break into groups of two to three. Each group should take the position of a supervisor and develop plans for rating the performance of each of the following restaurant jobs:

- Server
- Line cook
- Host

Each plan should address the following:

1. Who will rate the performance of each employee?
2. How will you rate the performance of each employee?
3. How often will you rate the performance of each employee?

Have each group share their evaluation plans for each job. The teacher should help to construct a table on the board that shows some of the similarities and differences between the proposed evaluation plans for each of the three different positions. The class should discuss the decisions made and consider how and why evaluation plans may differ for various jobs. The class should also consider the following discussion questions:

1. Would a blend of self-evaluations and standard supervisor evaluations be effective? Why or why not?
2. What categories are most common for evaluation employee performance? Why?
3. What are some advantages/disadvantages of frequent performance evaluations? Consider this from the perspective of a supervisor and also from the perspective of an employee.
4. Are there sources of bias that can enter the performance evaluation process? Describe them.
5. How can organizations reduce bias in performance evaluation?
6. Would it be useful to link compensation to performance evaluation outcomes? Why or why not?

Building Supervision Skills

Designing an Appraisal for Superiors

Divide the class into teams of four or five students. Each team will design a performance appraisal intended to evaluate the performance of either the president of the university or the president of the United States (or some other prominent person chosen by the class or the instructor). First, each team should choose which type of appraisal is best suited to evaluate the person's performance. Second, team members decide the content of the appraisal (what questions should be asked). Third, the class as a whole should discuss which types of appraisals were selected and why, and why certain questions were chosen.

Supervision Laws: Health and Safety, Labor Relations, Fair Employment

Where There's Smoke . . .

It's becoming common—the sight of workers huddled outside their office buildings, drawing the last bit of smoke into their lungs before they return to work from their furtive cigarette break. According to the National Cancer Institute, U.S. workplaces are rapidly becoming smoke-free, with 69 percent of respondents to a 1999 survey saying they worked in places where smoking is not allowed. In 1993, that number was only 46 percent.

More than three-quarters of states limit smoking in school buildings and health care facilities, but only 24 states limit smoking in private businesses. White-collar workplaces are more likely to be smoke-free than service-oriented or blue-collar workplaces. And there are more smoking bans in the North than in the South. What does it all mean for employees?

Some people believe the workplace has become a much healthier environment since the bans started. Even some smokers apparently don't want to be surrounded by smoke all day. Smokers bound by nonsmoking rules at work have been shown to quit at higher rates than in workplaces where smoking is allowed. As they quit, the air becomes cleaner not only for themselves but also for others.

But there may be a persistent backlash from those who cherish the right to smoke. According to the National Smokers Alliance, "Smokers have been unfairly characterized as second-class citizens who don't have the same rights as nonsmokers." The practice of smoking outside the workplace, some feel, forces workers into extreme cold and heat, which is seen as unfair and counterproductive.

Nevertheless, the evidence continues to mount that, in terms of employee health, where there's smoke, there's danger.

Most supervisors today are aware that maintaining the safety and health of employees is a major task. This responsibility is just one of many imposed by the federal government on organizations operating in the United States. Other chapters in this book have addressed additional responsibilities. Chapter 3 discussed labor laws that limit the ways in which organizations can use teamwork. Chapter 11 introduced the impact of the law on the scope of benefits organizations must offer employees. Chapters 15 and 17 explored laws intended to offer equal employment opportunities.

This appendix covers three areas in which federal laws govern the actions of organizations. First, it describes the role of the federal government in regulating safety and health in the workplace. It then describes safety and health hazards,

Sources: Amy Joyce, "Smoke-Free Workplaces Spreading Like Wildfire," Washington Post, November 15, 1998, p. H4; American Cancer Society, "Smoke-Free Workplace Encourages Smokers to Quit," news release, August 28, 2002, www.cancer.org; Minnesota Smoke-Free Coalition, "National Cancer Institute: Up in Smoke: Many States Lag Behind in Workplace Smoking Protections," news release, August 10, 2001, www.smokefreecoalition.org; National Cancer Institute, "Clean Indoor Air: Fact Sheet," State Cancer Legislative Database Program, Bethesda, Maryland, January 2002, www.scld-nci-net.

organizational programs for promoting safety and health, and the role of the supervisor in this area. Next, the appendix discusses unions—their impact and the laws that govern the interaction of organizations with unions and unionizing efforts. Finally, the appendix examines various ways in which the law has attempted to make the workplace fair and accessible to a diverse workforce. It introduces legal requirements for accommodating disabled employees, providing leave to workers who have family and medical needs, and keeping jobs open for employees who must complete military obligations. Finally, the appendix suggests ways to prevent the harassment of workers and respond when an employee claims harassment has occurred.

Government Regulation of Safety and Health

According to the Bureau of Labor Statistics, in 2002, more than 4.7 million occupational injuries and illnesses occurred among the almost 109 million workers in the private sector.[1] These problems are not limited to factory settings. Incidence rates were highest for workers in air transportation, nursing and personal care facilities, and the motor vehicle and equipment industry.[2] Figure B.1 shows the industries that reported the largest number (not rate) of workplace injuries and illnesses in 2002. Not only is the challenge of preventing these problems widespread, but many injuries and illnesses reported today are associated with modern technology—complaints such as injuries related to repetitive motion and the less-than-optimal design of workstations.

Many organizations recognize that safeguarding the well-being of employees in the workplace is not only ethical but also essential to attracting and keeping qualified personnel. Unfortunately, this view has not always prevailed. As a result, the government has stepped in to regulate the safety and health of the workplace.

Terrible accidents occurred when the industrial revolution brought together inexperienced workers with new and unfamiliar machinery. Beginning primarily in the early 1900s, state governments passed inspection laws and set up workers' compensation programs to provide benefits for employees injured on the job. In 1913 Congress created the Department of Labor, whose duties include the improvement of working conditions. Despite such actions, however, public sentiment in favor of further protection continued to grow.

FIGURE B.1 | Industries with the Most Occupational Injuries and Illnesses, 2002

Source: Bureau of Labor Statistics, "Workplace Injuries and Illnesses in 2002," Table 4, news release, December 18, 2003, www.bls.gov.

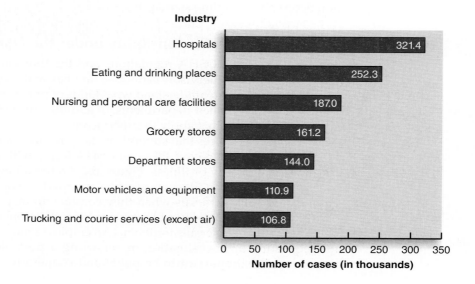

Occupational Safety and Health Act (OSHAct) of 1970

The most far-reaching of the laws regulating workplace safety and health is the Occupational Safety and Health Act (OSHAct) of 1970. The law is intended "to assure so far as possible every working man and woman in the nation safe and healthful working conditions and to preserve our human resources." The OSHAct sets up government agencies to conduct research regarding occupational health and safety, set health and safety standards, inspect workplaces, and penalize employers that do not meet standards. Penalties can be severe, including fines of $7,000 per day for failure to correct a violation and jail terms of six months for falsifying records to deceive inspectors.

OSHA and NIOSH

The OSHAct established two federal agencies to see that employers carry out its provisions. The Occupational Safety and Health Administration (OSHA), a part of the U.S. Department of Labor, is charged with setting and enforcing standards for workplace health and safety. People often think of OSHA standards as pertaining mainly to factory-related issues such as personal protective equipment (e.g., gloves, safety shoes) and guards on machinery. However, many OSHA standards pertain to health and safety issues that arise in offices, including recently proposed standards for air quality and the prevention of repetitive-motion injuries. (These topics are discussed later in this appendix.)

To ensure that organizations are meeting its standards, OSHA's inspectors may visit companies but must show a search warrant before conducting an inspection. "Between state and federal [inspections], we do about 85,000 inspections a year total, out of about 6 million workplaces," says former OSHA assistant secretary Charles Jeffress. The agency also hosts a Web site with special areas for small businesses and links to online advisers. It has placed compliance-assistance specialists in its regional offices and also hosts forums and training sessions around the country.[3] OSHA also operates a program of free onsite consultations through which independent consultants evaluate an organization's work practices, environmental hazards, and health and safety program. If an organization follows the consultant's recommendations, it bears no penalties for the shortcomings identified.

The National Institute for Occupational Safety and Health (NIOSH) is responsible for conducting research related to workplace safety and health. It is a part of the Department of Health and Human Services. NIOSH provides OSHA with information necessary for setting standards.

The Supervisor's Responsibility under the OSHAct

Given the extent of OSHA regulations and the thousands of pages interpreting those regulations, supervisors cannot be familiar with every regulation. However, supervisors do need to understand what kinds of practices are required to preserve health and safety in their departments. In addition, the OSHAct imposes some specific responsibilities that apply to supervisors.

The OSHAct requires that supervisors keep records of occupational injuries and illnesses. They must record these on OSHA forms within six working days after learning of the injury or illness. Figure B.2, on the following page, details which types of accidents and illnesses must be recorded. A supervisor also may have to accompany OSHA officials when they conduct an inspection. These inspections occur in response to a request by an employer, a union, or an employee, or when OSHA's own schedule calls for them. (An employer may not penalize an employee for requesting an investigation or reporting a possible violation.) During the inspection, it is important to be polite and cooperative. This is not always easy

FIGURE B.2 | Accidents and Illnesses That Must Be Recorded under OSHAct

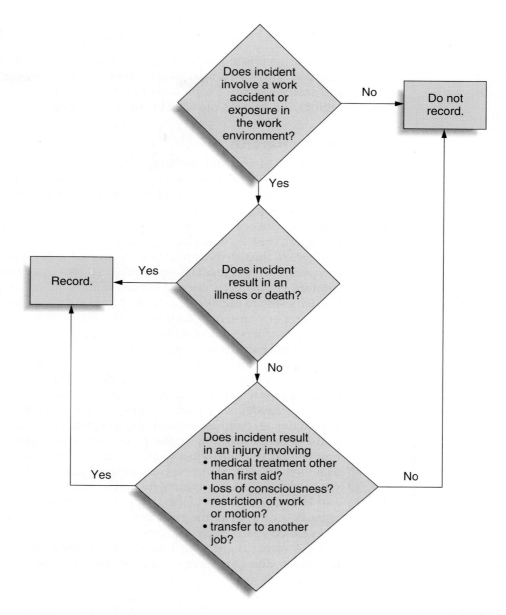

because the inspection may come at an inconvenient time, and a supervisor may view it as unwanted interference. However, being uncooperative is no way to foster good relations with the agency and could even lead the inspectors to be tougher than they otherwise might be.

Because chemical hazards are widespread in the modern workplace, OSHA has issued a right-to-know rule requiring that employees be informed about the chemicals used where they work. Each organization must have available information about what chemical hazards exist in the workplace and how employees can protect themselves against those hazards. The information must include labels on containers of chemicals and hazardous materials, as well as Material Safety Data Sheets (MSDS), both of which identify the chemicals, describe how to handle them, and identify the risks involved. A supervisor should make certain that this information is available for all chemicals that are brought into, used in, or produced at the workplace he or she supervises. If a supervisor finds that some information still is needed, the suppliers of the chemicals and other hazardous substances should be able to provide it.

Types of Safety and Health Problems

Because supervisors have an important role to play in maintaining a safe and healthy workplace, they need to be aware of problems that commonly arise, including health and safety hazards. People tend to associate both classes of hazards with factory settings, but hazards can arise in any work setting, from offices to police cars.

Health Hazards

As a result of stressful working conditions, an air-traffic controller developed a stomach ulcer. A clerical employee believes that sharing a poorly ventilated room with a photocopier has caused her dizzy spells. These are examples of conditions in the work environment that may gradually hurt the health of the people there. Such conditions are health hazards. In general, health hazards may be physical, chemical, biological, or stress-inducing (see Figure B.3).

Physical health hazards include noise, vibration, radiation, temperature extremes, and furniture and equipment that are not designed properly for the user's comfort. For instance, operating noisy equipment can impair an employee's hearing. Exposure to radiation can make a person more vulnerable to cancer.

Improperly designed furniture can contribute to muscle aches and repetitive motion disorders (described later in this appendix).

Chemical hazards may be present in dusts, fumes, and gases. They include chemicals that are carcinogenic (causes of cancer). Examples of chemical hazards are asbestos, coal dust, lead, and benzene. People in office buildings may be exposed to chemicals from synthetic carpeting, tobacco smoke, and other sources. OSHA has proposed guidelines for indoor air quality but has not implemented regulations. The guidelines emphasize providing adequate ventilation and requiring employees to use separate smoking rooms or go outdoors to smoke. Although studies have estimated that ventilation and other requirements could cost employers more than $8 billion a year, OSHA also has estimated that companies could save $15 billion a year from increased productivity and less absenteeism.[4] For this practical reason and to meet ethical standards, many businesses try to keep their indoor air clean, regardless of whether the government requires specific measures.

Enclosed spaces such as aircraft can pose health hazards when the air quality is poor. A recent flight from Los Angeles to the East Coast made an unscheduled landing in Chicago where paramedics met the crew and passengers, who suffered

FIGURE B.3 | Types of Health Hazards

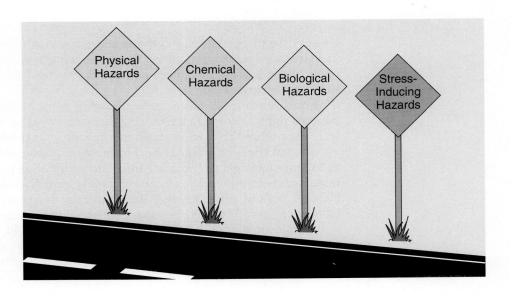

loss of motor skills and mental alertness, inability to judge the passage of time, apathy, and even loss of consciousness. The problems were attributed to bad air. Recycled air saves the airplanes $60,000 per plane per year, but some believe that these savings come at too high a price. The Centers for Disease Control and Prevention and NIOSH are looking into continued complaints about carbon dioxide levels, overly dry air, and other health hazards on planes.[5]

Biological hazards include bacteria, fungi, and insects associated with risks to people's health. Modern office buildings, which tend to be sealed tight against the elements, can be fertile grounds for such health hazards. Likewise, overwatering plants can encourage the growth of molds in the standing water, and those molds can circulate in air currents, making employees ill.

Stressful working conditions also may harm the health of employees. For example, employees may be more apt to suffer from stress-related illnesses if their work requires them to take risks, please an unpredictable supervisor, or witness a lot of suffering. (Chapter 13 describes the consequences of stress and ways to manage it.)

Safety Hazards

A safety hazard is a condition in the workplace that may lead to an injury-causing accident. Common types of injuries include cuts, broken bones, burns, and electric shocks. Figure B.4 shows several common job-related injuries and illnesses, along with corresponding days of work lost. At their most serious, injuries can lead to death. NIOSH reports that each day an average of 9,000 U.S. workers sustain disabling injuries on the job, 16 die from an injury sustained at work, and 137 die from work-related diseases. A NIOSH-funded study of the costs of such injuries and illnesses revealed that the direct cost to businesses is over $40 billion a year, plus about $200 billion in indirect costs.[6] In general, safety hazards arise from personal behavior (that is, unsafe acts) or conditions of the physical environment.

Types of Safety Hazards

Personal behavior as a safety hazard refers to practices by managers and employees that create an environment in which accidents may occur. This behavior may be as basic as carelessness or as obvious as drinking on the job. Sometimes employees

FIGURE B.4 | Common Job-Related Injuries and Illnesses and Corresponding Days of Work Generally Missed

Source: NIOSH, *Worker Health Chartbook 2000*, DHHS (NIOSH) Publication No. 2000-127, http://www.cdc.gov/niosh/pdfs/2000-127d.pdf.

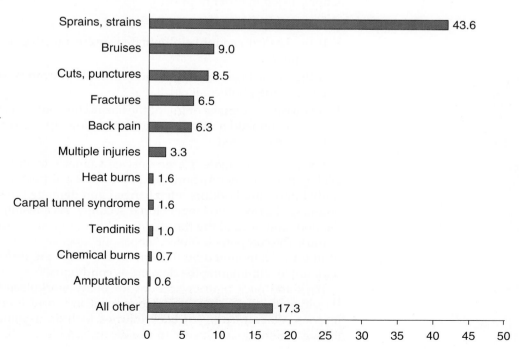

cause a safety hazard by refusing to follow proper procedures or use safety equipment such as goggles or gloves. Supervisors and other managers can contribute by failing to enforce safety measures or requiring employees to work such long hours that they do not get enough rest to think clearly. NIOSH's *Worker Health Chartbook 2000* reported that in 1997, motor-vehicle–related incidents were the leading cause of fatal workplace injury.[7] Therefore, supervisors should be especially concerned about encouraging safe behavior among employees who spend work time in vehicles— delivery personnel, salespeople, employees who take business trips, and so on.

Some employees are said to be accident-prone—that is, more likely to have accidents than other people. These employees tend to act on impulse, without careful thought, and do not concentrate on their work. Many employees who are vulnerable to accidents have negative attitudes about their jobs, co-workers, or supervisors. Perhaps they find the work boring. Sometimes people who are otherwise careful are vulnerable to accidents. When people are struggling with personal problems or do not get enough sleep, they may become accident prone. Therefore, a supervisor needs to pay attention to the behavior of all employees to recognize which of them are at risk for causing an accident on any given day. A supervisor may need to restrict the activities of an employee who is temporarily accident prone or even to send that person home. If the problem continues, a supervisor may have to use the counseling and discipline procedures described in Chapter 12.

Hazardous working conditions that can lead to accidents are as varied as a messy work environment, electrical cords where people might trip over them, poor lighting, and a lack of protective devices on machinery. A study by Liberty Mutual that used Bureau of Labor Statistics and workers' compensation data found that falls and slips were the second and third most costly types of worksite injuries in the United States in 1998.[8] Even language barriers can contribute to work hazards, as in the case of a young Hispanic worker who slipped from a wet roof and was paralyzed. His supervisor, who did not speak Spanish, said the worker did not speak English, so it had been difficult to communicate that the roof was dangerously slick.[9]

Responses

A supervisor who observes unsafe conditions should take one of the following actions, listed in order of priority:

1. Eliminate the hazard.
2. If the hazard cannot be eliminated, use protective devices such as guards on machinery.
3. If the hazard cannot be guarded, provide warnings, such as labels on the hot parts inside photocopiers.
4. If you cannot remove or guard the hazard on your own, notify the proper authority. Recommend a solution, and then follow up to make sure that the condition has been corrected.

For Frank Clemente, Cargo Service Center's facility supervisor at Chicago's O'Hare International Airport, one of the busiest airports in the world, safety is especially important. Forklifts often banged and damaged the dock doors at the warehouse, so the doors no longer closed securely. As a result, moisture would form on the floor and around the threshold, making the warehouse floor slippery and hazardous. The company installed "knockout" dock doors, which consist of panels that fit into tracks mounted on the wall. If the doors are dislodged, they can easily be remounted, eliminating the dangerous conditions.[10]

Back and neck injuries account for many workplace injuries, so a supervisor should especially seek measures to prevent and correct safety hazards causing such injuries. Ways to prevent back injuries include designing the job to minimize injuries, training employees to use lifting techniques that minimize strain on the back, reducing the size or weight of objects to be lifted, using mechanical aids, and making sure workers assigned to do a job are strong enough to do it safely. The position that puts the most stress on the back is sitting. Supervisors of office employees should be sure employees have comfortable chairs and enough opportunities to stand up and move around.

Common Concerns

Several common concerns about safety and health in the workplace are especially significant because they are widely occurring, or at least widely discussed. These include smoking, alcoholism and drug abuse, problems related to the use of computers, repetitive-motion disorders, and AIDS.

Smoking

An estimated 57 million individuals in the United States currently smoke cigarettes, risking serious health consequences such as cancer, heart disease, and high blood pressure. With about 440,000 deaths in the United States each year being attributable to tobacco use, smoking is the leading preventable cause of death and disease in the country.[11] Environmental ("secondhand") tobacco smoke contains more than 4,000 chemicals, of which more than 50 are known to be carcinogenic. Secondhand smoke is associated with a greater risk for lung cancer and coronary heart disease, as well as a variety of risks to children, including sudden infant death syndrome, asthma, bronchitis, and pneumonia.[12] As well as a health hazard, cigarette smoking is a safety hazard; lit cigarettes can cause burns, fires, or explosions when handled carelessly or near flammable substances.

Because the consequences of cigarette smoking are potentially serious, many organizations have restricted the amount of smoking allowed in the workplace, as seen in the opening story. In many locations, the restrictions also are required by state or local law. A 1999 survey of 17 states and the District of Columbia conducted by the American Medical Association found that official workplace policies that limited smoking in public, common, or work areas were in effect at 87–97 percent of firms. According to the National Cancer Institute, laws that restrict smoking at some or all work sites are in effect in the District of Columbia and 47 states, with smoking most often prohibited in school buildings and health care facilities.[13]

Supervisors can help minimize the effects of smoking in the workplace by enforcing the organization's restrictions and providing encouragement and recognition to employees who are trying to quit smoking.

Alcoholism and Drug Abuse

Alcoholism and drug abuse are serious problems in the workplace and can be costly to the organization. People who are under the influence of these substances are more likely to be involved in accidents. Many organizational policies therefore call for strong action when an employee is found to be under the influence.

Part of the supervisor's role in promoting safety is counseling and disciplining employees with these problems. (For more information on how supervisors should respond, refer to Chapter 12.)

Problems Related to Computer Use

A sizable majority of U.S. workers now use computers on the job. As computers have become increasingly common in all kinds of work environments, people have attributed some health problems to computer use.[14] Many of the concerns involve the use of video display terminals (VDT), the screens on which computers display information. Users of VDTs have complained that working with or near these screens causes a variety of health problems, including eyestrain and vision problems. Some reports have suggested that VDT use also is linked to pregnancy

FIGURE B.5 | Positioning a VDT for Comfortable Viewing

problems, notably miscarriages, through the radiation emitted by the VDTs, but research currently does not support a link between VDT use and pregnancy risks.

Fortunately, the problems associated with VDT use can be reduced or eliminated. Computer workstations should position VDTs to minimize glare (see Figure B.5), and lighting for screen viewing should be at a moderate level (20 to 50 foot-candles as measured by a light meter). Computer screens should be placed at least 16 inches from the user's eyes. Employees who use computers should take rest breaks; a break as short as three to five minutes each hour can alleviate eye discomfort. Occasionally glancing away from the screen toward distant objects relaxes the eye muscles. Those who are concerned about radiation also may wish to install radiation shields on their computers or use only low-emission VDTs.

Typing or staring into computers for long stretches can lead to sore muscles in the back, arms, legs, and neck. Many of these problems are associated with poor posture. The corrections may be as simple as adjusting the height and position of the user's chair, keyboard or mouse, and computer screen. Computer users may also be susceptible to repetitive-motion disorders, discussed next.

Repetitive-Motion Disorders

According to OSHA, musculoskeletal disorders, or MSDs (injuries and disorders of soft tissues include muscles, tendons, ligaments, joints, and cartilage and the nervous system), account for about one out of every three lost-workday occupational injuries and illnesses.[15] MSDs occur in all occupations and industries. In 2002, the main causes of MSDs were worker motion or position. In more than 50,000 cases, injuries occurred from workers performing the same motion over and over in a way that caused damage. Advances in machinery and electronic equipment have enabled workers to perform repetitive functions at an increasingly rapid pace. Unfortunately, the repeated application of force to the same muscles or joints can result in injuries known as repetitive-motion disorders.

An example of these disorders is carpal tunnel syndrome, which involves pain in the wrist and fingers. This is a common complaint among those who type at a keyboard all day or perform other tasks involving the wrist, such as making the same cut in chickens all day at a poultry processor. Some people in the newspaper business have speculated that stiff competition for jobs in that field has forced many reporters and columnists to try to cope with the pain rather than complain about it.

Back problems are another major cost to employees and employers, accounting for an estimated $50 billion per year in workers' compensation. An additional $50 billion is spent each year on indirect costs such as finding and training substitute workers and running physical conditioning and reduced-work programs to help ease employees back into their jobs. Reduced workplace productivity is a cause for concern. "If you look at lost work time," says Professor Alan Hedge of Cornell University's Department of Design and Environmental Analysis, "it's the tip of the iceberg. When you're hurting at work you're not as effective."[16]

To prevent repetitive-motion disorders, an organization can take several measures, including designing jobs and workstations to allow for rests, using adjustable furniture, and avoiding awkward movements and bad posture. This type of response to the problem is an application of ergonomics, the science concerned with the human characteristics that need to be considered in designing tasks and equipment so that people will work most effectively and safely. While supervisors need not be experts in ergonomics, they can cultivate an awareness of these issues. Another measure is to encourage employees who are in pain to seek medical attention right away. Supervisors should never tell their employees to work through pain, as this may aggravate an existing injury.

AIDS

Although other illnesses are more widespread, probably the most feared is AIDS (acquired immunodeficiency syndrome), caused by HIV, the human immunodeficiency virus. The biggest reason for this fear is that AIDS remains incurable and fatal. Fortunately, people cannot catch it from touching a person with AIDS or sharing a drinking fountain or restroom; the HIV virus is transmitted through the exchange of bodily fluids, which can occur through sexual activity, blood transfusions, and the sharing of contaminated hypodermic needles, as well as between an infected mother and a fetus.

Most of the activities involving the transmission of HIV would not occur in the workplace. The major exception is health care institutions where hypodermic needles are used. These institutions should have procedures for the proper handling and disposal of the needles to prevent the spread of AIDS and other serious diseases such as hepatitis.

In most work settings, the major concern about AIDS is how to treat employees who are HIV-positive or who have AIDS. Both fairness and federal anti-discrimination laws dictate treating these employees in the same way as anyone else with a disability. As long as the employees can perform their jobs, they should be allowed to remain. At some point, an organization may have to make reasonable accommodations to allow them to continue working, such as allowing an ill employee to complete job assignments at home.

When an employee has AIDS, a supervisor must confront the fears that other employees are likely to have about working with that employee. With help from the human resources department, a supervisor may need to educate other employees about AIDS and how it is transmitted. Despite these efforts, some employees may shun a co-worker with AIDS. Therefore, the supervisor and others in the organization must do their best to protect the confidentiality of a person with AIDS. If an employee has AIDS, or the employee's co-workers are having trouble coping, the supervisor may wish to refer them to the organization's employee-assistance program, if one exists. (These programs are described in Chapter 12.)

Workplace Programs to Promote Safety and Health

Many employers have instituted formal programs to promote the safety and health of employees. The program may include training, safety meetings, posters, awards for safe performance, and safety and health committees. A typical committee includes operative employees and managers, perhaps with a membership that rotates among the employees. A recent study of occupational safety and health committees in the public sector in New Jersey found that committees with more worker involvement were associated with fewer reported illnesses and injuries.[17] The duties of a health and safety committee can include regularly inspecting work areas, reviewing employees' suggestions for improving health and safety, and promoting awareness about safety. The committee also might sponsor the organization's contests or awards for safe practices.

Many organizations have extended their safety and health programs to cover off-duty conduct by employees that contributes to health problems. These efforts may be part of a wellness program (see Chapter 13). For example, some wellness programs seek to discourage employees from smoking altogether (not just restricting smoking at work), and others seek to teach healthy eating and exercise habits.

Benefits

By reducing the number and severity of work-related injuries and illnesses, safety and health programs can cut the costs to organizations in a number of areas. These include health and workers' compensation insurance, defense of lawsuits, repair or replacement of equipment damaged in accidents, and wages paid for lost time. The savings can be significant. In addition, safety and health programs can motivate employees, reduce turnover, and help prevent pain and suffering among employees and their families. Finally, an organization that is a safe and healthy place to work is more likely to enjoy good relations with the government and community and should have an easier time recruiting desirable employees.

Characteristics of an Effective Program

A safety and health program is effective when it minimizes the likelihood that people will be injured or become ill as a result of conditions in the workplace, when all levels of management demonstrate a strong commitment to the program, and when employees believe the program is worthwhile. In addition, all employees need to be trained in the importance of safety and ways to promote health and safety in the workplace. This training should give employees an ongoing awareness of the need to behave in safe ways. Finally, an organization should have a system for identifying and correcting hazards before they do damage. In addition to those mentioned elsewhere in this appendix, workplace hazards can include pesticides, loose carpeting, cleaning products, toner, markers, correction fluid, artificial lighting, dark stairways, needles or syringes, lead-based paint (in older buildings), noise, carbon dioxide, radon, X-rays, perfume, radioactive materials and waste, biological waste, poisonous substances, and tools and equipment that are not the proper size for the employee.[18]

Role of the Supervisor

Top management's support of safety measures is important; the organization may even have a safety director or other manager responsible for safety programs. Nevertheless, it is up to supervisors to see that employees follow safety precautions. It is the supervisors who observe and are responsible for the day-to-day performance of employees. Unfortunately, some supervisors must witness a serious injury before they appreciate why they must enforce safety rules and procedures. Supervisors who avoid enforcing these rules because they are afraid employees will react negatively are missing the point of why the rules exist. They also are failing to recognize that they have an important role in maintaining a safe and healthy workplace.

Effective supervisors also go beyond simple enforcement of rules. They may encourage their employees to diagnose hazards and help them cut through red tape to improve unsafe conditions. A study of hospitals found that nurses who saw safety-related problems often could not bring about the changes needed to correct those problems.[19] A supervisor can be a necessary ally in this situation.

Training and Hazard Prevention

A supervisor needs to see that employees understand and follow all procedures designed to maintain safety and health. New employees must be well trained in how to do their job safely; more experienced employees need training when they take on new responsibilities or when the organization introduces new procedures, materials, or machinery. In addition, employees need reminders about safe practices. In addition to comments from the supervisor, the reminders could include posters, items in the company or department newsletter, and presentations by one employee to the others. Statistics about the department's performance, such as the number of accidents during the current year compared with last year, can be posted on bulletin boards or reported in the newsletter. In addition, OSHA requires that companies with more than 10 employees display the safety and health poster shown in Figure B.6, which provides information about employees' rights under the OSHAct.

FIGURE B.6 | OSHA Safety and Health Poster

Some special concerns arise with regard to educating workers who are or may become pregnant. A Supreme Court ruling prohibits employers from forbidding pregnant workers from holding hazardous jobs, a policy that, if permitted, could force women to choose between holding a job and having a baby. Nevertheless, women who remain in these jobs may sue an employer for damages if a child is born with injuries caused by hazardous working conditions. The acceptable way to protect female employees of childbearing age is to emphasize information. They should be informed of any pregnancy-related risks of work assignments. A supervisor also may encourage employees to ask for a reassignment to a less hazardous job if they become pregnant. (The organization may not reduce the employee's pay, benefits, or seniority rights.) If the employee cannot be reassigned, the organization can give the employee leave during her pregnancy, including full pay and a guarantee of getting the job back after the baby is born.

Another situation calling for special attention is the supervision of shift workers, who also need additional guidance in safe practices. Employees will be more alert and better able to concentrate if they adapt their overall lifestyle to working night shifts or rotating shifts. They must make an extra effort to get enough quality sleep during the day, seeking out a quiet, dark, cool place for doing so. People who are naturally alert late at night will probably sleep best if they do so right after working at night, whereas others will do better if they sleep just before going in to work at night. People who work a night shift also will be more comfortable if they eat relatively light foods during their shift, avoiding heavy, greasy items.

A supervisor should encourage all employees to participate in the promotion of safe and healthy conditions. One way to do this is to emphasize that employees share in the responsibility for creating a safe work setting. In addition, a supervisor should be responsive to employee complaints related to safety, seeing that the health and safety committee or the appropriate individual investigates these complaints. Any hazardous conditions should be corrected immediately.

Prompt Responses

A supervisor who observes a violation of health and safety guidelines should respond immediately and consistently. Failure to react is a signal to employees that guidelines are not really important. First, a supervisor should determine why the violation occurred. Does the employee understand what the proper procedures are? If the employee understands the procedures but still resists following them, the supervisor should try to find out why. For example, if an employee complains that some safety equipment is uncomfortable to use, investigating the complaint may turn up a more effective alternative, such as a greater selection of safety glasses or a way to set up a job so that less safety equipment is required. Despite complaints, however, a supervisor must insist that employees follow safety procedures, even when they seem inconvenient. If the safety rules are violated, a supervisor may have to take disciplinary action. (See Chapter 12 for a discussion of discipline.)

Quality of Work Life

By combating fatigue, boredom, and dissatisfaction, which can make an employee accident prone, a supervisor can promote safety and health. These efforts may include improving the quality of work life by making jobs more interesting and satisfying. Although no one has proved a link between quality of work life and employee safety and health, it seems reasonable to assume that interested, satisfied employees will tend to be healthier and more careful. (Chapter 11 offers some guidelines for expanding and enriching jobs.)

In the case of shift workers, a supervisor can help minimize fatigue by encouraging the organization to place employees on a single shift or rotate shifts so that employees go to work later and later, rather than earlier and earlier or in no steady pattern. Providing bright lighting also will help employees stay alert at night.

Setting an Example

As with any other area in which a supervisor wants employees to behave in a certain way, the supervisor must set a good example and follow safe practices. For instance, a supervisor who uses tools improperly, creates a tower of soft drink cans on a filing cabinet, or tries to troubleshoot a photocopier without first turning off the power is voiding the effect of even the most eloquent lecture on safety in the workplace.

The following guidelines are some other ways in which supervisors can set an example about safety. Most of these carry little or no financial cost.[20]

1. Be a fanatic about health and safety. Make it a top priority in your factory, shop, or office.

2. Establish a safety committee with responsibility for conducting periodic safety audits.

3. Heighten worker awareness through safety training programs, regularly scheduled safety campaigns, and celebration of National Safety Week.

4. Reward suggestions for improved health and safety measures.

5. Make cleanliness more than a virtue. Make it a requirement.

6. Distribute a safety and emergency procedures and instructions manual.

7. Post emergency phone numbers in prominent locations throughout the workplace.

8. Conduct safety evacuation drills where appropriate.

9. Insist that all hazardous substances and materials be tightly sealed and properly stored.

10. When you say that hard hats are required on the work site, mean it!

11. Install appropriate smoke detectors, alarms, and fire extinguishers.

12. Strictly enforce company no-smoking rules and introduce a no-perfume policy when necessary.

13. Clearly mark all hazardous items and zones.

14. Never condone or encourage safety shortcuts.

Labor Relations: The Supervisor's Role

Concerns related to health and safety are among the issues that spurred the formation of unions in the United States during the late 1800s. Employees, who then worked as long as 12 hours each day, banded together to persuade employers to shorten work hours, pay higher wages, and improve safety. Today unions continue to negotiate with organizations over similar issues.

In 1935, the federal government passed the Wagner Act (also called the National Labor Relations Act). This law aims to define and protect the rights of workers and employers, encourage collective bargaining, and eliminate unfair practices (for example, violence and threatening to fire employees who join a union). In 2011, the National Labor Relations Board issued a rule requiring companies to display a poster summarizing employees' rights under the act. The poster is supposed to be displayed in locations where the company posts other notices of rights and workplace rules, including on company Web sites for employees.

Following passage of the Wagner Act, union membership tripled (see Figure B.7 on the following page). As a percentage of the total workforce, union membership peaked in the 1940s. Union membership has since fallen to less than 12 percent of the workforce during the past decade.[21] This drop has accompanied a decline in the industrial sector of the economy, where union membership was traditionally strongest. The power of unions also has declined along with the numbers. During the 1980s, many unions made major concessions in negotiations with employers.

FIGURE B.7 | Union Membership as a Percentage of the Employed U.S. Workforce

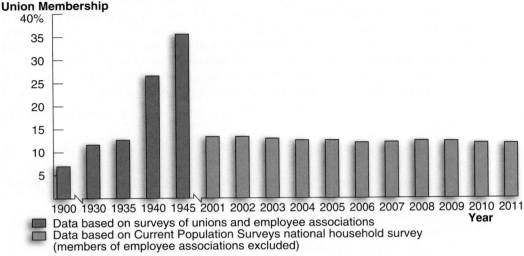

Source: C. Chang and C. Sorrentino, "Union Membership in 12 Countries," *Monthly Labor Review* 114, no. 12 (1991), pp. 46–53; L. Troy and N. Sheflin, *Union Sourcebook* (West Orange, NJ: Industrial Relations Data and Information Services, 1985); Bureau of Labor Statistics, Current Population Survey database, http://data.bls.gov, accessed February 27, 2012.

The processes by which supervisors and other managers work constructively with unions constitute the management discipline of labor relations. Effective labor relations cannot eliminate all conflicts between labor and management, but they do provide a relatively low-cost means of resolving conflict through discussion rather than confrontation. Labor relations occur through activities such as organization drives and collective bargaining.

The Organization Drive

An organization drive is the union's method of getting its members elected to represent the workers in an organization. Management typically resists these drives because it believes a union will interfere with managers' ability to make decisions in the best interests of the company. Managers also fear that the union will convert employees' loyalty to the company into loyalty to the union. The union tries to convince employees that management has never had their interests at heart and that they will be better off if they let the union bargain collectively with management.

The process of organizing begins when a few employees decide they want to be represented by a union or when union leaders target an organization as a likely candidate. Union representatives then go to the company to organize. If at least 30 percent of the employees sign an authorization card stating they want the union to represent them, the union may request an election. The employees vote by secret ballot. If a majority of the voting employees favor the union, the union becomes the representative of *all* employees in the bargaining unit.

Although managers generally want to keep unions out, federal law says supervisors and other managers may not restrain employees from forming or joining a union. Supervisors are allowed to state their views about unions, but they may not threaten employees with punishment for forming or joining a union, and they may not promise rewards for working against the union. A supervisor who is unsure about what kinds of comments are permitted should consult with the organization's human resources department. A union may not try to pressure employees into joining. Supervisors who think the union is violating this law should inform the human resources department.

Collective Bargaining

Typically, workers and managers have differing views on a variety of issues; after all, the fundamental reason for unions is to give workers a stronger voice when differences arise. The basic process for resolving such differences is collective bargaining—the process of seeking to reach a contract spelling out the rights and duties of unionized workers and their employer. Typically, bargaining begins when the union and management set forth their demands. Because the two parties usually differ on what is acceptable, they discuss how to resolve the major areas of conflict. If they need help resolving a conflict, they may call in a mediator, or conciliator, a neutral person who helps the two sides reach agreement.

A supervisor seldom has a direct role in collective bargaining. However, management may ask a supervisor to provide information that will help during the bargaining process. This is another reason the supervisor should keep careful records concerning employees.

The Labor Contract

A typical labor contract contains provisions such as guidelines for union membership; procedures for handling grievances; policies about regular and overtime pay, benefits (including vacations and holidays), and work hours; and agreements concerning safety and health. A supervisor must abide by the terms of this contract, so he or she must be familiar with it. A supervisor who is unfamiliar with the labor contract may unintentionally cause a problem by, for example, asking an employee to do something forbidden by the contract or using a procedure for discipline that is prohibited. Ignoring a provision in the contract, such as the length of rest periods, may be interpreted as an agreement to change the contract. A supervisor also should treat all employees fairly and consistently. This is good practice whether or not there is a union; plus, federal law prohibits supervisors and other managers from discriminating against union members.

Working with the Union Steward

Part of a supervisor's job under a labor contract is to maintain a good relationship with the union steward. A union steward is an employee who serves as the union's representative in a particular work unit. Employees go to the union steward with their contract-related questions and complaints.

To minimize conflict and resolve problems that arise, a supervisor needs to cooperate with the union steward. The supervisor should treat a union steward with respect and tell him or her about problems and upcoming changes. If the supervisor and union steward have a cooperative relationship, they often can resolve problems themselves rather than subject the organization and its employees to the cost and stress of an ongoing dispute.

Grievances

Employees who believe they have been treated unfairly under the terms of the labor contract may bring a formal complaint, or grievance. Typically, when an employee brings a grievance, he or she first meets with the supervisor and union steward to look for a solution. Most of the time, the three of them can resolve the problem. If not, higher-level managers and union representatives meet to seek a solution. If they cannot reach an agreement, both parties might agree to bring in an outside arbitrator, a neutral person who reaches a decision on how to resolve a conflict. Both parties must adhere to the terms set by the arbitrator.

To avoid this costly and time-consuming process, supervisors should make sure employees have a chance to be heard. In many cases, a supervisor can resolve conflicts before an employee even files a grievance. When a grievance is filed, a supervisor should take it seriously. This means gathering complete information and trying to resolve the problem as quickly as possible. Conflicts that are allowed to continue are likely to seem more significant to both parties.

Strikes

Occasionally, the parties are unable to reach an agreement during collective bargaining, so the employees vote to go on strike. During a strike, employees leave their jobs and refuse to come back until there is a contract. The use of strikes has been declining in recent decades. According to the U.S. Department of Labor's Bureau of Labor Statistics, there were 381 major strikes in 1970, 187 in 1980, 44 in 1990, and only 14 in 2003.[22] In general, striking during the term of a contract—a wildcat strike—is illegal.

The Supervisor's Role in Preventing Strikes

Although a supervisor has little control over any agreement reached during collective bargaining by union and management representatives, he or she does have a role in minimizing the likelihood of a strike. Treating employees fairly and reasonably fosters good relations between employees and management. In this kind of climate, employees are less likely to desire a strike. Good communication practices also enable employees to understand management's point of view and give them a chance to vent their frustrations while staying on the job.

The Supervisor's Role During a Strike

Once the employees have voted to strike, there is little a supervisor can do to resolve the conflict. If the circumstances of the strike do not involve unfair labor practices by an employer, the employer may hire replacement workers. Then the supervisor must tackle the challenge of training and getting to know a new workforce. The supervisor will have to adjust goals and expectations to allow for the new employees' inexperience.

When a wildcat strike occurs, a supervisor should follow the practices listed in Table B.1, notably, to observe carefully what is occurring and encourage employees to abide by the contract and return to work. At no time should the supervisor make agreements or even discuss the problem that led to the wildcat strike.

TABLE B.1 | Guidelines for Supervising During a Wildcat Strike

Source: Leslie W. Rue and Lloyd L. Byars, *Supervision: Key Link to Productivity*, 6th ed. (New York: Irwin/McGraw-Hill, 1999), p. 263. Copyright © 1999 by The McGraw-Hill Companies. Reproduced with permission of The McGraw-Hill Companies.

Stay on the job.
Notify higher management by telephone or messenger.
Carefully record the events as they happen.
Pay strict attention to who the leaders are, and record their behavior.
Record any lack of action by union officials.
Report all information as fully and as soon as possible to higher management.
Encourage employees to go back to work.
Ask union officials to instruct employees to go back to work.
Do not discuss the cause of the strike.
Do not make any agreements or say anything that might imply permission to leave work.
Make it clear that management will discuss the issue when all employees are back at work.

Notification about Plant Closings

Although unions no longer have their former strength in numbers, they do occasionally influence laws intended to protect workers. A recent law intended to mitigate the hardship caused by layoffs is the Worker Adjustment and Retraining Notification Act (WARN), which took effect in 1989. Under WARN, companies with at least 100 employees must provide at least 60 days' written notice of plans to close a facility for six months or longer or to lay off at least one-third of the workforce (or 500 or more employees, even if they are less than one-third of the company's workforce). The law makes exceptions for temporary facilities and temporary workers; if workers were hired to carry out a particular project, no notice is required when the project ends. Under WARN, companies are supposed to notify affected supervisors and managers, as well as nonmanagement employees.

The way WARN is applied may be complicated. Even so, supervisors should be aware of this law because layoffs and other kinds of reorganizations are a common feature of the modern business environment.

Fair Employment

Supervisors have an important role in helping their employers maintain fair employment practices. Fair employment goes beyond the initial decisions related to recruiting and hiring employees. Employers also have to provide a workplace in which employees can do their work free of intimidation and with equal opportunities to advance according to their abilities. Laws concerning fair employment cover the requirement to avoid harassment and provide reasonable accommodation. In addition, the government has passed laws intended to help employees keep their jobs when family, medical, and military needs arise. In all of these cases, supervisors can assist with compliance through planning and leadership aimed at keeping their group working effectively.

Sexual or Other Harassment

According to the Equal Employment Opportunity Commission (EEOC), the laws prohibiting discrimination forbid harassment of employees.[23] For example, Title VII of the Civil Rights Act forbids discrimination based on race, color, sex, religion, or national origin, including harassment of employees based on those characteristics. Likewise, harassment of employees for being 40 years or older or having a disability is forbidden because of the Age Discrimination in Employment Act and the Americans with Disabilities Act. In general, harassment does not mean an offhand remark or a little gentle teasing. Rather, it means conduct that is strong enough to make the workplace feel hostile or result in some employment action, such as an employee being demoted, moving to a less desired job, or leaving the company. However, it is risky for a supervisor to assume that teasing is lighthearted; a safer attitude is to encourage positive behavior.

In recent years, most attention has been directed toward sexual harassment, defined by the EEOC as "unwelcome sexual advances, requests for sexual favors, and other verbal and physical conduct of a sexual nature" that "has the purpose or effect of unreasonably interfering with an individual's work performance or creating an intimidating, hostile, or offensive work environment." It may include any of the behaviors listed in Table B.2 on the following page. The perpetrator and victim may be either male or female. (Less than 15 percent of complaints filed with the EEOC in 2003 were filed by men, but the percentage has been steadily growing over the past decade.[24]) The victim does not need to prove that sexual harassment caused psychological harm, only that it was unwelcome.

The number of sexual harassment charges filed with the EEOC increased dramatically during the 1990s and then fell somewhat in recent years. Whether or not

TABLE B.2 | Behaviors That May Constitute Sexual Harassment

Source: Based on Michael A. Verespej, "New-Age Sexual Harassment," *Industry Week*, May 15, 1995, p. 66.

Suggestive remarks.
Teasing or taunting of a sexual nature.
Unwelcome physical conduct or sexual advances.
Continual use of offensive language.
Sexual bantering.
Bragging about sexual prowess.
Office or locker-room pinups.
"Compliments" with sexual overtones.
A demand for sex in return for retaining a job or being promoted.

that decline is part of a trend, the problem continues to deserve serious consideration. Not only did penalties cost violators $50 million in 2003, but companies that permit harassment may be making their workplace inhospitable to some of their best people. In addition, ethics demands that people be treated politely and fairly.

Responding to Charges of Sexual Harassment

A sexual harassment charge is serious. Court decisions have held employers liable for the misdeeds of their employees unless an organization actively tries to prevent the misbehavior and responds effectively when it does occur. Therefore, when an employee charges a member of an organization with sexual harassment, a supervisor must take the problem seriously. There are no exceptions to this rule—not the attractiveness of the victim or the supervisor's opinion of a man who is offended by centerfold pictures.

A supervisor must see that the complaint is investigated properly. Generally, the investigation involves a third party, such as a personnel official, interviewing everyone involved. This official, the supervisor, and the parties involved should keep the investigation confidential. The supervisor must avoid expressing an opinion or imposing his or her interpretation on the situation.

Whether harassment occurs depends on how the behavior affects the recipient, not on the intent of the person performing the behavior. Thus, if lewd jokes and pornographic pictures create a climate that feels hostile and intimidating to an employee, it does not matter that the person who told the jokes and hung up the pictures thought only that they were funny. Perceptions vary from one person to another. This principle is especially important to supervisors evaluating their own behavior. Supervisors must appreciate that their position in the organization gives them greater power than the people they supervise. Behavior that might seem merely playful to a supervisor may seem more frightening in the eyes of someone with less power in the organization.

If the investigation indicates that sexual harassment did occur, the problem must be corrected. One approach that does *not* work is ignoring the offensive behavior in the hope that it will go away. The victim telling the offender to stop is effective more than half the time. Because of differences in perceptions, it may be helpful to describe not only the offending behavior but also the kind of behavior that would be acceptable. In addition, a supervisor needs to work with the human resources department to identify a prompt and firm response to charges that are proven. The response might be to move the offending employee to another department or shift or even to fire him or her. Discipline should be appropriate and swift, occurring the same day if possible or at least within a week.

Preventing Sexual Harassment

An employee who harasses another employee hurts the organization in several ways. The person who is being harassed is upset and unable to work as effectively as possible. If that person complains, disciplining the harasser may involve transferring or dismissing him or her, resulting in the loss of an otherwise qualified employee. And if the harassed person sues, the company faces the embarrassment and expense of defending itself in court. It is clearly in the organization's best interests to prevent harassment.

Accommodation of Disabled Employees

As we saw in Chapter 15, the Americans with Disabilities Act requires that employers make their facilities accessible to qualified employees with disabilities. People who qualify for this protection include those who have an impairment that substantially limits one or more life activities (including major bodily functions), or have a record of such an impairment, or are regarded as having such an impairment (for example, not being hired in the past because someone thought the person was impaired). Among many other possibilities, this definition covers people with hearing aids or prosthetic limbs, those with autism or an intellectual disability, and those with cancer or diabetes—assuming that, with reasonable accommodations, they can perform the essentials functions of their job.[25] Under this law, supervisors sometimes have to ensure that their company makes reasonable accommodations so that employees with disabilities can perform their jobs.

In the years since the passage of the ADA, the definition of what accommodations are "reasonable" has evolved through administrative decisions and court cases. Deciding what accommodations to make can be complex.[26] Supervisors should work with the human resources department to ensure that any actions taken meet the legal requirements. Supervisors contribute their perspective on which activities are required by the job, while human resource professionals contribute knowledge of what the law requires. Similarly, if an employee's performance seems to be declining and the supervisor believes a disability may be causing the decline, the supervisor should work with the human resources department to avoid discriminatory treatment. In general, supervisors should not convey to an employee their belief that he or she may be disabled; rather, they should focus on the work performance itself. Avoid casually using terms such as "manic" or "crazy," which may be interpreted as references to mental illness.

Family, Medical, and Military Leave

At times, employees must take time off work because they are ill or need to care for family members or fulfill military duties. In some situations, the organization must keep the employee's job available. Supervisors have to plan how the remaining employees will get the work done until the employee returns. They have to help the returning employee make a smooth transition back into the job. These responsibilities require strong leadership as well as good planning skills. Supervisors should be aware of the laws requiring these efforts.

Family and Medical Leave Act

Under the Family and Medical Leave Act (FMLA), employers with more than 50 employees must allow their eligible employees to take unpaid leave for up to 12 weeks for family and medical reasons. Although the law does not require paid leave, it does require that the employer maintain the employee's health benefits during the leave. When the employee returns, the employer must place the employee in the same or an equivalent position.

Reasons for which employees may take leave under FMLA include birth or adoption of a child; the need to care for an ill spouse, child, or parent; and a serious health condition that makes it impossible for the employee to perform his or her job. The Labor Department recently broadened the definition of "son and daughter" to cover any child under an employee's care. For example, that child could be a nephew the employee cares for while the child's parents serve in the military or a daughter cared for by the nonbiological, non-adoptive parent in a same-sex partnership.[27] In addition, unpaid leave is available to those whose family member became seriously injured or ill during military service or who need time off to make child care or other arrangements for a family member called to active duty in the U.S. armed services.

Employees who wish to take leave under FMLA must give the employer notice—30 days' notice if the reason is foreseeable. They also must comply with the organization's paperwork requirements. The employee's leave may be taken intermittently or in one absence. Each 12 months, the employee becomes eligible for another 12 weeks of unpaid leave. It is up to the employer to determine when each yearlong period begins and ends.

In some states, employers must meet state requirements that are stricter than the federal requirements of the FMLA. California recently became the first state to require paid family leave. Workers can earn up to six weeks of partial income, with the pay funded by a payroll tax of $4 per month per employee. Other states provide paid leave to low-income parents.[28]

The Department of Labor studied data on use of the FMLA during 1999 and the first half of 2000.[29] The department found that 23.8 million workers, or 16.5 percent, took some time off under FMLA. More than half took leave to care for their own health, and almost one-fifth took time off to care for a new child. Of the employees who took a leave, more than half were back at work within 10 days, and one-fourth took their leaves in installments as short as an hour. The main challenge for supervisors is to keep the work group organized when an employee's family or medical needs require time off. Through skillful planning and communication, supervisors can help to keep the organization running smoothly while also complying with the law.

Uniformed Services Employment and Reemployment Rights Act

In addition to family and personal commitments, many employees have made commitments to the military. And military campaigns in Afghanistan and Iraq have required that thousands of these employees serve their country for extended periods. That service has brought renewed attention to a 1994 law, the Uniformed Services Employment and Reemployment Rights Act (USERRA). Under USERRA, an individual who leaves a civilian job for service on active duty or for military training must be reemployed in the job that person would have held if he or she had not been absent for the military service. Along with the job itself, the returning employee must be granted the same level of benefits he or she would have received, including unpaid leave under FMLA. The law also requires that employers provide returning service members with reasonable efforts for training or retraining if needed, and the employer must make efforts to accommodate disabled veterans when they return. These obligations remain in effect for up to five years of military service. To receive the benefits, the service member must have been released under honorable conditions and report back to the employer in a timely manner.

In contrast to other employment laws, USERRA does not have an exemption for small organizations. Even a family business with a handful of employees is required to rehire returning service members. Complying with USERRA can be particularly challenging for small organizations, which acutely feel the absence of the service member yet may have difficulty affording an additional employee or finding someone to fill in temporarily. Still, most employees can be motivated to do extra because of their appreciation of the sacrifices being made by their co-workers in the military.

An additional challenge of reemploying veterans is that the stress of battle takes a heavy toll on some service members. The recent conflicts in the Middle East have required the largest and longest lasting mobilization of the reserve and National Guard since the Korean War, and the battle conditions have been traumatic for some who served. Some cope, while others experience posttraumatic stress disorder. Remember that supervisors should not even try to diagnose an employee's mental condition. However, if reemployed service members—or any employees— are having difficulty concentrating or getting along with their co-workers, the supervisor may need to intervene as described in Chapters 12 and 13.

One expert who has had plenty of experience with these challenges is Elaine Weinstein, senior vice president of human resources for KeySpan. More than two dozen of KeySpan's employees have been mobilized for military service since September 11, 2001. As they return, Weinstein plans what actions the company needs to take to help them make the transition back to civilian work. Sometimes a flexible work schedule is useful. Weinstein offers advice based on ethics: "Treat them as you would wish to be treated after leaving your family and supporting your country."[30]

Some people have complained about the challenges of complying with fair employment requirements. Family, medical, and military leave all pose hardships on organizations. And the need to avoid harassment feels like a minefield to some people. For example, fear of being accused of sexual harassment leaves some individuals feeling unable to pay friendly compliments. However, respecting the viewpoints, emotional comfort, and personal responsibilities of all employees simply makes ethical and practical sense. The same is true of ensuring employees' safety and health and practicing good labor relations. In each case, a supervisor recognizes that good employee relations are at the heart of cultivating the organization's most important resources: its employees.

Notes

1. Bureau of Labor Statistics, "Workplace Injuries and Illnesses in 2002," news release, December 18, 2003, www.bls.gov.

2. Ibid., Tables 1 and 4.

3. Christina LeBeau, "Breakway (A Special Report): Second Thoughts—Not Tough Enough? At Smaller Firms, Less OSHA Oversight and More Deaths and Injuries," *The Wall Street Journal*, March 19, 2001, pp. 14ff.

4. Aerias, "Standards and Guidelines for Indoor Air Quality (IAQ)," 2001, www.aerias.org/c_doc_149.htm.

5. Gayle Hanson, "In-Flight Air Recycling Fouls Friendly Skies," *Insight on the News*, February 17, 1997, p. 18; Julie Flaherty, "Flight Attendants Demand Cleaner In-Flight Air," Reuters, January 4, 2001.

6. National Institute for Occupational Safety and Health, "About NIOSH," www.cdc.gov/niosh/about.html; downloaded October 21, 2004.

7. "Worker Health Chartbook," *Professional Safety*, December 2000, p. 1.

8. "Watch Your Step: Workplace Injuries Cost a Bundle," *U.S. News & World Report*, March 26, 2001, p. 10.

9. Steven Greenhouse, "Hispanic Workers Die at a Higher Rate," *The New York Times*, July 16, 2001, p. A11.

10. "Safety on the Docks," *Warehousing Management*, July 2001, pp. 33–37.

11. U.S. Department of Health and Human Services, "Preventing Disease and Death from Tobacco Use," Fact Sheet, January 8, 2001, www.hhs.gov, downloaded September 20, 2001; U.S. Department of Health and Human Services, "New Surgeon General's Report Expands List of Diseases Caused by Smoking," news release, May 27, 2004, http://www.hhs.gov.

12. Centers for Disease Control and Prevention, "Secondhand Smoke," Fact Sheet, February 2004, www.cdc.gov/tobacco/factsheets/secondhand_smoke_factsheet.htm.

13. "State-Specific Prevalence of Current Cigarette Smoking among Adults and the Proportion of

Adults Who Work in a Smoke-Free Environment, United States, 1999," *Journal of the American Medical Association,* December 13, 2000, pp. 2865–66; National Cancer Institute, State Cancer Legislative Database Program, "Clean Indoor Air," Fact Sheet, January 2002, www.scld-nci.net.

14. See, for example, Oregon Occupational Safety and Health Division, *Evaluating Your Computer Workstation,* publication no. 440-1863, February 2004, www.cbs.state.or.us; Lori Eig and Julie Landis, "MSDs and the Workplace," *Journal of Employee Assistance,* 3rd Quarter, 2004, pp. 12–14.

15. Bureau of Labor Statistics, "Number of Nonfatal Occupational Injuries and Illnesses with Days Away from Work Involving Musculoskeletal Disorders by Selected Worker and Case Characteristics, 2002," Table 11, March 2004, www.bls.gov.

16. Robert J. Grossman, "Back with a Vengeance," *HRMagazine,* August 2001, pp. 36–46.

17. Adrienne E. Eaton and Thomas Nocerino, "The Effectiveness of Health and Safety Committees: Results of a Survey of Public-Sector Workplaces," *Industrial Relations,* April 2000, pp. 265ff.

18. Robert D. Ramsey, "Handling Hazards in the Workplace," *Supervision,* May 2000, pp. 6–8.

19. June Fabre, "Improve Patient Safety and Staff Retention by Mentoring Your Staff," *Healthcare Review,* July 1, 2003, downloaded from Look Smart's FindArticles, www.findarticles.com.

20. These suggestions are excerpted from Ramsey, "Handling Hazards in the Workplace."

21. Bureau of Labor Statistics, "Union Members—2010," news release, January 21, 2011, http://www.bls.gov/cps.

22. Bureau of Labor Statistics, "Work Stoppages Involving 1,000 or More Workers, 1947–2003," Major Work Stoppages: Detailed Monthly Data page, www.bls.gov, downloaded October 25, 2004.

23. See Equal Employment Opportunity Commission, "Questions & Answers for Small Employers on Employer Liability for Harassment by Supervisors," June 21, 1999, www.eeoc.gov/policy/docs/harassment-facts.html.

24. Equal Employment Opportunity Commission, "Sexual Harassment Charges, EEOC & FEPAs Combined: FY 1992–FY 2003," March 8, 2004, www.eeoc.gov/stats/harass.html.

25. Equal Employment Opportunity Commission (EEOC), "Notice Concerning the Americans with Disabilities Act (ADA) Amendments Act of 2008," Laws, Regulations, and Guidance: Statutes, http://www1.eeoc.gov, accessed January 10, 2012; EEOC, "Questions and Answers about Diabetes in the Workplace and the Americans with Disabilities Act (ADA)," last modified February 2, 2011, http://www.eeoc.gov/facts/diabetes.html; Office of Disability Employment Policy, U.S. Department of Labor, "The ADA Amendments Act of 2008," Accommodation and Compliance Series, Job Accommodation Network, http://askjan.org, accessed January 10, 2012.

26. The cautions in this paragraph are based on Jonathan A. Segal, "Throw Supervisors a Lifeline and Save Yourself," *HRMagazine,* June 2003, downloaded from InfoTrac, http://web2.infotrac.galegroup.com.

27. Wage and Hour Division, U.S. Department of Labor, "US Department of Labor Clarifies FMLA Definition of 'Son and Daughter,'" news release, June 22, 2010, http://www.dol.gov; Wage and Hour Division, "The Family and Medical Leave Act Military Family Leave Entitlements," fact sheet 28A, n.d., http://www.dol.gov, accessed January 11, 2012.

28. Jill Elswick, "FMLA Protects Seriously Ill Workers against Job Loss," *Employee Benefit News,* August 1, 2004, downloaded from Business & Company Resource Center, http://galenet.galegroup.com; Burt Helm, "California Offers Paid Leave for All Workers," *Inc.,* October 2004, downloaded from InfoTrac, http://web2.infotrac.galegroup.com.

29. Michael Prince, "FMLA Hasn't Been Big Burden for Employers," *Business Insurance,* September 29, 2003, downloaded from Business & Company Resource Center, http://galenet.galegroup.com.

30. Linda Wasmer Andrews, "Aftershocks of War," *HRMagazine,* April 2004, downloaded from InfoTrac, http://web2.infotrac.galegroup.com.

The Supervisor's Career Path: Finding a Career That Fits

Setting Career Goals

Many jobs exist, but finding a career that is rewarding and fits your personal needs and preferences can be a challenge. A career is a chosen pursuit; it is all the things you are doing at any given point to create a satisfying life while setting and working toward goals. A job is a regular activity performed for payment. You might have a job as a waiter for money but be interning in a law office and taking political science classes to develop your career.

Careers evolve over time—you will likely hold a series of jobs in a variety of industries that will eventually make up your career. Setting career goals is a crucial part of any job search. It lets potential employers know you are focused and goal oriented. Whether through letters, phone calls, or interviews, every moment of contact with prospective employers must convey that you have goals and that you arrived at these career goals thoughtfully. Determining your career goals involves some soul-searching and research, but it will pay off in a satisfying job that fits.

Step One: Self-Assessment and Your Personality Profile

The first step in finding the right career path is to have a solid understanding of yourself. What do you like? What do you do well? What do you care about? What motivates you? You can access numerous resources to assist you in uncovering your personal interests and values. The Myers-Brigg Type Indicator, mentioned in Chapter 13, is frequently used to assist people with self-assessment. Although you can't take the Myers-Brigg test online, you can access a number of these personality typing tests and get some insights into your preferences. Visit the following Web site for a list: http://www.jobhuntersbible.com/counseling/ptests.shtml. Formulate lists of your interests, your skills, and the values that comprise your personality profile. This profile will become the foundation for your job search, setting a direction for a career that will match your personality and your interests. Don't forget about your priorities. The Knowing Yourself quiz in Chapter 11, "What Motivates You?" may help you identify issues that are important to your career choice—issues such as work environment, prestige, and job security. In Chapter 15, "Would You Hire You?" helps identify what you value in your work environment. Priorities will help you focus on what is important. While you might have a strong interest in figure skating, you may value security and need money. If so, you'll need a job that is more stable and lucrative—maybe managing an ice rink would meet your interests as well as your needs.

Step Two: Establish Your Skills Inventory

On the basis of your education and job experience, compile a list of all the skills you've acquired. As discussed in Chapter 1, supervisory skills can be broken down into five skill categories:

- *Technical skills*—knowledge of particular techniques/procedures.
- *Human relations skills*—ability to communicate, motivate, and understand other people.
- *Conceptual skills*—ability to see relationship of parts to the whole.
- *Decision-making skills*—ability to analyze information and make good decisions.
- *Knowledge skills*—ability to use e-mail, voice mail, fax, intranet, and Internet to manage data.

Also refer back to Figure 1.5, "Characteristics of a Successful Supervisor," for a reminder of the skill sets demonstrated by successful supervisors.

Think about your skills and strengths in terms of:

- **Personality-related skills.** These are skills that reflect your personal capabilities, talents, and general areas of interest. These would include strengths such as being detail oriented, a good listener, artistic, or athletic. These tend to be skills that are broad and applicable to a variety of occupations.
- **Experience/education-related skills.** These are skills that you have acquired through education or experience and reflect your abilities. These skills would include things such as balancing a budget, speaking a foreign language, or typing more than 100 words per minute. These also can include very specific skills such as understanding a complex computer program or operating specific equipment.

Step Three: Research Employment Trends

Where will the jobs be in the future? Making informed career decisions requires not only careful self-assessment but also an assessment of the job market and an understanding of the industries that interest you. You may decide a career in manufacturing sounds intriguing, but knowing that overall employment in this sector is expected to decrease over the next 10 years may affect your pursuit of a career in manufacturing. The U.S. Department of Labor produces an *Occupational Outlook Handbook* that can give you insights about what the future likely holds for your areas of interest. At http://www.bls.gov/oco, you can find information about specific occupations or browse through a variety of "occupational clusters" such as management, sales, and production.

A few trends highlighted in the 2010–2011 handbook include:

- The long-term shift from goods-producing to service-providing employment is expected to continue in many industries. Service-providing industries are expected to account for about 14.5 million of the 15.3 million new wage and salary jobs generated from 2008 to 2018.
- Health care and social assistance occupations will grow the fastest and add more new jobs than any other major occupational group. Over the 2008–2018 period, a 24 percent increase in the number of health-care and related jobs is projected, a gain of 4 million. Workers in this industry provide services in hospitals, nursing and residential care facilities, and services to individuals and families.
- The U.S. workforce will become more diverse by 2018. Hispanics are projected to account for an increasing share of the labor force by 2018, growing from 14.3 to 17.6 percent.

On the basis of your personality profile, your skills inventory, and projected employment trends, you can target occupations and/or industries that will suit your preferences and meet your priorities.

Step Four: Finding the Jobs That Fit and Setting Your Career Objectives

Now that you've targeted industries and occupations that interest you, you can begin to narrow your search to specific jobs. By browsing through the help wanted section of any newspaper or visiting job search Web sites such as CareerBuilder.com and Monster.com, you can match your preferences to specific job listings. Using your personality profile and your skills inventory, look through the postings for occupations in the industries you've targeted. At CareerBuilder.com, you can even enter specific skills and receive a listing of jobs that require those skills.

Reviewing job postings and considering the occupations and industries available should lead to a fairly targeted list of jobs and careers that match your personality and skills. Separate the list into jobs that you are interested in and are qualified for today and jobs to which you aspire. The jobs that you aspire to will be the framework on which you can start to build your career. The training and education needed for these more advanced positions should be prominent in your decision-making process as you begin and continue your job search.

Preparing for Your Job Search

Writing Your Résumé

Now that you've done your homework and know the specific occupations and industries you plan to target for your job search, you need to prepare your résumé. Having a well-organized résumé that accurately highlights your strengths and experience is crucial to a successful job search. As discussed in Chapter 15, the selection process begins when candidates for a job send in their résumés. Résumés are typically screened or skimmed through by human resource personnel or, sometimes, résumé-reading software. In this screening process, the résumé is reviewed for specific skills, abilities, and education that will match the job specifications for the open position. Because your résumé will likely be put through this process, it is essential that it include specific language that matches the occupation or industry you have targeted.

Résumé Ingredients

All résumés must include basic information about who you are and what you have to offer a prospective employer. Start building your résumé by compiling the basics:

- **Name, address, phone number, and e-mail address.**
- **Career objective**—this is a brief statement that should read like a job description for positions that interest you.
- **Education**—include all degrees received, dates, and schools (be sure to include city and state for each school). If your GPA is good, include it. You can also include coursework that is relevant to the position.
- **Activities and honors**—list all awards, fellowships, scholarships, and memberships in professional organizations.
- **Experience**—list all positions you've held (including volunteer work and self-employment). For each position, include the job title, organization, city and state, dates of employment, and a brief summary of your duties. Be sure to highlight special responsibilities and activities that relate to the positions in which you are interested. Also be sure to specify results whenever possible.
- **Skills**—you can highlight skills you have developed through your education and experience by creating headings that focus on your qualifications. Job listings can give you ideas for these headings.

- **References**—be sure to get permission to use someone as a reference, choose individuals who can testify to your abilities, and make sure your references know when you've applied for a position and that they have a current copy of your résumé.

Formats

A résumé is a reflection of you and should showcase your individual style and talents. There are many ways to organize a résumé; the crucial issue is to create a résumé that best highlights your unique strengths and interests. Résumés are typically organized in one of two ways: chronologically or based on functional areas. A chronological résumé is best when your education and experience progress logically for the position you're interested in and you have impressive job titles to highlight. A functional résumé emphasizes skills and qualifications and works well if you are looking to switch fields or if you have gaps in your work history.

Visit job search Web sites for numerous examples of effective résumé styles and formats. Two helpful sites are http://resume.monster.com/ and http://www.collegegrad.com/resumes.

Depending on the scope of your job search, you may need multiple versions of your résumé in order to receive the best response possible each time you apply. At some companies, the reader of your résumé will be a human resources manager; at others, it will be the supervisor for the position. The reader may focus on specific skills defined by key words or may be looking for the most creative applicants. And often the first reader is not even a human, but software designed to eliminate résumés that lack the basic job requirements. The ideal résumé for a human resources reviewer may not trigger enough positive marks in scanning software, and vice versa. With so many different possibilities, job seekers must understand what each employer wants to receive. In many cases, submitting something other than what is requested will simply result in a rejection without further evaluation of the applicant.

Many resources are available to aid in building a conventional résumé. Word-processing software commonly comes with an assortment of templates. Many career Web sites, such as Monster (http://www.monster.com) and Dice (http://www.dice.com) provide examples. No single format is considered ideal for every situation. But as a general rule, the résumé should be laid out so it is easy for the human reader's eye to note your skill set and experience. You can use font styles such as boldface and italics, but use them sparingly as highlights. Avoid fancy font types, colors, wildly different font sizes, and large blocks of unformatted or unbroken text. These can cause the reader to focus on the formatting rather than the contents of the résumé.

Some employers accept or require electronic forms of your résumé. This is especially important if the employer mentions that the company uses résumé-scanning software or asks for an *ASCII, plain-text,* or *machine-readable* version of your résumé. When you write a résumé that will be read by software rather than people, use relevant keywords, industry buzzwords, and terms related to your area of specialty. These terms increase the chances that your résumé will be favorably scored. If possible, use phrases and keywords exactly as they appear in the job's description. Plain-text résumés contain no formatting or layout marks such as fonts, boldface, italics, and tabs. They are submitted online or via e-mail, and are usually interpreted and sorted by software rather than people. Simple formatting also is important with paper résumés, because employers often want to be able to scan them. To ensure that your résumé is scannable, follow these guidelines:

- Use a single, standard typeface in 12- or 14-point type.
- Use a ragged right margin (text aligned on the left only).
- Do not use italics, underlines, lines, boxes, script, bullets, or borders.
- Do not staple pages together or fold the résumé.

There are a number of resources for preparing an electronic résumé. Use a search engine such as Google or Bing, and search for "electronic resume tips," and similar topics. You can also visit career and job sites including Monster, Dice, and LinkedIn (http://www.linkedin.com/).

Proofread, Proofread, Proofread

Check and double-check your résumé for typographical and grammatical errors. Have friends and family check it as well. Errors, no matter how minor, are red flags to potential employers because they indicate a lack of attention to detail.

Job Application Letters

A job application letter, or résumé cover letter, should accompany every résumé you send to a human reviewer. A letter is generally not included as part of an online application, especially if it will be processed by software. However, if the employer's application Web page provides a way to include an application letter, you should do so.

The letter should briefly highlight your qualifications, but its greatest value lies in helping the reader understand specifically how you would fit ideally with and benefit your new organization. Therefore, adapt your letter to a specific organization. Visit the organization's Web site to research what the company does, what its goals are, and any other useful facts that might help you match your skills and experience to what the company values. In the letter, express enthusiasm for joining the company, identify a key activity or area in which you would be involved, and describe how your experience makes you a perfect fit for that part of the job. Every applicant will claim to be "diligent, hard-working, and enthusiastic," but surprisingly few people offer specific details: "With my background in news aggregation, I'll make it easy to find new content for your Web site."

Whenever possible, address your job letter to the hiring manager. A letter that includes a person's name will get more close attention than the standard "Dear Sir/Madam" letter.

Other Useful Job Search Tools

While your résumé is the key tool you'll need for your job search, some other items will come in handy and demonstrate your professionalism:

- **Voice mail:** Whether on your landline or your cell phone, voice mail is the best way to ensure you don't miss that important call. Potential employers confronted with busy signals or unanswered calls might not call back. Be sure your outgoing message is short and professional, and respond to any messages within one business day.

- **E-mail:** A permanent personal e-mail account with a reputable Internet service provider (ISP) is crucial to your job search. You will need an e-mail program that can transmit attachments, such as your résumé, quickly and easily. Make sure the e-mail address you choose is professional and easily recognizable.

- **Social networking sites:** LinkedIn (http://www.linkedin.com) can help you stay connected with past colleagues and forge new connections with people who share professional interests. To get the most out of social networking, make it an ongoing part of your career, not just a tool for job hunting. Become a valued colleague by posting encouragement, useful links, and answers to questions. The more visible you are to people in your professional circle over time, the easier it will be to see opportunities as they arise and reach out to others when you're looking for a job. Also remember that employers are increasingly looking at purely social sites including Facebook, Google+, and Twitter as a way to gauge the character of the people they hire. If your personal social sites contain information that would jeopardize your job search or career, make sure that access to that information is as restricted as you can make it. Better yet, simply remove the content from the site.

- **An information management system:** Throughout your job search, you will access a significant amount of information and contact a number of people. Keep yourself organized by establishing a system for tracking all the information you will acquire throughout your search. You'll likely need a system that will accommodate hard copy as well as electronic information. A set of file folders (both standard paper files and electronic files) will help you keep track of important information as you acquire it. Creating separate files for job hunting tips, your résumé and supporting material (such as work samples), jobs that interest you, and contacts might be a good starting point.

Job Hunting Resources

Once you've set some career goals and prepared your résumé, you can begin your job search in earnest. There are a variety of resources to assist you in this search.

College Career Centers

Most colleges have career centers that can provide job listings and information about companies and set you up with on-campus interviews. They may also have career counselors who can give you feedback on your résumé, assist you with interviewing skills, and advise you about openings. Many of these career centers will work with alumni as well as current students, so don't rule them out just because you've graduated.

The Internet

The Internet is an invaluable resource in your job search and an essential tool for connecting with many desirable employers. A large and growing number of organizations encourage or require applicants to apply online for certain positions. Thousands of Web sites provide access to information, tips, and services that can help you become more effective in applying and interviewing for jobs. Search engines can provide links to advice on topics such as résumé writing and job interviews. You can even find advice for the best ways to interview with certain companies.

Many sites provide lists of job opportunities. Some, including Monster (http://www.monster.com/) and CareerBuilder (http://www.careerbuilder.com/) maintain national job databases in almost every field. Others, including Dice (http://www.dice.com/), have a national database but focus on a single sector, such as technology. State and federal governments often post their job opportunities on their own Web sites, as do many companies of all sizes. If you are looking for local jobs, and especially for small-business opportunities, community-oriented sites like Craigslist (http://www.craigslist.org/) often list jobs that do not appear on the national search sites.

The Web also provides many resources for digging deeper into the operations of the organizations that interest you. You can search recent news stories for clues about the financial health of the organization. You can browse corporate Web sites for information about companies' activities and culture. You can even visit and follow social-media sites and accounts related to the company and its employees to better understand its current state and see how the larger community views the organization.

Classifieds

The proliferation of job-search Web sites has decreased the use of classified advertising significantly. This doesn't mean you should rule out this important source of job openings. Many companies advertise in local papers, trade journals, and industry magazines. As mentioned, reviewing the help wanted ads can give you insight into local companies and industries that are growing (and hiring).

Job Fairs

Many communities (including your college campus) will host job fairs to help local businesses recruit candidates for openings. These are typically industry specific but also can be more general. Attending job fairs is a good way to learn about companies that are hiring and make valuable contacts with people in your targeted industry.

Headhunters and Recruiters

Professional search firms often are hired by larger corporations to find candidates for open positions. Contacting professional search firms that specialize in your targeted industry can increase your visibility. Recruiters can be a good source of information in terms of trends in the industry and the types of positions available. They also can act as a sounding board, offering feedback on your résumé and advice on your job search.

Networking

In addition to your career center and job-search Web sites, you can use *networking* to boost your chances of finding that perfect job. Networking involves creating alliances and developing your list of professional contacts who may be aware of employment opportunities. An effective networking campaign will focus on connecting with as many associations, trade and industry groups, alumni chapters, and ethnic organizations as possible. Members of these groups are resources you can and should use. Prepare yourself with a simple statement about who you are and what you want: "I am a recent college graduate interested in a career in marketing. I've researched the industry and decided to focus my job search on openings in new product development. . . ." You may then follow up with a request for an informational interview or ask about job openings the individual contact may be aware of in the area you specified.

Be sure to keep track of your contacts. Whether you use index cards or a 4G phone, be sure to record names, addresses, phone numbers, and relevant information every time you meet a new contact.

Networking today also has an online component. Professional social-networking services like LinkedIn (http://www.linkedin.com) help you establish and maintain an active network of people with related professional interests. The service also hosts discussion forums and interest groups, which are an ideal place to ask questions, make suggestions, and gradually build respect and recognition among professional peers. Participants can write recommendations for the co-workers, supervisors, and employees they find exceptional. Ask for recommendations and write them for others. They become an enduring list of good marks and references that are easy for prospective employers to see and verify.

Informational Interviews

Informational interviews are an excellent way to tap into the hidden job market—those unadvertised jobs. In an informational interview, you meet with an individual who works in an industry or occupation you hope to enter. An informational interview can:

- Help you clarify your career goal.
- Uncover employment opportunities that are not advertised.
- Expand your professional network.
- Build confidence for your job interviews.

Look to your network of contacts for potential people to interview. If granted an informational interview, keep these tips in mind:

1. **Do your homework.** Good preparation involves researching the individual, company, and industry. Go to the interview with a goal in mind—are you more interested in finding out about growth areas in the industry or do you need information about the day-to-day responsibilities for a specific occupation? Come prepared with a list of questions and be sure to ask your contact how much time you have so that you can prioritize your list.

2. **Provide the context.** Remind your new contact which friend, acquaintance, organization, or affiliation you have in common. Then, briefly state your goals for the meeting and offer a brief overview of your background. You can then proceed with the interview, asking your contact the questions you've prepared. Be sure to ask about additional contacts that might be useful to broaden your network.

3. **Don't ask for a job.** Remember this is an informational interview—from the contact's point of view, a plea for work could be uncomfortable. If you impress your new contact and he or she knows of something suitable, that person will mention it.

4. **Follow up.** A formal thank you is mandatory, but you also should aim to stay in touch with your contacts. If you've met with someone to whom your initial contact referred you, send an e-mail letting him or her know, summarizing the conversation, and thanking that person. If you come across an article that you think might be interesting, forward it. By simply touching base with your contacts every four to six weeks, you greatly increase the number of people who are thinking about you and your job search. Be sure to let your contacts know when you've found a job and thank them again for their assistance.

Applying for Jobs Online

Companies that invite or require job hunters to apply for positions online generally provide the instructions on their Web site. Some also post a set of application pages to be completed and submitted. Others offer to accept and process a plain-text version of your résumé. If you submit a plain-text résumé, never trust the processing software to put everything in the right place. When the system displays the filled-out forms that result from scanning your résumé, edit the forms before you submit your application.

For any application method, provide exactly what the employer asks for, in exactly the way it is requested. A surprising number of applicants disregard instructions, and their applications are automatically rejected. For example, if a company requires that work experience be entered into text boxes on a Web page, it will not accept a note from you that says, "See the résumé I emailed to hr@yourcompany.com."

Often, employers gather information on Web forms so they can use software that automatically screens applications to make sure they meet minimum criteria. If a Web form asks for a list of skills or qualification keywords, try to make your relevant keywords exactly match the job description provided by the company, if you can truthfully do so. There is a reasonable chance that the software will be looking for those same keywords, and it may not catch variations.

Many online application systems will send an e-mail confirmation once an application is received and found to be complete. If you don't receive an expected confirmation, or if you receive an e-mail saying an error occurred, visit the application site again to correct errors or to seek out what went wrong. If the company provided a contact e-mail or phone number for support, you can ask for help, but make sure you already have tried to correct any problems you can find on your own. If you do get confirmation that your application was properly received, there is little left to do besides wait. A difficult economy and the ease of finding employers and job openings online have increased the flood of applications into employers' human resource departments. Sending follow-up inquiries to already-overwhelmed employers will almost never help your cause.

Interviewing Essentials

Preparing for Your Interview

Research

The preparation process for a formal job interview is similar to the process for an informational interview. It is crucial that your do your homework. Research the company, individual, and industry as well as the position for which you are applying. The company's corporate Web site is an excellent resource for this type of research, as are industry trade magazines and professional organization Web sites. Find out as much as you can about:

- The company—its corporate goals, financial position, competition, etc.
- The hiring manager—you might find a biography or press releases about this individual by doing a search on the corporate Web site.
- The industry—what trends and challenges is your chosen industry facing?
- The position—see if you can find a job description; do some research on salary ranges at the Bureau of Labor Statistics Web site: http://www.bls.gov/ncs.

The interview is about finding a good fit, both for the company and for you. It is your opportunity to demonstrate how your skills and experience will benefit the organization. It is also your opportunity to find out what you need to know about the job and the company for which you might work. Prepare questions that will assist you in the decision process should you be offered the job. Refer back to your personality profile and your priorities, and make sure any questions you have about the responsibilities of the job, the office culture, and so forth get asked. Three to five questions should be about the right number to prepare—more and it may feel like you are doing the interviewing.

Rehearse

Be ready to answer that tried-and-true question: "Tell me about yourself." Determine your greatest strengths relative to the position, and prepare a brief statement about what these are and why they will benefit the company with which you are interviewing. Think about your career goals and how the position for which you are applying fits into these goals. Also be prepared to address the "what is your greatest weakness" question. Practicing answers to common interview questions either in front of a mirror or with a friend will improve your ability to answer these effectively and confidently. Practicing also will give you some insights about your body language, facial expressions, and eye contact—all-important nonverbal clues that seasoned interviewers will pick up on.

Dress Appropriately and Bring the Essentials

If you are not sure about the dress code for the company, call the human resources office and ask. Stick with more conservative styles—avoid anything too trendy—and make sure anything you wear fits well and is clean and in good repair.

- Bring extra copies of your résumé, something to write on, and something to write with.
- If appropriate, bring work samples.
- Bring a list of your references if they are not included on your résumé. The list should include names, addresses, and phone numbers.

The Interview

You've done your homework and practiced responses to the standard interview questions about your strengths, weaknesses, and goals. Each interview you are granted will present its own unique set of challenges, as each is a reflection of the personal style of the interviewer. Your initial interview might be a phone interview or a video interview. It might be with the hiring manager, but it might also be with the team with which you will be working. You might be asked mainly straightforward questions about your skills and experience, or you might be asked more open-ended behavioral questions about how you would react to a variety of situations. The more prepared you are for the interview, the less likely you will get stumped by any of the questions or scenarios you meet. All the work you've done to assess your skills and your appropriateness for the job; the research you've completed on the company, industry, and hiring manager; and the responses and questions you've prepared should make you confident to face whatever challenges lie ahead.

Today more employers are trying to make hiring more efficient by conducting initial interviews on the telephone. Though phone and face-to-face interviews have the same goal, telephone interviews present a unique set of challenges. As a job candidate, you depend on the tone of your voice to convey everything you want to express about your competence and personality. Therefore, it is important to practice a pleasant, professional manner of speaking. Just before answering the phone or calling for the interview, smile at the wall as if you've just met the most delightful person on earth. Smiling elevates your mood and makes you sound energetic and cheerful. Some people find they sound more engaged and energetic if they stand for the interview. Test that idea with a willing friend ahead of time to make sure you don't move too much and sound as if you're running in place. Also, practice answering common interview questions ahead of time to be ready with concise, clear, and positive answers. Stay far away from sarcasm or sly humor; over the phone, no one sees your smile, so these remarks may fall flat.

You may also be asked to participate in an online video interview via Skype or a similar service. If so, you must prepare the visual environment as carefully as yourself for the interview. Make sure that the area behind your seat is professional and neutral—no beer cans, dirty laundry, broken furniture, or posters of questionable taste. Make absolutely certain that no people, dogs, or other distractions will wander into or through the room during the interview. Pick a chair that forces you to sit upright and look engaged; substitute a stool if your chair makes you slouch. Dress and present yourself on video exactly as if you were dressing for an in-person interview. And just before you connect online, make sure every other program on your computer, especially e-mail and chat systems, are completely shut off, so that you cannot be interrupted or distracted by them during the interview.

First Impressions

A crucial component of the interview is the first impression. Be on time! Plan to arrive at least 5 to 10 minutes early. Show respect to everyone you come in contact with, whether it is the security guard at the front door, the receptionist, or people you see in the elevator. Smile and make eye contact.

Mirroring is a great way to make a good first impression with your interviewer. Greet him or her with a smile and a handshake that mirrors his or hers—not overly firm or soft. Sit when your interviewer sits and look to him or her for cues on body language. Try not to be overly formal if your interviewer seems to be the more casual type. Sit up a little straighter if you are dealing with someone who seems more formal.

During the Interview

You and your interviewer might engage in small talk to start the interview, but this will likely be limited. The interviewer might begin with a brief explanation of the opening, or he or she might start with a question—let the interviewer lead the discussion. Listen carefully and respond accurately and briefly to each question. Look for opportunities to showcase your skills. Answer questions thoroughly, providing specifics wherever possible. Many successful interviewers use the STAR approach to emphasize not only their skills, but the results (benefits) of their skills:

S: Describe a *situation* where you relied upon a skill you have highlighted in your résumé.

T: What *tasks* were involved in the situation?

A: What *actions* did you take?

R: What were the *results?*

Don't be evasive; if you don't know the answer to a question, don't try to schmooze your way out of it. Admit what you don't know and ensure the interviewer you will find the answer as quickly as possible.

The salary question may come up, so be prepared to provide your requirements. If you've done your homework, you should know what to expect, and the range of the salary you require shouldn't be a surprise to the hiring manager.

Don't forget to ask your prepared questions. If the interviewer hasn't covered issues that are important to your decision to accept an offer if presented, you'll need to press for time to ask questions. If time doesn't allow, ask if you might follow up with a phone call or e-mail.

Closing

If you feel you are a good match for the position, be sure to make your case before the interview ends. Let your interviewer know you want the job and when you can start. If an on-the-spot decision isn't possible (usually the case), follow up will be needed. It's likely you'll be asked to interview with other members of the hiring team; try to determine who these individuals are and when you might meet with them. Find out what additional information might be useful to the interviewer and when you should follow up. Determine the timetable for filling the position. Make sure you know your interviewer's name, title, and mailing address. Thank the interviewer for his or her time and interest—and don't overstay your welcome.

After the Interview

Make some notes after your interview about the issues you discussed, what went well, and what didn't. Every interview is a learning experience and will enhance your preparation for the next interview. If there was a question that was particularly difficult, note it and make sure you have an answer for it at your next interview. Make sure you have the name, title, and address of your interviewers.

Follow-Up

Thank-you notes for all the individuals you interviewed with are crucial. If you can get them done within 24 hours, it will impress your interviewers and demonstrate your interest. In this e-mail age, a handwritten thank-you note is a nice gesture. Make it brief and courteous. Thank your interviewers for their time and interest, and if you want the job, say so again.

Use the timetable you were given in the interview as a guide for an appropriate amount of time for follow-up. You can follow up by phone or e-mail. Be persistent and keep asking for the next interview or, if appropriate, for the job.

Getting Hired

The Job Offer

Your hard work has paid off, and you are offered a job! Remember, impressions still count, so be sure to let your potential employer know how pleased you are to be offered the position. Avoid snap judgments about the offer by making your first question, "When do you need a decision by?" Ask for at least a day or two to consider the offer. Be sure you understand the offer explicitly and that you know:

- The job title and reporting structure.
- The total salary including any potential bonuses.
- The location.
- The hours (not all companies are 9 to 5).
- The expected start date.
- What expenses will be covered (that is, if you have to relocate, will your new employer pay for the cost of moving?).
- The benefits you qualify for—this is an increasingly important issue to consider. Benefits can add a lot to your base pay if they are comprehensive and include health care, tuition reimbursement, and paid vacation time.

A good job offer checklist is available through CollegeGrad.com, at http://www.collegegrad.com/jobsearch/jobofferchecklist.shtml.

Evaluate the Offer

Once you clearly understand the details of the job offer, you can carefully evaluate its appropriateness. The Bureau of Labor Statistics offers some excellent insights for evaluating job offers at its Web site: http://www.bls.gov/oco/oco20046.htm. Go back to your personality profile—do the duties and responsibilities of the job fit your interests and values? Does the work environment suit you? Is the position one that will contribute to your overall career goals? Will the salary meet your needs financially? While it may be tempting to accept the first offer, keeping your goals and interests in mind will pay off in long-term satisfaction. Compromises that seem small might grow as your satisfaction declines because the job doesn't match your interests or goals.

Negotiating

If you've decided the position fits within your career goals but there are details about the job offer that concern you, you may be able to negotiate some of these details. The key to successful negotiations is understanding that there is no such thing as "winning." Effective negotiating means reaching a decision that is mutually beneficial. If a company is interested enough in you to have made you an offer, then it likely will consider your reasonable requests for changes to that offer. Reasonable is the key word: Don't ask for a 50 percent increase in the salary that has been offered and expect a positive outcome.

Be respectful when making counteroffers and continue to demonstrate your interest in the company. Explain your rationale and offer alternatives: If you're asking for a higher salary, you might provide statistics on competitive salaries and demonstrate that your request is reasonable. If you need more vacation time for personal reasons, offer to work longer hours or cut back your salary to accommodate your needs. Be prepared for compromises and keep negotiations professional.

Acceptance

Once you have agreed to the terms of your employment, write a letter of acceptance outlining the details of your acceptance. This will ensure you accurately understand the offer and that your employer agrees to the terms. Be sure to reiterate your enthusiasm for the job and the company.

Building Your Career

Networking at the Office

Your job search may end with your acceptance of a job offer, but your *career search* should not. As discussed, your career evolves over time—the job you have accepted and started is but one step in the development of your career. Use your employment wisely. Search out individuals at your new company who hold positions you are interested in and enlist their assistance in the development of your career. These mentors can be valuable assets as you explore your career possibilities.

Take advantage of every opportunity presented to you to expand your skill set and network with colleagues. Volunteer for task forces, join company groups that interest you, participate actively in meetings—be visible and let colleagues know your goals and aspirations.

Professional Organizations

Every industry has professional organizations or associations. As mentioned in the discussion of networking, these organizations are a great career resource. Membership means opportunities for meetings in which industry trends are discussed and networking abounds. Membership also means access to industry leaders—people making a difference in the industry. There are large, broad associations such as the American Marketing Association (http://www.marketingpower.com) with its 38,000 members or the Society for Hispanic Professionals (http://www.nshp.org/?wf=goto) with its 7,500 members. There are also more specialized organizations such as the New England Direct Marketing Association (http://www.nedma.com). You can't join every group, so do some research to find the organizations that have the most to offer you professionally.

Continuing Education

Some industries, such as health care and insurance, mandate continuing education. To keep professional licenses active, individuals must complete a certain number of continuing education hours. Even if your chosen profession is not one that mandates continuing education, staying up-to-date on the technical skills associated with your position is key to a successful career.

There are numerous resources for continuing education. For more general skills such as computer or software training, your local community is a great place to start. Local libraries, community colleges, and even some school districts offer courses in which you can learn standard software applications such as PowerPoint and Excel.

Professional organizations are another good source for continuing education and professional development. Most organizations offer seminars and/or training. For example, the American Marketing Association offers a two-day "Marketing Boot Camp" for marketers new to the profession. Find seminars and training sessions that interest you and use these to expand your skill set and network.

Back to the Drawing Board (Sort of)

As you gain experience in your new position and network in your field, your career goals likely will shift. After about six months to a year in your position, you should get out your job search files and pull your personality profile, skills inventory, and résumé. Review where you were, where you've been, and where you now want to go. What has changed? Updating your résumé on a regular basis will keep you focused on your goals and ensure your career search does not end when your job search does.

Resources

http://www.collegegrad.com/intv

http://www.businessweek.com/magazine/toc/09_37/B4146career.htm

http://www.collegeview.com/articles/article/preparing-early-for-the-job-market

http://www.bls.gov/oco/oco2003.htm

http://www.quintcareers.com/STAR_interviewing.html

http://content.monster.com

http://www.rileyguide.com

Glossary

accountability The practice of imposing penalties for failing to adequately carry out responsibilities and providing rewards for meeting responsibilities. 15

action plan The plan for how to achieve an objective. 146

active listening Hearing what the speaker is saying, seeking to understand the facts and feelings the speaker is trying to convey, and stating what you understand that message to be. 261

affirmative action Plans designed to increase opportunities for groups that traditionally have been discriminated against. 439

ageism Discrimination based on age. 127

agenda A list of the topics to be covered at a meeting. 80

apprenticeship Training that involves working alongside an experienced person, who shows the apprentice how to do the various tasks involved in a job or trade. 465

aptitude test A test that measures a person's ability to learn skills related to the job. 434

authoritarian leadership A leadership style in which the leader retains a great deal of authority. 206

authority The right to perform a task or give orders to someone else. 183

average rate of return (ARR) A percentage that represents the average annual earnings for each dollar of a given investment. 51

Baldrige Performance Excellence Program An annual award administered by the U.S. Department of Commerce and given to the company that shows the highest quality performance in seven categories. 39

behavior modification The use of reinforcement theory to motivate people to behave in a certain way. 298

behaviorally anchored rating scales (BARS) A performance appraisal in which an employee is rated on scales containing statements describing performance in several areas. 492

benchmarking Identifying the top performer of a process, then learning and carrying out the top performer's practices. 39

biofeedback Developing an awareness of bodily functions in order to control them. 365

bona fide occupational qualification (BFOQ) An objective characteristic required for an individual to perform a job properly. 128

bounded rationality Choosing an alternative that meets minimum standards of acceptability. 231

brainstorming An idea-generating process in which group members state their ideas, a member of the group records them, and no one may comment on the ideas until the process is complete. 243

budget A plan for spending money. 150

burnout The inability to function effectively as a result of ongoing stress. 363

central tendency The tendency to select employee ratings in the middle of a scale. 498

chain of command The flow of authority in an organization from one level of management to the next. 189

challenge stressor A stressful stimulus that is viewed as an opportunity to grow and develop. 365

closed-ended question A question that requires a simple answer, such as yes or no. 433

coaching Guidance and instruction in how to do a job so that it satisfies performance goals. 471

code of ethics An organization's written statement of its values and rules for ethical behavior. 100

cohesiveness The degree to which group members stick together. 70

commissions Payment linked to the amount of sales completed. 302

communication The process by which people send and receive information. 256

compromise Settling on a solution that gives each person part of what he or she wants; no one gets everything, and no one loses completely. 385

conceptual skills The ability to see the relation of the parts to the whole and to one another. 6

concurrent control Control that occurs while the work takes place. 162

conflict The struggle that results from incompatible or opposing needs, feelings, thoughts, or demands within a person or between two or more people. 380

conflict management Responding to problems stemming from conflict. 384

conflict resolution Managing a conflict by confronting the problem and solving it. 386

contingency planning Planning what to do if the original plans don't work out. 147

controlling The management function of ensuring that work goes according to plan. 12, 155

corporate culture Beliefs and norms that govern organizational behavior in a firm. 122

corporate social responsibility Managerial obligation to take action that protects and improves the welfare of society and the organization's interests. 96

counseling The process of learning about an individual's personal problem and helping him or her resolve it. 329

creativity The ability to bring about something imaginative or new. 244

critical-incident appraisal A performance appraisal in which a supervisor keeps a written record of incidents that show positive and negative ways an employee has acted; the supervisor uses this record to assess the employee's performance. 493

cross-training Training in the skills required to perform more than one job. 306

decision A choice from among available alternatives. 228

decision tree A graph that helps decision makers use probability theory by showing the expected values of decisions in varying circumstances. 239

decision-making leave A day off during which a problem employee is supposed to decide whether to return to work and meet standards or to stay away for good. 336

decision-making skills The ability to analyze information and reach good decisions. 6

decision-making software A computer program that leads the user through the steps of the formal decision-making process. 239

delegating Giving another person the authority and responsibility to carry out a task. 191

democratic leadership A leadership style in which the leader allows subordinates to participate in decision making and problem solving. 206

demotion Transfer of an employee to a job involving less responsibility and usually lower pay. 333

department A unique group of resources that management has assigned to carry out a particular task. 177

departmentalization Setting up departments in an organization. 178

detour behavior Tactics for postponing or avoiding work. 49

directive counseling An approach to counseling in which the supervisor asks the employee questions about the specific problem; when the supervisor understands the problem, he or she suggests ways to handle it. 329

disability A physical or mental impairment that substantially limits a major life activity, a record of such an impairment, or being regarded as having such an impairment. 128

discipline Action taken by the supervisor to prevent employees from breaking rules. 331

discrimination Unfair or inequitable treatment based on prejudice. 123

dismissal Relieving an employee of his or her job. 333

diversity Characteristics of individuals that shape their identities and the experiences they have in society. 120

downtime See idle time. 49

downward communication Organizational communication in which a message is sent to someone at a lower level. 277

employee assistance program (EAP) A company-based program for providing counseling and related help to employees whose personal problems are affecting their performance. 339

employee handbook A document that describes an organization's conditions of employment, policies regarding employees, administrative procedures, and related matters. 459

employee involvement teams Teams of employees who plan ways to improve quality in their areas of organization. 34

empowerment Delegation of broad decision-making authority and responsibility. 192

Equal Employment Opportunity Commission (EEOC) The federal government agency charged with enforcing Title VII of the Civil Rights Act. 437

ethics The principles by which people distinguish what is morally right. 97

exception principle The control principle stating that a supervisor should take action only when variance is meaningful. 159

extrinsic reward Recognition or compensation that is extraneous to the task accomplished. 301

feedback The way the receiver of a message responds or fails to respond to the message. 257

feedback control Control that focuses on past performance. 162

financial incentives Payments for meeting or exceeding objectives. 302

flextime A policy that grants employees some leeway in choosing which 8 hours a day or which 40 hours a week to work. 294

forced-choice approach A performance appraisal that presents an appraiser with sets of statements describing employee behavior; the appraiser must choose which statement is most characteristic of the employee and which is least characteristic. 492

formal communication Organizational communication that is work related and follows the lines of the organization chart. 278

formal groups Groups set up by management to meet organizational objectives. 66

frustration Defeat in the effort to achieve desired goals. 380

functional authority The right given by higher management to specific staff personnel to give orders concerning an area in which the staff personnel have expertise. 184

functional groups Groups that fulfill ongoing needs in the organization by carrying out a particular function. 65

gainsharing A group incentive plan in which the organization encourages employees to participate in making suggestions and decisions, then rewards the group with a share of improved earnings. 304

Gantt chart Scheduling tool that lists the activities to be completed and uses horizontal bars to graph how long each activity will take, including its starting and ending dates. 152

goals Objectives, often those with a broad focus. 142

grapevine The path along which informal communication travels. 280

graphic rating scale A performance appraisal that rates the degree to which an employee has achieved various characteristics. 489

group Two or more people who interact with one another, are aware of one another, and think of themselves as a group. 64

group incentive plan A financial incentive plan that rewards a team of workers for meeting or exceeding an objective. 303

groupthink The failure to think independently and realistically as a group because of the desire to enjoy consensus and closeness. 241

halo effect The practice of forming an overall opinion on the basis of one outstanding characteristic. 433

harshness bias Rating employees more severely than their performances merit. 497

hindrance stressor A stressful stimulus that impedes an individual's ability to perform. 365

homogeneity The degree to which the members of a group are the same. 71

human relations skills The ability to work effectively with other people. 6

idle time, or downtime Time during which employees or machines are not producing goods or services. 49

inference A conclusion drawn from the facts available. 266

informal communication Organizational communication that is directed toward individual needs and interests and does not necessarily follow formal lines of communication. 278

informal groups Groups that form when individuals in the organization develop relationships to meet personal needs. 66

insubordination Deliberate refusal to do what the supervisor or other superior asks. 324

interactive multimedia Computer software that brings together sound, video, graphics, animation, and text and adjusts content on the basis of user responses. 469

internal locus of control The belief that you are the primary cause of what happens to yourself. 204

intrinsic reward Personal satisfaction that comes directly from performing a task. 301

ISO 9000 A series of standards adopted by the International Organization for Standardization to spell out acceptable criteria for quality systems. 39

job description A listing of the characteristics of a job, including the job title, duties involved, and working conditions. 420

job enlargement An effort to make a job more interesting by adding more duties to it. 306

job enrichment The incorporation of motivating factors into a job—in particular, giving the employee more responsibility and recognition. 306

job rotation Moving employees from job to job to give them more variety. 306

job sharing An arrangement in which two part-time employees share the duties of one full-time job. 294

job specification A listing of the characteristics desirable in the person performing a given job, including educational and work background, physical characteristics, and personal strengths. 421

laissez-faire leadership A leadership style in which the leader is uninvolved and lets subordinates direct themselves. 206

lateral communication Organizational communication in which a message is sent to a person at the same level. 278

leading Influencing people to act (or not act) in a certain way. 11, 203

learning organization An organization that does well in creating, aspiring, and transferring knowledge and in modifying behavior to reflect new knowledge. 182

leniency bias Rating employees more favorably than their performances merit. 498

line authority The right to carry out tasks and give orders related to the organization's primary purpose. 183

management by objectives (MBO) A formal system for planning in which managers and employees at all levels set objectives for what they are to accomplish; their performance is then measured against those objectives. 147

mentoring Providing guidance, advice, and encouragement through an ongoing one-on-one work relationship. 472

motivation Giving people incentives that cause them to act in desired ways. 292

negative reinforcement Removal of something unpleasant after a desired behavior has occurred. 159

nepotism The hiring of one's relatives. 104

network organizations Organizations that maintain flexibility by staying small and contracting with other individuals and organizations as needed to complete projects. 182

noise Anything that can distort a message by interfering with the communication process. 256

nondirective counseling An approach to counseling in which the supervisor primarily listens, encouraging the employee to look for the source of the problem and propose possible solutions. 330

nonverbal message   A message conveyed without using words. 269

norms   Group standards for appropriate or acceptable behavior. 70

objectives   The desired accomplishments of the organization as a whole or of part of the organization. 142

on-the-job training   Teaching a job while trainer and trainee perform the job at the work site. 465

open-ended question   A question that gives the person responding broad control over the response. 433

operational planning   The development of objectives that specify how divisions, departments, and work groups will support organizational goals. 143

organic structure   Organizational structure in which the boundaries between jobs continually shift and people pitch in wherever their contributions are needed. 181

organizational politics   Intentional acts of influence to enhance or protect the self-interest of individuals or groups. 397

organizing   Setting up the group, allocating resources, and assigning work to achieve goals. 11, 175

orientation   The process of giving new employees the information they need to do their work comfortably, effectively, and efficiently. 455

overhead   Expenses not related directly to producing goods and services; examples are rent, utilities, and staff support. 48

paired-comparison approach   A performance appraisal that measures the relative performance of employees in a group. 491

parity principle   The principle that personnel who are given responsibility must also be given enough authority to carry out that responsibility. 189

payback period   The length of time it will take for the benefits generated by an investment (such as cost savings from machinery) to offset the cost of the investment. 51

peer reviews   Performance appraisals conducted by an employee's co-workers. 495

perceptions   The ways people see and interpret reality. 267

perfectionism   The attempt to do things perfectly. 358

performance appraisal   Formal feedback on how well an employee is performing his or her job. 484

performance report   A summary of performance and comparison with performance standards. 163

personal power   Power that arises from an individual's personal characteristics. 397

piecework system   Payment according to the quantity produced. 302

planning   Setting goals and determining how to meet them. 10, 142

policies   Broad guidelines for how to act. 145

position power   Power that comes from a person's formal role in an organization. 397

positive discipline   Discipline designed to prevent problem behavior from beginning. 336

positive reinforcement   Presentation of something pleasant after a desired behavior has occurred. 159

power   The ability to get others to act in a certain way. 185, 397

precontrol   Efforts aimed at preventing behavior that may lead to undesirable results. 162

prejudice   A preconceived judgment about an individual or group of people. 123

prejudices   Negative conclusions about a category of people based on stereotypes. 268

probability theory   A body of techniques for comparing the consequences of possible decisions in a risk situation. 238

problem   A factor in the organization that is a barrier to improvement. 160

procedures   The steps that must be completed to achieve a specific purpose. 145

process control   Quality control that emphasizes how to do things in a way that leads to better quality. 31

procrastination   Putting off what needs to be done. 357

product quality control   Quality control that focuses on ways to improve the product itself. 30

productivity   The amount of results (output) an organization gets for a given amount of inputs. 28

proficiency test   A test that measures whether the person has the skills needed to perform a job. 434

profit-sharing plan   A group incentive plan under which the company sets aside a share of its profits and divides it among employees. 303

program evaluation and review technique (PERT)   Scheduling tool that identifies the relationships among tasks as well as the amount of time each task will take. 152

proximity bias   The tendency to assign similar scores to items that are near each other on a questionnaire. 498

psychomotor test   A test that measures a person's strength, dexterity, and coordination. 434

punishment   An unpleasant consequence given in response to undesirable behavior. 298

Pygmalion effect   The direct relationship between expectations and performance; high expectations lead to high performance. 307

qualified individual with a disability   Person with a disability who, with or without reasonable accommodation, can perform the essential functions of a particular job. 129

quality control   An organization's efforts to prevent or correct defects in its goods or services or to improve them in some way. 30

recency syndrome   The tendency to remember more easily those events that have occurred recently. 233

recruitment   A process of identifying people interested in holding a particular job or working for the organization. 422

reinforcement A desired consequence or the ending of a negative consequence, either of which is given in response to a desirable behavior. 159, 298

responsibility The obligation to perform assigned activities. 185

role conflicts Situations in which a person has two different roles that call for conflicting types of behavior. 69

role-playing A training method in which roles are assigned to participants, who then act out the way they would handle a specific situation. 470

roles Patterns of behavior related to employees' positions in a group. 69

rules Specific statements of what to do or not do in a given situation. 146

scheduling Setting a precise timetable for the work to be completed. 152

self-managing work teams Groups of 5 to 15 members who work together to produce an entire product. 73

sexism Discrimination based on gender stereotypes. 125

sexual harassment Unwanted sexual attentions, including language, behavior, or the display of images. 126

similarity bias The tendency to judge others more positively when they are like yourself. 498

Six Sigma A process-oriented quality-control method designed to improve the product or service output to 99.97 percent perfect. 35

span of control The number of people a manager supervises. 190

staff authority The right to advise or assist those with line authority. 184

staffing Identifying, hiring, and developing the necessary number and quality of employees. 11

standards Measures of what is expected. 156

statistical process control (SPC) A quality-control technique using statistics to monitor production quality on an ongoing basis and making corrections whenever the results show the process is out of control. 33

statistical quality control Looking for defects in parts or finished products selected through a sampling technique. 33

status A group member's position in relation to others in the group. 70

stereotypes Generalized, fixed images of others. 125, 234

strategic planning The creation of long-term goals for the organization as a whole. 143

stress The body's response to coping with environmental demands. 359

structured interview An interview based on questions the interviewer has prepared in advance. 430

supervisor A manager at the first level of management. 4

suspension Requirement that an employee not come to work for a set period of time; the employee is not paid for the time off. 333

sustainability An organization's ability to meet its present needs without compromising the ability of future generations to meet their needs. 108

symptom An indication of an underlying problem. 160

task groups Groups that are set up to carry out a specific activity and then disband when the activity is completed. 65

team A small group whose members share goals, commitment, and accountability for results. 73

team building Developing the ability of team members to work together to achieve common objectives. 77

technical skills The specialized knowledge and expertise used to carry out particular techniques or procedures. 6

Theory X A set of management attitudes based on the view that people dislike work and must be coerced to perform. 304

Theory Y A set of management attitudes based on the view that work is a natural activity and that people will work hard and creatively to achieve objectives to which they are committed. 305

Theory Z A set of management attitudes that emphasizes employee participation in all aspects of decision making. 306

360-degree feedback Performance appraisal that combines assessments from several sources. 495

time log A record of what activities a person is doing hour by hour throughout the day. 350

time management The practice of controlling the way you use time. 350

total quality management (TQM) An organization-wide focus on satisfying customers by continuously improving every business process for delivering goods or services. 36

training Increasing the skills that will enable employees to better meet the organization's goals. 454

turnover The rate at which employees leave an organization. 52

Type A personality A pattern of behavior that involves constantly trying to accomplish a lot in a hurry. 361

Type B personality A pattern of behavior that focuses on a relaxed but active approach to life. 361

unity of command The principle that each employee should have only one supervisor. 189

unstructured interview An interview in which the interviewer has no list of questions prepared in advance but asks questions on the basis of the applicant's responses. 430

upward communication Organizational communication in which a message is sent to someone at a higher level. 277

value The worth a customer places on a total package of goods and services relative to its cost. 40

variance The size of the difference between actual performance and a performance standard. 159

verbal message   A message that consists of words. 269

vestibule training   Training that takes place on equipment set up in a special area off the job site. 466

wellness program   Organizational activities designed to help employees adopt healthy practices. 369

whistle-blower   Someone who exposes a violation of ethics or law. 106

work-standards approach   A performance appraisal in which an appraiser compares an employee's performance with objective measures of what the employee should do. 494

zero-defects approach   A quality-control technique based on the view that everyone in the organization should work toward the goal of delivering such high quality that all aspects of the organization's goods and services are free of problems. 34

Photo Credits

Index

Note: Page numbers followed by n refer to notes.